MUSICAL JOURNEYS IN
SUMATRA
MARGARET KARTOMI

University of Illinois Press
Urbana, Chicago, and Springfield

759909943

🛡 MONASH University

*Production of this book was made possible by publication
subsidies from the Faculty of Arts, Monash University,
and the Australian Academy of the Humanities.*

Cataloging information is available from the Library of Congress

ISBN 978-0-252-03671-2 (cloth : alk.)
ISBN 978-0-252-09382-1 (ebook)

CONTENTS

Most non-English terms in this book are given in a speech variety of Malay, Minang-kabau, Batak Mandailing, Acehnese, or Latinized Arabic, with an appropriate abbreviation in parenthesis—Ma., Mi., and so on, or in the Indonesian language (I.). The spelling of Indonesian words conforms to the official system of 1972 and the Javanese spellings as in Javanese newspapers from 1974. Words and names in use before the new spellings were introduced are given in the old spelling, for example, *dj* and *tj* (old spelling) are rendered *j* and *c* respectively (new spelling). Use of local vernacular spellings are noted directly in the text (e.g., Besemah is abbreviated as Be.). Place names are given in their official Indonesian spellings, while terms and genres usually appear in their local spellings.

Diacritics are given mainly for Acehnese and Javanese words, because they are less familiar to readers than the Malay, Indonesian, and most other foreign words used in this book.

ABBREVIATIONS

Languages

Ac.	Acehnese, Aceh
Angk.	Angkola
Ar.	Arabic
BB	Bahasa Besemah
Be.	Besemah Malay
Bengk.	Bengkulu, Malay people of Bengkulu descent
BI	Bahasa Indonesia
BJ	Bahasa Jawa
BM	Bahasa Melayu/Malay
I.	Indonesian, nationals of Indonesia, and their lingua franca
Jav.	Javanese
La.	Lampung, people of Lampung descent who live in areas where Lampungic speech varieties are dominant
Ma.	Malay
Mand.	Mandailing
Me. Pa.	Melayu Pasisir (Coastal Malay)
Mi.	Minangkabau
M-m.	Muko-muko dialect
Sa.	Sanskrit

Regions and Maps

OKI	Ogan Komering Ilir, the lower reaches of the Ogan and Komering Rivers in South Sumatra
OKU	Ogan Komering Ulu, the upper reaches of the Ogan and Komering Rivers in South Sumatra
W-H map	Map of Sumatra compiled by W. A. Foley in Wurm and Hattori 1981, available online at http://tinyurl.com/44porat.
Ethnologue map	Map of Sumatra. From Lewis 2009.

NOTE ON INFORMAL LEARNING, MUSICAL NOTATION, AND TRANSCRIPTION

Throughout Sumatra, people traditionally learn to perform music, dance, and theater by trial and error and by listening to and watching experienced artists. Normally they perform either in free meter or in fixed two-, four-, or six-beat meter, adopting a more extemporaneous approach when in free meter. Whatever the meter, they frequently vary the rhythmic motives, pitches of tones and melodic ornamentation (Ma. *bunga*). Drummers in Sumatra teach the rhythmic-timbral motives by uttering onomatopoeic syllables in standard rhythms to represent the sounds while they play. Clearly a notation system is neither necessary nor desirable for the traditional learning process.

In order to facilitate discussion, however, the musical examples in this book are transcribed either in solfa notation or in an adapted form of Western staff notation, with the drum timbres depicted by the abbreviated onomatopoeic syllables used to refer to them. For example, in some areas the drum syllable *tum* or *tung*, notated "t," designates a deep, resonant, undamped sound beaten with the left hand near the center of the drum head, while the drum syllable *ba*, notated "b," denotes a sharp, relatively high-pitched right-hand stroke near the rim. Other syllables are used in other areas. Cyclic (or repetitive) drum and frame-drum rhythms or rhythmic motives are notated with a time signature and repeat marks: //:, and a dot designates a rest. A quarter note/crotchet value is given two spaces in a notation, while two eighth note/quaver values are given one space each with a line drawn below the note, for example, two high-pitched *ba* drum sounds are notated as bb. If, say, a drummer plays a repetitious rhythmic motive containing whole, half, and quarter notes on two main timbral pitches, for example, high and low (b and t) pitches in the *tumba* drumming system of the northwest Pasisir (chap. 10) in quadruple meter, the performance is notated as follows: 4/4 //:t b̲ b̲ t̲ b̲ t̲ b̲ ://, in which the pair of eighth notes are shown by a line drawn under them, and the four sixteenth notes by two lines enclosed with repeat signs //: and ://.

Traditional Sumatran artists and audiences do not normally adhere to a concept of "in-tuneness," or fixed pitches, as classical Western musicians tend to. Nor do they insist that a given set of actual or relative pitches is the one and only correct one. In this respect they differ from certain Javanese musicians and audiences who prefer to play or listen to *gamelan* tuned to the pitches they grew up with, or who only approve of particular *gamelan* tunings that are influenced by the courts of, say, Surakarta or Yogyakarta in Java.

As the vocal and instrumental tunings—even of fixed-pitch instruments such as gong chimes—tend to vary considerably between and within neighborhoods, I have chosen not to measure the pitches down to the last cent or cycle per second. Such an exercise would distort local aesthetic attitudes, forcing on them an uncharacteristic concept of in-tuneness in place of the artists' and audiences' usual tolerance of pitch variability. Sometimes, on revisiting a village twenty or thirty years after my first visit, I found that a gong chime or other instrument had changed pitch slightly, but the musicians easily accepted the change, feeling no need to retune the instrument.

In the musical transcriptions, therefore, I have chosen to notate each tone to the nearest diatonic semitone and have summarized the tonal palette used in some items as ascending intervallic successions or scales.[1] The tones in melodies sung or played are denoted by capital letters, with the symbol "♭" denoting a halftone "flat" and the symbol "♯" denoting a halftone "sharp." A few indications of the exact tunings and tone systems that singers and instrumentalists employ are given to the nearest Western quarter-tone frequency as a preliminary to much more detailed studies being made of each musico-lingual group. Until all the facts are in, the aurally perceived tunings given cannot, of course, be regarded as typical. Tonal systems and scales are notated as capital letters, for example, tones D E F♯ G A B C♯ in the case of a Western major scale, and with flat (♭) or sharp (♯) signs following the appropriate notes, and + or − above or below notes that are an approximate quarter tone higher or lower than written, respectively. The major scale pitched an octave above the scale beginning with "middle C" is notated C^I D^I E^I and so on, and two octaves above as C^{II} D^{II} E^{II} and so on, while the scale an octave below it is notated C_I D_I E_I and so on, and two octaves below as C_{II} D_{II} E_{II} and so on. In some chapters, the scales of musical examples given are transposed to the same notional pitch (in C or C minor) to facilitate ease of comparison, followed by the actual pitches heard or recorded, which are given in curly brackets, for example, {C D♭ E F G A♭} becomes {G A♭ B C^I D^I E♭^{I}} with C^I as the tonal center, with an asterisk (*) inserted next to notes that have been so transposed.

The transcriptions use the Western notational convention of placing the bar line in front of a metric stress instead of after it as is conventional in Javanese *gamelan* notation.

MUSIC EXAMPLES

FIGURES

MAPS AND TABLES

Mas Kartomi and I have many warm memories of Sumatra. Our most moving experiences were of economically poor but culturally rich villagers everywhere who gave unstintingly of their warmth and hospitality, invited us to their weddings, circumcisions, and religious celebrations, and organized performances at our request, often with little notice. Male and female clan elders, religious leaders, government officials, musicians, bards, actors, and comedians demonstrated or explained the techniques, meanings, social functions, and historical significance of the music, dances, art of self-defense, theater, legends, and bardic arts.

My most vivid recollections of Sumatra's still-unspoiled natural environment in the 1970s are of towering volcanoes in the mountain ranges—Bukit Barisan—that run along Sumatra's west coast; jagged ridges with white mist hanging over crater lakes; the fresh scented air after the rains while I walked along the forest paths; the short, rocky streams that cascade down to the narrow plains of the west coast; and the magnificent long, navigable rivers that flow eastward from the mountains through the foothills, alluvial plains, and coastal mangrove marshes to empty finally into the Strait of Malacca. The sections of each river, ranging from the young and vigorous to the old and slow, have their own soundscapes, ranging from the brilliant bird sounds on the glittering middle reaches of the Kampar to the calm, slowly washing sounds and currents of the lower reaches of the Musi River as it passes sluggishly from Palembang and Bukit Siguntang through the delta to the ocean. We explored the magnificent Buddhist temple complexes, including the Saivite-Mahayana Tantric temple ruins at Muara Takus in the upper reaches of the Kampar Kanan in Riau, an area periodically visited by herds of elephants (Schnitger 1964, 33–37); the Candi Muaro Jambi ruins located a few score kilometers up the great Batang Hari River from the Jambi coast; and the Candi Portibi complex in Padang Lawas, North Sumatra, all probably built during the eleventh through thirteenth centuries as part of the Melayu kingdom that centered in Jambi.

I tried hard but never managed to encounter a Sumatran tiger, elephant, or crocodile, or even a mischievous little squirrel, deer, or pig in the wild. However, I stepped over many snakes in the forests and learned to like the *cicak* (I., "geckos") and even the rather harmless spiders in the houses. I met several men who had befriended potentially dangerous tigers by turning into weretigers themselves, and a number of *pencak silat* (I., "art of self-defense") performers whose forebears had learned to imitate the tiger's long, stealthy steps and techniques of attack and defense and had developed them into moves and gestures in their displays and fights. I also met male and female shamans who had an impressive knowledge of the local magic, lore, and arts for ritual occasions, and specialist male shamans who performed mystical rituals deep in the forest before felling a tree to make some mystically powerful drums, for example, Aceh's *rapa'i Pasè*.

I remember with trepidation some of the adventures that we had on Sumatra's great lakes. One evening we were in a small boat on Lake Toba during a storm as the thunder and lightning flashed and gusty winds blew the heavy rain in the wrong direction, and the boatsman asked us for foreign cigarettes and other offerings to throw to the spirits of the lake to calm the waves and to help him steer between and around the rocks back from Simanindo to Tomok on Lake Toba's Samosir Island.

I vividly remember listening to local legends told and sung to us before we fell asleep under the stars on sacks of copra on our all-night sea voyage from Sibolga to the southern shore of the island of Nias, where we heard the soaring music of the powerful *hoho* choirs, watched the ultraslow female welcome dance, and witnessed the young men learning to jump over a high stone barrier to show their manliness before they were allowed to marry.

One unforgettable river voyage took us all the way from the temple complex at Muara Takus on Riau's Kampar River of the Malay Pelalawan palace and countless riverside villages, to the river mouth and offshore islands out at sea. On the way we canoed around a maze of riverlets that led off from near the village of Betung in the middle reaches of the Kampar. We passed under low bridges on which small huts had been built by some seminomadic Petalangan fisherfolk who prefer to live with the forest fairies (*orang bunyian*) rather than join the semisettled communities (see fig. 6.8). On that side voyage we also saw honey-collecting shamans singing to the venerated spirit of a tall *sialang* tree on a bank of a riverlet in order to gain the tree spirit's protection from the bees before scaling its heights to collect their honey. About sixty kilometers before reaching the end of our voyage on the Kampar, our boat paused near a partly submerged tree branch in a shallow part of the river to await the onslaught of a mighty three- to four-meter-high tidal wave—the so-called Bono, which swept upstream twice a day from the Kampar's twelve-kilometer-wide mouth, crashing against the banks with a thunderous sound and destroying everything in its path except for boats piloted by experienced navigators like ours, who knew how to throttle fast and furiously into the seven roaring walls of water that rolled in at us with a misty spray, and finally to bring us out safely through the wide river mouth into the sea.

After disembarking on the island of Penyelai beyond the river mouth in the Malacca Strait, we met some Suku Laut women in their fifties and sixties who could still perform the Malay *joget* song-dances of their youth. In the 1950s they used to sail up and down the Kampar with their male manager and musicians to present *joget* nights. They sang flirtatious Malay *panton* verses in response to verses sung by their male partners, who pressed coins into their hands for the privilege of dancing and singing with them in couples, without touching (see chap. 10).

From Penyelai we sailed to the Siak Sri Indrapura palace on the Siak River, where we saw a royal Malay *nobat* (drum-oboe) ensemble and the meeting outhouse where it was performed until the late 1930s in the presence of the former sultan or on the occasion of his death. We then drove over mud roads to Rengat on the Indragiri River, which flows from Lake Singkarak in the Minangkabau highlands across eastern Sumatra to the sea. There the descendants of the Indragiri royal family showed us their royal *nobat* drums and other *pusaka* (inherited regalia) and introduced us to their loyal Suku Mamak servant-musicians, who performed for us in their forest village that they inhabit when not wandering in the forest.

Sometimes we came across material objects of indigenous religion. One day in 1976 we were walking in the coffee tree gardens on the outskirts of a forest owned by local members of the Lubis *marga* (genealogical unit) in the Mandailing Batak *huta* (village) of Pakantan, and we stumbled on a stone relic carved with a lingam-yoni design. It marked part of the border of the village and was believed to sound protective warnings at times of danger, including during the Japanese occupation in World War II. The next day we saw another pair of lingam-yoni carvings, this time in wood, resting permanently on the wall of the chieftain's (*raja*'s) platform in a ceremonial house in which the clan elders, including descendants of the *raja*, customarily dance at indigenous religious ceremonies with nine-drum-ensemble accompaniment (see figs. 11.4 and 11.5). Drums and gongs in the ceremonial ensembles occur in "male" and "female" pairs, sometimes with the smallest, "child" drum or gong representing the product of the dualism, which thereby becomes a ternary unit. Together the three components symbolize the creative unity that is believed to pervade all aspects of existence and the harmony that needs to exist between the natural environment and human society.

From the 1980s onward, Sumatra's pristine natural environment has been deteriorating. Illegal logging of the forests began in earnest, and some species of fauna and flora became endangered. At the same time, the nomadic groups and even the settled peoples were losing their musico-lingual diversity and traditional way of life.

From the early 1970s, Mas Kartomi and I focused on collecting the most endangered species of the musical arts—genres attached to the rituals of ancestor and nature veneration that were under attack by the state and some adherents of the world religions for being "backward" and "primitive." They included the vocal and bardic repertories, shamanic invocations, Jew's harp and other solo instrumental music, rice-stamping music, funeral laments and dances, genres featuring mixed gender performances, various kinds of ritual ensemble music for drums with optional gong-chimes and/or a wind or bowed string instrument, syntheses of Malay-Portuguese music and dance, and arts associated with former petty royalty. In the past two decades some genres that we recorded in the 1970s and 1980s have virtually disappeared or have been changed in their very essence due to religious and governmental and commercial pressures.

||||

After our first few field trips in the 1970s, I decided I would work toward writing a book on the musical arts of Sumatra and its offshore islands, if only to help orient future observers and scholars who might join me in researching this virtual musical terra incognita. No monograph had appeared to match the first substantial books on the music of Java (Kunst [1949] 1973) and Bali (McPhee 1966), nor was there one on the horizon. The rest of Indonesia was similarly bereft of sizable studies, except for a book-length article on the music of Madura (Brandts Buys and Zijp Brandts Buys 1928) and another on the music of Nias (Kunst 1942).

However, I greatly underestimated the time it would take to traverse greater Sumatra and to analyze the musical and ethnographic data. It is only now, forty years later, that I have been able to produce this, my first, book on Sumatra, and it deals with aspects of only six of Sumatra's ten provinces and a few offshore islands, based on thirty-two field trips throughout all of Sumatra's provinces between 1971 and 2011. Whenever possible we returned to places we had already visited in order to observe and record changes in the practices and styles of the musical arts and to collect data on the consumption of commercial popular music and dance. However, there is no space to deal with the popular music in this book. It needs and deserves detailed coverage in its own right.

ACKNOWLEDGMENTS

An island whose people have been as kind and hospitable as those of Sumatra places me under an obligation to document, analyze, and bring the extraordinary artistic expressions and achievements of its peoples to public attention. Hundreds of musicians, instrument makers, dancers, poets, storytellers, shamans, headmen, fisherfolk, farmers, merchants, and corporate and government officials have helped us record, photograph, and study the wealth of traditional musical arts that we encountered on our journeys. At the time of writing I am still doing more fieldwork and writing, and my team of researchers and I are slowly digitizing the recordings and visual data and making them publically accessible, though there is still a mass of material that urgently needs to be processed and published.[1] I hope that other students of Sumatra will be able to use, reuse, and add to the data that we have been privileged to gather.

The many individuals who have informed, advised, and critically discussed their musical cultures with me are too numerous to name, though some are mentioned in the acknowledgments in the chapters. First and foremost I am deeply indebted to the many Sumatran artists, scholars, teachers, and government officials whom I have acknowledged in the chapters. During the decades the book was taking shape, I had the benefit of a succession of research grants from the Australian Research Council funding body (formerly the Australian Research Grants Committee) that enabled me to travel and meet countless artists in Sumatra and international scholars at conferences, provided research assistance for the archival processing and preservation of my field recordings and other data, and above all, time to think about the critical issues involved in writing this first book on Sumatra and to work them into publishable form. Monash University's School of Music-Conservatorium, Centre for Southeast Asian Studies, and Monash Asia Institute also supported me generously in my team's research over the decades.

I am fortunate indeed to have been aided in the preparation of this manuscript by two fine musicologists, Bronia Kornhauser and Paul Watt, whose scholarly dedication and research skills are quite complementary to each other, and who provided a critical backdrop on which to test my ideas. Thanks to Laurie Matheson of the University of Illinois Press for waiting for me to finish and then publishing the book with such care, to Aline Scott Maxwell and Gregory Hurworth for transcribing some of the music, and to Kay Dreyfus for her ideas in the early stages. Thanks also to Petrus Voorhoeve, Lode Brakel, Sander Adelaar, Paul Lewis, and Karl Anderbeck for their valued linguistic advice; Olaf Smedal for his ethnographic assistance; Michael Bakan, David Harnish, and Greg Barton for critically reading my early drafts; Jane Drakard for her comments on chapter 10; and Artur Simon, Megan Collins, Noerdin Daood, Marzuki Hassan, Edmund Edwards McKinnon, Iwan Amir, Judith Becker, David Harnish, Anne Rasmussen, Mohd. Anis Md. Noor, Veronica Doubleday, Stephen Blum, Richard Yale, Barbara Leigh, Anthony Reid, Anthony Milner, Leonard Andaya, and Barbara Andaya for our discussions of concepts and approaches over the years. Gary Swinton and Phil Scamp of Monash's School of Geography and Environmental Science drew the maps and some of the illustrations, and Iwan Amir helped make audio and video recordings of some of the performances in the field.

I owe a great debt to my loving and agreeable life companion and husband, Mas Kartomi, who made most of the recordings, took most of the photographs, and was my constant companion on my field trips except in 2008–10 when he had grown too frail. Our daughter, Karen Sri Kartomi Thomas, PhD, who herself researched the theater of Sumatra's offshore island of Buguran in Riau's Natuna Archipelago, was always there with Damien, Jesse, James, Antony, and Josef to support me. Finally, I owe an enormous debt to my late parents, George and Edna Hutchesson, who played violin and piano chamber music together, introduced me to Indonesians at the age of eleven, and took me to Indonesia aged nineteen. They would be happy to know that the first "big Sumatra book" is now complete.

||||

My thinking about Sumatra's musical arts has evolved over four decades. Some materials in the book have appeared in different form in journals, books, and encyclopedia, and I am grateful to the publishers for their kind permission to reproduce sections of my writings. They include "Tiger-Capturing Music in Minangkabau, West Sumatra" (1972, in *Sumatra Research Bulletin* 2.1:24–41); "Dualism in Unity: The Ceremonial Music of the Mandailing Raja Tradition" (1981, in *Asian Music* 12.2:74–108); "Muslim Music in West Sumatran Culture" (1986, in *World of Music* 28.3:13–32); "*Kapri*: A Synthesis of Malay and Portuguese Music on the West Coast of North Sumatra" (1987, in *Cultures and Societies of North Sumatra*, ed. Rainer Carle, 351–94 [Hamburg: Dietrich Reimer Verlag]); "*Dabuih* in West Sumatra: A Synthesis of Muslim and Pre-Muslim Ceremony and Musical Style" (1991, in *Archipel* 41:33–52); "The Paradoxical and Nostalgic History of *Gending Sriwijaya*" (1993, in *Archipel* 45:37–50); "The Royal Nobat Ensemble of Indragiri in Riau, Sumatra, in Colonial and Pre-Colonial Times" (1997, in *Galpin Society Journal* [March]: 3–15); "Conflict and Synthesis in the Development of Music of South Sumatra" (1998, in *All Kinds of Music: Festschrift for Andrew McCredie*, ed. David Swale, 15–41 [Adelaide: University of Adelaide]); "The Music-Culture of South-Coast West Sumatra: Backwater of the Minangkabau 'Heartland' or Home of the Sacred Mermaid and the Earth Goddess?" (1998–99, in *Asian Music* 30.1 (Fall/Winter): 133–82); and "If a man can kill a buffalo with one blow he can play a *rapai Pasè*: How the Frame Drum Expresses Facets of Acehnese Identity" (2004, in *Min Su Qu Yi / Journal of Chinese Ritual, Theater and Folklore* 144:39–88).

Unless otherwise stated, all photographs, drawings, and transcriptions are owned by Margaret Kartomi and Mas Kartomi. Every effort has been made to trace and acknowledge the reproduction of copyright material in this book. We would be pleased to hear from any copyright holders whom we have been unable to contact.

MUSICAL JOURNEYS IN SUMATRA

1

SUMATRA'S PERFORMING ARTS, GROUPS, AND SUBGROUPS

This book is an introduction to the traditional musical arts of Sumatra, the sixth largest island in the world and home to an estimated 44 million Indonesians.[1] It aims to document and explain the ethnographic, cultural, and historical contexts of the performing arts that contain music, and to trace some of the changes in their style, content, and reception from 1971 when our field travels began.

The musical arts, or performing arts containing music, include the vocal, instrumental, and body percussive music, the dance and other body movement, the art of self-defense, the bardic arts, and the musical theater performed at domestic ceremonies, as well as the arts performed during religious rituals and processions, and the adaptations of traditional genres that are performed on government and commercial occasions, during artistic tours and missions, and on the media. Besides the related historical, mythical, religious, and social-contextual issues, some chapters refer to stylistic aspects of the music-dance relationships, the dance syntax, and the musical syntax, including melody, tempo, rhythm, meter, formal structure, melodic ornamentation, improvisation, and instrumental and body percussive interlocking techniques.

The book could have been structured in various ways. On our journeys along Sumatra's rivers, seacoasts, offshore islands, and in the mountains we found common themes across the arts, including an emphasis on identity, rituals and ceremonies, religion, foreign contact, musical instruments and ensembles, pitch variability, social class, gender issues, and education in the performing arts. We found that constructs of a group's artistic identity were related not only to its music, dance, and lingual factors but also to the geographical terrain: whether its members lived in the mountains, the plains, or the upstream, middle-stream, and/or downstream reaches of the many rivers. They were also related to the political divisions of Sumatra into provinces, metropolitan cities, regencies, administrative districts, village complexes, and hamlets. Guided by these complexes of factors, the chapters are grouped in a way that I think most effectively brings out the common themes and connections between them, though of course the reader need not feel bound to follow that order. Moreover, each chapter is a self-contained essay that may be read on its own if the reader so wishes.

As this is the first book on Sumatra's musical arts, it cannot cover all of the island's ten provinces. It has space for discussion of parts of only six—South Sumatra, Bangka-Belitung, Riau, West Sumatra, North Sumatra, and Aceh, making brief references in passing to the other four provinces—Lampung, Bengkulu, Jambi, and the Riau Archipelago. The chapters focus on select subgroups from four of its major population groups—the Minangkabau, the Malay, the Batak, the Acehnese—and one minor population group, the Chinese Indonesian, which is only discussed in respect of communities on Bangka Island. Sumatra's Javanese transmigrant and other immigrant communities are not included.

Beginning in the province of West Sumatra, the book discusses the performing arts of the Minangkabau hinterland and coastal areas. It then moves to the Indragiri Hilir and Suku Mamak Malay subgroups in the province of Riau, and south to some upstream and downstream Malay and Komering subgroups in South Sumatra and three Malay and two Chinese Indonesian subgroups on the offshore island of Bangka, which has been part of a separate province from 2000.[2] The chapters then move north to the Mandailing Batak and west-coast Malays in the province of North Sumatra and finally to the western and northern Acehnese in the province of Aceh on Sumatra's northernmost tip.

Space limitations have also prevented discussion of the changing popular music scene, which needs separate study in its own right. However, some chapters refer to the history and performance of a few popular genres.

THE MUSICO-LINGUAL GROUPS OF SUMATRA

In order to distinguish musically between Sumatra's population groups and subgroups, I have privileged their sung genres over the instrumental ones and classified the population groups and subgroups first and foremost on the basis of the musico-lingual attributes of their vocal musical genres. The ethnographic identity of each subgroup's songs, theater, and sung comedy pieces can readily be recognized through their lingual or textual qualities, while the musical instruments that they play move readily across the porous borders of the subgroups and are therefore relatively unreliable markers of difference.[3] For example, the highly portable end-blown bamboo flute is found in virtually every group and is therefore unsuitable as a signifier of distinctiveness between them. However, different types of bamboo flutes can help distinguish musico-lingual subgroups from one another at the secondary (instrument-based) level of classification, such as between Minangkabau's whistle-block flute (*saluang Pauah*) of the *rantau* (Pauah area) and the ring flute (*saluang darek*) of the *darek* (heartland).

Thus, map 1.1 and figure 1.1 show samples of what I have called the musico-lingual groups and subgroups of Sumatra, by which I mean population groups and subgroups that are primarily distinguished from one another on the basis of the lingual attributes of their vocal-musical genres (including songs, ritual/religious chanting, song-dances, and intoned theatrical monologues or exchanges), and only secondarily on the basis of their musical instruments. Other musico-lingual groups and subgroups may of course be added as more detailed knowledge of these and other groups comes to light. Map 1.1 is based on the Wurm-Hattori map of Sumatra's languages (compiled by W. A. Foley, 1981, henceforth cited as W-H), and the Ethnologue map of Sumatra prepared by the Summer Institute of Languages (SIL) as explained in appendix 1, modified slightly by my own field experience of the speech varieties in the performed genres.[4]

As fig. 1.1 and map 1.1 indicate, the Sumatran peoples discussed in this book may be divided into five musico-lingual groups: the Malay/Melayu, the Minangkabau, the Batak, the Acehnese, and the Chinese Indonesian, which may be subdivided into thirty-three subgroups.

Around two-thirds of Sumatra's population speak varieties of Malay, including a few nomadic or seminomadic Malay subgroups that the government refers to corporately as Suku Terasing (Isolated Peoples). They are divided into the Suku Dalem (People of the Interior), who prefer to live in the forest, and the Orang Suku Laut (Sea Peoples), who prefer to live on houseboats at sea when weather permits. The former include the Suku Kubu (in South Sumatra and Jambi, chap. 7), the Suku Lubu (near Mandailing), the Suku Sakai (in northern Riau between the Rokan and the Sakai Rivers), the Suku Mamak (south of the Indragiri River in Riau, chap. 6), and the Suku Lom (in northern Bangka, chap. 9), while the latter include the Suku Sekak (around Bangka's coast, chap. 9), the Suku Muara ("People of the River Mouth," for example, from Penyelai Island in the mouth of Riau's Kampar River, chap. 10), and others.[5]

In addition to the subgroups shown in figure 1.1, there is at least one cross-regional subgroup. My field experience suggests that Sumatra's west coast possesses a high degree of cultural unity, which is due to its Malay lingua franca, its coastal-Sumatran and international trading contact from the early centuries C.E., its animist-Hindu and Sufi mysticism and acceptance of Islam, its common legends and associated music and dance, and its history of indigenous courts (from the seventh century C.E.) and colonial European contact (from the sixteenth century). Thus, the western coastline may be said to be inhabited by a cross-regional, west-coast Malay subgroup, which subdivides into five parts: (1) the west Acehnese coast (approximately between Calang and Tapaktuan), (2) the Aneuk Jamée or Jamu district (between Singkil [including Pulau Banyak] and Natal), (3) the north Minangkabau district (between Natal and Painan), (4) the south Minangkabau-north Bengkulu district (between Painan and Muko-muko), and (5) the Bengkulu-Lampung district (between Muko-muko and

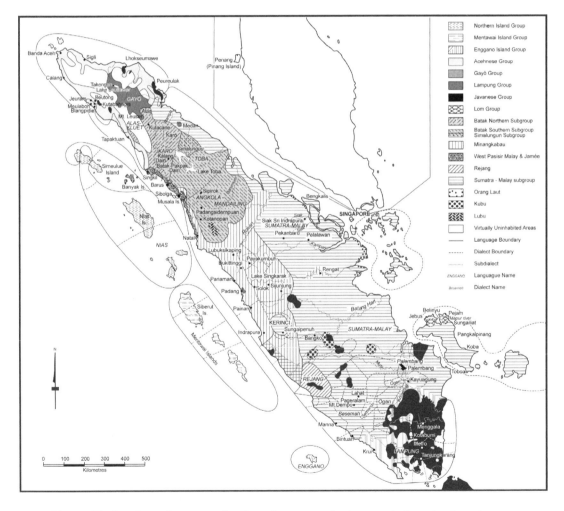

Map 1.1 The locations of some musico-lingual groups and subgroups in Sumatra, based on Foley, 1981

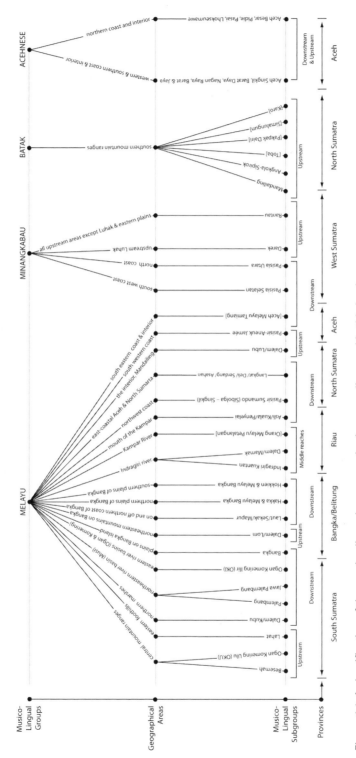

Figure 1.1 A classification of the musico-lingual groups and subgroups discussed in this book

Krui), of which only 5 is not discussed in this book. The populations of the five parts speak and sing in similar, though by no means identical, varieties of Malay.

Lingually the Minangkabau are closely related to the Malay, but over recent centuries they have forged a largely separate cultural and artistic identity for themselves. Some Minangkabau musical, dance, storytelling, and art of self-defense genres resemble the equivalent genres in Malay areas, but the two musico-lingual groups differ stylistically and in their artistic terminology. Moreover, each shows a preference for different genres. The Minangkabau's most prized genres are the flute-accompanied vocal music, the plate dance (*tari piring*), and the brass gong-chime ensemble music (*talempong*), while the Malays tend to single out their many repartee singing forms and *joget*-style dances with violin-drum ensemble accompaniment. The two groups' musical theater forms, for example, the Minangkabau *randai* and the Malay *bangsawan* and Abdul Muluk (*Dul Muluk*), also differ radically from each other in performance style and content.

The Batak group in North Sumatra divides into six related musico-lingual subgroups: the Toba, the Karo, the Pak-pak Dairi, the Simelungun, the Angkola, and the Mandailing, of which only the latter is discussed in this book. Some of the other Batak subgroups have been well researched by ethnomusicologists such as Liberty Manik, Artur Simon, Mauly Purba, Ben Pasaribu, and Lynette Moore. Due to a history of contact between the palaces and among the commoners, some of the legends and songs of the east and west-coast Malays are related to some of the Batak examples, and the east- and west-coast Malays also share a substantial number of music and dance forms with each other.

The Acehnese musico-lingual group divides into two main subgroups: the Acehnese in north-coastal Aceh and Aceh Besar, and the Acehnese on the western coast and interior, that is, in the Kabupatens Aceh Daya, the Aceh Barat, the Nagan Raya, and the Barat Daya (ABDYA). The other five musico-lingual groups in Aceh are the Aneuk Jamée or Jamu people on the southwestern coast; the Kluet, the Gayo Luwes-Alas, and the Gayo in the southwestern and central interiors; and the Tamiang in the southeast. The latter four are not discussed in this book.

THEMES

I shall now briefly introduce some of the major themes that recur throughout the chapters—identity, rituals and ceremonies, religion, the impact of foreign contact on the performing arts, the musical instruments and pitch variability, the dances and music-dance relationships, social class, gender issues, and arts education.

Identity

Since Indonesia declared its independence in 1945, and especially since the implementation of its decentralization policy after Suharto's downfall in 1998, the various provinces and some musico-lingual groups within them have become acutely aware of the need to distinguish themselves from others for their own economic, political, and cultural advantage, including for local tourist development. The concepts of identity of the Malay, Minangkabau, Acehnese, and Batak subgroups discussed in this book feed on the cultural memory of past hegemonies, the *kerajaan* (kingdoms) and sultanates, and the long-term process of their ethnicization (Kahn 1993; L. Andaya 2008); and the groups and subgroups tend to include select items of their musical arts in their statements of concepts of identity (I. *kepribadian*).

Each subgroup's construct of identity is, of course, continually changing as it adapts to the effects of modern technology and globalization on rituals and their associated performances and the popular, commercial, and media arts. However, these matters are only occasionally touched on in this book.

Rituals and Ceremonies

All traditional Sumatran societies perform rituals with music and dance.[6] By ritual is meant rites of passage, including a baby's first wash/haircut, weddings, male circumcisions, and funerals; agricultural cycle rites for planting, harvesting, and grain winnowing; honey collecting, tiger capturing, healing, and clairvoyant and other shamanic rites; morale-boosting rites for self-defense or going into battle; and rituals to celebrate Muslim holy days.[7] In traditional practice, a whole community of relatives and neighbors in a hamlet, village, or suburban street takes part in a ritual, either as host, clan elder, master teacher/performer, musician, dancer, organizer, food preparer, relative, neighbor, or a combination of these roles, that is, with the whole community "performing" in it (Schechner 1993, 353). Thus the rituals induce a kind of performative behavior that unifies and satisfies the community aesthetically, spiritually, and socially, as in the case of traditional Mandailing funerals (chap. 11). Each ritual may comprise several "ceremonies" (i.e., the smallest configuration of a rite that constitutes a meaningful whole [V. Turner 1982, 80]), and any number of musical performances. For example, a traditional wedding may include a proposal ceremony comprising spoken and sung dialogue between the groom's and the bride's parents; a tuneful henna party for the bride before the wedding; a ceremonial bridal bathing and dressing ceremony with song (chap. 12); a procession of the bridegroom and party to the bride's parents' house with a self-defense display or dancing accompanied by portable instruments; and the legal wedding ceremony proper, usually held at home or in the local place of worship.

After the wedding, artists are frequently engaged to entertain the bridal couple as they sit in state on their bridal throne (Ma. *pelaminan*) for up to three days or nights (and for weeks at traditional royal or merchant weddings). In more religiously liberal times, mixed Malay social dancing called *joget* was performed at many such celebrations by semiprofessional female singer-dancers with paying male partners who wanted to dance and sing *pantun* (quatrain verses) with the partner of their choice, usually for a small payment, accompanied by male instrumentalists (chap. 10). *Joget* once had the mystical status of ceremonial entertainment at weddings and other functions, as the singing of mantra and performances could attract benign spirits to bless the community, but a *joget's* performance is now regarded as a sin by its orthodox Muslim detractors in many areas.

The government also holds ceremonies for election campaigns; to celebrate national, regional or local events; and on other occasions that require displays of local identity.

Religion

The great majority of Sumatrans today are traditionalist or modernist Shafi'i Muslims. Although a tiny number of families in Bengkulu and Pariaman profess to be Shi'a Muslims (chap. 4), they are statistically insignificant. There are also several substantial Christian (Catholic or Protestant) communities, especially in Batak North Sumatra, and some smaller Confucian communities, especially in rural and urban Bangka. Many people are mystically inclined and retain a veneration of the spirits of nature and the ancestors.

Indigenous religions or cosmologies (*kepercayaan asli*, "traditional beliefs"; *animisme*, "animism") are intimately related to many forms of the performing arts practiced by members of Sumatra's musico-lingual groups.[8] The belief systems vary in the detail, but they are all based on the notion that spirits (*roh halus* or *jin Islam*, "Muslim spirits") exist in humans (alive and deceased), animals, rocks, plants, mountains, rivers, the sea, thunder, and other objects of the environment; and that various spirits inhabit the sources of food, shelter, and fertility, and constantly involve themselves in people's lives. In highland South Sumatra, people refer to the age of the deities (*zaman diwe diwate*) and the age of the ancestors (*zaman puyang*) (Barendregt 2005, 407).

Male and female shamans (Ma. *dukun*; Ma. *datuk*; Mand. *sibaso*) are believed to possess "inherited mystical knowledge" (*ilmu pusaka*) or "unseen knowledge" (*ilmu gaib*), which they can use to improve their clients' lives by exorcizing evil spirits, performing healing rituals, telling fortunes, and using their magic to prepare the *sajen* (incense and other spirit offerings) for a séance, or hot chains and broken glass for a *dabus* ceremony (chap. 5). Some male shamans are also *guru pencak silat* (masters of the art of self-defense) who demonstrate and teach the philosophy and techniques of the martial arts (*pencak silat*) and the associated drum playing, with optional melodic oboe and colotomic gong parts. Some shamans double as professional musicians who regularly use their knowledge to protect themselves and others, especially at night-time performances or while on a journey away from home when disruptive spirits (*iblis, jin kafir*) are believed to be more active. In traditional belief, it is also a moral imperative to treat potentially dangerous animals with esteem, even to befriend them, and if they threaten human life to capture them with respect, in some cases with poetry and music (chap. 2).

Early proselytizers in many areas were strongly influenced by Sufi ideas, which provided artists with opportunities to adapt aspects of the local indigenous-Hindu-Buddhist ritual arts to the new Muslim culture and to broaden the traditional methods of educating the young. For example, masters of the Minangkabau art of self-defense reinterpreted and adapted the old indigenous religious ideas to the new Sufi philosophy and Muslim religious concepts, thereby offering a broader approach to education of the young (Barendregt 1995).[9]

Although some Muslim leaders rejected the *adat* rituals and the "heathen path," many artists saw no contradiction between worshipping Allah and performing the rituals and associated arts, especially if Muslim prayers or sayings were inserted at structural points in a performance and gave it a Muslim flavor. There is insufficient space here to discuss the controversy about whether or how the *adat* arts should have been preserved after the conversion to Islam. Suffice it to say that many of the *asli* arts survived until the 1970s and 1980s, when we observed them, and some have survived in more isolated areas to this day.[10]

The so-called modernist Muslims tend to adhere to a literal interpretation of scripture and approve only of the Islamic-related performing arts, while the "traditionalists" tend to enjoy not only the Islamic arts but also the mystical ancestral arts to which Muslim attributes (e.g., prayers) are often added, and they find ways to resolve the religious ambiguities while maintaining local religious ideas and artistic genres.

However, most people continue to fuse their conviction in a world religion with indigenous beliefs in ancestral and nature-spirit veneration, which are expressed in mystical rituals attached to various social situations. Every musico-lingual group and subgroup has its own indigenous belief system and associated practices, which it shares in some respects with other groups, though each differs in its detail.

This book deals mainly with indigenous religious and Muslim communities and refers briefly to a few Christian villages in upstream South Sumatra and to some Confucian communities belonging to the Peranakan Indonesian Chinese minorities on the island of Bangka.[11]

Foreign Contact

Over the millennia, Sumatrans' extensive contact with China, the Perso-Arabic world, India, Java, the Malay world (including the Malay Peninsula and west Kalimantan), mainland Southeast Asia, Europe, and in recent decades America has had a significant impact on the music, dance, and theater of various parts of the island. This book mentions some of the results, but a thorough investigation of such extensive contacts over such a long period of time awaits future research, which will likely be hampered by the loss of most of the documentation. Chinese contact is probably the oldest, and although most of the specific artistic influences have long since been absorbed into indigenous culture, some clear signs remain: for example, many Sumatran myths and legends mention links with Chinese emperors and princesses, and Chinese musical instruments are included in the Palembang palace's ensembles. Moreover, despite experiencing many difficulties, Chinese Indonesian communities in Bangka and a few other areas still perform traditional Chinese genres. Some instances of artistic Perso-Arabic and Indian contact are detailed in this book, for example, the transplantation of *zapin* dance and music from the Hadhramaut/Yemen and the adoption of the *tabut* arts and the *Dul Muluk* theater from North India, Iran, and Iraq. However, it is the contact with Europe that is best documented.

Sumatrans' contact with European colonial powers, initially the Portuguese, had a lasting impact on their musical arts scene, resulting in the introduction of European plucked and bowed strings, especially the violin (Ma., I. *biola*), the European major and minor scales, musical harmony, and implied harmony, and the development of various hybrid genres of music and dance. The Portuguese, who conquered Malacca in 1511 and stayed in Southeast Asia until 1641, brought European string, wind, and percussion instruments into their households for their slaves to play (chap. 10).

Mainly for technical ease in performance, the violin eventually replaced most of the existing bowed strings (*rebab, hareubab, arbab*) throughout Sumatra, as in the case of the *rabab pasisia* on the southern coast of Minangkabau (chap. 3) and the *biola Aceh* in Aceh (M. Kartomi 2005). Slave musicians of the Portuguese who were freed in the seventeenth century may have been among those who spread hybrid Malay-Portuguese music and dance genres and the violin between the many Malay kingdoms, including those on the west coast of the Malay Peninsula and the east and west coasts of Sumatra. The genres included the west-coast North Sumatran *kapri* and east-coast *ronggeng/joget* dance music with *pantun*-verse response singing (chap. 10). The latter may well have spread along the well-established river trade routes between the east and west coasts. Itinerant *joget* music and dance troupes who travel from village to village up- and downriver from the east coast are now obsolete (chap. 10), but in recent decades permits were sometimes issued for troupes to perform at weddings in such cities as Medan and Tanjung Pinang.

From around the 1890s various popular Malay music genres developed, including diatonic *gamad* music for a vocalist and hybrid Malay-European bands with couples dancing along the Minangkabau and Bengkulu coasts, and *bangsawan*, Abdul Muluk (*Dul Muluk*), and other forms of Malay theater with Malay-European bands along Sumatra's east coast and on the offshore Bangka and Belitung islands. From the 1920s, popular bands playing diatonically tuned instruments became standard fare for people who listened to the radio and went to the movies, and the consumption of television, prerecorded commercial cassettes and VCDs in the latter decades of the twentieth century strengthened the exposure to diatonically tuned music, which influenced many new creations by Sumatran artists.

Not even the *asli* gong-chime ensembles were exempt from the adaptation to diatonic tuning. From 1967 onward, composers such as Jusaf Rahman wrote works for the diatonically tuned *talempong kreasi* (*talempong* ensemble [for] new creations) that had been developed at the Academy of Traditional Music (ASKI) in Padang-panjang, encouraged by its head, Boestanoel Arifin Adam (M. Kartomi 1979). Ever since then, most traditional Minangkabau dances performed at weddings at home and in the diaspora have been accompanied by this music, or if the *talempong kreasi* is not available, on keyboards and pop band instruments.

The impact of the other colonial powers on the performing arts of Sumatra—the British in their brief interregnum (1810–23) and the Dutch from the seventeenth century (in some areas) until the Japanese invasion in World War II—was apparently minimal compared to the Portuguese. The music and dance styles that the British and the Dutch transplanted consolidated the effects of the tunings and genres that the Portuguese had introduced. In the highlands of Bengkulu and South Sumatra the British introduced the Maypole Dance ("Tari Inggeris," "English Dance"), which is still performed in a few areas and is sometimes included in overseas tours; in 1981, I saw it performed by dancers and a *biola*-drum ensemble of the Misi Kesenian (Indonesian Cultural Mission) in Melbourne. When the British left Bengkulu in 1823, the Indian Sepoy soldiers whom they had brought there to defend their fort transplanted the Shi'a *tabut* ceremonies that they performed annually in Bengkulu to other west-coast towns, including Pariaman (chap. 4), where each year it attracts thousands of tourists, and to Bengkulu.

The effects of the Dutch on Sumatrans' artistic life in the areas where they were operating, in some cases from the early nineteenth century, still need to be researched. My field travels left me with the impression that Dutch officials were frequently invited to attend ceremonies in the palaces and great houses of the aristocratic elite, with whom they were often on good terms, and that the *controleur* (administrative "commandant") sometimes reported on the traditional arts where he was stationed. For example, the *controleur* W. Willer described some Mandailing ensembles in Kotanopan in his official report in the late nineteenth century (chap. 11). Local elites were also invited to Dutch events where they learned to perform Dutch social dances such as quadrilles and the Tari Langsèr Madam maze dance that I saw performed with gusto in the former court town of Haloban in offshore Aceh's Pulau Banyak Barat, in 2010. In southeast Sumatra, Dutch mine and plantation owners during the nineteenth century and the twentieth century promoted outdoor *tanjidor* brass and percussion bands among their workers, who played military marches and popular songs (e.g., "La Paloma") in their wedding processions and receptions, and still occasionally do so in eastern South Sumatra, Bangka and Belitung. *Tanjidor* takes its name from the Portuguese word *tangedor* (player), a derivative of *tanger* meaning "to make a twang" (as on a guitar) (Heins 1975; Yampolsky 1994a, CD 5).

Musical Instruments, Ensembles, and Pitch Variability

Most traditional Sumatran-Malay instrumental ensembles consist of drums, a vocal and/or melodic instrument (a flute, an oboe, or a bowed string instrument), and an optional pair of thick-rimmed gongs, which are played to accompany social dancing at rituals and celebrations. The further north one goes, the fewer gongs one finds, but even in Aceh the main drum and oboe ensemble may include a small gong. A notional classification system for Sumatra's instruments will be presented in chapter 14.

Similar types of instruments and ensembles are found in the Malay and Minangkabau groups, but the latter are more famous for their gong-chime ensembles. The Batak ensembles stand out because of their tuned drum chimes, while the Acehnese are remarkable for their large range of frame drum types. The Suku Dalem peoples feature Hindu bells (*gento*, Sa.), flutes, and drums or frame drums, and the Orang Suku Laut play conch shells, flutes, and drums, and the above-mentioned Malay ensemble for their social dancing. Indonesian Chinese ensembles comprise bowed strings, a range of percussion instruments, and a flat gong. Most ensembles are played in both religious and secular contexts.

Among the instruments played informally by women or men at home or in the fields are the bamboo tube zithers, Jew's harps, oboes, and flutes. In some areas the bowed strings (*rebab* etc. and the violin) are played by bards. The great hanging bronze gongs found in Java are very rare, found only in the *gamelan* of the former palace in Palembang, though smaller hanging metal gongs are played in the *gamelan* in some Javanese transmigrant villages in various parts of Sumatra.

Singers and instrumentalists throughout Sumatra have a high tolerance of pitch variability; indeed they relish subtle variations of pitch in their solo vocal and instrumental music and between their sets of instruments. Unlike in Java and Bali, there is no set of typical scales or tunings found in large areas of the island.

Dance

Virtually all dance performances in Sumatra are accompanied by music. The discussions of the dances in this book focus on their relationships with the music, myths, legends, and performance contexts rather than the syntactic details of dance design, floor plans, and movements, for which specialist choreological research is needed. Some dances that are performed to welcome guests or facilitate the social mixing of the sexes are associated with indigenous religious rituals, while others express an Islamic (*Islami*) devotional content or are perceived as having an Islamic flavor (*yang bernafaskan Islam*). A few other forms of music and dance were introduced by colonial European powers and adapted to local conditions, while since the late 1960s, many traditional forms have been affected stylistically by genres shown in the media.

Social Class

From the early first millennium C.E., indigenous Malay societies throughout Sumatra and neighboring Malaya divided into three social classes. The highest class comprised the hereditary rulers and lesser aristocrats, with their state-centered trading activities supported by the religious and military leaders. The two subservient classes were the common people who lived at subsistence level in settled agricultural communities, and the seminomadic or nomadic Suku Terasing (Isolated Tribes), who were either semisettled farmer-gatherers or nomadic collectors of forest or sea products (the Suku Dalem and the Orang Suku Laut), some of whom served the local king from a cautious distance. Examples of the first class were Riau's Indragiri and Siak Sri Inderapura palace aristocrats, while an example of the second class was the settled farming communities along the upper reaches of the Indragiri River. The two categories of the third class were exemplified by the semisettled Petalangan people along the middle reaches of the Kampar River, who still spend some months of each year in the forests, and the nomadic members of the Suku Mamak, who still live south of the former Indragiri palace (chap. 6).

A new, racially based class structure emerged in Indonesian societies during colonial times from around the seventeenth century. The highest rung was occupied by the Dutch and other Europeans, the second rung by the "foreign Orientals," who were mainly the Peranakan Chinese Indonesians, and the bottom rung by the "natives" (*pribumi*) (M. Kartomi 2000). The Dutch, who established and maintained power in part by collaborating with the sultans and chieftains in the towns and rural areas, generally treated the foreign Orientals as a pariah group and tried to settle the forest and sea peoples, giving some privileges to the native aristocracy.

Under Sukarno (1949–65), leftist art organizations promoted some of the performing art forms of the working class and the peasantry.[12] Though the traditional elites no longer possessed unchallenged access to wealth and political power, some of their members, for example, the late Malay Serdang palace descendant Tengku Luckman Sinar and the late Batak Mandailing descendant A.P. Parlindungan in Medan, actively promoted the arts of their particular former palace or great house.

Social stratification in the Suharto and post-Suharto eras has been more complex. The powerful military generals and capitalists in the Suharto era were not a unitary group, nor did a clear lower class of poor workers or peasantry emerge. Some economists argue that alliances of the poor have had less to do with class than economic, religious, and community ties, and that a complex mosaic of middle-class groups who were united by patterns of consumption rather than political vision or economic interests lay between the poor and the privileged classes (Dick et al. 2002, 34).[13] The artistic implications of these changing class structures are, of course, distinct from those of the divisions between the musico-lingual groups and subgroups.

Gender Issues

The roles of men and women in the rituals and the performing arts and the social rules governing their interaction vary from subgroup to subgroup. In some communities, for example, in the Lahat area of South Sumatra (chap. 7), mixed couples are allowed to dance together at chaperoned celebrations if they are still single. In other areas, for example, the former east-coast kingdoms, the male and female artists are not normally allowed to mix, though the young unmarried women may sing and dance together while men of any age play the musical instruments. In some parts of Minangkabau, groups of married and single women traditionally play the *talempong* gong-chime ensembles, either in sitting position or standing position in processions, while in other areas only groups of men play.

Several couples' dances are performed by pairs of men wearing male and female garb respectively, because married women are not allowed to appear on stage, for example, in the *sikambang* song-dances in northwest-coastal Aceh and North Sumatra (chap. 10). Erotic song texts are often inserted into the exchanges of verses between male and female—or male only—pairs in the many forms of *joget*-style couples dancing, including *sikambang*. In the colonial era, the boy who took the leading part in *seudati* performances—the *aneuk seudati* (*seudati* child)—wore female garb; and he and the leader of his company, the *dalém*, reportedly sang texts that were erotic and possibly even pederastic in character (Snouck Hurgronje 1993–94, 2:222). Modernist *ulama* banned *seudati* in Aceh in the late 1950s (though morally acceptable versions were revived in the 1960s), and they almost destroyed its female version, *seudati inong*, which by the 1980s had been replaced by the Muslim-texted, female *laweut* dance. The most commonly stated objection to *seudati* was that mixed couples met in the dark at performances.

Gender separation of hosts, guests, and artists at rituals is traditional in some Muslim communities, for example, in Aceh, where men and women sit in separate rooms to partake of the festive meal and enjoy all-male performances for a male audience and all-female performances for a female audience. In other areas, strict gender segregation has been imposed more recently. With the rise of a more assertive Muslim piety from the late 1980s, many more communities have segregated their male and female performers and insisted on Islamizing the costumes worn by female performers. In South Sumatra, for example, female artists from the 1990s on have dispensed with their bare-shouldered traditional costumes and flower-decorated hair buns, covering their bodies with clothing (usually a *kain kebaya panjang*, "sarong and long blouse") and wearing a *jilbab* (head scarf).

Education in the Performing Arts

To date Sumatra's formal performing arts education is largely unresearched, and my field impressions are largely circumstantial. After Indonesia's independence in 1949, many primary and secondary schools taught children to sing national and regional songs, apparently with only a few schools teaching local dances and music where a teacher was available. From the 1950s artists were encouraged to develop semiprofessional or professional dance troupes (*sanggar*, lit. "workshops"), which also often offered dance lessons for children. Some new Western classical music schools were established, mainly within the Chinese Indonesian communities in the cities. Many musicians taught themselves to perform international popular music, which, after being banned by Sukarno for a few years in the early 1960s, quickly became very popular. By the 1980s Sumatra had become a booming market for international, Sumatran, and other Indonesian popular music performance and sales.

Since the late 1960s, the Department of Education and Culture encouraged its employees to engage in research into the regional performing arts and to publish encyclopedia.[14] Tertiary institutions in the performing arts were established relatively late compared to Java, where the first Konservatori Karawitan (Music College) was established in Solo in 1950. The pioneering institution was West Sumatra's Konservatori Karawitan, which opened in Padang Panjang in 1965, became the Akademi Seni Karawitan Indonesia (Academy of Indonesian Performing Arts), and achieved tertiary status as the Sekolah Tinggi Seni Indonesia (Indonesian Academy of the Arts) in 1999. Artistic practices in the institution had a far-reaching effect on "ethnopolitical entrepeneurship," including the development of a standard "ethnic Minangkabau" wedding culture (Fraser 2007, 306–57). The second institution was the Jurusan Etnomusikologi (Ethnomusicology Department), founded in the University of North Sumatra in Medan in 1979. The two institutions used a combination of indigenous and Western pedagogical methods in the training of students, developed new creations and styles based on the traditional arts, combined Sumatran and Western instrumentations and stage production techniques in performances, and encouraged staff and students to engage in research into the arts. However, these developments go beyond the scope of this book.

||||

Many commonalities are to be found between the musical arts of the various Malay subgroups, especially around Sumatra's coast. They share some artistic genres with one another, including certain types of female welcome dances, instrumental ensembles, bardic legends, and Muslim *dhikr*-based forms. Likewise, the Malay-speaking peoples who live in the inland areas of all the provinces except Aceh, West Sumatra, and North Sumatra practice similar rituals and arts, though their popular theater forms are now virtually obsolete. People living in the partly swampy eastern coastal areas, including along the banks of the long eastbound rivers and in the former kingdoms, share many similar rituals, songs, dances, myths, legends, and instrumental ensembles, while inhabitants of the west coastal plains, including those living on the banks of the relatively short rivers and in the former kingdoms, practice another related constellation of rituals and arts. Everywhere there is local and individual diversity in the details of the performances and a tolerant attitude toward variations in musical tunings.

Although the music and dance of the nomadic and seminomadic forest and sea peoples are under-researched, they appear to resemble each other in some respects due to their partly similar lifestyles, which include shamanic healing and exorcistic ceremonies, portable musical instruments, and songs and legends on similar kinds of themes.

The coastal Minangkabau subgroups share some music and dance forms with Malay-speaking subgroups, such as the umbrella dance with its vocal, violin, and drum accompaniment, which is also performed along much of Sumatra's west coast. However, there are also many distinctive upstream Minangkabau genres, such as the *talempong darek* gong-chime and drum ensembles, and other forms that are associated with Islam, such as *salawak dulang* (duo singing with tray-beating accompaniment).

The other main musico-lingual groups and subgroups discussed are artistically distinctive from one another and from all other Sumatran groups. For example, the Mandailing Batak musico-lingual subgroup, whose male and female dancers perform ritual *tortor* dancing at various ceremonies and whose musicians play sets of up to nine tuned drums (*gordang sambilan*) that somewhat resemble those of other Batak subgroups, nevertheless have a unique constellation of music and dance. Members of the Acehnese musico-lingual group perform song-dances in standing and sitting positions (e.g., *seudati, ratôh duek*) with improvisatory-worded singing and elaborate body percussion techniques; and they play a great variety of types of frame drum, some of which are likewise quite distinctive in the Sumatran context as a whole.

The few similarities that exist between genres of otherwise very distinctive musico-lingual groups, for example, the Minangkabau and the Acehnese, are usually attributed to possible historical contact between them. Thus, the late ethnomusicologist Mursal Esten of the Arts Academy (STSI) in Padangpanjang hypothesized that the frame drum played in Minangkabau's Pariaman area, where it is called *rapa'i*, is a transplant from Aceh, where *rapa'i* is the generic name for its family of frame drums. In particular, the *rapa'i* may have been transplanted in the seventeenth century by artists associated with Pariaman's legendary saint Syéh Burhanuddin, who is said to have been a pupil of the famous Abdur'rauf of Singkil in Aceh (Mursal Esten, pers. comm., November 1990).

Today the traditional forms of Sumatra's genres are performed mainly in the context of the indigenous religious and Muslim celebrations of the farmers, coastal or river fishermen, and small traders in the villages and towns. Some are also performed by the few surviving nomadic or seminomadic hunters and gatherers in the forests or on the beaches, or in their government-supplied community houses. However, it is mostly in their modernized, standardized versions that the traditional arts are now seen in the media and on the government and commercial stages.

I

WEST SUMATRA AND RIAU

The Minangkabau- and the Malay-speaking peoples of the central region of Sumatra live in three provinces—West Sumatra, Riau, and the Riau Islands (Kepulauan Riau), of which only the first two are relevant to part I (i.e., chaps. 2–5 about West Sumatra and chap. 6 about Riau).[1] In colonial times all three provinces were part of one province: Central Sumatra.

Since the early first millennium C.E., the people of West Sumatra and Riau have spoken varieties of Malay (apart from the western offshore Mentawei islanders, who are not discussed in this book).[2] In recent times the volcanic soils of the Minangkabau and Riau highland valleys supported large populations who directed their goods down a network of rivers to maritime ports on the Strait of Malacca and the west-coast.

Not surprisingly, therefore, the Malay and Minangkabau performing arts have many stylistic aspects in common. For example, their songs are mostly set to secular *pantun or syair* quatrains, of which thousands have been collected, and many have been published and translated. The quatrains largely determine the form of the songs, which are essentially strophic but allow a high degree of improvisatory freedom on the performer's part, including the insertion of melodic phrases (with or without repeated textual phrases) or sections of percussive rhythms, and the insertion of incidental ornamentation, largely at whim. When performed, the verses are not normally attached to specific melodies; indeed, the same texts can be sung with minor adaptations to other Malay melodies in circulation. Many melodies are set to four to seven selected notes of the international major or minor scales, though they often contain intervals such as lowered seconds or sevenths that suggest Arabic modal influence. The fact that many also contain harmonic implications is attributable to Sumatran-European contact, which began at least five centuries ago.

THE MINANGKABAU IN WEST SUMATRA

Although the Minangkabau language is closely related to the Malay, the Minang-kabau people have long insisted on their distinct cultural identity, which served "to maximise economic and political advantage" (L. Andaya 2008, 82). In earlier centuries the most recognizable marker of their identity was the upstream Pagaruyung palace (near Batusangkar) in the *darek* (highlands) (ibid.). Today the main boundary markers are their matrilineal/matrilocal customs, the *merantau* out-migration of their young men, their buffalo horn–shaped longhouses, and their performing arts, including the *déndang jo saluang* (classical song with flute), standing and sitting *talempong* gong-chime ensembles (figs. I.1 and I.2), the musical *kaba* storytelling with bowed-string accompaniment, and the dances associated with the agricultural cycle and courting such as the plate and candle dances (figs. I.3 and I.4).

The first written record of the name Minangkabau appears in a list of the Malay suzerains of the Javanese Majapahit kingdom dated 1365.[3] Thus, the Minangkabau

Figure I.1 A *talempong pacik* (ensemble that includes small handheld kettle-gongs and drums) played in procession in Sisawah, 1985

Figure I.2 A *talempong duduak* (gong-chimes played in sitting position), traditional dances associated with the agricultural cycle and courting such as the plate and the candle dances and the *randai* theater, Padang, 1972

Figure I.3 *Tari piring* (plate dance) in Batasangkar, 1985

Figure I.4 *Tari lilin* (candle dance), Heni Gustina, Padang Panjang, 1986

have been recognized as a hill-culture polity for no less than six hundred years, spreading out from their highland heartland (*luhak nan tigo*) into the *rantau* (lit. "place of migration," that is, the areas surrounding the heartland) and sending its forest and mining products down to the east and west coasts for export. For two centuries, from the late 1660s to 1833, Pagaruyung was the locus of Minangkabau identity (L. Andaya 2008, 104), receiving tribute from courts throughout Sumatra and Malaya.

Islam came to Minangkabau in the 1500s (Hadler 2008, 19), displacing the indigenous religion and Buddhism only gradually, and never completely. In the early 1800s, the Padri war began as an internecine conflict between Wahhabi reformists and *adat* traditionalists, after which it became a war against colonial occupation. Using peace talks as a ruse, the Wahhabi slaughtered the royal house of Pagaruyung in 1815 (Hadler 2008, 24), and brought a proselytizing jihad to the neighboring Mandailing Batak in the north. After the Wahhabi movement in Arabia was disgraced and the Padri war came to an end in 1838, the Dutch colonial state was established in 1846, and it administered Minangkabau and Mandailing as a single colonial unit (Hadler 2008). Despite those and many other subsequent upheavals, including the Indonesian war of independence, Minangkabau's matrilineal, matrilocal customs persists to the present, as Jeffrey Hadler's study of Minangkabau Muslims and matriarchs has concluded (Hadler 2008, 847), and as my field-based studies of the music culture from the 1970s onward have shown.

THE MINANGKABAU MUSICO-LINGUAL GROUP AND SUBGROUPS

The Minangkabau musico-lingual group may be divided into two upstream and two downstream subgroups (see fig. 1.1). The upstream groups live in (1) the *darék*, that is, the above-mentioned *luhak nan tigo*, which comprises three regional divisions—Agam, Tanah Datar, and Lima Puluh Koto, and (2) the remaining upland areas. The downstream groups live in the *rantau*, that is the downstream "coastal area" (Mi. *pasisia*; I. *pasisir*), which comprises two regional divisions—the northern *pasisia* and the southern *pasisia*.[4] The *darék* and the *rantau* groups differ from each other in their speech varieties, vocal music, and instrumental types; for example, the standard *saluang* in the *darék* consists of a long open bamboo tube, while the *saluang Pauah* found in parts of the *rantau* is a whistle-block flute.

Chapter 2 focuses on an aspect of the artistic tradition of the *darék*, that is, the mystical tiger-capturing songs sung by a shaman and accompanied by his partner shaman on an oblique bamboo flute (i.e., the abovementioned *saluang jo déndang* music). As orthodox *ulama* do not approve of pre-Muslim tiger music and rituals, the shamans begin their performances with Muslim prayers.

Chapter 3 discusses the traditional pre-Muslim music, dance, and legend of the southern *pasisia*, where descendants of local royalty claim descent from the *luhak nan tiga* heartland. Yet the style of their key songs and dances is quite different, based on locally told legends such as the pan-Sumatran west-coastal Sikambang legend about a mermaid (Sikambang) and the Minangkabau south-coastal legend of the Earth Goddess. The culture is also typified by its bardic *kaba* singing accompanied on a *rabab pasisia* (a bowed four-string instrument), and in the extreme south by its female *nenet* dances, which it shares with the northern coast of Bengkulu province.

Chapter 4 describes the northern *pasisia* version of the ten-day Shi'a *tabuik* (Mi.; I. *tabut*) in Pariaman, which was formerly the site of an important Shi'a *tarekat* (Hadler 2008, 119). Though generally regarded as heterodox, Shi'a families in several towns along Sumatra's west and north coast still performed this ceremony in the colonial era, including around Lake Maninjau (fig. 1.5). Today it is performed only in Pariaman and Bengkulu. Normally every year scores of *tabuik* musicians take part in the street processions in Pariaman, playing the *dol* (Mi., *tambua*) and *tasa* (Mi.) drums of Persian origin, while villages in which Shi'a-believing families live (or lived till recently) build a model of the heavenly bird (*burak*) that is believed to have carried the martyr Husein and his brother Hasan to heaven, and carry it in procession to the sea. The Pariaman area is also typified by its predilection for the sitting *indang* song-dances; the three-string *rabab* that accompanies the bards' singing; the presence of a *dol* in some local *talempong* ensembles; and the *tasa* and *dol/tambua* drumming competitions, the latter also found in the Lake Maninjau area.

Chapter 5 discusses four Minangkabau genres based on Sufi Muslim practices, including *dabuih* (Mi.; Ar. *dabus*), a devotional genre that was probably borrowed from Muslim India, in which a group of men continuously repeat the ninety-nine most beautiful names of Allah and vigorously play their frame drums (*rabana*) as some of them rise and stab themselves with an awl (*dabus*) to show their religious devotion and invulnerability. Unlike in Aceh, *dabuih* is not normally performed in a competition between two groups who try to destroy the drum rhythms and thereby the religious concentration of the other side (see chap. 13).

The other genres are *indang*, in which a row of men or women sing devotional or secular songs in "sitting" position (actually kneeling on their heels) while performing

Figure I.5 Lake Maninjau

concerted body movements; *diki Mauluik* (Mi.; I. *zikir* [*dhikr*] *Maulud*), in which a group of men sing about the Prophet in the month of Muhammad's birth, Maulud; and *salawek/salawat dulang*, in which two male vocalists sing devotional or secular texts to their own percussive brass-tray accompaniment.

THE MALAY PEOPLES OF RIAU

The ecology of the province of Riau is dominated by its magnificent river systems, which have provided the people with their main means of communication and trade over the millennia. The Indragiri, Kampar, Siak, and Rokan Rivers flow eastward or northeastward from the Minangkabau highlands through the lush tropical rainforests of the foothills and the alluvial piedmont plains to the swampy coastal mangrove forests before finally emptying into the Strait of Malacca.

The mainland Riau Malays are mostly farmers or swidden farmer-gatherers (e.g., the Petalangan Malays on the Kampar River), though a small minority of nomadic or seminomadic Suku Dalem/Mamak and Suku Sakai peoples traditionally live an isolated life in the forest where they practice their indigenous religion and rituals, and grow dry subsistence crops on the forest outskirts. From around the sixteenth century, Malay rulers built palaces on the rivers, for example, at Siak Sri Indrapura, Pelalawan, and Indragiri, with the main palace located at Daik in the Riau-Lingga archipelago. Chapter 6 deals with only two of Riau's musico-lingual subgroups: the Indragiri-Kuantan Malays, represented by the descendants of the Indragiri palace at Rengat, and their loyal Suku Dalem or Suku Mamak supporters.

Probably founded in the late sixteenth century, the Indragiri dynasty was involved in the lucrative trade in gold, pepper, and other products that were brought from the Kuantan area down the Indragiri to the Strait of Malacca in the sixteenth and seventeenth centuries.[5] As Indragiri's royal descendants told us in 1984, all trading boats moving downstream from the highlands and Kuantan were visible to the royal family and their tax and tribute collectors from the palace compound. In Kuantan, local Malays and *perantau* from Minangkabau established their mixed Malay-Minangkabau culture, with its healing ceremonies, elaborate drumming genres (fig. 3.5), *rabab*-accompanied *sijobang* storytelling (figs. 3.3 and 3.4), and Muslim devotional genres, which gave Kuantan its unique identity.

In the late sixteenth century, the palace paid tribute to the sultanate of Johor, then to Siak, founded in 1722 (Barnard 2003, 73). In the eighteenth and nineteenth centuries, Siak's founder, Raja Kecik, and his successors attempted to gain control of the trade network in the strait by uniting Indragiri and the other palaces under its sway via marriage alliances, warfare, raiding, trade, and mythic storytelling (ibid.).

By 1900, however, Siak's multiple centers of authority had declined, due to the rise of the British trading communities in Singapore and Penang (Barnard 2003, 172).

The small trading kingdoms in the precolonial- and colonial-era Malay world shared a hierarchical system of *adat* customs and rituals. A ruler's most important regalia (*pusaka*) and symbol of his sovereignty was his *nobat* orchestra; indeed, a ruler without his mystically potent *nobat* lost his right to rule. Chapter 6 describes the role of the *nobat* in the former Indragiri palace at Rengat, based on our discussions with descendants of the *istana* (palace) and their forest-dwelling Suku Mamak subjects who were the king's trusted musicians, instrument makers, and servants.

The first *nobat* orchestra in the Malay world (*alam Melayu*) was probably acquired from Moghul North India by the first sultan of Malacca in the fifteenth century. When Johor eventually emerged to replace Aceh as the center of the Malay world (*alam Melayu*) in the late seventeenth century, it adopted the *nobat* and other court customs of the Malacca period as well as the Muslim arts and customs that had been instituted by Aceh's Malay sultanate as symbols of Malay identity. Indragiri's royal descendants claimed that their *nobat* was a gift from Johor in the seventeenth century, but that the instruments were maintained and if necessary remade by their loyal Suku Mamak (Orang Terasing) followers. For centuries Suku Mamak men had been the king's favored musicians and most loyal servants, who assisted at ceremonies and still came to visit on special occasions such as the Muslim holy day of Idulfitri. As we discovered on our visit to Rengat, the royal descendants still treasure their hardy set of antique *nobat* drums, having lost the set's oboes and other instrumental components. However, on our visits to Siak and the museum in Tanjung Pinang in the 1980s, we saw the wind and percussion instruments of similar complete *nobat* orchestras of the former Siak and Riau/Lingga sultanates.[6]

The Malay sultans in Sumatra lost their legitimacy when Indonesia declared its independence in 1945. However, some of the royal descendants secretly kept their regalia, including in some cases the remnants of their *nobat* orchestras (e.g., Langkat and Asahan in east Sumatra). Under President Suharto's regime (1965–98), descendants of the royal houses were allowed openly to seek funding to rebuild their palaces and display their regalia and other possessions to tourists, though in Riau, only Siak Sri Indrapura managed to do so. In the twenty-first century, the descendants of Indonesia's sultans have been lobbying for power; and in 2008 a Council of Sultans with a political agenda was founded.

UPSTREAM MINANGKABAU
Music to Capture Tigers By

Associated with a veneration for the ancestors and spirits of nature, the repertory of tiger-capturing songs (*dendang marindu harimau,* or *dendang manangkok harimau*) belongs to the most evocative of the traditional vocal music (*dendang*) of the Minangkabau highlands. Singing with great respect for the tiger in freely ornamented chant-like melodic settings of beautiful poetry, and accompanied by an imitative but elaborately ornamented flute part in a prolonged series of tiger-capturing rituals, the lead shaman renders the basic melodic idea of a song without any essential changes lest the magic power of the song be lost, as tradition holds it would be if the tiger cannot immediately recognize it. On the one hand, tradition holds that each song's essential poetic and melodic ideas have remained the same over the generations. On the other hand, tradition requires that the shamans who sing and play it improvise to produce a creatively varied yet supremely calm rendition of its fixed musical-poetic ideas for each performance.

There is a long-standing conflict between nominal and devout Muslims in the area over such matters as tiger-capturing songs and other shamanic activities. Nominal Muslims immersed in tradition have needed to adapt their ancient customs to the requirements of the Muslim era, in which many devout religious leaders and their followers have demanded strict obedience to the religious tenets of Islam. Little is known as to the exact dates of the period of Minangkabau conversion to Islam, but it possibly occurred during the period of Acehnese domination of the coast in the late sixteenth and early seventeenth centuries, following Minangkabau's Hindu-Buddhist era (ca. ninth to fifteenth centuries).

Before Minangkabau adopted Hindu-Buddhist concepts, nature- and ancestral-spirit belief pervaded its musical arts. For example, the *pancak silek* (I. *pencak silat*) martial art tradition encapsulated the belief in tiger spirits, with the *raja macan* (king of tigers) serving as its patron. Vestiges of these beliefs remain to this day among the isolated Suku Mamak people, who live in the forests south of Rengat in neighboring mainland Riau, where every martial art lesson begins with evoking one or several tiger spirits (Barendregt 1995, 117–18).

ART OF THE SHAMAN

The art of the shaman (*ilmu pawang*) is still a potent force in many Minangkabau villages. Black magic is practiced by the *guna-guna* ("black" shamans) in some areas, despite the fact that it is banned. It is generally conceded by believers that black magic is more powerful than white magic, and that black magic needs to be used only as a last resort. "Black" shamans are sometimes employed to use their magic in revenge against an enemy or to force someone to fall in love with a client. It is forbidden for anyone to hear, much less to record, songs of black magic, because of their potency and the likelihood that the magic will harm the listener. Moreover, the practitioners of black magic try to keep their activities secret, for fear of recrimination.

There are several grades of shaman. For example, a *pawang dabuih* who presides at a mystical *dabuih* (I. *dabus*) performance is a man of great religious strength with a developed ability for Sufi-style religious concentration, but he is skilled in the arts of white magic only. Special crocodile shamans (*pawang muara*) are employed to capture crocodiles, and snake shamans (*pawang ular*) capture snakes. But the most powerful shaman of them all is the *pawang manangkok harimau*, a gifted person who has already mastered the arts of black and white magic and who then learns from another such shaman (often his father) the supreme art of capturing the king or queen of the jungle—the tiger.

Such a shaman is greatly respected in rural communities as a figure of spiritual strength, extraordinary ability, personal bravery, and fortitude. Usually he is an expert player on the *saluang* (a long bamboo flute) and is an accomplished singer, able to improvise melodic variations for hours, an entire night, or a succession of many nights (see fig. 2.1). Sometimes he will play nightly for months on end. Like all Minangkabau specialist *pantun* singers (*tukang pantun*), he must be able to remember the poetic texts of thousands of *pantun* and sing them in an improvisational manner, with melodic ornamentation.[1]

Figure 2.1 A *pawang* singing accompanied by *saluang* music played by his son, who is also a *pawang* (shaman), Nagari Panyakalan, 1972

Like most other Minangkabau men, the shaman must also be trained in the art of self-defense (Mi. *pancak silek*). A tiger-capturing shaman in particular must have complete mastery of the art, since he may have to use it when he encounters a tiger far away from human contact.

Not surprisingly, only a few men, and even fewer women, achieve the status of *pawang manangkok harimau*. During our visit in 1972 in the district of Solok, for example, there were only two such shamans. Their services were in demand all over the *darek* (hinterland) including, on occasion, as far afield as the east Jambi coast.

There were many more tigers in Sumatra during the early part of the nineteenth century than now. William Marsden, secretary for English possession in Sumatra,

Figure 2.2 An *aluambek* (self-defense-based) dance on a loosely-strung floor in Pariaman, 1972

wrote in *The History of Sumatra* (first published in 1783), "The number of people annually slain by these rapacious tyrants of the woods, is almost incredible. I have known instances of whole villages being depopulated by them" (Marsden [1811] 1966, 184–85). He further noted, "The size and strength of the species (of tiger) which prevailed on this island are prodigious. They are said to break, with a stroke of their fore paw, the leg of a horse or a buffalo; and the largest prey they kill is without difficulty dragged by them into the woods" (Marsden [1811] 1966, 185).

A tiger may be killed only if she or he is found to be guilty of having eaten a human being or an animal. There is evidence in mythology that the Minangkabau people have held the tiger family, including the tiger's relative, the cat, in great respect. There is, indeed, an aura of ancestor veneration around the Minangkabau tiger. A tigress is the legendary female ancestor of the people of Agam, one of the three original districts (*Iuhak nan tigo*) of the Minangkabau heartland. Popular legend relates that Sri Maharajo Dirajo, the first of the three ancestral kings, arranged marriages with animals from various parts of Minangkabau, and the present inhabitants are said to be the offspring. According to one version of the legend as recounted by P. E. de Josselin de Jong (1951, 99), the inhabitants of Agam district are the descendants of the king and a tigress (*harimau Campu*), whereas the people of Lima Puluh Kota are descendants of a the king and a cat (*kucieng Siam*), while the people of Tanah Datar (including those living in the Solok area) are descendants of the king and a dog (*anjieng Moalam*).

CAPTURED WITH SONG AND RESPECT

The tiger and tigress are regarded as the king and queen of uninhabited jungle areas, while man is the king of settled areas. Tigers are differentiated by the shamans not only according to sex but also according to humanly attributed moral qualities, as referred to by their poetic song texts. If a tigress "trespasses" from her area into the rightful domain of man and consumes an animal or a human being, she is said to have committed a sin (*salah*), and the penalty is death. Her "guilt feelings" are played upon by the shaman before her capture. The shaman eventually uses moral pressure to "force" the tigress to enter a cage set for her in the jungle. He may even entice her with sexual references, mentioning for example that her lover has already bowed to the shaman's will and entered the cage, and asks why she does not follow him.

Alternatively, the tigress may be addressed respectfully in such terms as "Rudiah, rich widow" and be asked, in song, to step onto a beautiful tiger island (a metaphor for "tiger cage") to rejoin her late husband. The shaman treats her as if she possesses the emotions and motivations of a human being. The tigress is not captured and killed in a brutal way. If the shaman needs to defend himself physically from the tiger, he opposes her with the sacrosanct and elegant art of self-defense. Moreover, the songs he sings to entice the tiger into the cage belong to the sweetest and most classical of the Minangkabau tradition, accompanied by the gentle, soft-toned bamboo flute *saluang*. Only to a crazed tiger may one speak roughly.

The beautiful vocal melodies, set to elegant poetic meters and containing delicate allusions, metaphors, and polite points of etiquette, are in keeping with the indigenous religious Minangkabau belief that the character of the tiger family is one of diplomacy and elegant cunning. This anthropomorphic attribution to the tiger of moral feelings, sexual love, and artistic feelings is an ancient practice.

Moral feelings are also attributed by a *pawang ular* to snakes that have "sinned." If such a shaman finds a snake in the forest, he stands calmly alongside it and, in ceremonial song, commands the snake to remain still if it is guilty, while the shaman goes away. Several hours later, the shaman returns. If the shaman finds that the snake has not moved, he deems it guilty and expects no resistance from the snake as he kills it. If, on the other hand, the snake has departed by the time he returns (that is, the snake has not been seemingly transfixed to the spot in guilt), the snake is believed never to have been responsible for harming a human being or a domestic animal. Snakes, like tigers, are highly respected in Minangkabau tradition. No one is allowed to accompany shamans on their professional expeditions into the jungle. However, I was told what happens on such expeditions by two shamans, a father and son from Nagari Panyakalan: Kecamatan Kubung and Kabupaten Solok, who are known as Djabur Datuk Radjo Taduang and Haliman Datuk Radjo Campo (fig. 2.1). The son, Haliman, who claims to have captured over a hundred tigers, said he learned his craft from his father, who said he had caught more tigers than he could remember.

It sometimes happens that a roaming tiger may trespass into human territory and consume a child, an adult, or a domestic animal. There are many "good" tigers who never make such an error, but tigers who have sinned, like everyone else, must pay the penalty. A village plagued by a roaming tiger may, through its council, decide to employ the services of a tiger-capturing shaman, who is usually paid a comparatively large fee for his services (e.g., 100,000 rupiah, worth approximately $US270 in 2012). It may take only a night or two to capture a tiger, but in difficult cases it may take up to nine months. If a tiger cannot be caught, this indicates that it never committed the sin of eating a human being or an animal and thus can never be made to feel guilty.

The shamans always work in pairs. They bring a tiger cage into the forest at night, to an area the tiger has been known to frequent. A young goat or lamb is tied as bait inside the cage, and the door is left open. Night after night, the shamans sit near the cage waiting for the tiger to come. Each night, they begin their watch by burning incense and singing prayers in Arabic, asking for Allah's blessing. The prayers are interspersed with chant-like songs (strings of repeated tones on the main tone and the fourth above) in the Minangkabau language, describing the reasons for their having to capture the tiger.

According to one song we heard, a tiger had eaten several nieces and nephews of a villager called Harmaini, and it was therefore urgent that it be caught. In microtonal ornamented melodies marked by a strongly descending direction of melodic movement, and ending on a string of repeated tones on the lowest note of the range, the older shaman sang prayers in Arabic alternating with Minangkabau, requesting help and strength from Allah and the angels to perform his difficult task (audio example 2.1; see appendix 6, p. 383).

After a few minutes, the older shaman began to sing classical tiger-capturing songs in a subdued, calm voice, in slow tempo and relatively free rhythm, with Bp. Haliman playing a countermelody on the four-holed end-blown *saluang darek*, which he played sideways (see music example 2.1). The surface of the bamboo flute, which was seventy centimeters long and two centimeters in diameter, had been burned in a pattern to look like tiger skin (Mi. *adok*). Sometimes the two men performed pieces of "flute with song" (*saluang jo dendang*) in unison. They shut their eyes and hid their faces with *salawek dulang* (brass trays) as they performed, in order to help them concentrate as they sought supernatural assistance in their task.

The long series of songs performed for us comprised only the least potent *dendang* that are sung night after night in the tiger-capturing process. There are eleven grades of *dendang*, each of which possesses progressively more powerful degrees of magic. If the first few grades of songs fail to capture the tiger, then more-potent songs are sung. We were not allowed to hear the more potent of the songs because, we were told, they were powerful enough to prevent us from ever leaving the area.

When we first requested permission from these two famous *pawang* to record their tiger-capturing songs, they were loath to discuss the matter at all. They said they feared for their safety, as well as ours, because any knowledge of their songs, talismans, and practices could be dangerous. We were not allowed to hear the magical and very powerful sound of the buzzing disk—which they swing on occasions between the more powerful grades of songs—but only permitted to see it. Eventually, they agreed to show us some of their other talismans, but only briefly, and allowed us to record some of the songs.

If a tigress appears during one of the shaman's sojourns in the forest, the shamans sing highly potent songs of black magic (*dendang jimat*). They brandish their talismans and, if necessary, fight her or simply frighten her with a display of the art of self-defense. The movements of this version of the art, which is called *silek harimau* (Mi., "tiger self-defense") are the most violent, dangerous, and *kasar* (rough) of all forms of Minangkabau *silek*.[2] The most powerful talismans used include the protruding tooth of a tiger (the *sayiyang*), which is said to be as strong as a diamond and very useful in combat. Another potent talisman is a piece of a human skull, particularly that of a deceased little boy.

The buzzing disk is the most potent talisman of all. It consists of a piece of human skull threaded on to a string and induces the tiger to enter the cage. Tradition has it that a tiger dies as soon as the string of the buzzing disk has been worn out through swinging. It is believed that anyone who hears the sound of a buzzing disk, including a tiger, will go mad, and when it is in this state the shaman is in complete control. If the tiger enters the cage when the shamans are not there, they know immediately, they say, and go back to shut the door on the tiger.

It is said that the tiger never eats a live lamb or goat tied in the cage as bait. For one thing, the tiger becomes crazed with guilt by the time it enters the cage; for another, it is by then too terrified to feel the pangs of hunger. After the tiger has been killed, the shamans generally sell the tiger skin or stuff it for sale at a good price.

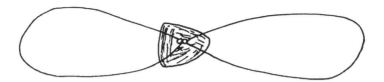

Figure 2.3 A sketch of a Minangkabau buzzing disk (*manggasieng*)

Bp. Djabur told us that shamans would not dare to alter the songs for fear they would lose their potency and that probably no changes had been made to the songs for generations. Indeed, it is believed that only the faithful rendition of the songs can compel a guilty tiger to enter a cage. Although some degree of improvisatory freedom is allowed in performance, no basic changes may be made in music or text.

Tiger-capturing songs are notable for their lack of passion, indeed, their calmness and quietness. This is partly because of their spiritual purpose, which is to create an atmosphere conducive to contact with the benevolent supernatural. Loud singing may attract dangerous spiritual forces and frighten away beneficial ones, whereas beautiful, soft singing attracts the good forces to help in a difficult situation, such as having to capture a dangerous, man-eating tiger.

Many classical Minangkabau songs have a melancholy character and introspective texts and are performed in a soft, subtle manner. Sad, slow songs are called *sadiah* (compare with I. *sedih* meaning "sad"), whereas happy, fast songs are called *gembira bagurau* (Mi., "happy," or compare with Mi. *bagurau* meaning "joking" at a *malam bagurau*, "evening of joking"). There are several categories of sad songs, for instance those dealing with the traditional Minangkabau practice of young men going *marantau* (Mi.), that is, leaving home and seeking fortune in a faraway place. According to an ancient Minangkabau custom, a professional mourner is engaged for a funeral; she cries uncontrollably and works herself into an extremely emotional state as she sings the saddest of songs: *ratok manangisi kamatian* (Mi., "crying songs for a death"). This custom, however, is now banned by Islamic law. Sad songs are also sung by palm sugar collectors, who believe that the more tears they shed as they collect the sweet liquid from the *arenga* palm tree, the greater their harvest. The songs they sing are called *ratok manangisi anau* (Mi., "crying songs for a palm tree"). *Ratok* is the general term for extremely sad songs, sung while crying; it compares with *ratap* in Indonesian, meaning "lament." Many *dendang* texts deal with sad events, unfortunate love experiences, loneliness, and other melancholy subjects.

Tiger-capturing songs, which are set to poetic texts (*syair, pantun*, and others) that belong to this expressive, classical vocal tradition, are often particularly beautiful and imaginative. The songs are accompanied by one of the most widespread and popular of all Minangkabau instruments, the sweet-toned *saluang*, a long open-ended, end-blown bamboo flute, with four, five, or six finger holes. The *saluang* is played sideways because the instrument is longer than an arm's length and the player's breath can be used more economically when the instrument is played in this position.

The player produces a continuous sound by circular breathing, performing vibrato by continuously pushing the bamboo tube to and from the mouth. In the example reproduced (music example 2.1), the *saluang* plays a countermelody, to the melody of

Music example 2.1 Transcription of the first of a cycle of tiger-capturing songs (*dendang marindu harimau*)

the singer, and fills in pauses between phrases and lines of the song text with melody. Its dynamic swells and abatements are often independent of the vocal dynamics.

The two shamans perform the song in relatively free rhythm (*dendang bebas*) in a basically quadruple meter at a slow tempo. With a fairly moderate degree of rhythmic, intonational, and ornamental freedom, the singer improvises a continuously variable melodic line set to the continuously changing poetic text. He improvises on a simple musical idea that he imaginatively transforms into a unique series of renditions.

The crux of this basic musical idea is the irregular overlap and interplay of two main tones in the vocal part and, simultaneously, two other main tones on the *saluang*. Whereas the *saluang* uses a total of five pitch levels of which tones 5 and 3 are most important, the vocal part uses only four with a variably pitched lowest tone, emphasizing tones 6 and 2, Interestingly enough, my Minangkabau informants insisted that only two tones were used by the *saluang* player. By not mentioning the other three tones, they implied that they lacked tonal importance.

On the basis of musical analysis as well as on the advice of informants, then, the two main tones in the vocal part form a horizontal interval of a fourth, while the two main tones in the *saluang* part produce a horizontal interval of approximately a (minor) third. The two main vertical intervals, on the other hand, formed by combining the vocal and the *saluang* parts, are the fourth and fifth, as can be seen from the skeletal outline, which consists of the prolonged notes only:

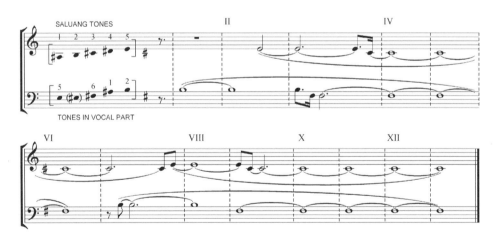

Music example 2.2 Skeletal outline of music example 2.1

The structural importance of these two sets of main pitch levels is underlined by the fact that they always constitute the final and highest tones in each part. The long duration of the final fifth endorses its prominence as the most important vertical interval, but the imitative entries by the *saluang* in bars II and VII emphasize the interval of the fourth.

Within these main intervallic relationships of alternating fourths and fifths, the variable nature of each performance results in the occurrence of thirds and sixths, but even an occasional seventh and a second too, due to the melodic ornamentation occurring simultaneously in the two parts and the rhythmic delay between the overlapping parts.

Integral to the melodic style and improvisational technique of the performers is the *ola-ola* (ornamentation, such as melodic turns) and vibrato.[3] Vibrato in the vocal part is of a small amplitude, lightly applied, and reserved mostly for notes of prolonged time values. Such prolonged notes always occur on one of the four main pitch levels, a fact that further endorses their importance. The ornaments used include an acciaccatura-like feature, turns, shakes, and anticipatory tone repeats, all lending a quality of subtlety and continual variability to the performance.

In all the variants, the melodic line of the *saluang* is more highly ornamented than the vocal line. The vocal part, on the other hand, contains more tonal repetition (61 percent) than the *saluang* part (33 percent), thereby having more limited opportunity for melodic ornamentation. A degree of chant-like tonal repetition in the vocal part and a higher degree of melodic variability in the instrumental part is also in accordance with the prevalent view that the texts must be comprehensible to the audience. A *tukang pantun* (a singer of *pantun* quatrains) is admired for his musical ability but esteemed even more for his ability to remember and improvise large quantities of fascinating poetry.

||||

The character of the tiger-capturing procedure, with the exception of the Islamic prayers at the beginning, suggests that it originated from indigenous religious beliefs and practices of ancient origins, imbued with a mystical respect for nature (especially the tiger) and the spirits, and containing an element of animal-ancestor veneration. The details of its mysticism are a very serious matter to believers. This complex process of tiger-capture by means of *ilmu batin*, calm improvisational song, the art of self-defense, and baiting a cage is simply the most viable way of solving a difficult problem. And the fact that the music is essentially unchanging has both a mystical and a practical function that does not detract from its beauty.

Perhaps there is a large degree of truth in the claim that the shaman's highly developed gift for singing poetry is an essential part of the impressive act of capturing dangerous tigers. There is possibly a twofold relationship between the skill of the musical performers and the capture of the tiger, namely, the calming effect the music may have on the tiger and the calming influence of the music on the nerves of the *pawang* in the process of capturing the tiger. Possibly no one but the shaman will ever know for sure whether—or to what extent—the music really has the effect of relaxing and taming the tiger and inducing it to enter the cage, since no one is allowed to accompany the shamans into the forest on their tiger-capturing expeditions.

That the music has a psychological effect on the shamans is more certain. These calmly beautiful, subtly ornamented songs set to imaginative poetic texts and accompanied by the sweet sound of the *saluang* are eminently suitable for their function of settling the nerves and giving moral and psychological strength to those skilled artists, the shamans who work for long nocturnal periods in the forests of the Minangkabau.

POSTSCRIPT

Unfortunately, despite the careful capturing procedure and moral judgment of the Minangkabau people, the Sumatran tiger is seriously threatened. According to the World Wildlife Fund in 2007, only a few hundred remain in the dense forests, which are fast being cleared. The fund has organized an international campaign to finance conservation of the tiger throughout Asia (its habitat ranges from Siberia to Sumatra) and is cooperating with the Indonesian government to provide sanctuaries for both the Sumatran and the Javanese tigers. The Bali tiger seems to have disappeared altogether. One of the few areas where Sumatran tigers and other endangered species are protected is the World Heritage Site in Aceh on the tip of Sumatra, but it has already lost 20 percent of its forest cover to illegal agriculture, according to the World Wildlife Fund.[4]

"DENDANG MARINDU HARIMAU" (SONG TO ATTRACT A TIGER)

O buai buai buai O buai yo harimau buai	Sway, sway, O tiger sway,
Maudaki ka bukik oi	While climbing the mountain,
Kok nan gadang yo harimau oi	O tiger, you are great,
Kok dipikia tanah nan ka dibari ka harimau	Mind how much land has been given to you, tiger.
Disinan kayu nan kami katuakkan	There, where the branches are twisted,
Sinan janji badapati	Is the place where our vow will be fulfilled,
Ho dibukik kayu gadang harimau ye	There on the hill where a tall tree grows, O tiger.

Ho kok tidak di ulang-ulang ye
Dimano kiambang kikaji harimau ye
Kok tidak utang dibaia ye
Dimano kok ka dibarikan harimau e

O lenggang biduak lenggang papan
Lenggang dikujua nak nyo hampai
    harimau
Ye kok kami malapeh buah pitanggang
    harimau
Tanggang duduk, tanggang makan,
    tanggang lalok,
Harimau juo nan kami tanggang ye

O lah rampak karambia bagai

Luruik sabatang ateh muru

Balun tampak janjilah sampai
Harimau lah patuik pulo, harimau
    kanai parindu

O karambia diateh munggu
Runduah jalan ka Malako
Untuang dahulu balun babai ye
Harimau kini jan dianduah pulo ye

Oi, sibadaruah sibadarang e
Sibadaranglah ka pulau harimau ye
Oi pulau cantiak si mangganih si
    manggeong ye
Si mangganih dongok pandai e

Ondeh Rudiah rando kayo
Dino kok lai talari kini-kini
Marilah datang malam-malam
Kadalam pinjangaro

O . . . anak sinantun sigunantun
Taringaik matonyo putiah harimau

Hati kok matohharikan . . .

O duduk harimau lah gilo

A place not often visited,
Where the plants grow, tiger,
If the debt is not paid this time
Where do you want to surrender, tiger?

The boat sways, so do its planks,
The sways are quieter now, tiger.

We are using our magic rites, tiger,

Without sitting, eating, or sleeping,

It is you, tiger, whom we want to trick.

The coconut tree has coconuts of
    many sizes,
They all fell down into (a bowl of)
    sour milk,
Our vow has not yet been fulfilled,
It is high time (you) tiger submit and
    be caught.

The coconuts are on the earth heap,
Many people take a trip to Malacca,
The debt has not yet been paid,
Don't put off the capture until
    tomorrow.

O spirits of the charm,
Go to the tiger island,
That beautiful island, full of spirits,

Spirits who look silly but are really
    very clever.

O Rudiah, rich widow,
If you can, run away now,
Then come at night
Into the cage.

O child, whoever you are,
Remember the whites of the tigress's
    eyes,
They warm your heart.

O tigress, you are staggering when you
    sit down,

Tagak harimau lah gilo	You are staggering when you stand up,
Balan mamandang harimau ka pinjangaro	Even before we see you enter the cage, tiger.
Harimau lah gilo	The tigress is already crazy,
Tariah diparang sibilang deh	As if her front teeth were cut with a knife
Kanai miang manggalagek yo	And gripped by a wire, itching hot.
Ao ka tenggang dayo lai	What else can she do?
Tirai kulambu lah tabaka	The mosquito net has been lifted,
Aruah kami kuruang dalam pinjangaro	Her soul has already been caught in the cage,
Lautan sajo yo bakuliliang	Only the sea surrounds her.
Apo ka tenggang dayo lai	What else can be done?
O si gampak si gampo rayo	O people in the whole wide world,
Anak si Tuleh bangso dalam	Son of Tuleh, an aristocrat,
Nak kami turunkan doa kami dari siko	We are sending our prayers from here,
Kami arak harimau pinjaro tangah malam	We are sending the tigress into her cage in the dead of night.
O buai buai . . . si harimau buai	O sway, sway, tigress sway,
Hangoh padi, hangoh pandan e	Look at the rice field, look at the *pandan* tree,
Hangoh kapayo tumbuhyno	Look, they are growing near the pool,
Inyo angoh badan angoh lah tabantang tubunhnyo harimau	Look at the tigress's body spreading over the ground.
Nampak di lende-lende hatinyo	Seen in the membrane of her heart,
Angah ditangah matohari	Breathing under hot sun rays,
Mati nampiak mati mangarabang harimau	The dying tigress rejecting death,
Bakisai tulang jo urek	The bones are separated from the muscles.
Abih urek bapaluik tulang	Her muscles no longer cover her bones,
Abih dagiang bakariengi darah	Her flesh runs out of blood,
Hilang karano rupo jo tampan pupuah balangnyo	Her features are lost, the stripes of her skin are fading away.
Angkekkan kuku, bacukkan tariang sabalun utang dibaiya	Raise your claws, tiger, bite before the debt is paid.

ACKNOWLEDGMENTS

I am grateful to the Wedana (administrative head) of Solok, Bp. Zacharia Latief Datuk Nanbatuah; the head of the Education and Culture office in Solok, Bp. Amzar

Shafei BA; and Bp. Boestanoel Arifin Adam, director of the Konservatori Karawitan (Conservatorium) in Padang Panjang, for helping us contact artists in the Solok area during our fieldwork in 1972. I also wish to thank Bp. Purnama Raja Zakir and Ibu Fardia Zakir for help in transcribing and making free translations of the song texts. Above all I wish to thank the pair of tiger-capturing shamans, Bp. Djabur Datuak Radjo Taduang and Bp. Haliman Datuak Radjo Campo, for allowing us to record their performances and for their skill and patience in explaining the basis of their skills and procedures. In the 1970s their fame extended far and wide, even across to the province of Riau.

THE MINANGKABAU
SOUTH COAST
Home of the Mermaid and
the Earth Goddess

To many West Sumatrans and observers, the Minangkabau south coast (Mi. *pasisia salatan*) is a cultural backwater of the much better known heartland (Mi. *darék*; I. *darat*), with its historical palace at Pagaruyung.[1] As this chapter aims to show, however, the people of the south coast have their own distinctive heritage of rituals, music, dance, and epic storytelling based on their connection to the sea as well as the land, as opposed to the single environmental focus of the land-bound *darék*, and they too had a main palace, at Indrapura.

The people are a mix of Malay-speaking, west-coast Sumatran traders and fisherfolk, on the one hand, and descendant of immigrant, *darék* Minangkabau-speaking farmers, on the other. Over the centuries young men in the *darék* were encouraged to seek their fortunes in the coastal *rantau* area (Mi. "the area abroad," Naim 1973), and many never returned to their *kampuang halaman* (Mi. "original village"), as is recounted in many sad songs and stories. Malay-speaking people also migrated up and down Sumatra's west coast, with some settling in the south coastal area of Minangkabau. Both the coastal and the upstream peoples brought their artistic genres with them.

Whatever their ancestry, south-coast dwellers believe fiercely in their cultural identity separate from that of the hinterland. Their dual focus on the sea and the land is reflected in their two main legends: one about the mermaid Sikambang, performed along most of Sumatra's west coast, and the other about the Earth Goddess, Bundo Kanduang, performed both in the heartland and on the south coast. The people in the *darék* claim that Bundo Kanduang was born in the heartland, but south-coast dwellers believe she was born near the main former court of Indrapura at Lunang on the south coast, and that she is continually reincarnated in the body of a mystically gifted woman who lives in Lunang.[2] The Bundo Kanduang legend is also known as "Cindua Mato," the name of a commoner who became a heroic adjutant of Bundo Kanduang's son, the first monarch of the Minangkabau heartland (*luhak nan tigo*), and eventually replaced him as the legendary first king of both the *darék* and the *pasisia salatan* (mi.), and *utara* (south and north coast) that is, of all Minangkabau.

Another important legend in the southernmost part of the south coast and the north-coast Bengkulu province is "Malin Deman," about the Seven Angels who descended to earth and accidentally left their youngest sister there without her wings, so she was unable to return to heaven. She married a mortal and gave birth to a son before escaping back to heaven. (For other versions of this legend, see chaps. 7, 12, and 14.)

In addition to the south coast's shamanic arts, including the rain-rejection (*mono-lak hujan*) ritual, the overwhelmingly Muslim population of the coastal areas practices a range of locally developed Muslim devotional genres (*kesenian Islami*), including several *dikia* (*zikir*)-based genres. They are usually performed at boys' circumcisions (*sunat rasul*), boys' and girls' celebrations on mastering the recitation of the Qur'an (*tamat Qur'an*), farewells to pilgrims going on the *hajj*, and welcomes on their return, accompanied in each case by a devotional frame drum–playing procession (*arak-arakan mangaji*) or session. Both the traditional religious and the Muslim genres are performed at ceremonies presided over by the traditional elders (*niniak mamak*) and the *ulama*, such as weddings, a baby's first haircut, a ritual to appoint an elder, and celebrations of Muslim holy days. They also developed a local version of Malay vocal music with violin and percussion accompaniment known as *gamad* or *gamaik*, and popular music with Minangkabau song texts called *pop Minang*.

This chapter, however, focuses mainly on the *asali* (Mi. "original, authentic") genres, reserving discussion of the Muslim genres for chapter 5. First, the chapter surveys the music-related history of the former palaces and the common people on the south coast. It then describes the shamanic rituals and dances; the bardic art of *kaba* (epic) performance; the songs and song-dances attached to the three main legends: "Sikambang," "Bundo Kanduang"/"Cindua Mato," and the "Seven Angels"/"Malin Deman"; some other dances, and finally the south coast's main musical instruments and ensembles. Most dances are accompanied by the drum-oboe (*gandang-sarunai*) ensemble, but the Sikambang song-dances are accompanied by a violin (*biola*) and frame-drum ensemble in a hybrid Malay-Portuguese style, the roots of which date back to Portuguese-ruled Malacca in the sixteenth century, whence it spread to coastal Sumatran and other Malay areas (see chap. 10).[3]

HISTORY OF THE PERFORMING ARTS IN THE FORMER
SOUTH-COAST PALACES AND VILLAGE COMMUNITIES

Minangkabau's south coast divides into two parts: the northern area between Painan and Sirantih, with its two former courts at Tarusan and Painan, and the southern area between Indrapura and Muko-muko, with its former palaces at Indrapura and Muko-muko (the latter located in north-coastal Bengkulu province, map 3.1). The harbor towns of Indrapura and Painan were among the eight outposts (*bab*) of the main Minangkabau kingdom of Pagaruyung (Loeb [1935] 1972, 98), the others being the seaports of Padang, Pariaman, and Bengkulu on Sumatra's west coast, and Jambi, Indragiri, and Siak on the east coast (ibid.). The ruins of the palace at Indrapura still exist in coastal Muaro Sangkai village, and a subsidiary of the palace is maintained in the village of Lunang, near the location of the royal graves. The remnants of a stone fortress said to have been built by Portuguese soldiers in the sixteenth century can be seen near Painan, but other material remains of the past have been lost, as has detailed knowledge of the Painan and Tarusan palace arts.[4]

Descendants of the Indrapura palace—Pandekar Sutan Sabarudin and Tengku Regen of Kp Muara Sakai—told me in 1986 what they knew about the arts that were practiced in the Indrapura palace. They included the coastal Sumatran Malay arts based on the Sikambang legend, on the one hand, and the Minangkabau song-

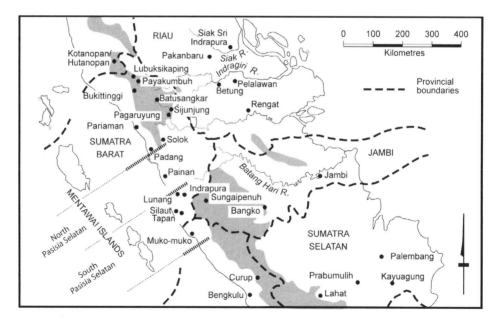

Map 3.1 The province of West Sumatra, after Foley 1981

dances based on the Bundo Kanduang legend, on the other. Bards, musicians, and dancers from far and wide came to perform whenever the reigning king held a royal celebration. As in other Malay palaces, the people were expected to contribute their dance and music performances in return for the mystical blessings bestowed on them through their temporary proximity to the king. Although village artists were not allowed to perform on the palace grounds, they provided a *ramai* (I., "lively") atmosphere by performing their music and dance and setting up food stalls just outside it. They presented male dances and *pancak silek* art-of-self-defense displays, all-night bardic performances, Sikambang couples song-dances with violin and frame-drum accompaniment, Seven Angel *gandai* dances by women with *gandang-sarunai* (frame drum-oboe) accompaniment, magic and humorous dances by men, and various mixed-gender dances associated with the agricultural cycle.

Forty-one generations of kings reigned until the Indrapura kingdom's demise in the mid-twentieth century. The thirty-seventh king, Raja Marabaki Gele Tuanku Belindung, who died in 1890, contributed most to the performing arts. A *biduan* (palace servant) named Sikambang, who was a fine dancer, chose some of the local village dances such as the plate dance (*tari piriang*) to be refined (Mi. *diperhaluih*) for princesses to dance and designed some beautiful dance costumes. From the Sikambang legend, she developed the "Sikambang Air Tejun" ("Waterfall Sikambang") dance and the "Sikambang Air Haji" ("Sikambang Water Pilgrim") dance, which were accompanied by a solo vocalist singing Malay *pantun* verses, a *biola*, and pair of frame drums (*gandang*). The male palace dances were developed by Sikambang's husband, Silameh, including an elaborate palace version of the *silek*-based *dampieng* (Mi.) dance prepared in a bridegroom's procession and the circular *galombang* (Mi. "wave") dance performed on arrival at the wedding celebrations. Twelve male dancers performed local art-of-self-defense-based dance movements while rhythmically clapping on the material of their baggy trousers between their legs and periodically singing in chorus.

The Indrapura palace's descendants also claimed that the south coast's other main legendary hero, Malin Deman, was born near Lunang and died there. He married the youngest of the legendary Seven Angels. Songs and dances based on the Seven Angels and the Bundo Kanduang/Cindua Mato legends are widely performed in and around Indrapura, Lunang, Silaut, and Tapan, where they resemble the genres of the northernmost *kabupaten* of Bengkulu province, especially around Muko-muko, Rejang Pasisir, and the south coast diaspora in Solok (audio example 3.1).

Because the version of the Cindua Mato legend helps to clarify the south coast's relationship with the dominant Minangkabau *darék* court in Pagaruyung, I shall outline it below. The following is based on an account by *kaba* performer Bp. Aslim of Pasar Salido:

> In the beginning the primal Queen of Minangkabau, Bundo Kanduang, gave virginal birth to her son Dang Tuanku, the substitute for Allah on earth and the primal Minangkabau king who ruled the *luhak nan tigo* hinterland at Pagaruyung with his mother. As it happened, he shared his soul with a poor, uneducated commoner called Cindua Mato, who agreed to carry out most of his wishes, including capturing his future wife, Puti Bungsu, from a distant kingdom. This led to war with Dang Tuanku's rival in love, Raja Imbang Jayo, whom he fought and eventually had executed. When Dang Tuanku died, Cindua Mato went into exile on the south coast at Indrapura. Eventually he returned to Pagaruyung but found he had to kill Imbang Jayo's father, who was seeking revenge for his son's death. The way was then open for Cindua Mato to become the first king of the hinterland and the coastal areas of Minangkabau. Meanwhile (according to the legend's *darék* version), the three other members of the royal family had either ascended to seventh heaven or (according to the south-coastal version) had fled by river and sea boat to Lunang, near Indrapura, where they died and were buried, leaving the son and daughter of Dang Tuanku and Puti Bungsu (Sutan Alam Dunia and Puti Sri Dunia) to rule the Minangkabau and Rao kingdoms respectively. The Sutan married a princess from Aceh but soon divorced her without paying the full bride-wealth, whereupon the king of Aceh punished him by forcing him to surrender the coastal area of Minangkabau to Aceh. (Aceh actually took over the Minangkabau coastal trade outlets in the sixteenth century and is said to have helped Islamize the people in the early seventeenth century.)

The last part of this account of the legend also captures the south-coastal people's ambivalence toward the Acehnese, whom they despised as overlords but respected for their knowledge of Islam, missionary zeal, and some devotional music and dance that they say they learned from them.

SHAMANIC RITUAL ARTS

Besides the dances developed by commoners for palace use, the common people on the south coast have a tradition of shamanic ritual arts. They include the *rantak kudo* dance, which has given rise to many modern variants.

It is in villages like Kampuang Sungai Kuok, discussed below, that *dukun belian* (healing rite practitioners), *tegenai* (multipurpose shamans), and other kinds of shamans still practice the most intimate and personal of the pre-Muslim rituals and the associated music and dance forms. Despite the disapproval of the *ulama*, clients approach the shamans to use their white magic (Mi. *ilmu aluih*) or black magic skills (Mi. *ilmu sihir*) for particular purposes, such as attracting a lover, capturing a tiger, and solving family problems.[5] Such skills are also used to conduct rituals that include singing magically potent songs, reciting mantras, brandishing talismans (Ar. *azimat*), and playing potent instruments such as Jew's harps (*rinding*), ring-stop flutes (*saluang*, fig. 3.2), and bullroarers (*gasieng*).[6] Analysis of the melodic performance style of ten magic songs sung by local shamans indicates that they tend to use small half- and microtonal intervals, turns and other melodic ornamentation, stepwise melodic movement, and leaps of a fourth or a fifth within the usual range of a fourth or a fifth, rendered in a slow, introspective manner.

The buzzing disk (fig. 2.3, chap. 2) is one of the most powerful talismans used in magic rituals. It is believed to be possessed by an *ibilih* (Mi.; I. *iblis*), a spirit who lives in the center of the earth. Ideally it should be made from part of a hero's skull bone, preferably incised from his forehead seven days after his death, and into which a long circular piece of string is threaded through two holes. The player holds it taut and swirls it around swiftly for minutes on end, making a humming sound that is taboo because it can kill a victim, even a baby in the womb, at the behest of a mystically powerful shaman.

As in the *darék*, a village head may employ a pair of male shamans to catch a marauding tiger if it has killed one or more people or domestic animals. Traditionally, a trap is set for the tiger in its jungle haunt, and beautiful, calm songs are sung to the animal with *serdam* (ring or fipple flute) accompaniment, praising the tiger for its beauty and intelligence and inviting it to enter the cage to pay its debt to society for having committed the sin of eating a human being or an animal (chap. 2). The following is the text of a pantun sung by a shaman after capturing a tiger in Nagari Lagan on the south coast:

Lagan ketek Lagan gadlang	Small Lagan (village) to big Lagan
Dari ketek sampai gadlang	From small to large
Bandaraso anta nyo	Bring (it) to the madrasah
Untuang badan macan iko yo	Luckily, this is the corpse of the tiger

The first couplet mentions the remarkable growth of Lagan village over the lifetime of the elderly singer, and the second couplet the shaman's remarkable success in capturing and killing a marauding tiger and bringing it to the local madrasah (Muslim school) before it is brought to its burial place.

Bamboo flutes are associated with a wide range of magic practices, including attracting a lover and capturing dangerous animals, and they may also accompany nonshamanic songs of love or admonition or be played solo. Unlike their *darék* counterparts, south-coast shamans and other musicians like to play a short bamboo duct flute called *bansi* (I. *bangsi*), which is also used to accompany traditional solo singing and story-telling (see fig. 3.1).[7]

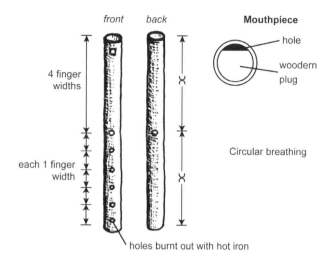

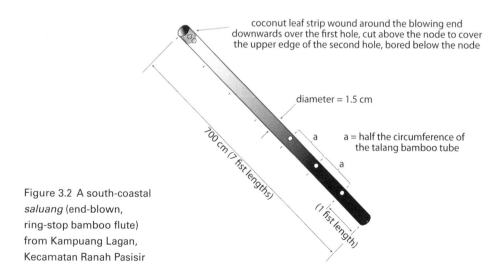

Figure 3.1 A *bansi* (bamboo duct flute) in Painan, showing the mouthpiece

Alternatively, they play a ring-stop bamboo flute (*saluang*) such as the one from Lagan village shown in figure 3.2, which is blown obliquely and has a complex mouthpiece "with a double sound orifice and external air duct" (Kaudern 1927, 243).[8] Like the longer *saluang* of the *darék*, the player of this type of *saluang* blows into it obliquely with his head held on a slant, so that his breath is directed diagonally into the tube and he can use the technique of circular breathing. In both *pasisia* and *darék*, the sound of the *saluang* is regarded as mystically potent and introspective, especially when combined with shamanic singing.

Figure 3.2 A south-coastal *saluang* (end-blown, ring-stop bamboo flute) from Kampuang Lagan, Kecamatan Ranah Pasisir

THE *GILO LUKAH* DANCE

One of the most popular of the south-coast shamanic dances is the *gilo lukah* (crazy fish trap) dance, which is performed in and around such towns as Painan, Pasarkuok, Buahbatung, Sirantih, Lakitan, and Balaiselasa. According to the shaman Bp. M. Noerdin of Kp Painan Timur, this divination dance originated in a hermit's hut in nearby Gunung Segirik and may be performed only in response to a formal request from a client, for example, if he wants to entice a reluctant girl to marry him or to know whether his son will pass an examination. In the former case, it is believed that if the procedures of the ritual are properly carried out, the couple will eventually marry, but if due process is not followed, the couple may go crazy or encounter other misfortunes.

In a *gilo lukah* séance in Kampuang Pasar Sirantih in 1986, a *dukun* (shaman) and his assistant dressed a fish trap to look like a woman.[9] Her "head" consisted of a dried pumpkin gourd with her face painted on it, and her fish-trap body was dressed in a *kain/kabaya* (wraparound skirt and long-sleeved blouse) with a *salendang* (Mi., "long shawl") around her neck. The shaman knelt and chanted a mantra based on four tones in the range of a fourth (C D E F, where F was the keynote), whereupon he and his assistant picked up the *gilo lukah* fish trap and moved it up and down rhythmically, entering a state of trance. Then it seemed as if a female spirit possessed the fish trap and forced it to move about violently and irregularly of its own accord. The bodies of the *dukun* and his assistant kept bobbing up and down as they tried vainly to hold the *gilo lukah* still, while members of the audience yelled out in fright or laughter whenever they found the *gilo lukah* performers' movements to be startling or funny. Eventually the *dukun* resumed his chanting, asked the spirit to answer his clients' queries, and passed on her response to them.

THE *RANTAK KUDO* DANCE

Along the Minangkabau coast until the late 1980s, it was common to mark a baby's death by poignant lament (Mi. *ratok*) singing and dancing. In the *darék*, on the other hand, a professional mourner sang laments for days and nights in the home of the deceased. In both areas the rituals provided therapy for the bereaved parents. Such rituals became rarer from the late 1980s onward, however, as cassette recordings of traditional and Muslim music increasingly replaced live performances at ritual events.

Apart from the Sikambang song-dances with violin and frame drum accompaniment (described below), the main coastal lament song-dance was the *rantak kudo*, accompanied by the dancers' rhythmic foot-stamping on the loosely strung floor boards of the traditional houses, or, if performed on the ground or a hard floor, their drum-rhythm equivalents. *Rantak* (Mi.; I. *serentak*) means "dancing in time to a drum rhythm," and *kudo* means "horse." The male dancers represented the deceased baby's father and his male relatives and friends. As some performers danced until they entered a state of trance, they were customarily overseen by a shaman (*dukun*), whose mystical power (*kasakten*) was symbolized by his headdress, made of horse skin.

A *rantak kudo* performance on a loosely strung floor (in Kampuang Laban, Salido, Kecamatan IV Jurai, near Painan) began with the lead vocalist singing a four-tone melody (on D E♭ F G) with a tight throat in free meter, while the lead dancer performed a *sambah* (bow) with his left foot stretched backward and the palms of his hands held together at chest level. As the singing continued, he stamped out a sparse rhythm that was also tapped out on the wooden body of a drum. He and his eight companions moved around the arena in diagonal and square formations performing an odd number (seven, nine, or eleven) of jerky movements called *kudo merentak* (lit. "horse stamps"), derived from the art of self-defense (Mi. *pancak*). They sounded like the stamping of shod horses' feet on a stable floor. At first, one of the dancers sang in uncoordinated free meter, changing to strict meter as the three drummers played their interlocking rhythms on a pair of *adok* (heavy frame drums) and a *gandang* (double-headed drum).

Then the mother (played by a male dancer) appeared, modestly hiding her face behind her shawl. She laid the baby's "corpse" (a doll) on a cushion with a cloth underneath it on the floor and then picked him up and danced the *tari salendang/ kain* ("shawl" or "cloth" dance) with him, performing intricate hand movements that were accentuated by the swirling ends of the long shawl held in her hands. She made a vain attempt to restore him to life as she sang a *ratok* to express her sadness, sometimes improvising verses on other themes, such as the misery of poverty. She was accompanied by three musicians, one of whom played a fixed rhythm (*irama tatap*) on an *adok*; the second played a variable rhythm (*irama kutera*) on another *adok*, and the third played a variable rhythm on a *gandang*. Then the *adok* player softly and slowly sang a lullaby, "Dang Kumbang" ("The Bee") to texts such as "A, o, buai" (Ah, oh, [baby] sway).

Her husband reentered the arena as she laid the baby's corpse on the cushion again. With their eyes downcast, the parents performed a powerfully emotional couples dance around the corpse of their baby son (*anak kanduang lanang*), with the husband's arms outstretched behind his wife to shield her. The three drummers sang poignant songs accompanied by the pair of *adok* and *gandang*, with a local *saluang* (ring-stop flute) played to accompany the most tragic verses. The couple expressed their grief by singing a *pantun* couplet about a baby monkey followed by a couplet about their baby's corpse lying in a sling, with the next verse referring to the baby by name and to his burial. As is standard practice in the *pantun* form, the first couplet of each quatrain contains an allusion (*sampiran*) and the second couplet the poet's real intent, as in the following:

Ditabiang batuang basilang	Chopped, cross-shaped, young bamboo
Anak baruek diateh rabo	A baby monkey is on top of the branch
Kain pendukuang nan pamalang	The unlucky one is in a sling
Tangan mamaluek nan cilako	(My) arms cuddle the blighted one
Sajak Galundi rabah mudo	Since Galundi has died young
Dulak batu ndo ka tapian	Push the [burial] stone to the bank
Sajak rang anak hilang dim*ato*	Since the child is lost to sight
Lah samak jalan katapian	The path to the bathing place is overgrown

Another quatrain offered consolation to the parents by referring to the support of their community:

Tabang si ramo-ramo	Fly big butterfly
Inggok ka ateh dulang	Swoop down onto the tray
Kalo tampak urang basamo-samo	If [we] see people congregating together
Raso nampak urang nan hilang	It feels as if a lost person is found

The *rantak kudo* dance then resumed, performed by four male couples. They assumed the *balabeh* posture of an art-of-self-defense performer facing his opponent, lowering the body and resting its weight on the knees while holding one hand in front of his chest and concentrating his mind on his task (also known as kudo-kudo [Mi., "horse stance"]). They performed art-of-self-defense routines while stamping out *rantak kudo* rhythms on the floor. The *dukun* watched over the dancers in case they entered a state of altered consciousness and harmed themselves. He also controlled the dancing by uttering the signal "Psst!" to direct the men to stamp out the *rantak cuku* (Mi., "walk in zigzag fashion") rhythm and then to change to other routines or formations, such as the *rantak selisi* ("the couple swap places" rhythm), the *rantak beniti batang* (the "climbing up a tree" rhythm), the *rantak serong* ("diagonal formation" rhythm), and finally the *sambah* (bow of respect) to the audience (audio example 3.2). In some episodes the lead musician played the heavy *adok*, giving rhythmic signals to the *gandang* player to start and end each piece and play along with him according to the time span of each dance episode, as decided by the *dukun*.

Another *rantak kudo* creation myth is told in Silaut as follows:

> One day a young mother, Sibentan, was singing a lullaby to her baby in her hammock. Her singing was so beautiful that her husband and son, who were outside cutting the grass, left their work and came into the house to listen. Then they started to dance and attracted others to join in. The sound of the floorboards moving beneath them resembled the sound of horse hooves stamping, so they called the dance *rantak kudo* (Mi., "horse stamping"). Sibentan also danced, wearing a long dance scarf (*salendang*).

Some south-coast artists believe that Sibentan was the daughter of the legendary hero Cindua Mato and that the creation of the *rantak kudo* dance was inspired by her and her husband's suffering at the death of their newborn baby, while others claim that Sibentan is another name for the mermaid Sikambang.

Unlike the above shamanic items, many of the song-dances performed at celebrations are based on episodes from local legends.

BARDIC PERFORMANCES

When bards (*tukang kaba* or *tukang cerito*) perform their detailed versions of the legends in all-night performances, they accompany their chanting and singing on the unique south-coastal type of string instrument (*rabab*) and an optional frame drum (*adok, rapano,* or *rapa'i*) as in figs. 3.3 and 3.4. They embroider their improvised episodes with detail that audiences find fascinating and at times uproariously funny.

A well-known bard in the 1980s was Bp. Aslim of Pasar Salido, Kecamatan Painan. He accompanied his narrations on his south-coast-style *rabab* (see fig. 3.3) and a frame drum, with his assistant and apprentice sometimes taking over the narration and frame-drum playing to give him a rest.

Unique in Southeast Asia, the south-coast *rabab* resembles the shape of an early European alto violin, but it is played in a totally non-European, *asali* way. Made of light wood, it is cut into shape and glued together with sap.[10] It has four strings tuned in fifths with one often used as a drone or ignored altogether, and it has a wooden or plastic wheel-shaped bridge. While it is being played, its horsehair bow is tautened with the second finger of the player's right hand.

In 1986, a host in Kampuang Lagan hired Bp. Aslim to perform a *kaba* for several nights at his son's wedding, paying his transportation costs as well as giving him food and drink throughout his performances.[11] On the first night as he sat cross-legged on the floor tuning his *rabab* resting on his left foot (fig. 3.3), Bp. Aslim chose to chant the story of Sutan Pangaduan, a Saudi Arabian–born knight who sailed to Minangkabau and fought battles there against the Portuguese, the Dutch, and the English, with help from his brother.[12] In all poignant scenes he accompanied his chanting on

Figure 3.3 A bard (Bp. Aslim) chanting a story (*kaba*) while accompanying himself on a south-coast, four-string *rabab*, with his assistant playing a frame drum, Pasar Salido, Kecamatan Painan, 1986

Figure 3.4. A bard (Bp. Asri) chanting a story while accompanying himself on a south-coast *rabab*, with his assistant playing a frame drum, Kampuang Surantih, Kecamatan Batang Kapus, 1986

the *rabab*, often moving members of his audience to tears, and reserved the frame drum (usually the *adok*, with the *rabano* for variety) for cheerful or action scenes.

As he chanted he played long held tones on the *rabab*, focusing on the keynote and the fourth and fifth degree of the major scale. Mostly, however, the *rabab* melody was more highly ornamented than the vocal part, containing vibrato and tremolo (*garitik*), turns, and other ornaments.

Music example 3.1 Melodic ornaments in the playing of Bp. Aslim

A feature of his *rabab* style was his extensive double stopping. Sometimes he played a drone at the octave and the fifth or melodic passages with turns and other ornaments.

Music example 3.2 Double stopping in the playing of Bp. Aslim

Within and between narrated episodes, he sang songs or played melodic episodes on the *rabab*, and his assistant played varied rhythmic-timbral patterns on an *adok*. They included the sound *tak* produced by a sharp, high-pitched, left-hand rap near the rim of the head, the deeply resonant low-pitched *tum* produced by beating the palm of the left hand about three centimeters from the rim, and the high-pitched *tĕ* produced by a soft right-hand tap on the rim, as in music example 3.3:

Music example 3.3 A rhythmic-timbral pattern played on an *adok* (heavy frame drum)

The audience particularly enjoyed the episodes of humorous and often bawdy verses that he inserted into the narration at strategic points without warning, and they laughed uproariously and called out comments in response. One amusing *pantun* that he sang described a four-string south-coast *rabab* with a broken string, followed by a pungent comment with a double meaning about replacing one's partner with someone else after a broken marriage:

Rabab batali ampek	The rabab has four strings
Putuih salai tinggal tigo	One broken, three left
Nan hilang indak kadapek	What is lost can't be got back
Cari nan lain kaganti nyo	Look for a replacement

Bp. Aslim's devotees said that the later the hour, the more interesting the *kaba* episodes became and the more beautiful the *rabab* sounded (I. *makin malam makin bagus ceritanya dan makin merdu suara rababnya*).

DANCES BASED ON THE MERMAID AND EARTH GODDESS LEGENDS

Over the centuries, the south coast developed a song-dance culture based on the pan-west-coast Sumatran legend of the mermaid Sikambang, including the umbrella and shawl (*payuang* and *salendang*) dances, some of which are happy love song-dances, while others express the grief of parents if their baby were to fall dangerously ill or die. The song texts are in Malay. Other items derive from the legend of the Earth Goddess, Bundo Kanduang, and the associated legend of Cindua Mato, the hero and first king of all Minangkabau. The song texts are in Minangkabau.

Sikambang

In the southernmost coastal version of the Sikambang legend (between Indrapura and Lagan), the mermaid Sikambang gives birth to baby Otik just after her husband, Sutan Pamenan, has sailed overseas. On his return several months later, he sees his baby for the first time. According to one version of the story, the baby has just died, and the grieving parents sing laments, performing the appropriate ceremonies for days and nights to express their sorrow. According to another version, the child recovers from his illness, whereupon his parents make offerings to the spirits and celebrate with thanksgiving rituals, music, and dance, which continue for many days and nights.[13] The tragic song-dances performed in response to parents' worst nightmare—the fatal illness or death of their baby—serve as therapy as the parents try to adjust to the situation.

As is usual in Malay-speaking villages along Sumatra's west coast, the Sikambang dance role is played by a man dressed as a woman in a *kain-kebaya* (a blouse and wraparound skirt) and long dance scarf (Ma. *salendang*; I. *slendang*).[14] One performance that I saw outside a home in Kampuang Sirantih, Kecamatan Batang Kapas, consisted of two scenes, one portraying Sikambang dancing solo, and the other the couple Sikambang and Sutan Pamenan dancing a duo. In the first scene, titled "Lagan Gadis Basanai" ("Lagan Village Girl Basanai"), the dancer performed a highly expressive dance of a mother's grief at her baby's death, as "she" danced sorrowfully around a baby doll representing Otik lying on the ground swathed in a shawl. She was accompanied by a male *ratok* (lament) vocalist singing an anhemitonic pentatonic melody with ornamentation (*bungo*), a violin (*biola*, I., as opposed to a *rabab*, Mi.) player who doubled as a *ratok* singer, and an *adok* drummer, who played only in the less sad sections of the dance. The *rebab* player used only the three upper strings, which he tuned in fifths on D, A and E^1, with the second (D) string serving as a drone, and he liberally ornamented the melody on tones D^1, C^1, B, and A. At times the *biola* player sang in approximate unison with his *rebab* playing, and at other times another singer took over from him.

The dancer portraying Sikambang held her long *salendang* in front of her face to preserve her privacy, given the intensity of her feelings. All her emotions were expressed through her body and hand movements as she held and moved the ends of her *salendang*. After paying her respects to her audience of humans and spirits in the opening *sambah*, she danced in a circular formation, stepping forward on each drumbeat as she swung her *salendang* from side to side and stamped out a rhythm from the *rantak kudo* dance. Then she knelt and observed her baby lying on the floor, and the music momentarily stopped. Rising again as the music resumed, she acted as if he were still alive. She bowed over the child, unable to believe that he had died, picking up his corpse and dancing with him in her arms while fanning him with one end of her scarf. Another dancer then came and relieved her of her baby, whereupon she stood still with feet wide apart, lay on the floor, and began to roll on the ground in agony at her child's death, her face still covered with the scarf. Finally she bowed in the four directions, stood still, and departed from the arena.

In the second scene, the *biola* player began to play again without any singing and was joined by a frame drum (*adok*) player, who played cyclic rhythms such as the following (music example 3.4):

Music example 3.4 A cyclic rhythm played on an *adok* in the second scene of a *sikambang* dance

A dancer then entered the arena portraying the child's father (Sutan Pamenan), who had just returned from overseas. He danced closely together with his wife without touching her, while she broke the news to him (in mime) that their child had just died. He then danced by himself, hiding his grief by covering his face with his hands. Together the couple danced slowly around and around their baby's corpse. Sikambang's expressive hand and finger movements were accentuated by the swirling ends of her *salendang*, which she held in the fingers of each hand. She picked up her dead son and fanned him with her *salendang*, while her husband danced behind her. He picked up an umbrella and swayed it from side to side as he danced the umbrella dance (*tari payuang*), stretching his arm out protectively behind his wife and baby, after which they made their exit.

Bundo Kanduang/Cindua Mato

In both the *pasisia* and the *darék*, most ceremonies at weddings, installations of an elder (*batagak penghulu*), a baby's first haircutting ceremony, the erection of a new house, or thanksgiving after a good harvest are opened by welcome dances representing Cindua Mato or Bundo Kanduang. The primal ancestress of each Minangkabau clan, Bundo Kanduang, leads the welcome processional dance with her two maidservants each holding a *carano* (ceremonial vessel), one of which contains burning incense and the other a bowl of betel-nut preparation to present to elders and honored guests. On the south coast, the dance is usually followed by a local version of the Minangkabau *galombang duobale* (lit. "twelve wave") dance, with twelve men dancing movements derived from the art of self-defense in a circular formation while performing their own vocal music and percussion, mainly clapping their baggy trousers between their legs. Like other south-coast dances, the Bundo Kanduang welcome dance is usually accompanied by one of the two typical south-coastal instrumental ensembles: the *gandang-sarunai* (Mi., "drum-oboe," see fig 3.5) or the *sikambang* (violin and drum) bands, which will be described in the last section of this chapter.

In the southernmost coastal area, song-dances related to the Bundo Kanduang/Cindua Mato legends include a series of sacred, ancestral female eagle dances (Mi. *tari-tari alang*) performed after a ritual procession "to go down to the river [to bathe]" (Ma. *arak-arak turun ke air/turun mandi*), that is, when a bride is given her last ceremonial wash before her wedding, or a baby is given his or her first ceremonial wash or haircut (as in the Malin Deman legend described below).[15] During a procession that I witnessed in Silaut, a group of men played a *gandang-sarunai* ensemble comprising several large and/or small frame drums (*adok* or *rapano)* and an oboe (*sarunai* or *nenet*) interspersed with group singing of Muslim texts.[16]

After *magreb*, a shaman directed a performance of the eagle dances in an open arena. He sang a classical song (*padendangan*) about Bundo Kanduang's son Dang Tuanku, who asked Cindua Mato to capture the beautiful princess Putri Bungsu (Ma.; Mi. Puti Bungsu) as his bride. However his rival, Raja Imbang Jayo, kidnapped and imprisoned her. Cindua Mato created a diversion by giving alcoholic drinks to the prison guards, which enabled the princess to fly down past the drunken guards and escape. Imbang Jayo attacked Cindua Mato, but Cindua Mato killed him while riding his buffalo and succeeded in his mission to deliver the princess to Dang Tuanku. A group of girls then entered the arena and performed three eagle dances, accompanied by a male singer and a *gandang, adok* and *rapano*. Wearing long shawls, they performed birdlike flying movements.

Staged Bundo Kanduang/Cindua Mato Song-Dances

The first two of four dances staged at government events on the south coast between Indrapura and Muko-muko in 1985–86 were performed by young women and the last two by men.[17] The following description of the series, known as "Tari Sibentan" (or "Tari Bentan"), is based on a performance near Painan, at Kampuang Laban, Salido, Kecamatan IV Jurai.

The first dance, "Tari Sibentan," portrayed the young mother Sibentan (the subject of the second version of the *rantak kudo* legend told above) wearing a long shawl around her shoulders and dancing the *tari salendang/kain*, while a vocalist sang the verses of a lullaby accompanied by a pair of *adok* and a *gandang*. In the second dance, "Tari Tambo Sikanduang," the singer referred to the mythic history (*tambo*) of Bundo Kanduang. Typically, a young female dancer representing the primal female ancestress entered the arena in a stately procession followed by her two maidservants, each holding a *carano* (ceremonial vessel), one of which contained burning incense and the other a betel-nut preparation. At the end of the dance, the maidservants welcomed the elders and honored guests by presenting them with a betel-nut preparation wrapped in a leaf.

In the third dance, "Tari Adau-Adau" (Mi., "Fight Dance"), or "Tari Padang" (Mi., "Sword Dance"), a pair of male dancers prepared to engage in their mock-fighting skills while the singer, with *adok* and *gandang* accompaniment, sang verses about the heroic exploits of Cindua Mato as he captured Putri Bungsu from prison. Playing the role of palace guards (Mi., I. *hulubalang*), the pair elegantly raised and lowered their swords and then placed them on the floor so that they were free to stand facing each other in the *balabeh* position adopted by self-defense performers. Then the music stopped and the atmosphere changed as the two men fought a lengthy *silek* duel. Whenever a *pasilek* (Mi., "performer") succeeded in driving his opponent into a tight corner, he called out, "Hai!" or "Huh!" In accord with traditional polite behavior, however, there was no clear winner, for each *pasilek* allowed his opponent to win some skirmishes, and they performed a closing *sambah* together at the end.

The fourth dance, "Tari Badinding," comprised two parts: "Tari Rantak Kudo" and "Tari Sikambang," both of which portrayed the tragic feelings of the bereaved parents of the baby son of the hero Cindua Mato, Galundi. In the "Tari Rantak Kudo," a bereaved father (or in another version an older son) moved around the arena in diagonal and square formations performing an odd number of jerky *kudo merentak* (horse stamps) movements. Then the mother appeared (played by a male dancer), arranged her baby's "corpse" (a doll) on a cushion, picked him up, and danced with him as she sang a lament (*ratok*) to express her tragic feelings. Both parents then performed a powerfully emotional dance around the corpse of their baby son lying on the floor, with the vocalist accompanied by a pair of *adok* and a *gandang*.

The Seven Sisters/Malin Deman Dances: *Gandai*

According to Pandekar Sutan Sabarudin, a holy (*kramat*) man named Bujang XI could talk like an adult from the age of two months and had eleven fingers. He told him the definitive version of the Malin Deman legend, which lies at the base of the set of *gandai* dances performed in the area around Silaut. The legend is as follows:

At Batang Muar (in Ipo, Bengkulu), the wife of the Tuanku Raja—whose name was Putri Mayang Sani—gave birth to a son. The couple named him Malin Deman. As is the custom, when he was ten days old he was carried in a procession to the river for the *turun mandi* (lit. "go down to the water") ceremony. While his nurse was washing him, using a bowl of holy water containing a piece of lemon, she was distracted by a loud noise and did not notice until later that a piece of the baby's hair, which had stuck to the piece of lemon, had floated down the river. The hair actually possessed magic properties, including an ability to grow three times its length of its own accord. Eventually the hair lodged under a rock in a deep part of the river at Lubuk Dusun Rami.

Meanwhile the baby prince was brought to the palace at Indrapura and was reunited with his father, Tuanku Raja. When the prince reached sixteen years of age, his father became ill. On his deathbed, his father told him that his future depended on his finding the piece of hair that had been lost when he was a ten-day-old baby because it was actually the source of supernatural strength. If, for example, the piece of hair were to measure one depo (the length of an outstretched arm), it would magically become three depo in length.

After the last rite of his father's funeral ceremony had been carried out, the prince decided to go on a journey to find the piece of hair. Carrying a *bansi* (bamboo duct flute) with him, he traveled for months and eventually reached a place called Urai. There he happened to meet a lady standing at the door of a little house in the *ladang* (dry rice field). She asked him, "Who are you?" He replied, "My name is Malin Deman and my mother is Mayang Sani." She then asked, "Where are you going?" He replied, "To find the lady who nursed me as a baby and who, I think, has a piece of my hair." The lady at the door of the house was actually Dewa Indurjati, who had nursed Malin Deman as a baby. She was one of the seven beautiful angels who descend from heaven every seventh day to bathe naked in the lake, surrounded by a flower garden, after leaving their clothes and wings on the bank. Dewa Indurjati realized that Malin Deman was the baby whom she had nursed, and she immediately told him that the piece of hair had lodged in a deep pond in the river.

After he found the pond, Malin Deman dived in and eventually recovered the hair, which restored his magic power and enabled him to see the other six angels by the lake. Dewa Indurjati then asked Malin Deman to play the *bansi* to her *rapano* accompaniment. Her six sisters emerged and danced to this music, and after a while she too joined in the dancing as her frame drum began to play of its own accord. Malin Deman fell in love with Dewa Indurjati. He stole and hid her clothes and wings so that she could not fly back to heaven with her six sisters that night. Then he married her, and she bore him a child. Eventually, however, she managed to find her clothes and wings and returned to heaven.

The *bansi* mentioned in the Malin Deman legend was once a common instrument in the area, played mainly by shamans for love magic. However, it possessed magic qualities only if made from a rare yellow species of bamboo called *buluh parindu*, found deep in the forest. If someone asked a shaman to help him attract a member of the opposite sex, the shaman would play a special magic *bansi*, recite mantras, and use *ilmu pitunang* (magic to ensure an engagement), which would suddenly make it possible for the loved one, whether near or far, to hear the *bansi* sound and be attracted toward it.

Bansi vary between eighteen and thirty centimeters in length (fig. 3.1). The mouthpiece has a wooden plug with a square blowing hole and an open bottom end. The second of its six finger holes is bored out with a hot iron four finger-widths down the front of the tube, and there is a single hole halfway down the rear. *Bansi* players perform song melodies to accompany vocalists who sing poetic texts such as "Lagu Onde Mak Oi" ("Oh Mother Song"), "Malereng" ("Walk up a Hill"), and "Mudik Arau" ("*Arau* Branch from Upstream").

In the area between Indrapura and Muko-muko, the main female dances are based on the Malin Deman/Seven Angels legend when the youngest angel was living on earth. Six girls representing the six older angels performed the whole set of *gandai* dances in the yard of a home in Silaut in 1986. In some dances all six performed as a single group, while in others they broke into groups of four plus two, two groups of three, or three pairs, and formed varying circular and line formations.

The first of the set of nineteen *gandai* dances that we recorded was the "Tari Lori" (M-m., "Opening Dance") in vigorous art-of-self-defense style with fast, loud music performed by a female singer and a male oboist and frame-drum player. In modern practice the *bansi* is usually replaced by an oboe named *nenet* or *sarunai*, because, we were told, the sound of an oboe carries better than a *bansi* in a large assembly. The oboe player began to play in free meter; then the *rapano* (frame drum) player joined in and established quadruple meter with a fast cyclic rhythm, alternating between loud and soft sections, whereupon a female vocalist entered singing the *lori* song in near unison with the oboe. The six girls then entered the arena and danced in a series of formations, performing very intricate hand movements, with their eyes modestly downcast. Local artists described their intricate hand movements as resembling those of birds and angels flying; indeed their most characteristic movements included waving both arms gracefully up and down over slightly crouched legs.

In the second dance, called "Tari Nenet" (M-m.), the oboe dominated the accompaniment. The six girls danced slowly in a circle performing various arm and finger movements while sweeping their long scarves around their necks from side to side, as in the above-mentioned coastal Malay-style handkerchief dance (*tari saputangan*). In the next song, titled "Lagu Hari Paneh" (M-m., "Hot Day"), the lead dancer sang about her sorrow at the prospect of being parted from her mother on her upcoming marriage, while the other girls danced with her in sympathy. The lead dancer then repeated the "Oh Mother Song," while the other five dancers repeatedly raised and lowered their arms as if they were bird wings; they subsequently clapped and performed elegant hand movements while holding their handkerchiefs, forming two circles of three dancers. The leader then sang, and her companions danced the "Tari Salisiah air" (M-m., "Waterplay," lit. "Play in Shallow Water Dance"), in near unison with the *nenet/sarunai* line set in the lower part of the range; this dance depicts the Seven Angels bathing in the lake.

Many song-dances followed, accompanied by oboe and drums. They included the fast "Tari Tanjuang Sikabu" (the name of a nearby peninsula), which depicts women tilling the fields; the slow "Tari Totok" ("Indigenous Dance"), which depicts a mother caring for her child and a text offering advice on how to look after a baby; and "Tari Kasih Sayang" ("Love Dance"), with five of the girls dancing with their left hand on their hip, clapping their hands, or sweeping their long dance shawls alternately to the right and the left as the sixth dancer sang advice about love. One of the *pantuns* offered couples advice on their relationship:

Kalo ado jarum nan patah	If a needle is broken
Jangan disimpan dalam peti	Don't store it in a box.
Kalo ado kato-kato nan salah	If wrong words are said
Jangan disimpan dalam hati.	Don't store them in (your) heart.

The musical ensemble changed to a quick tempo for the next dance. The fast "Tanjuang Karang" ("Coral Peninsula") dance began with the dancers dividing into two groups of three, after which each group danced in a circle, then a triangular for-mation, and finally in two parallel lines facing the audience. In the fast "Menjong Anabek" (M-m., "Stop Running Away") song-dance, five of the girls performed art-of-self-defense movements as they tried to stop the oldest angel from flying back to heaven. In the "Tari Mimpi" ("Dream Dance"), the six girls moved slowly and quietly around a circle, swaying their arms as if they were birds flying. In the "Sasuah Julan Babiduk" (M-m., "Boat Moves with Difficulty") song-dance, the girls repeated the "Salisiah Air" ("Waterplay") movements while holding the ends of a handkerchief between their hands, and the singer described a boat in distress. In the fast "Tari Biduk Teleng" (M-m., "Boat Sways"), the dancers portrayed a boat tipping over precariously after hitting a huge wave, depicting the near disaster by movements of their handkerchiefs. In the very fast "Tari Rantak Kudo," the dancers added vigorous stamping movements to the boat-swaying dance movements. The "Kuau Letok" (M-m., "A Bird Crows") dance was even faster, with the dancers again putting their left hand on their hips, swaying their arms up and down as if flying, and delicately clapping their hands in between. A repeat of the "Biduk Teleng" dance followed with a low-pitched oboe accompaniment, then a new version of the "Oh Mother" dance with its *rantak kudo*–based movements, and finally, the fast, newly created "Tutung Sayak" ("Throw the Angels' Drinking Vessels [half-coconut-shell containers] Away") dance.

Some of the men at Silaut said that as the night progresses the *gandai* dancers look more and more beautiful. They said that after a while the *nenet/sarunai* and *gandang* musicians play magically of their own accord without human intervention, the girls sometimes enter a dreamlike state of trance, the sound of the music makes the girls seem even more attractive late at night, and the men in the audience tend to fall in love with and marry them.

OTHER DANCES

Some kinds of music and dance are associated with agricultural rituals, especially the plate dance and rice-stamping music, while others are associated with humorous folk stories. Both the *darék* and the *pasisia* are well known for their versions of the plate dance (*tari piriang*), one of which may have been developed by the female dancer Sikambang at the Indrapura palace for the princesses of the palace to perform, as mentioned above.

According to Bp. Aslim, the plate dances originated from the time-worn Minang-kabau practice of women bringing food on many small plates for their families to eat when harvesting in the rice field. Eventually the women are said to have picked up a pair of empty plates after the evening meal and to have entertained themselves by rotating them in their hands while rhythmically clicking their finger rings on the plates, thereby creating the basis of the plate dance. Eventually they added various athletic movements to the dance, such as rolling on the ground while holding a plate in each hand or walking on a row of plates without breaking them. Another origin story holds that a girl lost her betrothal ring in the rice field, and she developed the plate dance with ring-plate percussion as she searched for it. On the south coast the plate dances are usually accompanied by a *gandang-sarunai* ensemble (audio example 3.3).[18]

Some women said that they used to dance the plate dances during the weeks of backbreaking work stamping the husks off the rice grain, when they also played rice-stamping music by beating heavy wooden poles down on tonally different parts of the troughs (Mi. *lasuang*) of raw rice, producing intricately interlocking rhythmic music called *lasuang* for hours, days and nights on end. However, the introduction of machines to do this work since the 1970s has resulted in *lasuang* music being performed only rarely.

A number of humorous dances are based on movements of domestic animals. In Sungai Kuok, Kecamatan Batang Kapas, for example, the *tupai jonjang* dance tells the story of an elderly prince named Anak Rajo Tuo Sutan, his wife Puti Lindung Bulan, and their two sons, the older of whom is named Sutan Tupai Jonjang and the younger Kuciang Sabun (Soap Cat). A young man dances the naughty "soap cat" solo, scaring the audience by leaping about and jumping onto a table, breaking all the tableware and ruining the cooking utensils in the kitchen. With a reputation for being a glutton, he consumes large quantities of fruit and cake. His antics and athletic displays based on art-of-self-defense movements are accompanied by a *gandang-sarunai* ensemble, with the musicians taking turns singing amusing *pantun* about impossible, unlikely, or comical events, such as:

Ciang balang baranak balang	A striped cat gives birth to a striped snake
Bagolek-golek tia teniru	While rolling on the ground,
Urang gayek coma di lamang	An old man greedily eats glutinous rice cooked in a bamboo tube
Lulo bibir dek sambilu.	(His) lips are pierced by the sharp bamboo blade

Meanwhile, the father becomes angrier and angrier as he tries to control his athletic little soap-cat son, but to no avail. Finally Anak Rajo Tuo Sutan threatens him with expulsion. His father asks him in *pantun* song form: "Do you want to be expelled?" "Yes," replies the son, "but only if I am sent to Pulau Agar-Agar (Jelly Island), where I can eat all I want!" The father then sings: "You'll be hanged if you're not careful!" "I don't mind being hanged," the son replies, "as long as it is from a banana tree!" "Do you want to be shot?" "Yes, I don't mind, but only if the bullets are made of *onde-onde* (cakes)!" "Do you want to be struck with a sword?" "Yes, but only if it is made of sugar cane." Eventually, his father starts to laugh and forgives him, and he is lovingly accepted back into the family. The repartee singing is dramatic and humorous, with the singers frequently changing dynamic level from loud to soft, alternating in the athletic scenes with bouts of purely instrumental drum and oboe music

INSTRUMENTAL ENSEMBLES THAT ACCOMPANY SONG-DANCES

South-coastal song-dances are usually accompanied by one of the two typical instrumental ensembles: the *gandang-sarunai* (Mi., "drum-oboe," fig 3.5) or the *sikambang* violin and drum (i.e., *biola-gandang*) bands. The latter type only accompanies local versions of the pan-west-coast Sumatran *sikambang* song-dances. As the following examples will show, instruments are arranged differently in different villages, which is not surprising given that the inhabitants of most south-coastal villages lived in relative isolation for centuries, until roads were built between them in the past two to three decades.

The main instruments in a *gandang-sarunai* ensemble are the drums, that is, double-headed drums with rattan lacing (*gandang*), large frame drums (*adok*) and small frame drums (*redap*), and an oboe: either a *sarunai kayu* (Mi.) or *nenet* (Mi.) made of wood (as in figs. 3.7 and 3.8), or a *katopong* or *sarunai batang padi* (Mi.) made of rice stalk (as in fig. 3.9). Figure 3.5 shows a *gandang-sarunai* ensemble in Painan Timur that has two *gandang*, a wooden oboe (*sarunai*), and a gong chime, while Figure 3.6 shows a similar ensemble in Pasar Salido (near Painan) that has a rice-stalk oboe. Both types of oboe are played by circular breathing.

The large *adok* frame drum has a heavy wooden base and wooden tuning pegs that are held in place around its circumference by rattan cord lacing. Its goat- or buffalo-skin head, which varies between approximately forty-two and fifty centimeters in diameter (fig. 3.10), is tightly stretched by hammering its tuning pegs, after which the head is heated beside a flame. A *redap* is a small frame drum that is also made predominantly of wood. Its goatskin head is laced to its body with rattan cord, and its sixteen wooden pegs serve to tauten its skin head. The two drummers produce a range of timbres, such as the sharp sound referred to onomatopoeically as *tak* (played by the fingers of the left hand near the rim of the head) and the deep resonant sound *tum* (played by the palm of the left hand midhead), as mentioned above. Other timbres include the double sound *tumba* (with the resonant *tum* sound followed by the sharp resonant *ba* sound played by the right hand), and the double sound *tĕbum* (a

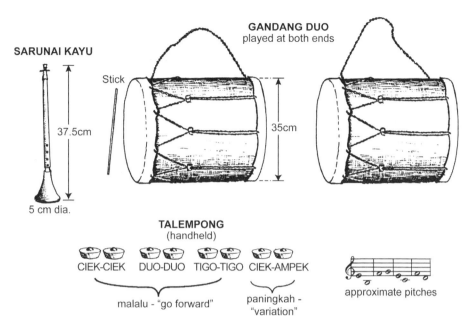

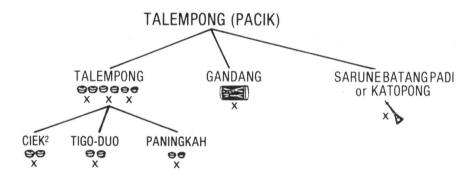

Figure 3.5 A *gandang-sarunai* ensemble comprising a pair of *gandang*, a *sarunai kayu*, and four pairs of *talempong*, Kampuang Lagan, Kecamatan Ranah Pasisir, Kabupaten Painan

Figure 3.6 A *gandang-sarunai* ensemble comprising a *gandang*, a *katopong* (rice-stalk oboe), and three pairs of *talempong*, Pasar Salido

short, soft, damped sound called *tě* played on the edge of the head by the player's left hand followed by a fully resonant sound called *bum* played by the left hand).

In both the northern and the southern subdistricts of the south coast, musicians use the *sarunai* as the main melody instrument, even if *talempong* are present. The *sarunai* is regarded as a remarkable instrument because it looks elegant and is attributed with magic power. It is also conveniently portable. Its body consists of five interlocking tubes of different sizes that can collapse into the widest tube for

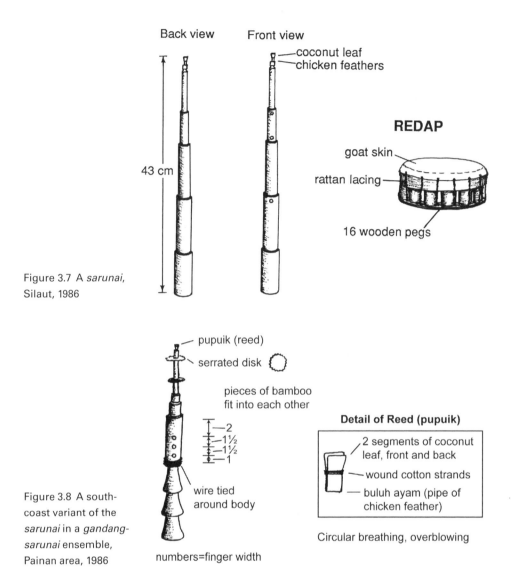

Back view   Front view

—coconut leaf
—chicken feathers

REDAP

goat skin
rattan lacing

16 wooden pegs

43 cm

Figure 3.7 A *sarunai*,
Silaut, 1986

— pupuik (reed)
— serrated disk

pieces of bamboo
fit into each other

—2
—1½
—1½
—1

Detail of Reed (pupuik)

2 segments of coconut
leaf, front and back

—wound cotton strands
— buluh ayam (pipe of
chicken feather)

wire tied
around body

Figure 3.8 A south-
coast variant of the
sarunai in a *gandang-
sarunai* ensemble,
Painan area, 1986

numbers=finger width

Circular breathing, overblowing

transportability (fig. 3.7). To make the instrument, it is necessary to measure (with precise lengths of leaf) the distance between its three widely spaced front holes and the position of its single midrear hole. Its double reed (Mi. *ayam buluh*, "bamboo chicken") is made of coconut leaf with a chicken feather attached. The player dips the reed in water to soften it before playing the instrument, using the technique of circular breathing. Figure 3.7 shows five pieces of bamboo tubing, of increasing width, which fit into each other to form the main body of the oboe, with the reed mouthpiece attached. Its main accompanying instrument is a *redap* frame drum.

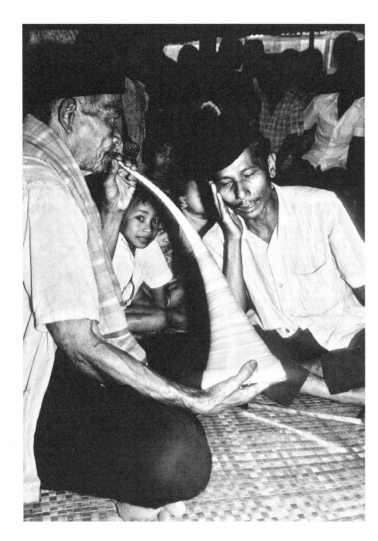

Figure 3.9 A rice-stalk *sarunai* or *pupuik* player, Solok, 1985

Figure 3.9 shows another ensemble arrangement in Pasar Salido, where the wound-leaf rice-stalk *sarunai* is preferred to the wooden type. About thirty-five centimeters in length, its six-centimeter-long rice stalk reed fits vertically into the body of the instrument, which consists of a tube made of lengths of coconut leaf wound in a tubular shape and flaring out gradually to produce a cavity of ten centimeters in diameter at the lower end. When the cavity is partly covered and uncovered in regular motion by the player's hand, it produces a "wowing" sound. The player produces a continuous stream of melody based on four tones: F^1, D^1, E^1, C^1, with half- and microtones in between and much ornamentation (*bungo*). The photo in figure 3.9 was actually taken in the *darék* at Solok, but the south-coast instrument is basically similar.

Some *gandang-sarunai* ensembles add gong-chimes (*talempong*), as in figure 3.10, but they are not considered essential instruments. When present, they are played either in sitting position (*duduak*) or in standing position (Mi. *pacik*, "held by hand"). Normally each musician plays a pair of *talempong*, which are often tuned to the approximate hemitonic-pentatonic pitches: E and B, F and G, and E and C respectively. The first three pairs interlock to play the main melody, or melodic patterns. If there is a fourth musician, he plays the rhythmic *paningkah* (Mi. "that accompanies, varies, improvises") part on a pair of *talempong* tuned to F and D. All together this produces a hexatonic scale: B C D E F G (audio example 3.4).

If there are only three pairs of *talempong* players, as in figure 3.10, the first pair, known as *ciek-ciek* (one-one), plays the main melody (*malalu*, lit. "go forward"). The second, called *tigo-duo* (three-two), plays a moderately dense part. The third, known as *paningkah*, plays the densest part. If there are four pairs, the fourth is referred to as *ampek* (four).[19]

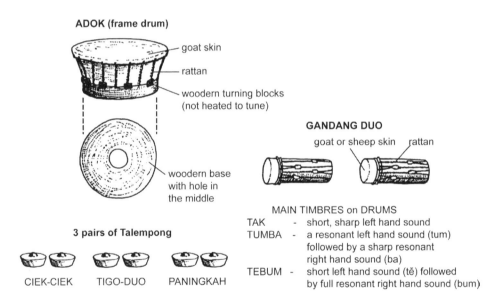

Figure 3.10 A *gandang sarunai* ensemble comprising a pair of *gandang*, an *adok*, and three pairs of *talempong*, Painan

If playing in a wedding or other procession, the *talempong* players use a stick in their right hand to beat one or two gong-chimes held on their left arm and hand, and two drummers also use a stick to beat one end of the drum suspended around their neck and the other with their hand. Sometimes, however, the musicians play inside a building, for example, at a circumcision ritual or a government ceremony, in which case they play sitting cross-legged (*duduak*) or kneeling on the floor (audio example 3.5).

The lead *gandang* or *talempong* player in a *gandang-sarunai* ensemble usually gives the rhythmic signal to start a piece as well as to end it, though in some areas the drums enter after the *talempong*. The order of entry and terms designating the pairs of gong-chimes also vary. For example in Kampuang Lagan (fig. 3.5), the *gandang* player starts and the first three gong-chime players then enter in turn, establishing the main interlocking melodic-rhythmic pattern, or *malalu* (go forward, continue), on their pairs of kettle-gongs The first player, called *satu-satu* (one-one), plays on every beat, as in the following:

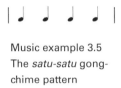

Music example 3.5
The *satu-satu* gong-chime pattern

The second gong-chime pattern, called *duo-duo* (two-two), plays one or two notes on every beat, as in the following:

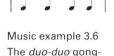

Music example 3.6
The *duo-duo* gong-chime pattern

The third gong-chime pattern, called *tigo-tigo* (three-three), plays three notes on every beat, as in:

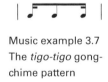

Music example 3.7
The *tigo-tigo* gong-chime pattern

After the first three players have established their basic pattern, the fourth player enters, improvising an irregular-rhythmic *paningkah* part that may contain several musical surprises. The *sarunai* player then enters, assuming the greatest degree of melodic and rhythmic freedom of all, and leavening his basic melodic line with microtonal and tonal ornaments, such as turns and tremolos. However, in the *gandang-sarunai* in Kampuang Painan Timur, the *tigo-duo* player combines the *duo-duo* and *tigo-tigo* players' roles (cf. the ensemble in Lagan, fig. 3.5), after which the improvisatory *paningkah* player enters, as usual playing the densest texture of all the pairs.

The *gandang-sarunai* repertory includes many pieces with animal and bird titles, such as "Lagu Tupai Begaluik" ("Fighting Squirrel Piece") and "Lagu Alung Babega" ("Eagle-Circling Piece"), or images of human activities, such as "Lagu Kecimpuang Mandi" ("Busily Bathing in a River Piece") and "Lagu Lenggang" ("Walking Song"). Although different tunings and interlocking melodic-rhythmic patterns are used, some south-coast pieces have the same titles as pieces in upland Minangkabau. For example, a popular piece called "Lagu Siamang Tagagau" ("Surprised Monkey Piece") is found in many *darék* villages as well as in the south-coastal Kampuang. South-coast song-dances are generally accompanied by a drum-oboe (*gandang-sarunai*) ensemble that sometimes contains gong-chimes (*talempong*), though the *rantak kudo* dance is traditionally accompanied by the dancers' foot-stamping rhythms, to which episodes of drumming may be added. Also unique to the south coast is its bardic performances of the legends accompanied by the unique south-coast *rabab*, with its European shape and south-coast Minangkabau playing style, plus an optional frame drum.

||||

Over the centuries the inhabitants of the south coast accepted a variety of foreign groups into their midst, including traders and settlers from Aceh, west-coastal Sumatra, India, the Middle East, Portugal, England, and the Netherlands. However, apart from the Muslim genres, the only apparently enduring external influence was the couple dances and songs with violin (*biola*) and frame-drum accompaniment that probably originated in sixteenth-century Portuguese Malacca, which were transformed on the south coast into the *sikambang* song-dances, and from which the *gamad* song-dances developed in the early twentieth century and *pop Minang* in the latter twentieth century.

Inhabitants of the south coast differ from their *darék* neighbors in that their traditional music, dance, and bardic arts derive from their dual orientation to the sea and the land. This dualism is reflected in the south-coast versions of the two main legends; the sea-oriented Malay legend of the mermaid Sikambang and the land-oriented Minangkabau legend of the Earth Goddess, Bundo Kanduang, and the hero Cindua Mato. The Sikambang legend inspired the tragic lament song-dances and the happy couples dances and songs, the latter with violin and frame-drum accompaniment, while the Bundo Kanduang/Cindua Mato legend serves as the basis of the main welcome dance and the set of *alang* (eagle) dances and songs.

Also important in the southernmost district is the Minangkabau-Bengkulu version of the widespread Sumatran legend of Malin Kundang and the Seven Angels and associated song-dances. Some genres, such as the plate dances and rice-stamping music, are associated with fertility and agricultural traditions. Other dances are based on amusing folk stories and athletic display. All are accompanied by an oboe and drum ensemble (*gandang-sarunai*).

Most south-coastal artists claim a lack of interest in the *darék* hinterland genres such as *randai* theater, *indang* song-dances, and *talempong* ensembles, and in the north coast's *tabuik* festivals. They focus for their sense of identity on the Sikambang song-dance laments and love dances, *gandang-sarunai* ensemble music, the Malin Deman–associated *gandai* dances, the Cindua Mato eagle dances, and their claim that the Minangkabau ancestress Bundo Kanduang and hero Cindua Mato originated in Lunang. Also unique are the south coast's *kaba* performances accompanied by the south-coast *rabab*, with its European shape and local Minangkabau playing style.

As in the *darék, pasisia selatan* young men like to perform the art of self-defense with its many local stylistic variations and associated etiquette behavior. Movements of many of their dances are based on it, including the male *dampieng* and *galombang duobale* dances, performances of which are normally followed by the *pasisia selatan*'s *rantak kudo* dance, with its foot-stamping rhythms. Some *darék* artists also perform the *galombang* dance, but usually in the context of their *randai* theater. Also as in the *darék*, the southern shamanic art forms are associated with feats involving "black" and "white" magic as in the case of the love magic–associated *gilo lukah* (crazy fish trap) dance and music and the tragic lament genres. Some healing and other shamanic rituals are preceded by Muslim prayers that create a spiritually more potent mystical and artistic setting and serve to please some Muslim leaders in the community.

Most female dances feature elegant hand movements that are emphasized by swirling the ends of their long dance shawls held in each hand. Only men normally play instruments and perform the *dikia*-based arts. They also sing and dance both the male and the female roles in couples dancing, for example, in the Sikambang dances. Girls take part in group dances until they are married, with men playing the instrumental accompaniment, but married women often serve as the lead singers, respected for their knowledge of texts and traditional singing style.

South-coast musical instruments of *asali* Malay or Minangkabau origin include the various local forms of drums, oboes, and optional gong-chimes in the *gandang-sarunai* ensembles; the viola-shaped *rabab*; the large *asali* frame drum called the *adok*; and the shamanic Jew's harp, bullroarer, and local forms of *saluang* and *bansi* flutes. The instruments of Malay-Portuguese or European origin used in the *orkes Malayu* and *gamat* ensembles include the *biola* (violin), the harmonium, guitars, drum kit, and maracas, sometimes with an Indian harmonium and *tabla* added, as in other Malay areas. *Asali* Muslim musical forms are accompanied by instruments of Middle Eastern or Acehnese origin, including large and medium-sized frame drums and brass percussion trays (*dulang*).

Asali narrative songs and some healing and other magic songs (e.g., as used in tiger capturing) usually have a narrow melodic range and are highly ornamented, while Portuguese-Malay songs for couples dancing (e.g., Sikambang) are mostly in major or minor scales with a range of over an octave and less melodically ornamented. The oboe melodies played in instrumental dance music usually have a range of a fourth or a fifth and use many half- and microtones in between. Muslim devotional songs are set to heptatonic, hexatonic, or pentatonic Arabic-sounding scales and are accompanied by frame drums, rhythmic body movement, clapping sounds, and other body percussion. Most songs combine a metrically free solo introduction with unison main melodies in quadruple meter. The music and dance forms belonging to each of the three strata have their own singular stylistic elements that are combined or transformed in different ways.

Clearly, then, the south coast should not be regarded as a cultural backwater of the Minangkabau heartland. The people have their own artistic identity, resulting from their own mixes of locally diverse forms and external influences. Their former palaces, fishing and farming villages, trading communities, and specific responses to foreign contact give them a singular identity, which is most concretely symbolized by its versions of the pan-Sumatran coastal sacred mermaid myth and the Minangkabau Earth Goddess myth and their expressions in the performing arts.

ACKNOWLEDGMENTS

I wish to acknowledge the assistance of many artists in the south-coastal district of Minangkabau and in the city of Padang who played a part in the preparation of this chapter.

During our fieldwork along the south coast in December 1985–January 1986, I was assisted and informed by the musicians Bapak Zainul Basri and Bapak Shaminau in Kampuang Painan Timur, Kecamatan Empat Surai, who played *asali*-Malay and/or *asali*-Malay-Portuguese music. Bapak M. Noerdin, a shaman (*tegenai*) from the same village explained the meaning and styles of *rantak kudo, dabuih*, the rain-rejection (*monolak hujan*) ceremony, and other shaman-led mystical performances. In Pasar Salido, the *tukang kaba* and south-coastal-style *rabab* maker Bapak Aslim and the elders were extremely informative and generous in allowing us to record his *kaba* performances. In Kampuang Luar, Kecamatan IV Jurai, I was fortunate to have discussions with the *sarunai* maker and player Bapak Arlis Sahur Jamasli. In Sungai Kuok, Kecamatan Batang Kapas, Bapak M. Anas performed and explained the amusing *tari* "Tupai Jonjang." In Kampuang Pasar Sirantih, Kecamatan Batang Kapas, Bapak Sjamsun, and colleagues gave me an overview of the richly varied *asali*-Malay, *asali*-Malay-Portuguese, and *asali*-Muslim forms performed in the Sirantih area (especially the *rabab* playing, the local center of which had moved there after the death a decade before of the leading *rabab* master in nearby Kampuang Kambung). Also in Pasar Sirantih the *saluang* player and maker Bapak Jutar and singer Bapak Yung Ambus performed and explained the texts and functions of their repertoire of coastal flute and vocal music (*saluang jo dendang pasisia*).

In Kampuang Kepala Banda, Sungai Kuok, Kecamatan Batang Kapas, a *pawang* and *kalipah* (caliph) named Bapak A. Mils gave me secret information about the mantras and magic rituals he performed accompanied by a buzzing disk (*gasieng*) and then a Jew's harp (*rinding*). In Kampuang Lagan, Bukit Pulus Dalem, Kecamatan Ranah Pasisir, and Bapak Tamar led and explained a number of local *asali*-Malay performances.

My main informants in Indrapura were the royal descendants and musicians Pandekar Sutan Sabarudin and Tengku Regen of Kampuang Muara Sakai and the local *camat* Bapak Ashar P., while in Lunang my main contact was the musician Bapak Pain. In Silaut, Kecamatan Pancung Soal, I was assisted by the head of Pasar Sebelah village, who was also a musician, Bapak Dahlil, and other elders who discussed the *asali* and other music and dance with me. In Silaut, Kecamatan Pancung Soal, I was informed by Bapak Jamaludin (group leader), *sarunai* player Bapak Saroden, *gandang* player Bapak Tamar, and *redap* player Bapak Takwin, and the *gandai* dancers: Nona ("Miss") Roslaini (leader), Nona Ramdani, Nona Sarini, Nona Megawati, and Nona Rosmi. Some other artists requested not to be named in print.

I would like to thank Bapak Azwar Anas, the former governor of West Sumatra, and officials of the Department of Education and Culture for their permission and assistance in the field.

TABUT

A Shi'a Ritual Transplanted from India to Minangkabau's North Coast

number of historians have observed that Islam came to Indonesia largely by way of India, indeed that it was "filtered through the religious experience of India" (Benda 1958, 12) and "had thus acquired mystical elements that fitted it to operate within the Indonesian setting" (Legge 1964, 49).

That Sumatran Islam was not just of the orthodox Sunni variety but also had Shi'a elements in early as well as fairly late times has not, however, been widely discussed, presumably because the available evidence for it is scant. This chapter contributes to the evidence by describing an elaborate Shi'a mourning festival of music and spectacle of Persian and Indian origins called *tabut* (Ar., "coffin"; Mi. *tabuik*, Bengk. *tabot*, Ac. *tabut Hasan Hosen*), which was transplanted, probably more than three centuries ago, from India to Pariaman and some other coastal Sumatran towns and had such an impact in Pariaman's hinterland that aspects of it were absorbed into its indigenous non-Muslim arts.

Shi'a Islam is not officially allowed in Indonesia today. The government and most of the *ulama* regard Shi'ism as heretical and potentially a threat to the peace.[1] Yet a few families of Shi'a believers who claim descent from British Indian sepoys (lit. "soldiers," called Mi. *orang sipahi*, I. *orang Kling*) live in the west-coast Sumatran towns of Pariaman and Bengkulu, where *tabut* festivals are held, if the government gives permission, every year.[2] The families' beliefs and practices are tolerated by local *imam* prayer leaders, who pray and chant in Shi'a style every year during *tabut*. Similarly in the Acehnese port town of Sigli, some *orang Kling* descendants of Shi'a believers performed their style of *tabut* annually in the colonial and early postcolonial eras whenever government permission was granted. However, it was banned there after 1953.[3]

Other Shi'a-related rituals and performing arts of Perso-Indian origin are also practiced in several provinces of Sumatra, though their practitioners are no longer Shi'a believers. The partly historical, partly legendary Shi'a-oriented story of the martyrdom of Hosan and Husen (Mi. Husen, Sigli Hosen), grandsons of the Prophet Muhammad, is still sung by storytellers in Aceh and mainland Riau, examples of which we recorded in 1982 and 1984 respectively. A major Shi'a literary work, the *Hikayat Muhammad Hanafiyah*, was translated into Malay from the Persian not much later than the fourteenth century (Brakel 1975b, 62–63). As Brakel commented, "The mere fact that a Shi'a text of the more extreme kind was received into Malay literature at all to thrive there up till the present day, is . . . of great significance. It provides strong proof . . . of . . . the heretical character [to Sunni believers] of early Indonesian Islam" (60). In both Aceh and Java, the simple rituals of voluntary fasting and eating "holy porridge" (*bubur Asyura*) on the tenth day of Muharram still commemorate Hosen's violent death while defending the faith. The first month of the Muslim year, Muharram (Mi. Muharam), is known as Asan-Usen in Aceh and as Sura in Java.

The *tabut* festival described in this chapter is much more elaborate than the simple Asyura-related rituals. Besides the coastal Minangkabau towns of Pariaman and Bengkulu, it was sometimes held until recent decades in other coastal Sumatran towns, including Sigli, Kutaraja/Banda Aceh, Meulaboh, Trumon, Singkil, Barus, Sibolga, Natal, Padang, Painan, Krui, and even the inland Minangkabau towns of Maninjau and Solok, according to some Dutch sources and my informants in these towns (see map 4.1).

The two west-coastal Sumatran towns that practice *tabut* to this day are, of course, only distant outposts of the Shi'a world. Their versions of *tabut*'s origins must be traced to important Shi'a centers in Muslim North India and ultimately to Iran, where Shi'ism became the state religion after 1500 and Muharram mourning festivals became very important events. They are generally called *ta'zia* (lit. "tomb") in Iran, Iraq, and North India, where they developed into forms of theater called *ta'zia* but are called *tabut* in South India, *tazia* in western India, and *taja* in Surinam. Although Shi'ism originated in Arabia and its mourning processions date back at least as far as the tenth century (Burckhardt-Qureshi 1981, 64), Shi'ism only attained "its full development in Persia after 1500" (63), and the evidence suggests that *ta'zia/tabut* in Iran developed considerably later than that.

From the sixteenth to the eighteenth centuries, strong cultural links between Iran and India were forged through the various Shi'a dynasties in both North and South

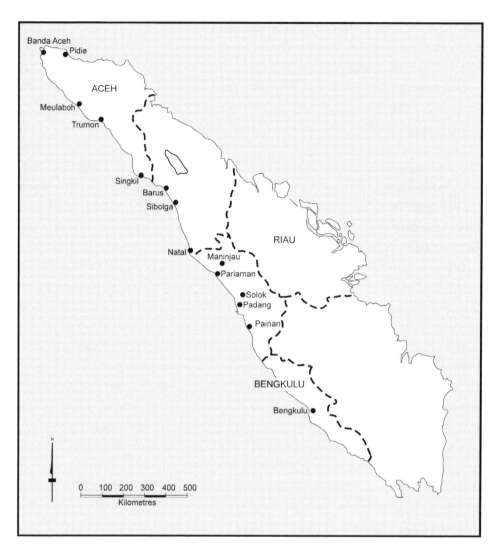

Map 4.1 Distribution of *tabut* and other Shi'a performing arts in Sumatra in the early twentieth century

India, as exemplified by the development of the Urdu language, which is used in the Shi'a *majlis* chant. It included the *matam* (*mahatam*) dirge sung in *ta'zia/tabut* in India, and later in coastal West Sumatra too, though the Urdu words sung in forms of *matam* in Pariaman are no longer fully understood there. Urdu, which became the language of the Muslim courts and the lingua franca for Muslims in India in the eighteenth century, developed as a result of contact between speakers of Persian—the court language spoken at the early Indian Muslim courts—and speakers of the North Indian version of Hindi (Burckhardt-Qureshi 1981, 42). This long period of contact is

Figure 4.1 An early-twentieth-century *burak* (*tabuik*) procession with *dol* and *tasa* drummers in Maninjau, West Sumatra (Joustra 1915, 124). Other early photos of West Sumatran tabuik may be found in the KITLV archives at Leiden: KLV001049773, dated 1939, and KLV001009626, dated 1948 (Paul Mason, pers. comm., 2010).

also the reason for the essential similarity between *ta'zia/tabut* in India and its Iranian counterpart. The published descriptions of *ta'zia/tabut* in Iran, North India, and South India show, however, that its various forms contain many differences of detail.[4]

How old is *tabut* in Sumatra? Christiaan Snouck Hurgronje has suggested that the festival originated during either the first or the second "wave" of Shi'a influence in Indonesia (1906, 2:216). Probably the simple Javanese and Acehnese Shi'a rituals mentioned above were developed and the *Hikayat Muhammad Hanafiyah* was translated into Malay during the first wave, around the fourteenth century (Brakel 1975b, 60–61). The British colonial power brought Indian sepoy troops (*orang sipahi* or *orang cipahi*, Tamil pronunciation) to build and maintain their fort at Bengkulu during the second wave, beginning in the late seventeenth century.[5] Snouck Hurgronje gathered this information from informants in the late nineteenth century, and it is confirmed by the fact that present-day *tabut* rituals are led by those claiming sepoy descent. As Brakel has argued, the early Shi'a influences and associated rituals in Indonesian Islam probably "facilitated the introduction of a more splendid type of ritual (i.e., *tabut*) from India and/or Persia" from the late seventeenth century onward (Brakel 1975b, 61).

TABUIK'S HISTORICAL AND LEGENDARY BACKGROUND

When Husen the martyr died on the Karbala battlefield at the hands of Yazid's troops in 680, Islam was split into two sects that differ not only in dogma but also in style. The Shi'a believe in the divine right of the Prophet's family to rule, and the suffering of their leaders led to the introduction of the passion motif into their brand of Islam. The Sunni, on the other hand, reject divine right, and passion is conspicuously absent from their brand of Islam. In Iran, where the official religion is still Shi'a Islam, grief at the death of Husain and his relatives is expressed in passion plays, moving orations in the mosques, and processions marked by the beating of the breasts and self-flagellation. *Tabut* belongs to this passionate tradition.

As has been mentioned, the story of the martyrdom of Hasan and Hosen (Pariaman spelling) in Sumatra is partly historical, legendary, and mythical. Not surprisingly, it resembles the story in Shi'a India, as recounted, for example, by J. Shurreef and G. A. Herklots ([1832] 1895, 98–108). This account assumes that both Hosen and Hasan were martyrs. Thus the dirges sung during *tabut* at Pariaman (in Minangkabau or Urdu) mention both brothers; for example, singers exclaim: "Kasihan [poor] Hasan, kasihan Hosen!"

The account is also reflected in the *tabuik* myth at Pariaman, which asserts that an ancestor of the sepoys happened to be present on the Plain of Karbala on the day that the army of Hosen was defeated, when his body was chopped into pieces by the enemy of the faith. The ancestor of the sepoys was amazed to witness the descent to earth of a heavenly bird-shaped chariot of angels to pick up Hosen's remains and those of his brother Hasan. The sepoy managed to hang on to the chariot as it began its ascent to heaven, but when the angels noticed his presence, he was promptly dropped back to earth. Every tenth of Muharram since then, he and his descendants and followers have attempted to commemorate the wondrous vision of Hasan's and Hosen's ascent to heaven with a *tabut* festival, during which the faithful build a model of the beautiful bird-shaped chariot that carried Hosen's funeral bier. This model is either called *tabut* (lit. "coffin") or *burak*, the latter meaning a mythical bird that can move with the "speed of *burq*" (i.e., lightning; hence the derivation of its name, *booraq* [Shurreef and Herklots (1832) 1895, 122]) (fig. 4.2a and b).[6]

The myths about the dissemination of *tabut* in Sumatra mention Bengkulu as its place of origin in Sumatra. One holds that *tabut* was brought to Bengkulu from India by its first Muslim inhabitant, Imam Senggolo, alias Syek Burhanuddin. Another has

a   b

Figure 4.2a and b *Taboot* or *tazeea* and *booraq*. Models of parts of a complete "Taboot or tazeea" from the Deccan in early nineteenth-century India (Shurreef and Herklots [1832] 1895, plate 1). The goblet-shaped funeral bier resting on a square tomb is placed on top of the *burak* and carried in procession to the sea on the tenth of Muharram.

it that a Muslim leader named Kadar Ali brought *tabut* to Pariaman from Bengkulu. Informants in Aceh indicate that discharged sepoys brought *tabut* with them when they sailed from Bengkulu to Kuta Raja and Sigli. Some details of the rituals and performances in each town differ, but the musicians all played local as well as Indian musical instruments. The varied forms of *tabut* in Sumatra's towns are probably the result of several processes of transplantation and local development.

The passionate atmosphere of a full-scale *tabut* festival in Pariaman is created largely by the military sound of teams of drummers playing up to a hundred large drums (*dol*) at once, led by one small drum (*tasa*) per team, and playing a repertory of up to about fifty rhythms, which are classified locally as slow, medium, or fast. The names of these two types of drums clearly point to their Indian origins. At least as long ago as the early nineteenth century (see fig. 4.3), drums called *dhol* and *tasa* were used in Lucknow and other areas of North India from which *tabut* was transplanted to Sumatra. The *tasa* has a bowl-shaped earthenware body and goatskin head laced with rattan to a thick rattan ring around the base of the bowl. It is beaten with a pair of wooden sticks to produce a sharp, high-pitched sound that penetrates the sound of scores of *dol* and is therefore suitable to serve as the rhythmic leader.

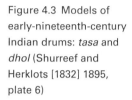
Figure 4.3 Models of early-nineteenth-century Indian drums: *tasa* and *dhol* (Shurreef and Herklots [1832] 1895, plate 6)

The Indian *tasa* dates from pre-Muslim times, and its name probably derives from Persian (Dournon and Kartomi 1984, 532).

Like the *tasa*, but unlike the Indian *dhol* or Iranian *dohol*, the Sumatran *dol* is suspended around the player's neck and is beaten with only a pair of wooden sticks. Its goatskin heads are attached with perpendicular and triangular rattan lacing to the wooden body, which is cylindrical in Pariaman and barrel-shaped in Bengkulu. Though the *dol* is very heavy to carry, the Persian *dohol* is even larger and heavier (During 1984, 580). According to Nelly Caron (1975, 4, 9), the *dohol* is one of the instruments played in the *ta'zia* of Iran, while according to Dournon and Kartomi (1984, 532) the *tasa* is played in the *ta'zia* of North India. However, the literature is unclear about the geographical distribution and extent of the use of these drums in Muharram.

TABUIK PROCEEDINGS IN PARIAMAN

We were told in Pariaman in 1982 that all faithful sepoy descendants were expected to play an active role in the *tabuik* proceedings, and that only they were allowed to play the major ceremonial roles. Until the 1970s, members of several neighborhoods in Pariaman took part, each constructing a magnificent *burak* and carrying out the other required rituals. However, in the 1982 festival, Syiah (local spelling of "Shi'a") families from only two neighborhoods participated—Perak and Jawa, who became symbolic rivals in their representations of a side in the Karbala war.[7] The sepoys are known not only as *orang Kling* (descendants of India) but also as *anak pisang* (banana people), a term that refers to the symbolic Syiah revenge expressed by the "slaughter" of the banana stalks ritual in *tabuik* (see below).

First, the two families requested permission of government to hold the festival. They were represented by their respective *pawang tabuik* (*tabuik* shamans), who happened to be women. The government officials came to their houses and discussed the financial aspects of the event, with the two families offering to pay some of the costs, as was their religious duty. Because the officials hoped the event would attract many tourists to Pariaman, they requested that the festival be held four days late, that is, from 4–14 Muharram instead of 1–10 Muharram, so that the climax of the festival would occur on Sunday, 14 Muharram. The officials argued that a large number of tourists would shop in Pariaman's roadside stalls and shops, that the travel and accommodation industry in general would profit considerably, and that the event would bring big economic benefits to the population at large.

Being passionate Syiah believers, the two female diviners were very upset at the proposed change of dates, which, they warned, could result in illness, death, and other disasters. Forced to compromise, however, they decided secretly to hold two *tabuik* rituals: one on 1–10 Muharram according to Syiah regulations at home, and the other on the dates proposed by the government. Despite promises of considerable governmental assistance, most expenses were nevertheless borne by the two families, whose religion forbade their making a profit from their *tabuik* activities.

In the days before the festival began, scores of *dol* and a few *tasa* drums were collected from the store outside town and brought to the two *tabuik* homes (*rumah tabuik*) to be tuned and repaired if necessary (fig. 4.6). The drums are said to have once accompanied the military exercises of the sepoys during the period of British rule in Sumatra. Their exceedingly loud, military-style rhythms lent a sense of great excitement to the proceedings as their players rehearsed each day in different parts of town and played in the street processions at specified times. Meanwhile, the materials and tools to make the *daraga* (funeral shrine, fig 4.4) and the elaborate, high funeral bier *burak* were brought to a shed outside the two *tabuik* homes, ready for the two teams of artists to construct the shrines and biers in the allocated ten days under the watchful eyes of the two female shamans, who made sure they were decorated properly. The term *daraga* is derived from *dargah*, a Persian loan word to Hindi meaning "sacred shrine" (Ronkel 1914, 337).[8]

For each of the ten days of the festival, a set of ritual requirements had to be fulfilled. Any variance from the rules could prompt disaster. The first day saw the men construct the first stage of the *daraga* on a clay mold in the nearby yard and build a bamboo fence around the *daraga*. Groups of women in each *tabuik* house began to decorate umbrellas with scores of white paper flowers to be placed on the *daraga* and to decorate the high *burak* itself on the tenth day. "Roofs" of white cloth were then attached horizontally at three vertical levels between four bamboo poles standing around a clay mold (representing a grave) at the base of the *daraga*. Throughout the festival, various offerings were added to the *daraga*, and incense was burned. Meanwhile, the *tasa* and *dol* players in each village tautened the drumheads by holding them close to the flames of a small bonfire to make them sound *nyariang* ("clear and bright"), and to rehearse and process around the streets (fig. 4.5). The bonfires, which are reminiscent of the bonfires in the *tabut/ta'ziya* festivals in India (Shurreef and Herklots [1832] 1895, 113), burned around the town throughout *tabuik*.[9]

On the afternoon of the first day, both villages held their first main procession: Mangambil Tanah (Take a Clod of Earth), keeping the exact timing and place secret in case they were disrupted by members of the rival *tabuik* neighborhood. Led by their *pawang tabuik*, about a hundred people on each side walked in procession to the accompaniment of slowly played *dol* and *tasa* dirge rhythms to the bank of a river. The two *tabuik* families sat in separate enclosures; ate a special *tabuik* snack of boiled banana, coconut, and sugar; and drank a traditional cooling ginger drink called *sarobat* (in Indian *tabut* this is called *shurbut*; see Shurreef and Herklots [1832] 1895, 123). After Ashar prayers (the third of the five daily prayers at around 4:00 P.M.), the crowds on the riverbank watched one of two sepoy descendants representing each family dive into the river. While still submerged, each diver put a handful of earth from the riverbed into a piece of white cloth and then pressed and tied it into a pudding shape so that no one could see the earth when he reemerged. Kneeling beside the wrapped clod and a bowl of burning incense near the riverbank, the *imam* of the local mosque and his assistant then said prayers that included reference to the deaths of Hasan and Hosen. With loud dirge drumming, the processions then moved back to the *daraga*. The wrapped clod of earth was ceremonially placed in it alongside the burning incense, and appropriate prayers were said. The clod of earth symbolized the bodies of Hasan and Hosen, dust to dust.[10]

On the second day, both *pawang tabuik* said that the chairs on the veranda of their houses had begun to shake because the ceremonies had begun late. Even though they had secretly commenced the rituals at the correct time, they had had visitations from their sepoy ancestors in their dreams that night. They felt sick and uneasy during the entire ten days.

The second to fourth days were intended to be silent days, serving as "the calm before the storm," while shifts of craftsmen worked around the clock to finish building and decorating the two *burak*, protecting each section with plastic covers when it was finished. In Bengkulu these three days are called *hari gam* (from the Hindi *gramm* meaning "sorrow" or "condolence"; see Ronkel 1914, 338). The drummers were supposed to remain quiet, though we could in fact hear them rehearsing.

Figure 4.4 A decorated *daraga* (shrine) in the Perak neighborhood of Pariaman during *tabuik*, 1982

Figure 4.5 *Tasa* and *dol* players in Pariaman during the *tabuik* procession, 1982

Figure 4.6 Tuning a *dol* in Pariaman before performing in the *tabuik* procession

Figure 4.7 The ceremonial cutting of the banana stalks in Pariaman during *tabuik*

Two major rituals were held on the fifth day. The Turun Panja (The Outspread Hand Comes Down) ritual took place at noon. *Panja* (*penja*), also known as *jari-jari* (fingers), derives from the Persian *panjah*, meaning "hand with fingers outspread" (Ronkel 1914, 339). Made of gold, silver, or zinc, it symbolizes the dismembered hand of Hasan. Kept hidden in white cloth all year in the ceiling of the *tabuik* house, it is brought down for this ritual every fifth of Muharram and given its annual purification wash in lemon water. Sales of the holy water, used for healing purposes, go toward the considerable cost of holding a *tabuik* festival.

The purified *panja* was then placed in a half-hemispherical frame covered in white lace and carried in procession around the *daraga*. The *pawang tabuik* circumambulated the shrine many times while singing heartrending dirges at her own independent tempo. She was followed by crowds of mourners who alternately raised and lowered their hands in grief to the rhythm of the drums.[11] Her singing, called *maratapi jari-jari* (Mi., "mourning the hands"), stylistically resembled local indigenous *ratap* singing on sorrowful or mystical occasions.[12] She sang such texts as "Ah, ah, Hosen, Ali bidansyah [holy] Ali kasihan [pity], Hosen, kasihan Hasan, Hasan Allah mati [dead], hoyak Hosen, mahoyak Hosen [lit. 'sway Hosen, or long live Hosen'])."[13] Meanwhile the crowd continually chanted: "Hasan, Hosen" as they encircled the *daraga* to the accompaniment of the *dol* and the *tasa*. The drummers played slow dirge rhythms called "Daraga" and "Ali Mahatam" ("Ali Dirge") or "Matam," which according to Philippus van Ronkel (1914, 338) derives from the Sanskrit *matta* meaning "foggy" or "cloudy" and is also the Muslim Indian name of a *majlis* chant rhythm (Burkhardt-Qureshi 1981). Meanwhile, mourners threw yellow rice grains and coins, sprinkled scented oil on the shrine, and bought the ashes of the burning incense to use as medicine.

A variety of symbolic objects were carried in the procession, including flags of four colors—black, white, red, and yellow, with the red flags symbolizing Hosen and the green flags representing Hasan. They also carried yellow paper fish, the symbolic meaning of which had been forgotten by the participants.[14] There was also a model of the real *jari-jari*, that is, a hand-shaped cloth object with a skirt attached that was black on one side and either yellow (in the Jawa neighborhood) or white (in Perak) on the other.

Late that afternoon, the ceremony called Mamancang Batang Pisang (Cut the Banana Stalk) was carried out simultaneously in both villages. Beforehand, crowds of people followed the two teams of drummers who were parading along the streets to their own medium-tempo drumming. Each aimed to take a secret route to a clump of banana plants, trying to avoid the other side, for if one side happened to meet the other, a mock battle would ensue. On reaching a patch of banana plants, they stopped, and a few smiling men who were in a trancelike state chopped off the stalks near the roots in one sweep with a magically potent sword, *pedang Jenawi* (fig. 4.7), symbolizing the revenge for Hosen's death at the hands of Yazid.[15] The stalks were brought back to the *daraga* and placed in the earth on each side of it, together with military flags (black and white for Perak's *daraga* and black and yellow for Jawa's). Citrus branches (which symbolize purity), with white *melati* flowers (which symbolize funerals) and a knife (symbolizing the dismembering of Hosen's body) hanging from them on each side were also planted alongside the *daraga*. The ceremony ended with *ashar* prayers said by the *imam* at the nearest mosque.

The intensely emotional experiences of the fifth day were followed by light entertainment on the next. In the afternoon of the sixth day, the *tabuik lenong* (small model *tabuik*) processions took place around town. A decorated tower about one and a half meters high was carried above the head of a participant on each side and was swayed from side to side like the swaying of the great *tabuik* on the tenth day. In former decades, artists belonging to the *tabuik lenong* groups could be hired to perform popular Minangkabau *gamad* music (with violin, accordion, and drums), a mask dance, and other local dances in front of people's homes in the evenings, in return for contributions toward the cost of *tabuik*. Until the 1960s, a dancer wearing a goatskin mask still performed during *tabut* in Barus, and we know that a masked dance was associated with *tabuik* in Solok during the early part of this century (see fig. 4.8). These performances are called *maradai*.[16] It is possible that *maradai* in Pariaman once included folk games featuring large paper models of animals like the *ikan-ikan* (fish) and *gajah-gajah* (elephant) games, which are still played during *tabot* in Bengkulu.

At noon on the seventh day, the Maarak Jari-jari (Procession of Hands) took place, and the passionate atmosphere returned. In doleful processions around the street, each side paraded its *panja* and chanted phrases such as "Hasan, Hosen, kasihan Hasan, kasihan Hosen!" as its drummers played the "Ali Mahatam" drum rhythm. Meanwhile, the craftsmen in both the Jawa and the Perak neighborhoods had finished making the tower of their *tabuik* cenotaphs (fig. 4.9) and had covered the bird-shaped structure with velvet. The cenotaphs in 1982 were not very different from their counterparts in 2009 (see figs. 4.10 and 4.11).

By evening the feeling of tragic excitement had risen to fever pitch, and the *beruji* (i.e., *dol* drums) or m*anjara* (ritual visits to rival *tabuik* groups) mock war scenes began, symbolizing the *perang jihad* (holy war) of Karbala. Hundreds of people accompanied the lead *tasa* drummer and scores of *gandang tabuik* drummers as they played the fast, exciting *irama basosoh perang* (warring battle rhythm) while processing down the streets of Pariaman's Tandikat neighborhood, periodically building up to a fever pitch of intensity and tempo as they moved from one area to another and

Figure 4.8 An early-twentieth-century Hasan-Hosen or *tabuik* procession in the inland town of Solok, West Sumatra (Lekkerkerker 1916, 171; Joustra 1923, 140)

Figure 4.9 The tower of a *burak* wrapped in plastic for protection before being mounted on a portable frame in the Jawa neighborhood, Pariaman, 1982

Figure 4.10 A *burak* or *tabuik*
in procession on the last day of
tabuik, Pariaman, 1982

Figure 4.11 A *burak* or *tabuik*
in procession on the last day of
tabuik, Pariaman, 2009 (photo:
Paul Mason)

pausing every half hour or so to rest.[17] As the various groups of drummers played in different areas, the soundscape took on an aleatoric character.

Then the two sides converged at a wide crossroads corner, and the violence began. Some men began to throw stones, and eventually someone was blinded in one eye, whereupon the police interrupted the electric atmosphere and dispersed the crowd. Everyone then went home.

On the eighth night, the Maarak Saroban (Turban Procession) was supposed to be held to celebrate Hosen's heroism, with models of Hosen's turban and severed hand carried by members of each side to commemorate the beheading of Hosen by Yazid's soldiers, who are said to have cried out: "We have won! Here's the head (the turban) of Hosen!" Memory of this scene stimulates bitter emotion and feelings of revenge, which are then normally vented in a *tabuik* mock war scene between the two sides in the streets. However, because several men had suffered injuries on the previous night, the chief of police issued a ban on drumming in the town for the rest of the festival, and the procession could not, therefore, take place. Some disappointed people argued that the ban should be applied only to young drummers, who were more likely to inflame the crowd with their amazingly fast, exciting rhythms, and that elderly drummers should be allowed to play their stately rhythms. Nevertheless, the total ban prevailed.

The *tabuik* families stayed up all night on the ninth night to finish making the *tabuik* cenotaphs. In the Jawa neighborhood, the *burak*'s solid, rounded buttocks, legs, and body were covered in black velvet, and in the Perak neighborhood with dark green velvet. Like the Indian *booraq* described by Shurreef and Herklots ([1832] 1895, 122), each *burak* had the breast and neck of a swan, the loins of a lion, two wings, the tail of a peacock, and the stature of a mule. The main difference was that the neck supported the head of a tiny lady with Indian features and long black hair, as opposed to a man's head and face in the 1832 Indian example they described. The trapezoidal tower had long, rectangular windows and was covered in red, white, and black velvet with gold trimmings. Both tower and "bird" had red, gold, white, or green Chinese shiny paper designs of crabs and fish attached here and there, recalling the patronage of *tabuik* by the Chinese Indonesian population in Pariaman before 1966. About fifteen umbrellas covered with white paper flowers were "planted" around the bases of the tower and the bier. Around midnight the construction reached full height after its various parts were mounted on top of each other. An approximately 1.5 meter high tower was placed on top of the 3 meter high *burak*, and a funeral bier, almost half a meter in height, was mounted on the tower with an open, upright umbrella placed right on top. The red and green flags that projected out of it symbolized Hosen and Hasan, respectively.

On the morning of the tenth day, around sixteen men on each side mounted the high *tabuik* cenotaphs on their shoulders and paraded them around the streets (fig. 4.12), taking care to avoid the power lines. The constructions were shaken—*dihoyak*— in elegant motion to symbolize the battle of Karbala. However, on the very day when emotions were supposed to be released, the drumming was banned, turning the long-awaited occasion into an anticlimax. The accompanying crowd was supposed to scream out expressions like "Mahoyak Hosen" ("Long live Hosen!") and other antagonistic cries against the other side. Instead, there was virtual silence, and the procession was curtailed after only half an hour.

By noon the streets of Pariaman were packed with about two hundred thousand people who had arrived by road from all parts of the province; some had even flown in from as far away as Jakarta. The two *tabuik* went on parade and arrived at oppo-

Figure 4.12 A "dancing" *burak* during the final procession on the tenth of Muharram, Pariaman, 1982

site ends of the main street. Political figures gave speeches about the government's contribution to the occasion and its significance in terms of the state philosophy, Pancasila, to which the crowd listened politely. Then the two *tabuik* began to move on their final journey down to the sea. Without the drumming, however, the antagonistic excitement that was supposed to be built up between the two sides was entirely absent. The event was like a film with its magnificent soundtrack missing due to a technical hitch. Without the music, the occasion had lost most of its meaning. The two giant *tabuik* moved silently across the beach, where an exciting *perang pasir* beach "battle" was supposed to take place. The sculpted ladies' heads were removed from each *tabuik* so that their power would be dismantled (*diamankan*) and they could be used at the next *tabuik* festival. At Magrib prayers just after sunset, the *tabuik* were thrown into the waves. There was a moment of excitement as adults and children swam in to retrieve parts of the *tabuik* to serve as good-luck charms; then everyone went home.[18]

The enmity between the two sides had officially ended now that the *tabuik* had been thrown into the sea, symbolizing the ascent of Hasan and Hosen to heaven. But for the *tabuik* families the ceremonials had not yet ended. In Pariaman (but not in Bengkulu), the eleventh to thirteenth days of Muharram are days of *kanduri* ritual feasts, prayers, and the burial of the remaining *tabuik* equipment in the local graveyard.

The unprecedented government ban on the drumming to stop the violence in 1982 changed the character of *tabuik* in Pariaman during the following decades.

THE *DOL-TASA* MUSIC

The *gandang tabuik* drum rhythms played in Pariaman in 1982 may be divided into four categories based on tempo. The first consisted of the very slow, dirgelike rhythms, exemplified by *irama daraga*, which was played while the participants were encircling the *daraga* funeral shrine to mourn the death of Hasan. The second comprised slow rhythms, such as "Ali Matam," performed while an elderly *pawang tabuik* sang a mixed Minangkabau-Urdu text that mourned the death of Hosen's and Hasan's father, Ali. The third comprised rhythms in medium tempo, such as *irama dua-dua*, played during routine processions. And the last were the very fast rhythms, such as *irama basosoh perang*, reserved for the most passionate mourning processions.

Another *tabuik* performance, which was part of a *dol-tasa* competition that we recorded in 1972, serves to demonstrate the characteristic *basosoh perang* rhythmic patterns. The performance began with a solo *tasa* introduction, followed by the entry of the *dol* drummers playing straight, syncopated, and at times interlocking rhythms, with the concluding passage played by the *tasa* and the *dol* in unison. Displaced rhythms resulted in some metrically ambiguous passages. The rhythmic structure of the piece comprised fourteen sections, the first ten of which may be heard in audio example 4.1, while section 14 is shown in music example 4.1.

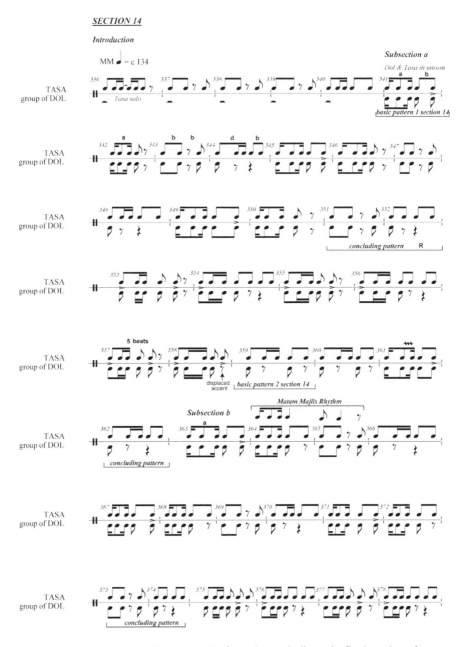

Music example 4.1 A transcribed sample of *gandang tabuik* music; final section of an extended performance of *irama basosoh* (war rhythm) led by Bp. M. Jarang (recorded by H. and M. Kartomi in Tandikat in 1972 and transcribed by Aline Scott-Maxwell)

As may be seen in music example 4.1, the structure consists of several sections linked by transition passages that contain many internal repeats or variants of their distinctive rhythmic-timbral motives. The performers continually increased the dynamic level and the tempo from ♩ = 108 to ♩ = 134, and then allowed it to subside in intensity and tempo.

The section begins with a short introduction on the *tasa* using motives a and b (♫♩♩ and ♩♩), followed by subsections *a, b,* and *c* on *tasa* and *dol* in duplicative or interlocking rhythms, with the first subsection based on *a* and *b*, followed by a concluding passage based on motives b and d in the first subsection. After being repeated, it varied the rhythm the third time, followed by a combination of additive five-beat and six-beat patterns repeated once, and led via a displaced accent into a statement of the section's basic pattern ♫♩♩ ♩♩, with another displaced accent occurring before the concluding pattern (bar 362). This was followed by subsection *b*, beginning with motives *a* and *b* (bar 363), followed by a variant of the *matam majlis* rhythm (bars 364–65, repeated at 368–69 and 372–73), after which it continued in a similar manner. The *matam majlis* rhythm, which is quoted by Burkhardt-Qureshi in her article on *majlis* in Iran (1981), resembles the rhythm of the same name in *dol* and *tasa* playing of Persian origin.

TABUIK'S IMPACT ON THE HINTERLAND

The passionate drumming, dirge singing, and crowd chanting in Pariaman's *tabuik* contrast strongly with the local Minangkabau styles of indigenous music and ritual. Despite its foreign Muslim origins, however, *tabuik* has made a substantial impact on the indigenous musical culture of the Pariaman hinterland. In most parts of West Sumatra, the main ritual ensemble, the *talempong*, consists minimally of a gong-chime and one or more small double-headed drums (*gandang*) or frame drums, but in the *talempong* of the Pariaman hinterland, the small drum or frame drum is replaced by a large *dol*. It is played resting on the ground as opposed to being carried in procession in *tabuik*, but the fact that it was adopted at all in the conservative *talempong* tradition is unusual. The titles of some pieces in its repertory, for example, "Ali Mahatam" ("Ali Dirge") and "Gajah Muharam" ("Elephant Muharram"), suggest that foreign Shi'a elements had a deep influence on the music of the hinterland, including that of the main ensemble *talempong jao* (Javanese *talempong*), which normally comprises five small bossed gongs in a frame, a *dol*, and an optional *lasuang* rice-stamping block.[19]

Perhaps the reason for the successful transplantation of Indian Shi'a musical elements into the domestic ceremonies of a conservative Sunni Sumatran community is the long-standing predilection for competitions between teams of virtuoso play-

Figure 4.13 Part of a troupe of *dol* players led by a *tasa* player in a competition in Kampuang Pincuran Songsang, a village outside Pariaman, 1982

ers, in this case, of *dol-tasa* players. Such competitions are still sponsored by local government officials today, and not only around *tabuik* time. At the competitions the *tasa* player stands on a decorated portable stage and leads the twenty to forty *dol* players of his team, who stand below the stage in military formations while they play (fig. 4.13). They have a repertoire of about thirty works ranging from the slow and dirgelike to the medium fast and the very fast, and they are played with alternate ultraloud and relatively soft dynamics.[20] Because a *tasa*, with its rounded earthenware body, is more difficult to make than a *dol*, and as hundreds of *dol* need to be made for each *tabuik* festival, it is perhaps not surprising that it was the *dol* and not the *tasa* that became the main drum in Pariaman hinterland culture.

THE SURVIVAL OF *TABUIK*

Clearly, *tabuik* in Pariaman has had a checkered political history. Because of its relatively great expense and alleged threat to the peace, the Dutch colonial authorities frequently banned or discouraged it, especially in the 1920s and 1930s, and it disappeared altogether during the stringencies of the Japanese occupation. In the 1950s and early 1960s, it was revived again as an instrument of the political parties, particularly the Nationalist and Communist parties (PNI and PKI), with the main Muslim party (Nahdlatul Ulama) turning a blind eye to the Shi'a elements. With Chinese Indonesian business support, the two big parties funded increasingly elaborate *tabuik* festivals, painting their own political slogans on the wings of the *burak* that they sponsored.

Tabuik was also banned in the political turmoil of 1965–66. As Suharto's New Order regime tried to establish its power, Pariaman's once-substantial Chinese Indonesian population fled or was killed, and with it one of *tabuik*'s main sources of sponsorship disappeared. *Tabuik*'s former association with the PNI, the PKI, and local Chinese Indonesian sponsorship did not endear it to the new regime.

Meanwhile, theologians in the Muhammadiyah movement were arguing against the Shi'a elements in *tabuik*. They opposed the alleged heretical belief in the divine right of Ali, Hasan, and Hosen to inherit the caliphate and pointed out the historical error of believing that Hasan, like Hosen, died a martyr's death. However, the *ulama* were eventually persuaded by government officials and the New Order's political party–like organization of "functional groups"—Golkar (Golongon Karya)—that *tabuik* should be allowed to revive again, though in a secularized and tourist-oriented form. Everyone saw the potential economic benefits to Pariaman of allowing its unique, colorful *tabuik* tradition to come before the public eye again, thereby attracting large numbers of visitors to West Sumatra and media coverage of the province, and swelling the coffers of a range of local businesses.

Tabuik officially resumed in Pariaman in 1974, with around two hundred thousand or more tourists attending each time. Government officials enjoyed their association with the popular festival, taking advantage of the opportunities it offered to display their social organizing skills and political speech making. The stone throwing in the 1982 festival, however, prompted the authorities to plan the event differently. They wanted to make it safer and to learn from the experience of *tabot* organizers in Bengkulu, who seemed to have defused the violent element more successfully than they had.

In Bengkulu the authorities had encouraged a much larger number of villages than in Pariaman to construct *tabot* cenotaphs and to take part in the processions, with at least eleven villages producing a *tabot* each year. In 1979, the State of Bengkulu's twentieth-anniversary year, a total of fifty *tabot* floats took part in the street processions and *tabot* competitions and attention was diverted away from the passionate, potentially dangerous expression of emotions aroused by thoughts of the holy war at Karbala and feelings of revenge. The two nights of *tabot* war scenes had been replaced by *dol-tasa* competitions, with local *gamad* music and dance entertainment performed within the circles of *dol-tasa* players.

So Pariaman's *tabuik* organizers decided to increase tourist audiences and prioritize performances of the Minangkabau arts. Performances of the art of self-defense, dramatic comedy sketches, and dances such as the plate and *galombang* dances replaced the scenes of stone throwing and violence that had induced the Bupati to ban live drumming in the last part of *tabuik* in 1982. In the twenty-first century, the Department of Culture and Tourism ensured that various items of Minangkabau music, dance, and theater were performed in the streets to entertain the tourists and keep them in Pariaman for the full ten days of the festival. Paul Mason's video clip of the *tabuik* festival in Pariaman in 2009 (http://paul.sobriquet.net/publications/fieldnotes) includes street performances of many Minangkabau performing arts for tourists between the *tabuik* rituals, including the final procession of the cenotaphs and their dissipation after being thrown into the sea at sunset.

The cost of the artistic diversions in *tabuik*, of course, is that the element of passion—the distinguishing feature of Shi'ism—is lost. But this is precisely what the prevailing religious and political authorities want. The chances of *tabut's* survival, then, will presumably be proportional to its ability to adapt to the will of the authorities. If this means that it loses its essential character, little can be done to prevent it, for the lines of contact between the few Shi'a believers in Sumatra and the centers of Shi'ism overseas are now too weak to have an effect on this generation.

In any case, the important elements for the local population are the festival's splendid spectacle, stirring drum processions, and the health- and luck-bringing relics. It is these artistic and mystical elements, filtered long ago through religious experience in India and Iran, that will continue to attract throngs of Sunni adherents from all over the countryside and beyond to converge on Pariaman for the experience of *tabuik*.

ACKNOWLEDGMENTS

Our *tabut*-related fieldwork in Pariaman in 1972 and 1982, Bengkulu in 1981, and Sigli in 1982 was assisted by the Australian Research Council and the Department of Music at Monash University. I am grateful to Dra Chalida Fachruddin of the anthropology department, University of North Sumatra, and her father Bp. Guru Bakar, a respected *ulama* who lives near Pariaman, for their friendship, advice, and help while in Pariaman, and to the Bupati of Padang Pariaman in the 1980s, Bp. Anas Malik. Paul Mason kindly updated my knowledge of *tabuik* in Pariaman on the basis of his recent fieldwork and agreed to allow me to use his photo of the *tabuik* event in Pariaman in 2008 (fig. 4.11). Unless otherwise noted, the other photos were taken by Mas Kartomi in 1982.

FOUR SUFI MUSLIM GENRES
IN MINANGKABAU

This chapter examines four genres of the Muslim-associated performing arts as Mas Kartomi and I experienced them in Minangkabau during the 1970s and 1980s: *indang, salawek dulang, dikia Mauluik,* and *dabuih.* They are believed to have been developed centuries ago by local Sufi brotherhoods as part of *dakwah*— the early proselytization of the faith and the deepening of piety among believers, even though the songs of *dikia Mauluik* and *dabuih* are set to mainly secular texts on many occasions.

Indang is a song-dance performed by a row of men or women in *duduak* ("sitting," actually half-kneeling) position with rhythmic body movement, clapping, and frame-drum playing. *Salawek dulang* (or *salawek talang;* I. *salawat dulang*) is performed by a pair of alternating male solo singers, each of whom accompany themselves on a brass percussion tray (*dulang*). *Dikia Mauluik* (I. *dhikr Maulud,* lit. "remembering Allah in the month of Maulud") is a group vocal-instrumental form with mostly Sufi-oriented Muslim song texts based on *dikia* (Mi.; Ar. *zikir*) texts that are sung with body exercises and frame-drum accompaniment in the month of the Prophet's birth.[1] *Dabuih* (Mi., Ar., I. *dabus*) is a ritual form involving acts of self-harm as a demonstration of one's faith and physical invulnerability from pain (and sometimes in the colonial era in Aceh, readiness for battle). Though probably developed in part from transplanted genres, all four are regarded as *asali* (I. *asli,* "authentic") Minangkabau forms, and they all reflect clear Sufi aims and attributes.

Two of the genres—*dikia Mauluik* and *dabuih*—have only religious texts that are based on *dikia*; thus, some local religious leaders and academics classify them as "arts with a Muslim flavor" (*kesenian yang bernafaskan Islam*).[2] The other two genres—*indang* and *salawek dulang*—reputedly have agricultural origins, as reflected in their largely secular and topical song texts and the fact that the title, *indang*, means "to winnow"; however, as the performing groups normally add Muslim phrases (such as *Bismillah*, "in the name of Allah") at the beginning and the end of some sections, even the most devout *ulama* find them acceptable and classify them, with the academics, as "arts with a Muslim theme" (*kesenian Islami*).

The "Muslim sound" of three of the genres that use instruments is attributed in part to their use of the Muslim instrument par excellence, the frame drum, and the *salawek dulang* genre to the pair of brass trays played in rhythms similar to those of the frame drums.[3] Normally a frame drum has a skin head made from a goat, snake, or other animal, which is pinned to a ring-shaped wooden frame and tautened with a piece of rattan inserted in the inside rim. Musicians refer to the three main pitch-timbres played on the frame drums by onomatopoeic syllables. In the Pariaman area, *tum* denotes a low-pitched sound beaten midhead on the downbeat, *tak* a high-pitched sound tapped with the fingers near the rim of the head on an offbeat, and *darap* a medium-pitched double sound beaten near the middle of the head with the hand supported by the thumb on the edge. Sometimes both the high and the low sounds are played simultaneously on the same drum.

Although traditional Minangkabau society is matrilocal and affords special privileges for women, the main exponents of the four genres have traditionally been groups of men.[4] Besides singing lullabies and baby-thanksgiving and other songs, women usually perform traditional, non-Muslim dances such as *tari lilin* and *tari piriang* (Mi., the candle and plate dances with brass gong-chime ensemble accompaniment) and *tari payuang* (Mi., the umbrella dance with violin and frame-drum accompaniment) in mixed or single-sex couples at harvest festivals, and in some areas (e.g., Pariaman and Payakumbuah) they play the *talempong* gong-chime ensembles.[5]

From the late 1970s onward, however, separate female *indang* groups became common. While male performers usually wear a sarong over a trouser suit plus a *peci* (Muslim-associated hat), the women of the *darek* mostly wear traditional Minangkabau horn-shaped headdresses, long blouses, and skirts consisting of cloth containing gold or silver thread (*songket*). Women of the *pasisia* areas often wear velvet bridal costumes with a lavish number of gold hair ornaments.

Suharto's New Order government directed both male and female civil servants as well as children to perform *indang* song texts on festive occasions, with more virtuosic choreographies than previously, which required significant time devoted to group practice. It also became mandatory for *indang* and *salawek dulang* troupes to sing political propaganda texts in election campaigns and at government ceremonies. Many groups participated in performing art competitions, and some were featured in the local and national media. *Indang* groups were especially prominent, but other female devotional singing groups were also formed to perform modern *kasidah* and *nasyid* songs learned from commercial cassette recordings, with optional frame-drum playing.[6]

Another recent change involved the disappearance of the mosque drums. Until around the 1980s, each village mosque (fig. 5.2) yard had a long, single-headed drum called a *tabuh* (fig 5.1), housed respectfully in its own roofed pavilion. It was beaten five times daily to call the people to prayer or to warn them of impending danger such as a fire or invasion.

Recently, most mosque drums have fallen into disrepair, as their role was replaced by a *mu'adhdhin* (Ar.) who calls worshippers to prayer in amplified melodic strains of Egyptian or Turkish origin (fig. 5.3).

Figure 5.1 A long, single-headed drum (*tabuh*) in a Minangkabau mosque, traditionally used as a means of communication and to call people to prayer

Figure 5.2 A traditional
Minangkabau mosque

Figure 5.3 A Minangkabau
mu'adhdhin from Talang Maur

HISTORY

To understand the styles, content, and history of the traditional Muslim-associated genres, it is necessary to revisit the early history of Minangkabau Islam. Scholarly and popular belief holds that the Minangkabau people were converted at the beginning of the sixteenth century (Dobbin 1974, 319–56). The Portuguese traveler Tomé Pires, who visited Minangkabau in 1512–15, wrote that only one of the kings in Minangkabau was Muslim (Pires, in Cortesão [1944] 1967), which suggests that the local conversion to Islam was just beginning at the time.

The local Muslim arts may have begun to develop and spread from the seventeenth century onward as part of the *dakwah* activity of traveling religious leaders. The religion may have been spread by seaborne missionaries, soldiers, and merchants from Aceh, especially during and after the reign of Aceh's powerful king Iskandar Muda (1613–36), who controlled much of the west Sumatran, east Sumatran, and Malayan coasts. The Pariaman area in West Sumatra became part of Aceh's military zone in 1636. It is also probable that the religion was spread up the Indragiri and Kampar Rivers by traveling religious teachers from Sumatra's east coast.[7]

Besides the preaching of sermons in the mosques, one of the main early methods of spreading adherence to the faith was to establish Sufi-oriented *tarekat* (brotherhoods) in the villages, members of whom followed the *ilmu tassawuf* (Sufi knowledge). They learned to perform new rituals expressing the Sufi mystical path that may have been grafted onto existing indigenous religious and Hindu/Buddhist practices. Indeed, it stands to reason that the members of the brotherhoods would not have abandoned their old beliefs and practices entirely in the course of their conversion and that they would have adapted them to their changing beliefs. They met in one another's homes to sing, including Sufi texts that cite the ninety-nine names of Allah and praise the prophet Muhammad and the other prophets and saints of the mystics, a practice that remains today in some villages. The rhythmic motion and intoning of the *zikir/dikia* (Ar., Mi.) helped transport the men into a state of religious ecstasy (*seluk*) or perceived union with Allah, as in Sufi genres the world over.

The first Minangkabau *pesantren* (religious school) is believed to have been established by a Minangkabau missionary named Syéh Burhanuddin, born in 1646 in Padangpanjang, Pariangan, and a former pupil of the famous Sufi scholar 'Abdurra'uf of Singkil in Aceh. Soon after returning to Minangkabau from Aceh, he established the school at the present-day pilgrimage site of Ulakan, near Pariaman (Bp. Rasyid Manggis, pers. comm., 1978). He and his followers and Acehnese contacts may have been responsible, at least in part, for the spread of the Minangkabau genre *dabuih* (known as *dabôih/dabôh* in Aceh), and variants of the frame drum, known as *rapa'i* in Aceh but as *indang, indang rapa'i* (in Pariaman) or *rabana* (Ma.; Mi. *rabano*) in Minangkabau.

Indang may then have been transformed by contact with Islam into a new genre that combined pre-Muslim and Muslim elements. Even today, some of the songs used in *indang* performances have an affinity with pre-Muslim mystical singing in Malay *pantun* quatrains, and the interlocking *indang* frame-drum rhythms played resemble those of the drum and gong parts of the traditional *talempong* gong-chime ensembles, as will be exemplified below.

In the early days of conversion, the *tukang kaba* (storytellers) are said to have been encouraged to sing ancestral legends with added Muslim phrases to give them a Muslim flavor, and to sing new stories about Muslim heroes. Moreover, as Taufik Abdullah suggests, the ancestral Cindua Mato legend was probably created in the sixteenth century when Islam was still being integrated into the countryside (Abdullah 1970, 10), that is, at a time when "custom was based on religion, and religion was based on custom" (Collins 2003, 43). Similarly, in the month of Maulud, members of the various *tarekat* sang *barzanji* songs about the Prophet's birth and life to their own accompaniment on their large and medium-sized frame drums (*rapa'i, rabana,* and *rabano*), thereby creating the *dikia Mauluik* genre that is discussed below.[8]

The traditional art of *dabuih* also combines Muslim elements with local ones. *Dabuih* devotees perform movements from the traditional Minangkabau art of self-defense: *silek* (I. *silat*). Barendregt has argued that *silat* was once based on the ideology of the veneration of nature and ancestral spirits, and that around the fifth to the ninth centuries its philosophy and practice were enriched by adopting the Hindu-Buddhist idea of "the inner being" (*tenaga dalam*) and associated martial art techniques.[9] *Silat* philosophy and education were then adapted in the early sixteenth century to mystical Sufi concepts that influenced the customary law (*adék*) and represented the outer (physical movement) form of the inner life (Barendregt 1995, 113).

INDANG

Indang, also known as *indang rapa'i* in the Pariaman area, is a sitting song-dance with religious or secular poetic texts and frame-drum (*indang*) accompaniment that is popular throughout Minangkabau. Usually it is presented as a separate genre, but it is also performed as part of the *dabuih* ritual described below. In the 1960s, several troupes of artists developed *indang* into a modern art form that could be performed on stage, such as for weddings, circumcisions, and government functions. Some groups also perform the *alaambek* dance with vocal accompaniment (audio example 5.1).

Women have been allowed to create and lead *indang* performing groups since the 1980s, and there are now scores of female groups. Some rehearse thoroughly and perform in a highly virtuosic manner. In a performance, a group of male or female vocalists, holding a frame drum (*indang, rabano*) each, sit cross-legged in a row with their shoulders touching, led by the *tukang aliah* (overall leader).

A complete group usually comprises around eleven to fifteen artists called *tukang indang* (*indang* players). The lead vocalist, who is referred to as the *tukang dikia* (I. *tukang zikir*), sits separately behind the row and begins by singing a Muslim greeting, after which the group sings a response. She or he then sings a solo devotional text (*dikia*) or a secular verse leading into another response sung by the group. The group continues to sing alternating solo and chorus sections, with or without their own frame-drum accompaniment, as instructed by the *kalipah* (frame-drum leader). The members of the group begin to move their bodies in concert, or they break into two or more subgroups, each alternating with one or two of the other subgroups.

After the group enters the stage or arena, they lower their heads as a sign of respect to the audience. They then sit cross-legged on the floor or ground and beat out a series

Figure 5.4 A row of teenage girls performing the *indang* sitting dance, Nagari Mandahiling, Kabupaten Pariaman, 1982. In their repetitive routine the odd-numbered girls bend forward, while the even-numbered girls reach upward and clap in regular, interlocking patterns.

of interlocking rhythms on the frame drums in a loudly carrying (*nyariang*) fashion, building up to a very fast tempo (*irama capek*). Every second player makes identical movements in the opposite direction to those of his two immediate neighbors. If one group sways forward, the other group sways backward; if one sways diagonally back to the left, the other sways diagonally forward to the right. If alternate players bend backward and raise their drums in the air, the others bend forward, lowering their drums (fig. 5.4). Sometimes the left half of the group moves in one direction while the right half moves in the other. They place their drums on the floor in front of them and either weave identical rhythmic patterns in the air with their hands, or they snap their fingers or clap their hands in regular rhythm.[10] Meanwhile, they make strenuous efforts to concentrate on Allah, periodically playing very loudly to express their fierce religious desire.

The virtuosity of a performance demands discipline and organization, which is facilitated by the performers sitting very close together (see fig. 5.5a). In Nagari Mandahiling, Kabupaten Padang Pariaman, the "overall leader" (*tukang aliah*), sits in the middle of the row of players, with the pair of "chorus leaders" (*tukang tiang gadaik*) on either side. The "drumming leaders" (*tukang apik*) sit on each side of the chorus leaders, with thethe "assistants of the overall leader" (*tukang pangga*) on each side of them. The "body movement leaders" (*tukang bunga salapan*) sit on each side of the "protectors" (*tukang karang*) at both ends, ensuring that the pressure of the row of moving bodies does not force them to fall off the edge of the stage (fig. 5.5a).[11]

Different arrangements of players are found in some villages (fig. 5.5b). In Kecamatan Sungai Pandahan Village, Lubuk Sikaping, Kabupaten Pasaman, the overall leader enters first on the largest frame drum (called *induk*, lit. "mother"), followed by the smaller frame drums called *maimbau* (second entry) and *untuk lapak* (third entry).[12] In addition there are several frame drum players called *panuruik* ("followers").

After the intensely virtuosic instrumental introduction that accompanies the first set of movements, the players put their drums on the floor and rest from their exertions while the *tukang aliah* sings a welcoming song. Then the *tukang dikia* commences a long melodic passage based on the beginning of the confession of faith (*Al-Fatihah*, the first chapter of the Qur'an). The *indang* players perform movements while she or he sings, beginning in free meter (*irama palairan*) and ending in strict quadruple meter (*irama datar*). The last phrase is repeated first by the assistant leaders (*tukang pangga*) and then by the leader and the whole chorus, who sing an octave lower. The choral melodies, which are sung several times to different *pantun* in Minangkabau, are mostly symmetrical, frequently containing melodic sequences and triplets. They occur in cycles of sixteen-beat phrases and are mostly based on five to seven notes of a major or minor scale, such as the melody in music example 5.1.

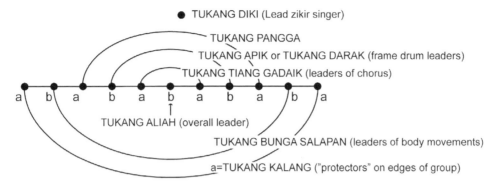

Figure 5.5a The frame-drum (*rapa'i indang*) players designated "a" perform identical body movements, while those designated "b" perform complementary movements.

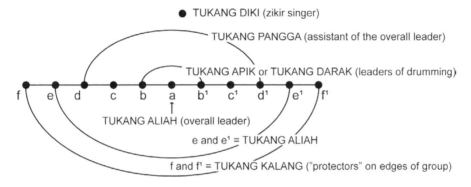

Figure 5.5b The frame-drum (*indang*) players who are designated "b/c/d/e/f" perform identical body movements, while those designated "b1/c1/d1/e1/f1" perform complementary movements under the headship of "a," the overall leader.

The performance of alternating solo and chorus singing, with or without frame-drum accompaniment, continues at varying dynamic levels and tempi for as long as the occasion requires. At the end, the *tukang aliah* sings an apology for any inadequacies in the performance.

Indang groups perform at life-event ceremonies and in competitions, for example, to raise money for community projects. A group at a wedding usually sings texts that offer moral and religious instruction to the bridal couple, and they also entertain their audiences with amusing poetry about romantic love, adventures, and everyday experiences.

In addition to serious texts, humorous texts about daring subjects such as sex are prevalent at *indang* competitions organized between village troupes during rice-

Music example 5.1 An *indang* melody

planting and harvesting seasons, as we witnessed at a night-time performance in the Pariaman area in 1982. The verbal battle may continue all night for several nights. Funds raised by selling tickets to the thousands of enthusiastic spectators from surrounding villages are used to finance infrastructure developments such as a new bridge or road.

This night's performance was broken into a series of approximately forty-minute periods, during each of which a minimum of three songs were sung to eight *pantun* verses each. The troupes sat in a triangular formation. While two of the troupes competed against each other, the third rested and thought up the questions it was going to ask its opponents during its turn. First, group A posed a question in *pantun* verse, asking where the Prophet Muhammad was born. Group B was required to give an acceptable answer, preferably a correct one, but as it happened not to know the answer, a cleverly evasive, witty one was offered, and the group waited to see how intense the audience's applause would be, for the degree of applause decides whether the answer is acceptable. On this occasion the evasive answer was judged to be adequate. Then group B asked a question of group A, also in *pantun* form. This time the audience judged that it had given an inadequate answer, so a new group, C, had to replace group A and try to answer the questions of both groups A and B, as well as posing its own questions to group D. Thus the number of questions requiring answers may increase as time goes on. At the end of the night, the audience's applause finally decided which side won the competition.

Indang drumming and body movements have become faster and increasingly virtuosic in recent decades, especially in the Pariaman region where intervillage competitions are frequently held. Musicians in most areas play large frame drums measuring between twenty and forty-five centimeters in diameter, but in Pariaman much smaller frame drums (ten to fourteen centimeters) are used, and are known by the Acehnese name of *rapa'i*. The smaller drum is easier to hold and play than a large one while performing body movements, and especially when its players choose to rotate its rolling edge on their left hand. The smaller drums are also said to produce a clearer (*lebih nyariang*), more beautiful (*lebih rancak*), louder, and higher-pitched sound, especially after their skin has been heated and thereby tautened near a flame.

INDANG ORIGIN LEGENDS

There are several legends about the origin of *indang*, two of which deal with *indang* as an instrument, and one with *indang* as both a genre and an instrument.

One holds that the frame-drum *indang* was first played in a sampan at sea by a Minangkabau mystic and scholar named Kalipah Taher, which suggests to some that this religious proselytizer returned with his frame drum from Aceh and that the *indang* genre therefore has Acehnese origins. Another legend contends that the *indang* instrument was transplanted to Pariaman from Aceh with the name *rapa'i*, which is the generic name for all frame drums in Aceh. The name is said to have stuck and is still used in the coastal and inland Pariaman area of Minangkabau.

According to a third origin legend, the frame drum's *adék* name, *indang*, suggests that both the genre and the frame drum itself derive from a pre-Muslim Minangkabau ritual with music and dance called *indang* that was performed at harvest festivals when farming families were winnowing large quantities of rice. When the people converted to Islam, *indang* adopted a partly devotional character, though retaining many of its secular or indigenous religious song texts. The name *indang* derives from the *pusako* (ancestral) expression *mahindang manampeh bareh bipiliah atak siek-ciek*, meaning "winnow the rice on the bamboo tray, pick out the remaining grains one by one," where *indang* means "to winnow" (Toorn 1891). Thus, the *indang* genre and frame drum are believed to be indigenous Minangkabau. Although frame drums are played in devotional genres in many parts of the Muslim world, the instrument actually appears in Mesopotamian art from around 3000 B.C.E. and of course could have spread to Sumatra from there long before the people's conversion to Islam.

A fourth legend is sometimes attached to the third. One day a Minangkabau named Chatib Sangko traveled to Meulaboh (in west Aceh) to study Islam from a member of the Sufi Rifa'iyyah sect, Tuanku Rifa'iyyah, who had assumed the name of the sect to which he belonged. Carrying his frame drum, Tuanku Rifa'iyyah sailed from Aceh with Chatib Sangko to Minangkabau and helped him convert the people to Islam. They did so partly by teaching them a devotional sitting dance with religious song texts that became known by the Minangkabau name of *indang*. Tuanku Rifa'iyyah's name was written inside his frame drum, and the two men called it by the Acehnese term, *rapa'i*. However, eventually the instrument became known as *indang*, the same name as the genre. In some respects, the *indang* genre resembles Aceh's *rapa'i geurimpheng* and *rateb meuseukat*, though its body percussion component, if present, is much less prominent and complex than in Aceh.

SALAWEK DULANG

The word *salawek* derives from the Arabic *salawat*, meaning "blessings" (on the prophet Muhammad), and *dulang* means "tray." In performances of *salawek dulang*, a pair of male vocalists alternate or overlap with each other as they sing improvised or composed poetic texts on sacred or secular topics in Minangkabau and accompany their singing by rhythmically tapping on a round brass tray (*dulang* or *talam*) held in each performer's left hand, producing rhythms that partly resemble those played on frame drums (audio example 5.2).

They also tell stories, comment humorously on topical events, and make jokes about normally forbidden subjects. The main purpose is to entertain and instruct people in religious and moral teachings performed at *kenduri* (feasts) on the occasions of weddings, circumcisions, the departure or return of a pilgrim, hundredth-day commemorations of a death, national or religious holidays, and government functions.

Most of the trays that are played are antique objects, fashioned from high-quality brass, with circular designs raised at two different levels around the circumference, and a simple leaf pattern etched around the edge. Some trays have been locally made, while others are said to have been imported long ago from India.

In a performance, the two players sit cross-legged on the floor or a raised stage wearing a sarong over their trousers, a shirt, and a *peci*. Each player holds a brass tray upright on his left foot so that his two hands are free to beat out rhythms on the tray. The lead singer begins the performance by asking members of the audience, both supernatural and human, to forgive any mistakes they may make. He then sings the salutation *Assalamū' 'alaikum* (peace be with you) in free meter, following this with the first part of the Muslim confession of faith: *lā ilāha illā 'llāh* (there is no God but God), and addresses the prophet, *O Nabi Muhammad* (O Prophet Muhammad).

Both singers shut their eyes and hide their faces behind their trays as they sing in an attempt to reach a state of religious concentration or altered consciousness. They then discover that they can effortlessly remember hundreds of religious phrases and can recount long stories about the prophets and a number of local legends. After the first vocalist has sung a few phrases, the second enters, beginning either at the unison or at the fourth above him, whereupon he sings the same melody as the leader but with different ornamentation. Sometimes he staggers his entry, which can produce two-part, imitative singing. Then the first singer may pause to breathe, thinking up his next song for a few moments. During the pause, the second singer takes his turn to sing, then to rest, as his partner sings again. The staggered entries produce continuous melody in one part or occasionally two.

Throughout a performance, the singers choose from many well-known metered rhythms with their own titles, such as *guguah talam* (tray rhythm) or *guguah tokoh* (leading rhythm). A rhythm in slow tempo is chosen to begin with, and after a few minutes a new fast rhythm is selected. Subsequently, various other rhythms are performed in alternating fast, medium, or slow tempo. The most talented singers may include elaborate melismatic ornamentation (*bungo*) in their performances. Some melodies are three-toned (based approximately, e.g., on solfa major-scale tones 1, 2, and 3) with halftones gradually added to expand the range in the course of the partly improvised singing. Other melodies are basically four-, five-, or six-toned, with halftones commonly added in melismatic passages that, in some cases, expand the range above the tonal palette established to that point. The singing style involves either very slight vibrato or none at all. The verses, in *pantun* quatrains, are in the Minangkabau language, with some standard Arabic phrases inserted at various points.

As in the case of the *indang* genre, *salawek dulang* competitions are popular. One pair of performers may ask questions in *pantun* form of another pair, who must reply correctly and wittily, or at least in a manner that satisfactorily entertains the audience, and without any hesitation. Members of the audience may ask the competitors for advice or information, pose religious or secular questions, and ask them to improvise answers to their choice of topics. A member of the audience may, for example, compose a *pantun* that asks whether his child will pass a certain examination, or whether—and when—his son will return home after leaving for many years to seek his fortune. One of the *salawek dulang* performers then improvises a response, also in *pantun* form, which may involve several sung verses. Audience applause punctuates each question and answer and finally decides which pair of *salawek dulang* performers wins the contest.

DIKIA MAULUIK

As has been noted, in many areas *dikia* singing focuses on an important religious event such as the birth of the prophet Muhammad, which is celebrated in the third month (Ar. Rabii' ul-awal; Mi. Mauluik) of the Muslim calendar. *Dikia Mauluik* performances are performed nightly in different homes throughout the month of Maulud, after a harvest, at a feast (*kenduri*) to celebrate a life event such as a birth, a circumcision, or a wedding, or to mark success in a Qur'an-reading examination or on winning a contest. As the women of a neighborhood prepare food for the feast, a *dikia Mauluik* group plays long into the night in return for food and drink, and sometimes money. They also play to bid farewell to a pilgrim bound for Mecca, followed by a ceremonial procession in which people process with the pilgrim under a black umbrella (symbolizing protection) to his point of departure (audio example 5.3).

In the Payakumbuh area, *dikia Mauluik* is as popular as *indang* in other areas. Performances resemble *indang* in that the artists sit cross-legged while singing religious texts to their own frame-drum accompaniment, but there are no body exercises. Instead the focus is on chanting passages from the Qur'an in Arabic, sometimes from memory and at other times by reading copies lying open on the floor. Frame drums, usually called *rabano*, vary in size, but are all relatively large (ca. 50 to 54 cm in diameter, 12 to 15 cm deep). Their goatskin heads are pinned to hardwood frames whose backs are partly closed, leaving an open space of approximately twenty-four centimeters in diameter. The players mainly beat on or near the edge and near the middle of the heads, which are tautened by pressing rattan into the inside rims as well as by heating their skins. Other sounds are produced by beating or tapping other parts of the drumhead (figs. 5.6 and 5.7).

Figure 5.6 A group of *dhikr* performers led by Bp. Zakaria Dalimunthe, Padang Sidempuan, Angkola, 1972

Figure 5.7 A dikia Mauluik ensemble led by Bp. Islamidar, Talang Maur, Payakumbuh, 1985

The leader (*tukang dikia*) begins a performance by singing the words, in Minangkabau or Arabic: "Let us sing to celebrate the birth of the Prophet." He chooses a page
from the Qur'an and initially sings two lines of the text for all to join in, in unison.

All performers note the number of the page to discover which rhythm they should
play on the *rabano*. If page 4 is chosen, for example, they play a slow rhythm associated with the number four, called *guguah ompe*, "fourth rhythm." Two lines from the
chosen page are sung over and over again to the same drum rhythm, though some
players do not really need the Qur'an in front of them as they know the texts by
heart, and some of them cannot read Arabic script anyway. Next they sing a *pantun*
verse in the local language in praise of the Prophet, after which the leader chooses
another text, say from page 12, whereupon the relatively fast "twelfth rhythm" (*guguah duobale*) is played to accompany the singing of the text. Some *rabano* players
concentrate on playing a basic rhythm over and over again, while others play more-
complex rhythmic variations (*getah* or *bungo*) in interlocking fashion.[13] A fast, fairly
complex rhythm imitates the sound of water hand-play in a river (when people while
bathing produce a stream of interlocking rhythmic timbres by forming air pockets
in the water and making them explode).

DABUIH

In January 1972, we attended a *dabuih* (Mi.; I. *dabus*) performance under the mystically potent banyan tree in the middle of Nagari Sungai Pandahan, a village in the
Lubuk Sikaping district of West Sumatra. It began just before midnight, lit by a
full moon and a bonfire. The musician-devotees, who had been tuning their frame
drums by inserting bamboo rings in the rim and heating the skins near the fire, were
members of a loosely organized fraternity (*tarekat Qadiriyyah*) that met about once
a month for devotional exercises. At these sessions the performers sometimes accompanied their unison choral singing of religious formulas with repetitive unison
or interlocking rhythmic passages played on the frame drums, which they held in
their hands usually with the leader, the *syéh*, singing a religious text followed by a
group-sung refrain. They also served clients who wanted them to present a *dabuih*
performance for a special occasion (audio example 5.4).

Preparations for the performance had begun several hours before and a crowd of
men, women, and children had gathered in a circle to watch. More than thirty male
performers, wearing sarongs, long-sleeved white coats, and either local-style folded
head-cloths or *peci* were sitting close together in a half-circle near the fire.

In charge of the ritual was a middle-aged man who was well-known not only for
his knowledge of magic and skill as a shaman (*pawang*) but also for his ability to
take charge of a *dabuih* performance, in which role he was referred to as the *kalipah*.
This term derives from the Arabic, *khalifah*, which in this context means a person
responsible for carrying out the teachings of the order (*tarekat*).[14] One of his tasks was
to ensure that the *syéh* and the novices among his followers did not harm themselves
during a performance.

At about 11:00 P.M., the *kalipah* read aloud a verse from the Qur'an as he sat cross-
legged and blessed a bowl of water containing leaves of *asam* (tamarind). A group of
children tried to dip their fingers in the water, for it was reputed to bestow power and
strength on them, but they were shooed away. The *kalipah* had also lit some incense,
which was smoldering in the shell of half a coconut. The water and the incense are seen
to link the natural and the supernatural worlds. They are normally prepared before an
indigenous religious ceremony when a request is made to contact the spirits of nature
or ancestors, or in this case, to contact the Muslim spirits (*jin Islam*) for blessings.

Other equipment assembled for the ritual included awls (wooden-handled iron
spikes), which the Minangkabau call *si giriak*, iron knives, thorny branches, plates
of broken glass, large stones, and white-hot chains that had been heated during
the previous two hours or so. The *dabuih* performers would later place these items
against their own bodies after reaching a state of altered consciousness. Their ultimate

aim was to achieve "religious concentration," leading to the highest stage of mysti-cal ecstasy on achieving union with Allah, and in this state their bodies would be invulnerable and immune to pain. To attain this union, they performed songs called *indang* or *dikia* (lit. "remembrance of God") that repeated the names and attributes of Allah or the syllable *Hu* (meaning "He") over and over, playing their frame drums (*indang* or *rabano*) with a vigor that reflected their intense religious concentration.

The proceedings opened with an enthusiastic recitation of the first verse of the *Al Fātiha*, which begins with the words *Al-hamdu li'llāhi Rabbi'l-'ālamīn* (Praise be to God, Lord of all the Worlds) and is believed to exert a protective, healing power on all present. The men were sitting closely together in a row with their heads bowed and their hands stretched out to rest on their frame drums, which they had placed on the ground before them. The *kalipah* walked around the semicircle of musician-devotees, sprinkling them with the blessed water and passing between each of them the half coconut shell containing burning incense. The musical leader was the player of the large frame drum called *induk* (mother), who sat at the head of the semicircle of players, with the *paimbau* (second-entry drummer), the *untuk lapak* (third-entry drummer), and the *panuruik* (follower) drummers seated on each side of him (as shown in fig. 5.8).

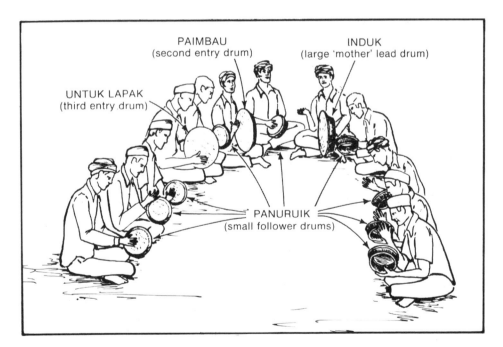

Figure 5.8 Arrangement of frame-drum (*indang* or *rabano*) players in a *dabuih* performance. Different arrangements of the drummers are found in different areas.

Some of the *indang* players slowly raised their hands, then lowered them again to pick up their instruments, and began to play while singing a request for Allah's blessing. The rest of the men knelt, bent over to touch the ground in supplication, and began to concentrate their thoughts on Allah. The musicians began to sway their heads, torsos, and arms to the right and then to the left, moving on every fourth beat. Their bodily movements and singing accompanied their strenuous efforts to concentrate their thoughts on Allah. Then the *indang induk* player suddenly began to sing a loud descending melody to the word *Hu!* (He), short for *Huwa* (Ar.), which stands for the exulted name of Allah (see music example 5.1).[15] *Huwa*, like *Alāhu Allāhu Akbar* (God is great), often occurs in song texts in other parts of the Muslim world, including Turkish dervish songs. Periodically, they stopped singing and beat their frame drums very loudly in interlocking rhythms.

Meanwhile, the *kalipah* was slowly rubbing the *asam* water onto the knives and awls, and the arms and bodies of the *syéh* and his followers, whose dazed facial expressions told of their gradual withdrawal from physical sensation. The tamarind water was intended to make a participant invulnerable to injury and to act as a disinfectant in case someone wounded himself.

The frame-drum playing, choruses, and regular head and body movements of the participants eventually transported the participants and some onlookers into a mesmeric state, whereupon some entered the space in front of the musicians and started stabbing their flesh with awls provided by the *kalipah* and under his watchful gaze. The musicians continued playing a mesmerizingly repetitive rhythm on all the *indang* in unison. Holding the drumheads by their rims in their left hands and beating with their right hands on the rim and center of the drums, they produced two clear pitches approximately a fifth apart, in an interlocking rhythm as in music example 5.2.

Following an introductory passage, the players of the large and small drums established another interlocking rhythm, which they played for several minutes. After a break of a few minutes, they played a second *indang* piece, beginning in a

Music example 5.2 A transcribed example of an interlocking rhythm (approximate pitches given) (recorded by H. and M. Kartomi in Nagari Sungai Pandahan, 1972)

slower tempo, with the small frame drums beaten midframe and near the rim to produce two pitches (notated F-sharp and D, music example 5.3). While the players of the *induk* and *paimbau* frame drums, beating midframe, produced a fairly steady stream of fully resonant interlocking textures broken irregularly by musical rests, the players of the small frame drums divided into two groups to produce their main musical pattern:

Music example 5.3 A transcription of a
main musical pattern of small frame drums

The self-stabbing stopped during the third *indang* piece, which was rhythmically more repetitious and even slower in tempo than the second one, yet more melodically active. Its interplay of five pitches,

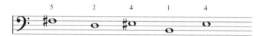

arranged in an alternating pattern of open fifths, fourths, thirds, and (from bar 13) halftones, is shown in music example 5.4. It should be noted, however, that such a combination of pitches happens only occasionally in a performance, because it

Music example 5.4 A transcription of pitch patterns used in an *indang* performance

is difficult to tune heat-tuned frame drums to precise pitches and even harder to maintain them. Thus a great variety of pitch combinations may occur. The Dutch observer A. L. van Hasselt (1882, 104–6) referred to certain other pitch combinations in his description of frame-drum playing in *badikiye, barodah*, and *basanji* (*dhikr/ zikir, rodat*, and *barzanji*) performances around 130 years ago.

Meanwhile, the *syéh* held his forehead with one hand, and pressing his right temple with the other as he focused his thoughts, he submitted to the effects of the music, the incense, and the holy water that the *kalipah* had sprinkled around again. Gripped by emotion, the *indang induk* player began to sing in a style that resembled the traditional Minangkabau "crying songs" called *ratok*, which are usually sung either while weeping and collecting palm sugar—in which case they are called *ratok manangisi enau* (lament for a palm tree)—or to mourn a death, in which case they are called *ratok manangisi hamatian* (lament at a death). These songs are banned by orthodox Muslims today and are therefore seldom heard outside the more acceptable *dabuih* context. The main drummer's loud, emotionally charged singing of Minangkabau (no longer Arabic) phrases exhorted his listeners to abide by the religious laws. His performance was marked by gasps, vocal glides, and vibrato, and the melodic line revolved around a few small intervals, as in the phrase shown in music example 5.5:

Music example 5.5 A transcription of
a melodic phrase of narrow intervals

In some cases he featured strings of repeated notes, touching now and then on neighboring notes (up to a tone above or below the repeated tones). Finally, he sang a long, wailing glide on the last syllable of *As-salāmu ʿalaikum*, in a style reminiscent of the funereal *ratok*.

Holding their awls, the *syéh* and his followers then stood up and performed movements resembling the art of self-defense. The music changed in style and mood. The drummers sang a pious *indang* hymn to a melody comprising four symmetrical melodic phrases and in strict meter based on the words *Allāhu Akbar*, repeating this and other phrases to their own frame-drum accompaniment. The mood of emotional restraint marked by the use of regular meter and unison melodic phrases was psychologically appropriate for the moment, just before the self-stabbing was to begin. The *syéh* and his younger companion were in such an exulted state by now that they did not notice the musical change.

Again the musicians began to beat on the frame drums and to sing verses about the prophet Sulaiman, followed by verses referring to Hasan and Hosen (local spelling, grandsons of the Prophet). However, only when they mentioned the name of the prophet Muhammad did the drumming become very loud and fast, and the self-stabbing began again. Using all their force, the *syéh* and his followers stood and stabbed their arms, necks, and tongues with awls, all the while performing elegant movements resembling those used in the local art of self-defense. At first they stabbed themselves only on the heavy *induk* drumbeats, and then more quickly and irregularly. Despite their savage stabbing, they suffered no wounds, nor did any blood spurt out. Their skin showed only a few puncture marks.

Another young devotee then picked up a knife and began to carve into his flesh on the side and front of his elbow. Some blood spurted out. The *kalipah* took away the knife to prevent the devotee from doing himself serious harm and wiped his wounds with the holy tamarind water, which helped to stop the bleeding and disinfect the wound. The young man was led away to rest awhile. He had been an unsuccessful *dabuih* performer, it was explained, because he had not yet been able to reach a sufficient degree of religious concentration or trust in God.

The men continued their choral singing to the words *Allah Alah Arao* ("It seems I see God"), repeating the words many times, accompanying themselves vigorously on the frame drums. Another performer stood up and stabbed himself many times, but such was his control of mind over matter, I was told, that the awl could not penetrate his flesh. He cut into his neck and the inside of his mouth with a knife, yet no blood appeared.

The group chanting in Minangkabau and Arabic continued for an hour or so. After the group singing of the names of the martyrs Hasan and Hosen, the lead singer broke into a lament, signaling to the *indang induk* player for everyone to stop playing. The *ratok*-like lament combined Arabic and Minangkabau texts and was sung melismatically, breaking the rules of orthodoxy not only by mixing the languages but also by moving away from the simple chanting style, which allegedly made it harder for the listeners to comprehend the religious message conveyed. The singing style closely resembled the highly melismatic and melodically ornamented style of free-metered singing of traditional laments (*ratok*), as in music example 5.6.

The *syéh* and another of his *dabuih* followers were now in such an altered state of consciousness that they were able to pick up the white-hot chains from the fire with their bare hands and place them on each other's backs and shoulders without wincing. When they removed the chains again and threw them into a bowl of water standing nearby, the water immediately boiled. The men were singing a melody set

Music example 5.6 A transcription of a free-metered highly ornamented *ratok* (traditional lament)

to a text with four symmetrical phrases per verse based on the words *Ja nara kum bardun wa salaman ala Ibrāhim Yā nāru kûnī bardan wa salāman ʿalā Ibrāhīm* ("O fire, be thou cold, and a security unto Abraham!"; *Surāh* 21:69, translated in Hughes [1885] 1976, 5). The Qur'an indicates that Allah spoke these words to save Ibrāhīm (Abraham) when he was thrown into a fire for destroying his people's idols and urging them to worship the one true God. Just as Abraham's life was saved by his faith, which caused Allah to turn the fire into which he had been thrown cold, so the *dabuih* performers' trust in Allah prevented them from being harmed by the white-hot chains. The mesmerized men were making uneven vocal entries but achieved some metrical regularity by clapping on the beat at the ends of phrases. As shown in the four phrases in music example 5.7, each entry made similar melodic ascents and descents, ending in unresolved fashion on the leading note in phrases 1 and 3, and on the tonal center in phrases 2 and 4.

Music example 5.7 A transcribed excerpt of *dabuih* singing

The *dabuih* performers then began to wipe their feet on the thorny branches nearby, without drawing blood. They stabbed themselves again quite ferociously, which began to alarm the *kalipah*. Fearing that he might not be able to control them when necessary, the *kalipah* decided to halt the performance and led them back to a corner to rest.

The *indang* performers once more became the center of attention. They stood up close together in a row, beating their frame drums vigorously. By now the frame drums had lost some of their tautness and their pitch had dropped from to (see music example 5.8).

Every second performer repeatedly bent down from his torso in regular rhythm as his neighbor on each side stood upright, and the resulting wavelike motions of the performers continued for a few minutes. Then they sat close together on the ground in a row, still playing their frame drums as they raised them, lowered them on every

Music example 5.8 A transcription of a lower-pitched section of *indang* in the later stage of the performance

second beat, with each alternate performer moving backward as his neighbor moved forward, and vice versa. Half of them then moved diagonally backward as the other half moved diagonally forward, and they repeated these rhythmical movements many times. Placing their instruments on the ground in front of them, they sang another hymn and, still moving in these formations, vigorously yet gracefully wove patterns in the air with their hands.

After half an hour or so of *indang* movements, the *syéh* rose again and in a seemingly effortless fashion picked up a very heavy stone wrapped in white cloth. Its pure whiteness was believed to give the performer supernatural strength. The *syéh* wiped his hands in the plate of broken glass, lay on it, and rolled around so that the sharp glass pierced his back and chest. He clutched some pieces of glass tightly in his hands, whereupon another performer pressed some more glass pieces into his back. He suffered minor wounds, but they did not bleed.

He and a young devotee rose from their kneeling position, picked up an awl each, apologized to all present for possible past wrongs, and made a bow (*sambah*) to the north, the south, the east, and the west, using movements resembling those used in the local art of self-defense (*basilek*).

The *syéh* and his companions continued this ritual till dawn. After some final prayers had been said, they all went home, and some were working in the fields an hour or so later.

THE RELIGIOUS AND LEGENDARY BACKGROUND OF *DABUIH*

Dabuih is the Minangkabau form of the Arabic word *dabbus* (I. *dabus*), meaning "awl," the name of the main implement used by devotees to show their faith and invulnerability by stabbing themselves. The Sufi ritual *dabuih* just described was in fact transplanted originally via Banten or Aceh, perhaps via India and the Arab peninsula. It derived from one of the oldest Sufi fraternities, the Rifa'iyyah, an order founded by the mystic Rifa'i who died in Arabia in 1183. (Few Sumatrans know of this connection, in my experience.) Like the Sadi, Nevlevi, and other Sufi fraternities, Rifa'iyya is an order that has been operating for centuries in the Muslim world. Its members characteristically meet to express their religious enthusiasm and achieve exultation through group exercises, led by a *khalifah*. Their devotional exercises comprise the singing or chanting of religious phrases (*dhikr, zikir*), instrumental music and dance, and displays of invulnerability through faith. Their concerted repetitions of religious phrases comply with the Qur'anic injunction: "And remember Allah often."

Sufi fraternities were most active between the twelfth and the nineteenth centuries but declined in the twentieth century. The spiritual idea behind *dabbus/dabus* is that ultimate truth can be attained only by losing one's identity and becoming one with God, specifically by reaching a state of divine ecstasy through group exercises and by playing and "listening to music (*al samā*), for it is only then that the heart is stirred to seek Allah"; so spoke the Sufi mystic Abu Said Ibn al-ʻArabi, who died around 952 (Farmer 1952, 65). The principal occupation of the Sufi while still in the body is meditation on the *wahdānīyah*, or Unity of God, the remembrance of God's names (*zikir*), and the progressive advancement in the *tariqah*, or "journey of life, so as to attain unification with God" (Hughes [1885] 1976, 609). These Sufi ideas are all contained within the *dabuih* ritual. The fervent—and at times even frenetically intense—frame-drum playing, together with the emotional singing of religious phrases that are repeated many times; the rhythmic bodily movements; the incense and other ritual adjuncts all reflect the intense desire of participants for unification with Allah.

C. Poensen mentioned in the 1880s that members of the Charijiten brotherhood in Mecca still held the ritual "*daboes*" during zul Hijjah, the last month of the Muslim year when the faithful make their pilgrimages (Poensen 1888, 254). G. A. Herklots and Jaffur Shareef described a *dabus*-like ceremony called "*Rufaee*" or "*Goorz-mar*" among Deccan dwellers, in which an awl ("*goorz*" or "*dhuboos*") was used, that is, "a sort of iron club, pointed at one end and having a knob at the other, covered with spikes" (1895, 193). A drawing of an awl used on the Deccan (ibid., plate 6) resembles awls used in Aceh and Minangkabau.

The account of Acehnese *dabôih* performance given by Snouck Hurgronje (1906, 2:249–57) somewhat resembles the Minangkabau *dabuih* case as well as aspects of *dabôih* performances that I witnessed in West and East Aceh (Kartomi 1982). In both the Acehnese and the Minangkabau cases, the ritual commences with the *kalipah* uttering salutations. The frame-drum playing, group choruses, and regular head and body movements of the participants produces giddiness, excites holy visions, and eventually transports them—and even some onlookers—into a mesmeric, ecstatic state. In both areas, the devotees sing about and use the element of fire associated with the prophets Abraham and Sulaiman.[16] In both areas, some performances are serious religious affairs in which the self-wounding is believed to be a real expression of religious invulnerability, while other performances, especially at weddings and other feasts, serve primarily as a form of entertainment, which Snouck Hurgronje describes as "mere theatrical representations, in fact . . . mere conjuring, where nothing but the name" (of the *rapaʻi* drum) "and a few formalities recall its connection with mysticism" (1906, 2:250). Some participants only pretend to deal themselves heavy blows and actually "only momentarily press the point of the awl or dagger against some hard portion of the skin" (ibid., 252), though this interpretation of fraudulent intent is disputed by J. Vredenbregt (1973, 318–19).

The Minangkabau performance that I described above differs from the Acehnese in many of its small details. In West Sumatra, holy water is used to facilitate recovery from the brethren's self-inflicted wounds, not the leader's saliva as in Aceh. More importantly, *dabôih* performances in Aceh are frequently staged as competitions between two groups, each of whom tries to disrupt the rhythm of the drumming by the other in order to win, which has a major effect on the music performed (Kartomi 1982).

The legendary origin of *dabuih* in Minangkabau is popularly attributed to the Acehnese Muslim scholar Dalim Maulah. He is said to have accompanied his Minangkabau student Chatib Sangko, who had visited to study religion from him, on his return journey from Aceh to Minangkabau and to have brought *dabus* skills (Ac. *ilmu dabôih*) with him to use as a means of spreading the Muslim faith in West Sumatra (informants in Nagari Tandikat and Padang, pers. comm., 1972). *Dabuih* may then have spread throughout Minangkabau during the sixteenth and early seventeenth centuries when Aceh controlled the coastal areas.

The task of the Muslim missionaries was probably facilitated by the fact that the Minangkabau already had their own traditions, including *randai dampeng*, a ritual in which nine men (*bujang sembilan*) performed the art of self-defense in a circular formation to drum and song accompaniment, sometimes entering a state of trance in which they could perform abnormal physical feats and could contact the spirits of nature and the ancestors for the common good (Rasjid Manggis, pers. comm., Bukit Tinggi, 1972). Both *adék* trance dancers and *dabuih* performers who attained union with God gained personal spiritual satisfaction and social prestige for their abilities and contributed thereby to the social cohesion and confidence of their community. Moreover, *dabuih* performers symbolized the basic religious conflict in Minangkabau society by combining elements of Islamic and pre-Islamic belief, art, and ritual into the one art form.

Despite the fiercely monotheistic creed of Islam, the gentle Sufi mysticism of the brotherhoods must, to a degree, have tolerated the spirit worship of the indigenous Minangkabau religion, allowing elements of local belief and ceremony to be combined with the tenets and practices of Islam. In *dabuih*, the Muslim role of *kalipah* replaced the animist role of shaman of pre-Muslim ritual, yet their tasks of preparing holy ritualistic materials—inducing a mesmerizing atmosphere through music, aromas, and the like, and controlling their subjects when in an altered state of conscious-ness—were almost identical. In some villages, for example, Nagari Sungai Pandahan, *kalipah* still also act as shamans and continue to use pre-Muslim ritualistic adjuncts in *dabuih*. Female *kalipah* even lead *dabuih* performances in at least one village: in

1972 the elderly Ibu Taksiah was well known in Nagari Tandikat for her skills both as a *kalipah* and a shaman. However, she is atypical of the male-dominant Sufi tradition.

Though based on different belief systems, then, *dabuih* and pre-Islamic trance ceremonies are remarkably similar in their ultimate spiritual purpose, the means employed to achieve it, and the details of the structure of the ceremonies. The aim of contacting the supernatural is achieved in both cases through repetitious drum music, song, bodily movement, and incense and other ceremonial adjuncts that allow participants to achieve a state of altered consciousness and anesthesia. In this state they are able to perform abnormal physical feats that seem to them to indicate that they are in contact with, or possessed by, divine power.

In Minangkabau today, some orthodox leaders reject *dabuih* and other Sufi artistic genres for being "heterodox," allowing only the call to prayer and simple chants of the Qur'an to be performed. They avoid traditional music, dance, and theater, banning performances from areas near mosques, and reject all music and dance associated with magic or for display for its own sake, citing the fact that the official, puritanical Wahhabi doctrine in Arabia regards *dabus* as unorthodox too, while Sufi fraternities in Egypt have been held in official disfavor since the 1920s and 1930s, when the property of some orders was confiscated.

Yet *dabus* has managed to survive to the present day not only in Minangkabau and Aceh but also in such areas as Banten in West Java (as *debus* or *gedebus*; see Poensen 1888, 259; Vredenbregt 1973, 129), Bugis and Makassan Sulawesi (as *daboso*, noted in my fieldwork in 1984), Ternate (M. Kartomi 1993a), and Malaya (as *berdabus*), or in Negri Sembilan (*dabuih*; see Kartomi 1992) and Muslim South Africa (as Rifa').[17] However, it is reportedly less popular and widespread now than it was in the 1970s.[18]

||||

The local Minangkabau adaptations of Sufi Muslim artistic styles and themes discussed in this chapter were probably transplanted into West Sumatra from the early period of conversion around the sixteenth century. Besides adopting some transplanted Muslim attributes, the converts clearly retained some aspects of the preexisting local indigenous religious belief system in their art forms. For example, some of the *indang* song texts still refer to the ancient agricultural rite and deities involved in the seasonal practice of winnowing the husks off the rice grain. The local *pancak silek* martial arts still express elements of Hindu-Buddhist philosophy and nature mysticism as well as Muslim values, whether performed as part of *dabuih* or at self-defense displays and fights.

All four Muslim-associated genres have a distinctively Minangkabau performance style. Except for the mostly Arabic texts sung in *dikia Mauluik* and some parts of *dabuih*, the singers and choruses primarily use the Minangkabau language in their poetic song texts and repartee. One local characteristic is the witty repartee for which the Minangkabau people are famous, including the partly improvised sung response verses in *indang* and *salawek dulang* performances and competitions and the partly improvised formal speeches at *adék* and other events. At extended village performances of *indang* and *salawek dulang*, the lead singer improvises song lyrics that may deal with political critiques, nature, the forest, animals, the sea, romance, and marriage; and he frequently indulges in sung repartee that includes ribald sexual references or poses questions as part of the religious and secular quizzes that are a standard part of *indang* competitions between villages. *Dabuih* was clearly transplanted into Minangkabau from another Sufi-associated area, perhaps Aceh or Banten, but it was then transformed into a local performance practice that retains some of the pre-Muslim Minangkabau characteristics. Likewise, a form of *dikia Mauluik* is said to have been taught to converts in Minangkabau by overseas members of a Sufi brotherhood who visited or settled in West Sumatra, or by local pilgrims who had learned the form from a Sufi brotherhood leader in the Hadramaut or elsewhere on the Arabian peninsula or Muslim India (Rasjid Manggis, pers. comm., 1972). Moreover, the cyclic structures and rhythms of the frame drums, vocal melodies, and solo-group response structures in *indang, dabuih*, and *dikia Mauluik* clearly belong to Minangkabau tradition, given that these musical features also belong to the *talempong* gong-chime and drum ensembles and other non-Muslim traditional genres. At social functions where performances are heavily invested with *adék* behavior and etiquette, traditional Minangkabau costumes are still worn by the local elders, artists, guests, and their families, with some preferring to wear Islamic or combined Islamic-Minangkabau dress.

Performances are especially popular at planting and harvest time, holy day celebrations, weddings, circumcisions, departing or returning *hajj* pilgrim processions, performing art competitions or festivals, and government or commercial functions. They are performed in people's homes, *surau* meetinghouses, marketplaces, and in the case of *dabuih*, in an outside venue, such as under a banyan tree in the middle of a village. From around the 1980s, when the people became more devout Muslims, mixed-gender performances became rare, but an increasing number of female groups began to perform *indang* and other songs and dances in domestic and school settings and on certain political occasions, retaining and developing their distinctive Minangkabau style.[19]

Because *indang* and *salawek dulang* performers normally add some Muslim phrases to their largely secular texts, *ulama* and scholars describe them as "arts with an Islamic flavor." The *dikia Mauluik* and *dabuih* performances, on the other hand, mainly use Islamic texts and serve a devotional or religious-educational purpose, so they are classified as "Islamic arts." Both classes of genre serve as continuing *dakwah* as well as entertainment and artistic expression among the common people in the villages. Whatever characteristics the genres may have adopted from external sources, they express a distinctive regional identity that is not replicated anywhere else in the Muslim world.

ACKNOWLEDGMENTS

I am grateful to Bp. Usman Burak of Nagari Jorong Sawah Mansi, Kecamatan Lubuk Alung, Kabupaten Pariaman and his *indang* troupe in 1982; Bp. Sidi Burak of Tujuh Koto, Nagari Mandahiling, Pariaman, and his *indang* troupe, also in 1982; Bp. Moh. Effendy and the *dabuih* performers in Nagari Sungai Pandahan and Nagari Tandikat, Lubuk Sikaping, for assisting us in recording and studying performances of *dabuih* and other elements of traditional musical culture in 1972, as well as the various government officials and musicians who helped us record *ratok* singing in Solok in 1972 and Payakumbuh in 1985. Many thanks to Bp. Islamidar and his troupe in Nagari Talang Maur, Payakumbuh, for allowing us to record their performances of *dikia Mauluik* in 1985, and the *salawek dulang* performers Bp. Mandjo Bungsu (leader) and Bp. Ho in Nagari Sisawah, Sijunjung district, in 1985. I am indebted to Bp. Rasyid Manggis of Bukit Tinggi, who gave me his ideas about the history of his forebears at the court in Payakumbuh and the meaning of many Minangkabau Muslim and pre-Muslim genres in 1976, and Prof. Dr. Daryusti MH and his team of Sekolah Tinggi Seni Indonesia (Padangpanjang) artists and scholars who performed at Monash University in 2009.

6

THE RIAU INDRAGIRI SULTANATE'S
NOBAT ENSEMBLE AND ITS SUKU
MAMAK STALWARTS

This chapter deals with the *gendang nobat* ensemble in the former Malay palace of Indragiri, located at Rengat between the middle and upper reaches of the Indragiri River. It belongs to the court traditions of the group of Malay sultanates that once ruled in Sumatra, the Malay Peninsula, and Brunei.[1] Tradition holds that ever since the Malay palace at Malacca was founded in the fifteenth century C.E., the *gendang nobat* (*nobat* drums) have served as an indispensable symbol of the regalia that authorized the ruler's sovereignty. If a *nobat* was stolen or lost, the sultan who had owned it lost all his power. The *Sejarah Melayu* ("Malay Annals") mentions that the king of the Riau island kingdom of Bentan was the first ruler to use the *nobat* (Brown 1953, 28), and that the instruments (also referred to as "the drums of sovereignty") played a role in the *adat istiadat* (traditional customs) and state functions in Malacca under Sultan Mohammad Shah (1424–41).[2]

The instrumental components of *nobat* vary, but they normally contain a single-headed drum called a *nekara*, which symbolizes the ruler; a pair of double-headed drums called *gendang nobat*, which lead the ensemble; a *nafiri*—a flared silver oboe up to eighty centimeters long (figs. 6.1 and 6.5); and *sarunai*—a quadruple-reed, flared oboe; and in some cases, one to three suspended *gong*. The terms *nobat*, *nekara* (*nengkara*), *nafiri*, and *sarunai* (*serunai*) or *sunai* are Malayo-Indonesian variants of the Indian/West Asian terms *naubat* (Arabic root *nawbah* [plural form *nawbat*] meaning "turn, rotate"), *naqqara, nafir*, and *surnay* (Flora 1995, 52–53, 60; al-Faruqi 1981).

Taboos (*pantang larangan*) surrounded these priceless sets of instruments. Only the sultan was allowed to handle them, though he usually appointed a group of trusted musicians to care for and play them in his presence. A *nobat* could only be played at the sultan's installation, to announce his arrival at a meeting or function, to announce an important royal decision, to awaken him on the morning of the Muslim holy days of Idulfitri and Iduladha, and at life-event rituals for him or members of his family at his command.[3]

In postcolonial Indonesia (after 1945), the Malay sultans in Sumatra lost their sovereignty, and their palaces were sacked by antifeudal revolutionaries, while in nearby Malaysia, a rotating system of nine kings was established, with a *nobat* always being played in the presence of the Yang di Pertuan Agong (Paramount Ruler) of Malaysia. Since only hereditary members of the main royal descendant (*keturunan raja*) or his appointed group of hereditary musicians were allowed to play a *nobat*—and then only in the presence of the sultan—the performance traditions have virtually disappeared, except at the home of the descendant of the sultan of Indragiri at Rengat. The *nobat* tradition at the former palace at Pagaruyung totally disappeared long ago,

Figure 6.1 A *nafiri* trumpet from the *nobat* of the former Riau-Lingga court at Daik, Riau Archipelago, housed in the museum in Tanjung Pinang

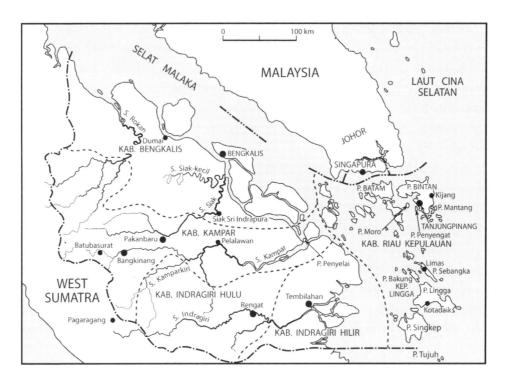

Map 6.1 The province of Riau and the river islands, showing the town of Rengat on the Indragiri River, where the descendants of the royal family of the former kingdom of the Indragiri live, and the other great rivers of Riau, the Kampar and the Siak (Map: Gary Swinton)

Figure 6.2 Restored former Malay palace at Siak

while the one at Pelalawan disappeared during the Japanese occupation in World War II (Ashley Turner, pers. comm., 1984).[4] However, we photographed the remnants of the Riau-Lingga *nobat* ensemble at Tanjung Pinang (see fig. 6.4), the Siak palace (see fig. 6.2; for its location see map 6.1), and the home of the former royal family of Indragiri at Rengat. We visited this family in 1984, and it is their *nobat* that is the topic of this chapter.

THE *GENDANG NOBAT* ENSEMBLE AT INDRAGIRI

The most striking aspect of the royal Malay *nobat* drums at the home of the descendants of the former sultan of Indragiri is their rough, natural tree-trunk appearance, with one of the main pair of drums being much squatter and more irregular in shape than the other (fig. 6.3). Most other Malay sultanates in the Malay Peninsula or former sultanates in Sumatra possess much more finely crafted *nobat* ensembles that are made with much more expensive materials and with consummate craftsmanship as is believed to befit a monarch. How is it, then, that the drums of the *nobat* of the kingdom of Indragiri are so rough looking? Indeed, how is it that this *nobat*, with its history of Malay feudal and European colonial associations, should have retained any significance at all as a sacred object in postcolonial, postrevolutionary Indonesia?

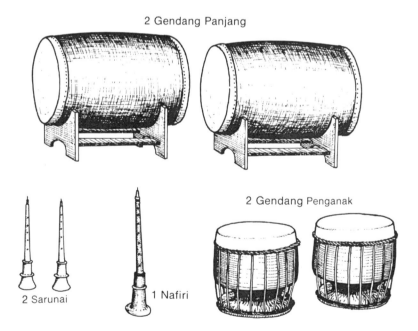

Figure 6.3 A *nobat* of the former Riau-Lingga court: two *gendang panjang*, two *gendang penganak*, two *sarunai*, one *nafiri*

From the sixteenth century onward, the *nobat* of the lndragiri kingdom could only be played by musicians whom the sultan designated to the task. In Indragiri these musicians happened to be from among the sultan's most loyal subjects, the shy, forest-dwelling Suku Mamak, who long ago made the drums as a gift and symbol of their loyalty to and spiritual reverence for their sultan. The Suku Mamak still maintain close links with Indragiri's royal descendants, much as they have done for centuries.[5]

The drums' rough shapes indicate that they were made from materials gleaned from the local forest by Suku Mamak craftsmen, who made them under the direction of one of their mystically gifted shamans, the *gumantan* or *wakil batin*. The Suku Mamak, like the Suku Batin or Sakai who live in the interior around and beyond the Siak River, may be among the oldest of the Malay peoples; certainly they preserve elements of archaic Malay culture.

The Suku Mamak are still rotational *ladang* (dry field) cultivators, who live mainly on the sweet potatoes and vegetables they plant in tiny settlements in or on the edge of the forest. Every ten years or so they normally move to a different part of the forest. They revere ancestral and nature spirits, and their diviners possess the power (*ilmu*) to call birds, tigers, and elephants. Even today the Suku Mamak avoid the towns, shun government interference in their lives, and trade only in village markets on the edge of the forest. They help maintain the ancestral royal graves, which consist of tiered white stone constructions resembling the ancient Malay graves found among other pre-Muslim, or nominally Muslim, Malays in some other parts of Sumatra. The terraced royal lndragiri and subsidiary graves of white stone are still to be found near Kota Lama, a village outside Rengat.

Royal funerals were always marked by the sounding of the *nobat*. In general, Malay communities believe drums to be the most ancient and sacred of instruments, as in most of Southeast Asia. Gongs are also fairly widespread and revered, but all the evidence supports the local view that drums are much older. Certainly in Suku Mamak society today it is the drums—in various shapes and sizes—that dominate the local instrumentarium. Their hierarchical concept of instruments is headed by the drums; indeed all instruments are seen in relation to their leading musical and sacral role. The three drums called *gendang nobat*, like the *gendang ketabung* (or *ketebung*) used in local Malay Petalangan healing ceremonies, are at the top of the hierarchy, followed by the *gedombah* (fig. 6.4), followed in turn by the truncated conical double-headed drums (*gendang*) used in the art of self-defense and other genres.

The Indragiri *nobat* ensemble currently comprises two double-headed drums and one single-headed drum. Formerly a bamboo oboe (Ma. *sarunai*), called *sunai nobat* in the palace and *su'unai nobat* among the Suku Mamak, was part of the ensemble, but it has been lost; it was used to provide a melodic line. According to the *silsilah*

Figure 6.4 The drums (*gendang nobat*) of the *nobat* ensemble at the former Indragiri court at Rengat, Riau, with a royal descendant and the single-headed drum (*gedombah*)

(family tree) kept in the household of the former royal family, the two main drums in their *nobat* are six centuries old, believed to date back twenty-five generations. Their roughly cylindrical bodies are twenty or twenty-four centimeters in diameter at the larger head and either eighty or eighty-six centimeters in length respectively. They were hewn from an irregularly shaped tree trunk that was then hollowed out. Only *kayu pulut* (sticky wood) trees are allowed to be used. Their double heads are said to be made of buckskin, which is laced by rattan cords to their heads. Their mainly diamond-shaped lacings are looped to a bamboo ring covered in a spiral of wound rattan and attached to the outside circumference at each end to hold them firmly in place and to tauten the drumheads, which can also be more finely tuned by heating them alongside a naked flame or by hammering the rattan ring stretched around their circumference.

To learn to play the instruments, members of the *nobat* ensemble first had to learn the sixteen basic rhythms (*ragam*) that determine the tempo, then to play the relatively regular rhythmic part, and finally to play the difficult interlocking part using the mnemonics "dik" and "dum." Each of the two principal players, called *penghulu gendang* (lit. "drum chief"), rests his double-headed drum horizontally across his knees and on his extended left foot as he sits cross-legged. According to the sparse evidence I was able to obtain about this obsolete music, they beat one or both ends by hand or with a rattan stick, emphasizing the downbeat and always playing in quadruple meter. The single-headed drum has an hourglass shape and was made locally in 1960 from hardwood by the Suku Mamak. Its single head, attached by rattan lacings, measures thirty-one centimeters in diameter, with its lower end measuring twenty-one centimeters. Its lacing patterns are identical to that of the drums (*ketabung*) used for healing ceremonies (fig. 6.6).[6] Its player also holds it horizontally across his crossed knees, with the head resting on his extended left foot. He is expected to produce sharper drum sounds than the players of the pair of main drums and to interlock with them rhythmically. The players of the pair of double-headed *nobat* drums perform the *penengkah* (lead) music role, while the player of the single-headed drum plays the *penyelalu* (continuous) musical role.

Figure 6.5 A silver *sunai nobat* (oboe) from the *nobat* at the Siak Sri Indrapura palace, situated near the mouth of the Siak River in Riau

Before the Indonesian revolution in 1945, the installation of a king always had to be accompanied by special pieces played on the *nobat* in the presence of all the other regalia. The *nobat* was also frequently played in a royal *balai* (pavilion on stilts) where the elders met to make decisions about political, legal, and ritual matters. When the *nobat* was heard from the pavilion, the people knew an important decision had been made. Presiding at the meetings was the sultan and in attendance were the Raja Muda (the crown prince, his right-hand man), administrative nobles (Datuk Mangkumi, Datuk Bendahara, and Datuk Bintara), and the representative of the local Malay people (Datuk Temenggung), who was also the head of customary law, called the *pemangku adat*.[7]

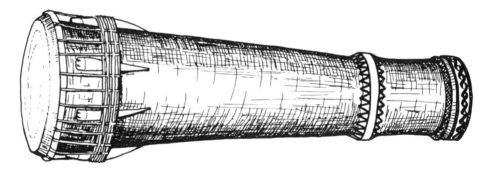

Figure 6.6 A *ketabung* drum played at healing ceremonies among the Suku Mamak forest-dwellers near Rengat, Riau

Also at births, weddings, and funerals and on Muslim feast days—Idulfitri and Iduladha—the *nobat* was sounded in the presence of the sultan and his family, elders and their families, and the Suku Mamak devotees. Their leading representative at court was the Datuk Patih Mamak-mamak, who represented the five Suku Mamak villages. Also present were a group of Batin-Batin Suku Mamak (diviners) called Batin, Antar-antar, and Gumantan (the healing shaman); the Bintara (head of security); and the Munti (heads of each of the five neighborhoods).

Sometimes the sultan commanded the appropriate shaman to conduct ceremonies to exorcise the bad spirits (*hantu*) and to conciliate the good ones (*roh halus, jin*), involving the performance of *nobat* music. The rituals were for the good of the kingdom, for example, to heal a patient and to ask for protection when signs of danger appeared. The Suku Mamak shamans also ritually cleansed the regalia each year. As the *nobat* instruments are the main surviving regalia now, they are the objects of the cleansing ceremony still carried out annually by the Batin-Batin Suku Mamak.

At rituals, the Suku Mamak musicians traditionally wore a white *teluk belanga* (Malay trouser suit) with a black *peci* (Muslim hat) and a locally made red-and-blue checked sarong, which contrasted with the costumes of the various nobles. Presiding at the ceremonies was the sultan, who normally wore a black or white gold-trimmed coat over his *teluk belanga*. The last time the *nobat* of Indragiri was "played" is reputed to have been at midnight when the last sultan, Mahmud Indragiri, died in 1963. On this occasion the spirits of the royal ancestors are said to have sounded the drums, whereupon everyone in the palace woke up. They all said the music was beautiful and mysterious and was based on a continuous repetition of the following drum rhythm, with variations:

Music example 6.1 A
repetitious drum rhythm
on a *gendang nobat*

HISTORY OF THE INDRAGIRI KINGDOM AND ITS *NOBAT*

According to the *pehabaran* or *nyanyi panjang* (lengthy songs), which are still sung by Suku Mamak bards at social gatherings, the Indragiri sultanate was founded as an outpost of the great Malay kingdom of Malacca, which in turn was founded in the fifteenth century and fell to the Portuguese in 1511 (audio example 6.1).

The name of the first sultan of Indragiri was Sultan Narasinga.[8] His father—Raja Gedombah of Indragiri—had refused to accept Islam, despite the efforts of the sultan of Malacca to encourage, indeed force, him to do so. After having established the palace at Indragiri, Raja Gedombah reportedly succeeded in defeating a Portuguese fleet that had invaded Indragiri. Nevertheless, his success was aborted, and he subsequently died in prison in Portuguese Malacca. The Indragiri kingdom was only nominally Muslim; the people continued to adhere to their own ancient beliefs in the spirits of the ancestors and of nature. Meanwhile, the sultan of Malacca educated Raja Gedombah's son in the Muslim religion, and on his conversion he sent him with a fleet of ships—under Commander Dang Purnama and the Kebun Bunga guards—to maintain the Indragiri kingdom around the upper reaches of the Indragiri River. He settled near the present-day town of Rengat. At first, only the Suku Mamak forest-people recognized his power, and they were extremely loyal to him. Some Portuguese traders are said to have sailed up the Indragiri River and to have worked in league with the sultan for a few decades, and some died there and were buried at Kota Lama. As with other Malay kings, the symbols of the sultan's sovereignty included a *nobat* ensemble, several Portuguese cannons, flags, sacred krises, swords, and other metal weapons. The objects of the regalia were ritually cleaned each year. On Muslim feast days such as Idulfitri and Iduladha and at palace ceremonies such as the installation of a sultan, the only workers (*abdi dalem*) trusted enough to be allowed to enter the palace were the Suku Mamak. At an installation only they would be allowed to play the *nobat*.

The last king of Indragiri was Sultan Mahmud Indragiri, who was installed in 1916 and died in 1963. In postrevolutionary Indonesia (from 1945), the national government refused to recognize the power of the Malay, or most other, local kings. However, in New Order Indonesia (1965), Sultan Mahmud's son-in-law Tengku Hamat has been able to use the title of Datuk Tumenggung, beginning in 1970. Every two years in his home in Rengat, he still carries out the ceremony for the purification of the royal *pusaka* (heirlooms), including the three *nobat* drums. Like his father-in-law before him, he presides at such rituals, sitting on his throne next to that of his wife, who performs the role of the *permaisuri* (queen).

Every two years in colonial times, a *semahan* (large-scale celebration) was held in the palace for a day and a night, at which a diviner (*kadhi adat*) would burn incense, say mantras, recite Muslim prayers, and call the *roh halus* (auspicious spirits) to come and bless the *pusaka*, the palace, and the people in and around it. At such purification ceremonies, the king sat on his throne next to that of his *permaisuri* in front of the crown prince, administrative nobles, the representative of the local Malay people, and the representatives of the Suku Mamak people. All present feasted on *nasi kuning* (yellow rice) and other delicious dishes. Music and dance performed in the palace by the sultan's Malay (Muslim) subjects included the *tari inai* (henna-

Figure 6.7 *Obab*, Kp Talau, 1984

stained-fingernail dance), *zapin* dancing with large and small frame-drum (*rabana* and *marwas*) accompaniment, *bediki* (*zikir* in Arabic, which are Malay versions of Arabic religious singing by a group of men accompanied by small frame drums), and songs accompanied by *marwas* and a *gambus* (a pear-shaped lute of West Asian origin), while the nominally Muslim Suku Mamak performed music such as "Lagu Gadiombi" in their healing and other ceremonies on the *obab* (a bowed string instrument with a fish-skin-covered coconut-shell body, fig. 6.7), (see audio example 6.2).[9]

At coronations and on other important occasions, all the people from far and wide were also invited to attend. They brought gifts, offerings of food, or performances of music and dance, including *pencak silat* (self-defense), to make the celebration *ramai* (cheerfully vigorous).

Displays of the Suku Mamak art of self-defense are usually accompanied by a pair of double-headed drums, an oboe, and a *tetawak* (gong), which is about thirty-seven centimeters in diameter and plays cyclic rhythms such as:

Music example 6.2 An example
of cyclic rhythm played on the
tetawak (gong)

The rhythms/pieces played by the musicians include the slow *irama silat main adat* (traditional art-of-self-defense rhythm), the fast *irama serama angin* (magic wind rhythm), the slow *irama serama* (magic rhythm), and the fast *irama siamang menjawat* (the monkey scratches his chest rhythm). The *su'unai* (oboe) comprises a wooden tube and flair with six small front finger holes and a coconut-leaf double-reed. The larger *gendang ibu* (mother drum) is usually about sixty centimeters long and thirty-five centimeters in diameter, while the smaller *gendang anak* (child drum) measures about forty-five centimeters in length and thirty centimeters in diameter.[10]

At palace celebrations in the colonial era, a special group of Suku Mamak artists usually performed just outside the palace, contributing music and dance, which they still normally perform at their weddings. They often involve two or more couples or groups at a time and are usually held in September. In the past, they entertained the sultan with the *tari berarak* (wedding) "processional dance" accompanied by *celempung* and *tekelek* (bronze gong-chimes), *kelintang* (xylophone), and *gandang* (double-headed drums), which are strictly only part of the nonpalace culture and can be used nowadays to accompany *pencak silat* (audio example 6.3). On such occasions too, storytellers from the villages would sing or tell their *pehabaran* (legends) for nights on end about the ancestors, the royal animals of the forest (tigers and elephants), and about the three rivers (Batang Hari, Indragiri, and Kampar) that flow from the central western highlands of Sumatra eastward through Jambi and Riau to the sea.

Other mystical, secret, or private musical expressions of the Suku Mamak still performed today—but not at the former palace—include the music played on a *gumantan*'s (healer's) large *ketebung* drum with a small gong, end-blown *pupuik* (a multi-reed stalk oboe enclosed in a bamboo tube), and Jew's harps (*genggong*). In addition they sing crying songs at funerals (*ratap*), love songs (*lagu bedondong*), and other vocal music.

Unlike the double-headed *ketebung* of the royal *nobat* ensemble, a shamanic *ketebung* is a large single-headed, low-waisted cylindrical drum that is usually suspended from a beam in the house of the *gumantan* (shamanic healer) in a Suku Mamak village and is allowed to be played only at healing ceremonies.

About 135 centimeters long and with a head measuring 25 centimeters in diameter, it is made of heavy *ruyung ibil* (sugar palm–tree trunk). Its deerskin or goatskin head is attached to its body by a very intricate pattern of rattan cords laced over seven wooden wedges. It is stored with a white cloth wrapped around it. The player, sitting cross-legged, rests its head on his leg and beats it with two hands.[11] When it is played loudly, the sound is called *lantung* (strong); when played softly it is called *lembut* or *lempek* (soft); and when beaten with medium intensity the sound is called *lunak* (medium loud). One of the less potent but well-known rhythms played on the *ketebung* is the *irama siamang menjawat* mentioned above, also played to accompany displays of the art of self-defense.

In the heyday of the court, a Suku Mamak diviner was often called from his home (e.g., fig. 6.8) to use his power at times of adversity or to mark an important event. If a member of the royal family or attendants was seriously sick, a *belian duduk* (sitting healing ceremony) with *ratip* (healing songs) would be performed by a local Suku Mamak healer, using his sacred *ketebung* drum (audio example 6.4).

Figure 6.8 A shaman's house over a riverlet near Betung

When a king died, a special funeral rhythm was played on the *nobat* from 4:00 P.M. to 6:00 P.M. (i.e., ending before Magreb prayers) and from 8:00 P.M. to midnight. Meanwhile, the *penghulu istana* (palace religious leader) led the singing of praises of the dead king and *sempelong* (flute, fig. 6.9) accompanied laments (*ratap*) at his death, with the elders joining in. Islam forbids the performance of such songs of praise and laments, but the palace allowed it to mark the death of its king.

The immediate problem following a king's death was the need for another king to be installed as soon as possible, preferably the next morning, because the corpse was not allowed to be buried till a successor had been appointed. The new king was installed (*dinobatkan*) with all his subjects present, or represented, and the appropriate prayers said by the *penghulu istana* and/or the *imam* of the palace mosque, with the *nobat* sounding and all the other regalia assembled nearby.

When a king married, Muslim prayers were said and the *nobat* was played with specific rhythms associated with weddings. The king's subjects brought gifts of food

Figure 6.9 A *sempelong* flute, played in Talang Jerinjing, a Suku Mamak village

or presented performances of female welcome dances such as the *tari inai* (henna-stained-fingernail dance) and of *nyanyi panjang* (long story-songs).[12]

||||

The roughly hewn, intricately laced *nobat* drums of Indragiri, preserved with such reverence to this day, are a relic of a feudal and colonial time and worldview. As such, they have largely lost their musical and social significance, except among the kingdom's royal descendants and their loyal forest-dwelling Suku Mamak "subjects," most of whom continue to resist the efforts of the postcolonial government to alter their seminomadic ways, convert them to Islam, and encourage them to live in towns. Even though petty royalty has officially been abolished in Indonesia, the Suku Mamak still consider it a religious duty to revere their ancestors and to be loyal to the descendants of the Indragiri royal family, to whom their ancestors paid homage for centuries. To continue to pay such homage is also a form of protest at the government's attempted interference with their way of life and the threatened destruction of the natural environment that gives them sustenance. They know the palace can no longer protect them or assist them in the marketing of their forest and agricultural products, and that it can no longer invite them to take part in large ceremonies that previously symbolized an ordered, mystically oriented existence. Likewise, members of the present generation of Suku Mamak musicians have only a dim memory of the different *nobat* rhythms that they used to play at the various types of palace ceremonies.

Followers of the former Indragiri palace, especially the Suku Mamak people, still feel a warm nostalgia for the old palace culture, even though it represented a repressive feudal tradition overlaid with an even more repressive colonial system. The virtual extinction of the Indragiri *nobat* tradition is but one of many examples of the impoverishment of the Suku Mamak musical lifestyle in recent decades, a loss that cannot be redressed. The fast pace of change forced on the Suku Mamak by the present government and big business is much more threatening to them than the effects of colonial rule, which was less pervasive and allowed them to live in the forests, as they and their forbears had done for countless generations. With such rapid change in recent times, many other cultural treasures have also been irretrievably lost. Although the details of the royal *nobat* rhythms may largely have been forgotten, it is likely that aspects of them may live on in Suku Mamak drumming in other ritual contexts, as future research may show. One hopes they will be allowed to adapt and transform their way of life creatively, despite indications that their culture and the environment that sustains it will soon be destroyed forever.

ACKNOWLEDGMENTS

In 1984, H. Kartomi and I joined Ashley Turner, a PhD student at Monash University, who was carrying out music fieldwork among the Petalangan people in Riau, especially in and around the village of Betung on the Kampar River. After traveling along the Kampar and part of the Siak Rivers, we visited the Rengat area on the Indragiri River where the *nobat* discussed in this article is located. All along we were fortunate enough to be accompanied by the Riau-born poet, author, and scholar Tenas Effendy, who has family connections among the descendants of the former Malay sultanate of Pelalawan, on the Kampar River in Riau, but lives in Pakan Baru. Tenas Effendy was born in Kuda Pandang, Kecamatan Kuala Kampar. His father, Syek Said Umar, was secretary to the ruler of the Pelalawan kingdom. We wish to thank him for sharing his deep knowledge of the Riau culture with us, to thank both him and Turner for their companionship and contacts while in the field, and to thank Turner for his critical comments on this chapter.

For assistance in obtaining data for this chapter, I wish to thank the descendants of the Indragiri royal family whom H. Kartomi and I met in Rengat, especially Tengku Hamat (son-in-law of the last sultan, Mahmud Indragiri) and Encik Oemar Syarif (the Datuk Temenggung).

I also wish to thank the many musicians and dancers and the village leader at the Suku Mamak village of Talang Jerinjing, Kecamatan Rengat, who performed for our whole party. These people prefer to remain anonymous and to live in as much isolation from outsiders as possible.

II

SOUTH SUMATRA AND BANGKA

The southern region of Sumatra is divided into five provinces: Lampung, Beng-kulu, South Sumatra, Bangka-Belitung, and Jambi, of which only South Suma-tra and the Bangka part of Bangka-Belitung (which separated from South Sumatra in 2000) are discussed in this book.

Ecologically South Sumatra is dominated by the Bukit Barisan mountain range in the west where the mighty Musi River and its maze of tributaries begin, dissecting the descending plains across to the coastal marshes and the sea in the east.

South Sumatrans speak an estimated thirty-two varieties of Malay (Barendregt 2005) and varieties of the Lampungic language group, and the people of Bangka speak at least three Malay varieties plus local variants of Chinese (Hakka and Hokkien).

The Malay musico-lingual group in South Sumatra and Bangka may be divided into at least three upstream (*ulu*) and twelve downstream (*ilir*) subgroups. The up-stream subgroups are (1) the Besemah Malay in the central-western Bukit Barisan mountain range, (2) the people of the Lahat foothills east of the ranges, and (3) the Ogan Komering Ulu (OKU) subgroups, who speak the Ogan variety of Malay and/or the Komering variety of Lampungic in the Ogan and Komering basins and southwest foothills. The mid- and downstream (*ilir*) groups in the other foothills and plains are (4) the Ogan Tengah (Middle Ogan) Malay, (5) the nomadic Malay Kubu (alias Suku Dalem) forest-dwellers in the Rawas and Musi Banyuasin river basins and around and across the South Sumatra-Jambi border, (6) the Musi Banyuasin Malay in the north, (7) the Malay and/or Komering-speaking Ogan Komering Ilir (OKI) subgroup in and around the lower Ogan and Komering river basins, (8) the Palembang Malay, and (9) the Javanized Palembang Malay of the former palace in Palembang.

Chapter 7 surveys six of the above musico-lingual subgroups living in South Sumatra; however, subgroups 4, 6, and 7, the upstream Rejang (who speak a language
isolate), and the Javanese and other transmigrant communities are not discussed.
Chapter 8 discusses the province's official musical symbol, Gending Sriwijaya. Chapter 9 discusses the Malay, Suku Lom, Suku Laut, Peranakan Hakka and Peranakan
Hokkien (Chinese Indonesian) people living in Bangka. All three chapters are based
on field recordings and other data collected in the 1970s, 1980s, and 1990s. For an
explanation of instrumental tunings and vocal scales in South Sumatra, see appendix
4; for a discussion of the former Palembang court *gamelan*, see appendix 5.

HISTORICAL OUTLINE

It was in South Sumatra, probably at Bukit Seguntang near the present-day capital
of Palembang, that Southeast Asia's first major old Malay-speaking kingdom, Sriwijaya, was founded in the seventh century C.E. Many subsequent Malay kingdoms in
Malaysia's Malay Peninsula and Sumatra trace their descent from its royal house, but
the former Palembang sultanate itself, which was founded in the fourteenth century
and is of Javanese Demak ancestry, does not, nor do the former chieftains on Bangka.
The town of Melayu, on the Batang Hari River in Jambi, served as the subsequent
center of the prosperous and powerful kingdom of Sriwijaya, as confirmed by an
inscription dated 1286 left by the conquering Javanese in the upper reaches of the
Batang Hari River. It refers to the people as the inhabitants of the kingdom of Melayu
(Krom 1931, 335–36). As Chinese, Arab, and Old Malay records and iconographical
evidence indicate, its ruling elite built a number of palaces and Saivite-Mahayana
Tantric Buddhist temples, most of the remains of which are now lost, though some
have been found especially at sites on the Jambi River and further north. Between
the seventh and the fourteenth century, Sriwijaya was the center of the international
trade route from northwest Sumatra to Arabia and India and northeast to China.
The name Melayu persisted into the fourteenth century in inland Jambi, where a
1347 inscription attributed to Adityawarman refers to Melayupura (the town of the
Melayu) located in the Minangkabau highlands.

The historical evidence suggests that the concept of Malay ethnicity and class that
developed among the Sriwijaya and other palace elites spawned the creation of the
seminomadic Suku Laut (Sea Peoples) around the coasts of Bangka and Belitung,
consisting of various communities who preferred to live in houseboats at sea for
part of each year, and the nomadic or seminomadic Suku Dalam and Suku Lom,
who preferred to live in the isolation of their forest environment in South Sumatra

and Bangka respectively. These peoples provided valuable sea or forest products respectively and services to their local Malay chieftains. In return they were rewarded artistically, spiritually, and economically by their rulers, who encouraged the maintenance of their lifestyle (L. Andaya 2008, 4).

7

SOUTH SUMATRA

"The Realm of Many Rivers"

This chapter will show how South Sumatra's topography—the mountains, plains, rivers, and seas—can serve as a key interpretative grid for understanding the historical distribution of its musico-lingual groups, and how the region's environment and associated cosmology, *adat*, and the history of religion and foreign contact have shaped its music, dance, and theater.[1]

South Sumatra's magnificent network of rivers and tributaries—known as the Batang Hari Sembilan (lit. "Nine River Branches")—has governed its peoples' travels, worldviews, *adat*, legends, and musical arts for well over two millennia (see map 7.1).[2] From the early centuries of the Common Era, local and foreign traders, envoys, religious teachers, and artists from China, Java, India, the Middle East, and other overseas places traveled up and down the great Musi River and its many major tributaries. Flowing from their sources in the mysterious Bukit Barisan in the west, the rivers enabled the people to move about and settle in the highlands, foothills, plains, swampy east-coast lowlands, and towns located on the river estuaries, and they served as routes for the disseminations of artistic ideas, bardic arts, musical pieces, songs, dances, theater forms, and musical instruments. The rivers also facilitated the nomadic lifestyle of the Orang Suku Dalem/Kubu and Suku Lom in the forests.

For at least the past fifteen hundred years, the ancient court and market capital of Palembang on the Musi River some 140 kilometers from the sea dominated communications, trade, migration, and government. Along the coast and offshore islands of Bangka and Belitung, the Orang Laut (Sea Peoples) moved about by sea and river

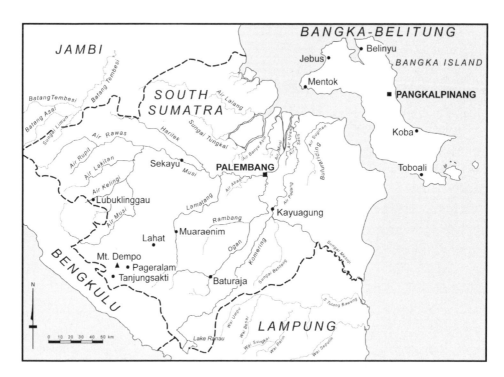

Map 7.1 Network of rivers in South Sumatra

in their houseboats, returning to land to live in makeshift houses on the beaches during inclement weather when they held their major rituals.

The great majority of the population of South Sumatra are Sunni Muslims, with a few Christians. Many members of the Sufi-oriented Sunni Muslim communities are influenced by the ancestral spirit world as well as the Muslim doctrine of souls (*jin*), while the strictly monotheistic, fundamentalist Muslims reject Sufi and other mysticism and all the mystical rituals and arts. The Orang Laut in coastal South Sumatra and Bangka base their cultural identity on belief in the ancestral sea and beach deities, and the mainland Orang Dalem or Suku Kubu in the local ancestral and forest spirits. They have mostly resisted efforts by a succession of Dutch and Indonesian authorities to convert them to Islam or Christianity and settle them in government-built houses. Bangka's *peranakan* Hakka and Hokkien peoples honor the deities of their ancestors, especially the goddess Ibu Dewi Kwan Yin, protectress at sea.

The people of South Sumatra and Bangka can trace their musical heritage back to the prehistoric era. Fragments of waisted bronze "kettledrums" (*nekara*) and other megalithic remains found in South Sumatra's Bukit Barisan and on Bangka (Ooi Keat Gin 2004) indicate that a society influenced by the Dōng-son culture of the Annam-

Tonkin region (northern and central Vietnam) lived in Sumatra's southern highlands from around five hundred to one thousand years before the Common Era.[3]

Entering southern Sumatra via the Musi River system, the bearers of Dōng-son culture traveled upstream to the fertile mountainous valleys and plateaus. Among the megaliths found near Pagar Alam in Besemah Lebar is a human figure depicted with a waisted bronze kettledrum (of the Heger I type) strapped to his back as he rides an elephant (Thomassen à Thuessink van der Hoop 1932, 90) (see fig. 7.1). Remains of other bronze Dōng-son drums have been found on South Sumatran soil and in many other parts of mainland and insular Southeast Asia (Kunst 1949, 105–6).[4] We can only guess at the extent of the musical and religious significance that the drums doubtless possessed in prehistoric times. Dōng-son kettledrums have ceased to form any part of living musical culture, though remains of these instruments are still regarded as sacred objects by the people of the region, and the megalithic sites are still used as shrines at which to propitiate the ancestors. There is no evidence that the *kromongan* and other bronze instrumental ensembles played in South Sumatra during recent centuries and to this day derive from megalithic times, though the ergological bronze-working skills of local blacksmiths are so old as to be legendary.

Figure 7.1 The "Elephant Stone" (ca. 200–300 c.e.), showing a Dōng-son drum on the back of a warrior riding an elephant, originally found in Besemah and subsequently situated outside the State Museum in Palembang

From the seventh to the thirteenth century c.e., the maritime Buddhist kingdom of Sriwijaya (Śrīvijaya), with its center initially located near the modern capital, Palembang, came to control the shipping in the Strait of Malacca and became the region's major port of international trade. As the first Malay kingdom in Southeast Asia, it pursued military, trade, and marriage ties with kingdoms or chiefdoms in Java, the Lake Ranau area in southwestern South Sumatra, Jambi (where its capital moved in the eleventh century), the state of Kedah on the Malay Peninsula, southern Siam, and China.[5] Inscriptions in Old Malay found from as early as 683 c.e. attest to the importance of Old Malay as Sriwijaya's official state language (Coedès 1968, 82–83). As documented by Chinese, Arabic-Persian, Malay, and other sources from the seventh to the tenth century, Sriwijaya was a major center for Mahayana Buddhist learning (see chap. 8).[6]

After the decline of Sriwijaya, Muslim proselytizers and merchants came to eastern South Sumatra via the seas and lower reaches of the Musi River, moving up to the highlands centuries later.[7] The king of Palembang converted to Islam in the seventeenth century, and the princes and commoners in his constituencies followed suit. Some of the Suku Kubu and Suku Laut, who preferred to live a largely isolated existence in the northern interior and/or on the eastern coastlines of South Sumatra and Bangka, enjoyed a special complementary relationship with members of the aristocracy, providing artistic and other services to the sultan on ceremonial occasions (Bp. Usman Effendy, pers. comm., Burai Baru, 1971). Religious leaders from the Arabian peninsula who were influential in the palace banned all dancing but allowed Demak-Javanese *gamelan* and shadow-puppet theater and some Muslim devotional arts to develop. Rural communities added the Muslim arts to their ancestral ritual dances and musical genres. Chinese middlemen in Palembang helped develop the sultan's trading activities in South Sumatra and beyond. Chinese princesses who married into the sultanate brought Chinese cloth designs, furniture, and other cultural artifacts into the court, including the *so na* (oboe) into the *gamelan* (Raden Moh Husin [RMH] Nato Dirajo, pers. comm., Palembang, 1988). The sultans became patrons of local craftsmen and craftswomen who made textiles, dance costumes, gong-chimes, and other musical instruments and art objects (Colombijn 2002, 289). The textile industry in and around Palembang included providing *songket* cloth for the aristocrats and merchant class to wear, and for export (ibid.).

South Sumatran *songket* is an important element of identity in the dancing and wedding rituals in both the upstream and the downstream areas. *Songket* is a luxury silk or cotton brocade featuring a basic color (e.g., red or violet), with its interwoven motifs containing a supplementary metal weft to give it a shimmering effect (Uchino 2005, 205). Though Palembang *songket* became famous in the eighteenth century, it probably originated there in pre-Muslim times, perhaps influenced in part by Indian and/or Chinese cloths (ibid.). Whether in the mountains or on the plains, female dancers wear *songket* as a full-length wraparound sarong and a long, matching shoulder scarf (*selendang*; see fig. 7.2). Traditionally dressed brides also wear this costume, and bridegrooms wear matching sarongs made of *songket*, though orthodox Muslims since the 1980s have rejected this "Hindu-Buddhist" look in favor of Muslim-style costumes that cover the whole body apart from the face. To this day, the female textile artists in the Palembang and Ogan-Komering areas are well known for their special local colors and designs, which differ from those of their counterparts in the Minangkabau highlands, Aceh, west Malaysia, and elsewhere.

In 1832, long after the Palembang sultanate's conversion to Islam, the Dutch government abolished the Palembang sultanate and established its own colonial administration in the town. However, resentment of their overlordship served only to strengthen and spread the Islamic faith. Although the Dutch and their English rivals were aware of the economic potential of South Sumatra (especially in the highlands) from the seventeenth century (B. W. Andaya 1995, 543), colonization and Christian proselytization developed slowly. English Protestants who came to the highlands during Raffles's governorship around 1818 did not make a lasting impact. After local revolts against the Dutch 1823 to 1850 had been quelled (Barendregt 2005, 145–50), the first Dutch Catholic priests arrived in the 1880s and the first Dutch Protestants in 1910, but their efforts met lasting success in only a few communities, for example, in parts of Tanjungsakti and Pagar Alam (discussed below). These communities practiced a local hymn-singing and harmonium-playing culture in the churches and at local life event ceremonies (pers. comm., Moh. Saman, Tanjungsakti, 1988).

In the highland villages, the traditional customs and arts began to decline in the early twentieth century as the Dutch began to supplement the traditional modes of communication on foot and by boat by building railways and, later, motorways. In the 1920s, a strongly orthodox form of Islam spread in the highlands (Barendregt 2005, 138), by which time virtually the whole province had converted to Islam, and their ancestral and nature-based worldviews and cultural life were overlaid with local interpretations of a Muslim worldview (Bowen 1993). Yet even after Indonesian independence had been declared in 1945, many aspects of the *adat* ceremonial arts remained in practice. In the mid-twentieth century, members of the nobility who had lived across the countryside in the colonial period were largely replaced or supplemented by Indonesian public servants; however, some were descendants of the former aristocracy, and they patronized the arts. Yet for the masses of subsistence farmers or swidden farmer-gatherers, little had changed. The Dutch and subsequently the Indonesian provincial government attempted to settle some of the nomadic forest/interior and sea peoples in South Sumatra and Bangka, but they were generally unsuccessful, for most continued in the nomadic or seminomadic lifestyles of their ancestors.[8]

THE UPSTREAM PEOPLES

Of the many musico-lingual groups among the Orang Ulu (People of the Headwaters), this chapter focuses only on two groups: the Besemah in Tanjungsakti and Kayuagung (see map 7.1), and the Ogan-Komering Ulu (OKU) Malays in Burai, both of whom live on the east side of the Bukit Barisan mountain range.[9] Some musical arts in the Lahat foothills are described, and then the musical arts of the plains.

As indicated by the extensive megaliths and other archeological remains found around Lahat and Lake Ranau, the Besemah occupy the oldest settled area of South Sumatra (beginning several centuries before the Common Era), despite the fact that one of their legends claims that they descended from the ancestor Atung Bungsu of the fourteenth-century Javanese kingdom of Majapahit (Barendregt 2005, 57).[10] The legends, which refer to the megaliths and other cultural artifacts, are most clearly told in the form of the bardic arts and dance.

BESEMAH'S BARDIC LEGENDS

In the 1980s, the hosts of some weddings and other rituals and celebrations in Besemah were still frequently employing semiprofessional singers to perform the ancestral narratives (*cerite puyang*, Barendregt 2005, 8) and legendary *guritan* (oral epics), such as "The Story of Radin Guane" (W. A. Collins 1979).[11] In colonial times these performances lasted for several nights on end, but from the 1980s onward they were commonly reduced to two nights (Bp. Toyeb, pers. comm., Pagaralam, 1989). In the performances, the bards frequently pay respect to the highest mountain, Dempo (see map 7.1), the home of Betare Guru (Vishnu), the "Lord of Souls," and refer to other local variants of Hindu beliefs, including the tale of the cosmic egg, to explain the origin of human beings (Barendregt 2005, 40–41). The performances also invoke local deities, deified ancestors, and other supernatural beings (Barendregt 2005, 41) and specify the established relationships between the mostly patrilineal clans, who are divided into the bride-giving and the bride-taking moieties.[12] The narratives, which may also be written on bark manuscripts (Surat Ulu), refer to the social customs, adages, genealogies (*silsilah*), and secret cosmologies of the ancestors.[13]

In our recording of a *guritan* performance in Tanjungsakti in 1971, the bard first addressed the ancestral spirits, then sang a story about his people's ancestral origins using the anhemitonic pentatonic tonal $\{5_1\ 6_1\ 1_1\ 2_1\ 3\ 5\ 6\}$ $\{E_1\ F\sharp_1\ A_1\ B_1\ C\sharp\ E\ F\sharp\}$ (see audio example 7.1). Beginning on $\{5\}$ or $\{E\}$ and descending to the main tone $\{1_1\}$ $\{A_1\}$, he sang the phrase

Music example 7.1 A phrase excerpted from a
guritan performance

and then chanted part of the story on $\{E_1\}$, ending with a melodic flourish, as in music example 7.1.

In another *guritan* performance in Tanjungsakti in 1989, Ibu Sri Cik Timah, a middle-aged woman of the Pumi clan from Kampung Negeri Kaja, sang "Lagu Tangis Ayam" ("The Crying Chicken Song"), the text of which gave a female view of male-female relations as expressed in the Bujang (bachelor) Indaran legend. She began each verse on the lowest note (D) and rose in pitch on and around the tones of the hexatonic scale $\{1\ 2\ 3\ (4)\ 5\ 6\}$ or $\{D^*\ E\ F\sharp\ (G)\ A\ B\}$, using a little vibrato on the long notes, melodic ornament, and glides between some tones, with tone 4 acting as an inessential passing note.

An important ancestral narrative tells how the culture hero, Atung Bungsu, traveled upriver, "weighed the earth and water" at each suitable estuary, and founded settlements on those sites.[14] However, the major highland legend told by bards describes the deeds of the primal male ancestor Puyang Serunting Sakti, alias Lidah Pahit (Bitter Tongue), so named because whatever he said became instant reality. This was due to a gift—actually a curse—received from a deity who lived on Palembang's Seguntang Hill, the sacred center of the Sriwijaya-Palembang Empire. One version holds that Bitter Tongue was the ruler of Java's Sailendra dynasty, while another says he came from Java's Majapahit kingdom. One day, Bitter Tongue is said to have turned a human being playing a slit drum into a stone figure, while on another occasion, his words immortalized a pair of tigers caught copulating by turning them into a stone megalith (Thomassen à Thuessink van der Hoop 1932; Barendregt 2005, xiv–xv).

The most famous part of the legend, however, describes how Bitter Tongue happened to see the youngest of seven beautiful angel-sisters, Puyang Bidodari/Putri Bungsu, bathing in the lake. Falling in love with her, he hid her shawl (*selendang*), which prevented her from flying back to heaven with her sisters, leaving her no choice but to marry him and bear his child. Another part of the legend tells how Putri Bungsu and her six sisters guided Atong Bungsu in his choices of estuaries along the Musi, where he founded settlements for his people (Barendregt 2005, 54–58).

However, members of the wife-receiving Semidang clan, who claim direct descent from Serunting Sakti, feuded with the wife-giving Penjelang clan who owned the area, and the feud continues to this day, as told in the legend that accompanies the dance (Barendregt 2005, 112–14). The Youngest Angel story, which is told in countless forms in many parts of Sumatra and other parts of Southeast Asia, is the basis of the most classical of Besemah's ancestral dances, *tari kebar* (wave dance), or *tari lang* (eagle dance) (henceforth *tari kebar*).

BESEMAH'S CLASSICAL AND SOCIAL DANCES AND ENSEMBLE MUSIC

The Besemah tradition is rich in classical, *adat* dances, the most sacred of which is *tari kebar*, usually performed by a pair of young female dancers, as in fig 7.2. Their eagle-like flying and hovering movements simulate the flying away of the Youngest Sister/Angel in the Bitter Tongue legend. Each female dancer wears a sarong made of shimmering *songket* textile and matching *selendang* (long scarf), holding its ends with the fingers of each hand, the movements of which emphasize her intricate hand and arm movements. Most dances (as in audio example 7.2) are performed at weddings,

Figure 7.2 *Tari kebar*, Tanjungsakti, 1989

accompanied by a *kenong* (or *kelintang*) gong-chime and drum ensemble, though sometimes a "Malay ensemble" comprising a *serunai* (oboe) or a *biola* and frame drums is played instead.[15] Both are centuries-old ensemble traditions.

The classical *kebar* dance is based on the following episode from the Bitter Tongue legend:

> Bitter Tongue and his wife, the Youngest Angel, were guests at a wedding. At the height of the celebrations, the revelers requested that the Youngest Angel dance in the arena in front of the chieftain's house. She refused but was eventually persuaded to agree on one condition: that her husband return the silk shawl (*baju rambut*, lit. "hair cloth") that he had stolen from her. At first Bitter Tongue refused, but after the people implored him to comply, he had to agree. With a heavy heart, he took her to the place where he had stuffed the shawl into a bamboo tube (*tepang*), and returned it to her. To fulfill her end of the bargain, she began to dance. Her scarf billowed as she performed wondrously elegant movements with her outstretched arms, like an eagle hovering in the sky. Her movements were more refined and exquisite than anyone had ever seen. All who watched were speechless, as if in a trance. Eventually, it seemed, she was no longer dancing on the earth. The longer she danced, the higher she floated; it seemed she was no longer dancing on the earth. Finally she flew home again to highest heaven.

In Tanjungsakti two young female dancers normally perform three main *tari kebar* routines.[16] They are the *nendang* (lit. "move" [on earth]), simulating the angel's movements while still dancing on earth; the *ngebar* (spread out) movements, as she begins to fly and to test the reactions of her entranced onlookers; and the *betaup* (meaning unknown), when she simulates flying back to her home in the sky. In the first routine the two dancers take twelve steps to the right, three steps back, circle to the right, and repeat the routine to the left, holding their right arms and hands up at a right angle (*siku*). In the second routine, they take twelve steps forward, circle to the right, take three steps back, and repeat the routine to the left; then with both arms simulating flying movements, they take three steps back. In the third, they circle widely in the middle of the yard with their arms and hands in the *siku* position, move to the right and then to the left, and take three steps back. If any young men take part, they combine select movements from the art of self-defense and the *gandai* dance, the latter of which is normally performed by a group of girls in the Serawai area of South Sumatra, Bengkulu, and on the southern coast of Minangkabau (described in chap. 3).

The *kebar* dance was frequently performed in the colonial era but almost died out during the Japanese occupation. It was revived again in the 1950s, but even in the late 1980s only a few dancers could perform it, as it requires the ability to execute very slow movements, with a degree of bodily control that is difficult to learn (Bp. H. I. Majusuf [b. 1911] and village head Bp. Sahumi Munir, pers. comm., Jokoh, 1989).

Another classical highland dance that is performed in the Serawai area (on the border of Bengkulu and South Sumatra) is the *tari Inggeris* (English dance), or *tari adat*, which resembles an English maypole round dance. Men and women, or women only, hold a long ribbon attached to the top of a pole and dance in a circle around it, accompanied by an *orkes Melayu* that minimally comprises a *biola* and frame drums.[17] The dance is apparently an artistic residue of the period when the British East India Company ran its colony in Bengkulu (1685–1824). Sir Thomas Stamford Raffles, who was appointed the governor-general of Bencoolen (1818–24), visited parts of Serawai, Rejang, and Besemah, including Tanjungsakti, in 1818 (Raffles 1835, 337), accompanied by some Protestant missionaries (whose proselytizing influence, however, did not last; Bp. Mahmid Semidang, pers. comm., Sukajadi, 1989). However, the dance could, of course, have been introduced in the highlands long before Raffles's tenure in Bengkulu.

In the highlands there is also an array of mixed dances that follow codes of moral behavior prescribed by customary law (W. A. Collins 1979, 52; Barendregt 2005, 9). In some areas of Besemah, clan exogamy is so strong that members of the same clan are forbidden to dance together or exchange sung poetry (Barendregt 2005, chap. 15). However, unmarried couples or groups of three who are not blood relatives are allowed to dance a social version of the *kebar* dance (alias *tari melayang-layang* ([eagle] floating in the air dance) and exchange sung *pantun* verses at a wedding or guest-welcoming ceremony, as long as the first female dancer to appear is the bride, or an important guest.[18]

At a wedding in 1989 that we attended in the village of Jokoh in Kecamatan Paga-ralam, the bride arrived in a procession from her parents' home in another village. She danced in the yard outside her bridegroom's house with two men from the clan into which she was marrying. However, the groom was not permitted to take part, as most of his potential female partners present were from his clan. After that, other couples or trios could join in the dancing and exchange singing. The male dancers performed protective, expansive arm movements and other "distinctively male" gestures while stepping forward and backward in various formations, while their female partner danced in front of them, performing more spatially confined and intricate "female" movements, especially of the fingers and hands. At times both the male and female dancers' arms and shoulders spread open (*melebar*) and fluttered up and down like the movements of an eagle flying, with the men raising their arms above their shoulder level to "protect" their female partners, who were allowed to raise their arms only up to shoulder level.

Two musicians accompanied the performance on an ensemble called *kenong*, which comprised a framed set of four horizontal gong-chimes (also called *kenong*) and a frame drum called a *redap*. First, they played the relatively fast piece "Cacing Pembuka" (based on a rhythmic motive called *cacing* [worm]), after which the "Irama Joget" ("*Joget* Rhythm") was played to accompany the Malay *tari Musi* (Musi River dance), ending with a return to the first piece, "Cacing Penutup" ("Closing *Cacing*").[19] One musician beat out a melody with a pair of sticks on the set of gong-chimes, the largest of which measured five by thirty-four centimeters in height and diameter respectively, had a three-centimeter boss, and was tuned (from left to right) to tones {$^{\flat}2$ 2 3 $1^{!}$} or {D$^{\flat}$ D E C$^{!}$}. The other played a *redap* that measured seventeen centimeters in diameter and ten centimeters in height. *Kenong* tunings are substantially variable; for example, in 1989 one *kenong* ensemble in Sukajadi village was tuned (from left to right) to C^{1} D^{1} G^{1} A^{1}, while another in nearby Jokoh village was tuned to the hemitonic four-tone palette {$^{\flat}2^{1}$ 1^{1} 3 2} or {D$^{\flat 1}$ C^{1} E D}.

Such *pantun* exchange singing and dancing in couples or groups of three was still a popular courting practice in the 1980s. However, as some Muslim leaders disapproved of the gender mixing, a new version of the dance was choreographed for three girls to perform as a guest-welcoming dance.[20] Renamed *tari elang* (I., "eagle dance"), it has replaced the *tari kebar* and *tari joget* in official circles.

A range of traditional "social mixing" (*pergaulan*) dances for young people is performed across the Besemah highlands. In Kecamatan Pagaralam, they may be accompanied by a gong-chime ensemble called *tabuhan, tale,* or *kelintang*, which usually comprises a framed set of four horizontal bossed gongs (also called *tabuhan, tale,* or *kelintang*) and a frame-drum *redap* (about 32 cm in diameter and 15 cm in height).

The same dances are sometimes accompanied by an *orkes Melayu*, comprising a violin (*biola*), frame drums (*redap*), cylindrical drums (*gendang*), and an optional gong (*gung*). It plays Malay melodies such as "Lagu Lancang Kuning" ("Yellow Boat Song"), "Perang di Aceh" ("War in Aceh"), "Tari Tanggai" ("Long-Fingernail Dance"), and "Tari Piring" ("Plate Dance"), the latter of which possibly originated in Minangkabau or Kerinci.

In the South Sumatran Rejang area, the *kelintang* ensembles contain a set of gong-chimes (*kelintang*) comprising four, five, six, seven, or nine small bronze or iron gongs arranged in a row in a horizontal wooden frame; a *gendang panjang* (cylindrical drum); two *redap* or *deb* (frame drums); and a suspended gong, with a *serunai* (oboe) or a *biola* substituting at times for the gong chime.[21]

In the lower hills of Kecamatan Lahat, the main traditional courting dance, called *gegerit*, is named after the typical shoulder-raising dance movements that imitate an eagle flying. Both the music and the dance combine pre-Muslim movements and instruments with those that "have an Islamic flavor." Two unmarried men in *adat* ceremonial dress wear a small dagger (*keris*) with which to protect their partners and dance behind two unmarried women wearing elaborately ornamented red velvet bridal costumes.[22] They are accompanied by a *tabuhan* ensemble consisting of a gong-chime (tuned in one case to {5¹ 2¹ 1¹ 5 1¹ 2¹} or {G¹ D¹ C¹ G C¹ D¹}, with a melody played partly in octaves); a suspended bronze gong (*gung*) measuring forty-four centimeters in diameter playing a cyclic rhythmic pattern; a double-headed *gendang*; and two instruments associated with the holy land, that is, a set of four small double-headed drums (*marwas*, plural *marawis*) and a lute (*gambus*).

In both the Pagaralam and the Lahat areas, the *tari erai-erai* (lemongrass dance) is popular.[23] Mixed unmarried couples or pairs of women play both the male and the female roles of a couple dance while exchanging *pantun* verses about such topics as love, poverty, wealth, and homelessness.[24] They are accompanied by a three-stringed violin (*biola*) played with double-stopping, a flute (*suling*), a frame drum (*terbangan*), a two-headed drum (*gendang* or *drem*), and a chorus, the members of which sing Malay songs in diatonic or Arabic scales. Among the *erai-erai* songs that we recorded at Merapi village near Lahat in 1988 was the famous Malay song "Rasa Sayang-é" ("The Feeling of Love, Ah!"), set in a major scale (see music example 7.2).[25]

While some children are taught to perform all the dances, others are allowed by their parents to learn only the *kesenian Islami* songs and dances that are taught in the Muslim schools (*madrasah*). In Tanjungsakti and many other parts of South Sumatra, the most popular of these items is the *tari ya dana* or *rebana* dance, in which groups of boys or girls kneel on their heels closely together in a row, moving from side to side and back and forth in unison, or in twos or threes, while singing songs about the five laws of Islam and other Muslim themes to their own *rebana* (frame drum) and *kicikan* (frame with jingles) accompaniment. This dance, which somewhat resembles the Minangkabau *indang* dance (see chap. 5), may have been transplanted and developed in the highlands from Kerinci or West Sumatra in the 1960s, or earlier (Haji Teman, pers. comm., Jokoh, 1989). Groups of dancers sometimes participate

Music example 7.2 A transcription of "Rasa Sayang-é"

in locally organized competitions to raise money to build a mosque or a road, or serve another communal need, hence the name *tari ya dana* (dance [for] funding). Its other name, *tari rebana*, emphasizes the dancers' frame-drum playing as they sing the confession of faith (e.g., *Lā ilāha illā 'llāh*, "There is no God but God"), or other Muslim phrases, and secular texts.

Throughout the highlands, various forms of the art of self-defense (*silat*) associated with Islamized *adat* beliefs are performed by pairs of mock combatants. Usually an elegant martial arts display is followed by a bout of agile mock combat with knives and daggers, accompanied by an ensemble comprising a small gong and a double-headed drum or a large gong with a set of three cylindrical drums. In Lahat, the main martial art display takes the form of a *keris* (dagger) dance, accompanied by a *rebab* (bowed string instrument) and doubled-headed, cylindrical drums.

VOCAL MUSIC

In our journeys during the 1970s, shamans in the more isolated Besemah musico-lingual subgroups still performed rites and made offerings of burning incense, rice, eggs, and forest products to attract and appease the spirits. They sang mystical invocations (mantra) before tackling such tasks as curing a patient, clearing forest land, planting, or harvesting a crop. Honey-collecting shamans (*plawang medu*) still sang a large repertory of mystical songs to quiet a swarm of bees (*lagu ngalaka medu*, lit. "songs to defeat the honeybees") while they carried a burning torch up a tall *sialang* tree to collect honey from a hive hanging from a branch (Goldsworthy 1978). A *plawang* also performed rituals to commence a rice-stamping performance, when groups of women rhythmically stamped the husks off the grain with poles on troughs at harvest time. A pair of shamans who could befriend "the king or queen of the forest" sang magic spells (*jampi*) to entice a tiger who had consumed a person to enter a cage containing meat bait set up for his or her capture (see chap. 2).

One of the main vocal genres in Besemah is the *rejunk*, in which men and women sing partly improvised rhyming quatrains (*rejunk, cang-incang*) for a special ceremony or to help themselves or one another solve everyday problems. The singing is often accompanied by a small *gembos* (*gambus*) or a guitar (*gitar tunggal*) (Barendregt 2005, 390).[26]

At a wedding feast, which *adat* decrees must begin with the ancestral *kebar* dance of the Youngest Angel (Van Rees 1870), marriageable young men and women from different Besemah villages traditionally exchange *rejunk* verses, flirting and entertaining each other for hours after midnight. As has been noted, only men and women from different villages may dance and sing together and marry, to avoid interbreeding. Thus, young men and women may formally offer each other advice about how to cope with love and other problems, adding local proverbs (*andai-andai*; see Voorhoeve 1985, 35) to their exchanges if they wish, usually delivered with humor. If they come from different villages, they may even exchange verses about whether they should get married.

Sometimes a couple may sing long sessions of very refined *cang-incang* verses (a *rejunk panjang*, "a long *rejunk*") to see if they are suited for marriage, as in an excerpt of a session that we recorded in Tanjungsakti in 1971.[27] A male vocalist, Bp. Lesai, sang that he had lost his appetite because of the unrequited feelings of love buried in his heart, to which a female singer (Ibu Sri Cik Timah) replied with friendly advice about how he should deal with this emotional problem. The man began by singing a verse about how humble he felt, to which the woman replied that she felt humbler still, but as they both liked each other, they sang a verse that stated, "The Chinese never make wrong calculations because they are so clever." Everyone understands that the verse implies that the couple are particularly suited to each other, and eventually they found the words with which to accept each other (Guru Anang of Pasar Lama, pers. comm., Tanjungsakti, 1971). The pair sang a pentatonic melody (*petikan*) that approximated tones {D E F♯ A B} over a range of two octaves, with leaps of fourths and fifths between the main tones (D and A) and frequent glides. Sri Cik Timah said that such verses and their melodies change every few years; the one they sang was well known in the early 1940s, and they also liked to perform a song that was popular in 1936.

Some singers insert turns and other ornamentation (*ligut*) in the melodies they sing, as in a performance of *cang-incang* verses recorded at a wedding in Kayuagung in 1971. The melody is based on the hemitonic pentatonic scale {1^{*1} 2^1 3^1 5 6 (7)} or {$F\sharp^1$ G^1 A^1 $C\sharp$ D (E)}, with phrases focusing on tones {1_1 2_1 3_1}, and {3 5 6}, with an occasional tone 7 added for variety (music example 7.3).[28]

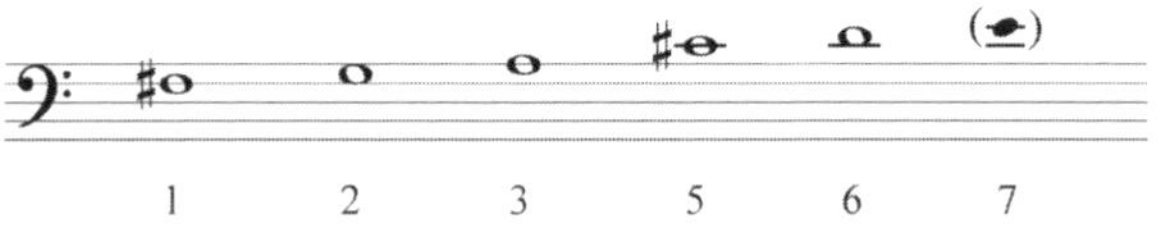

Music example 7.3 Basic tones for *cang-incang* verses in *rejunk* performance

The melodic outline of the piece is transcribed below (music example 7.4), with the text of lyric 1 sourced from audio example 7.3 (verse 3) and translated as

From the market and the villages, elders and people
All gather for the ceremony happily.

Note the term *rejunk* included in lyric 2. Both text and translation of this second lyric have been sourced from Barendregt (2005, 382):

Here is the news, hear the tidings.
There probably are junks at sea right now.[29]

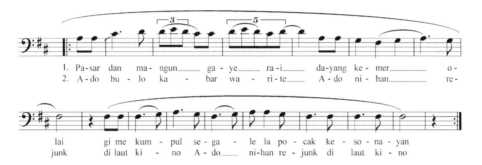

Music example 7.4 A transcribed excerpt of a *cang-incang* verse from a *rejunk* performance recorded at a wedding in Kayuagung, 1971

Rejunk can also serve a mystical aim, for example, when a shaman sings praises of a patient as a healing device. It can also have a psychological purpose, for example, when a man relieves his feelings of loneliness or distress by singing loudly in the forest. At the induction of an elder (*pasirah*), a man may describe the inductee's extraordinary attributes or good deeds in *rejunk* verse, whereupon the elder's wife may sing a response on behalf of her husband and the people of the village. The verses may contain metaphors about the local river, thus articulating the group's relatedness to streaming water and a particular soil (Barendregt 2005, 384).

In Besemah's more mountainous areas, where communications have been difficult, each musico-lingual subgroup whose singing we recorded had its own exclusive scales or tuning, a factor that may also be related to the different intonations of the local dialects (Barendregt 2005, 385). There is a great variety of tunings (*petikan*) and rhythms (*alunan*) between vocal and instrumental performances in different areas, as Barendregt also noted (384). Yet several groups describe their music in terms of river metaphors. For example, plucked string passages in the piece "Petik Tabuh Musi" ("Musi [River] Rhythm") on a *gembos* (*gambus*) or on a Jew's harp are compared to the slow, rushing sound of the river Musi. Some *alunan* are described as being calm and slow, while others are "rushing through landscape" rhythms; both musical expressions are metaphors for young rivers. Thus the sound of water is seen as shaping melody, rhythm, and tuning, and the link between particular groups and songs is articulated in sound and the geographical imagery of the texts (384–85).

Finally, lullabies are believed to have an efficacious effect on a baby's well-being. Semiprofessional singers at baby thanksgiving ceremonies sing lullabies ("Ngayun Buai," lit. "Sway and Sing to Sleep"), sometimes softly and calmly and at other times quite loudly to entertain their audience. In Burai and some neighboring hilly villages of Ogan Komering Ulu, lullabies are sung in five- or six-tone scales with frequent changes of tonal center and considerable melodic ornamentation.[30]

SOLO INSTRUMENTAL MUSIC

Music played on a Jew's harp (*ginggung*) is based mainly on the melodies of courting songs and is therefore related to the vocal music. The *ginggung* consists of a very thin, rectangular bamboo lathe with a split to accommodate its long, vibrating tongue. The player holds it by her left hand in her half-open mouth while the second finger of her right hand vibrates the other end by tugging a small cord attached to it. The fluctuating size of her mouth cavity keeps changing, producing harmonics that can produce a melody or, more typically, a series of melodic fragments, as in the courting song "Mantau Kundang" (see audio example 7.4). In the audio example 7.4, the fundamental note is $\{E^{\flat}_1\}$ and the harmonics are variants of $\{B^{\flat} \ G \ F \ E^{\flat} \ B^{\flat}_1\}$.

Traditional practice allows a young man to go to the home of his would-be partner at night to attract her attention by playing "Plucked Music to Call a Friend" ("Petik Mantau Kundang") on a Jew's harp, often mouthing words of love while playing an octave drone passage, as in music example 7.5. If the girl likes him and her parents are absent or asleep, she signals her assent to meet him by mouthing an answer on her own Jew's harp and opens the door to him. Even if her father and mother are present, they may have already agreed that they may marry, in which case they discreetly depart while their daughter sees her lover. Other titles played are "Petik

Music example 7.5 A fragment of the
piece "Mantau Kundang" played on
a *ginggung* (Jew's harp)

Bidodari Berkindun" ("Angel Rocks a Child") and "Petik Tabuh Musi" ("Musi [River] Rhythm"; Bp. Saman, Bp. Y. Herman Jentamat, pers. comm., Burai, 1989).

Another important solo instrument, usually played only by men, is the *serdam*, an end-blown ring flute around forty centimeters long with three front holes and a back hole.[31] Some *serdam* melodies are associated with happy feelings, for example, when playing melodies of songs about friendship, love, and weddings, but most are perceived as being sad. A *serdam* player often accompanies a professional *rejunk* singer who is called to the home of a deceased person on the first, third, seventh, and fortieth day after a death in order to sing appropriate verses, usually interspersed with sobbing. Continuing all night for several nights on end, the music therapeutically stimulates the open expression of grief among the mourners. However, due to the disapproval of orthodox Muslim leaders who believe that death is the will of God and should be celebrated rather than mourned, this practice became rare from the 1980s onward.

Whatever the sentiment, the flute is played with the technique of circular breathing. The player produces long-held notes, interspersed with elaborately ornamented passages of microtonal and semitonal melody and leaps of octaves and fifths, and he usually employs strong dynamic contrasts. Tunings vary, but anhemitonic pentatonic palettes are widely found, such as in our 1971 recordings of *serdam* playing in Tanjungsakti. In the following example, the *serdam* player improvises in a relaxed fashion, basing his performance on standard vocal melodies using tones {G A B D ¹E¹}, featuring actively moving melodic sections alternating with long-held tones, and with standard melodic cadences such as

Music example 7.6 Example of a
standard vocal or *serdam* cadence

In Tanjungsakti, some vocal melodies are also played on a German-made *harmonika*, known locally as a *ramonika* or *regen* (fig. 7.3). In their attempt to convert the Tanjungsakti population to Christianity in the early twentieth century, German Protestant missionaries introduced this idiosyncratic, diatonically tuned instrument for local musicians to play Christian hymns. The musicians also adapted their traditional Jew's harp and *serdam* melodies to this instrument. Although it is called a *harmonika*, it is actually a chromatic button melodeon with four knobs and ten buttons, made around a hundred years ago by the German firm Höhner.[32] Bp. Mesulut said that musicians play "sad" pieces on it, such as "Tangis Anak Belai Jauh" (lit. "The Cry of a Young Child Comforted from Afar"), and "happy" pieces, such as "Mantau Kundang" ("Call a Friend").[33] Using an anhemitonic pentatonic scale {1 2 3 5 6} or {D E F♯ A B}, "Mantau Kundang" features fifths (A_1 E), thirds (D B_1), and octaves (A_1 A), and short rhythmic figures such as in music example 7.7 (bar 3) and audio example 7.5:

Music example 7.7 "Mantau Kundang" fragment
on *harmonika*

Various standard melodic figures focusing on the tonic octave and fifth were developed. In our 1989 visit to Tanjungsakti, the female village head, Ibu Ida Menalis, played the following *harmonika* figure (music example 7.8) in "Lagu Tari Tanggai," a song-dance performed to welcome guests (see also audio example 7.6):

Music example 7.8 Excerpt from "Lagu Tari Tanggai" played on
a *harmonika*

Rice-Stamping Music

Until the 1960s, it was common for groups of women to spend weeks at a time stamping the husks off rice grain placed in round wooden troughs (ca. fifty centimeters wide) that contain two main stamping holes (fig. 7.4). They lightened their task by turning the heavy work into a musical game, making interlocking music known as *cintuk* (sounds of poles beating) or *lisung* (rice-stamping trough) music.

In 1971–72, when we visited Tanjungsakti and Burai (northwest of the river Ogan), a group of four elderly women performed the interlocking *cintuk* rhythms at a wedding, each beating one pitch with her pole and with another adding a melody on a guitar (*gitar tunggal*). The three main tempi/rhythms (*irama*) played were (1) the slow-tempo *palit* ("touch a little" or "move the stamping pole from here to there"; see music example 7.9), in which the first two players alternated to play the highest tone and the other two played successively lower tones, (2) the medium-tempo *madang* (lit. "stop to rest and think"; see music example 7.10) and (3) the fast-tempo *siaman jauh* (music example 7.11) (audible from far away):

Figure 7.3 A ten-key, single-row *harmonika*, Tanjungsakti, 1988

Figure 7.4 A *cintuk*, Tanjungsakti

Music example 7.9 Slow
tempo *cintuk*

Music example 7.10 Medium tempo
cintuk

Music example 7.11 Fast tempo
cintuk

Decades ago, such rice-stamping music accompanied the ritual *gandai* or *kebar* dance at mystic rituals before planting and after harvesting. By the 1970s, however, rice-stamping and other music associated with mystical agricultural rites was becoming rare, not only because some Muslim leaders disapprove of these non-Muslim rituals but also because machines were increasingly replacing the need for human rice-stamping (Bp. Lesai, pers. comm., 1971).

THE PEOPLE OF THE INTERIOR: *KUBU, ANAK DALEM*

The Anak Dalem (People of the Forests) or Kubu (lit. "place of refuge") are nomadic or seminomadic hunter-gatherers who prefer to live in the rain forests (Sandbukt 1984, 97). In South Sumatra, they inhabit the largely swampy regencies of Musi Banyuasin (the Jani area), the Musi Rawas (along the Rawas River), and the upper Lahat (Ringgan) area, but substantial numbers live across the provincial border in Jambi. Like the seminomadic Sakai and Suku Mamak peoples in Riau, some Kubu subgroups once paid deference to princes of the local sultanate, with which they reportedly traded in silent barter. Like the Suku Orang Laut (Sea Peoples), they are not an ethnic category but rather a Malay dialect–speaking subgroup that came into being with the emergence of the Malay States in premodern times, contesting the settled existence imposed by the state (Benjamin 1976).

There is a close linguistic and cultural similarity between these tribal Malays and the Malays proper (Benjamin 1976, 37), but some Kubu still live in virtual isolation from the surrounding Malay society and maintain drastically sanctioned taboos against contact with outsiders. The cosmology on which the healing rituals of a Kubu group in Jambi are based distinguishes between upstream and downstream spirit-entities that are considered divinities, and with whom relationships of rational, if symbolic, interaction are perceived to exist (Sandbukt 1984, 85, 98).

Although Kubu music culture has been little studied, it is clear that these nomadic forest people play a few small, portable instruments, especially frame drums and flutes.[34] According to a group of Kubu people whom we visited in 1981 in a government-provided settlement at Lubuk Regis (near Tampino in Jambi), their honey-collecting and other shamanic singing, courting songs, Jew's harp music, and vocal and end-blown ring flute (*damuk Kubu*) music for mourning, are all performed in the context of reverence for the spirits of nature and the ancestors.[35] During their spiritual journeys, the healing shamans (*belian salek* or *malim*) perform an elaborate system of ceremonial dances and healing songs (*saleh*) while periodically shaking sets of bronze bells (Sa. *genta*) that mark stages in their spiritual journey. According to Edwin Loeb ([1935] 1972, 288), the shamans in one unspecified area sing thirty-three songs at their healing ceremonies. They strike "tambourines . . . and the people stand up. This is followed by a round dance, in which all present at first partake, but which is ended by the *malims* alone. The dance becomes wilder and wilder and the *malims* fall into a swoon" (ibid.).

The Dutch and Indonesian governments tried to persuade these tribal people to live in settled areas and the Indonesian government tried to Islamize them, with some limited success (M. Afiff, pers. comm., Jambi, 1987).

THE OGAN-KOMERING ILIR (OKI) RIVER BASINS

South Sumatra's southern plains are traversed by long tributaries of the Musi, the Ogan, and the Komering Rivers, which flow in parallel toward the south and the southwest. Members of the ethnic groups who live on the lower banks of the two rivers speak Ogan Malay and several other Malay dialects, while the inhabitants on both banks of the Komering River and in the Komering basin (stretching to the sea in the east) speak Kayuagung-Malay and/or Abung Malay, and often one of the two main Lampung languages: Bahasa Komering and Bahasa Lampung. Many of the people are wood-carvers, goldsmiths, and stone, tin, and ironworkers, including makers of brass-iron or bronze gong-chimes and other instruments.

At weddings of the Abung people in the Kayuagung and Mesuji districts of Ogan-Komering Ilir Regency and northeast coastal Lampung, tradition demands that unmarried young couples dress in their best traditional costumes and parade down the street with members of a *tanjidor* band, as we witnessed in Kayuagung in 1988 (see also Yampolsky 1975).[36] Men playing trumpets, trombones, and drums march behind the bridegroom's party as it moves from the groom's parents' house to the bride's parents' house, playing Malay songs such as "Terang Bulan" ("Full Moon") and Western songs such as "L' Amour" ("Love") that were popular on the radio and in the theater before and during the 1930s, the heyday of itinerant *bangsawan* theater troupes, which developed in the late nineteenth century (Tan 1993). *Tanjidor* bands were introduced into plantations in South Sumatra, Bangka, Belitung, Java, and western Kalimantan by the Dutch in the late nineteenth century and were still played by aging musicians in those areas in the late 1990s. Abung people, who originated in the districts of Kayuagung and Mesuji in Ogan Komering Ilir Regency and now mainly live along the northeastern coast of Lampung Province, speak a language similar to Melayu-Riau.

TARI TANGGAI

In Ogan-Komering Ilir (henceforth, OKI), bronze *keromongan* or *tabuhan* ensembles accompany various dances at weddings, elder installations, and guest-welcoming ceremonies, the main dance being the *tari tanggai* or *tari penguton* (figs. 7.52 and 7.56), the long-fingernail dance, also called *tari inai* (lit. henna-rubbed-fingernail dance).

Figure 7.5a *Tari penguton* dancers with part of a *tabuhan* ensemble in the background, Burai, 1973

Figure 7.5b Standing *tari penguton* dancers, Burai, 1973

Local opinion holds that *tari tanggai* and the accompanying bronze ensembles derive from a traditional, royal bridal custom. Unlike some other Sumatran-Malay groups whose brides decorate their hands and feet with red henna, brides at most OKI weddings attach to their fingers long, golden-colored fingernails that turn upward at the ends and symbolize virginity. Some think the fingernail practice derives from the Abung culture in neighboring Lampung province, where young women customarily wear a gold or silver fingernail on the little finger of their right hand to symbolize their virginity (Bp. Haji Muchtar Ahmab, pers. comm., KayuAgung, 1988). Legend has it that parts of OKI were colonized in Sriwijaya times by the Hindu kingdom of Tulung Bawang, centered near Menggala in Lampung.[37] Some families claim that their revered old *keromongan* ensembles are ancestral heirlooms (*pusaka*) that were formerly owned by princes of Menggala (ibid.).

The focus of the *tari tanggai* dance is on the elegance of the dancers' intricate arm, hand, and wrist movements, emphasized by the long fingernails (fig. 7.6).

Like the local bridal dress, their costumes are made of locally woven silk *songket* brocade featuring a basic color and gold or silver thread and worn with heavy heirloom jewelry. They perform with slow, exquisitely controlled movements in standing,

Figure 7.6 A *tari tanggai* dancer in a *mudra* pose, showing her attached long fingernails

then crouching, positions as they present the betel nut to elders, a bridal couple, or important guests, after which they rise and complete the last section of the dance.

An elaborately choreographed version of this dance, reminiscent of sultanate times and created in the Kayuagung area in the 1970s, is called *tari penguton* (guest-welcoming dance). The lead female dancer carries a box of betel nut and accessories to offer to an honored guest accompanied by six "ladies-in-waiting" who carry a bronze betel-spitting vase, fans, and umbrellas, and with male attendants who carry weapons. The dance is accompanied by an ensemble comprising a gong-chime, gongs, cymbals, and drums (audio example 7.7).

The names of the ensembles that accompany these dances vary from region to region and town to town. In Kayuagung, they are called *k(e)romongan* or *tabuhan*, in Burai Lama *tabuhan* or *gamalan*, and *kelenongan* in Menggala, Lampung.[38] The ensembles usually consist of a bronze gong-chime comprising a set of small tuned kettle-gongs that rest on soft cloth in a carved wooden frame, plus drums and gongs.

The bronze gong-chime, which is called *keromongan* or *ngeromong* in Kayuagung, *canang* in Burai Lama, and *kelitang* (also *kulitang, kulintang, keromong, tabuhan*) in the Menggala area of Lampung, is the main melodic instrument. A pair of performers is required for the instrument, one to play the main part (*ngeromong*), the other to play the interlocking part (*ngelitung*). One or two two-headed drums (*gendang*) may be used with the gong-chime, accompanied by colotomic patterns on suspended gongs that may be large (*tale*) or medium-sized (*tawak-tawak*), a small medium-pitched gong (*canang*), and cymbals (*rujih*). Audio example 7.7 illustrates the interaction of these instruments in the short excerpt of *mayok* rhythm, followed by the *penguton dik* section.[39] Fragments of these rhythms are shown in music example 7.12.

Music example 7.12 Rhythmic elements in *irama Mayok* and *penguton dik*

In Kayuagung, *keromongan* gong-chimes that we encountered comprised between seven and sixteen small kettle-gongs. In the Menggala area the *kelitang* ensemble consisted of the *kelitang* comprising nine to twelve kettle-gongs, a pair of large suspended gongs (*talo balak* and *talo tanggung*), a small suspended gong (*bende*), a pair of cymbals (*gujih*), a cylindrical drum (*ketipung*), and a frame drum (*terbang*) (Kartomi 1984; 1998a, 623). In Burai Lama, a set of *canang* (or *tabuhan*) consisted of eight or nine kettle-gongs playing the main (*lurus*) melody, while another played a much denser interlocking part (*ningkah*) on the *canang*, with one of a pair of gongs (*gung*) beaten alternately on every fourth beat and a small *canang* kettle beaten on every second beat.[40] The *gendang* player performed a rhythmically elaborate cycle that assists the gong-chime players to control the rhythm of their playing during the opening and the ending phrases and establishes and changes tempo as he sees fit.

In Kayuagung, on the other hand, half of the kettle gongs in the fourteen-piece gong-chime ensemble produced the main melody (*ngeromong*) and the other half the interlocking part (*ngelitak*), with the pair of suspended gongs (*tale balok* or *tawak-tawak*) alternating on every fourth beat, and the pair of small horizontal gongs (*bebondi*) beaten twice as frequently as the suspended gongs. In each ensemble, the pair of cylindrical drums (*gendang*) is optional. They are essential, however, to accompany the art of self-defense (*pencak silat*, fig. 7.7), which comprises two sections. In the first part (called *pencak*), the drums are played calmly and softly as

Figure 7.7 A wedding procession with a *pencak silat* display and frame-drum players, showing a wedding guest (the author) in Kayuagung, 1972

the performer presents the prescribed body exercises that aim to develop his "inner energy," a term that different people interpret either in a non-Muslim animist sense or as a Sufi Muslim mystical experience of the soul (*batin*). In the second part (called *silat*), the drums are played loudly and dramatically, especially if a pair of performers engage in a duel, either with or without daggers.

The bronze ensembles in Burai Lama and other parts of the Ogan-Komering area are also used to accompany the *tari piring* (plate dance), in which female dancers walk on a row of plates while holding and sometimes rotating a saucer containing a lighted candle in each hand. The ensemble also accompanies the *tari benang setukal* (weaving dance) in Kayuagung, in which female dancers in bridal costumes dance to the accompaniment of the interlocking *rapdorap* rhythm (where the onomatopoeic term *rapdorap* suggests the sound of a moving loom) played on the fourteen-kettle-gong *keromongan*; and the *tari sabung* (cockfight dance), in which a female dancer searches for a lost flower (a symbol of romance) and a male dancer eventually presents her with a betrothal ring. Cockfighting and gambling, which are banned, are nevertheless still practiced in the area, serving as a metaphor in the dance for the tribulations and joys of love (Bp. Kasno, *tanggai* troupe leader, pers. comm., Burai Lama, 1971).

ARTS WITH A MUSLIM THEME OR FLAVOR IN THE UPLANDS AND THE LOWLANDS

The musical arts associated with Islam are divided into two groups: those "with an Islamic theme" (*kesenian Islami*), in which Muslim texts are sung in Arabic or Malay; and those that are mainly secular or pagan-animist-related but nevertheless "have an Islamic flavor" (*kesenian yang bernafaskan Islam*), with secular texts and occasional religious phrases. They are normally performed by separate male or female groups who wear costumes that cover most of the body and are perceived to accord with Muslim values and changing fashions. Since the 1970s, the devotional genres with an Islamic theme (*kesenian Islam*) have increased in popularity in the uplands, the Ogan and Komering basins, the greater Palembang area, and the offshore island of Bangka, as have several dance-music genres and a theater form with an Islamic flavor (*kesenian yang bernafaskan Islam*). They became even more popular with the general rise of devotion to Muslim orthodoxy in the 1990s and early 2000s (Osman Effendy, pers. comm., Jakarta, 2003).

Hadra (fig. 7.8), the main genre with a Muslim theme, is practiced regularly in some village homes on Thursday nights and on holy days of the Muslim calendar, especially in the lowlands. Led by a solo singer, a group of men belonging to a Sufi brotherhood (*tarekat*) kneel or sit cross-legged on the floor and periodically sing responses to the soloist's lines sung in Arabic or Malay. They keep singing selections from the ninety-nine names of God (including epithets such as "God the Merciful," "God the Omnipotent") while performing coordinated body movements that sometimes build up to a strenuous level. This Sufi-derived form aims to deepen its participants' rapturous feeling of unity with Allah, including in some cases entering a trancelike state. Another genre with a Muslim theme is *barzanji*. Its performance style is similar to *hadra*, but the texts sung deal specifically with the birth and life of the Prophet.

Genres with an Islamic flavor include the *rodat, serapal anam*, and *zapin Melayu* dances (fig. 7.9), the instrumental *orkes gambus* (*gambus* ensemble; fig.7.10), and the *Abdul Muluk* (*Dul Muluk*) theater form (fig. 7.11). *Rodat* (Ar. *roddat*) is a vigorous form of *hadra* for young men, who kneel close together in a line and repeatedly move back and forth and to each side, either simultaneously or in pairs or groups of three, while singing standard or improvised texts on secular or religious themes, sometimes enhancing their body movements by rhythmic clapping.

They may also be commissioned to welcome particular named guests on religious, formal governmental, and corporate occasions. Like *serapal anam* (holy prophet [art]) groups, who limit themselves to singing praises of the Prophet, they are led

Figure 7.8 A *hadra* performance, Liwa, Lampung, 1983

Figure 7.9 A *Zapin Melayu* ensemble, Kayu Agung, 1988

Figure 7.10 Part of an *orkes gambus*, including a violin, a *gendang*, and a more recent style of *gambus*, Palembang, 1988

Figure 7.11 A *Dul Muluk* theater ensemble with an old-style *gambus, gendang, biola, bas,* and *bende*, Kayu Agung, 1988

by a solo singer. Standards of performance have traditionally been maintained by community- or government-organized competitions. In *rodat* and *serapal anam* competitions, members of a group take turns singing appropriate phrases while performing synchronic body movement, and then pose questions (religious or secular) in *pantun* form to their rival group, which is required to improvise immediate answers to them. The team that attracts the loudest applause wins.[41] The leader of a *gambus* ensemble is the player of the *gambus*, a pear-shaped, fretless, double-course plucked lute (Ar. *ud*), accompanied by a set of four or more small, two-headed hand drums called *marwas* (plural *marawis*). The homemade *gambus* instruments have relatively slender bodies, with goatskin covering the resonating chamber, and they are plucked with a bone plectrum.

An *orkes gambus* usually employs seven-tone modes with a "Middle Eastern flavor," as well as major and minor modes that may include a raised or lowered second, third, sixth, and/or seventh and a raised fourth. They contrast strongly with the mainly large-interval four-, five-, or six-tone palettes of the gong-chime ensembles. Sung in Malay or Arabic, the song texts tend to convey a moral message about matters of daily life, sometimes adding Arabic phrases. Their titles include "Lagu Serapal Anam," "Asik Santai" ("Relaxing"), "Merdeka Bangun" ("Freedom Arise"), and "Selamat Datang" ("Welcome").

Besides being a separate instrumental genre in its own right, an *orkes gambus* often accompanies dance genres such as the *tari tanggai* ("long-fingernail dance"; audio example 7.8) and the *zapin Melayu* dance. An example of the latter is "Tari Zapin Lagu Alaika" ("Alaika" is a girl's name), which begins with a free-metered instrumental introduction (*taksim*; Ar. *taqsim*), followed by a group of teenagers, then their male teacher singing the melody to accompany their dance performance (audio example 7.9).[42]

In the older, rural *zapin Melayu* dances, groups of men are the only participants. From the 1950s onward, women have also participated, either separately or (in the cities) together with a male partner in a group (Bp. Kasno, pers. comm., 1971). Performances are usually accompanied by a vocalist who sings memorized and improvised *pantun* verses, a *gambus* soloist and a *biola* player who follow and sometimes double the vocal line, one or more *rebana* (frame-drum) players, and a group of *marwas* players. The music and dance are in three parts: the *taksim*, the dance proper, and the *tahtim*. During the free-metered introduction (*taksim*), the *gambus* player displays his improvisation skills and virtuosity, while the dancers pose in the salutation position (*sembah*). During the body of the song or instrumental piece, the dancers begin the *salam pembukaan* (opening greeting) dance, with steps (*langkah*) linked by the basic dance motives (described in Nor 1993, 32–33), which are performed to a repeating melody with loud *marwas* drumming at the end of each repeat. The dancers step forward, backward, and diagonally in fast-moving formations at moderate to very fast tempo while performing intricate hand movements. After the dance proper, they conclude by dancing the phrases of the final section, the *tahtim* (coda, or an adaptation called *tahto*), which comprises "skips, turns, low *plié*, and standing and squatting positions" (Nor 1993, 62), while the *marwas* quartet provides brilliant, loud, interlocking rhythmic episodes, as can be heard in audio example 7.10 "Tari Zapin Lagu Pulut Hitam" ("*Zapin* Dance Black Sticky Rice Song").[43]

The basic *zapin* rhythmic pattern on the lead *rebana* is 4/4 //:d t tt t d t d :// , where "d" and "t" represent the instrument's main medium- and high-pitched sounds, and another *rebana* may double the first note for metric stress. Such a recurring rhythmic pattern establishes the meter, determines the tempo of the ensemble, and cues the vocalist's entry.

In addition to *zapin*, singers perform popular *lagu Melayu asli* (authentic Malay songs) with a "Malay ensemble" (*orkes Melayu*) that comprises a *biola* (violin), *harmonika, gitar* (guitar), *strengbas* (large string bass), *tambrin* (round frame with jingles), *seruling*, and *dramkit* (drum kit). In Palembang and OKI during the 1980s, the repertoire included the song "Lancang Kuning" ("Royal Yellow Barge"), which is said to have first become popular through its standard performance in the annual royal barge processions on the Musi run by the *kraton Palembang* (Palembang palace) until its demise in 1823.[44] This is the quintessential *zapin* song in many Malay areas of Sumatra.[45] Other songs were "Gajah Berjuang" ("The Fighting Elephant"), "Perang Aceh" ("War in Aceh"), "Senandung" ("Sad Song," sung slowly), and "Serampang Laut" (lit. "Harpoon Dance," sung at fast tempo) in *lagu dua* (lit. "two song," slow then fast) form, often in triple or triple-duple meter. Like the *orkes gambus*, an *orkes Melayu* ensemble can be used to accompany the long-fingernail dance and other traditional dances. Some South Sumatrans say that these songs do not have a Muslim flavor, as they are an offshoot of the pre-Muslim *gebos* lute and *ronggeng* and *joget* songs, while others say they possess a peripheral Muslim flavor by association, because they are Malay.[46]

The Malay theater form *Abdul (Dul) Muluk*, on the other hand, has an undoubted Muslim-Middle Eastern and early-twentieth-century Western pop song flavor. Between the late nineteenth century and the 1990s (Dumas 2000), troupes performed plays from *One Thousand and One Nights* and *Hikayat Abdul Muluk* ("Abdul Muluk Epic") in OKI and Palembang and on Bangka, as well as in west Kalimantan (from where it spread to West Java), with itinerant troupes from Java visiting occasionally.[47] A performance of a song about the heroine Siti Zubaidah in Kayuagung featured violin and *gendang* playing short interludes between songs and scenes and accompanying male vocalists singing Malay-style melodies to *pantun* verses and borrowed Western songs set in Arabic-sounding harmonic and melodic minor and major scales, often doubling the vocal line but with improvised melodic gestures and some double-stopping as in the four excerpts in audio example 7.11.[48]

The *Dul Muluk* shows that we saw in Palembang and Kayuagung in 1971 and 1989 had around twenty-five actors who sang, danced, and spoke the dialogue. In local shows, males always took the female roles but did not imitate a female voice in their dialogues. Their repertory included more than twenty songs with Malay or "Middle Eastern-sounding" melodies, accompanied by an all-male *orkes Dul Muluk* that comprised three violins (*biola*, placed on the player's left shoulder), a bass drum (*jidur*), a pair of *gendang*, and a small gong (*ketawa*), which played within and between the dramatic scenes.[49] The plots were taken mostly from the first of two sets of adventures in the *Hikayat Dul Muluk* when Abdul Muluk was married to his first wife, Siti Rochma, while the second set of stories dealt with his adventures when married to his second wife, Siti Ropea, which were only occasionally played. While the western archipelago's other main theater genres—*komedie stambul* and *bangsawan*—reached their height of popularity in the late nineteenth and early twentieth centuries, *Dul Muluk*'s heyday was in the 1920s and 1930s, when troupes traveled widely in Java, eastern South Sumatra, Bangka, Belitung, and western Kalimantan. Since the late 1950s, radio and television shows largely replaced the performances of theater troupes in South Sumatra, though *Dul Muluk* and *bangsawan* performances were still being presented in some areas, such as on Bangka (see chap. 9), during the 1990s (Dumas 2000).

PALEMBANG

The history of Sumatra's second largest city and present-day provincial capital, Palembang, may be traced back to the late seventh century, when the great maritime empire of Sriwijaya established its capital in or near the present-day city site. It was home to over a thousand Buddhist monks, who attracted pilgrims from China to study there while en route to the holy land of India. Archaeologists have discovered a few Buddhist statues, Hindu shrines, and Sanskrit stone inscriptions on and around the sacred Siguntang hills in southern Palembang, which may have been the location of Sriwijaya's capital. According to legend, however, this hill was sacred ancestral territory long before the coming of the Hindus and the Buddhists (Schnitger 1964, 8), and it remains a site of ancestral pilgrimages to this day. Sriwijaya's capital remained near the Musi River till the late eleventh century, when the center of power moved north to Jambi, which was conquered by the Javanese in 1377.

Modern South Sumatran choreographers imagine that Palembang's famous long-fingernail dance—*tari tanggai*—derived from Sriwijaya times, and they therefore developed a version of it named *tari sriwijaya*, with *kromongan* ensemble accompaniment (see chap. 8). In fact, most of Palembang's performing arts, including other Malay dances, *orkes Melayu*, and gong-chime ensembles, are borrowed from the rural areas or from Arabic sources, including the *zapin Melayu* accompanied by an *orkes gambusan Melayu* band comprising a *gambus*, a *biola*, and a set of four *marawis*, and the *Dul Muluk* and *bangsawan* theater (though the latter has become virtually obsolete since the 1980s).[50]

Palembang is also heir to a music and theater culture that was transplanted from northern Java into its former sultanate. According to *kraton* (palace) descendant RMH Nato Dirajo (pers. comm., 1988), the kingdom of Palembang was a vassal state of the Hindu-Javanese kingdom of Majapahit from the year 1365.[51] After a Javanese official named Ki Gedhé Ing Temayan moved to Palembang in the sixteenth century, the Javanese language became the lingua franca of the palace community. Terms of state were in Javanese; for example, the *kraton* was referred to as the *negara agung* (great state), and the *pangeran* (princes) headed the petty princedoms in the downstream and upstream *mancanegara* ("provincial areas" [of South Sumatra], including Besemah). Around 1670, a prince named Ki Gedhé Ing Suro fled from Surabaya and established the dynasty that was to become Palembang's sultanate until the Dutch abolished it in 1823 (Taal 2002, 172–200). In the early eighteenth century, the sultan of Demak in Java had rendered support to the king of Palembang in the struggle against his enemies, and at that time the Hindu-Buddhist king had converted to Islam and assumed the title of sultan. The sultans of Demak and Palembang had cemented their mutual support by exchanging a shipload of valuable gifts. The ship from Java, according to legend, contained a *gamelan sléndro-pélog* (a *gamelan* tuned in both the pentatonic *sléndro* and heptatonic *pélog* tunings) and a set of *wayang kulit purwa* (ancient leather shadow puppets), also known as *wayang kulit Palembang*, for the sultan of Palembang.[52] The legend also holds that visiting Demak-Javanese artists taught their Palembang counterparts how to perform the *gamelan*-accompanied theater form, after which it was adapted over the centuries to its new Palembang environment.

The Palembang palace prospered through trade in forest products and textiles until 1823, when the Dutch destroyed it and established control.[53] A Dutch impression of the sultan's palace in the midst of the city on the Musi River in 1823 at the moment before they sacked it is shown in Figure 7.12.

Unlike the Malay courts of Riau, Jambi, and east-coast North Sumatra, members of Palembang's former palace regard themselves as descendants of the Javanese, not

Figure 7.12 A Dutch impression of Palembang city on the Musi River, at the moment before the Dutch sacked it in 1823 (Source: Algemene Rijksarchief)

the Malay, aristocracy. To this day, some people living in and around the former palace in Palembang speak Javanized Palembang Malay at two levels: one with loan words from High Javanese (Krama Lugu) and the other from Low Javanese (Ngoko).[54] Although citizens of Palembang have no connections with Java, some bridal couples in Palembang Ilir wear Javanese costumes and follow Javanese customs at their weddings to this day.[55]

What was life like for artists who were attached to the palace during the prosperous sultanate reign? The ultra-Muslim *kraton* banned all dancing on religious grounds but accepted the all-night Hindu-Javanese *wayang kulit purwa* and *gamelan* performances partly because the puppeteers sang some religious phrases in Arabic and mentioned names and deeds of Muslim heroes and saints, including the Wali Sanga (nine saints who are widely credited with having spread Islam in Java), whose exploits were depicted within the stories featuring characters from the Mahabharata or Ramayana epics (RMH Nato Dirajo, pers. comm., 1988).[56] Descendants of the royal family in and around the former *kraton* complex still have occasion to patronize such *wayang* performances, which are usually in greatly shortened form.

A great mosque was built on the *ilir* bank of the Musi River in 1748 by Sultan Mahmud Badaruddin I (1724–58) next to the palace, while the palace complex was completed by his son, Sultan Mahmud Badaruddin (1776–1801) (Colombijn 2002, 288–89; Taal 2002, 173). As the *kraton* was the highest building in the town, palace officials could easily spot and collect tax from riverboats carrying cargoes to the market further downstream, and the sultan could easily retreat from it to the highlands in times of danger. According to a description of the working population by the Dutch resident C. F. E. Praetorius (1832), female breadwinners made textiles, including the valuable silk *songkets*, which were worn by local royalty, brides, and dancers and were also a lucrative part of overseas trade, while some of the men worked as blacksmiths, probably making *kromongan*, kettle-gongs, and other metallic musical instruments.[57] Praetorius (1832) mentioned that twenty-five musicians earned their living by performing the *gamelan* in the *kraton*. As in other Malay palaces (e.g., in Ternate; see Kartomi 1993a, 191–93), these artists would have been deferential royal musician-servants living in a village near the *kraton*, who were appointed by the sultan to maintain, play, and teach performance on the court *gamelan* in return for the privilege of contact with his perceived spiritual power. They would have worked in tandem with the village blacksmiths who forged replacement instruments for the court *gamelan* and noncourt *kromongan* on command, tuning them to the correct pitches and with the correct timbre.

During our visit to the former palace remains in Palembang in 1988, RMH Nato Dirajo showed us a set of *wayang purwa* puppets, some other royal artistic objects, and the royal Palembang *silsilah* (family tree), which recorded Palembang's close ties with Java in the seventeenth century through intermarriage with the Javanese courts at Banten, Surakarta, and Yogyakarta, and with the Malay-Sumatran court at Jambi. The set of puppets originally comprised 150 thick, carved coarse-leather puppets, but a hundred or so were lost in a fire.

Wayang performances were held in a Javanese-style open pavilion (*pendopo*, BJ) in the palace, according to an 1811 drawing (now in the possession of RMH Nato Dirajo) of its buildings by a Major William Thorn. As in Java's similar all-night shows, a bronze oil lamp was used to cast the shadows on the screen, and a mystical ceremony was held before a performance.[58] The *wayang* stories tell only of Javanese, not Malay, heroes and of Javanese clowns such as Semar, Petruk, and Gareng. The most popular stories performed were from the Mahabharata epic, especially the so-called *Pandawa Lima* ("Five Pandawa") stories, which deal with the exploits of the five Pandawa brothers versus the ninety-nine Kurawa brothers, and stories from the Ramayana were also performed (RMH Nato Dirajo, pers. comm., 1988).[59] Although Praetorius in 1832 referred to the ensemble from Demak as a *gamelan*, palace descendants sometimes refer to it by the local South Sumatran names of *kromongan* or *tabuhan* as well.

Though the former Palembang palace's *gamelan* is said to have been a complete set tuned in both *sléndro* and *pélog* tone systems, the *gamelan* that we recorded in 1988 comprised only the *sléndro* half.[60] Its metallophone tuning approximated {C E$^\flat$ G A$^\flat$ B}, numbered {1 2 3 5 6}, with the *kempur* (a horizontal gong) tuned to low B$^\flat_1$.

In audio example 7.12, "Wayang-Lagu Bertempur" (lit. "War Piece"), the low B$^\flat_1$ (tone 6) on the *kenong* is sounded with the *saron* on A$^\flat$ (tone 5), emphasizing the interval of a seventh, as in the *tari Adat Besemah* music (audio example 7.2; see also fig. 7.13). After beating out tone 5 several times, the *saron* plays various melodic formulas, with the gong beaten every two beats, the *kenong* sounding on every beat, and the drums playing rhythmic figures while establishing and leading changes in tempo. The music moves from a moderate to a fast tempo as the *dalang* prepares for a fighting scene on the puppet screen, ending suddenly with the statement of the final cadential formula: {3 4 5 3/ 4} or {G A$^\flat$ B$^\flat$ G/ A$^\flat$} (see music example 7.13).[61]

Figure 7.13 A *saron* from the former Palembang palace's *gamelan*

Music example 7.13 A transcription of "Wayang-Lagu Bertempur" ("War Piece") played on the *gamelan Palembang* in a *wayang kulit* performance

Formerly, when there were enough musicians to play all the instruments, the leading melody (*kepala lagu*) was usually played on the *gambang* (xylophone) or the *saron* (keyed metallophone), punctuated by a pair of hanging gongs (*gong panimbul*, or "main" gong, and *gong penuntun*, or "follower" gong) and a pair of horizontal gongs resting on crossed cords in a box (a *kenong* and a *kempur*). The pair of players on the *kromongan* (a gong-chime comprising two rows of six small gongs each) improvised the relatively dense melodic parts (e.g., four notes to each note on the *saron*). The pair of truncated conical, laced drums (*gendang induk* [mother drum] and *gendang peningkah* [follower drum]) with goatskin heads established the ensemble's tempo. Three bowed string instruments (*rebab*), a Chinese oboe (*terompet Cina*), a two-string zither (*kecapi*), and a male singer (*sintrèn*) completed the ensemble. In the performances that we heard in 1988, the musicians could no longer play those instruments or sing the songs, nor could the dancers perform the ritually important *sintrèn* (*serimpi*) dance (Dalang Sukri Rasjid, pers. comm., Kampung 28 Ilir, 1988).[62]

Although *wayang* with *gamelan* used to be performed in the former palace to lend luster to weddings and other celebrations, it never became a people's art. It has survived in Palembang mainly due to its royal descendants' efforts to keep it alive.

As mentioned above, the Palembang palace, like the Siak Sri Indrapura palace on the river Siak in Riau, also organized an annual rowing competition on the Musi River, preceded by an aquatic procession by the royal yellow barge, *Lancang Kuning*, carrying the sultan and his entourage. Malay melodies such as the standard "Lagu Lancang Kuning" ("Yellow Boat Song") were played by a violin and drum ensemble on the royal barge, but without the usual Malay dancing. Indeed, the *kraton*'s Arabic religious teachers (*ulama*) strongly discouraged dancing on moral and religious grounds, and the palace consequently banned all dancing. A substantial number of Arabs intermarried with the local population, as their family trees (*silsilah*) from the eighteenth century confirm; indeed, many families of Arab background live in the Arab quarters of Palembang to this day (RMH Nato Dirajo, pers. comm., 1988).[63]

Over the centuries, Chinese arts and patronage were also important (until 1965, when Suharto banned the culture and language). Marriages between Palembang royals and Chinese princesses brought Chinese visual art motifs into the designs of Palembang's *songket* brocade and other art objects. However, apart from the *terompet Cina* (Chinese *so na* oboe) in the palace *gamelan*, no Chinese musical influences remain (RMH Nato Dirajo, pers. comm., 1988).

Arguably Palembang's main contribution to the performing arts is not its *gamelan/ wayang* but its style of *zapin Melayu* dances. It is widely believed that these dances, traditionally performed by men to the accompaniment of a *gambus*, violin, drums, *zap* (tambourine with jingles, elsewhere called *marwas*), and an optional gong, were transplanted into Palembang by families of Arabic or part-Arabic heritage whose descendants live to this day in the city's Arabic quarters, and whose family trees indicate that their ancestors moved there from the Hadramaut in the latter part of the eighteenth century. This view gained further credence when M. A. M. Nor (1993) and Charles Capwell (1995) found that *zapin* performances in Malaya and Yemen shared similar terminologies (e.g., *zapin*, cf. *zafana*; *gambus*, cf. *qanbous*; and *marwas*, plural *marawis*).[64] They argued that *zapin*, which enjoys some of the prestige of Islam itself, had come to mark the identity of Malay culture.[65]

Zapin performances usually grace ceremonies such as weddings, circumcisions, a baby's first haircut, the completion of the Qur'an-reading exercise, and community fundraisers for mosque or road building. However, some elaborate contemporary versions performed on official occasions in Palembang add an extra violin that soars melodically above the *gambus* and main violin parts, along with an accordion, a flute (*seruling*), a keyboard, a *zap*, a *tambrin* (round frame with jingles), a *ketipung* (small two-headed drum), a *hajir* (bass drum), and optional bongos, guitars, cylindrical drums (*gendang dua*, "a pair of drums") and a *gung* (gong).

||||

As this chapter has attempted to show, the environment—especially the rivers and forest surrounds in South Sumatra, like the forests and seas on nearby Bangka Island—serves as a grid for understanding the distribution of the twelve indigenous musico-lingual groups in the region and the spread of certain musical genres among them. Historical factors, on the other hand, explain the main external artistic influences. Thus, Palembang's relationship with early-seventeenth-century Java resulted in the development of the *gamelan Palembang* and *wayang Palembang* arts. South Sumatra's oldest musical symbol—the bronze Dōng-son drums covered with geometrical figures and designs of heavenly bodies and animals, which were originally transported from South Vietnam—still reminds South Sumatrans of their ancestral veneration for the environment and the cultural contributions of countless traders, military leaders, religious innovators, and artists from India, China, the Arab lands, and beyond.

The musico-lingual group with the deepest veneration for its forest environment is the isolated Orang Kubu or Orang Suku Dalem people, who express their beliefs in the spirits of nature and the ancestors in many aspects of their lives, including their spiritual healing ceremonies (*belian salek*), during which a *malim* performs songs and dances on his spiritual journey to other worlds after reaching a state of trance. Being nomadic or seminomadic, these people carry only musical instruments that are light and portable, such as bamboo flutes and small drums, and their only bronze instruments are bells (*genta*) that a shaman sounds during spiritual ceremonies.

The Besemah, Rejang, and other upstream agricultural subgroups lived in relative isolation until the introduction of modern communications in the early twentieth century. Yet even in the 1970s, they still practiced their nature- and ancestor-venerating rituals and arts, which included shamanic songs to control dangerous animals, ensure a good harvest, or assist a desired romance, with would-be lovers mouthing secret messages to each other through their Jew's harps. Agricultural rites still included rice-stamping music and other arts performed to ensure successful planting activity and harvests, which were celebrated with mixed social dancing (*gegerit*). Bards were still singing the ancestral "Bitter Tongue and the Youngest of the Seven Sisters" legend, with women dancing the related *kebar* dance about the return of the seventh sister to heaven. Supernatural and human guests were still welcomed at celebrations with the female *penguton* dance, accompanied either by the bronze gong-chime ensembles—variously called *kenong, kelintang, tale*, and *tabuhan*—or the *orkes Melayu* with its *gambus* lute and *marwas* drums of Arab origin plus bowed strings and other local instruments, and with flutes and oboes being used for various other ritual and musical purposes. However, by the late 1980s, these practices were becoming rare. The female semiprofessional singing of sobbing, mourning songs (*ratok*) at funerals, which had long been banned by orthodox Muslim and Christian leaders, had almost died out.

Meanwhile, downstream subgroups still practiced some of their *adat* genres, including the female dance that depicts silk *songket* weaving for which the area has been famous since at least the nineteenth century. Their *adat* versions of the long-fingernail dance (*tari tanggai*) were also popular, with bridally dressed dancers wearing the long metallic nails that symbolize virginity, accompanied by a bronze ensemble that is variously called *kromongan, tabuhan*, or *gamelan*. Containing a larger number of instruments than their upstream counterparts, and differentiated by their twelve-kettle gong-chime (*kromongan* or *canang*) and drum interlocking techniques, these bronze ensembles may have spread across downstream South Sumatra from Lampung's Menggala kingdom at the height of its power in the thirteenth century. The frame-drum-accompanied Muslim arts remain strong to this day, including those "with an Islamic theme" such as *barzanji* and *hadra*, and those with "an Islamic flavor" and secular or religious texts such as the male *rodat* (sitting dance), which is taught to young people in the Muslim schools and performed at family celebrations and communal fund-raising competitions, and the *zapin* dance with *gambus* ensemble accompaniment.

Palembang has played a pivotal role in the region's culture for the past fifteen hundred years or longer. It was from Siguntang Bukit in that city that the Buddhist

Sriwijaya monarchs controlled the Strait of Malacca and pursued trade and diplomatic relations with China, Thailand, India, and the Middle East, and from which the Malay sultans and rural princes in the fourteenth to nineteenth centuries pursued their political, trading, and artistic activities. The *orkes Melayu/gambus, Dul Muluk* theater, *tanjidor* bands, and *zapin* dances introduced by Arabs are performed there to this day, but interest in the remnants of the Palembang sultanate arts is declining. Other local artists perform the *tanggai* and other dances from the Ogan-Komering Ilir basin, either to bronze ensemble accompaniment or, more commonly, pop bands. However, South Sumatra's provincial government chose a relatively modern creation—the song-dance "Gending Tari Sriwijaya"—to represent the province's artistic identity (see chap. 8).

ACKNOWLEDGMENTS

Space allows mention only of those individuals who helped us most. I am grateful to local government officials, especially the Camats (subdistrict administrative heads) in the Basemah, Lahat, Palembang, and Ogan-Komering, and northern areas for help in making our initial contacts during our field trips in November–December 1971, January 1988, January 1989, and in Jambi in January 1988. In South Sumatra, they include (1) artists Bp. Lesai and Ibu Tjiek Timah in Desa Masambulau, Marga Pumi, Tanjung Sakti, Besemah; Bp. Mochtar in Kayuagung; Bp. Usman Effendy, Bp. Ahmad Batarrudin, and Bp. Ibrahim Anang Tahar in Burai Lama and Burai Baru (near Palembang); and Hadji Wan Cik of Dusun Kedaton, Baturaja, in Ogan Ulu in 1971; (2) *wayang kulit gamelan* artists Bp. Husin Dato Dirajo and *silat* master Bp. Djohan Hanafiah in Palembang, 28 Ilir; (3) *Dul Muluk* artists Bp. Md. Hardjo and Bp. Abdul Hamid and troupe leaders Bp. and Ibu Hadji Muchtar Ahmad in Kelurahan Pemulutan, Kabupaten Ogan-Komering; former *bangsawan* artist Ibu Ernie in Kayuagung; Dr. S. Z. Hadisutjipto of Balai Pustaka and traditional dance and music specialist and choreographer Ibu Erna Nun Cik Aladin of Bom Baru, Palembang, 5 Ilir, in January 1988; (4) Bp. Rumshah Amasin, Bp. Senamit, Bp. Jaris, and eighty-one-year-old Bp. Toyeb of Desa Endikat Ilir in Tanjung Sakti and surrounding villages; Ibu Emma Majusuf and Bp. Sahumi Munir in Desa Jokoh; *tabuhan* musicians Haji Dur and Bp. Bujang and Bp. Saman Loear in Desa Endikat Ilir; Bp. Y. Herman Jentamat and Grup Tarian Adat Pasemah "Burung Binang" in Desa Sukajati and Desa Jokoh, Pagar Alam; *guritan* singers Bp. Cik Ait and Bp. H. Suhin in Tanjung Larang and Bp. Haji Raden Mustari in Tanjung Sakti; *harmonika* player Ibu Samina and singer Ibu Suliam and Bp. Dr. Burlian Muham (Camat) in Tanjung Sakti, Besemah, in 1989.

THE WARTIME CREATION OF
"GENDING SRIWIJAYA"
From Banned Song to South Sumatran Symbol

When I long for the glory of the past
I sing a tune again, the Sriwijaya song
In art I enjoy again that happy era
I recreate from the womb of that great time
Sriwijaya, with the great hermitages of the glorious masters.
The words of Dharma Pala, Shakya Khirti, Dharma Khirti
Resound from the summit of the holy Siguntang Hill
Spreading the holy guidance of the sacred Gautama Buddha.

"Gending Sriwijaya"

The subject of this chapter is the history of a single song-dance, the text of which is translated above.[1] Created in 1945 by a team of artists in wartime Palembang, the song "Gending Sriwijaya" was first performed with its accompanying dance "Tari Gending Sriwijaya" ("Sriwijaya Dance Piece") as an ironic joke at the expense of the Japanese invaders, who had been led to believe that its nostalgic reference to the glory of the Sriwijaya-Palembang kingdom in the seventh to eleventh centuries C.E. (Manguin 1993) represented their support for the Japanese wartime ideology of "Asia for Asians," as opposed to the idea of "Asia for the Dutch colonialists." As secret supporters of the nationalist leader Sukarno, the team of artists actually intended the new song to serve the cause of the Indonesian independence movement, in the hope that independence would lead to a return of the prosperity of the glorious Sriwijaya past.[2]

THE WARTIME POLITICS BEHIND THE PREMIERE

The first performance of "Tari Gending Sriwijaya" was presented at a function on 4 August 1945 as part of the Japanese propaganda effort to win over the hearts and minds of the people of Sumatra in general and Palembang in particular. After deciding in 1942 that the islands of Sumatra and Sulawesi were to be governed from the Japanese naval base in Singapore, the Japanese invaders established their All-Sumatra Advisory Council (Chuo Sangi In) in Bukittinggi, West Sumatra, planning thereby to consolidate their control throughout the island. The Japanese required the council chairman—the educational reformer Mohammed Sjafei—and the head of the council's secretariat, Adinegoro, to make "laudatory speeches" about the Japanese on their tours. On his tour to Palembang, they had to discuss "government questions about how best to further this war effort" with local functionaries, including Dr. A. K. Gani, the chairman of the Japanese-organized Palembang Council (Reid 1979, 139–47). The catch for the Japanese was that the team of artists was also secretly hatching plans for Indonesia's independence and designed their new song-dance to further this purpose.

On 26 July 1945, Sjafei and Adinegoro departed from Bukittinggi on their tour of Sumatra (Reid 1979, 140) and were scheduled to reach Palembang to conduct discussions with Gani in early August. Members of the Japanese wartime Propaganda Unit (Hodohan) in Palembang, which apparently included Palembang citizens as well as Japanese, asked Gani to commission a new artistic work to celebrate South Sumatra's past glory and to promote the "Asia for Asians" ideology. The work's premiere was intended to grace the special political event on 4 August at which Sjafei and Adinegoro would speak.

So Gani asked his friend Nungtjik A. R. to set up a team to create and perform a new South Sumatran work that would seem to the Japanese to support their Asia for Asians concept while in fact rallying underground support for the cause of Indonesian independence (Hadji Wan Tjik, pers. comm., 1971).

Born in Palembang in 1910, Nungtjik A. R. was employed as a journalist in the Japanese Department of Information, but he was also a radical socialist and active underground member of the Partai National Indonesia (PNI, "Nationalist Party of Indonesia"). In consultation with two friends—Salam Asterokusumo and M. J. Suud, who were members of the PNI and the Sarekat Islam Party respectively—he decided to write a poem, a translation of which heads this chapter, about the ancient kingdom of Sriwijaya for the occasion, and then to ask a composer, a choreographer, and a group of musicians to create a collaborative work for performance (Hadji Wan Tjik, pers. comm., 1971).

The team did not choose the theme lightly. Like most South Sumatrans, they were extremely proud of their ancestors' maritime kingdom of Sriwijaya. For around five centuries (seventh to eleventh century c.e.), Sriwijaya-Palembang had served as the major entrepôt and political center of Southeast Asia, hosting merchants from West, South, and Southeast Asia who were pursuing trade with the region and with China. Its prosperous trading activity had also brought it continuing contact with other royal states in the archipelago, and it controlled the international sea trade in Sumatra's river estuaries, across the Strait of Malacca, and in the southern Thai isthmus.

Nungtjik believed that if his fellow South Sumatrans could only become independent of foreign hegemony—the Dutch and the Japanese—they could start to redevelop their society economically and politically and even possibly regain their past standing as a major economic, political, religious, and artistic center in the region.

As mentioned in the song text,[3] the Sriwijaya-Palembang kingdom once counted among its *maha guru* (professors) the great Buddhist scholars Dharma Pala, Shakya Khirti, and Dharma Khirti. As its unearthed stupas and stone inscriptions (dated 683 c.e.) indicate (Coedès 1968), the Sriwijaya metropolis was originally centered around or near the Segantung (alias Siguntang) hill mentioned in the lyric, located just outside Palembang (Barendregt 2005, 59).[4] It was believed to represent the Buddhist-Hindu concept of Mount Mahameru, the abode of the gods and the axis of the world. As an internationally renowned center of Mahayana Buddhist learning, Sriwijaya attracted students from various parts of Asia, including Java, India, Tibet, and China (Becker 1993, 182). It was first mentioned in the writings of I-Ching, a Chinese Buddhist pilgrim who visited the kingdom in the late seventh century while en route to the great Buddhist teaching center of Nalanda in Bihar, northeast India. Nungtjik and his team chose to expound their feelings about ancient Sriwijaya in the song text as a surreptitious expression of their own nationalist feelings, having convinced the Japanese propaganda department that it reflected the Japanese wartime ideology of Asia for Asians.

When the lyric had been written, Nungtjik A. R. invited the versatile Palembang composer and musician Ahmad Dahlan Mahibat, who was a sympathizer but not a political activist, to set his lyric to a melody and arrange the music for performance. He advised the composer that it was politically unsafe to compose for ensembles of which the Japanese propaganda officials disapproved—namely, the *orkes Melayu* (Malay ensemble), which accompanied *bangsawan* operas, and the *tanjidor* brass bands, which the Japanese thought symbolized Dutch colonialism (Hadji Wan Cik, pers. comm., 1971). He and Nungtjik decided that the Japanese would approve of a work that had artistic associations with South Sumatra's obsolete *kraton* and the Sriwijaya kingdom, because it supported their Asia for Asians idea. Believing that a bronze ensemble of some kind was performed at the Sriwijaya court in its heyday, Mahibat decided to write in the tone system of the Demak-Javanese-style *gamelan pélog* played in the former Palembang court in its second incarnation (1690–1873).[5] Mahibat could, of course, have chosen to write "Gending Sriwijaya" for a rural or urban *kromongan*, *tabuhan*, or other South Sumatran gong-chime ensemble, but he chose instead to write a song in *pélog* that could easily be played on the diatonic instruments of an *orkès Melayu*, and to call it "Gending Sriwijaya" to suggest the association with the *gamelan pélog* in the former Palembang palace. The term *gend-*

ing, used in the former Palembang court, derives from the Javanese word *gendhing,* which in its broadest sense means *"gamelan* work."

When the music had been written and rehearsed on an *orkes Melayu,* Nungtjik requested the dancer Ibu Delima Rozak, who was a daughter of the *residen* (regent) of Palembang, Hadji Abdul Rozak (d. 1984), to choreograph a new dance for the 4 August event. She chose to create a variant of the traditional Ogan-Komering-style welcome dance for a bride at a South Sumatran wedding: the *tari tanggai* (long-fin-gernail dance) (Ibu Erna Nun Tjik Aladin, pers. comm., Palembang, 1988). Naturally she could not have chosen a dance from the former palace because its resident *ulamas,* who were of orthodox persuasion and Arabic heritage, had banned all dancing on the grounds that it was either pagan or Buddhist inspired.

Unfortunately there is no record of the details of the dancing in the first performance. It was intended to resemble performances of *tari tanggai* performed at rural weddings around and to the south of Palembang. A group of bare-shouldered female dancers perform slow movements based on the *mudrās* (hand and finger gestures) and poses used in Buddhist and Saivite meditation (Ibu Erna Nun Tjik Aladin, pers. comm., Palembang, 1988). They wear exquisite costumes comprising a *dodot* (sarong) and *salendang mantri* (long scarf across one shoulder) made of the *songket* brocade for which South Sumatran weavers are famous in gold, red, violet, and other colors, with elaborate *aesan gede* ("antique decoration," I. *hiasan gede*) jewelry, including necklets, bracelets, anklets, and scores of golden pieces rising from their hair buns.[6] The dancers' four fingers (but not their thumbs) are *ditanggai,* that is, they have long cone-shaped brass fingernails (*tanggai*) with upturned ends attached to the ends of their fingers, which emphasize their intricate wrist, hand, and finger movements.

The opening *sembah* movement, with each dancer's hands pressed together at chest level, is a gesture of respect to the spirits and the audience. The dance proper focuses on exquisite rotations and other movements of the hands and fingers as the performers move from standing to kneeling positions and back again. They swivel their hands on a base formed by pressing their two wrists together and rotate their hands in opposite directions, with their fingers elegantly bent upward and outward. They take eight small footsteps for each complete hand rotation, a routine that is varied or repeated many times. Near the end of the dance, they present golden containers of betel nut to the guests present (as in a performance that we photographed in Kayuagung in 1971; see fig. 8.1).

When the choreography was ready, all that remained was for Nungtjik and Ma-hibat to choose the singer and the musicians for the first performance of "Gending Sriwijaya." Through Residen Hadji Abdul Rozak, they sought the services of the famous Hadji Gung, a (nonpolitically active) film and *bangsawan* theater singer and

Figure 8.1 *Tari tanggai* (fingernail dance) performer holding a box of betel nut

actor, as the singer at its premiere. He came with his own *orkes Melayu*, comprising a *viol* (viola), *akordion*, saxophone, trombone, double bass, guitars, *gendang* (a pair of double-headed Malay drums), and a drum kit, which required that the choreographer partly redesign the dance and retrain the dancers to perform with him. The band played the work in a lightly harmonized style (as in music example 8.1) using chords on the tonic, dominant, subdominant, and relative minor, with dominant sevenths.

The rich irony that lay in the Japanese approval of the performance by a crooner and his Malay band of which they had disapproved ideologically was not lost on Hadji Gung's friend, the musician Hadji Wan Tjik, whom I interviewed in Palembang in 1971. Although the Japanese originally disapproved of the *orkes Melayu* because it was allegedly "colonial influenced," they favored the personage of Hadji Gung because of his public popularity and usefulness as a propaganda tool and therefore came to tolerate the music he made.

Hadji Gung was born in Palembang in 1898, the son of a Semando father and a Palembang-born mother.[7] He had learned to act in his youth when he joined several *bangsawan* troupes in Singapore, including the Dardanella Opera troupe, which

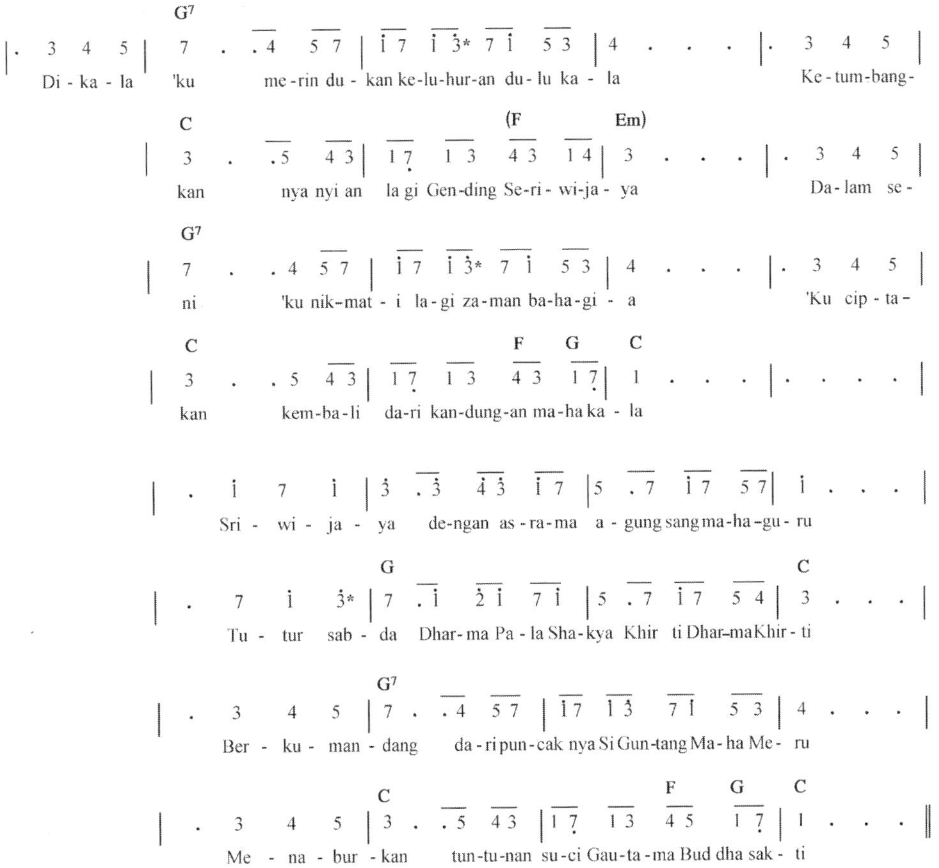

* some performers substitute tone 2 for tone 3 at these moments

Music example 8.1 A number script notation of "Gending Sriwijaya"

toured Java and many villages in and around Palembang. After starring in a feature film made in Singapore in 1936–37, he became very well known, and in 1942–43 he formed and toured his own *bangsawan* troupe, named Caya Matahari (Rays of the Sun), which referred to the Japanese rising sun symbol and was designed, of course, to please the Japanese. Capitalizing on his fame, the Japanese made Haji Gung a public servant and allowed his troupe to perform "information theater on Asia for the Asians," that is, performances of *bangsawan* theater accompanied by an *orkes Melayu* of which they had initially disapproved. They required that his company sell tickets for such performances and pay tax on the takings.[8] In 1944, Hadji Gung renamed his troupe Bintang Berlian (Diamond Star), and it was under this name that his troupe of musicians presented the first performance of "Gending Sriwijaya" (Hadji Wan Tjik, pers. comm., 1971).

And so it was that a South Sumatran *kreasi baru* (new creation)—"Tari Gending Sriwijaya"—received its premiere performance at a Japanese-organized function in Palembang along with speeches urging that Asia should be run by Asians, just days before the Japanese surrendered and World War II came to an end.

FROM PROVINCIAL SYMBOL TO INDONESIAN REGIONAL SONG

After the war of independence (1945–49) that finally forced the Dutch to leave the archipelago, the "Gending Sriwijaya" melody was arranged for various ensembles, including the traditional *tanjidor* brass and percussion bands that customarily played Malay and Western popular songs such as "Rasa Sayang-é," "La Paloma," and "Auld Lang Syne" for wedding processions in the Kayuagung area and other parts of the Ogan-Komering basin (see chap. 7). *Orkes Melayu* and pop bands played harmonized versions of the song on social occasions, especially at weddings held in a rural village or a city hotel. The number of *orkes Melayu* ensembles was declining, however, partly because the theatrical contexts in which they had often performed were disappearing. Most *bangsawan* troupe presenters, such as Hadji Gung, were poverty stricken after the war, unable any longer to afford the necessarily large cast of actors, singers, backdrops, stage properties, and *orkes Melayu* ensembles needed for the stage presentation.[9] Since the early 1960s, *bangsawan* has largely been replaced by the *Dul Muluk* theater troupes, which, with a minimum of resources, performed the stories of the adventurer Abdul Muluk, on the South Sumatra mainland and offshore Bangka. By the 1950s, Hadji Gung had sufficiently recovered his fortunes to be able to present a few simplified *bangsawan* performances in Palembang, but as his health declined, he lost the momentum of regular performance and died in 1976. South Sumatran *bangsawan* performance never properly recovered.

"GENDING SRIWIJAYA" AS PROVINCIAL SYMBOL

Spurred on by the official installation of Hadji Abdul Rozak as *residen* (regent) of the Palembang area and environs in 1958, government authorities in Palembang began to make a serious search for a song and dance that would adequately reflect the glory of South Sumatra's past and symbolize the current cultural identity of the province in newly independent Indonesia. They did not choose an item from the former sultanate because "feudal" arts were not in vogue in the antiroyalist 1940s–1950s; also the palace *ulama* had banned all dancing. Nor were they able to agree on a traditional song from the diverse ethnic groups.[10] So Rozak recommended to

President Sukarno that the recently composed "Gending Sriwijaya" be chosen for the purpose, and his proposal was formally approved. Even though the song had been created during the Japanese occupation, its expression of a wistful longing for the restoration of South Sumatra's greatness was seen as appropriate for the moment and for the future. The fact.that it had been created by members of the Indonesian Nationalist Party and Sarekat Islam, whose nationalist sentiments were undisputed, assisted its case.[11]

However, the song soon fell on hard times. In the first years of the frantically anti-Communist era of President Suharto (1965–98), "Gending Sriwijaya" was banned because of Nungtjik's alleged Communist associations. By 1955, Nungtjik had joined the "red" branch of the Socialist Party and in 1962 the Indonesian Communist Party (PKI). In 1963 he was diagnosed with tuberculosis and went to Peking for treatment, thus surviving Suharto's coup in 1965 and the mass killings of Communists and others that followed.[12] His family in Palembang believes that he died in China in August 1970 (Hadji Wan Tjik, pers. comm., 1971).

However, the officials in Palembang really wanted "Tari Gending Sriwijaya" to remain the provincial symbol, and in 1968 they urged Suharto to reconsider his decision. They claimed that Nungtjik was at heart really a nationalist, not a Communist, and that in any case he had written the lyric as just one member of a collaborative team of artists who were not members of the PKI. In 1970, the then-governor, Asnawi Mangkualam, formally recommended that the song be reinstated, and Suharto's ban was subsequently lifted (Hadji Wan Tjik, pers. comm., 1971).

From then on, "Tari Gending Sriwijaya" was frequently performed on official as well as unofficial occasions, accompanied either by a bronze *kromongan* ensemble, a Malay ensemble (comprising a *viol* (violin), *gendang* (drum), *gong*, and *akordion*), a *tanjidor* brass and percussion band, or an *orkes dangdut* consisting of Malay, Indian, Arabic, and Western popular music instruments. Sometimes the melody was performed on a solo Western instrument or by a pop band, and once it was recorded on the Javanese *gamelan pélog* at Radio Republik Indonesia in Jakarta (Mochtar Embut, pers. comm., Jakarta, 1975). Examples of arrangements of the song for piano and for voices are presented in music examples 8.2 and 8.3 respectively and are analyzed below.

FROM "TARI GENDING SRIWIJAYA" TO "TARI PENGUTON"

In the 1960s, the "Gending Sriwijaya" dance was further developed into a new, more elaborate and theatrical version (*kreasi baru*), called "Tari Penguton." It usually substitutes for the original dance at the most important government ceremonies, such as when welcoming a *bupati*, where custom now demands that five female dancers appear. Seven dancers are required to welcome a governor, and nine dancers to welcome the president of Indonesia. This hierarchy was established by a team of government officials in consultation with the choreographer of the dance.

The choreographer was Ibu Erna Nun Tjik Aladin of Bom Baru, the best-known dance teacher in Palembang in the 1960s. Based on movements from both the Besemah and the Ogan-Komering long-fingernail dances, it portrays the legendary seven heavenly angels from the Sipahit Lidah legend (see chap. 7) as they danced on earth in an imaginary court scene from Sriwijaya times. As in previous versions of "Tari Gending Sriwijaya," Ibu Erna's choreography consciously suggests Buddhist meditative practices, characterized by the slow, controlled movements of the dancers' hands and fingers emphasized by the attached long bronze fingernails (fig. 8.1). If the occasion demands, the dance can be performed in front of a theatrical backdrop with copies of royal *pusaka* (heirlooms) placed on pedestals, and it can be extended to include excerpts from *joget* and other South Sumatran dances and even some movements from modern dance.

The dance begins with a procession of female dancers wearing long fingernails and holding fans, with their female (or sometimes male) dancer-"protectors" carrying a spear, each holding an umbrella over the lead dancer or dancers. If nine female dancers are to appear, they enter and stand in four rows within a triangular formation, with one dancer in front carrying a square box of betel nut preparation (*sekapur sirih*) followed by a pair of dancers carrying spittoons (*peridonan kembar*), a pair of dancers in each of the next two rows, and another two at the back carrying a protective umbrella and spear respectively. They wear three kinds of local bridal jewelry, said to be differentiated according to rank in a former Palembang court (some assume it was Sriwijaya, but this cannot be proved, of course). Five dancers wear the *aesan gede* jewelry, which has the highest status and is said to have once been worn by a ruler's daughters, while the sixth and seventh dancers wear the *aesan salendang mantri* jewelry, which was once worn by royal ministers' daughters, and the eighth and ninth dancers wear the *aesan pak sangkong* jewelry, which was worn by daughters of ordinary officials (Wagirah, pers. comm., 1971).

After entering and moving diagonally across the stage, the female dancers take up their positions in the middle and front of the stage and then adopt a series of formations. Eventually the lead dancer and two attendants advance and present an elaborately carved box of betel nut preparations to important guests seated below, after which all the male and female dancers form a procession again and depart in state.

IBU ERNA NUN TJIK ALADIN'S IDEAS ABOUT
SOUTH SUMATRAN DANCE

I shall now momentarily digress to discuss Ibu Erna's life experience and ideas about South Sumatran dance, as they are the creative source behind her versions of "Tari Gending Sriwijaya" and "Tari Penguton." Ibu Erna learned to perform many South Sumatran regional dances as a child and young woman in the 1950s, and she also studied ballet, modern dance, and traditional Balinese and Javanese dance at Selekta in Malang (East Java). After opening her own dance school, she created new versions of many traditional South Sumatran dances for her star pupils, including the *songket* (gold- or silver-thread brocade-weaving) dance, the *dayung* (rowing) dance, the *gadis turun mandi* (girls go down to bathe in the river) dance, the *melati* (a flower) dance, and the *pukat* (fishing net) dance. Although her choreographies maintained the intricate arm, hand, and finger movements that she believed had survived from Buddhist-Hindu antiquity, she rarely used the Sriwijaya-associated bronze *kromongan* ensemble to accompany them. Instead she featured the *orkes Melayu* (comprising a *viol*, a *gendang*, an *akordion*, and a *gong*) in recognition of the fact that South Sumatrans had now replaced their Buddhist-Hindu heritage with a Malay-Muslim ethos.

Ibu Erna's interviews with various elders and clientele in rural and urban areas led her to distinguish two layers of South Sumatran dances: the autochthonous regional dances of the common people, performances of which had formerly been sponsored by the minor princes (*pangeran*) in their country houses, and the transplanted *zapin* dance, probably hailing originally from the Arab peninsula and which became popular in the eastern areas of the province in the early twentieth century (see chap. 7). Despite the *kraton*'s disapproval of dancing, she found that the descendants of the minor princes (who were often given the position of *bupati* after 1945) had promoted various rural versions of the long-fingernail dance, other female and male dances, and the self-defense arts at their official and family ceremonies, especially in Lahat, Tanjungsakti, and Kayuagung. She found that the most widespread social dance among commoners was *joget* or *ronggeng*, an ancient pan-Malay and pan-Javanese dance in which professional female dancers danced and sang witty, sexy response poetry (in *pantun* quatrains) in couples with paying male customers to *orkes Melayu* accompaniment.[13] These female professional dancers were often members of itinerant troupes who sailed with a group of male musicians and a manager along the Musi and other rivers, and in some cases to and from the offshore islands across the Bangka Strait; they used to stop at trading posts and in the villages to dance and improvise verses in couples with local men (see chap. 1). Due to orthodox Muslim sensitivities, however, *joget* troupes became very rare from the mid-1960s onward. Ibu Erna borrowed some movements from *joget* and *zapin* for use in her versions of "Tari Gending Sriwijaya" and "Tari Penguton."[14]

Ibu Delima Rozak's dance costumes, like those of other dancers—and brides—throughout the province, also changed as the community became more orthodox Muslim. Until the mid-1980s, Ibu Erna supported the view of her predecessor, Ibu Delima, that female dancers should wear the traditional bare-shoulder bridal costumes and the elaborate sets of gold hair adornments in their buns, despite their probable Buddhist origin (Ibu Erna, pers. comm., 1988). Since the late 1980s, however, many dancers have followed the trend of wearing costumes that cover their arms and shoulders and substituted Muslim *jilbab* head scarves for the golden hair decorations that were previously the norm.

THE MUSIC OF "GENDING SRIWIJAYA"

As singers normally learn the song melody aurally, or via numbers script (as in music example 8.1), "Gending Sriwijaya" has been interpreted and performed in many versions. Ibu Erna mentioned that she and many other South Sumatran artists recognize that when the melody is performed solo, it "sounds both South Sumatran Malay and Javanese"; when it is played on a *kromongan* ensemble, it "sounds South Sumatran Malay"; when it is played on an *orkes Melayu*, it "sounds Malay"; and when it is played with harmony by a pop band, it "sounds Malay-Western." As the reasons behind their statements are somewhat obscure, a description and analysis of the melody and select arrangements of it are presented below.[15]

Although the melody can be played on a suitably tuned *kromongan* ensemble, the form of the melody is not typical of *kromongan* style. Instead it resembles a typical form of *orkes Melayu* melodies. Its first two phrases (and repeats) comprise a variable series of eight (or sometimes seven) mostly isorhythmic four-bar phrases, each of which ends on a relatively long held note, as is typical of the *langgam* (slow) type of melody sung to *orkes Melayu* accompaniment (such as *lagu dua*), with violin, guitars, and drums providing rhythmic "filling-in" movement.[16] After beginning with a three-note anacrusis on solfa tone 1 or 3 in regular or "dotted" rhythm, each phrase changes melodic direction several times and ends on solfa tone 1 or 3, its sense of finality provided either by a gong stroke on the last tone or by a harmonic cadence. When played on a bronze ensemble such as a *kromongan* or a Javanese *gamelan*, a colotomic (punctuating) gong stroke is sounded on the final tone of a section, and when played on a piano or by a Western ensemble, a long-held low tone that simulates a low gong sound plus a harmonic cadence are played on the relevant instrument or ensemble instead.[17] The colotomic function belongs both to *gamelan* and *kromongan* norms, while the simulated gong and harmonic cadence belong to *orkes Melayu* and Sumatran pop styles.

The fact that the first two phrases of section 2 have a higher tessitura than the other phrases is the composer's decision rather than a typical South Sumatran or Javanese stylistic attribute. The undoubtedly Javanese attributes of the solo melody include the fact that the first section uses the tones of the main (lower) modal scale in *pélog bem* mode: the pentatonic tones {1 2 3 5 6} (which I shall now convert to solfa script numbers: {3 4 5 7 1¹}, equivalent of tones {E F G B C¹}). Also reminiscent of Javanese practice is the use in the second section of the higher modal scale in *pélog bem*, that is, (solfa) tones {4 5 7 1¹ 2¹} ({F G B C¹ D¹}), in which tone 4 replaces tone 3. Each phrase ends with a distinctive melodic contour that could occur in Javanese *pélog bem* mode (e.g., solfa tones {7 5 4 3}). The contour {4 3 1 7₁ 1}, which occurs at the end of phrases 4 and 8, possesses the greatest air of finality, while the contour {4 3 1 4 3} at the end of phrase 2 and {1¹ 7 5 7 1¹} at the end of phrase 5 has an intermediate degree of finality (according to Javanese tradition) and the contour {7 1¹ 5 3 4} at the end of phrases 1, 3, and 7 has the least degree of finality. Such features are also reminiscent of Javanese practice.

Arrangements of the song for (1) two-part choir and (2) piano are presented in music examples 8.2 and 8.3 below, and a performance of the latter is included in audio example 8.1. When the melody is arranged, say, for an *orkes Melayu, tanjidor* band, pop band, symphony orchestra, choir, or piano, two- or three-part harmonies and harmonic cadences of Western origin are dominant. Thus the opening phrase of the first section ends with a transient cadence in the relative minor (on tone 3, with some other versions just extending the C-major chord), followed by its repeat, which ends with a strong close: a IV–V–I cadence. Normally such a cadence is also played at the end of the sixteen (or sometimes twelve) *gatra* (Jav., "four-note units" or a four-tone section of a *saron* melody) or "bars" that make up section 2. Some performers use only the original solfa tones {3 4 5 7 1¹} (i.e., diatonic versions of the *pélog* tones), while in harmonized performances tone 2 is sometimes substituted for tone 3 (as in music example 8.1, marked *) for tonal variety or to suggest a modulation to the dominant.

The two-part diatonic writing in music example 8.2 moves mostly by step, as is to be expected given the partly gapped nature of the basic tonal material in *pélog pathet bem*. Though basically pentatonic, it consistently adds upper tone 2¹ as a substitute for upper tone 3¹ in phrase 1 and its repeats, giving it an overall hexatonic palette. Apart from its unison passages, it makes a feature of the intervals of a third, a fourth, a fifth, and a sixth.

Music example 8.2 A transcription of "Gending Sriwijaya," arranged by Ishak Mahmuddin

Music example 8.2 Cont.

Versions 8.2 and 8.3 have similar structures, but the melodic variant shown in music example 8.2 is in the form of {abab_1//cdab_1} plus a final coda—b_2—while in example 8.3 it is {abab_1//cdb_1}. The part writing in both versions loosely follows Javanese *pélog bem* modal practice (*pélog* in *bem* mode), using solfa tones {34 571^1} and {45 71^1 2^1}), but the performance shown in example 8.3 is melodically and rhythmically more varied, especially in the phrases ending with the long-held tones in the main melody. The number and order of phrases vary in different versions generally, but the first two phrases in section 2 of the piece tend to feature a slightly different variant of the isometer. In example 8.3, rhythmic movement is added below the upper part's long-held tones in the other or sometimes two other parts, which is a commonly used interlocking practice in bronze ensemble music, whether in Sumatra or in Java.

The two-part writing in the piano version by Mochtar Embut presents a Javanese composer's view of the interlocking, rhythmic, and melodic multiphony of *gamelan* music in a diatonicized idiom (audio example 8.1).

The interlocking relationship between the two independent melodic lines, which feature canonic devices and phrases in both similar and contrary motion, is based on two-voice rules that are neither Javanese, Malay, or Western but are unique to this composer. The upper part of the first section is set to four-bar, arch-shaped ascents and descents in the lower pentatonic mode: {E F G B C^1}, where F, C, and E serve as

Music example 8.3 "Gending Sriwijaya," arranged for piano from a performance by Mochtar Embut, 1975

the long-held end tones. The mode's F in the lower part is replaced by F♯ as a passing tone in one instance (bar 8). The lower part of the first section generally features distinctive repeated syncopated rhythms, with a more active line appearing in places where the upper part is less active (e.g., bar 5) and a less active line in places where the upper part is more active (e.g., bar 3). In the higher-pitched second section, C^1, C, E, and C_{11} are the long-held end tones in the more undulating four-bar melodic phrases set to tones {G B $C^1 E^1 F^1$}. The section begins with three-part multiphonic movement, after which the lower part again supplies the movement while the upper part is still. The upper melodic line resembles the beating out of the main melody of a piece played on a *gamelan* or *kromongan* ensemble, while the lower lines together suggest the texture of a pair of interlocking drum parts, and the final octave on low C_{11} resembles a gong stroke that marks the most important structural point: the end of a cycle, and apart from the final repeat, the end of the performance. The multiphony is specific to the arranger, Mochtar Embut.

In summary, the stable elements in most performances of "Gending Sriwijaya" are the basic melody, which hardly ever varies (even in pop song performances of it), the slow to medium tempo, the subdued dynamics, and the syllabic Malay-poetic text (Hadji Wan Tjik, pers. comm., 1971). Whether performing the piece on an *orkes Melayu, kromongan, gamelan*, or piano, South Sumatran artists are expected to perform the music in a quiet, thoughtful manner that expresses respect for the ancestors. The Malay markers of style in *orkes Melayu* performances include the Malay quatrain text sung by the soloist in a crooning style with ornament (*bunga*); the adding of occasional vocal tones between the original melodic tones; the violinist's florid, implied-harmonic melodic line with melisma added between the singer's long-held tones; the strummed chords of the guitarists; the cyclic Malay-drum part by a pair of drummers; and an optional drum-kit part. In "Malay-style pop" performances, a band aims to play in a "Malay-Western sound," which resembles that of an *orkes Melayu* but has a much louder dynamic level, percussive backbeat, and a more aggressive vocal style. Adapted Javanese-like attributes in the unaccompanied melody include the diatonicized Javanese tonal materials and modal formulae used and, in some performances, the use of interlocking techniques and the colotomic (punctuating) sound of a gong or simulated gong at the end/beginning of a melodic line. Pop performances of the piece are perceived as having a totally different, Western aesthetic.

New choreographies of the dance are still appearing in South Sumatra, for example, by *penata tari* Elly Rudi in Palembang on 7 July 2008. Novel arrangements of the song for various Indonesian ensembles keep being made in many parts of Indonesia, for example, an arrangement for a set of diatonic *angklung* (bamboo idiophones) that was played at the official opening of the new museum in Yogyakarta on 31 October

2008 (as reported by *Harian Yogya*, 3 November) and an orchestral arrangement played at a concert by the Institut Teknologi Bandung's ITB Studio Orchestra (*ITB News* 8, no.5, December 2008). Other arrangements are made to mark political events, for example, at a speech made by President Susilo Bambang Yudhoyono at the Jakarta Convention Centre (*Berita Utama*, 11 July 2007), and for commercial entertainment, for example, one that was sung at an indie concert by popular singer Guruh Sukarnoputra with his band in July 2007.

||||

The creative partnership between the song lyricist(s), composer, choreographer, singer, instrumentalists, and dancers in 1945 worked well because members of the team could unite in their opposition to Dutch and Japanese imperialism. It also provided them with a unique and powerful opportunity to create an important new work of music and dance while surreptitiously working against the enemy in wartime. When the lyricist wrote about Palembang's acclaimed Sriwijaya past, he inspired the team's and eventually the local audiences' confidence in a possible glorious future for South Sumatrans if there were to be a power change. The composer followed suit by setting the lyric to a melody proudly reminiscent not only of Palembang's former sultanate but also of the bronze-chime *kromongan, orkes Melayu*, and other musical ensembles that helped identify South Sumatra's culture, which meant that singers and other musicians in both the towns and the villages could learn to perform it. Likewise the choreographer's new creation built on South Sumatrans' pride in their traditional, Buddhist-*mudra*-style long-fingernail dance and dancers' famous brocade costumes, despite the devoutly Muslim sultanate's ban on dancing. Finally, the premiere performance led by a popular singer-actor who crooned the song to the accompaniment of a South Sumatran–style string and drum band (*orkes Melayu*) at an official function espousing Japanese Asia for Asians propaganda was deliciously ironic for the team and led eventually to the work's performance by many dance troupes and *tanjidor* and other bands.

Over the next few decades, artists in South Sumatra continued to collaborate as they developed new versions of "Tari Gending Sriwijaya," including the pageant-like "Tari Penguton." After being recognized in 1958 as the province's official song-dance, "Tari Gending Sriwijaya" achieved notoriety by being banned in 1965–70, after which it became so well known as a standard, Indonesian-language item in the repertoire of countless artistic groups throughout Indonesia that it was regarded as a regional song of national significance like, for example, the song "Bengawan Solo." The success of "Tari Gending Sriwijaya" has been due not only to its connections with Indonesia's nationalist movement and South Sumatran arts but also to the fact that its diatonicized-*pélog* melody is readily singable by other ethno-linguistic groups such as the Javanese, the Sundanese, and the Balinese, whose traditional music include *pélog* tunings.

First and foremost, however, "Tari Gending Sriwijaya" is not a regional Indonesian song. It is the official expression of South Sumatra's pride in the glory of its Sriwijaya heritage and an inspiration for creating a better future. Its birth during a radical time of disorder (*jaman gila*), the paradoxes in the twists and turns of its political reception, and its stately melodic and choreographic beauty make it a rich object of reflection and an appropriate symbol of the identity of the people of South Sumatra.

ACKNOWLEDGMENTS

I wish warmly to thank the musicians and dancers who helped Mas Kartomi and me research "Tari Gending Sriwijaya" and its cultural context in Palembang in 1971 and 1988. The musician Hadji Wan Tjik, who knew the song's composer, Ahmad Dahlan Mahibat, and the Bupati of Lahat—Bp. Mochtar Madji—informed us about the collaborative creation and first performance of the work under the Japanese during our visit in 1971. The choreographer Ibu Erna Nun Tjik Aladin and her husband, Bp. Nun Tjik Aladin of Bom Baru, Palembang, updated our knowledge of "Tari Gending Sriwijaya" and its offshoot "Tari Penguton" in 1988. In the same year, we learned about the history of *kraton* culture in Palembang from the royal descendant, Bp. R. M. Husin Nato Dirajo, who also gave me copies of rare drawings and typescripts about the *kraton* that were in his possession. I am grateful to Bp. Mochtar Embut for allowing me to play and record his piano arrangement of "Gending Sriwijaya" and to our daughter, Karen Sri Kartomi Thomas, for translating the text of "Gending Sriwijaya."

THE ISLAND OF BANGKA

This chapter discusses the performing arts of Bangka's four main musico-lingual subgroups: the Bangka Malays, the Suku Lom forest-dwellers, the Suku Sekak sea-boat-dwellers, and the Bangka Chinese Indonesians.[1]

According to some performing artists and community elders whom I interviewed on Bangka in 1981 and 1994, today's Bangka Malays are descendants of former Bangka Malay chiefdoms,[2] while the Suku Mapur or Suku Lom (where *lom* means *belum* [BI], i.e., "those who do not yet adhere to a world religion") are animists who prefer to live in relative isolation in the forests, and the Suku Sekak are also animists who, like other Orang Suku Laut (Sea Peoples), prefer to live in boats at sea when the weather permits. The Bangka Malays, the Suku Lom, and the Suku Sekak speak varieties of Malay, while the Chinese Indonesians normally speak varieties of Hakka or Hokkien as well as Malay.

The artists and elders also recognized that Bangka's artistic history is linked to the exploitation of its rich natural tin and pepper plantations. As vassals of the sultans of Palembang in the sixteenth–eighteenth centuries, the former small Malay chiefdoms in Bangka were forced to assist the sultans and later the Europeans (the British and the Dutch) in their exploitation of Bangka's tin and cash crops.[3] However, they practiced their own *adat*-based customs, legends, music, and dance, and they bartered forest and sea products with the Suku Lom and the Suku Sekak respectively. It is widely believed that these two so-called Suku Terasing (B.I., "Isolated Peoples") originally fled deep into the forests or out to sea to escape the endemic piracy and slave trade that operated along the coast until the late nineteenth century, and that by resisting attempts by the Dutch and later Indonesian governments to settle and "civilize" them, they have maintained at least some of their customs and arts to this day. The Chinese Indonesian culture, on the other hand, is maintained by the descendants of the Hakka- and Hokkien-speaking immigrants brought to Bangka to work in the tin mines and pepper plantations from the seventeenth to the nineteenth centuries. Bangka's population has a greater proportion of Chinese Indonesians than any other part of Sumatra (Census 2001).

Bangkan performing artists are proud of their cultural identity, expressed through their unique musico-lingual mix. They recognize the affinity between some of their Malay songs and dances and their counterparts in the Riau Islands and east-coast North Sumatra, and that they share a few genres—such as *Dul Muluk* theater and *tanjidor* brass-band music—with South Sumatra to their west. However, some Bangkans are hesitant to emphasize the latter link (Sakai 2003) because of their perception that the sultans in Palembang collaborated with the Dutch to exploit their resource-rich island, and that they also received the short end of the economic and political stick when they were still part of the Indonesian province of South Sumatra. Bangka and its twin island of Belitung broke away from South Sumatra in 2001, when they were reconstituted as the separate Province of Bangka-Belitung.

To understand how Bangka's four musico-lingual subgroups came into being it is necessary briefly to consider the history of foreign exploitation of their tin and cash crops by the sultans of Palembang (seventeenth–eighteenth centuries), Britain (1812–16), Holland (ca. 1817–World War II), and Indonesia (1949 to the present).

HISTORICAL BACKGROUND

The existence of Bangka's rich tin reserves was known from the late seventeenth century or earlier (B. Andaya 2003, 185), when Bangka's Malay chiefdoms were vassals of the sultan of Palembang (Smedal 1989, 10) and were handling forest and sea products collected by the Suku Lom and the Suku Sekak (Muh. Tanjung, pers. comm., 1987). When the first European settlers arrived in the late seventeenth century, they found the island to be sparsely populated (Wertheim 1964, 43–45). From the 1720s onward, Palembang's Sultan Mahmud controlled Bangka's tin commerce via a network of Chinese Indonesian traders who had allied themselves with both his and Jambi's royal families (B. Andaya 1993, 184–91). These traders brought in an influx of skilled Hakka tin miners from Yunnan, western Borneo, and other parts of Southeast Asia, especially in the 1740s. The great majority of the four thousand people of Chinese descent in the mid to late eighteenth century were Hakka-speaking miners in the north and Hokkien-speaking plantation workers in the south who transplanted their homeland temple rituals and arts to the island.[4] The large quantities of tin and pepper that they produced were exported to China and beyond (B. Andaya, 1993, 184–91).[5]

As pirates operated along the coast and European powers began to exploit the tin and archipelago-wide slave trade, the ancestors of the Suku Lom fled deep into the forest of north and central Bangka to escape abduction, pestilence, epidemics, and local Chinese Indonesian rebellions against the Dutch, for example, in the 1850s. Indeed, their fear of outsiders remained a cultural trait (Smedal 1989, 10), and their distinctive artistic expressions developed in the isolation of the forests. Likewise, for much of the year the Suku Sekak preferred to remain in isolation at sea during good weather.

From 1812 to 1816 the governor of Java, Thomas Stamford Raffles, tried to revitalize Bangka as a center of tin production for the British (Somers Heidhues, 1992, 82–89), after which the Netherlands East India Company took over the exploitation of the tin and cash crop plantations, run directly from Batavia. The "coolies" in the state-owned tin mines and the plantations were almost exclusively descendants of Chinese immigrants. The Dutch increased the number of imported Chinese laborers, whom they required to work very hard for small compensation. Isolated from the rest of the population, they were highly political and rebelled against Dutch rule more than once (Somers Heidhues 1996, 83). The Dutch allowed Chinese Indonesians to own land, and some became small farmers, fishermen, or clerics.[6] Bangka was Holland's most lucrative possession outside Java, noted for its exports to Europe and China until World War II (Somers Heidhues 1992, 82–89).

After Indonesian independence, Bangka's Malay population increased exponentially, though under Suharto the prices of tin and pepper fell and the economy declined until 1997, when prices surged again, coinciding with a rise in *hajj* pilgrimages, elaborate weddings (Sakai 2003, 199) and Muslim religiosity, expressed in part through an upsurge in the Muslim-associated performing arts.

Today, an estimated third of the population are descendants of Hokkien and Hakka immigrants, with the local Hakka speech variety being the most widespread.[7] Relations between the Chinese Indonesians and the Bangka Malays, the Suku Lom, and the Suku Sekak were cordial until the Suharto years 1965–98 (Amir Rasjid, pers. comm., 1994), as will be shown in the discussions of the arts of each subgroup below.[8]

THE BANGKA MALAY SUBGROUP

Among the surviving elements of the culture of traditional Bangka Malay chieftains and commoners are the legends (*hikayat*) intoned by storytellers and the custom of mutual help called *sepintu sedulang* (one tray, one door), according to which each household—whether Muslim, Confucian, or Buddhist—is expected to contribute a tray of food at a communal feast and to participate in or watch performances of Malay songs, dances, and bardic stories. In the modern dance named after that custom, *tari sepintu sedulang*, young female dancers in Bangkan bridal dress perform a series of elegant hand and finger movements as they step forward, backward, and to each side, and finally pick up and offer select guests a tray of fruit, flowers, or betel nut, accompanied by a *biola*, a *zap* (small tambourine), a *rebana*, and a small gong.[9] Another modern *adat*-based dance is the *tari pinang-pinang*, in which female dancers welcome guests with betel nut offerings.

At weddings, circumcisions, and other celebrations in the 1970s and 1980s, performances of the art of self-defense (*pencak silat*) accompanied by a pair of *gendang panjang* (long, two-headed drums) and a thick-rimmed Malay *gong* were common, as most Malay boys were expected to learn this skill and the associated Sufi-Malay philosophy. It was also still customary for mixed couples in Malay costumes at Bangka Malay village weddings, circumcisions, and other celebrations to dance *joget Melayu* while singing exchanges of *pantun* verses. However, when devout Muslim leaders in the 1990s declared the practice to be *haram* (forbidden), *joget* was usually replaced by single-gender song-dances with mainly Muslim texts such as *rodat* or *hadra*, which are performed in the sitting position reminiscent of Muslim prayers, with or without frame-drum accompaniment. Bangka's *rodat* repertory in 1994 included "Lagu Aini Pengasuh Nabi" ("Bringing Up the Prophet Song"), "Ya Ji Rotal" ("Calling the Prophet"), and "Sarip Nalai" ("Receiving a Returning Haji from the Holy Land").

Bangka's Malay population also enjoys performances of the classical regional songs on secular texts, which somewhat resemble those of the Riau Islands and east-coast North Sumatra. They include the paired slow- and fast-tempo songs on love or heroic themes called *senandung-lagu dua*, usually accompanied by a *gambus, biola, gendang, terbangan* (frame drum), small *gong*, and often a Chinese bowed-stringed instrument with a half-coconut shell body, a *rebab batok*, played by a musician of Chinese descent. The songs may accompany local variants of Malay dances such as the *serampang duabelas* (twelve-step) group dance and the *selendang* (scarf) couples dance. Since the early 1990s, these musical forms have often been replaced by pop band music.

A few elderly singers can still intone long Bangka legends at weddings and other celebrations, and the government has encouraged artists to dramatize them. In 1994 we saw a staged performance of a Bangka Malay legend that portrayed the creation of the island's landmarks—Mount Maras in north Bangka and Mount Menumbing in west Bangka—choreographed by Ibu Ermanila and performed by the Sanggar Mekulin (Mekulin Troupe) in Sungai Liat.

From the late nineteenth to the mid-twentieth century, the Bangka Malay and Chinese Indonesian communities supported three kinds of traveling theater troupes, *Dul Muluk, opera stambul*, and *bangsawan*, which attracted large audiences. The *Dul Muluk* shows came from Indragiri in mainland Riau (Dumas 2000, chap. 7). However, these genres are now virtually obsolete.

THE SUKU SEKAK "SEA PEOPLES"

The nomadic or seminomadic Suku Sekak operate mainly along Bangka's northeast coast and between its southeast coast and the neighboring island of Belitung.[10] They prefer to live on houseboats at sea, spending days or weeks at a time fishing and visiting their relatives and friends on other islands, returning in inclement weather to their makeshift beach houses on offshore islands (e.g., in the Pongoh area of Lepar Island) or in rocky outposts along the coast.

While at sea they entertain themselves by singing *lagu nelayan* (fishermens' songs), and they communicate with one another by singing very loudly at high pitch or by sounding a *tentuang* (trumpet) comprising a thirty-centimeter-long tube made of *betung buluh* (a variety of bamboo), with a hole cut at the nodal end. Audible two kilometers away, one short and two long blasts mean: "We are here, and there is no danger," while two long blasts mean: "We are nearing the beach with a load of fish, so come help carry them," and three long blasts mean: "We are in danger, help us."

Usually they perform their seasonal ceremonies or celebrations after a good catch on the beach. Shamans (*pawang*) present poetic speeches in a Sekak dialect and sing songs that either express the indigenous Sekak cosmology or address the sea and land spirits who control the elements, while the bards intone episodes from their legends. Men and women perform the *cakter, campale*, and *bedalong* (BM, *berdalung*) group circle dances. They also enjoy art-of-self-defense displays, the *silat*-based *kedindi* dance, and all-night sessions of mixed-couple *pantun* exchange-singing and dancing called *campak asli* (indigenous *campak*).

During the *musim barat* ("west [wet] season" from August to November), when the sea is rough, shamans sing magic songs to the sea spirits, asking them to quiet the waves and enable fishermen to go safely out to sea. An important two-day ritual to protect the people while at sea in the wet is the *taber laut* or *buang jung* (throw out the [model] boat) event. First, the *pawang* makes a model boat containing spirit offerings. After reaching a state of altered consciousness or trance (*kesurupan*), he performs the *berasik* ritual, intoning requests to the benign sea spirits to calm the wind and waves. He leads a performance of the *taberlaut* dance to exorcise the evil spirits, after which he allows the model boat to float out to sea with the offerings, and the local men, women, and children push their boats out to sea to catch fish and collect sea products. On their return, the Malay and Chinese Indonesian *orang darat* (land people) go down to the beach to wish them luck and exchange land-produced food products for the fish or other sea products. All present may then celebrate by joining in the Sekak *cakter, campale*, and *bedalong* circle dances with *campak asli* response singing.

At traditional all-night celebrations, professional female dancers may perform the *campak* couples dance with male partners, who throw money into a tin or put banknotes in their partners' blouses for the privilege of dancing and exchanging *pantun* verses with them. In 1994 during a daytime performance in the government-built *balai desa* (village pavilion) in Pejam and on the nearby beach, we recorded female campak vocalists singing "Lagu Nasi Dingin" ("Cold Rice Song") and "Cerai Kasih" ("Stop Loving"), accompanied by men playing a *biola*, a *gong*, and a *rebana* (audiovisual examples 9.1, 9.2, and 9.3a–b). They also performed the ritual *campale* and *taberlaut* dances with *pantun* response singing and a choreographed version of the *cakter* dance at a formal government event.[11]

On another occasion we recorded magic and celebratory dances in Pejem village (Kelurahan Gunung Pelawan, Kecamatan Belinyu) performed by some nonresident Suku Sekak who lived on the beach along Bangka's northeast coast, approximately twenty-one kilometers north of Pangkal Pinang. Some of them claimed to be descendants of Suku Mapur, whose parents had been moved by the government from Mapur Island (in the Riau Islands off Bintan's east coast) to the Suku Sekak area in northeast-coastal Bangka to stop their involvement with tin smuggling to Singapore (Bp. Purwadi, Head Department of Education and Culture, pers. comm., Pangkal Pinang, 1987). The government also tried to settle some of the Suku Lom in the same area.

THE LOM/MAPUR SUBGROUP

Bangka's small indigenous Lom (alias Mapur) population, who speak the distinctive Malay-related Bahasa Mapur (Lom), prefer to be called Suku Mapur rather than Suku Lom because of the term's perceived connotations of primitiveness.[12] Mapur is the name of the local river and of their language, and their traditional customs are called *adat Mapur* ("Mapur customs," Smedal 1989, 8). However, the administrative and academic literature still refers to them as Suku Lom because the term is widely known. Moreover, a Suku Laut group claiming descent from Mapur island to the north call themselves Suku Mapur as well. The people have traditionally lived in the hilly northeastern forest area of Kecamatan Belinyu around the Mapur River, and also more recently in the north-coastal fishing village of Pejem.

Like the colonial-era Dutch, the Indonesian authorities have tended to regard the Suku Lom as heathens who indiscriminately eat pigs, frogs, and the like and are "lazy" (Hagen 1908b; Smedal 1989, 14). Yet in fact they practice an elaborate cosmology, *adat*, and culture of their own. Their custom of mutual help (*besao*) bears some resemblance to the *sepintu sedalang* (mutual help) custom cherished by the Muslim Bangka Malays, whom the Suku Lom call Orang Selam, meaning "Muslims." Their *adat* customs apply not only to humans and their families but also to deities, other celestial beings, ghosts (*hantu*), animals, rivers, mountains, trees, and many objects of the natural environment. The Lom's creator-God—Gajah Mada (Roh Kuasé, "The Mighty One")—has a daughter named Isa and sons named after the prophets (Nabi) Rasul, Baginda Ali, Adam, Wahabi, and Mohammad, the latter being Gajah Mada's last born. Gajah Mada prohibited the building of houses of worship and schools in Suku Lom areas on pain of death and natural disaster (Smedal 1989, 24–30), which has served to limit social change among them and protect their culture.

Suku Lom funerals and grave burials are distinctive. An elder intones a funeral speech, and a procession circles three times around the grave, followed by a communal performance of the *campak* dance and a performance of the art of self-defense (*mencak*) accompanied by a *gong* and a double-headed *gendang* drum (Smedal 1989, 128). A ritual speech at a Lom funeral mentions "a large crowd [having] fun" (*dedak suka ramai*) "to the right of a communal house" (*de kanen balai besak*) with people enjoying a *mencak* display, *gong* and *gendang* music, and *campak* dancing (translation by Smedal 1989, 127–28). Marriage customs involve either an elopement or bride-wealth rituals, a celebration, and a feast (ibid.). Their traditional male and female clothes were made of bark, while male costumes for daily wear today consist of home-sewn, flyless trousers tied around the waist and a large plaited basket (*kerontong*) strapped with bark string to the barefooted individual's back (Smedal 1989, 16).[13]

Over the past century or so, the Dutch and Indonesian governments have made efforts to settle and modernize the Suku Lom, and as a result some moved to north-coastal Pejem to become sea fisherfolk or small gardeners. Others, however, preferred to stay in the forest, swiddens, and gardens and to practice their own *adat* and cosmology. Their strategy to avoid government interference is to occasionally spend the night in government-provided houses, as expected of them, but not make the effort to maintain them, and as a result the houses become virtually uninhabitable, and the projects fail.[14] Many Suku Lom are now engaged in slash-and-burn dry rice swidden agriculture and pineapple cash cropping, selling produce to Chinese

Indonesian middlemen. In some areas they can no longer engage in their traditional river-fishing and game-hunting pursuits due to the widespread depletion of the rivers and forests.

In the 1970s, some elders passed on their knowledge of *campak Lom* dancing, bark costumes, and ritual funerary processions to government choreographers, who developed a *kreasi baru* of the traditional performances in a show that purported to present a modern view of traditional Suku Lom life for visitors and tourists. A staged version that we saw in Sungai Liat in 1994 presented male warriors wielding spears and performing *mencak* self-defense movements against a painted forest backdrop. Men and women wearing fanciful costumes of red, white, and black cloth, bark head-dresses, headbands, and forest-product jewelry performed the *campak* dance as they processed in a circle to the accompaniment of a *batok* (a stick-beaten coconut-shell timekeeper), several *gendang*, and a small gong. The director used smoke bombs to suggest the Suku Lom reverence for the forest spirits. Olaf Smedal also saw a small group of Lom from Air Abik performing a staged dance accompanied by a violin, a set of drums, and a gong at a dance competition in Sungailiat in 1983. However, they did not win (Smedal, pers. comm., 2010).

Some Suku Lom who barter or sell their produce to Chinese Indonesian middle-men have a cordial relationship with their community and accept their invitations to their festivals. Indeed, the Chinese Indonesians on Bangka occupy a special place in the cosmology of the Suku Lom, who are grateful to them for saving them from starvation in World War II (Smedal 1989, 14).

THE CHINESE INDONESIAN MUSICAL ARTS

Beginning around 1910 or earlier, the Dutch encouraged the Chinese Indonesian laborers in many areas of north and south Bangka to play Dutch-inspired *tanjidor* band music at government functions and in military corps competitions. It became fashionable for families to employ *tanjidor* bands comprising trumpets, saxophones, trombones, tubas, clarinets, string basses, kettle drums, and cymbals to play at their weddings and funeral processions, and bands were still operating during our 1994 visit. They played Chinese favorites such as "Ai Cinde Kus Eu" (Mandarin, "Story of Love"), popular Western melodies with Malay texts such as "Auld Lang Syne"/"Janji Tua" ("Old Promise"), and Malay songs such as "Saputangan" ("Hand-kerchief") that had been popularized by touring Malay *bangsawan* and *komedie stambul* theater companies.

In southern Bangka between Toboali and Koba, the descendants of the pep-per plantation laborers who speak a Hokkien dialect are noted for their elaborate mass weddings, which were traditionally held after a good pepper harvest. Scores of couples were married at once with daytime performances of the female welcome dance—*tari sambut*—as the hundreds of guests arrived, *tanjidor* brass-band music was played, and the Chinese Indonesian and Malay male guests could enjoy all-night *joget* dancing and sung exchanges of *pantun* verses with their chosen female partners for small payments. Malay and Chinese string and wind instruments were often combined in the ensembles. However, in years when the harvest was poor, or when the pepper price dropped, only one couple would be married at a time. The "Lim Hom Satun" song is played by *tanjidor* bands at Chinese Indonesian mass weddings in southern Bangka when the community can afford it (Kartomi 2000, 305–8). In audio-visual example 9.4, a trumpeter leads the performance playing in a hexatonic major scale ({E F♯ G♯ A B C♯¹} or {5 6 7 1 2 3¹}) that sometimes reverts to a lowered 7th degree when in descending motion (as shown in music example 9.1).

Music example 9.1 Two *tanjidor* fragments demonstrating the lowered seventh degree (G) change

For centuries Chinese Indonesian artists have performed the local Bangka versions of the Khonghucu (Confucian) and Buddhist temple-related arts to honor the deities of the ancestors at the many temple festivals held throughout the island, such as at Chinese New Year and the midyear Pecun water festival. Since the early twentieth century in both north and south Bangka, their musicians also played *tanjidor* brass-band music at their weddings, with especially elaborate mass wedding celebrations in the south. Many also attended commercial performances by visiting Chinese opera, Chinese marionette theater (*wayang gantung*) and Malay-Chinese *bangsawan* theater troupes, as well as Malay *Dul Muluk* theater shows presented by visiting troupes from other parts of Sumatra (Dumas 2000).[15] At such theater shows and when the colonial or Indonesian governments allowed them to hold their festivals, they have mostly been able to mix freely with Bangkan Malays, Suku Lom, and Suku Sekak, as all were invited to participate, and this practice normally served to maintain good relations between them.[16]

However, Chinese Indonesian culture was severely repressed under Indonesia's anti-Chinese Suharto regime (1965–98), which banned all Chinese Indonesian arts and cultural expressions in Indonesia. To discourage large Chinese Indonesian festivals from taking place, a number of temples on Bangka were literally downsized when sections of the temple lands were seized by officials for other uses.

In 1994, we attended a greatly reduced festival inside the grounds of a temple in Jebus, north Bangka. Half of its land had been seized, and there was little space in which to situate the required effigy (as described below) and for the artistic performances, which in the past had included Chinese theater, music, and dance. The street procession could not take place because the permit had been refused, so there was a small, crowded procession inside the temple walls.

It was the annual Raja Jin (alias *rebutan*, "free-for-all") festival, held during the seventh month of the Chinese lunar calendar (Cit Gwee). At this time, worshippers honor the deity Ibu Dewi Kwan Yim, who is a reincarnation of Buddha the Merciful and protectress of people at sea, which is especially important in Bangka given the thousands of boatloads of arrivals from China and other parts of Southeast Asia over the centuries.

For weeks before the event, members of the local temple community had worked together to build the nine-meter-high bamboo construction that depicts a seated giant variously called Raja Jin (lit. "King Satan"), Raja Setan (BI), or—in Hokkien dialects—Bong Fi, Bong Fehi, or Bong Fai, with the king of all Raja Jin also being called, in Malay, Panglima Perang (War Commander). Members of the community covered the immense body and black trousers of this potentially wicked deity with shiny red, gold, and green paper and attached high up on his chin a paper drawing of Ibu Dewi Kwan Yim, as he sat in front of a wall in the temple yard.

During the festival, a group of musicians entertained the crowd in an ensemble consisting of a *sarunai* (a shawm with a funnel-shaped body and a reed mouthpiece comprising two membranes that vibrate when blown), a flat Chinese gong, a *tambur* (local two-headed drum), cymbals, and Chinese bowed-string instruments. Each worshipper was expected to bring an offering such as candles, incense (BM, *kukus menyan*), boiled sweet potato (BM, *ubi rebus*), and fresh vegetables to the temple to appease the deity. Some worshippers from other islands sent ultra-large red candles that were lit and would last for a whole year.

Finally, all present took part in a free-for-all, trying to crawl up to touch the face of the Raja Jin effigy and to grab part of the paper drawing of Ibu Dewi Kwan Yim. Those who succeeded believed this would attract good luck. Before 1965, local Chinese *tanjidor, kroncong*, or pop bands were often hired to play for dancing on a portable stage outside the temple, but such activities were still banned in 1994.

After Suharto's fall in 1998, some artists gradually began to perform again and teach young people to perform at the Raja Jin and other festivals; because the temples are now so small, however, activities still have to be carried out at a diminished level. In 2002 under Megawati Soekarnoputri's presidency, Chinese New Year again became a national Indonesian holiday, and the performing arts regained some of their former prominence, including on Bangka.

||||

Traditional Bangka Malay performance genres include the intoning of *hikayat* legends and local variants of the pan-Malay practice of *joget* couples dancing accompanied by a vocal solo, violin, drums, and gong. Others are the local art of self-defense accompanied by drums and a bossed gong and *rodat* and song genres with mainly Muslim texts accompanied by a *gambus* lute, drum and gong ensemble, and/or frame drums. New dances created since the early 1980s include the *sepintu sedulang* (one tray, one door), based on a local Bangka Malay *adat* custom, and the *tari pinang-pinang*, in which female dancers welcome guests with betel nut offerings

Although the forested areas inhabited by the Suku Lom are radically decreasing, communities in Bangka's northern forests perform their ritual dances and music, sing, and tell stories in their Mapur language. They also present intoned speeches at funerals, followed by art-of-self-defense displays, gong and drum music, and group circle dancing. The texts of some of their solo songs express their feelings of alienation at the creeping ecological destruction of their forest environment and the government's pressure on them to conform to sedentary living.

Suku Sekak communities frequent Bangka's coasts and offshore islands, communicate at sea with loud, high-pitched singing or *tentuang* trumpet playing, and perform their shamanic rituals, songs, and dances in their boats at sea, except in inclement weather, when they camp on the coast and perform their spiritual ceremonies for protection from the elements, to cure the sick, and to celebrate a fine catch or other good luck. Their group circle or couples song-dances are normally accompanied by a vocal soloist, violin, drums, and a small gong. Some songs express their sadness at the continuing loss of aspects of the traditional lifestyle. Most still prefer to live in relative isolation at sea if they can and try to resist government attempts to settle them on land. Like the Suku Lom and the Bangka Malays, their relations with the Chinese Indonesians are cordial, and they accept invitations to their temple ceremonies and feast days.

Bangka has the largest proportion of Chinese Indonesians of any area in Sumatra (Census 2001). From the turn of the nineteenth century till the Sukarno era, they enjoyed visits by traveling Chinese opera troupes with *pa tim* ensemble accompaniment and Malay-language *bangsawan* theater performances, which were also attended by the Malays. They continue to practice their Khonghucu temple arts on holy days in and around their temples throughout the island and to play *tanjidor* brass-band music. The exception was in 1965–98, when Suharto banned all forms of Chinese culture, and Bangka's temple grounds were forcibly reduced in size, resulting in a severe reduction in performance frequency and quality, and street processions, for example, at Chinese New Year, were forbidden. However, sometimes they managed to celebrate Bangka's special Raja Jin festival within limited temple space. The Chinese Indonesian arts began to regain some of their former prominence during Megawati Soekarnoputri's presidency (2001–4), when their festivals attracted increasing numbers of visitors and tourists from around Southeast Asia.

In 2001 many Bangkans welcomed their separation from the province of South Sumatra, which they felt had always overshadowed them culturally, politically, and economically. Modern Bangkan Malays like to promote their own heritage of customs, music, and dances on ceremonial occasions and to add "new creations" (*kreasi baru*) based on contemporary musicians' and choreographers' perceptions of traditional Bangka Malay, Suku Lom, and Suku Sekak music and dance. Now that the various *suku* can again join in the Chinese Indonesian celebrations, they can regularly renew their ties with them and one another and between their different spirit worlds in a way that promotes social harmony.[17]

ACKNOWLEDGMENTS

Thanks to the community elders and musicians in the Jebus/Belinyu district of northern Bangka and the artists and government officials in Mentok and Pangkalpinang for helping us record and interview artists in 1987 and 1994. I am grateful to the group of Suku Sekak dancers and musicians led by Bp. Muh. Tanjung, including Bp. Matahid, Cholid Ahmad, M. Nizar, Ibu Aan, Nona Zarina, and Nona Vitriana in Dusun Pejem, Kecamatan Belinyu, in 1994; the Lom artists led by Bp. Zamban and Bp. Karim in Desa Pejem, Kelurahan Gunung Pelawan, Kecamatan Belinyu; the *tanjidor* group led by Bp. Rusdi in Dusun Bawa, Desa Puput, Kecamatan Jebus; Raja Jin celebration leader Bp. Lak Sak Soi in Desa Parit Empat, Kecamatan Sungailiat; and the dance troupe leaders and choreographers Bp. Taufik Karya, Ibu Su'eryanti, and Ibu Ermanila in Sungailiat and Mentok, also in 1994. Thanks also to Olaf Smedal for his correspondence about the Suku Sekak and the Suku Lom and for sending me his tape-recordings of Suku Sekak music performed by a singer, a violinist, two drummers, and two gong players in Pejem in 1984.

III

NORTH SUMATRA

The province of North Sumatra is home to two main musico-lingual groups: the Pasisir Melayu (Coastal Malays) in the western and eastern coastal plains, and the Batak, who live between the coast and the foothills of the Great Dividing Range to the east. Although most people on the Pasisir are devout Muslims, they still retain some traditional coastal Malay customs based on local indigenous religion. Culturally and lingually they are quite separate from their Christian or Muslim Batak neighbors. The Pasisir's eastern land border has continually changed over the past century as impinging Batak populations expanded, settling closer to the coast in the Christian north than in the broad plains of the Muslim south. Both the Pasisir and the Batak people have a strongly patrilineal culture.

Chapter 10 discusses the west-coastal Pasisir Malays who live between Singkil and Natal and border on the territories of the Batak Pakpak, Toba, Angkola/Sipirok, and Mandailing subgroups, while chapter 11 discusses one of the six Batak subgroups, the Mandailing, making brief mention of the neighboring Lubu forest-dwellers, who speak a variant of Malay.

PASISIR-SUMANDO MALAY CULTURE

Because many west-coastal Pasisir Malays are descendants of out-migrants from West Sumatra, they are also known by the Minangkabau term Sumando or Pasisir Sumando, while their kin in south-coastal Aceh are known as Aneuk Jamée (Ac.) or Jamu (Ma., "guests"), a term that refers to the many guest workers who migrated over the centuries to south-coastal Aceh and offshore islands from other west-coastal areas of Sumatra.[1] The Pasisir Sumando and the Jamée speak varieties of a Malay-Minangkabau patois called Pasisir Malay, Jamée, or Jamu, though some also speak a variety of Simeulue or Niasan.

A key town on the Pasisir is Barus. Since the second half of the first millennium, it was mentioned in Chinese and Arab sources as a major world supplier of camphor. With its long history of commercial contacts with foreign countries, Barus was the seat of two palaces from the seventeenth century onward. As the two Barus court chronicles show (Drakard 1990, 2003), the royal *nobat* orchestra and other Malay and Batak music and legend graced the royal ceremonies in the palaces, which met their demise, however, in the nineteenth century.

The Pasisir Sumando forms part of Sumatra's entire west-coastal cultural area, which stretches from around Krui in Lampung to around Calang in Aceh and includes the offshore Pulau Banyak islands (see map 10.1). Its cultural unity, which resulted from centuries of trading contact, migration, and intermarriage, was recognized as early as 1512–15, when the Portuguese traveler Tomé Pires wrote about "the very rich kingdom of Baros [Barus], which [was] also called Panchur or Pansur. . . . [It was] bounded by Tico on one side and on the other side by the . . . kingdom of Singkel" (Cortesão [1944] 1976, 1:161–62.

A key term in the Pasisir Sumando performing arts is *sikambang*, which is not only the name of the cycle of major pan-west-coast Sumatran legends about the mermaid Sikambang but also the name of two musical genres: (1) the "original Malay" *sikambang asli* songs and (2) the hybrid *sikambang kapri* songs and dances with violin and frame-drum accompaniment that are widely thought to be a Malay-Portuguese patois of sixteenth-century origin. Chapter 10 also attempts to reconstruct the history of *sikambang kapri* music and dance, presenting a hypothesis to explain the initially surprising fact that the European violin and its associated harmonic *kapri* style were long ago accepted into the Pasisir's most intimate domestic ceremonies, even though the west coast lacks a history of substantial contact with the Portuguese, the region's first colonial power (1511–1641).

Pasisir Sumando culture shares its *kapri*-style music and *joget*-style dances with the Malay subcultures of the east coast of North Sumatra and parts of Riau, which may be explained by the centuries of trading contact and royal intermarriage between those regions.

BATAK CULTURE AND THE MANDAILING SUBCULTURE

The Batak peoples comprise a major ethnic and musico-lingual group in North Sumatra who speak several varieties of the Batak language.[2] Their cultural features include extensive lineages (*marga*), funeral rituals, and sets of tuned and untuned drums in their ritual ensembles. Though they live in the interior, they have inter-acted and exchanged ideas with the eastern and western coastal Malays for at least a millennium (L. Andaya 2008, 169).

The Batak peoples' associations with their Malay neighbors were established mainly through trade. Origin legends and linguistic evidence suggest that in the early to mid-first millennium c.e., they became major collectors and suppliers of camphor, benzoin, and other forest products, which they transported by forest paths and rivers south to Sriwijaya, where they were crucial to that kingdom's prosperity. As international trade opportunities developed in Sumatra's west- and east-coastal entrepôts, the products were shipped and sold to China, India, the Arabic lands, and beyond in return for luxury cloth, salt, and other goods (L. Andaya 2008, 114). As they migrated toward the west and east coasts, they formed Batak kinship networks in their new settlements that were distinguished from those of their Malay neighbors (ibid.). The main west-coastal entrepôt for Batak collectors was the above-mentioned town of Barus, where a population of Malay, Batak, and foreigners resided since around the seventh century c.e. or earlier.

Besides their indigenous ancestor- and nature-spirit-based religion, the Batak adopted Mahayana-Buddhist, Hindu, and Tantric beliefs from India that were pro-moted at the temple site of Padang Lawas, a strategically located ceremonial center of the Panai polity at the confluence of three rivers in the southern interior where several trade routes converged. The site was one of the distribution centers of over-land trade in forest products that the Batak people collected and transported. In the early second millennium c.e., one of their forest paths led from Padang Lawas to the southern kingdoms of Sriwijaya-Palembang and Melayu-Jambi, while a little earlier another path went via Padang Sidempuan and Hutanopan in Mandailing to Rao in Minangkabau (L. Andaya 2008, 150). When the Cholas from India attacked and destroyed Sriwijaya in 1024–25, the polity of Panai located among the Batak was also destroyed. However, by the late eleventh century, the Batak were active again in supplying resins to the east Sumatran port of Kota Cina (McKinnon and Sinar 1974, 63–86).

Beginning around the fourteenth century, they established new settlements along the land routes, and their clans became known as the Batak Karo, Toba, Pakpak-Dairi, Simelungun, Angkola-Sipirok, Mandailing, and Alas-Kluet (the latter residing in southwest Aceh).

In the fifteenth century, the sultanates of Aceh, Palembang, and Jambi increased production of a new cash crop for export to China and then to Europe, black pepper, creating a heavy local demand for rice production on the east and west Sumatran coasts, in Upper and Lower Mandailing, and in the Padang Lawas and Serdang hinterlands, with the Batak people providing the labor (L. Andaya 2008, 156–58).

It was apparently not until the sixteenth century that the Batak found it to their economic and cultural advantage to develop a separate Batak identity based on language, religion, and ritual. From that time onward, references in the historical literature to the Batak began to be made quite frequently (L. Andaya 2008, 156–58). Their ethnicization involved further development of their *perbegu* (*pelebegu*) religious beliefs based on the concepts of the soul (*tondi*), the ancestral spirits (*begu*) of humans, animals, and plants, and the associated patrilineal lineages and rituals, while retaining vestiges of Mahayana-Buddhist, Saivite, and Tantric beliefs associated with the twenty-six Buddhist temples and stupas at Padang Lawas (fig. 11.1), which provide evidence of the thriving Buddhist center in that region in the eleventh to fourteenth centuries.

Music at the elaborate Batak funeral ceremonies and other rituals was played on mystically potent, tuned drum sets (rare in Sumatra) and pairs of untuned drums. Each Batak subgroup had its own distinctive, though related, ritual vocal music, instrumental ensembles, and group dancing styles. In the more isolated mountainous areas, as in the hamlet of Pakantan in Upper Mandailing, communications between villages were minimal, and each hamlet acquired its own partly distinctive rituals, legends, dancing, and styles of instrumental and vocal music.

MANDAILING

Chapter 11 focuses on the music culture of the hamlet of Pakantan. It aims to reconstruct the historical and aesthetic context of its pre-Muslim ritual orchestral music in the eighteenth and nineteenth centuries, when the village was ruled by a chieftain (*raja*) of the original Lubis clan. The three ritual orchestras, which are differentiated by their respective sets of either five or nine tuned *gordang* drums or two untuned *gondang* drums, possess indigenous religious and aesthetic meaning. They were still frequently played in Pakantan in the years of our visits, 1971–72 and 1978, but much more rarely from the 1990s on. The musical rituals and aesthetic ideas discussed in the chapter are characteristic of the one village of Pakantan.

Although the majority of the Mandailing and neighboring Angkola-Sipirok people are Muslim and the other Batak sub-groups—the Toba, the Simalungun, the Karo, and the Pakpak Dairi—are mainly Christian, they all subscribe to the belief that they are part of a single Batak identity that arose from their common mythical ancestor, Si Raja Batak, born on the western shore of Lake Toba in the early first millennium C.E. (L. Andaya 2008, 169). Indeed, the main kinship clans in Pakantan—Lubis and Nasution—acknowledge that their founding ancestor, Namora Pande Bosi, originated from Lake Toba.

FROM SINGKIL TO NATAL

Sikambang, a Malay-Portuguese
Song-Dance Genre

The dominant musico-lingual subgroup along Sumatra's northwest coast between Singkil and Natal is called the Pasisir Melayu (Coastal Malay) or Sumando. This group inhabits the Pasisir coast, a narrow strip of land between the ports of Singkil and Natal along Sumatra's mid-northwest coast and including the former twin-court town of Barus (see map 10.1).[1] Mainly comprising fisherfolk, sailors, small traders, and descendants of aristocrats whose wealth was made from the local camphor and benzoin trade, these sea-oriented Muslims keep themselves culturally and lingually separate from their land-bound Batak Christian and Muslim neighbors who live between the *pasisir* area and the foothills of the Great Dividing Range to the east.

However, the genealogies of the rulers of Barus's former twin courts—the Raja di Hulu (upstream ruler) and the Raja di Hilir (downstream ruler) in the ancient town of Barus—specify that their ancestors were a mix of Malay, Minangkabau, and Batak, and that their kings possessed considerable cultural power till their demise in the nineteenth century.[2] The royal *Asal* Barus Chronicle also reported that royal life events were celebrated with a mix of "Batak, Malay, Arab, Hindu, and Islamic traditions" (*adat Batak, adat Melayu, adat Arab, adat Hindu dan adat Islam*; Drakard [1988] 2003, 161), thus stressing the town's cosmopolitan character. In colonial times, the two palaces promoted their local artistic pursuits, requiring groups of village artists to perform the *sikambang* and other genres on the outskirts of the palaces as contributions to a *raja* installation or other royal events, sometimes with Dutch administrators invited, and village men sang *sikambang kapri* songs and danced with itinerant troupes of female *joget* singer-dancers for their entertainment (102-year-old Bp. Tamar Sinaga, pers. comm., Bottot, 1981).

This chapter analyses and contextualizes the two main musical genres performed at northwest-coastal Sumatran weddings and baby thanksgivings between Singkil and Natal, the: *lagu sikambang asli* (original *sikambang* songs) and *lagu sikambang kapri* (*sikambang* songs with violin, harmony, and couples dancing).[3] It investigates the vocal style of the *sikambang asli* songs and how the harmonically generated violin accompaniment is blended with the Malay vocal style and frame-drum part in the *sikambang kapri* songs, as in some other hybrid genres in Southeast Asia (such as *kroncong* and *dendang sayang*).[4] It also hypothesizes that the genre's harmonic ele-

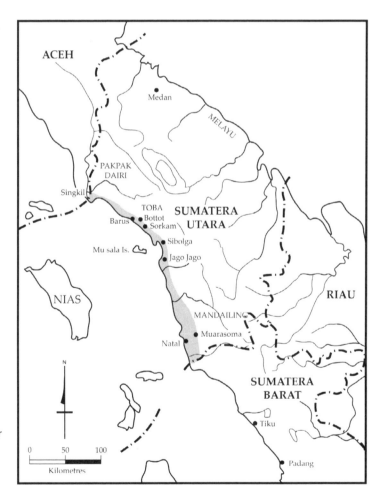

Map 10.1 The Pasisir area of western North Sumatra (shaded area)

ments and use of the violin are derived from Malay-Portuguese contact during the Portuguese colonial era in Southeast Asia (1511–1641).[5]

The *pasisir asli* genre, believed to be the older of the two, is associated with local ceremonial *adat* (custom) and veneration of the ancestral and nature spirits. *Sikambang asli* songs are sung by storytellers as they recount parts of this and other legends in *talibun* or *gurindam Barus* poetic form, by semiprofessional singers of ceremonial lullabies and laments (*ratap*), and by sea shamans (*pawang laui'*), who sing requests for protection from the sea or land spirits, call the wind, or simply express the feelings of lonely or frightened fisherfolk on boats at sea.[6] The *sikambang kapri* song texts derive from the main local legend, "Sikambang," named after a mermaid-angel who has a beautiful voice and brought the prototypical *sikambang* song down to earth. *Sikambang kapri* songs are sung by a vocalist with a violin (*biola*) player and two or more frame-drum (*gandang*) players (see fig. 10.1). They usually accompany couples dances such as *tari saputangan* (kerchief dance) and *tari slendang* (shawl dance), the latter shown in figure 10.2.[7] The song texts, musical style, and performance context are similar to *dendang sayang* (love song) and other harmonized Malay songs found throughout the Malay-speaking world, scattered as they are over the coastal areas of

Figure 10.1 A *gandang* player and a singer, Bottot, 1981

Figure 10.2 *Tari slendang* (scarf dance) by two male dancers, Barus, 1981

Sumatra, Malaya, and many other islands of the Indonesian archipelago. However, *sikambang kapri* has its own *pasisir* identity, based on its incorporation of elements of the local, pre-Muslim musical style of the *sikambang asli* and the lullabies, and the fact that they are performed in the two main ceremonies of the area.

Good performers sing loudly and at high pitch with great carrying power over water or land. They mostly sing unaccompanied, but decades ago shamans usually accompanied their songs to call the wind or for love magic on the now-obsolete bowed string instrument, *arbab*, a Jew's harp (*rinding*), a side-blown flute (*bangsi*), or a duct flute (*singkadu*) made from a rare variety of bamboo that has floated downstream (Bp. Darus, pers. comm., Sorkam, 1981) (see fig. 10.3).[8]

Both *sikambang* song genres may be performed at the most joyous of Pasisir occasions: baby thanksgivings (held on the forty-fourth day after birth; see fig. 10.4) and weddings, which traditionally involved buffalo sacrifice and lasted several days. A local *bidan kampuang* (village shaman and healer) blesses the opening proceedings with burning incense and leads a procession "to go down to the water" (*upacara turun ke ai*) for the ritual wash of the baby or the bride respectively, sprinkling holy water over them.[9] At weddings, which till recent decades lasted a week or longer, some men of the bridegroom's party (*anak sikambang*) perform self-defense-based *dampeng* dances as they process to the yard outside the bride's home. Upon their arrival, they

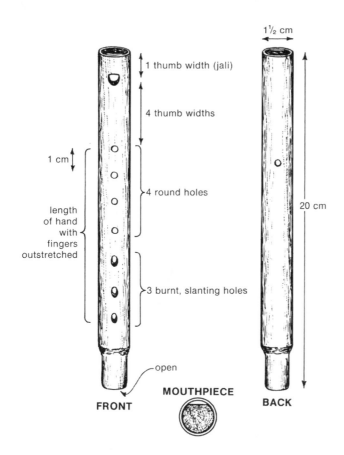

1½ cm

1 thumb width (jali)

4 thumb widths

1 cm

length
of hand
with
fingers
outstretched

4 round holes

3 burnt, slanting holes

20 cm

open

MOUTHPIECE

FRONT

BACK

Figure 10.3 A *singkadu* flute made of rare *buluh cino* bamboo, with three front finger holes burned out with a hot iron

perform *rondai* or *galombang duobale* (Ma., "twelve wave") circle dances around a *limau* (a mystical mango flower offering), singing *sikambang asli* songs between episodes of rhythmic clapping on the cloth of their loose trouser legs, sometimes continuing all night.

The lullaby texts sung at a baby thanksgiving welcome the spirits of the ancestors to the event and express wonder and enthusiasm for the future of the newborn baby, with the shaman and the prayer leader, the elders, the parents, and other relatives formally snipping off a piece of the baby's hair. *Sikambang* lullabies sung at a baby thanksgiving may comment on the baby's path to adulthood, while those sung at a wedding celebration offer advice to the bridal couple as prospective parents, while they sit in state as bridal "king and queen for a day" (*raja sehari*). Later the guests bless the bridal couple or the baby by sprinkling them with yellow rice grains (*beras kunyit*). After *magreb* prayers, a pair of repartee singers, a violinist, and a pair of frame-drum (*gandang*) players (fig. 10.1) may then perform the *sikambang kapri* songs in *pantun* or *syair* quatrains, with dancing in (all-male) couples (fig. 10.2).

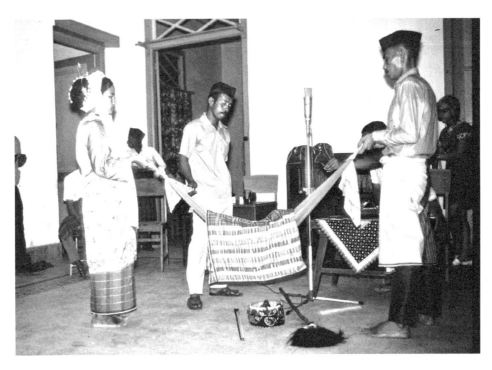

Figure 10.4 Two singer-dancers at a baby thanksgiving feast, Sibolga, 1972

Alternatively, the male guests may spend the night singing *dikir/rateb* (the liturgy) to their own frame-drum (*gandang*) accompaniment.

The section of this chapter titled "Three Sample *Sikambang* Items" discusses the contemporary styles and social contexts of the two main musical genres performed at Pasisir Sumando celebrations and mentions some other Malay areas where they are performed. The section titled "The Enigma of *Sikambang Kapri*'s Source" presents a hypothesis to explain the initially surprising fact that the violin and its associated thinly harmonic style, first introduced to Southeast Asia by the Portuguese, were long ago accepted into the Pasisir's most intimate family ceremonies, even though the area lacks a history of substantial contact with the former Portuguese colonial power, centered in Malacca from 1511 to 1641.[10]

THREE SAMPLE *SIKAMBANG* ITEMS

Transcriptions of three sample songs or song-dances will now be analyzed, beginning with a Malay ceremonial lullaby in the *sikambang asli* style, followed by a *sikambang kapri* song-dance, and finally a modern, rechoreographed *sikambang kapri* song-dance suitable for a government reception, festival, or media appearance.[11]

The first two examples were performed at a baby thanksgiving and the third at a government function in 1972. The second (*sikambang kapri*) item was danced by all-male couples, while the third example was danced by a mixed couple. Potentially erotic dancing and *pantun* singing performances by male and married female partners was prohibited beginning in the 1950s; married women were allowed to perform only in front of other women (Bp. Rizal, pers. comm., 1972). However, mixed teenage dancing is allowed, and since the early 1950s, the ban on mixed adult dancing was relaxed in government-sponsored performances in the towns (as in the third example: music example 10.9), outside the Pasisir region, and in the media.

Song 1: "Buai" ("Bue," local spelling)

This ceremonial lullaby (*lagu berayun anak*, "child swaying song," music example 10.1) is an authentic Malay *sikambang asli* song that possesses no harmonic implications or other European traits whatever, nor any Muslim tonal or modal characteristics such as those found in the Muslim songs of praise or the call to prayer. A semiprofes-

Recorded by H. and M. J. Kartomi
in Sibolga, January 1972

Music example 10.1 A transcription of "Bue" ("Buai," local spelling), Sibolga (recorded by H. and M. J. Kartomi, January 1972; transcription by Bronia Kornhauser)

sional singer, Ibu Roswani Anwar, sang the song in the strong, high-pitched vocal style (*suara jantan*) with melisma and other ornamentation (*kembangan*) as she swayed a baby boy to sleep in a hammock at a baby-thanksgiving ceremony held in a house full of people in 1972.

Free to improvise within the limits of the style, she sang the free strophic verses melismatically (Ma. *dengan aluk-aluk*), moving in tones, halftones, and microtones. Her ornate melodic phrases were separated by musical rests as she breathed in deeply in preparation for the next phrase. Her mainly semitonal and microtonal ululations around the dominant tone (E) in phrases 1 and 2 were followed by an embellished statement of a melodic formula (E D♯ C B) in phrase 3, but she inserted different embellishments in the repeat that followed, after which the melody expanded to a range of six semitones. The heartfelt intensity of her singing moved her attentive audience, who kept exclaiming: "*O, lamak benar!*" ("Oh, very nice!"), or "*Aduh suara!*" ("What a voice!"). The passion in her voice "made her voice moan" (*mendayukan suara*).

The first lyric she sang addressed the spirits of nature and asked for their blessing. She then addressed the baby as she swayed him in his hammock and presented him with an imagined Pasisir view of distant Palembang, telling him he would grow up and plant his crops successfully:

Bue buyung bue o bue	Rock, little boy, rock
anak mudo dibuekan	Young child being swayed
tanjak tanjak Palembang dari jao	Palembang seen protruding from afar
ayun anak buekan bue	Rock, child, rock
anak mudo dibuekan, salamo ado	Young child in the cradle, some day
banyak-banyak batanam ubi, tanah taleh keladi	You will plant a great deal of cassava and taro

Song 2: The Penang Island Song and the Umbrella Dance

The vocal *suara jantan* style is also employed by *sikambang kapri* singers with a violin playing a harmonically generated, Malay-style melody and a frame drum (*gandang*) playing a Malay cyclic rhythm, as in the next song to be discussed.[12] The vocal line of *sikambang kapri* songs is usually set in a European major or minor key; thus their melodic invention must comply with Western rules of harmony as well as Malay rules of violin–frame drum interaction and cyclic form.

In the performance of "Lagu Pulau Pinang" (music example 10.2; audio example 10.1), a male singer (Bp. Badul Nifa) sang the main melody accompanied by a violin (*biola*) player (Bp. Rizal), who performed an independent melodic line with implied harmonic color, while a pair of drummers (Bp. Abdullah and Bp. Beni) provided a Malay-style rhythmic pattern and cyclic sixteen-beat structure on the frame drums.[13]

Music example 10.2 A transcription of "Lagu Pulau Pinang Tari Payung" (recorded by H. and M. Kartomi, Sibolga, December 1971; transcription by Gregory Hurworth and the author)

Music example 10.2 Cont.

The *payung* (umbrella) dance, usually performed by all-male adult couples was performed for us by a mixed male-female couple (fig. 10.5). The lyrics refer to a Sumando man saying a sad farewell to his wife before making a voyage to the former British colonial port on the island of Penang (founded in 1780) in northwest Malaya.

The complete text of the song told a story, which is summarized as follows:

One day a newly married man from Pucang Gadang (an island off Sumatra's west coast) broke the news to his wife as they walked along the beach that he was about to sail to faraway Penang to sell a load of coffee. Though feeling apprehensive and sad at their approaching separation, she did not try to dissuade him. On his return home nine months later, he was delighted to find that his wife had just given birth to his daughter. However, the baby fell ill, so her parents took her to a healer who performed the appropriate rites with offerings that included bowls of blessed water and burning incense. A few days later the relieved parents saw that their daughter was becoming well and

Figure 10.5 *Tari payung* (umbrella dance), Sibolga, 1972

took her to her grandparents' home, where they presented a baby thanksgiving feast with music and dance for the whole community.

The vocalist sang in the high *suara jantan* (lit. "male voice") register, aiming to produce maximum sustainable volume and carrying power, with long stretches of melismatic melody (as many as twenty-seven notes to a syllable in bars 12–13) and incidental melodic embellishment, tremolo (bar 31), and glottal stops (as in bar 36). Like the lullaby performance, the intervals sung are mainly whole, half-, and micro-tones, with only rare use of intervals larger than a third (but note the fourth in bar 36). As in other *kapri* performances, vocal phrases sometimes begin with a small glide instead of a clear attack (as in bar 30) and terminate with a glide (bars 51, 57, 58). The vocalist freely varied and repeated words of the text, but unlike in the lullaby, his freedom to embellish the melodic line was constrained by the accompanying, sixteen-beat-long drum cycle. Yet he was able to vary the length of each strophe according to the number of melodic phrases he chose to set to each syllable, word, or phrase; for example, the first strophe lasted twenty-one bars (bars 11–31), while the second lasted twenty bars (43–63), with each strophe set to a varied melodic restatement of the descending melody. Typically the ranges of phrases sung in *kapri* style are larger than in the lullabies and other animist-associated Malay songs. While Bp. Badul Nifa frequently extended the range of a phrase to more than an octave, Ibu Roswani's phrases ranged more narrowly between one and five tones.

The strophes in *sikambang kapri* music normally occur in *pantun* ("abab" rhyme) or *syair* ("aaaa" rhyme) quatrain form. In the performance of "Lagu Pulau Pinang," the first two strophes were *pantun* quatrains, with the first couplet referring to the route of the voyage and the second presenting the intended core meaning of the verse:

Kok balai ke pulau Pinang	If (you) sail to Penang island
Ambuik aluan sitimur laui'	Take the northeastern course
Kok balai ati indak sanang	If (you) sail, (my) heart will be sad
Ai mato sapanjang lawik	(My) tears will be as full as the ocean
Pulau Pinang ainyo dareh	On Penang Island the streams run fast
Banyak batang lintang bulintang	Many logs floating across
Pulau Pinang bunyi nyo kareh	Penang Island sounds bad
Banyak dagang pulang barutang	Plenty of traders go home in debt

Unlike a spoken *pantun* recitation, a sung *kapri* performance may contain repetitions or variations of words or phrases at the whim of the singer and use different melisma and embellishment in each performance, as in the first *pantun* sung in music example 10.2. However, this singer's choices were somewhat restricted by the vertical musical relationship between the vocal and the violin part, though they remained fairly independent of each other. Sometimes the vocal and the violin lines anticipated or followed each other, but mostly they coincided at cadential points. In contrast to the fixed melodic formulas and restrictions of range that governed melodic invention in the lullaby, harmonic constraints govern the melodic invention in the violin and the vocal parts. Thus the vocalist tended to sing altered pitches soon after the violin produced its distinct modulations. The vocalist also raised tone 4 (F-sharp) in bar 18 to match the pitch on the violin as it modulated from C via its pivot note (raised tone 4) to the dominant key of G major. He also sang a lowered tone 7 when the violin modulated to the subdominant. However, the implied harmonies in the vocal and the violin parts did not always coincide; for example, the voice anticipated the modulation in the violin part in bars 12–13, producing a harmonically determined melodic sequence.

Modulations, in fact, are always more fully stated in the violin than the vocal part, with the singer needing to blend with the violin part by producing alternating raised and natural fourths and flattened and natural sevenths. Most violin modulations are fully established via a pivot note, but sometimes they are merely suggested without being stated, as in the tonic-dominant modulation in bars 25–27. The lowered seventh (B-flat) pivot note occasionally (in a sixth of cases in this example) occurs to establish modulations to the subdominant.

In other *kapri* songs most modulations are made to the dominant, a few to the subdominant, and none to any other key. The harmonic style is governed by the use of the rising or lowering leading note, violin double-stopping, and implied harmonies in the melodic lines. Though the violin sometimes double-stops in fifths and thirds above the tonic, the harmonic texture is relatively thin, and horizontal triads are only very rarely stated. Broken triads occur mostly on tones 1, 4, or 5, and mainly just before cadential points, for example, in the broken triads in bar 5 of "Lagu Pulau Pinang" in music example 10.3 (followed by a cadential formula on G F D C, ending on the tonic C in bars 6–7).

Music example 10.3 Broken triads
with a cadential formula on the *biola*

Within the ensemble, the violin produces continuous melody, playing the most active role of all not only during the singing but also in the vocal silences between verses, sometimes holding a tone over two or three bars (e.g., in bars 11–12 and 43–44) as the vocalist enters at the beginning of a strophe and producing sequential melodic patterns leading up to cadential points, as in the sequence of two-tone slurs in bars 7–8.

Music example 10.4 Sequential slurs
on the *biola*

The violin also provides the melodic introduction, a constant countermelody to the vocal line, melodic interludes between strophes and vocal phrases, and a postlude, which may include a melodic signal to the singer and frame-drum players to end the performance. Three common signals are shown in music example 10.5:

(a)

(b)

(c)

Music example 10.5 Three examples of cadential signals on a *biola*

Another structurally important aspect of musical interaction in the ensemble lies in the relationship between the violin and the frame drums, with the violin modulations marking the beginning of each frame-drum cycle, despite the fact that the latter start a little early or a little late at times. Each complete statement of the cyclic drum rhythm in music example 10.2 is marked by a modulation, which divides the overall musical form into four-bar sections.[14] These frame-drum cycles are called *tumba* because they combine two drum sounds that are given onomatopoetic names, *tum* or *tung* and *ba*.[15] Theoretically, the main frame-drum (*gandang pokok*) rhythm consists of the following cyclically repeated formula:

Music example 10.6 Cyclically repeated formula played on a *gandang pokok*

In each verse, the *pokok* (basic) pattern of the *tumba* part (shown in six variants in music example 10.2) varies more in the cycle's second half than in the first, and the opening bar is the least variable. The deep *tung* tone plays a punctuating role, like a gong marking the end of a cycle in some bronze ensembles in Sumatra. The *tumba* establishes a strict meter that offsets the greater rhythmic freedom of the voice and the violin. It also determines the tempo for the other members of the ensemble and, with the violin, provides cues for the vocalist's entry, which usually occurs after the third *tung* beat (see bar 11, example 10.2). The *tung* stroke frequently coincides with a cadential point or modulation on the violin, or in the voice, or both (see bars 21,

22, and 25). The *tumba*, then, is a temporal unit of great structural importance, and the most important structural point within the *tumba* is the *tung* stroke.

The low-pitched *tung* sound is made by the player's left hand beating on the middle of the left-hand skin, while *tang* is a high-pitched sound beaten by the right hand on the edge of the right-hand skin, and *ba* is a combination of left-hand and right-hand sounds. Variations (*paningkah*) to the rhythmic cycle are provided mainly by the *tang* and *ba* sounds, as well as by a fourth sound *kĕ*, which is a high-pitched left-hand sound. All four drum timbres were used in the *tumba* of a recorded piece of local *tari piring* (plate dance) music, as follows:

tang tung ba kĕ tang tang tung ba kĕ tang tang tung ba kĕ tang tang tung   tang

Music example 10.7 The *tumba* of a segment of *tari piring* music

Many other rhythmic patterns are used in different areas. A common sixteen-beat *pokok* rhythmic cycle called *irama kapri* used in the Jago-jago area is shown in the following example:

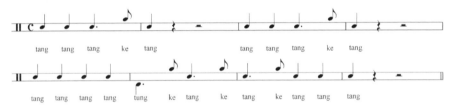

tang tang tang kĕ tang   tang tang tang kĕ tang

tang tang tang tang tung kĕ tang kĕ tang kĕ tang tang tang

Music example 10.8 *Irama kapri*

Song 3: "Lagu Sikambang Tarian Anak"

The performance we recorded was an arrangement of "Lagu Sikambang Tarian Anak" ("Sikambang Song-Dance [to celebrate the birth of a] Child," music example 10.9) made by order of the Department of Education and Culture branch in Sibolga for a festival in the early 1970s and was often used subsequently to welcome official guests.[16] A mixed couple sang and danced this stylized *kapri* version of a baby thanksgiving ceremony, accompanied by violin and frame drums. Rechoreographed to suit government, festival, and media occasions, it lasted less than thirty minutes and featured glamorous costumes and realistic stage properties, including a baby doll and a hammock (see fig. 10.4).

The singer sang in a musical style similar to that of example 10.2, freely inserting vocables in the text such as *a ule*, or exclamations such as *adu sayang* (oh dear).

Music example 10.9 A transcription of "Lagu Sikambang Tarian Anak" (recorded by H. and M. Kartomi, Sibolga, January 1972; transcription by Gregory Harworth and the author)

Music example 10.9 Cont.

The song's formal structure is determined by the cyclic nature of the drum pattern (*tumba*) and the whim of the singer, who may choose to lengthen sections and insert a large amount of textual repetition, melodic embellishment, and melisma, thus varying the number of cycles performed. As in harmonic Western music, the structure is also determined by the implied harmonic momentum in the violin melodic line. The three levels of structure consolidate one another.

The text of music example 10.9 presents part of the legend about the mermaid Sikambang, who is renowned for her beautiful singing. The story is a favorite of local storytellers from Singkil to Natal and is found in different versions right along Sumatra's west coast. A version recorded in Barus tells of the legendary origin of the Sikambang song as follows:

> Once upon a time the mermaid Sikambang was combing the hair of her renowned mortal mistress, the Maharani or Tuan Putri Rundu on Musala Island (off the coast of Sibolga), and she accidentally dropped the golden comb in the sea. The queen exclaimed: *Kambang! O Kambang e! cari, Kambang, cari!* ("Oh Kambang, look for it!"). The mermaid searched for the comb, but the tide took it out to sea and she could not find it. She searched day and night and, feeling forlorn, began singing an extremely emotional song. A passing fisherman heard it and was so impressed by her voice and her beautiful, sad song that he sang it wherever he went, and it spread along the coast of Sumatra.[17]

Professional storytellers sing episodes from the Sikambang story at all-night sessions, interspersing their episodes with poetic images and well-known Malay jokes, riddles, fables, and proverbs for light relief, such as the provocative image of girls wearing see-through blouses in the following:

Anak dara dua sepasang	A pair of young maidens
Pakai baju sutera jarang	Wear blouses of wide-meshed silk
Sebiji nanas sebiji pisang	One is a pineapple and the other a banana
Itulah sudah resmi musang	That's the natural prey of the civet cat.[18]

The image and moral proverb in the first and second couplets respectively refer to the *pantun* verse sung in example 10.9:

Pulo pandan jau ditangah	Pandan island far out to sea
Dibalik pulo si Angso duo	Return to the Angsa islands
Hanca badan dikandung tana	When mortal remains return to dust
Budi baik dikana juo	Good deeds are still remembered.

In this newly choreographed version of the dance, however, several male vocalists took turns singing a series of verses, while male and female couples mimed and danced the parts of a traditional baby thanksgiving ceremony. First, the female dancer playing the mother role entered, wearing a long blouse (*kebaya panjang*), a wraparound skirt (*kain*), and a *slendang* (shawl), as in figure 10.6.

She knelt on the floor and arranged a long piece of cloth (*kain gendong* or *kain candai*) around her on three sides. Raising her hands, she made a bow of respect (Ma. *sembah*) to the onlookers. The "baby" (a doll) lay beside her on a cloth alongside a sword of protection, a bowl of holy water containing a bottle, and a broom that symbolized the cleanliness of the baby's house (the latter two properties being modern additions), while the dancer portraying the father, wearing a *teluk belanga* (Malay trouser suit with wraparound waist cloth), sat cross-legged on the other side of the objects. The mother then rose, picked up the *kain gendong* (hammock cloth), wrapped it around the baby, and cradled it in her arms, whereupon the father held the baby and the bottle and danced while the mother held one end of the hammock cloth and gave the other end to him, and they swayed the child together. Finally, six mixed couples took turns swaying the baby and throwing yellow rice grains (*beras kunyit*) over the baby to symbolize their good wishes for the child and his parents.

Figure 10.6 *Tari anak* (child dance), Sibolga, 1978

Some Song-Dances Shared with Other Malay Areas

Some Pasisir song-dances are also performed by artists in and around North Sumatra's former east-coast court areas (Goldsworthy 1979; Sinar 1986), though evidence of cultural contact between Sumatra's west- and east-coast palaces is more limited than contact between west Malaya and east Sumatra (Sinar 1986, 11; 1993).[19] In the seventeenth through the nineteenth centuries, some people were in contact with their kin across the Strait of Malacca, especially in Johore (Langenberg 1977, 83), while others were involved in bidirectional migration across the strait when formal political contact had been made with the kingdoms of Johore and Riau-Lingga (L. Andaya 1975b, 1–11; Matheson 1975, 12–21).

The resemblances between west- and east-coast baby thanksgivings and weddings and their *joget*-style song-dances are striking, however. On both coasts, a royal yellow umbrella is placed over the baby, who lies in a crib placed in a small house construction with similar palm and coconut leaf decorations, as formal lullabies are sung.[20]

The ceremonial wedding and baby thanksgiving feasts in both areas feature a pyramid of rice decorated with hard-boiled eggs, chicken, and other morsels and the giving of sticky-rice cakes to the children. Several song-dances performed on both coasts are so similar that their artists seem likely to have been in direct or indirect contact for a considerable time. Some items performed on the Sumando coast were apparently transplanted from the former sultanate in Riau and/or the east coast of North Sumatra, where they are still performed, including *joget* couples song-dances such as the slow "Sinandung" and the faster "Inang" and "Lagu Dua" ("Second Song"), "Lagu Makan Sirih" ("Song for Chewing Betel Nut"), and "Lagu Kapri Bangsawan" ("Royal *Kapri* Song") (Nor 1993, 3; Goldsworthy 1979, 256–68).[21] The harmonic Malay *lagu/tari Melayu* with *biola* and drum accompaniment are also performed in Minangkabau, Bengkulu, Lampung, and areas around the former sultanates in Aceh and Palembang.[22]

Other Sumando-coast *kapri*-style songs that are sometimes sung in various versions along Sumatra's entire west coast or North Sumatra's east coast are "Lagu Kapri Pembukaan" ("Opening *Kapri* Song"), "Lagu Sampai Hati" ("Have a Heart Song" to accompany the kerchief dance *tari saputangan kapri*), "Lagu Kapri Tari Piring" ("*Kapri* Song Plate Dance"), "Lagu Sampaya" ("*Sampaya* Song" to accompany the *sampaya* circle dance), a number of low-pitched song-dances with sad texts in *talibun* poetic form called *tari lagu sinandung* (from *berhanyut*, "to call the wind," Sinar 1997, 59), and "Panutup Lagu Kapri Syamsir" ("Closing Syamsir *Kapri* Song," in which Syamsir is a man's name). "Lagu Sikambang Laui' Angkola" ("Sea *Sikambang* Song from Angkola") is also sung in the Natal and Angkola areas, and "Lagu Serunai Aceh"

("Acehnese Oboe Song") in western Aceh. *Tari piring* (the plate dance) is believed to have been transplanted from Pagaruyung to the Barus kingdoms and Sumando coast in the early nineteenth century (Bp. Tamar Sinaga, pers. comm., Bottot, 1981), and also at an unknown date to the east coast, where a sultan of Serdang married a Minangkabau princess (historian Tengku Luckman Sinar, pers. comm., 1981).

THE ENIGMA OF *SIKAMBANG KAPRI*'S SOURCE

How, then, did the stylistically hybrid *sikambang kapri* repertory become so prominent a part of the people's ceremonial life along the Sumando coast?

As hybrid musical styles such as *kapri* or *kroncong* normally only result from prolonged contact between musicians in two or more cultures (M. Kartomi 1981b), it follows that *kapri*—or at least its violin and harmonic components—could not have originated on the *Sumando* coast itself.[23] Although some Portuguese ships are reported to have sailed along the coast in the sixteenth and seventeenth centuries, and local legends in Barus peripherally mention local resistance to the Portuguese and their former fort on Nias, there is no evidence that Barus and other Sumando ports experienced substantial contact with Southeast Asia's first colonial European power in the sixteenth and seventeenth centuries.[24] Like other harmonic *joget* couples genres, the stylistic origin of the *sikambang kapri* genre is enigmatic. It must originally have been developed somewhere else and then have been transplanted and transformed into the local Pasisir style.

The nearest area of prolonged Portuguese contact to the Sumando coast was Malacca, which had been an important Malay sultanate and trading center from around 1400 until it was conquered by the Portuguese in 1511 (Ma [1433] 1970, 109). Malay music and dance that had developed in the pre-Portuguese sultanate of Malacca may already have spread via trading contact and intermarriage to the Malay courts in outlying areas to the east and west of the Strait of Malacca before Malacca's fall (Nor 1993, 20). In colonial households, however, European music was the preferred form of entertainment. From the early days of the Portuguese empire, slave musicians played European instruments that had been transplanted to Malacca and other colonial centers by ship.[25] The transported slaves included full-blood African and Indian *cafre* (heathens) (Boxer 1969, 305), the term from which the word *kapri* probably derived, and they were asked to play European string, wind, and possibly percussion instruments at their masters' social functions.[26]

Thus, for example, a lavish dinner provided by slave labor in 1637 in the Portuguese colony of Macao was accompanied by "indifferent good music of the voice, harp and guitar" (Mundy, quoted in Boxer 1969, 307). In 1689, a bride in Batavia who had fifty-nine slaves mentioned in a letter that there was "a slave orchestra which played the harp, viol, and bassoon at meal times" (Boxer 1965, 240). Indeed, "Dutch slave households," as Charles Boxer comments, "were unnecessarily large, and were maintained for ostentation and status-seeking" (ibid.). Further, "one feature of [South African] Cape life which impressed many visitors was the musical talent of the 'Malay' slaves and the skill with which they played entirely by ear on instruments such as the flute, violin and 'violincello'" (ibid., 260–61). As a Mr. Lichtenstein wrote:

> I know of many great houses in which there is not one of the slaves that cannot play upon some instrument, and where an orchestra is immediately collected together, if the young people of the house, when they are visited in the afternoon by their acquaintances, like to amuse themselves with dancing for an hour or two. At a nod, the cook exchanges his saucepan for a flute, the groom quits his curry-comb and takes his violin, and the gardener, throwing aside his spade, sits down to the violin-cello. (quoted in Boxer 1965, 261)

The Portuguese apparently brought bowed and plucked string instruments with them to Malacca from the early days of the empire, including alto violins called *piola* in Portuguese and *biola* in Malay, which were played by slave musicians in Malacca's Portuguese households.[27] The four-string violin, developed in Italy around 1550–1600 (Apel 1970, 908), was probably first used in the Iberian Peninsula in the early seventeenth century and presumably replaced the alto violin in Southeast Asia from the mid- to late seventeenth century (Goldsworthy 1979, 421). After spreading widely throughout the Malay world, it has long been regarded as an authentic Malay instrument. Its presence on Sumatra's west coast was noted in a book by William Marsden published in 1783 (Marsden [1811] 1966, 195–66), and both the violin and the viola were observed on North Sumatra's east coast by John Anderson in 1823 (Anderson [1826] 1971, 292).[28] In Portuguese Malacca, the violin accompanied the hybrid Malay-Portuguese musical style known as *branyo*, with couples dancing. The similar *dendang [dondang] sayang* (lit. "love song") genre, with its Malay vocalist accompanied by an ensemble of Malay, European, and Indian instruments, eventually spread throughout the Malay world, including coastal east Sumatra, where it is known under the umbrella term of *lagu/tari Melayu asli* (authentic Malay song/ dance) and by a variety of other local names in Sumatra and Malaysia, including *joget, ronggeng, japri* (in west-coastal Lampung), and *kapri*.

How, then, did harmonic Malay music and the associated dances spread throughout the Malay areas of Sumatra and other parts of Southeast Asia? Eventually, loyal Portuguese household slaves—including musicians—who had converted to Christianity were offered their freedom and the formal status and privileges of Portuguese nationals.[29] Referred to as Portugis (or if of African or Indian origin, as black Portugis), the freed slaves scattered and settled in various parts of the archipelago, including the nearby Malay sultanates in Johore, Singapore, the Riau Islands, and Sumatra's east coast during the seventeenth century. Some of the freed slaves married local women. Of all the European colonial powers, only the Portuguese encouraged their men to settle down with local wives, for "by taking root in their new homelands, they would at the same time plant roots for Portuguese interests" (Abdurachman 1982, 1). Indeed, "by the end of eighty years of Portuguese contact with the Southeastern Islands, a very hybrid population had come into being" whose culture combined "local ethnic forms and strains from African, Indian, Malayan and Portuguese origin, as is still apparent in the folk-lore, song and dance" (ibid., 28).

The freed slave-artists who had played European instruments in Portuguese households would have been well placed to form troupes and to play and teach their modern music, especially as played on the highly portable violin. Some worked as servants in the east-coast Sumatran Malay palaces at Peureulak, Langkat, Deli, Serdang, Asahan Siak Sri Indrapura, and offshore Lingga (see map 10.2), where they developed various local music and dance styles. In east Sumatra, the traditional *rebab* (bowed lute) and *serunai* (shawm) were probably replaced by the European *biola* and *akordion* (accordion) in transplanted genres such as *dendang saying*, and the Malay *gandang ronggeng* (drum) and *tawak* (deep-rimmed gong) were maintained in *ronggeng* and *joget* ensembles as in the past (Sinar 1997, 85). Some freed slaves from Malacca settled in Tugu, an enclave in Batavia on Java, where a style of the Malay-Portuguese *kroncong* genre developed (Kornhauser 1978, 112–15).[30] Like *kroncong* and other related genres, Malay *kapri*-style melodies that were (and remain) in European major and minor keys and featured mainly tonic and dominant harmonies were played on the European violin or sung in Malay style to partly improvised Malay quatrain verses and were punctuated in fixed Malay-style cycles by (frame) drums, and in some non-*kapri* genres, by gongs.

Thus, from the seventeenth century onward, genres that had their genesis in Malay-Portuguese contact expanded their repertory throughout the Malay world, including in the main rulers' courts on the coasts of north and east Aceh, North Sumatra's east and west coasts (see map 10.2), and in insular Riau, as well as in the many subsidiary great houses of the petty royals. They were adapted to local conditions in each center and are still performed as *Melayu asli* genres to this day.[31] The culture of the Portuguese, the region's first European colonial power, apparently had a much more extensive impact on Malay music and dance than the later colonial arrivals, the Dutch and the British.[32]

Map 10.2 Past royal centers in and around the Strait of Malacca

THE SPREAD OF THE VIOLIN AND COUPLES
DANCING TO THE PASISIR SUMANDO COAST

Given the probability that the violin and its harmonically generated melody with *ronggeng*-style couples dancing originally developed in west-coastal Malaya, how was it then transplanted to east Sumatra and thence to Sumatra's west coast?

There are several possible scenarios. The oldest known Malay reference to the *biola* is a clause in an early-eighteenth-century Acehnese literary work (*Hikayat Malem Dagang*), which reads: "They struck up the *kudang* [drums] and the *kucapi* [plucked zither] and the *biola* gave a wailing sound."[33] The violin could have been transplanted to Barus from Aceh, under whose hegemony Barus and other west-coastal towns labored in the seventeenth and eighteenth centuries.[34] However, the context described in the quotation does not suggest it was played in a *joget*-style performance.

The violin could also have been introduced to Barus directly from Malacca by sea, given that foreign traders living in this multicultural port are known to have visited Barus over the centuries (Van Basel 1761, in Kielstra 1887, 508–9).[35] However, there is little reason to believe that temporary residents such as traders exerted much energy in the development of local ceremonial and artistic pursuits, whereas the very legitimacy, mystical aura, and power of the courts in Barus depended on their promotion of the arts and ceremony. Normally only princes and their followers could afford to travel for adventure or to a new homeland, and only royal messengers could normally bear letters and diplomatic gifts for other royal personages. There may have been two-way artistic exchange between troupes of artists who traveled with their superiors between Barus and other Malay courts such as in Aceh, east Sumatra, Riau, or even Johor, where it was customary to have *joget* troupes perform couples dancing after a raja installation, wedding, or other ritual.[36] East- and west-coast Sumatran artists may have learned each other's repertory through their involvement in royal intermarriages and diplomatic missions between the two coastlines. A legendary Minangkabau princess once married into the east-coast court at Serdang, bringing West Sumatran *tari lilin* and *tari piring* (candle and plate dance) artist-servants with her, which explains why Serdang artists still perform the two dances to this day (Tengku Luckman Sinar, pers. comm., 1981).

The former twin courts at Barus were also in contact with the major Minangkabau and other Malay courts. The *sutan* or *kuria* of Barus Hilir, along with the rulers of Jambi, Palembang, Padang, Banten, Rokum, Aceh, Siak, Sungai Paguh, Inderagiri, Inderapura, and Pariaman, claimed mystical descent from the Yang Dipertuan of Pagaruyung (Drakard [1988] 2003, 212–16). The Barus Hilir *sutan* also claimed to have royal relatives in the courts at Mukomuko, Tarusan, Sorkam (ibid., 215), Lubo Tua, Surdang, and Tapus (ibid., 191).

Another strong possibility is that troupes of ordinary *joget/ronggeng* artists sailed up the great east-coast rivers from the villages around the east-coast Sumatran and offshore Riau palaces, then took the forest paths to the nearby palace of Pagaruyung, settling nearby, with a later generation eventually migrating to the west coast, and then sailing north to settle on the Pasisir Sumando. Indeed, the sources of the great Siak, Kampar, and Indragiri Rivers are located not far from the Pagaruyung palace, to which so many Sumatran courts paid special tribute from the seventeenth to the nineteenth century. Itinerant *joget* troupes regularly traveled up the Kampar River until the 1950s to perform in the villages along their banks (see below). Over the centuries the violin spread throughout West Sumatra, where villages in the highlands even accompany their plate and other dances on the violin and frame drums rather than the *talempong* (gong-chime) ensembles (see fig 10.7), as do many villages on the west coast.

Not surprisingly, *kapri* artists on the Pasisir Sumando coast share some of their repertory with similar ensembles along Sumatra's entire west coast, including the *gamad* bands in West Sumatra and the *badendang* and *japri* ensembles in the provinces of Bengkulu and Lampung respectively.[37] Possibly some song-dance troupes in the highlands migrated (*merantau*) to Pagaruyung's sister court at Indrapura on the southern Minangkabau coast. Moreover, the *Sejarah Chronicle* attributes the primal ancestor of the Raja di Hulu to Indrapura's subsidiary court at Tarusan (Drakard [1988] 2003, 283). From Indrapura the *joget* style could have spread up and down the west coast by sea, including to the famous port of Barus.

In support of this hypothesis, I need to digress momentarily and describe an itinerant *joget* troupe of four elderly female singer-dancers and four male instrumentalists who could still perform *joget* with a *biola* ensemble when I visited them in 1984 at Desa Teluk Bunga Ros, a village of Orang Melayu Pulau/Asli people on Penyelai Island at the mouth of the Kampar River.[38] These people are noted for their

Figure 10.7 Minangkabau plate dance with violin, Lubuksikaping, 1975

mystical powers and indigenous religion with a Hindu tinge.[39] During the 1930s, the then-young artists earned their living by sailing in a small boat up the Kampar River as far as the Pelalawan palace and thence to the river's source in Minangkabau, up the Kerinci River to the Kerinci palace, and across the sea and along the river Siak to the Siak palace. On the way they performed *joget* music and dance nightly in many villages, turning many male heads, and earning considerable amounts of money for their male manager.[40] Though they refused to admit it afterward, princes from the three palaces often danced with the female performers, and a Pelalawan prince even fell in love with a charismatic artist named Minah, following her for many weeks as she traveled and performed (Bp. Tenas Effendy, who heard the story in Betung and near Pelalawan, and from Mak Minah herself in 1984, pers. comm., 1984). Part of the proceeds of the performances had to be paid to the palaces when their tax collectors visited their village.

The artists at Bunga Ros described how in their youth they had heard *orkes Melayu* ensembles and learned to play the violin, *gambus* (plucked lute), *akordion* (accordion), and the gong. They accompanied some visiting "Malay opera" (*toneel Melayu*, *bangsawan*, and *Dul Muluk*) troupes that included *joget* and *zapin* folk dancing in their shows, and they learned the song-dances by imitation and later invented their own. Their *joget* ensemble comprised a *biola* (played resting on the left side of the chest), *ketawak* (small gong), *ketapung* (drum), and frame drums (*tamur* and *bebana*).[41] In the 1980s, they still performed *begendong* (lit. "swaying in a hammock") lullaby rituals and songs at weddings and baby thanksgivings, including *kapri*-style songs titled "Dendang Sayang," "Serampang Pantai," "Mak Inang," "Lagu Dua," and "Lagu/Tari Piring Topeng" ("Plate Mask Song/Dance"), variants of which are also performed on Sumatra's east and west coasts.[42] However, beginning around the 1950s the government frequently banned such traveling troupes from operating on the grounds that they caused marriage breakups and even riots. In Deli (in present-day Medan) and areas around other former palaces along the east coast, it was still common until the 1980s to request and receive a permit for *joget* entertainment at weddings (Goldsworthy 1979; Teuku Amin Ridwan, pers. comm., 1990). Today *joget* permits are given only for Indonesian Independence Day celebrations (17 August) under strict police control (Mauly Purba, pers. comm., Medan, 2006).

At least until the 1950s, then, troupes of *joget* singer-dancers and *biola* ensemble players sailed up Sumatra's east-coast rivers to Minangkabau, enjoying an exciting life of travel as they entertained local men from palace and village who wanted to sing and dance with the female *joget* singer-dancers in couples, with violin and Malay drum music accompaniment.[43] From West Sumatra, as my Orang Melayu Asli informants said, some troupes eventually took sea boats to the Pasisir Sumando coast, thereby introducing the Malay *joget* genre and repertory in such towns as Barus, where it became known locally as *sikambang kapri*.

Since the early 1960s the government has chosen to develop the *sikambang kapri* genre in towns such as Sibolga, Barus, and Singkil to become one of the main cultural symbols of the Pasisir Sumando population. Not only does the genre display distinctively local artistic qualities but it also shares parts of its repertory with the greater Malay world. Government, the media, and corporations have found *kapri* attractive because it presents young men and women in traditional Malay costumes who dance gracefully and politely in couples and exchange entertaining, witty, or erotic verses in Malay, a language that most Indonesians understand. It comprises scores of songs performed in slow, medium, or fast tempo; tuneful vocal and violin melodies with typical Malay rhythms and cyclic drum patterns; varied juxtapositions of dance sequences; standard dance motives and steps; and exquisitely elegant hand and wrist movements. *Sikambang kapri* is an attractive Pasisir Sumando identity marker.

Over the decades, new floor plans and choreographies have continually been created, including for story-based dances such as the Sumando umbrella dance accompanied by the "Penang Island Song." The substitution of all-male for mixed adult *kapri* couples dancing, which aims to preserve social decency and female modesty, is maintained in most rural and urban villages at the time of this writing. Some modern choreographies that focus on novel hip movements or are otherwise influenced by international pop dance styles are seen by some as verging on the unacceptably erotic, while the more restrained choreographies are broadly regarded as touchingly *halus* (refined, pure, harmonious), *lembut* (soft, polite, gentle), leisurely, and acceptable.

||||

Besides the Muslim devotional forms, the two main music and dance genres—the *sikambang Melayu asli* and the *sikambang kapri*—are performed at local life-event celebrations to this day. In colonial times village artists performed both genres on the outskirts of the palaces as contributions to a *raja* installation or other royal event, and village men danced with itinerant troupes of *joget* singer-dancers for their entertainment.

From the 1950s onward, religious sensibilities ensured that only adult male couples would perform the *kapri* repertory. At the same time, government corporations and the media made efforts to redevelop select mixed-couples song-dances for official functions. The *asli* genres—including the emotional *sikambang laui'* songs that are sung at high volume and high pitch at sea, the formal lullabies sung at weddings and thanksgivings, the laments sung when a baby dies, the all-night storytelling, the shamanic music for various kinds of magic, and the instrumental music—were still performed in the 1970s and 1980s, but mainly by elderly artists who had only a few young students and followers. But it was the mixed-gender *sikambang kapri* song-dances that the government chose as the main Pasisir Sumando identity marker in the 1970s, and they continue to represent the area in national and regional celebrations and tours with the support of corporations and the media.

Pasisir Sumando culture has distinctive musical attributes, especially the loud, high-pitched, melismatic *suara jantan* singing style and some items of the repertory, including the *asli* songs associated with the local Sikambang legend and the *kapri*-style songs that tell the Penang Island and other love- or baby-centered stories. The *sikambang kapri* genre shares some stylistic characteristics and repertory items with the harmonic Malay music and dance of some other parts of the Malay world, including the rest of Sumatra's west coast, North Sumatra's east coasts, the Riau Archipelago, and southwest-coastal Malaya. The ceremonies at which the songs and song-dances are performed reflect the people's historical orientation toward the sea, outward-looking attitudes and pursuits, links between the former dual courts of Barus and other courts in Sumatra, and the mix of populations, especially from coastal Minangkabau.

Of the various scenarios that can explain the enigma of *sikambang kapri's* origin and history, the most likely is the following. The genre's prototype developed from Malay-Portuguese contact in Malacca during the Portuguese colonial era, when Malay solo or duo-response singing and cyclic drum rhythmic patterns were combined with Portuguese violin and harmonic ideas and a mix of Malay and Portuguese dance forms. Freed Portuguese slave-musicians who settled in areas around the many small Malay courts to the south and east of Malacca spread the style in the courts and villages of the western Malay world. Over the generations the style was transformed into various regional genres that eventually became known under the umbrella term *lagu/tari Melayu*. Adventurous East Sumatran princes, their diplomats and/or village *joget/ronggeng* troupes transported the genre with the *biola* up the great rivers to the palace at Pagaruyung, around which they settled and developed a local style appropriate to the area. From there the genre spread westward by land to the Minangkabau coast and northward by sea to the Sumando coast, where it developed further variants of the style based on local *sikambang asli* singing, with yet further variants of the style, including *gamad* and *japri*, developing to the south. Thus interaction between the courts, trading and migrant communities, and itinerant artistic troupes resulted in continual exchanges of repertory and development of new songs and dances. In this way, select songs and dances from the various Malay coastal areas of Sumatra may have spread, in continually varying forms, around the Malay world of Sumatra and beyond.

ACKNOWLEDGMENTS

I am grateful to Bp. Djohan Arifin Nasution of the Department of Education and Culture office in Medan, who helped organize and accompanied us on our field trip to Sibolga and other parts of North Sumatra in December 1971. On our visit along the coast from Sibolga to Barus in 1981, we were assisted by Prof. Dr. A.P. Parlindungan, rector of the University of North Sumatra, USU; dean of arts Prof. Dr. Amin Ridwan; Bp. Nasrul Zahiruddin; and Bp. Kamarul Djaman. We warmly thank the *sikambang kapri* singers Ibu Rosihan Anwar and Bp. Badul Nifa; *biola* player Harris Fadila; frame-drum player Ayidin Efendi; and Bp. Daulai, Bp. Matondang, and Bp. Salihin of the Sanggar Kesenian Pesisir Tapanuli Tengah (Central Tapanuli West-Coast Art Troupe). During our 1981 fieldwork in Sibolga, Sorkam, and Bottot, we were privileged to be able to interview the 102-year-old musician Bp. Tamar Sinaga about the musical history of the palaces and the villages. Bp. Rajoki Nainggolan, and Bp. Jasmuni of the Sanggar Sikambang Sekata Bottot Sitilit Telukroban (Sikambang Troupe of Bottot and Telukroban, centered in Sorkam) helped us record *sikambang kapri* performances by male dancers in Bottot, including "Tari Pinang Lagu Pulau Pinang," "Tari Selendang Lagu Dua," and "Lagu Sampaya," which accompanied the "Tari Sapu Tangan" (alias "Tari Bungkus"), and a long session of *sikambang kapri* singing, with participants wittily answering one another's song verses (*membalas pantun*). Members of the Pasaribu family in Barus were very helpful, especially Bp. Zainal Arifin Pasaribu, Haji Syarif (chair of the Fansuri organization), Bp. Sidangtua, and Bp. Nawar Ramawie (the head of the local Radio Republik Indonesia office). I am also grateful to Bp. Maswar, an expert *singkadu* player born in Jago-jago, whose playing we recorded with Bp. Samsur in the University of North Sumatra's Department of Ethnomusicology in Medan. On the east coast, Ibu Maimunah Mochtar of Binjai, who in her youth was a professional singer and violin and Malay *rebab* (spike fiddle) player in theater performances, was most informative, as were her *gandang* player Bp. A. Manan and *akordion* player Bp. Tengku Rahmat Zainal Abidin in 1971. The late historian and descendant of the sultanate of Serdang, Bp. Dr. Tengku Luckman Sinar, who was also the patron of his Serdang-style performing arts troupe, assisted us greatly in our several recording trips from 1971 to 2003 in and around Medan. The choreographer and promoter of Lingga-Daik palace and village dances, Ibu Raja Katiga (alias Raja Kartija), was also a most helpful informant in Tanjung-pinang, Riau, in 1980 and 1981.

11

THE MANDAILING RAJA
TRADITION IN PAKANTAN

This chapter focuses on the social role, aesthetic thought, and ritual practice of the ceremonial music in the village complex of Pakantan in south Tapanuli, as we experienced it in 1971, 1972, and 1978. Much of its content is based on testimonies given to us by local female and male musicians and elders in 1978 and by members of the Pakantan diaspora in Medan, which we also visited several times during the 1970s and 1980s.[1] The testimonies were about their traditional philosophy, veneration of nature and the ancestors, visual art and design, and performing arts. I also draw on nineteenth-century colonial reports and on field recordings. Although the people wrote tree-bark books (*pustaha*) in their own script (*urup tulak-tulak*), historical records before the nineteenth century are rare. Mandailing bards, however, tell many myths and legends, some of which resemble those of their neighbors.[2]

Pakantan is situated in the Bukit Barisan mountain range near the provincial border between North Sumatra and West Sumatra and is part of the cooler upstream area known as Mandailing na Menek (lit. "Small Mandailing"), which contrasts with the warm, downstream alluvial plains in the north, called Mandailing Godang (lit. "Great Mandailing") (see map 11.1). Pakantan has all the hallmarks of an isolated valley of village hamlets (*huta*)—sweeping views of the surrounding mountains, crystal-clear streams, thick forests surrounding the people's small vegetable plots and coffee plantations, and moderately warm days and cool nights.[3] Unlike Mandailing Godang, villages in Mandailing na Menek were until recently connected to

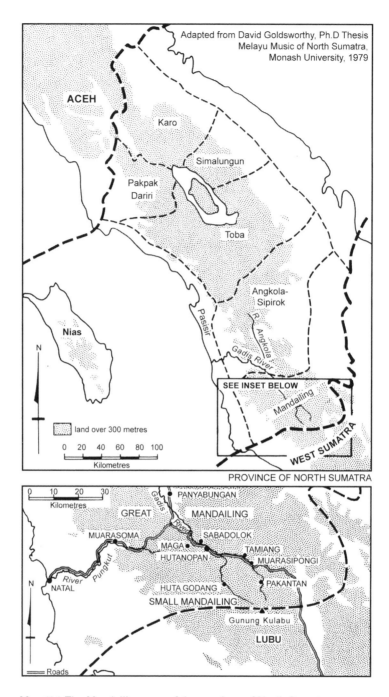

Map 11.1 The Mandailing area of the province of North Sumatra

the neighboring valleys only by footpaths and the occasional road. When neighbors from other valleys wanted to visit, they walked up the paths to the mountain tops and paused before descending to listen for the sound of a ritual orchestra below, which told them if a ceremony was in progress. If there was, the music (*uning-uningan*) drew them magically and irrevocably toward the source of sound. Even if they wished to resist, they could not, due to the alluring mystical power of the musical sound wafting from afar.

Indeed, music is perceived as being loveliest when it is heard from afar (*onak nidege siandao*), when its conflicting parts melt into a unified whole. On listening close up, one hears all the interesting detail of the interacting contemporaneous parts—the colotomic metallic percussion texture, the free-meter oboe melody, the calls of a human voice, and the rhythmic and tonal dualism, triadism, and other diversity of the drum sounds within the overall unity of the ensemble sound.

Like human beings, the ancestral and nature spirits are drawn like a magnet to the source of sound, but they are most attracted by the series of cyclic drum rhythms (*irama*) that they recognize in successive pieces. It is forbidden to change the basic rhythms and their sequence in a ceremony, lest the spirits not recognize the ancestral rhythms and fail to attend. Each *irama* is designed to address either the spirits or the spirits and a group of humans. Thus, if *irama idengs ideng* (rhythm for the spirits to come down) is played, it fulfills the spiritual purpose of requesting the spirits to attend and bless the ceremony, while if the *irama gondang raja-raja* (chieftains' drum rhythm) is played, it welcomes both the spirits and the senior descendant of the *raja* (chieftain) of Pakantan's founding clan (*marga*), the Lubis, who dances in the presence of the spirits and acquires some of their *hasaktian* (mystical power).

According to the ceremonial leaders—the shamans, male elders (*namora natoras*), and male and female musicians—their weddings, funerals, and clairvoyant rituals in the *huta* are reenactments of the traditions of the ancestors as they were practiced in the eighteenth and early nineteenth centuries before the people converted to Islam and were colonized by the Dutch, that is, before the Padri war of 1816–33.[4] Thus the people refer to their ceremonial music, which is always performed by one of three types of drum ensemble—the *gordang sambilan, gordang lima*, and *gondang dua*—as "music transmitted across the generations" (*uning-uningan di ompunta na parjolo sundut i*) (Nasution 2007, 26).[5] Their beliefs combine the native *perbegu* veneration of the spirits or souls of the ancestors and nature with Mahayana Buddhist and Hindu ideas transplanted from India to the former Buddhist centers of the interior at Batunadua and Portibi in Padang Lawas, south Tapanuli, discussed below.

CULTURAL HISTORY

Communication between most upstream Mandailing village complexes was difficult until the latter part of the twentieth century; consequently, the upstream Mandailing na Menek communities varied from one another in some aspects of their rituals, music, and dance.[6] The style of the artistic and ritual practices in Pakantan, nevertheless, closely resembles those in Huta na Godang but differs in several ways from those in Tamiang and Panyabungan.[7] The *adat* (traditional customs) and history of the entire area, however, are essentially similar; for example, the Mandailing na Menek experience of Islamization and Dutch colonization parallels that of both Mandailing Godang and the neighboring Angkola and Sipirok. The rest of Mandailing also shares its cultural history with that of the Angkola and the Sipirok people living to the north and east of Kotanopan.

The members of the main Mandailing *marga*—the Lubis, Nasution, Lintang, Hasibuan, Kotalanca, and Hutagambir clans—speak dialects of the Mandailing Batak language.[8] While most other Batak groups (the Toba, the Karo, the Pakpak-Dairi, and the Simalungun) were converted to Christianity from the mid- to the late nineteenth century, the Mandailing, the Angkola, and the Sipirok are mainly Muslim, originally having been forcibly converted by the Wahhabi-inspired Padri forces who entered Mandailing na Menek from the Minangkabau heartland around 1810.[9] They therefore see themselves as quite separate from the northern Batak, though they recognize that their primal ancestor was born there, on the western shore of Lake Toba.

The Dutch military arrived in 1821, took administrative control in 1835, and a Dutch *controleur* assumed administrative and judicial charge in 1895 with Kotanopan as the administration's center. Gradually, many *raja* lost their political and administrative power to the Dutch, retaining only their ceremonial authority and the trappings of power.[10] Despite this power shift, many cultural expressions of the customary law and kinship system Dalian Na Tolu (*adat*) were still apparent in the villages of Mandailing na Menek when we visited them in the 1970s. The "three pillars" (*dalian natolu*) of the exogamous kinship system are emphasized on ritual occasions by the division between the host and party (*kahanggi*), the wife-givers and kinship superiors (*mora*), and the wife-receivers and workers at the ceremony (*anak bora*).

In fact, in the 1980s the pre-Muslim culture in Pakantan was still alive and well. The culture was tinged with linguistic and popular religious elements of Saivite Buddhism and coexisted with Muslim-associated culture and arts of the Buginda (a petty royal descendant). The Buddhist "spiritual home" of the Mandailing, the Angkola, and the Sipirok at Batunadua and Portibi (in Padang Lawas, south Tapanuli) left ruins of at least sixteen brick temples and stupas that survive today (e.g., see fig.

Figure 11.1 Mural of dancing girls at Bahal 2, Portibi

11.1). It was probably part of the ancient kingdom of Panai (on the river Panai) and a dependency of Sriwijaya, which became independent in or before the thirteenth century (De Casparis and Mabbett 1992, 322).

Before the impact of European settlement and the Islamization of the area, the people comprised three social classes: the nobility, commoners, and slaves, the last of whom were usually members of the tribal, nomadic Lubu people, who lived in forested areas (H. Mangaraja Oloan, b. 1904 in Panyabungan, and Haji Abdul Aziz, b. 1911 in Tamiang, pers. comm., 1978).[11] The peoples' lives revolved around a system of rituals that included weddings (*horja siriaon*), funerals (*horja siluluton*), and clairvoyant ceremonies led by the *sibaso* (a male or female shaman). The patrilocal society confined women to the home, and their artistic pursuits included ritual dancing, lullaby (*bue-bue*) singing, and the playing of *gambang* (xylophone) and Jew's harp music. Young women were cloistered in their *bagas podoman* (traditional homes) under the watchful care of an elderly woman (*raja bujing*). Around his chosen girl's home at night, a young man traditionally played the soft, magically powerful *tulila* (*padi*-stalk flute) to attract her attention, if she was of the right *marga*, after which the courting couple would sing love poetry (*ende-ende*) to each other (Ibu Haji Maksum Lubis, pers. comm., 1978).[12] Males also learned the art of self-defense (*poncak sile*) from a young age. Men and women told legendary stories (*turi-turian*) in chant-like melody. A range of Muslim-associated songs and dances were also popular, including *nasit* and *kasidah* since the 1960s, with their devotional song texts and optional frame-drum accompaniment by male or female groups.

As leader of the *adat* and owner of the *pusaka* (heirlooms of the ancestors), the *raja* was the ceremonial, administrative, and judicial head of the small, local community. His grazing lands supported herds of buffalos, which were sacrificed at important ceremonial functions. His "great house" (*bagas borlang* or *bagas na godang*) was situated in a position high in the village complex to catch the freshest water from the stream that ran down the slope past the house. His symbolic color was gold or yellow, which contrasted prominently with the traditional Mandailing color system (*bona bulu*) of white, black, and red. One of his many functions was to preside over rituals and interclan meetings in a decorated, open-walled council hall (*sopo godang* or *sopo gordang*) situated next to a square in an elevated position in the village where the judicial court was located.

This council hall contained the *gordang sambilan* (nine drums) orchestra, comprising nine tuned drums in addition to metal percussion and double-reed wind instruments (see fig. 11.2). When the *raja* died, he was entitled to a large-scale funeral at which many buffalos were slaughtered and the highest orchestral status symbol, the *gordang sambilan*, was played for the dancing. Only the *raja* or his descendant could

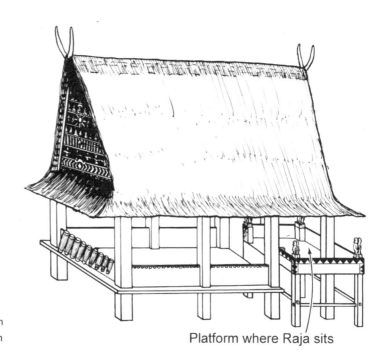

Figure 11.2 A *sopo gordang* showing a set of nine drums (*gordang sambilan*) and a raised platform for the *raja*, Pakantan

Platform where Raja sits

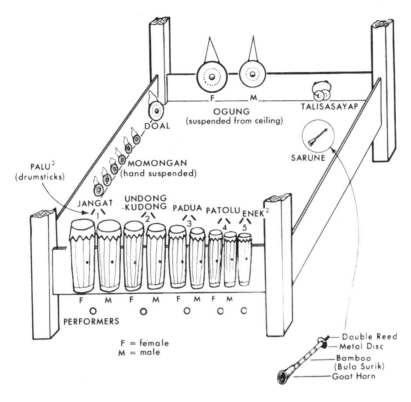

Figure 11.3 Detail of a *gordang sambilan* ensemble, Pakantan

give permission for a buffalo sacrifice and for a *gordang sambilan* performance on great ceremonial occasions (*horja na godang*). At minor ceremonies of commoners (*horja na menek*), only lesser animals such as goats and chickens were permitted to be consumed and only the two-drum *gondang* orchestra played. Shamans (*sibaso*) interpreted the *pelebegu* beliefs based on the veneration of the ancestors and the spirits of nature, pantheism, and the practice of magic. The rituals aimed to serve the supernatural beings, the *raja*, the clan elders (*namora natoras*), and the wider community.

Before the twentieth century, the lack of mobility and communication between villages meant that the people led a relatively isolated and culturally intact life. They adhered to a self-sufficient mystical worldview that pervaded and explained all aspects of experience. Musical expression, for example, was inseparable from ancestral religious belief and ceremony, the social hierarchy, the political and judicial systems, and the other traditional artistic expressions: the visual arts and dance and associated symbolism. Religious thought and practice were based on a belief in the essential unity of existence and in the dualistic and ternary aspect of reality, which explained the processes of creation and re-creation.

The pre-Muslim cosmology and social organization in Mandailing embody the notion that life is characterized by eternal tensions between sets of dualisms that are both opposite and complementary, though in some cases a third structure is added to the dyad to make a triad. The anthropologist Claude Lévi-Strauss studied dualism across cultures and concluded that its structure was either diametric or concentric (1963, 133), with the latter actually having a ternary nature, since an outer circle enclosing an inner circle contrasts with the open space encircling it.[13] This kind of dual organization is "in many instances (and perhaps in all) actually an inextricable mixture of the three types. . . . Triadism and dualism are inseparable, since dualism is never conceived of as such, but only as a 'borderline' form of the triadic type" (Lévi-Strauss 1963, 151). Although the terms "dualism" and "ternary structure" are not used in Pakantan, the people refer to dualistic and ternary ideas, which are imbued in their culture.

The most basic dualism in Pakantan thought is the male-female relationship associated not only with people but also with animals and even inanimate objects such as musical instruments, especially drums and gongs. It is symbolized by the ancestral lingam-yoni stone in the main graveyard on the outskirts of Pakantan (see fig. 11.4) that rumbles in warning when danger approaches (which reportedly occurred during World War II). The stone is probably a survival of Indian cults that were once active in the area, as evidenced by the remains of the Mahayana Buddhist temples and stupas at Portibi. Paul Mus (1933) proposed that the Hindu cult of Siva, with the lingam as his icon, was molded onto the tradition of local earth gods. The yoni on which the lingam stood received sacral fluid poured over the lingam, and together they symbolized the fertilized earth.

The dualisms and triadisms that the village elders and artists choose to emphasize in their explanations of the structure and aesthetics of the performing and visual arts are exemplified in the structure of the three instrumental ensembles and the visual arts, for example, in the pair of "female" and "male" flutes (*suling boru* and *suling jantan*) and the dualistic and triadic groups of drums explained below.

The concept of dualism in unity is also represented in the continuous geometric designs painted on traditional Mandailing houses and in many other aspects of Mandailing life.[14] The two pairs of two-faced protective ancestral figures carved in wood or in stone on the platform of Parlindungan Lubis's *sopo gordang* in Pakantan possess qualities of sexual ambiguity or dualistic unity (see fig. 11.5). They possess "the enigmatic quality of an embryo" (Holt 1967, 25), with their relatively large heads and only vaguely differentiated limbs.

The most complete symbol of pre-Islamic thought in Pakantan is the artistic design on the gables (*tutup ari*) of a ritual or other traditional house (see fig. 11.6). The design and its attributed meanings vary from village to village, but it is always based

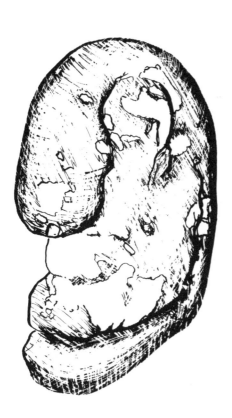

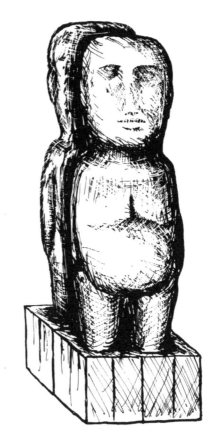

Figure 11.4 An ancestral lingam-yoni stone in a graveyard, Pakantan

Figure 11.5 A wooden ancestral figure on a *sopo gordang*, Pakantan

on the idea of dualism in unity. This includes the dualism of the earth, on the one hand (as symbolized by the design's mountain shape and the motifs of the buffalo head, the half coconut shell, and the scales, together with their low positions on the gable, their blackness, and their femaleness), and the heavenly bodies, on the other hand, namely, the sun, the moon, and the stars (together with their high positions, whiteness, and maleness).[15] The half coconut is a symbol of prosperity, hospitality, water, and the earth's fecundity. The scales are an earthly measuring agent, representing justice, security, and harmony on earth and in the cosmos. But the single most important symbol is the buffalo, which is represented twice on the gable design, both as a stylized buffalo head and as a pair of horns at the vertex of the gable. The buffalo, portrayed in black, is a symbol of the earth and its fertility.[16] Its moon-shaped horns are compared to an umbrella, which gives protection from the sun.[17] It is also a symbol of vital power, a link between heaven and earth, for the buffalo is believed to serve as a mount upon which important deceased people are transported to the

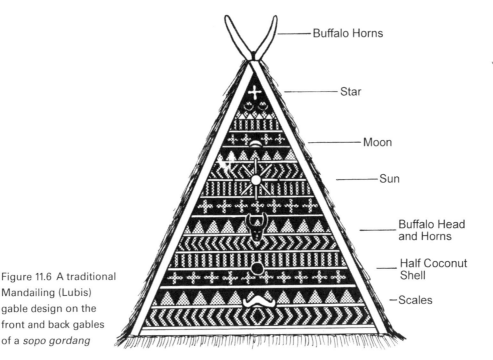

Buffalo Horns

Star

Moon

Sun

Buffalo Head
and Horns

Half Coconut
Shell

Scales

Figure 11.6 A traditional
Mandailing (Lubis)
gable design on the
front and back gables
of a *sopo gordang*

world of the spirits. The main sacrificial animal at important funerals is therefore the buffalo, which is symbolically linked to the *gordang sambilan* drum set.

With dualistic forces continually at work, the potential for instability and overt expressions of conflict are inherent in all contexts, including the artistic and the social. Individuals therefore have the moral responsibility to subsume conflicting elements into a *damé* (well-ordered, harmonious) state. Music, especially ensemble music, reflects the prevailing philosophical and belief system and exemplifies how conflicting musical-syntactical elements and emotive connotations aroused by the instrumental sounds may be resolved into a state of musical order and unity.[18]

Ritual was, and is still, based on a cosmological worldview and is geared to the agricultural cycle. The main transcendental rites are associated with death and fertility. Initial contact between human beings and the spirits/souls (*tondi*) of the ancestors and nature are the sets of drums, which play specific rhythms of invocation. Music, with its precise religious and social-hierarchical connotations, plays an integral part in ceremony, which is seen as a means of normalizing a discordant situation or event.

In the event of a death, a well-organized series of ceremonies enables the community to come to terms with loss. Traditionally, these ceremonies also provide the means for the soul of the deceased to journey to the next world. In cases where it is believed a supernatural being has been offended, thus allowing sickness or other calamities to occur, the offense is appeased by contacting the spirit world with music on the most sacred of instruments, the drum, under the guidance of a shaman or his or her representative. After providing the spirit with offerings (e.g., the masticatory *sirih* with lime and leaves of the piper betel, fried corn, and banana-leaf tips), specific cyclic drum rhythms are played in a strictly repetitive fashion with interlocking melodic patterns on the metallophones, a solo wind instrument and, optionally, a vocalist, with the latter two components being governed to a much higher degree than the others by the improvisational whim of the performer. The main musical dualism, then, occurs between the rigidly unvarying tunings and rhythmic patterns of the drums and metallophones, on the one hand, and the ornamented, variably intoned, and rhythmically free wind and vocal parts, on the other.

The three ceremonial ensembles are believed to act as an intermediary between the divine and the human worlds. As has been mentioned, the deities, who are said to recognize the special sonic power of the loudly piercing *sarune buluh* (single-reed "bamboo *sarune*"), or *saleot,* and the set ritual drum rhythms and kettle-gong cycles, are thereby attracted and may decide to descend and be present at the ceremony.[19] To be efficacious, the ensembles have to be complete, and the basic drum and gong rhythms have to be played in exactly the same way as each generation learns them from the other: change is not tolerated.

The Mandailing *sarune buluh* (bamboo *sarune*), which is played in the *gondang* and the two types of *gordang* ensembles, denotes a single-reed instrument, although the *sarune* in other Batak areas denotes a double-reed instrument. A percussion lamella reed is cut into the mouthpiece above a disk made of bone, and the lower part of the bamboo tube, into which four front finger holes are cut, fits into a conical flare made of buffalo horn.

The main ensemble repertoire for all the major ceremonies comprises the same five main musical rhythms/pieces (*irama*), while six other rhythms are reserved for specific parts of funerals, weddings, and morale-boosting ceremonies. All may be played on the three different grades of orchestra, the choice of which is governed by the class and social status of the feast-giver. The basic difference between these three ensembles is the type and number of drums used and therefore the dynamic intensity attained in performance: the orchestra with the highest status has the greatest carrying power and thus the highest potential to attract people and spirits from afar to travel to the source of the sound.

As the drums are the only distinguishing component of the three ensemble types, they are clearly the most important of all the instruments, musically and spiritually.[20] All three instrumental groups are otherwise identical, consisting of the *sarune buluh,* an optional vocal part, and a metallophone section comprising a pair of relatively large

Figure 11.7 A Mandailing *gandang dua* group, Medan, 1977

suspended gongs. The gongs are an *ogung induk* or *ogung dadaboru* "female" gong of about forty-eight centimeters in diameter and an *ogung jantan* or *ogung pangiring*, a "male" "accompanying" gong of about forty-three centimeters in diameter. The larger size of the "female" instruments may be due to the lingam-yoni connection: that the human vagina, being a potentially large cavity, can be penetrated by the relatively small lingam.[21] The groups also contain a small suspended kettle-gong (*doal*); two to six hand-suspended, narrow-rimmed, small kettle-gongs of varying pitch (*momongan* or *mongmongan*); and a pair of hand cymbals (*talisasayap* or *talisasayat*).

MAJOR CEREMONIES

As only the *raja* normally had the authority and wealth to sacrifice buffaloes, the *gordang sambilan* was played only at major ceremonies, funerals, and weddings, in the presence of the *raja* or his descendant. From the early twentieth century onward, however, rich merchants were occasionally given permission to sacrifice buffaloes, wear relatively high grades of traditional dress and ornaments, and employ *gordang sambilan* ensembles for weddings (audio example 11.1) and funerals of family members. To this day, the choice of the appropriate ceremonial level for a prospective feast-giver is decided at a formal meeting of clan elders (*namora natoras*) in the *sopo gordang*, presided over by the *raja*, who sits on his special layers of mats on a raised platform, with a protocol officer loudly announcing the series of events.

The nine wooden drums of the *gordang sambilan*, which are attached to the low wall of the *sopo gordang* (see fig. 11.2), are beaten with thunderous intensity by four or five performers with a drumstick in each hand.[22] In keeping with the idea of dualism in unity, the drums are arranged in four "sexual" pairs (with the larger drums designated "female" and the smaller ones "male"), plus a single drum (*enek-enek*, meaning "the little one," or "the child") to represent the unity—or product—of each pair. The largest, leading pair of drums is called *jangat* (lit. "to do something with pleasure"), while the second largest pair is called *undong kudong* (beginning to sound); the middle pair is called *padua* (the second) and the next smallest the *patolu* (the third).[23] The *undong kudong* pair usually begins a piece, followed by entries by the *padua* and the *patolu*; then the *jangat* comes in with its largely syncopated rhythmic variations, and finally the *enek-enek* enters with its more diverse, relatively free variations.

Pakantan musicians say that sets of *gordang* have always been made up of an odd number of drums, just as the number of buffaloes sacrificed at a ceremony has always amounted to an odd number. None cares to say how old the practice of playing nine, as opposed to five or seven, *gordang* might be. Nor does the literature clarify this point. In 1846, the Dutch East Indies representative T. I. Willer wrote that he had seen a set of drums of various sizes hanging in the hall of a headman's house, plus a valuable set of gongs and cymbals, and a *sarune*, but he did not specify how many drums constituted a set.[24] In 1895, another Dutch administrator, H. Ris, described an orchestra consisting of *gordang* "with nine different tones," plus an "agoeng," a set of "momongan," "talisasajah," and a "saroenei" (Ris 1895, 532). We know for certain, then, that the *gordang sambilan* assumed its present-day form at least as long ago as the late nineteenth century. Yet it presumably developed long before that, considering the time it would take for such an ensemble type to develop and become musically and symbolically established in the worldview and musical life of a community.

Some elders believe that the nine-*gordang* ensemble in Pakantan is an enlargement of an earlier norm of a seven-*gordang* set (*gordang pitu*), which are still said to exist in some areas today. The names of the second and third smallest pairs of drums in the *gordang sambilan*—*padua* (the second) and *patolu* (the third)—suggest that the *undong kudong* were once the largest pair, the *padua* the second largest, and the *patolu* the third largest. In the latter part of the nineteenth century, then, but possibly long before that, a pair of large *gordang* called *jangat* were probably added to the set of seven *gordang* without changing the original names of the drum pairs.

Since each single drum is seen to represent one clan or subclan, the addition of a pair of drums symbolizes the social acceptance of two new clans or subclans under the *raja's* jurisdiction. Thus the *gordang lima* (see figs. 11.8 and 11.9; an orchestra with five drums that is still occasionally played today for ceremonies involving magic) represents an early stage in the settlement of Pakantan, the *gordang pitu* a later stage, and the *gordang sambilan* the supposed final stage of clan settlement.

Five of the nine single drums of the *gordang sambilan* in Pakantan are said to represent the Nasution, Lintang, Hasibuan, Kotalanca, and Hutagambir clans, while three drums represent the dominant Lubis clan, including the Lubis Hutanopan, Lubis Singasora, and Lubis Pakantan subclans. One drum, however, represents the clan of the common overlord of them all—the *raja* or, today, his descendant or representative—who must also be a member of the Lubis clan, which dominates Pakantan society.

Funerals

The most important ceremony during the heyday of the *raja* institution was the funeral, a series of events intended to help the deceased reach the land of souls.[25] In 1783, William Marsden described the funeral of a Mandailing *raja* as follows:

> When a raja or person of consequence dies, the funeral usually occupies several months; that is, the corpse is kept unburied until the neighboring and distant chiefs or, in common cases, the relations and creditors of the deceased, can be convened, in order to celebrate the rites with dignity and respect. . . .
>
> When the relations and friends are assembled, each of whom brings with him a buffalo, hog, goat, dog, fowl or other article of provision, according to his ability, and the women, baskets of rice, which are presented and placed in order, the feasting begins and continues for nine days and nights, or so long as the provisions hold out. On the last of these days the coffin is . . . surrounded by . . . "howling ululantes" . . . whilst the younger persons of the family are dancing near it, in solemn movement, to the sound of gongs, *kalintangs*, and a kind of flageolet; at night it is returned to the house, where the dancing and music continues, with frequent firing of guns, and on the tenth day the body is carried to the grave, preceded by the *guru* or priest. . . .
>
> Mr. Charles Miller mentions his having been present at killing the hundred and sixth buffalo at the grave of a raja, in a part of the country where the ceremony was sometimes continued even a year after the interment; and that they seem to regard their ancestors as a kind of superior beings, attendant always upon them. (Marsden [1811] 1966, 387–89)[26]

When a *raja* died, the populace was informed by a musician beating a pair of *gordang jangat* to the rhythm called *bombat* (music example 11.1), repeated over and over, sometimes intensified by gunshots, until the members of the community arrived to extend their condolences to his family.

tong   tong   tong   tong   tong   tong   ge - dong

Music example 11.1 Bombat rhythm

When a free commoner died, however, a simple rhythm was played on a single *gordang*, a *tabuh* (a long mosque drum), or a gong.

accel............

f

Music example 11.2 Rhythm played to announce the death of a commoner. The same rhythm is still played in Pakantan today to announce a fire or a death.

In the sets of drum notations below (devised by A. P. Parlindungan and the author respectively), seven single timbres are shown (see music example 11.3), including two left-hand sounds, namely the *tampul*, literally a "blow" beaten with a stick in the performer's left hand, and a damped *tampul* where the right-hand side of the drum head is damped while the left hand beats the drum head with a stick. There are also five right-hand sounds, namely, the *topak* (lit. "be born") or hand-beat on the top of the right-hand drum head and damped on the left-hand end; a damped *topak* or sound made by finger-tapping the right-hand rim while the left-hand end is damped; an unnamed sound made by the fingers of the right hand double tapping near the head rim; an unnamed sound made by tapping the right-hand drum head; and an unnamed sound made by beating the shell with a stick.[27]

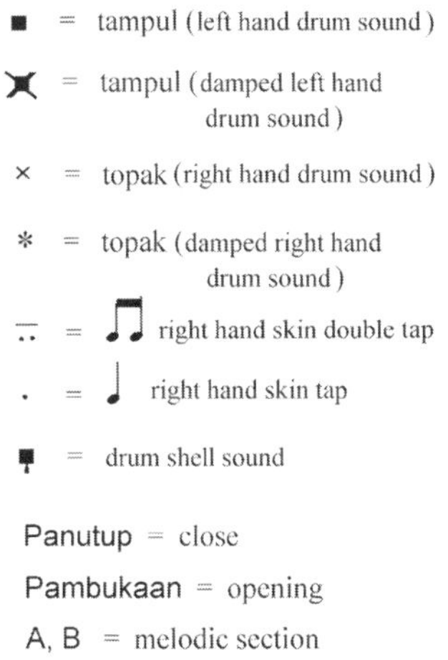

■   =   tampul (left hand drum sound)

✖   =   tampul (damped left hand
            drum sound)

×   =   topak (right hand drum sound)

✳   =   topak (damped right hand
            drum sound)

⁻⁻   =   ♫ right hand skin double tap

.   =   ♩ right hand skin tap

▮   =   drum shell sound

Panutup = close

Pambukaan = opening

A, B = melodic section

Music example 11.3
Legend of drum timbres
and structural terms
used in notations

Music example 11.4 shows the notation symbols used to identify and differentiate between each of the gong types, namely, the main gong (G1), secondary gong (G2), and *doal*.

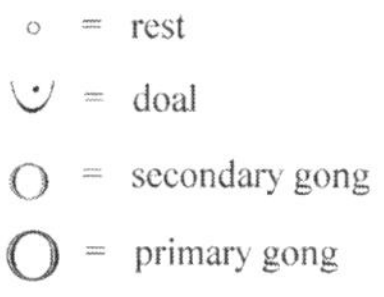

o   = rest

‿ = doal

◯ = secondary gong

◉ = primary gong

Music example 11.4 Legend of
gong symbols used in notations

During the days of feasting at a *raja*'s funeral, the clan members danced to the accompaniment of the *gordang sambilan* playing the standard repertoire. But when the *raja*'s corpse was finally carried in procession to the graveyard, a special "coffin rhythm" (*irama roto*, which also occurs as a piece called "Irama Roto-Roto"; music examples 11.5 and 11.6) was played; its basic motive (♪ ♩ ♩ ♩) was identical to that of the *raja*'s ceremonial dance (*tortor raja-raja*) when he was still alive.[28]

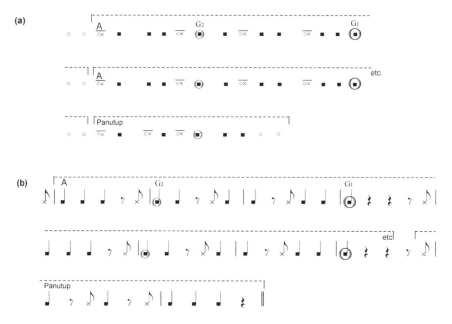

Music example 11.5 "Irama Roto-Roto" transcribed in (a) Parlindungan's script and
(b) the author's script

The other main motive (♪ ♩ ♩), comprising an upbeat followed by a unit of two notes, may be deemed incomplete, for it does not possess a third note as a "product" of the dualism as in the case of the main *raja* motive (♪ ♩ ♩ ♩).

Music example 11.6 "Irama Roto-Roto," as performed by a *gondang* ensemble in Pakantan (1978), transcribed in full music notation

Music example 11.6 Cont.

For light relief, a rhythm called "crazy tiger" (*irama sarama babiat*) is often played to accompany an amusing dance, called *tortor sarama*, by the *sibaso* or his representative (*bayo dato*). A fellow dancer serves as the shaman's chaperon, to make sure that when she or he enters a state of trance, nothing untoward happens—but if it does, the chaperon has to stop the dance immediately.[29]

"Irama Roto-Roto" is also played at "funerals" for tigers. Just as the *raja* is the king of a local settled area, so the tiger is regarded as the "king" or "queen" of unsettled areas, and therefore the tiger is entitled to have *gordang sambilan* music played at its funeral. When a dangerous tiger is caught, either by a hunting party or through shamanic practices, it is subjected to a ritual of judgment as to whether she or he has committed the sin (*salah*) of eating a human being or an animal, the verdict of guilt or innocence being originally pronounced by the *sibaso*, and then by the *raja*, or in modern practice, by the whole community led by the clan elders. If found guilty, the tiger is punished by being cut into pieces, which are buried (or, as it is termed, "planted") below a building constructed on stilts used for storing rice (*panje muran*), thereby transforming the tiger's body into an agent of fertility.

Clairvoyant Rituals

Second in status to the *gordang sambilan* is the *gordang lima* ensemble (audio example 11.2), normally kept in the house of the *sibaso* (a term that literally means "the word"), referring to a person who could read and write magic books and calendars, and who is a diviner and healer, a master of the arts of self-defense (*poncak sile*), a singer of legendary songs (*turi-turian*), and an expert in religious philosophy and white and black magic.[30] In addition to the usual wind, vocal, and metallophone instruments, the *gordang lima* consists of five single-headed drums that are graded in size and pitch, grouped into two pairs and a single small drum, and representing the Pakantan population when, generations ago, it comprised only five clans (see figs. 11.8 and 11.9).

Until the twentieth century, the *gordang lima* was used mainly for ceremonies held in the house of the *sibaso* or his or her representative, at the request of clients. She or he also chose propitious days for all important activities and officiated at life-event ceremonies at which the *gordang sambilan* and *gondang dua* were played. When the *raja* and the elders wished to obtain clairvoyant information, for example, about which side would win a certain local battle, the *sibaso* danced in a state of trance to the accompaniment of the *gordang lima* to drive out the *sibaso*'s own soul (*tondi*) and allow a *begu* (ghostly spirit) to enter him and answer the questions put through the medium of his or her voice. A piece of shredded bamboo attached to one of the drums sounded a magical buzzing noise as it was played. The *gordang lima* ensemble is still played, with the shredded bamboo buzzer, by Pakantan immigrants in the city

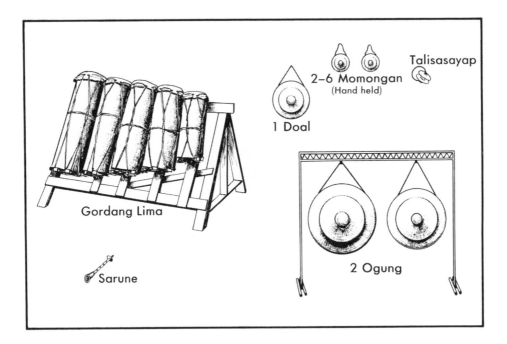

Figure 11.8 A five-drum ensemble, *gordang lima*

Figure 11.9 A *gordang lima* ensemble showing a set of 5 tuned drums played by a Mandailing group in Medan, 1972

of Medan today in a conscious effort to preserve their cultural heritage. However, since contacting the spirits through a shaman does not accord with Muslim beliefs, the *gordang lima* and associated mystical activity is, to all intents and purposes, virtually obsolete.

Free Commoners' Ceremonies

The *gondang dua* (alias *gondang*) ensemble was traditionally reserved for small weddings and funerals presented by free commoners (as opposed to slaves), at which the only animals consumed were goats, lambs, poultry, and/or fish, all of which cost much less than a buffalo. People of a variety of ranks and degrees of wealth also used the *gondang* for minor celebrations, for example, a baby's first birthday, a circumcision, or a house-warming ceremony, while the really materially poor, who could not even afford a *gondang* ensemble at their weddings and funerals, nurtured the spirits by hanging offerings from their houses.

Of the three ceremonial orchestras, therefore, the *gondang dua* (fig. 11.10) has the lowest social status. It comprises two small, double-headed drums (the female one being slightly larger than its male counterpart), again illustrating the religious theme of dualism in unity. Lacking a third drum to make up an odd number, however, it is philosophically less complete than the *gordang* ensembles.

Despite this association, some Pakantan musicians feel that this ensemble produces the most elegant balance of sound of the three. The *gondang dua* cannot, of course, rival the thunderous sonority of the *gordang* ensembles, which have the magical quality of being able to attract people from afar toward the source of the sound. But it is certainly superior to the *gordang* in terms of acoustic balance and clarity of sound texture. Moreover, its relatively subdued dynamic level allows the solo human voice to be heard above the instrumental sound, unlike in the *gordang sambilan* and *gordang lima*, where the dynamic intensity always drowns out any vocal part. The *gondang* ensemble also possesses greater potential than the *gordang* for musical subtlety and contrast of texture and dynamics between the drum, wind, metallophone, and optional solo vocal components therein.

Figure 11.10 A two-drum ensemble, *gondang dua*

Rhythms as Invocations

Each musical item on ceremonial occasions, whether played on a *gondang* or a *gordang* ensemble, is named after its *totop*, or fixed drum rhythm, and serves as an invocation. The first piece played at a ceremony is named after the drum rhythm called *irama jolo-jolo turun* (the rhythm asking the spirits to descend). If the basic rhythm of a piece is varied, it may not be immediately recognizable to its listeners, especially its transcendental listeners, and its effect of calling the spirits might therefore be lessened. Moreover, the repeated, unchanging drum patterns help provide a mesmerizing atmosphere in which the shaman can induce a state of trance, either in himself or in another mystically gifted individual who can then serve as a medium for the voice of a transcendental being. The basic drum timbres/rhythms of "Irama Jolo-Jolo Turun" as played on the *gondang dua* are notated below in A. P. Parlindungan's and the author's script (music examples 11.7a and 11.7b respectively) and a full musical notation of the beginning of the piece is given in example 11.8.

The piece is played in slow tempo. Its short motivic statements mostly contain an anacrusis: ♪♩. ♪♩♩♩ and ♪♩♩♩♩ with ♪♩♩ and ♪♩♩♩♩ being the most frequently used. A combined *tampul-topak* stroke (♩) occurs mainly on the first and third beats of the quadruple metric unit, the added intensity of this two-handed action reinforcing the metric beat. In line with the syntactic-musical dualism inherent in Pakantan's orchestral music, the relative freedom of the *sarune* line contrasts with the rigidity of the other parts in performance. Whereas the drums and the metallophones are stable and unchanging, the *sarune* line is whimsically variable in its intonation and rhythmic and melodic ideas, and alternation between long-held tones and ornamental passages.

The second piece played at a ceremony is "Irama Ideng-Ideng" (music example 11.9), meaning "rhythm praying that the spirits settle in." Its rhythm is based on the same motives as in "Irama Jolo-Jolo Turun," with ♪♩ and ♪♩♩♩♩ being the most prevalent. While the A sections of both "Jolo-Jolo Turun" and "Ideng-Ideng" are rhythmically the same, the B sections contain a different series of motives, with the same four timbres used in each motive. The double drum sounds ♩ and ♩ reinforce the meter by occurring mostly on the accented beat. As in all mystically potent pieces, the tempo is slow. When "Irama Ideng-Ideng" is played on the set of nine *gordang*, the basic rhythm played is the same as on the *gondang dua*, but it is accompanied by loud interlocking patterns on the other drums.

Only in the third piece does communal dancing begin, led by the host (*suhut*) and followed by his *mora* (the head of the relevant wife-giving clan). The piece is

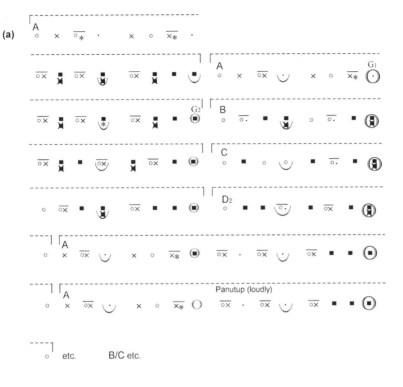

Music example 11.7 "Irama Jolo-Jolo Turun" transcribed in (a) Parlindungan's script and (b) the author's script

Music example 11.8 "Irama Jolo-Jolo Turun," as performed by Gunung Kulabu Kesenian Asli Mandailing, led by A. P. Parlindungan, transcribed in full music notation called "Irama Alap-Alap Tondi" (music example 11.10), meaning "rhythm calling the spirits." In this piece, only three motives (♪♩, ♪♩♩ and ♪♩♩♩) are used, in variable sequence, and the drum timbres are restricted to the *tampul* and the *topak* only. This strict prescription of motives and timbres, together with its slow tempo, strengthens the piece's function as a magic invocation (audio example 11.3).[31]

The simplest, shortest, and most aurally recognizable of all rhythms is the "Irama Raja-Raja" (music example 11.11), its title meaning "headman's rhythm." It consists of three motives (♩, ♪♩ and ♪♩♩♩), the last of which must be repeated. As the rhythm most firmly bound by traditional musical regulations, "Irama Raja-Raja" was regarded as very mystically potent. As in "Irama Roto-Roto," only the *tampul* and the *topak* timbres are played. In keeping with the previous four examples, the basic rhythm is almost never varied in performance and is always played in a slow tempo, in this case for the added reason of upholding the tradition of respect for and subservience to the office of *raja*. Its motivic character and restricted timbres closely resemble "Irama Roto-Roto" (discussed above), which is not surprising, as *roto* is the rhythm played at a *raja* funeral.

"Irama Raja-Raja" accompanies one of the most frequently performed Mandailing dances, *tortor raja-raja* (chieftain's dance). It is also called *irama saba-saba* (long scarf rhythm) because it is led (today) by a descendant of a *raja* wearing a symbolically important mystical and hierarchical emblem—the special *raja*-style shawl (*ulos*)—as he dances with the interclan elders (*namora natoras*). The *ulos* (an important symbol in all Batak ethnic groups) is draped around his neck and hangs below his knees. Holding the ends of the *ulos* loosely between his fingers, he moves it up or down on every second beat as he dances, lowering his legs slightly on the beat, and performing a variety of movements with both hands. After some time, the *ulos* is passed from one respected elder of the community to another, on receipt of which she or he is expected to dance.

The first four pieces are the most mystically powerful of all, easily recognizable by their distinctive drum rhythms. The fifth piece, "Irama Tua" ("Blessings Rhythm," music example 11.12), has a text that requests blessings from the spirits and is often performed with a tenor vocal part. Played in a moderately fast tempo, its *gondang dua* part contains the most complex rhythmic and timbral characteristics of the five pieces. One *gondang* player produces the basic (*totop*, "fixed") rhythm, while the other plays rhythms that vary (*mangalaluhon*) and interlock with one another. A comparatively wide range of *gondang* timbres (♩, ♩, ♩ and ♪) is used. In addition to the *tampul* and *topak* sounds, the drum stick strikes both the head (♩) and the shell (♩) of the drums. However, the shell-tapping mainly serves the rhythmic function of interlocking and stressing the offbeat.

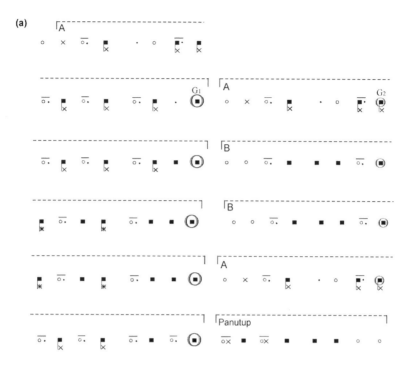

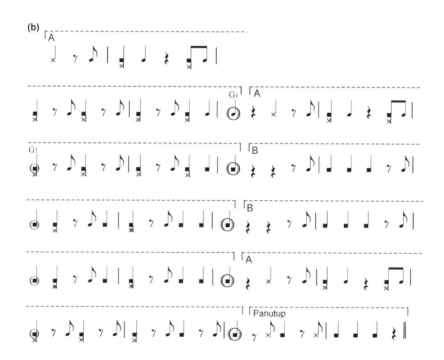

Music example 11.9 "Irama Ideng-Ideng" transcribed in (a) Parlindungan's script and (b) the author's script

(a)

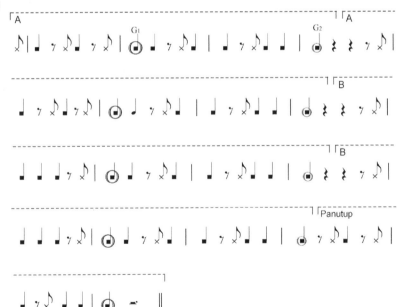

(b)

Music example 11.10 "Irama Alap-Alap Tondi"

(a)

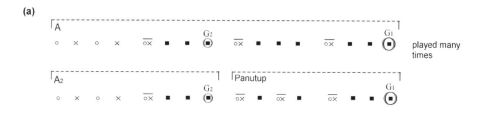

(b)

Music example 11.11 "Irama Raja-Raja"

(a)

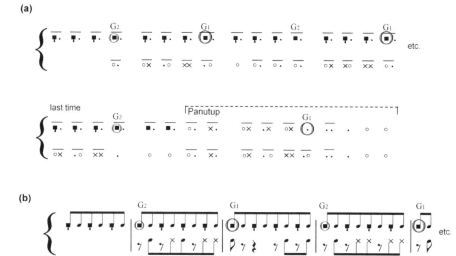

(b)

Music example 11.12 "Irama Tua"

The young unmarried members of the community then have the opportunity to take part in the ceremonial dancing, to the accompaniment of the piece "Irama Mandailing" (music example 11.13). The choice of partners is strictly regulated by a married woman (*raja bujing*), who sees to it that a woman does not dance with a man of the same clan, since marriage within the clan is taboo. While dancing, the women are *disembar* (protected) by the men, who dance in *manyembar* (protective) fashion; that is, they encircle the women "like an eagle encircling its prey." The female dancers, whose hands hold the edge of the long shawl (*ulos*) around their necks, are allowed to raise their hands to thigh, waist, or chest level, but no higher, while the men may raise their hands up to, or even higher than, shoulder level.

Music example 11.13 "Irama Mandailing"

As a dance (*tortor*) of great social importance because it may lead to marriage and human reproduction, *tortor Mandailing* is performed in a slow tempo. Its motivic structure is related to that of "Irama Raja-Raja," its similarity lying primarily in its use of the motive ♪ ♩ ♩ ♩. However, much more rhythmic variability is allowed in this piece than in "Raja-Raja," which should be regarded as the strict prototype of Pakantan-Mandailing cyclic rhythm. Moreover, it contains greater timbral variety than the others, using the ♩ ♩. ♩ stroke and the ♩ combination, mainly on the downbeats.

In the past, the *tortor Mandailing* was sometimes accompanied by a *gondang buluh* ensemble comprising two *gondang buluh* (stringed bamboo drums) and the usual *sarune*, cymbals, kettle-gongs, and gongs. Audio example 11.4 presents an excerpt of "Irama Mandailing" rhythm played by a *gondang buluh* at a ceremonial *tortor Mandailing* performance.

Before the end of the ceremony, the dance of the *raja's* wife (*tortor inanta soripada*) is performed. Unlike the other dances, this one is now almost obsolete. Ritually, it is regarded as relatively unimportant, as the descendants of a *raja's* wife are not counted in the lineage, which is patrilineal. After this dance, the young unmarried members of the community continue to dance to such rhythms as the lively *irama sampedang* (meaning unknown), and the stately *irama sorop-sorop ombun* (dew falling) rhythms. The popular dances *tua* and *raja-raja* are usually repeated several times before the dancing ends.

The other well-known rhythms are associated with specific parts of wedding ceremonies or for boosting morale in times of war. Special procession music that is played when a bride is "brought down to the stream" (*kehe tu aek* or *boru tu aek*) for her ritual wash or during a bridal procession to her husband's village is called *irama boru tu aek* (rhythm to go down to the stream) or *mangalo-alo* (glittering) in the former case and *irama sampedang* in the latter. The bride and her entourage are brought in procession to the local stream to be ceremonially shown the proper place where, as a married woman, she will bathe.

Unlike the five ritual rhythms, four subsequent rhythms are designed to be played at a fast, exciting pace to accompany general dancing at any ceremony. For example, the *katimbung* rhythm is an onomatopoeic name for the rhythmic sounds of a water game played by a group of children (according to one story) or the daughter of a *raja* and her friends (according to another story) in the river, as well as serving as a title for the piece of music based on its rhythms. In this popular game, players make sounds of varying pitch and loudness by forming air pockets in the water with their palms, thus causing the air in the hollows to explode. Each player produces a variety of rhythms that interlock with one another musically.

Another fast rhythm is *irama porang*, believed originally to have been played to raise the morale of troops before going into battle (*porang*). "Batta country," Marsden wrote, "[is] effectively . . . divided into number-less petty chief ships, the heads of which, also styled *rajas* . . . are . . . extremely jealous of any increase of their relative power, and on the slightest pretext a war breaks out between them" ([1811] 1966, 374). Even though a very small number of soldiers took part in the wars, morale-boosting was an important preliminary activity.

One of the *gondang* rhythms that is still popular today is the fast, exciting *poncak kutindik*, used for morale boosting, tiger funerals, and for accompanying performances of the local versions of the art of self-defense (*poncak*). Several types of *poncak* are still popular, distinguishable primarily by the stylized fighting movements (*gorak*) and the presence or absence of a weapon. In the most dangerous type, one participant tries to get hold of the knife brandished in the opponent's hand, at the same time fulfilling the aesthetic demands of the dance by elegantly performing the characteristic *poncak* movements (*gorak jago-jago*) and beginning and ending with a stylized bow of respect (Mand. *sombah*) to each other and to the audience.

||||

Until the advent of Islam in the early nineteenth century, belief in the dualistic/triadic yet unified nature of existence, as reflected in the *tutup ari* design and the three ritual musical ensembles, was the basis of Mandailing aesthetic thought and artistic practice. Social thought held that social conflict can be resolved by ritual contact with the spirits, who were contacted through invocatory drum rhythms and the actions of a mystically gifted individual, a shaman. The *raja*, who controlled the ritual symbols that linked the human and the spirit world—the drum and the buffalo—aimed to promote social cohesiveness through these symbolic forms, which guided and controlled the lifestyle, belief system, and arts.

Thus in the *gondang dua* ensemble, drums and gongs occur in gendered pairs, while in the five-, seven-, and nine-drum ensembles a relatively small drum is added that represents the product of the unity of the male-female drum pairs. The ensembles also represent the increasing number of ancestral clans that settled in the home environment in earliest times, just as the elders present at meetings in the *sopo gordang* represent the number of clans living in the village today.

For spiritual reasons, the most mystically potent rhythms or pieces have unvarying timbral-rhythmic drum patterns, while the less powerful rhythms or pieces have variable drum patterns and fast or moderately fast tempi. Syntactically, the music is characterized by simultaneous rhythmic, melodic, and intonational conflict between and within the parts, which are subsumed into a congruous unity at cadential points. Emotive connotations aroused by the various rhythms or pieces of the repertoire, such as sorrowful feelings aroused on hearing *irama roto*, are also resolved into a harmonious whole through the playing out of the musical, dance, and ritual process.

POSTSCRIPT

Since the 1970s, several Mandailingers who live in diaspora communities in Medan and Kuala Lumpur have assisted elders and artists in select homeland villages, including Pakantan, Huta na Godang, and Tamiang to revive the young people's knowledge of the *adat* and performance skills, providing funding and encouragement for their education and training and for organizing performances at home and festivals and performance tours to towns and cities in Indonesia and abroad. Thus for many years A. P. Parlindungan donated funds to maintain performance troupes in Pakantan and Medan, and Raja Syahbudin—an uncle of the Mandailing cultural promoter, Abdur-Razzaq Lubis—supported groups in both the Mandailing homeland and Kuala Lumpur. The head of the village of Tamiang in 1978, Muhamad Lubis, also promoted that village's local music and dance, partly in emulation of the lively Javanese cultural scene that he had witnessed during his long sojourn in Java. Moreover, Mandailing associations in Malaysia organized *gordang sambilan* festivals, which stimulated many young artists to acquire and develop the requisite performance skills.

Some Mandailingers, however, have felt severely discouraged by the destructive activities of illegal logging industries that burned large tracts of forest and caused severe water management problems in the Mandailing homeland from the 1970s onward, thereby destroying the traditional way of life and the intrinsic role of the arts and ritual in many areas. In the more regionally autonomous Indonesia since the fall of Suharto in 1997, the elders and the common people, who no longer control their land in face of such outside intrusions, need to be reempowered, writes Abdur-Razzaq Lubis. Effort needs to be made to redevelop and strengthen the sense of ethnic Mandailing identity that was expressed in the traditional arts and governance until the early 1980s.

ACKNOWLEDGMENTS

I wish to acknowledge the numerous elders, musicians, dancers, and storytellers who informed us so readily about their lives and arts, including the troupe of *gondang* and *gordang* musicians led by Zakaria Dalimunthe in Wele 1, Padang Sidempuan,

Mandailing Godang. I am especially grateful to the inhabitants of Pakantan, where I had discussions with Bp. Jumandailing, Bp. Ali Hamzah Lubis, Bp. Indrasanji, Haji Patuan Sayurmulia, Ibu Leila Lubis, and others, and recorded performances led by Bp. Nyabar Lubis with musicians Sarudin, Sikiron, and Sialim. I also had discussions in Tamiang with Haji Abdul Aziz and Bp. Raja Tamana Lubis, and recorded musicians Sarifudin, Darwin, Parman, and Saprin. H. Mangaraja Oloan (b. 1904) in Panyabungan gave me valuable historical information about the history of the performing arts, as did Raja Junjungan in Huta na Godang. In Sabadolok (Aek Kepesong), I was informed about the local Muslim arts by Ibu Haji Maksum Lubis. In the Mandailing diaspora in Medan, Raja Junjungan Lubis (former governor of North Sumatra) was helpful as was Bp. Burhannudin Nasution, the leader of the Pakantan-oriented Gunung Kulabu (Mount Kulabu) troupe; its lead musician, Bp. Amrul; and its patron Prof. Dr. A. P. Parlindungan, former rector of the University of North Sumatra and long-time promoter of the Mandailing performing arts.

Bapak A. P., as he was affectionately called, continually provided valuable assistance during our fieldtrips between 1971 and 1981, both among the Mandailing community in Medan, and in his home village of Pakantan. My transcriptions of the ensemble music, based on my adaptation of his number-based music-notational method, first appeared in my disk *The Mandailing People of Sumatra* (M. Kartomi 1983b), which contains recordings of Pakantan's Gunung Kulabu troupe and the Gunung Kulabu troupe in Medan. My research was greatly assisted by Bp. Johan Arifin Nasution of the Department of Education and Culture office in Medan.

ACEH

Aceh, the northernmost province of Sumatra, is largely mountainous and covered in dense tropical forest, with short rivers running down to the coastal areas (see map IV.1).[1] Chapters 12 and 13 center on Aceh's two largest musico-lingual groups: the western Acehnese (in Kabupatens Aceh Jaya, Aceh Barat, Nagan Raya, and Aceh Barat Daya) and the northern Acehnese (in Kabupatens Aceh Besar, Pidie, Bireuen, and Aceh Utara).

It is thought that the ancestors of the Acehnese migrated to coastal Aceh from the Chamic (Mon-Khmer) region of the Southeast Asian mainland in the mid-first millennium C.E. and around 1471 (Durie 1990, 111; Thurgood 2010, 38–39), and that they induced the earlier coastal populations to move up the rivers to settle in the mountainous interior.[2] Space prohibits discussion of these minority groups: the mostly upstream Gayo and the Alas peoples (living in the Kabupatens Bener Meriah, Aceh Tengah, and Gayo Lues), and the mostly downstream minorities, the Kluet (in parts of Kabupaten Aceh Selatan), and the Tamiang Malays in Kabupaten Aceh Timur (East Aceh).[3] Nor does this book discuss the western offshore islanders, including the Puloe people of Simeulue, though it refers briefly in chapters 12 and 13 to Pasisir Malays living in the Pulau Banyak archipelago.

Discussion of the western Acehnese group in chapter 12 necessarily touches on the minority Aneuk Jamée (Ac., "Descendants of the Guests") or Pasisir Selatan (Ma., "South Coastal") musico-lingual group, which is dominant in Singkil and the offshore Pulau Banyak archipelago in the extreme southwest and is found in pockets along Aceh's west coast. Since the early eighteenth century the colonial west-coastal plantations attracted immigrants from northern Aceh and Aneuk Jamée (Guests)

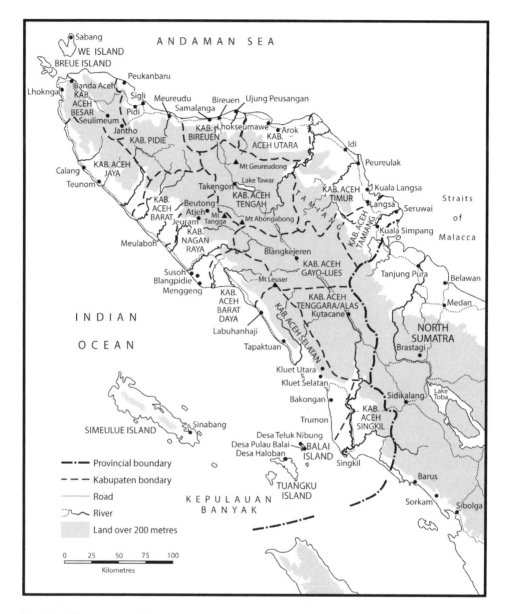

Map IV.1 The province of Aceh

from Sumatra's west coast to Aceh's west coast, with the Dutch-Aceh war (1883–ca. 1910) finally establishing Dutch control over Aceh until the Second World War. The western Acehnese accepted an Aneuk Jamée legend and associated song-dance genre into their culture.

Chapter 13 introduces Aceh's suite of male frame-drum (*rapa'i*) genres, one of which is performed in standing position and the others in sitting position. All genres have a solo vocalist and a chorus who accompany themselves on the *rapa'i* while performing upper-body dance movements and body percussion. The men consider their frame-drum genres and the *seudati* standing dance to be their main artistic contributions to Acehnese artistic identity, though the song-dance also occurs in female form: *seudati inong* (female *seudati*). Performed either in sitting (Ac. *duek*) or standing (Ac. *dong*) position, the genres break into three subclasses: (1) the standing dances with vocal music and body percussion (e.g., *seudati* [audiovisual examples IV.1 and IV.2]) (2) the sitting dances with vocal music and body percussion (e.g., *ratôh duek*), and (3) the sitting dances with frame-drum playing (e.g., *rapa'i geurimpheng* and *rapa'i pulot*, discussed in chap. 13).

Chapter 12 discusses the female lamentation song-dances that developed in western and southern Aceh and were transformed since Indonesian independence into a representation of an idealized view of female Acehnese identity in the modern *phô* song-dance. They are the standing dances with vocal music and body percussion (e.g., *manoe pocuk, phô,* and *malelang*) and the *seudati inong* (female *seudati*). They contrast with the area's standing protocol dances (e.g., *peumulia jamée*) to welcome guests, which were favored by the former *ulèëbalang* and the Dutch and Indonesian governments. They also differ strongly from the sitting dances that include vocal music and body percussion, for example, *ratéb meuseukat* and *ratôh duek* (M. Kartomi 2011a). The first two song-dance subclasses are associated with indigenous religion and the third (except for *ratôh duek*, which has mainly secular texts) with Islam.

A fourth subclass, which is not discussed, comprises the standing Pasisir Malay/ Aneuk Jamée couples dances with violin and frame-drum accompaniment in southwest-coastal Aceh, which were performed by mixed couples in some areas until the 1940s, after which men normally took both male and female roles. They are part of Sumatra's pan-west-coastal Pasisir Melayu art forms mentioned in chapters 3 and 10, including the Sikambang legend and the associated song-dances.

HISTORY

The people of Aceh have lived in a militarily contested zone for a good part of the past 137 years, and they have a fiercely proud and independent precolonial history.[4] As the historical records document, the coastal areas were visited by foreign merchants, diplomats, and religious leaders from the late first millennium C.E., and Pasai (in north coastal Aceh) in the 1290s was the first kingdom in Southeast Asia to embrace Islam. The Acehnese people's sense of identity is based on pride in their Islamic culture and their period of greatness in the sixteenth and seventeenth centuries, when Aceh had assumed political and cultural leadership of the Malay world (Ma. *alam*

Melayu), a century after the Portuguese conquest of Malacca in 1511. Through its thriving international trade with Muslim kingdoms in India and central and western Asia, Aceh became the leading Malay entrepôt in the Strait of Malacca, integrating Muslim belief and customs into the Malay oral and literary culture that it inherited from Johor (L. Andaya 2008, 108–9). At that time, Aceh's court *nobat* orchestra and drum-oboe ensembles linked it musically to the orbit of the Moghul court in India and the other Malay courts in western Southeast Asia.

Beginning around the fifteenth century, Aceh's devotional genres, including the song-dances in the standing and sitting positions and the frame-drum genres, are thought to have been developed and spread as instruments of *dakwah* (conversion) (M. Kartomi 2011a). They include the *ratéb meuseukat* dances that originated in western Aceh; their religious lyrics and body movements suggest that they derived from the practice of the litany.[5] In its prayerful form (*ratéb meuseukat*), a group of female devotees "sit" (*duek*) in a half- kneeling position and recite parts of the litany, sometimes while swaying or clapping, while in the *meuseukat* genre, a group of artists dressed in colorful dance costumes kneel close together in one or two rows perform-ing more elaborate songs, dance movements, and body percussion (see audiovisual example IV.3).[6]

For many Acehnese artists and scholars, the fact that Aceh's warrior-sultan Iskan-dar Muda (1607–36) conquered much of Sumatra's west, north, and northeast coasts and the coastal Malay Peninsula in the early seventeenth century explains some aspects of the musical history of other former kingdoms in Sumatra. For example, an Acehnese sultan in the eighteenth century marked his respect for a murdered king of Barus by sending his bereaved son off in state from the capital Kutaraja with drum-oboe music, and on his voyage back to Barus with royal *nobat* orchestral music (Drakard [1988] 2003, 246). The probable spread of the Acehnese arts along Sumatra's west coast in the sixteenth and seventeenth centuries is often attributed to Aceh's superior political and religious status at the time. Thus a legend tells of a Minangkabau religious leader who went to study Islam from a master in Aceh and on his return founded a Sufi brotherhood and an Islamic school in Ulukan, near Pariaman, in West Sumatra and introduced the associated arts, including the playing of the Acehnese *rapa'i* frame drum to accompany devotional singing.

Most Acehnese music and dance performances are gender segregated and per-formed before either male or female audiences. Until the late 1930s, however, it was common for female and male artists to perform together for mixed audiences at weddings and other celebrations with the support of the aristocratic administrative heads (*ulèëbalang*) who lived in their great houses throughout the countryside. Artists were encouraged to perform items in mixed couples, including the *joget* song-dances in East Aceh and the Sikambang song-dances in western and southern Aceh as well as the female *peumulia jamée* (guest-welcoming) dance and male or female *seudati* song-dances at the aristocrats' official and family celebrations and their own family's life events. All-night *hikayat* story reciting and performances were also frequently held in the villages, as well as male *rapa'i Pasè, rapa'i dabôh* and other frame-drum competitions, sometimes in the presence of the Dutch colonial administrators.[7]

After the 1945 Indonesian revolution, however, the *ulèëbalang* lost their power, and the *ulama* gained greater influence (Reid 2005, 325–28). From the late 1950s, some religious leaders preached an increasingly orthodox interpretation of Islam, and they discouraged men and women from performing together before mixed audiences, mainly on the grounds that such practices can encourage illicit sexual liaisons. With the religious revival in Aceh and other parts of Southeast Asia from the 1990s, gender segregation of performers and audiences gained further strength.[8]

Gender segregation in most of Aceh's other arts had begun, however, long before the late 1950s. Partly due to the custom of young *perantau* leaving their villages to seek their fortune elsewhere and leaving the women in charge of field and home, women throughout Aceh long ago developed their own genres or styles of music and dance. A whole lamentation tradition developed in the form of vocal music and song-dance to express grief at the death of a child, sorrow at the departure of a bride from her parents' home, fisherfolk's songs of loneliness or fear at sea, and crying songs for collecting sweet sap from a palm tree. The traditional Muslim separation of male and female worshippers and students of Qur'anic recitation in the mosques also led to the development of the separate female liturgical arts, such as *ratéb meuseukat*.

A CLASSIFICATION OF ACEH'S DANCE AND SONG-DANCE GENRES

Three elements of division come into play when classifying Aceh's traditional dances and song-dance genres (fig. IV.1): the gender of the performers, their body position, and the type of musical accompaniment. At the first level they may be classified into the male and the female, at the second into the standing (*dong*) and the sitting (*duek*), and at the third into the genres accompanied by vocal and body-percussion music as opposed to the genres accompanied by musical instruments.

Most traditional Acehnese music and dance performances are gender segregated, performed either before a male or a female audience. Women do not normally play musical instruments, but they have developed their own separate song-dances with body percussion in standing and sitting positions for the female components of their life-event rituals and celebrations and a separate category of dances with male instrumental or body-percussion accompaniment for welcoming guests at

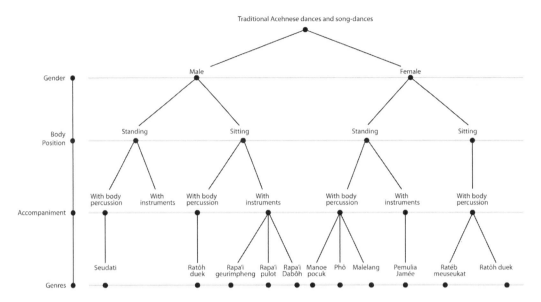

Figure IV.1 Classification of traditional Acehnese dances and song-dances

formal government events in the colonial (nominally under *ulèëbalang* rule) and postcolonial periods. The standard Acehnese ensemble minimally comprises a pair of drums, one or more cylindrical drums (*geundrang*) or frame drums (*rapa'i*), and an optional oboe (*seuruné kalée*).

The male and female standing genres are mostly performed in circular dance formations, while the male and female sitting dances are normally performed in one or more rows. Genres that feature music without dance (e.g., *rapa'i Pasè*), devotional genres (e.g., *rapa'i dabôh* and *dala'il khairat*), and genres created since the 1950s (e.g., *tari ranub lampuan*) are not included in figure IV.1. The various male and female forms of religious group-vocal music are regarded as religious expression, not art.

The standing dances, such as *seudati*, are widely believed to be older than the sitting dances, as suggested by their song texts, which contain references to agriculture, farmyard animals, indigenous religion, and Hindu themes, and by the type of body percussion used, especially the breast beating that is unique to male *seudati* and may have derived from Shi'a practices in sixteenth-century Aceh, as argued in chapter 12 (audiovisual examples IV.4 and IV.5).

Also the female song-dances performed in *dong* (standing) position, such as *phô* and *seudati inong*, use body-percussion techniques different from those of the sitting performers in *meuseukat*. The sitting song-dances, on the other hand, probably developed from the Sufi liturgical tradition in Sunni Islam before or after conversion, with performers chanting religious texts, often swaying from side to side after they feel they have achieved ecstatic union with God (M. Kartomi 2011a).

Aceh is rich in epics, proverbs, and other literary and oral forms, as Snouck Hurgronje showed in *The Acehnese* (1906). Besides *Perang Sabi* ("Holy War"), the main epics in northern Aceh are *Pocut Mohamet* ("Prince Mahomet," mentioned in chap. 12) and *Hikayat Aceh* ("The Story of Aceh," about the seventeenth-century Acehnese sultan Iskandar Muda), and in western and southern Aceh "Sikambang," "Malelang," "Malem Dewa" (Mi. "Malim Deman"), and "Cut Nyak Dhien" (the heroic female West Acehnese commander in the war against the Dutch). A bard may choose any episode from a legend to perform, formerly all night for a succession of nights, at a celebration. An Acehnese version of the Malem Dewa legend portrays the hero walking along a local river, whereupon he saw seven angels bathing naked in a local lake, with the youngest angel, Putri Bensu, sitting on a rock washing her hair. After meeting a kindly old lady—Nenek Kebayan/Inen Keben (who is mentioned in many Malay legends)—he learned that the angels bathed there once a week, so he kept observing them secretly. On falling in love with the youngest angel, he stole her shawl, which took away her power to fly back to heaven with her sisters. He married her, and she gave birth to their son in the Nenek's home, where they lived. Eventually the child found his mother's garment, and she flew back to heaven with him. Her forlorn husband followed her to heaven, and after fulfilling a series of very difficult tasks imposed by her father, he was reunited with her. This legend is also told in the Gayo mountains of Aceh, where it became the subject of a modern dance drama (Ara 2009, 154–55).

ACEHNESE ARTISTIC STYLE

Unlike in some other provinces of Sumatra, group performances are the norm in Aceh. Solo performances are restricted to bards, while solo and duo displays of the art of self-defense are presented only on Aceh's southeast and southwest coasts, where Malay culture is the norm.

Some instrumental and song-dance genres demand a remarkable degree of human strength and endurance. The great *rapa'i Pasè*—one of the largest frame-drum types in the world—can properly be played, it is said, only by a very strong man who can endure the physical demands of playing for hours at a time. Genres that include the performance of body percussion also demand a high degree of physical fitness and endurance in their performers. In their interlocking sections, they often reach a rhythmic-timbral complexity that is unprecedented outside Aceh. Less virtuosity is exhibited in the stamping and clapping episodes in song-dances discussed in chapter 12 than in the male and female *seudati* performances, but they are distinctive to the genre and may involve quite complex rhythms.

Given Aceh's turbulent history, the martial nature of the discipline expected of the performers of some Acehnese genres is perhaps not surprising. Both sexes perform song-dances that are noted for their martial precision, compactness, and climactic accelerations. For example, the male and the female *seudati* song-dances are led by a "commander" (*syéh*) with subsidiary dancers named according to a military hierarchy. They include the *apét syéh*, "assistant lead dancer"; *apét likot*, "assistant lead dancer at the rear"; *apét uneuen*, "assistant lead dancer on the right flank"; *apét wie*, "assistant lead dancer on the left flank"; *likot sago*, "dancer on the rear edge"; and several *sago*, "foot soldiers/dancers on the edge of a formation." The West Acehnese *phô* song-dance is also led by a *syéh* and two assistant commanders (chap. 12). The singing in both *seudati* and *phô* is led by an *aneuk syahé* (lit. "child of poetry"), assisted by an alternate singer. Performances depend heavily on the quality of the lead vocalist (*syahé*), whose partly improvised, ornamented melodic renditions of given or improvised texts set the tone of a performance. The *syahé* works in tandem with the *syéh* dance leader, who demands a high degree of precision from her group of performers and compactness in their choral singing, dance movements, and either *rapa'i* playing or body percussion, which must be copiously rehearsed.

Acehnese artists relish competitions between opposing groups and have done so in the villages since at least as early as the 1890s (Snouck Hurgronje 1906, 2:247). Usually audience acclaim decides who wins, but sometimes a jury is appointed. The competitive element partly explains the high standards and the degree of virtuosity that the performers attain. It also explains why the most virtuoso genres were chosen for further development on the national and international stage from the 1960s.

Government-organized festivals usually double as competitions. Due to the twenty-nine-year conflict between the Aceh Independence Movement (1974–2005) and the Indonesian National Army, however, only a few Aceh-wide arts festivals have been held since Indonesia's independence, for example, in 1958, 1972, 1987, and 2004. Frequent curfews have inhibited opportunities to learn and perform the arts. However, an upsurge in performances was observable in many rural and urban areas since 2006, and the fifth festival—PKA V (Pekan Kebudayaan Aceh V)—was held in 2009.

CHANGES IN THE LAMENT
DANCES IN ACEH
Phô as a Symbol of Female Identity

Remarkably, remnants of the ancient Acehnese culture of lament singing and dancing have survived among the women of western Aceh to this day. Traditionally they sang laments at funerals and at a bride's last ritual wash (*peusijuek* ritual), and they created three lament song-dances that feature solo and group singing, stamping dance routines around a ritual subject, and episodes of body percussion.[1] This chapter will show how aspects of religion, ethnicity, class, and gender; socio-political conditions; and the activities of some remarkable individual women have resulted in the survival of the song-dances—*manoe pocuk, malelang,* and *phô*—over the past three to four centuries, and how individual women changed the meaning and style of *phô* to become a symbol of female Acehnese identity.[2]

Lying between the mountain ranges and the sea, Aceh's western frontier was known historically as the *rantò* (Ac.) or *rantau* (Mi., I.), that is, a more or less unpopulated area to which young men traveled to seek their fortune, sometimes staying and bringing their families to settle (Snouck Hurgronje 1906, 2:235; Drewes 1980). Over the past three centuries, it became a magnet for two groups of out-migrants: Acehnese-speaking people from northern Aceh, and Aneuk Jamée (lit. "guests") speakers of a Malay-Minangkabau-Acehnese patois from along Sumatra's west coast.

Once "wild and inhospitable" (Snouck Hurgronje 1906, 1:275), the frontier was gradually settled around 1700 by immigrant plantation workers and others who produced pepper for the export market in such west-coast ports as Meulaboh and Susoh. The trade was initially under the control of the local aristocrats (*ulèëbalang*) and merchants from Muslim India and Arabia, and beginning in the late nineteenth century by Dutch administrators working partly through the *ulèëbalang*, who promoted local artists' performances at their functions. Today the *rantò* population comprises a mix of Acehnese and Aneuk Jamée farmers, fisherfolk, and small traders.[3]

One of the three vocalist-led ritual song-dances—*manoe pocuk*—can be performed without artistic training. *Malelang* and *phô*, however, are structured song-dances that require trained singer-dancers to perform episodes of body percussion and, above all, a skilled vocalist who can sing standard songs between the song-dance episodes and improvise witty question-answer song sessions for hours on end. When lead vocalists perform *malelang*, which belongs to the Aneuk Jamée musico-lingual subgroup, they sing episodes from the tragic Malelang legend and improvise in the Aneuk Jamée speech variety. When the vocalists perform *phô*, which belongs to the Acehnese musico-lingual group, they must sing from a large repertory of laments and other songs and improvise in Acehnese. Although the oldest known form of *phô* is north Acehnese (from Pidie), its modern form combines characteristics of western Acehnese and local Aneuk Jamée subcultures, which make it ethnically a hybrid form.

As this chapter will show, four hundred years ago *phô* was a passionately mournful funeral song-dance, which split at least a century and a half ago into two forms: female lament song-dances at a funeral, and flirtatious song-dances to entertain men at the end of a funeral; it was finally transformed in approximately the 1950s into a shortened song-dance medley that expresses an idealized, modernist-Muslim view of Acehnese female identity.

Before they converted to Islam, the Acehnese people adhered to a cosmology based on veneration of the ancestors and the spirits of nature—plants, animals, rocks, mountains, the sea, stars, and planets, combined with strains of Hindu culture.[4] It was in this context that the lament tradition developed. Studies by Christiaan Snouck Hurgronje, G. P. Rouffaer (1906), and Bertram Schrieke (1957) show that the seventeenth-century Acehnese state was strongly Islamic. However, Lode F. Brakel also draws attention to features of the state that "spring from original Indonesian civilisation itself," its Hindu remnants, its acceptance of influences from Moghul India (1975b, 56) and Shi'a as well as Sunni Muslim characteristics (60–63); and Denys Lombard (1967, 134–39) has documented the architectural and literary evidence of Hindu characteristics in the court culture.

Besides *phô*, which involved dirges and dances in a circle around a coffin (Siegel 1979, 147), the lament culture consisted of weeping songs (*ratapan*) by professional female mourners at funerals and the stylistically similar "crying laments for a palm tree" (I. *ratap tangis enau*) to extract the maximum yield of palm sugar from the tree. Fisherfolk at sea sang sea laments (*dendang lauiʾ*) loudly, at high pitch, and with elaborate melodic ornamentation so that their voices would carry over the water; they sang despondently about the size of their catch if it was small, or about longing, loneliness, or fear at times of danger. This style, which is still extant, has become typical of most lament singing right along Sumatraʾs west coast (see chaps. 3 and 5).

Over the centuries, the Acehnese and Aneuk Jamée immigrants in the *rantò* adapted their transplanted genres and developed new forms in their new environment. The women of Acehnese descent developed not only the female *manoe pocuk* and *phô* standing dances (and practiced the northern Acehnese *seudati inong* [female *seudati*]) but also the devotional Muslim *meuseukat* (M. Kartomi 2011a). The men developed their *rapaʾi* sitting dances (chap. 13) and the bardic *haba Dang Deuria* and continued to perform the standard Acehnese song-dances, including the *seudati agam* (male *seudati*).[5] The Aneuk Jamée people continued to practice their versions of the Sumatran west-coast *sikambang asli* and *sikambang kapri* repertory (chap. 3), the bards told the new Malelang legend, and the women created the *malelang* song-dance.[6]

The *manoe pocuk, malelang,* and *phô* song-dances are performed at life-event ceremonies such as weddings, baby thanksgivings, circumcisions, and vow fulfillment ceremonies, for example, when a childless couple sponsor a feast and a *malelang* performance in the hope that the shaman will help them conceive a child. A shaman also assists the host of the feast to engage the services of a group of singer-dancers by uttering invocations before the betel-nut preparations are exchanged with the groupʾs leader, whereupon she or he formally agrees that the group will perform. As will be shown below, references to the indigenous religion and Hinduism are made in some performances of the three forms, but with phrases and references added that reflect the peopleʾs strong adherence to Islam.[7]

THE *MANOE POCUK* SONG-DANCE

Manoe pocuk means "wash the peak," in which "peak" refers to the height of a ritual *manoe pocuk* bathing ceremony at a communal *kenduri* (Ac., "feast").[8]

In a performance, the lead *manoe pocuk* singers (*syahé* [*aneuk syahé*] and *apét*) take turns singing well-known verses and improvise lyrics of greetings and advice for the occasion, sometimes referring to the spirits of nature and the ancestors and the Hindu god Batara Guru (Ibu Murniati, pers. comm., March 2007), with a few Muslim devotional phrases inserted as well. The *rakan* (group of singer-dancers) sing standard responses in chorus and dance around the ceremonial subject, who sits on the ground or the floor. The members of the group perform various rhythmic body percussion routines, including clapping their hands and stamping their feet on the last (fourth or sixth) beat of a measure. On the four beats of one dance routine, they bend down inward toward the ritual subject and clap, stand upright, move outward again, and take a step around the circle, repeating the exercise many times. The dancers beat out various repetitive rhythmic patterns, including (in Blangpidie) one with a hand-clap on the first and second beats, a foot stamp on the third beat, and a rest on the fourth beat of each 4/4 measure. Then the shaman leads a ritual that symbolizes the subject's last liminal bath by sprinkling scented water containing flower petals and lime or *enau* (*arenga* palm) over her or him, after which select relatives and guests repeat the exercise.

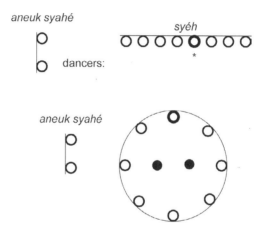

Figure 12.1 Designs of *manoe pocuk* dance formations

If the parents of a bride request a performance at a bridal *manoe pocuk/ turun ke air* (Ac./Ma.) ritual, the *syéh* sings laments (*meuba'eu*) at the bride's imminent change of status and frequently her departure from the parental home, and the female relatives and friends sing and dance around her, after which she is blessed with scented water (fig. 12.2).[9]

A similar *manoe pocuk* ritual is carried out if a boy is to be circumcised. Usually two boys are circumcised at once. Wearing the local variant of the Acehnese royal costume, the boys usually sit in state on separate thrones, resting their feet on a pair of thick banana stems beside a pair of bowls containing scented water, and a group of women perform the *manoe pocuk* song-dance around them, with a vocalist singing appropriate songs for hours on end, as in figure 12.3.

Figure 12.2 A *manoe pocuk* rehearsal danced around a mock bride, near Blangpidie, Aceh Barat Daya, 2007

Figure 12.3 A group of *manoe pocuk* performers led by Chèh Nurmulia of Jeuram, who dance and sing around a pair of boys who are about to be circumcised, Gampong Blang Seumoet, Kecamatan Beutong, Kabupaten Nagan Raya, 2007

MALELANG

Malelang is an Aneuk Jamée song-dance with more varied dance formations and body percussion techniques than in the *manoe pocuk* circle dance. It is attached to a powerfully emotional legend about slander that led to the death of a boy and a girl. The following descriptions of the legend and a song-dance performance are based on an account by the late dance leader Ibu Mariam, a *malelang* vocalist and farmer of Gampong Ujung Padang, Kecamatan Susoh, Aceh Selatan (Burhan and Idris 1986–87, 131–33), and on a performance that I saw in a former *ulèëbalang*'s residence, the *Rumôh Putéh* (White House) situated in Gampong Kuala Batée, Aceh Barat Daya, in 2007.[10] It was led by Ibu Nurhayati of Desa Gelanggang Gajah, who teaches the *malelang* dance to secondary-school girls in the Kuala Batée area.[11]

The legend, passed on from generation to generation, is told as follows:

In the kingdom of Kuala Batée on the border of South and West Aceh, a beautiful orphaned girl named Madion lived with her mother's brother's family. She had been brought up with her uncle's son Malelang, who had treated her as a young sister, but recently there had been talk of their betrothal.

A fine *inai* (red henna berry) tree, a *pinang* (betel nut) tree, and banana plants were growing in a garden on the edge of the nearby forest. One day Madion ran to the garden and told Malelang, who was working there, that their mother had asked her to fetch some betel nut for her. On her way to the *pinang* tree, she climbed over a fence, accidentally tearing her trousers and skin, which caused her to bleed a little. Then Malelang arrived to help her collect some betel nut, and they started to run home. However, the village chief's guard caught sight of them alone together and reported to the king that they had engaged in sexual intercourse under the tree.

On hearing of the charge, Madion ran confidently down to the palace to explain that she and Malelang had gone separately to the garden that morning to collect *pinang* for their mother and explained how she had wounded herself climbing the fence. The king, however, angrily told their mother that he didn't believe Madion's story and they would be sentenced to death for immoral behavior. The mother cried and begged him to reconsider, but he refused, so in desperation she asked that they be given seven days reprieve to be married. The *raja* agreed, and the mother hoped he would revoke the death sentence.

Madion and Malelang were dressed in beautiful wedding clothes and antique jewelry, their feet and hands were tattooed and stained with red henna, and they sat in state (*sanding*) as *raja sehari* (Ma., "king and queen for a day"). On the seventh day of the wedding, the mother was called to the palace and came home with the dreadful news that the king had stuck to his decision. The pair was made to walk into a glass casket in the village square, and the king's guard put them to death.

The mother cried inconsolably as she sang laments (*meuratap*) in beautiful poetry, day after day. Eventually the corpses of her two innocent children arose from the casket in an apparition, and they stood up together in the middle of a circle of light.[12]

The idea of the circular formation of the *malelang* song-dance is said to be linked to the apparition of the circle of light around Malelang and Madion in the legend.

In a *malelang* performance in Desa Padang, Susoh, the *syahé* stood apart and with tense vocal cords sang a *saleum syahé* (greeting) in the Aneuk Jamée language to those present, followed by a Muslim prayer based on the phrase *salam alaikom* for the well-being of all present.[13] The dance commander (*syéh*) and eleven other adult women entered the arena and performed the *saleum rakan* (group greeting) in two parallel lines, making their bow (*seumbah*) to the audience with their palms pressed together vertically in front of their chests "as the Prophet demanded."[14] They repeated part of the solo singer's greeting song and danced in a circle, snapping their fingers on the last beat of each measure as they danced.

The girls stopped dancing to kneel on their heels and enjoy their *syahé*'s performance of an episode from the tragic Malelang legend. She sang an opening verse from the legend, which was followed by a *rakan* circle-dancing episode with rhythmic stamping, and she continued to perform a series of *kisah* (story-singing) scenes interspersed with the *rakan*'s circle-dancing episodes. When the sung story episode called for the mother's lament, the *syahé* sang an emotional text to a highly ornamented melody in descending strains and with extremely tense vocal cords, while the group of dancers moved around the circle again, snapping their fingers, stamping their feet, and clapping their hands in cyclic rhythms (e.g., //: snap snap stamp clap://) while periodically singing responsive *panton* choruses.

At the end of the formal part of the performance, the popular *estra* (extra) section began, with the *syahé* posing questions or riddles and the *syéh* giving informative or witty answers, all in song performed with relaxed vocal cords. Sometimes the *syahé* improvised moral or religious messages for the audience's edification or sang amusing secular comments and jokes for their entertainment. Some *syahé* emphasize the message "Beware of slander" as the overriding moral of the story, while others point to the moral injunction that boys and girls should never be alone together lest disaster befall them.

The performers in Gampong Padang wore all-white costumes with flowers in their Acehnese-style hair buns (traditionally arranged slightly off center), but in the performance in the Rumôh Putéh in Gampong Kuala Batée, the performers wore pink long-sleeved dresses with pleated skirts that were probably Dutch-inspired in the colonial era (see fig. 12.4). After the *syahé* sang *kisah* sections in the latter performance, the girls danced slowly around a clockwise circle, swinging their arms, stepping forward and halting at each step to stamp the right foot lightly to the left and the right before returning to the same spot, then stamping forward onto the next spot. Repeating the routine on all the spots around the circle for as many rotations as

Figure 12.4 A *malelang* dance performance in the White House, March 2007, led by Ibu Ceh Nurhayati (b. 1952) of Desa Gelanggang Gajah, Kecamatan Kuala Batée, Kabupaten Aceh Barat Daya

the *syéh* decided time allowed, they sometimes swung their hips on the second and third beats of a measure (a nontraditional practice). In some routines they stamped on the first beat of a measure, rested on the second, slid their foot forward on the third, and clapped on the fourth.

Because *malelang* is a lament art form that was formerly performed at the death of a child, a *fatwah ulama* in the 1950s resulted in a call to ban the form, yet it is still performed in nonfuneral contexts in a few areas.[15] As *malelang* has not yet been transformed into a *kreasi baru* or performed in festivals, its future is uncertain, except as part of a standard modern *phô* performance to which a short *malelang* scene has been added. It has never been performed at festivals.

PHÔ AND ITS HISTORY

The name *phô* derives from *peuba-e pô*, where *peuba-e* means "singer of laments" and *pô* is a term of respect (Ac., Isjkarim et al. 1980–81, 179). Aboe Bakar defined *phô* in his dictionary as "song-dances at a mourning ceremony performed by young female

dancers/singers of *panton* with body percussion" (Bakar [1985] 2001, 716, my trans.).[16]
The verb *meuratap* (Ac.) means "to sing laments" (Isjkarim et al. 1980–81, 179).

Also according to the late dance leader and choreographer Mak Yan of Meulaboh, *phô* was a mourning song-dance performed on the occasion of a royal death. As a young girl in the late colonial era, she took part in a *phô* performance at a funeral in the great house of Meulaboh's last *ulèëbalang*, whose daughter, Ibu Cut Asiah, also remembers seeing it when she was a child (Cut Asiah, pers. comm., 2007).[17] Led by their *syéh*, a group of women circled the corpse slowly, lightly stamping as they stepped forward toward the corpse on every six or eight beats (in 6/8 or 8/8 meter), while their *syahé* sang laments, and the group periodically echoed phrases from them in chorus.

Mak Yan's reference to the early history of *phô* can be substantiated by literary evidence. The oldest Acehnese literary source that mentions the ritual *phô* song-dances at royal funerals is the mid-eighteenth-century literary epic *Hikayat Pocut Mahomet*, which describes an *ulèëbalang*-led war on Aceh's north coast.[18] It describes *phô* mourners circling around the corpse of the aristocratic warrior Lord Béntara from Pidie while singing laments and beating their breasts violently, reminiscent of the breast beating by Shi'a devotees during Muharram month in India, Iran, and Iraq. Lord Béntara's corpse was described as having been laid out in his mother's house, with fine curtains hung across the ceiling and over the walls:

> The corpse arrived and was laid out . . . [line 2212] . . .
> After that relatives arrived, encircling the coffin [2217] . . .
> Half of them wailed, and half struck themselves as they danced for the
>   dead one [2228]
> Their hair flew as they swung around the coffin [2229]. (trans. of *Hikayat
>   Pocut Mahomet*, in Siegel 1979, 147)

The poet continued:

> Now the corpse was inside the house; the crowd present beat their breasts . . .
> People beat themselves in a horrible way.
> Of some of them the rings on their fingers were broken owing to their beating and
>   pounding their breasts . . .
> Pidie resounded with lamentation. (Drewes 1979, 245)[19]

Although virtually all Acehnese are now Sunnis who adhere to the Shafi'i school of jurisprudence, this literary reference lends credence to the view that the Acehnese court and the royal *phô* ritual were once associated with Shi'a beliefs.[20]

The *Hikayat* also mentions the singing of mourning hymns:

The slave girls were singing mourning hymns (*muphô*) and the young lads wept
and lamented.
All the people of the village beat (*poh, peh*) themselves. (Drewes 1979, 193)

We know from the *Pocut Mahomet* epic, then, that mourners in northern Aceh once
danced in a circle around a royal corpse singing laments while weeping and beating
(*poh, peh*) their breasts. As Pocut Mahomet's mother said to her son: "Should you die
in the guest-room, I would sing mourning hymns [with dance] for three days and
beat my breast."[21] Elsewhere the poet wrote: "The maids of honour began crying in
their distress, and some of them beat themselves and struck their breast" (Drewes
1979, 203, line 2031), and "As if a dead body had been brought into the house, that is
how they lamented and beat their breasts" (ibid., 216, line 2204).

The grief-stricken, Shi'a-style breast beating in *phô* ritual song-dances at eighteenth-century funerals apparently diminished and eventually disappeared in Aceh
at some time during or before the nineteenth century; certainly there is no mention
of such practices in the late-nineteenth-century sources. However, the custom of
muphô ("to lament in music and dance," Snouck Hurgronje 1906, 1:424) was still being
practiced on the west coast, with women dancing flirtatiously and singing response
panton with men in the audience on the final day of a funeral.[22] Female singer-dancers
assembled in the house of a deceased person in front of male onlookers to dance
around a coffin singing love songs that seemed to adulate the deceased but were
actually addressed, flirtatiously and with ribald lyrics, to men in the audience:[23]

> On the West Coast [of Aceh] especially we meet with the *adat* [traditional custom]
> known as *muphô*, looked on with strong disfavour by the pious. Some five or six days
> after a death, men, women and girls assemble together in the house, the walls of which
> are partly removed. The women and girls perform a dance in which they raise one leg
> repeatedly. This is accompanied by the recitation of *pantons* [quatrains] which are often
> very far from decent in their purport. The performers keep by them ready-made *sirih*
> [betel nut] quids, which they distribute to their favourites among the male audience.
> (Snouck Hurgronje 1906, 1:424)

It is probable, then, that these *phô* performers danced sorrowfully around the coffin
on the first day or two of an *ulèëbalang*'s or other rich person's funeral, and that their
flirtatious dances were part of the final *lanie/estra* section of a lengthy performance at
the end of the week of mourning. Thus a form of *phô* from northern Aceh survived
in west-coastal great houses and rural villages till at least the second decade of the
twentieth century, even though some orthodox *ulama* disapproved of the form.

How and when was *phô* transplanted from northern to western Aceh, where it
has survived to this day, though in different form? As mentioned above, the former
ulèëbalang Putéh family in the Kuala Batée area of western Aceh believe that their

ancestors migrated to the west from the Kuala Batée area of Pidie in the early days of *rantò* settlement (from ca. 1700), bringing *ilmu phô* (the knowledge of *phô)* with them. They say that a descendant of Teuku Tjoet Putéh—the adventurer and fortune-seeker Teuku Cut Dhin—walked for weeks along forest paths to choose an unsettled area on the *rantò* into which his family could migrate. On finding a suitable area near Kutabahagia (northwest of Blangpidie), which he named Kerajaan Kuala Batée after his ancestral home on the north coast, he brought his family there, built a great house (the Rumōh Putéh, "White House"), and introduced the funeral art *phô*, which became part of local custom and spread, especially in the Blangpidie, Jeuram, and Meulaboh hinterland (Ibu Cut Putéh, pers. comm., Kuala Batée, 2007).[24]

During the war with the Dutch (1873–1910), the balance of political power, which had been shared in precolonial Aceh between the sultanate, the *ulèëbalang*, and the *ulama*, was shattered. The aristocratic leaders were polarized against the religious leaders, with the latter gaining prestige among the people for their more consistently anti-Dutch position. The Dutch forced the sultan to surrender in 1903, and the war ended around 1910.

The attitude of the *ulama* to artistic performances differed from that of the *ulèëbalang*. Some influential *ulama* had come to accept a rigidly monotheistic cosmology that may have been linked with a resurgence of Wahhabism in Saudi Arabia.[25] They argued that Muslims should not practice arts of non-Muslim origin and strongly disapproved of magic practices, pilgrimages to shrines, and the use of omens, all of which they labeled as heathen. They opposed weeping at funerals, because death was deemed the will of Allah and not to be regretted. They opposed females performing in front of males for fear that this might result in immoral sexual liaisons. Thus *phô* performance was discouraged in some areas. Meanwhile, a female sitting song-dance with an Islamic theme, *ratéb meuseukat*, was developing for female audiences at celebrations, and it came to rival *phô* in Seunagan and some neighboring areas of Nagan Raya. The culture memory holds that *meuseukat* songs, body movements, and body percussion were "invented" by a remarkable woman named T. Rukibah, daughter of the charismatic religious leader Habib Muda Seunagan, around the turn of the twentieth century.[26]

Until the 1940s, the *ulèëbalang* continued to sponsor entertaining performances of the traditional song-dances for their guests, including local Dutch functionaries. They invited troupes to perform at *kenduri* feasts before mixed or segregated audiences in the great houses on holy days, holidays, and at life-event ceremonies. Indeed, the 1920s and 1930s were marked by lengthy *ulèëbalang* weddings that featured elaborate performances of all the male and female musical, dance, storytelling, and theatrical arts (Ibu Cut Asiah, pers. comm., February 2007).[27] The *ulèëbalang* encouraged female circle-dance troupes to develop entertaining new choreographies and to wear attractive traditional Acehnese costumes, with their hair worn in a high Acehnese bun slanted to one side with cascades of jasmine flowers attached. In the 1930s, the *malelang* troupe at Kuala Batée even wore Dutch-influenced dresses and skirts, as they do today (see fig. 12.4).

Phô, malelang, and *manoe pocuk* song-dances continued to be performed at many kinds of functions, including a baby's first wash or haircut, and at circumcisions, weddings, and rituals to fulfill a vow or seek good fortune. Members of audiences at village feasts were entertained by *syahé* whose *kisah* and final *estra* (extra) components in some performances expressed subtle criticisms of the Dutch and mourned the deaths of the western Acehnese heroes Teuku Umar and his wife Cut Nyak Dhien in the war. The Dutch rejected some art forms that were permitted by the *ulama*, such as *dabôh* and the bards' *Hikayat Prang Sabi* (Ac., "Holy War Epic"), which expressed resistance to colonial rule.[28] The *syahé* also sang traditional or popular Aneuk Jamée or Pasisir Melayu songs, such as "Lagu Pulau Pinang" (chap. 10), and local adaptations of songs from the popular Malay film repertory. When an audience's attention finally began to flag, they sang the *saleum top* (Ac., "final greeting") including a request to the audience to forgive any inadequacies in the performance while the group stood in a row for the final bow and then made their exit.

The colonial era ended with the Japanese occupation (1942–45) and the war of Indonesian independence (1945–49), including Aceh's Cumbok war (1945–46), which resulted in the killing or exile of most members of the *ulèëbalang* class because they were believed to have collaborated with the Dutch (Meuraxa 1966). Like all the other performing arts, *phô* declined in this period of violent conflict. The ensuing vacuum of power was filled by the religious leaders, who continued to adhere to an austere form of Islam, banned the non-Muslim arts, and restricted female singing and dancing to female audiences in the home.[29] According to Amir, "These were dire times for the *ulèëbalang*-backed art forms, given that anti-royal, nationalist sentiments were so strong. . . . [They] returned to [their] roots in the villages, being performed only in those rural settings in which religious edicts were less strictly enforced" (2006, 134).

The quality of artistic life suffered again during the period of civil unrest between 1953 and 1957.[30] However, as a gesture of political reconciliation and to boost the credentials of the *ulama*, the first governor of Aceh, Ali Hasjmi, who was the leader of its largest *ulama* organization, PUSA (Persatuan Ulama Seluruh Aceh), opened the first, week-long Festival of Acehnese Arts (Pekan Kebudayaan Aceh [PKA I]) in the capital in August 1958. Troupes from all over Aceh presented performances, but they did not include western Aceh's *phô* nor the pan-Acehnese male genre *seudati*. "The *ulama* vetoed *seudati* and some even declared it to be *haram* ("forbidden") in Islam" (Amir 2006, 134), the implication being that only Muslim-associated forms should be allowed, for all "animist" expressions were deemed irreligious and backward. After a debate lasting about a decade, the local Department of Religious Affairs declared that the real problem was not the singing and dancing but the feared impropriety of mixed audiences that might lead to improper sexual liaisons and forgetting to pray (ibid.).[31]

Meanwhile, Acehnese and Indonesian government patronage of the arts had replaced that of the former *ulëëbalang* in the colonial period. Under President Sukarno, Department of Education and Culture offices tried to stimulate artistic activity in villages and towns by organizing arts festivals and competitions, collecting data on performing groups in rural and urban areas, and choosing troupes to take part in cultural missions in other parts of Indonesia and abroad. *Phô, malelang, manoe pocuk*, and *meuseukat* dances continued to be performed at village events, but they were neglected at the regency level.

Major changes in the arts and the demise of many artists occurred under Suharto's New Order (1965–98). Though Aceh's violent separatist unrest had subsided by 1962, it was followed by a huge purge of Communists and others during Suharto's ascent to power in 1965–66, which led to the deaths of many artists and further diminished grassroots artistic activity. It also induced the government to issue edicts that would standardize select art forms, discourage or forbid those that were out of favor, and exclude any antigovernment commentary (especially from the *estra* sections in *phô* and *seudati*), so that they could be used during election campaigns and at government functions.

Phô was one of the art forms that was redeveloped and controlled by codifying its sequence of song-dances, dance movements, costumes, and songs. It was excluded from the first All Aceh Arts Festival (PKA I) in 1958, but the Department of Culture officials in Jeuram helped the talented female singer-dancer Chèh Mak Yan of Desa Lama Inong train a troupe of *phô* singer-dancers to perform an abridged version for an appearance at the second all-Aceh arts festival (PKA II) in 1972 (Ibu Cut Asiah, pers. comm., 2007). She standardized the songs, movements, dance formations, body percussion, and costumes and rechoreographed the dances into a thirty-minute routine that could be shortened further if the protocol of the occasion demanded it, for example, at government or commercial functions. She included in the mix of Acehnese items two song-dances attached to the Aneuk Jamée legend "Malelang." The popular *estra* (*lanie*) section was standardized, curbing the opportunity for the *syahé* to comment critically on politically controversial topics and providing approved texts on government "development" policy for the *syahé* and *rakan* to sing.[32]

A modern *phô* performance normally lasts around thirty minutes, with each of its segments shortened to two to three minutes (audiovisual example 12.1). Usually a *syahé* and a group of eight women dance, sing, and perform body percussion. The *syahé* stands apart with her *apét* assistant and sings the standard verses to standard melodies, avoiding the traditional *phô* laments. She sings lullabies, a pair of lyrics about "Malelang," and texts on weddings, babies, and heroines. After the *rakan* enter the stage and form two parallel rows, they perform the *saleum bersaf* (opening greeting bow) and then dance a medley of eleven song-dances in circles, concentric circles, half-circles, and triangular, pentagonal, and boat-shaped formations (M. Kartomi 2004, 33–37).[33]

The first *phô* item—"the heavenly bird-flower procession" (*bineuih bungong rawatu*)—begins with the artists stepping meditatively around a circle as the *syahé* sings sad *panton* quatrains from the Malelang legend, sometimes drawing the moral that young men and women should never be alone together or that slander is destructive and wrong (audiovisual example 12.2). The next three song-dances depict the two major phases in a young woman's life, marriage, with the *syahé* singing *panton* that refer to a bride's sadness as she leaves the parental home and her ritual bath, and the birth and bathing of her baby.

In "the bride descends to bathe" (*tren dara baro*) item, a "bride" (danced by the *syéh/céh* [local spelling]) kneels in the middle of the rotating *rakan*, whose dance symbolizes a procession down to the river for a bride's ritual bath before the marriage ceremony. As the singer-dancers rotate slowly around the *syéh*, they pause at twelve progressive points in the circle while performing a *malelang* dance-like stepping routine, moving the right foot to the front and the back, diagonally toward the center and back, diagonally away from the center and back, and then to the front and the back again. In the "bathing of a baby" (*troun tajak manoe*) item, the kneeling *syéh* mimes the bathing movements, while four of the *rakan* kneel together in front and the others stand behind her.

In the following "baby swaying in a hammock" (*ayon aneuk*) item, the *rakan* portray the movement of swaying in a hammock, while the lead singer sings the lullaby "Jak Kutimang" ("Sway Back and Forth"). The *syéh* sings comments that are answered by the group, who snap their fingers on the second and fourth beats of a measure, then on each beat, after which they beat the sides of their thighs on the upbeats, followed by sharp hand-claps on the downbeats. The composite score of a segment of a performance of this song is presented in music example 12.1. In the transcription, the odd-numbered dancers (designated *uneun*) clap their right hand horizontally down onto their left palm, while the even-numbered dancers (*wie*) clap their left hand horizontally down onto their right palm. The transcription is from

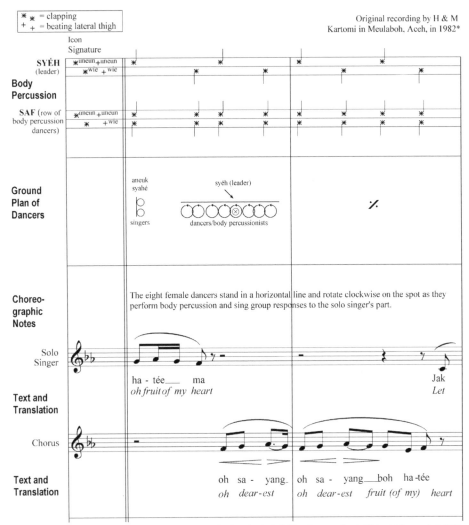

Music example 12.1. Segment of a transcription from a composite score depicting a performance of a lullaby, "Jak Kutimang," with vocal and body-percussion music in a modern *phô* performance, led by the syahé Cèh Siti Jeuram from Ibu Cut Asiah's Pho Cut Nya Dien troupe, recorded in Meulaboh in 1982.

a recording of "Jak Kutimang" on M. Kartomi 1998, CD 2. The text, which may be sung in the *phô* or the meuseukat song-dances, reads:

Jak ku dodo hai aneuk do do da i-di
O sayang boh hate kan kutimang
[Let (me) sing oh child sing to sleep, Si Kumbang
Oh dearest fruit of my heart]

Music example 12.1. Cont.

Finally, while members of the *rakan* stand still, the soloist sings a popular song as a signal to the group that the ritual section has finished and the *estra* (*lanie*) section is about to begin. Members of the audience look forward to this component, because they know the popular songs well, and the soloists constantly surprise and amuse them with the content and style of their suggestive, allusive verses.

The vocalist takes the limelight again and leads the section. First, she sings the *kisah* (storytelling) section in slow to medium tempo, with poetic texts that tell part of the tragic "Malelang" story, while the other artists stand at ease and listen. Occasionally they step forward around a circle or a pair of concentric circles, which serves as a structural device between sections. If there is time, the *syahé* may intersperse her lyrics with humorous or ironic commentaries on daily life experiences, current events, politics, religion, and sex, but normally the time is occupied with four or more standard *estras*, that is, (1) *peuleuet manok* ("cockfight," lit. "trimmed rooster"), that is, a vocal duel between the *syahé* and her *apét* that is reminiscent of the now-banned cockfighting duels; (2) *bineuih bungong rawatu* (the flowers procession) with a sorrowful text about the funeral procession of the hapless Malelang and Madion; (3) *thum bédék* (cannon shot), a scene with a text that refers to the killing of the anti-Dutch war hero Teuku Umar; and (4) *gr'um it-it manoe* (bathe to the sound of beating and prayer), a scene in which the dancers stand in a single row and rotate slowly on the spot while singing a prayer and performing body percussion.[34]

Unlike their forebears prior to the 1940s, female vocalists in the more devout villages refrain from improvising risqué *panton* texts; if allowed on stage at all, they sing only demure lyrics. However, some female *syahé* in more liberal villages improvise witty or telling lyrics on politics, sex, and religion, as in some of my video recordings of Syéh Indah's songs made in Beutong Ateuh in 2010.[35]

As the above description shows, the body-percussion techniques used in modern *phô* can include hand-clapping (*pok-pok jaroe*), finger-snapping (*geuteb jaroe*), and thigh-beating (*pèh pha*) or kneecap-tapping (*pèh teuot*), as well as the essential quasi-body-percussion technique of foot-stamping (*geud'am gaki*), with each technique realized in a variety of movements and sounds. In some performances the dancers borrow techniques from the *seudati* dance, such as lower shoulder-tapping (*pèh bahoe*), elbow-tapping (*pèh singkè*), and light backside-tapping (*pèh punggung*). However, *pho* never includes breast-beating (*pèh dada*), a technique reserved for male *seudati* performers. (see fig. 12.5)[36] Although the stamping and clapping around a corpse in *phô* used to express the dancing mourners' feelings of grief, the body percussion today has only aesthetic meaning. The stamping serves a rhythmic and colotomic (punctuating) musical role, that is, to mark the end of a rhythmic cycle and the beginning of its repeat, with the clapping and thigh-beating in some performances serving a subsidiary punctuating role.

In the 1980s, the newly transformed version of *phô* became popular in many parts of western Aceh, with the performers being encouraged to wear traditional Acehnese costumes, including shiny *songket*-cloth torso wraps around their trouser suits, ancestral jewelry, and flower-ornamented Acehnese hair knots (fig. 12.6). At a performance that I recorded in Meulaboh in 1982, the *syahé* sang lyrics about a wide range of topics, including Muslim themes, doomsday, earthquakes, exploits of heroes and heroines, endearments for a child, references to legendary princesses, descriptions of body percussion and dance movements, the loss of a best friend, various allegories, for example, about birds representing a class of school girls, and New Order/Suharto-era government propaganda (Kartomi 2003, CD notes).

Category I Body percussion sounds/movements

LOWER SHOULDER OR UPPER BREAST TAPPING (sitting)		
1	□	*peh bahoe [uneun, abbrev: un]*: right hand tapping on left or right shoulder
2	□	*peh bahoe [wie]*: left hand tapping on left or right shoulder
3	⊟	*peh bahoe [uneun/wie]*: right hand tapping on right shoulder and left hand tapping on left shoulder
4	▭✕▭	*peh bahoe [uneun/wie]*: double shoulder tapping with crossed hands
5	⌐	*peh bahoe [uneun]*: right hand tapping on neighbouring dancer's shoulder
6	┐	*peh bahoe [wie]*: left hand tapping on neighbouring dancer's shoulder
BREAST BEATING ON LOWEST RIB, male only (standing and stepping)		
7	○	*peh dada [uneun]*: right hand beating on left breast
8	○	*peh dada [wie]*: left hand beating on right breast
9	8	*peh dada [uneun/wie]*: double breast beating
ELBOW TAPPING (sitting)		
10	⌐	*peh singkè [uneun]*: right hand tapping on left elbow
11	¬	*peh singkè [wie]*: left hand tapping on right elbow
BACKSIDE TAPPING (standing, stepping or sitting)		
12	⊞	*peh punggung [uneun]*: right backside tapping with right hand
13	⊞	*peh punggung [wie]*: left backside tapping with left hand
THIGH BEATING (standing, stepping or sitting)		
14	+−	*peh pha [uneun]*: right hand beating on right outer lateral thigh
15	−+	*peh pha [wie]*: left hand beating on left outer lateral thigh
16	+	*peh pha [uneun]*: right hand beating on left or right front thigh
17	+	*peh pha [wie]*: left hand beating on left or right front thigh
18	‡	*peh pha [uneun/wie]*: right hand beating on right thigh and left hand beating on left thigh
19	+✕+	*peh pha [uneun/wie]*: crossed hand beating on opposite thighs
20	⊕	*peh pha [uneun/wie]*: back of right hand beating on right front thigh or back of left hand beating on left front thigh, or both
KNEE CAP TAPPING (sitting)		
21	◢	*peh teuot [uneun]*: right hand tapping just above left knee cap
22	◢	*peh teuot [wie]*: left hand tapping just above right knee cap
23	◢	*peh teuot [uneun/wie]*: both hands tapping both knees
CLAPPING (standing, stepping or sitting)		
24	✳	*pok-pok jaroe [uneun]*: right hand horizontal clapping down on left palm (sometimes as body sways to left), or clapping a neighbour's hand
25	✳	*pok-pok jaroe [wie]*: left hand horizontal clapping down on right palm (sometimes as body sways to right), or clapping a neighbour's hand
26	✳✳	*pok-pok jaroe*: vertical hand clapping to the front of the body
27	✳✳	*pok-pok jaroe*: vertical hand clapping above the head
28	✳−✳	*pok-pok jaroe*: clapping a neighbouring dancer's hand
FINGER SNAPPING (standing, stepping or sitting)		
29	✕	*geutèb jaroe [uneun]*: third finger and thumb snapping on right palm
30	✕	*geutèb jaroe [wie]*: third finger and thumb snapping on left palm
31	⦻	*geutèb jaroe [uneun/wie]*: simultaneous (double) finger snapping in both hands
32	−⦻−	*geutèb jaroe I [uneun/wie]*: double finger snapping with both arms outstretched or moving both hands in circular formations
33	✕− −✕	*geutèb jaroe II [uneun/wie]*: double finger snapping with raised elbows in front of body

Category II Quasi-body percussion sounds/movements taught with body percussion

FOOT STAMPING (standing or stepping)		
1	⚄	*geu'dam gaki [uneun]*: stamping or tapping right foot on the floor or ground, often with finger snapping to accentuate the sound
2	⚄	*geu'dam gaki [wie]*: stamping or tapping left foot on the floor or ground, often with finger snapping to accentuate the sound
FLOOR BEATING (sitting)		
3	˜	*peh aleue [uneun]*: beating right palm on floor
4	˜	*peh aleue [wie]*: beating left palm on floor
5	˜˜	*peh aleue [uneun/wie]*: beating both palms on floor

Category III Other movements taught with body percussion

SHOULDER SHRUGGING (standing)		
1	V	*nyet*: shrugging shoulders while lowering body by bending at knees
2	Λ	*nyap*: shrugging shoulders while standing up on one's toes

Figure 12.5 A classification of body percussion, quasi body percussion, and related movements in Aceh.

The then-governor (Ibrahim Hassan) encouraged government artists and officials to stimulate artistic activity and raise performance standards, partly via holding contests (*tunang*) between the regional art troupes and partly by offering opportunities to some groups to perform during government election campaigns.[37]

Ibu Cut Asiah (see fig. 12.7) led the troupe sponsored by the *bupati* (regent) of West Aceh in Meulaboh to perform the newly standardized version of *phô* at PKA III in 1987, and she also took part in the concurrently held seminar on *phô*. However, the seminar did not encourage creative innovation; on the contrary, it further codified it. Its report expressed the hope that its standard form would be learned and performed by many young troupes of artists in the region (Ibu Cut Asiah, pers. comm., 2007). Indeed, the official performance of *phô* by the *bupati*'s troupe that we

Figure 12.6 *Phô* dancers in traditional costumes and hair knots, Meulaboh, 1982

saw in Meulaboh in 2007 was remarkably similar choreographically to the one we recorded in 1982; Ibu Cut Asiah herself confirmed that there was little substantial difference. It was as if *phô* had been frozen for years during the worst of the conflict, only to reappear a quarter century later in the same, standardized, form.[38]

The relative resurgence of artistic activity in the 1970s and 1980s ended in 1989, when the government began a decade of serious military operations to suppress the separatist Free Aceh Movement (GAM). Village performances became rare, occurring only in the relative safety of day. Due to frequent military action, curfews, and poor security, family celebrations were postponed or held quietly, and female song-dances were performed only in safe rural environments and in protected government venues.

When Suharto lost power and the Indonesian Reform (Reformasi) era began in 1998, *phô* performances became even less frequent, as even the previously frugal government funding was reduced or ceased altogether, for a time. After the government imposed martial law again in 2003, *phô* was performed only at a few government-sponsored festivals, including the first and second Peyasan Pasè (Celebrations in Pasè) in Lhokseumawe in 2003 and 2004, and the Kutaradja Arts Festival and PKA-IV in Banda Aceh, with troupes being sent by all the *bupati*'s offices (including those in Jeuram and Meulaboh) to take part in the competitions. Security in the west and the

Figure 12.7 Ibu Cut Asiah
(b. 1930) in 2007

south was so poor that performances of the arts were virtually in abeyance, though some proseparatist (GAM) songs and traditional arts were performed in GAM-controlled areas. If *phô* was performed at all, the women modified their costumes in tune with the newly imposed *syari'a* law, moving away from the traditional Acehnese trouser suit and hair bun in favor of a long dress over trousers and a *jilbab* (Muslim headscarf) that covered their neck and hair.

During those decades of military conflict, Aceh was virtually forgotten by the outside world. Then the tsunami struck on 26 December 2004, the worst-hit area being in and around Meulaboh, and international pressure on the Indonesian government and GAM led to a peace agreement in 2005. The people had lived with the conflict and frequent curfews for so long that once peace was declared there was an explosion of artistic activity, dance schools were reopened, and new traditional and pop music groups were formed. On traveling around western Aceh in 2007 and 2010, I witnessed a joyous upsurge of celebrations and postponed life-event ceremonies in the countryside.[39] In 2010, I recorded a *phô* performance led by the talented singer-dancer Syéh Indah in Dusun Puuk, a hamlet in the isolated agricultural village Beutong Ateuh in the mountains of Nagan Raya.[40] Syéh Indah had her mixed audience in stitches of laughter as she set up a *kisah* with improvised *estra* sections at the end of her troupe's *phô* and *ayeun aneuk* (lullaby) performances, daringly referring in the latter case to the baby's penis and intimations of sex. In her songs she also mentioned the names of former *ulèëbalang* in their palaces and referred to the ancestors who had migrated from Pidie in northern Aceh. She used a seven-tone palette, but the *phô* dancers sang in the melodic range: D E F G A, while dancing in a steady, medium tempo throughout. When singing the "Jak Kutimang" lullaby, they performed cycles of movements with clapping and stamping in four-beat measures, including the routines //: clap—raise both hands—step—stamp://, and: step—step—sway foot on floor—stamp://.

Despite the serious decline in performances during the twenty-nine-year conflict, *phô* resumed its role as an insignia art form of western Aceh. Contemporary stage performances of *phô* comply not only with devout Acehnese religious leaders' continuing demand for female modesty, gender segregation, and propagation of Muslim morality, but also with the government's promotion of attractive female dancers as a symbol of West Aceh's identity. Meanwhile, some thoughtful present-day artists are considering whether they will be able to creatively redevelop *phô* in the future, now that its identity as a rural folk form and carrier of social critique has seemingly been lost, though perhaps not irretrievably.

||||

Four hundred years ago, *phô* was a funereal circle song-dance that featured passionate Shi'a-like breast beating and an indigenous religious atmosphere, after which it became a series of both sad and flirtatious dances at funerals, and was finally transformed to express an idealized Muslim view of Acehnese female identity. Changes from traditional to modern *phô* performance style—from mixed to female-only audiences, funereal to idealized feminine singing-dancing, expansion of the tragic stamping to include other body percussion, and the addition of a moral Aneuk Jamée story ("Malelang") to the Acehnese *phô* dance—clearly reflect the changes in religious belief, a trend toward stricter gender relations, and the mix of two ethnicities. Modern *phô* meets the desires of both government officials and religious leaders in their respective campaigns. Like the aristocratic *ulèëbalang* leaders in colonial times, government officials benefit from sharing the aura of attractive female artists at functions, and current religious leaders like to promote female performances that feature modest Muslim dress, express Muslim thoughts and greetings, and exude a moral message.

The history of *phô* in the twentieth century is the story of a number of talented women artists, some of whose names are recorded in the cultural memory. Due mainly to *phô's* association with pre-Muslim funeral laments, it was not allowed at the first all-Aceh arts festival, PKA-I in 1958. Rather than let *phô* die, however, Ibu Mak Yan transformed it in the late 1950s into a religiously and socially acceptable *kreasi baru* (new creation) that combined segments of the Aneuk Jamée *malelang* song-dance with several western Acehnese female song-dances, making it suitable for performance on official government occasions, exposure in the media, or even—if so desired—at a modern wedding or other feast. She also led a troupe to perform the newly choreographed *phô* at the PKA-II festival in 1972, while her former student Ibu Cut Asiah led performances of a similar choreography at PKA-III in 1987, PKA-IV in 2004, and PKA-V in 2008 (Ibu Cut Asiah, pers. comm., 2010). Ibu Cut Asiah's former student Ibu Rohani and her *syahé* Siti Jeuram from Calang in Kabupaten Aceh Jaya performed the same version at the festival in Lhokseumawe in 2003.

Of the three lamentation song-dances in western and southern Aceh, only *phô* has been sufficiently transformed to become an official symbol of female Acehnese identity today. Modern *phô* is a standard thirty-minute dance with a moral message and a fixed structure that can be imitated by any trained group if it possesses a lead singer who can perform the appropriate songs. *Malelang* is not regarded as an identity symbol because it is performed in only a few villages and its songs are in the Aneuk Jamée language. Nor is *manoe pocuk* suitable, as it is a simple circle song-dance that can be learned through informal observation by any group of willing females at a ritual, as long as a competent lead singer is available.

The general shortage of female lead singers is a major challenge to the future survival of all three circle-dance performances. In the more isolated villages, it is still fairly common for daughters to inherit their mothers' musical and dance skills, as in the isolated hamlet of Puuk in Gampong Beutong Ateuh, where the singer Syéh Nurulala (alias Syéh Lima) recently handed over leadership of the female performing arts to her daughter Syéh Indah (as I witnessed on a visit in 2010). However, in the towns and cities such a traditional mode of transmission is now rare.

ACKNOWLEDGMENTS

I was very grateful on our first field trip to Meulaboh in 1983 for assistance from the *bupati* of West Aceh, the late Teuku Tjut Mohamad Hoessin of Oedjong Kalak, Koetapadang, and the choreographer Ibu Cut Asiah with her late husband, Bp. Zakariah bin Hadi, as troupe promoter and lead singer Siti Jeuram. I also interviewed Ibu Cut Asiah in 2007 and 2010.

I greatly appreciated the opportunity to record performances by many troupes from Aceh Barat, Aceh Jaya, Nagan Raya, and Aceh Barat Daya who had gathered in Lhokseumawe in 2003 to compete in the Festival Tari dan Seuruné Kalée (Festival of Acehnese Dance and Oboes) organized by the festival director, M. Rizal and Bupati Tarmizi A. Karim in Lhokseumawe.

Of the many other artists consulted on our field trips between 2003 and 2010, the most experienced and informed were the late Noerdin Daood of Pidie and Jakarta (who accompanied us to Lhoksemawe in 2003) and the fine *seudati* dancer and choreographer Syéch Lah Geunta of Aceh Timur. Ibu Cèh Murniati, Ibu Cèh Nurmulia of Jeuram, and Ibu Rohani of Jaya Jalang village (near Jeuram) were also helpful, as were Ibu Céh Hanila Y.S. of Pasar Kota Bahagia and Ibu Céh Nurhayati of Desa Gelanggang Gajah, who led performances in the Rumôh Putéh at Desa Kasa, Kecamatan Kuala Batée in March 2007, and the *ulèëbalang* descendant Ibu Cut Putéh at the Rumôh Putéh. Ibu Rohani of Jaya Jalang village (near Jeuram), whose late singing teacher, Ibu Hasana of Daya Baro village informed her about *ulèëbalang* artistic practices in the 1930s, led performances that we recorded in the Lhokseumawe Festival in 2003. We are also grateful to the Culture and Tourism Department officers Bp. Nyak Cut Syam in Meulaboh in 2007 and Bp. Tabrani Usman and Dr. Sayid Saifullah in Jeuram in 2010. Also in 2010, we were assisted by Ibu Syéh Indah of Gampong Blang Seumoet, Kecamatan Beutong, Nagan Raya. In 2005 we were assisted by Ibu Céh Nurmulia of Jeuram and Ibu Murniati and Ibu Rasmiati in Desa Air Berudang, Kecamatan Tapaktuan Aceh Barat Daya.

Our most important colleague in western Aceh was the fine *syahé* and lament singer Marzuki Hassan, who accompanied us on our 2007 field trip in Aceh Barat Daya and Nagan Raya. Born in Gampung Muntai Gerung-Gerung, Blangpidie, he has a very deep practical knowledge of the performing arts. Since 2003 he has also assisted us several times in our research at the Jakarta Arts Institute, where he has taught West Acehnese vocal music and dances for the past thirty-six years, and in Jakarta's Acehnese diaspora community.

Finally, my warm thanks go to colleagues Lance Castles in Melbourne for his research advice and Iwan Amir for his research assistance and camera skills on our trips to Aceh in 2003, 2007, and 2010.

13

"ONLY IF A MAN CAN KILL A BUFFALO WITH ONE BLOW CAN HE PLAY A RAPA'I PASÈ"

The Frame Drum as a Symbol of Male Identity

RAPA'I CULTURE

The largest kind of frame drum in Aceh is the great *rapa'i Pasè*, with a skin head and heavy wooden body of up to a meter or more in upper diameter and up to thirty-two centimeters in body length.[1] The name is believed to derive from the Pasai (Ac. Pasè) district of North Aceh, where the first known Muslim kingdom in Southeast Asia—Samudera Pasai—was founded in the late thirteenth century.[2] Venerated as family heirlooms and associated with supernatural energy, *adat*, Islam, state political power, the historical greatness of Aceh, and male-human strength, the *rapa'i Pasè* was traditionally played in ensembles with the singing of improvised texts at life-cycle and religious feasts and in intervillage competitions and served as a signaling agent between villages in Pidie, Bireuen, and North Aceh. Because such strength and energy are required to play a *rapa'i Pasè*, it is said that only a man who can kill a buffalo with one sharp blow can do so, for he must produce a sound that reverberates like thunder, and it can carry as far as ten kilometers away.[3]

Besides the *rapa'i Pasè*, Acehnese men play several other variants of the frame drum and the tambourine (i.e., frame drums with jingles attached). All of them are known generically as the *rapa'i*, though some variants are also known as *rabana* in southeastern and southwestern areas.[4] The main Acehnese variants of the frame drum are differentiated from one another by name and approximate size, as shown in table 13.1 (see also figs. 13.2–13.6).

Table 13.1 The main variants of the Acehnese *rapa'i*

Instrument type	Size
Rapa'i Pasè	Large to very large (70 cm to 1.3 m in diameter and 18–32 cm in body length)
Rapa'i dabôh	Medium-large size (ca. 48–50 cm x 12 cm)
Rapa'i geurimpheng	Medium size (ca. 35–38 cm x 8–10 cm)
Rapa'i pulot	
Rapai geleng	Medium size (ca. 38 cm x 10 cm).
	Medium size (ca. 35 cm x 8 cm)
Dap, dab, or *rapa'i aneuk/tingkah*	Tiny (6–8 cm x 4 cm)

The *rapa'i* family of musical instruments occurs in a large number of artistic genres, both secular and religious. In the secular genres, between eight and twenty men play a single *rapa'i* each, while one or two play in a vocal and/or instrumental ensemble, with double the number played in competitions between two groups. In Sufi-style religious genres such as *rapa'i dabôh*, sixty or more men of a village and surrounding areas may take part. In group performances usually one or several *rapa'i* musicians repeatedly play a simple rhythm, mainly focusing on the downbeats, while another (or another group) plays more-complex, interlocking rhythms, focusing on a syncopated rhythmic commentary. The latter are called the *rapa'i tingkah* (interlocking *rapa'i*) players.

This chapter demonstrates the ways in which the ergology (making) and morphology of the variants of the *rapa'i* relate to its performance practice, the genres in which it is used, the cultural memory, and the sense of Acehnese cultural identity among its makers, performers, and audiences. It begins by considering the defining and distinctive elements of the Acehnese sense of identity in its connection to *rapa'i*. It also discusses the loss of thousands of *rapa'i Pasè* (which are by far the most valuable of the frame-drum types) during Aceh's recent armed conflict (1976–2005) and considers the attempts by Indonesian governments to appropriate, secularize, and aestheticize *rapa'i* and other forms of the traditional arts, and the various elite and nonelite views of identity.[5] Due to limited space, other *rapa'i* genres that are named after their accompanying performance style and song content such as *rapa'i kisah* (storytelling *rapa'i*) and *rapa'i hajat* (Ar. "(Muslim) message *rapa'i*") will not be discussed, nor will the organological variants of the frame drums of the Tamiang Malay, Aneuk Jamèe/Pasisir Malay, and Gayo musico-lingual groups in Aceh.[6]

RAPA'I AND ACEHNESE IDEAS OF IDENTITY

Given the important role of *rapa'i* performance at feasts and celebrations and the attribution of indigenous religious as well as Muslim-Sufi spiritual and social meaning to the instruments, many Acehnese—including the orthodox *ulama* and secular government–technocrat or community leaders at all levels—regard the instrument as a symbol of Acehnese unity and cultural identity.[7]

Ideas of identity are always, of course, in a state of flux as a result of changing social, religious, class-based, and cultural experience. Acehnese men, women, children, indigenous-religious mystics, traditionalist Sufi Muslims, modernist Muslim leaders, descendants of former aristocrats, government officials, artists, soldiers, and other groups within the community have their own colorings of that sense of identity. Doubtless, the complex effects of horizontal conflicts within the Acehnese elite and vertical conflicts between the Acehnese elite and the Indonesian government (and the Dutch colonial government before that) have influenced the changing definitions or symbols of identity.[8] However, most seem to agree that playing and listening to *rapa'i* and other traditional music—as well as dancing and other public representational systems—help to articulate their sense of identity as Acehnese. Only very few—if any—religious leaders subscribe to the Wahhabi-associated bans on musical instruments and dance found in the Middle East. Thus *rapa'i* culture is deeply embedded in the all-male devotional sessions in the men's communal houses (*meunasah*) and in the performances at celebrations or competitions.

As an Acehnese proverb puts it, the *rapa'i* is as much a symbol of Acehnese identity as is the well-known *timpan* cake, and together the two symbols represent communal unity.[9] The Acehnese verse and its Indonesian and English translations are as shown in table 13.2. To paraphrase the proverb: "Just as we need pure rather than muddy water (and rice), we should live not for ourselves but for our community, as symbolized by *timpan* cakes and *rapa'i* music that are contributed at celebrations." As it is the women who provide the refreshments and the men who provide the entertainment

Table 13.2 An Acehnese verse and its Indonesian and English translations

Acehnese	Indonesian	English
Ie, ie bit	*Air, air sesungguhnya*	Water, real water
Bu pi bu bit	*Nasi pun nasi sesungguhnya*	Rice, real rice
Peunajôh timpan	*Penyejuk timpan*	Refreshments are *timpan* cakes
Piasan rapa'i	*Alat perayaan rapa'i*	Tools of celebration are the *rapa'i*
Meukon ie leuhop	*Bukan air lumpur*	Not muddy water
Meukon droe gob	*Bukan diri sendiri, kaum sendiri*	Not ourselves but our community

(*rapa'i* music) at celebrations, the *timpan* cakes are seen as a symbol of the female view and the *rapa'i* as the symbol of the male view of Acehnese identity. For in traditional practice it is only the men who are regarded as having the physical strength and endurance to play the instrument, and they frequently do so for hours on end.

Thus only fit men can play a *rapa'i* and contribute to the team in the expected style, which is tightly organized, compact, and regimented. Like the *rapa'i Pasè*, men who play the heavy *rapa'i dabôh* need greater strength than the players of the smaller frame drums, though considerable physical endurance is required to play the medium-sized *dabôh* frame drums, especially at high, emotional points in performances when some participants enter a trancelike state of religious concentration as they seek "invulnerability" (*éleumèe keubai*) when preparing themselves for fighting. The *rapa'i* genres' emphasis on bodily and religious or mystical strength, endurance, and defensive capability is seen to express those facets of identity that are characteristically male and heroic. Women, who are viewed as ideally soft and gentle, are regarded as quite unsuited to *rapa'i* performance, even though the prophet reportedly allowed them to play frame drums, and despite the fact that famous warrior heroines and queens punctuate Aceh's history.[10] Gender is a significant socio-ideological divide in the Acehnese performing arts. Audiences are segregated, not only because the *ulama* forbid the uncontrolled mixing of the sexes but also because Aceh is traditionally a matrilocal society, with distinct rules about property ownership, the division of labor, and expectations of how each gender ought to behave. *Rapa'i*-linked performances belong to a male—not a female—coloring of identity.

Acehnese narratives about identity tend to emphasize the primordial aspects of the "glorious past." Known for centuries as Serambi Mekah (I., "The Porch of Mecca"), Aceh was widely regarded as a center of religious knowledge and as the last port of call for pilgrims from Southeast Asia traveling to and from the Holy Land.[11] Aceh's strategic location made it famous as a center for international trade, which attracted merchants from north, east, and west, including China, India, the Arabic-Persian lands, and Europe.

Historical awareness as a marker of Acehnese identity is expressed in many of the performing arts, including improvised song texts and bardic tales that tell of Aceh's pride in its rise to greatness as a Muslim trading empire under Sultan Iskandar Muda and his successors from the turn of the seventeenth century. Islam is widely believed to have first come to northern Sumatra with visiting Muslim traders in the late first millennium C.E., some of whom married local women, which resulted in minority, though lasting, communities of Muslims settling in areas that had previously espoused animist, Hindu, or Buddhist beliefs. Only beginning in the thirteenth and fourteenth centuries were some port principalities in northern Sumatra and the

Malay Peninsula ruled by Muslim kings. Thus some of the artistic expressions and worldviews of pre-Muslim Aceh, including those associated with old *rapa'i* frame drums that are treasured as heirlooms and believed to house spirits of the ancestors, survived in a subtly Islamized form. As the ergological methods described below will indicate, the beliefs surrounding the making and ownership of a *rapa'i* are pantheistic and ancestor venerating, though some myths surrounding the origin and function of the instrument have a predominantly Muslim hue.[12] Together these diverse belief systems combine and meld in most people's minds to make up the syncretic culture that typifies both the instrument and the people's identity.

Further clues about the ways in which the Acehnese people view themselves may be seen in the content of texts sung in the *rapa'i* genres, including love, mysticism, religion, and daily affairs. Some texts refer to heroes, heroines, soldiers, and ordinary people engaged in guerilla or other military activity against Aceh's neighbors and European trading or colonial powers over the centuries. They include the lengthy war against the Dutch colonial power from 1873 to around 1910, the feats of the anti-Dutch heroine Cut Nyak Dhien in that war, the pockets of anticolonial resistance that persisted until the Japanese invaded in 1942 and the Dutch were forced to leave, and subsequent periodic resistance to the Indonesian state from the 1950s to 2005.[13] Moreover, the song texts sound very different from those in other Sumatran languages, for Acehnese is historically related to the Chamic or Mon-Khmer language groups of Vietnam, Cambodia, and Hainan (China) through which the original ancestors are believed to have migrated to Aceh in the mid-first millennium C.E. (Daud and Durie 1999, 1).[14] Some performance traits suggest that the Acehnese may have retained some degree of artistic legacy from those lands. For example, as in mainland Southeast Asia, the north Acehnese use eggcup-shaped troughs on which to stamp the husks of their rice grain and to play rice-stamping music.[15]

Aceh's cultural uniqueness also lies in its use of the *sanjak* verse form with its internal rhyme (Snouck Hurgronje 1906, 2:73–74), its remarkably rich repertory of proverbs (ibid, 67), and the many references in the song texts to characters in Acehnese legends and to historical figures such as the remarkable sixteenth-century queen Putroe Phang and the heroine Cut Nyak Dhien (M. Kartomi 1998b (recording), Aceh CD notes).

If Acehnese *rapa'i*-based genres are compared with genres in other parts of Southeast Asia, such as in Java (which is ethnomusicologically well researched), five points of stylistic distinctiveness emerge. First, Acehnese *rapa'i* music frequently features fast, sudden cadential points and endings, unlike the slowing endings of most Javanese *gamelan* pieces. Second, the Acehnese favor vocal, frame-drum, body-percussion, and optional oboe music rather than the metal gong and drum ensembles that are dominant in Javanese, Balinese, Malay, Minangkabau, Thai, and some other Southeast Asian cultures. Third, Aceh has a much greater diversity of *rapa'i* types and performance genres than elsewhere in Indonesia and Malaysia. Fourth, most Acehnese genres are performed in groups rather than by individuals, unlike the solo as well as group performances of the Malay, the Javanese, and the Balinese. Fifth, only in Aceh is group *rapa'i* playing combined with vigorous body movement, alternating with solo and group singing and stylized group body percussion, and performed in such an enthusiastic, smiling, vigorous—even at times frenzied—way.[16]

The onomatopoeic names of the timbres produced on the various *rapa'i* are distinctive to Aceh, but they vary from place to place. In the Banda Aceh area, the high-pitched, undamped sound of a *rapa'i dabôh* is called *preung*, and the bass sound is called *tum* or *geudum* (the late Bp. Abdullah Raja, pers. comm., Banda Aceh, 1982). In North Aceh, however, the high-pitched, undamped *rapa'i* sound is called *ceureung* or *peureung*; the medium-pitched, damped sound *peureuk*; and the bass sound *meugeunton gum*. A good frame-drum sound should be either loud, clear, and high-pitched, or loud, resonant, and low-pitched; moreover, it is said, the later the hour, the more beautiful the sound of the *rapa'i*, especially if heard from afar (Ali Akbar, pers. comm., March 2003).

ORIGIN AND HISTORY OF *RAPA'I*

Many Acehnese believe that their frame drums were transplanted—along with Islam itself—from Arabia, Persia, Egypt, or elsewhere in the Middle East or central Asia at the time of the first Muslim Acehnese kingdom in the thirteenth century C.E. However, as Persian and other prototypical frame drums around the Mediterranean and western Asia existed at least as early as the third millennium B.C.E., the *rapa'i* could have been developed or—more likely—its importance strengthened far earlier than that, that is, in pre-Islamic times.[17] According to legend, merchants from the Middle East, India, and elsewhere frequently visited, traded with, and settled in Aceh from the late first millennium onward, exerting considerable religious and cultural influence on its people, who at the time subscribed to indigenous religious and Saivite-Buddhist thought.[18]

The belief is widespread that the *rapa'i Pasè* was named after the late-thirteenth-century Muslim kingdom of Samudera Pasai, located near present-day Lhokseumawe. It is probable that *rapa'i* spread as a result of the activities of a number of well-known *ulama* who traveled around various parts of Aceh. Members of the *tarèkat* brotherhoods were taught that the Sufi "way to closeness with God" included devotional singing with *rapa'i* playing as a means of disseminating the faith.

In the nineteenth century, some *ulama* who had made the pilgrimage encouraged the regular use of frame drums in their *ratéb* (religious exercises), which they had learned to perform in the holy land (Snouck Hurgronje 1994, 2:216–47).

One Acehnese *panton* verse mentions the widely held view that the *rapa'i* was transplanted into Aceh by the Persian-born saint Syéh Abdul Qadir al-Jilani (alias Bandar Khalifah 1077–1166 C.E.) and that it may have first been introduced in Kampong Pandée, Kecamatan Mesjid Raya, in Greater Aceh (Idris 1993, 79).[19] However, evidence to support this theory is hard to find. Abdul Qadir died about a millennium ago, though his influence still remains strong in Aceh and some other parts of Indonesia. The Sufi brotherhoods that operated in Aceh, such as the Qadiriyah, which he founded, and others—the Rifa'iyah, the Qushashi, the Shattariyah, and the Sammaniyah—aim to cultivate good conduct and the soul's relationship with the divine through vocal and instrumental music, especially the frame drum, of which the prophet Muhammad approved (Doubleday 1999, 109–12). Beginning in the early sixteenth century and still today, members of the brotherhoods have followed the *ilmu tassawuf* (body of Sufi knowledge) that was taught to them via the great mystical Arab, Persian Indian, and Acehnese saints. The lead singers in the *rapa'i-* or body-percussion- accompanied religious song-dances perform lyrics that are based on the *tassawuf* and promote the doctrine of the unity of being (*wahdat al-wujud*).

The name *rapa'i* itself, however, probably derives from the great twelfth-century "saint of the mystics" and founder of the Rifa'iyah brotherhood in Arabia, Syéh Ahmed Rifa'i (d. 1182, Snouck Hurgronje 1906, 1:63), which spread widely in Aceh, where Rifa'i was held in high honor (ibid., 2:49).[20] Among the outward forms of worship associated with Rifa'i are unaccompanied religious *liké* (*zikr*) singing with *rapa'i* playing that continues until the devotees attain a state of religious excitement, as in performances of *dabôh* described below, led by a *kalipah* (mystical leader) who is seen as a spiritual successor of Ahmed Rifa'i.

The earliest Muslim writers in Southeast Asia to be known by name lived in Aceh in the sixteenth and seventeenth centuries. They included the Malay scholar and poet Hamzah Fansuri, who had been initiated into the Qadiriyah order in Arabia and promoted the brotherhood's values and practices in Aceh, including the chanting of holy names and texts and *rapa'i* playing. In the seventeenth and eighteenth centuries respectively, the followers of the mystic teachers Ahmad Qushāshī' and Muḥammad Sammān also used the arts as *dakwah*. Qushāshī' encouraged his followers to become conscious of man's unity with Allah and recommended that their observances involve the repetitive chanting of the name of God and the prophets and the following of prescribed prayers (Snouck Hurgronje 1906, 2:216). Qushāshī''s disciples spread the mystical Shatarriyah *tarèkat* throughout Southeast Asia from around 1661 C.E., but it was his famous Acehnese pupil ʿAbdurraʾuf of Singkil who consolidated his teachings in Aceh, where he is revered under his popular name of Teungku di Kuala as the saint who brought Islam to Aceh (ibid., 2:17–20, 216). When Qushāshī's form of *dhikr* (*liké*) reached Aceh, it focused on a kind of mystical love of Allah combined "with a color of pantheism which satisfie[d] their craving for the esoteric and abstruse" (ibid., 2:216).

In the nineteenth century, Acehnese religious leaders from the Sammāniyah sect introduced a form of worship (*ratéb*) in the holy land that derived from the seventeenth-century mystic teacher, Muḥammad Sammān. Like other *ratéb*, it comprised repetitive group chanting of religious formulas, such as the confession of faith, epithets applied or names of Allah or praises of Allah and his prophet Muhammad.[21] Syéh Sammān held that noise and motion were "powerful agents for producing the desired state of mystic transport" as opposed to other teachers who made "quiet and repose the conditions for the proper performance of their *dikrs*" (Snouck Hurgronje 1906, 2:217). Followers of Sammān's ideas and practices in Aceh performed *ratéb saman* fast and furiously until their bodies were bathed in perspiration and they had reached "a state of unnatural excitement," which, as Snouck Hurgronje added, was "by no means diminished by the custom observed in some places of extinguishing the lights" (ibid., 2:218).[22] More than a century ago, the *saman* genre went further than other devotional art forms in expanding the dynamic range and intensity of performance, and it gradually influenced other devotional genres. Though *saman* (which is called *ratôh duek* today in Aceh and *saman* in the Gayo highlands) has never included frame drumming, the extraordinarily vigorous and continually evolving group body movements and postures of *saman* have had a strong influence on the style of group *rapaʾi* playing, not least in the popular, virtuoso form called *rapaʾi geleng*, which, with a set of head- and neck-turning movements, often reaches a frenetic state of excitement.

Religious and secular *rapaʾi* playing by members of informal Sufi brotherhoods, including the main twentieth-century *tarèkat,* Naqsyabandiyah (Bruinessen 1994, 144), still take place today in western Aceh and other areas, especially at night on Thursdays and holy days. Security conditions rarely allowed such activities to take place in the turbulent period from 1989 to 1998 (the DOM [Daerah Operasi Militer, Military Operations Area period]) through the Reformasi period (since 1998) until the Helsinki peace accord was signed in 2005. During those two decades, regular devotional sessions (e.g., *dalaiʾl*) could not be held in places of worship, and many valuable *rapaʾi Pasè* were commandeered or stolen. However, in 2005 regular devotional groups began to meet again, and instrument makers were commissioned to make new *rapaʾi*, mostly using traditional methods.

HOW *RAPA'I* ARE MADE

In traditional practice, making a *rapa'i*, which is a mystically potent object, is a dangerous process that involves rare spiritual and practical skills. The most difficult *rapa'i* to make and play is a large *rapa'i Pasè* (fig. 13.1), which is regarded as a great "instrument of the soul" (Daham 2003, 4).[23] As it is made, a *rapa'i Pasè* maker (*utôh*) and his assistant must address prayers to the appropriate ancestral or nature spirit, followed by a prayer to Allah.

Whereas it takes three or four full working days for a maker (*utôh*) to create a set of *rapa'i geurimpheng* or *rapa'i pulot*, it usually takes him and six assistants at least a month to create a single large *rapa'i Pasè*, once he finds the right timber and skin. The diameter of the cow- or buffalo-skin heads of the *rapa'i Pasè* vary from 1.3 meters (in the case of a *rapa'i Pasè cut*, "large drum") to about 70 centimeters (*rapa'i Pasè ubit*, "small drum"), while the waisted wooden bodies range from 18 to 32 centimeters deep, and the whole instrument may weigh up to 30 kilograms (Ibu Aisyah Daud, pers. comm., 1982).

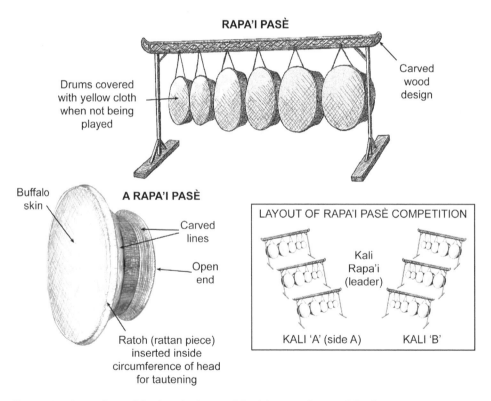

Figure 13.1 A set of *rapa'i Pasè*; a single *rapa'i Pasè*; layout of a *rapa'i Pasè* competition

Very few makers of this remarkable instrument are left in Aceh today.[24] One is reputed to live in Meulaboh, West Aceh, while another lives in North Aceh.[25] Like all the legendary *utôh*, Utôh Taleb—who lives in Buloh Blang Ara, Kecamatan Kuta Makmur, North Aceh—inherited his skills for making and playing *rapa'i Pasè* from his father and grandfather before him. His workshop, located in Larek Baloh, employs six or more men when a job is in hand.

To make a *rapa'i Pasè*, a great black hardwood (*kayu puno*) tree must be found. If low-quality wood is used, a drum will fail to produce a strong sound with significant carrying power. By far the most suitable wood comes from a *tualang* tree, which is the *endatu* (ancestor) of all good timber, but finding a suitable tree in the forest is not easy.[26] A maker and his assistant might have to search for up to two weeks to find a suitable tree that can be cut in an environmentally sensitive way so as not to destroy other trees and undergrowth. The pair invoke the spirits and pray at every step of the process. Before cutting the lower part (I. *bani*) or trunk (I. *akar*) of the tree, a mystical ceremony (*peusijuek*, lit., "cooling ceremony") must be performed, and a goat (at least) must be sacrificed, or preferably a whole feast (*kenduri*) given, in order to convince the spirit (*jén*) to allow the tree to be used for making an instrument. The belief is that to dispense with the ceremony or to hold it imperfectly would result in the wood becoming as hard as iron (*keubai*, "invulnerable"), and therefore unable to be cut with a hacksaw. Moreover, the *rapa'i* made may later be lost or disappear and return to its birthplace in the forest.

The best medium- and small-size *rapa'i* are made from the lower trunk of a hardwood *bak panah* (jackfruit) tree and the skin of a type of black monkey with long hands (*kulét himbèe*) (Idris 1993, 81), though due to its rarity, processed goatskin is mostly used nowadays.[27] Making a *rapa'i* involves two procedures. First, the skin is wrapped around the edge of the "head" and attached to the frame by jamming it in. Second, the tension of the membrane is increased or decreased in order to tune it. A further elaboration is to make a removable rattan hoop that is wrung in between the skin and edge for tautening before playing and removed afterward to allow the skin to rest; thus, unlike the *rabana*-variant, no lacing or stitching is needed.

The sound of a properly made *rapa'i Pasè* must be so penetrating that it can be heard many kilometers away. It is judged to be a good instrument if it "has a clear, ringing sound" (Ac. *nyaréng*; I. *nyaring*) when played at medium intensity, and if beaten very hard can sound "thunderous" (Ac. *reudôk*; I. *gemuruh*).

Some legendary frame drums that are believed to be centuries old and represent their owner's soul are given proper names. Bequeathed as heirlooms from father to son, they are sold only if the owner is in dire straits, when they may be exchanged for a cow or a buffalo (Daham 2003, 4). Because they are so valuable, some disappear; for example, the Rapa'i Brok (Large Monkey Drum) and the Rapa'i Boh (Fruit Drum) were lost from their storage place in Desa Beurandang (near Landing), Kecamatan Lhok Sukon, North Aceh (Daham 2003, 2) (see further proper names below).

In 2002 Utôh Taleb said that he was periodically receiving orders from the government and private companies to make new *rapa'i Pasè*, but production had been very limited. As he commented, the conflict had been destroying the arts in Aceh for many years, and festivals or competitions that would stimulate musical activity were very rarely held. He singled out the Indonesian Army's Operasi DOM (military operation) in Aceh (Daham 2003, 4) from 1989 to 1998 as the worst period, when orders were radically reduced to a tiny trickle.

Utôh Taleb said that he was trying to keep the playing skills alive in his area by leading his own troupe of players. The danger is, of course, that when the expert makers die, their skills die with them, as young men are not normally attracted to learn these skills and carry on the tradition. Even the best teams of makers look around for other jobs when the demand for *rapa'i* is low (Daham 2003, 4).

PERFORMANCE PRACTICE AND FUNCTIONS OF THE VARIANTS OF THE *RAPA'I*

All the variants of the *rapa'i* are standard frame drums except for the largest of the *rapa'i Pasè*, the deep, heavy, waisted body of which suggests that it represents a transitional form between a waisted double-headed drum and a single-headed frame drum.

Except for the *rapa'i Pasè*, all the *rapa'i* variants are normally played with the musician holding the instrument with his left hand in vertical position on his lap, the ground, or the floor. He beats it with his right hand to produce either a high-pitched or a deep bass sound. To produce the high sound, his right hand beats sharply on or near the upper edge of the head, while to make the deep bass sound his left hand beats midway between the lower edge and the center of the head. He can also make subsidiary sounds by left-hand beats on the front or back of the skin. He produces various rhythms, tempi, dynamic levels, and interlocking musical structures as he and the rest of the players simultaneously or alternately perform body movement (*likok*) and body-percussion routines.

Thus, the ergology and spiritual qualities of each variant of the *rapa'i* are closely related to its attributed value, functions, and performance practice.

Rapa'i Pasè

Sets of *rapa'i Pasè* are played mainly in the Pasai/Pasè area, especially in and around Aron and other parts of North Aceh and in Bireuen. Each heirloom drum is wrapped in royal yellow cloth for storage. If a new one is acquired, a ceremony must be held at which a shaman (*pawang*) sings or utters mantras to bond it, as a friend, to its owner. The anthropomorphic proper names of each *induk* ("mother," large) specimen include Raja Boh (Royal Ruler Fruit), Raja Kuneng (Royal Ruler Yellow), Si Mirah (Red Divinity), Putrou Ijo (the mythical Green Princess, known throughout Sumatra), Putroe Barén (Princess Barén), and Pang Lima (military commander) (Idris 1993, 80).[28] The title of the largest drum serves as the name of a whole set (see fig. 13.1).

Before a performance, the drumheads need to be tautened and tuned. If conditions are humid, the drums are tuned by holding the head over a fire to make the skin drier, tighter, and higher pitched. If conditions are dry, the skin is moistened with water, after which a rattan tautening hoop is inserted in the inner rim. The pitch produced by beating the head can be changed by directly pressing on part of it and damping the inner side of the head with the hand, thus picking up various overtones, or beating it on different parts of the head.

Until the late 1980s, when the conflict intensified, a set or sets of *rapa'i Pasè* were often played at an intervillage competition (*urueh*), a wedding, a circumcision, or a holy day celebration (e.g., Maulid Nabi, "Birth of the Prophet"). At the time of this writing, such performances are still held, albeit only occasionally. At a performance, each group of some five to ten *rapa'i Pasè* is suspended from a sturdy wooden frame (fig. 13.1) with a player standing in front, and a helper holding the back rim after it is beaten to stop it from swaying too far away from the player. After the leader gives the signal to start, each player beats the head with his right fist to produce either a sharp and loud sound, made by beating the hand near the upper rim, or a deep and resonant sound, made by beating the hand halfway between the rim and the lower mid-head. Some people say that a loud sound beaten forcefully on a great *rapa'i Pasè* can break a glass window ten meters away, while others say it can make the player's heart vibrate violently, making him feel that he is located "behind the sound" (Daham 2003, 4).

The mystical gift and physical fitness required of a *rapa'i Pasè* player are highly admired. After all, "only if a man can kill a buffalo with one blow can he play a *rapa'i Pasè*." Because these frame drums are so large and heavy, they demand great strength and endurance on the part of the player, especially in lengthy performances. They begin with the singing of religious *liké* or secular *panton* verses and responses in the early evening (after *Isya* prayers), followed by episodes of *rapa'i Pasè* playing from about 10:00 P.M. until dawn. In such performances, the drumming sections alternate with vocal episodes sung by one or two *aneuk syahé* (lit. "child of poetry"), who sing texts about religion, pose riddles, or make humorous comments on everyday matters. Until the early twentieth century, groups of *rapa'i Pasè* used to be played on important occasions to welcome the sultan, other members of the aristocracy (the *ulèëbalang*), and honored guests; and Acehnese officials continued the practice in colonial times. Today the drums are routinely played at government functions, including competitions and festivals.

On competitive occasions, teams of up to twenty *rapa'i Pasè* players on each side aim to win a prize. It is awarded to the group judged by the audience or a jury to have a good knowledge of the repertory played, the rhythmic/timbral sound quality and carrying power of the drumming, and the lead vocalist's singing quality and ability to improvise answers to the verses posed by the opposite side (*lawan*). If there is a jury, audience calls and clapping also influence the decision. Until the late 1980s, large numbers of drums—fifteen to twenty on each side—could still be assembled. A layout of a *rapa'i Pasè* competition between two villages is shown in figure 13.1, with three sets of suspended drums on each side. Until the 1960s, up to sixty *rapa'i* were suspended from several sturdy wooden frames on each side (pers. comm., Ibu Aisyah Daud, pers. comm., 1982).

In the early 1990s, more than two hundred *rapa'i Pasè* were registered in North Aceh.[29] In the uneasy temporary peace in March 2003, however, only two sets of three medium-size *rapa'i Pasè* and six players could be assembled to play at the opening ceremony of the festival in Lhokseumawe (audiovisual example 13.1) (fig. 13.2). There

Figure 13.2 Three medium-size *rapa'i Pasè* played at the Festival of Dance and Oboes, Lhokseumawe, 2003 (Photo: Iwan Dzulvan Amir)

were reports that many owners had hidden them in wells to avoid theft, as many had been commandeered by the military forces (M. Samsuddin, pers. comm., 1982).

Rapa'i dabôh

A *rapa'i dabôh* is a medium-large frame drum with a goatskin head of approximately forty-eight to fifty centimeters in diameter, a ten-to-twelve-centimeter-long tapered body, a fifteen-centimeter back diameter (fig. 13.3), and sometimes some in-built pairs of metal plates/jingles (*ngrieuk*). *Dabôh* (also pronounced *dabôih* in some areas) is an all-male devotional genre practiced in different styles in many parts of Indonesia, Malaysia, and other parts of the Muslim world under the name of *dabus, debus,* or *gedebus.* A *dabbus* (Ar., "an iron awl") is the main implement by which the *dabôh* dancers inflict wounds on themselves as they try to show their religious concentration and invincibility to pain.

Dabôh is a Sufi mystical performance with mass *rapa'i* playing and displays of religious concentration. It was transplanted to Aceh several centuries ago, probably from Muslim India or the Arabian Peninsula and developed various performance styles in different areas of Aceh, especially in West Aceh, where many gifted masters still teach the art. In the 1890s *dabôh* was also called *"rapa'i* (from Rifa'i)," a word that also designated "the tambourine which [was] used in this as well as other dikirs" (Snouck Hurgronje 1906, 2:251). Performances embellished feasts or formed part of competitions between groups, often lasting from after *Isya* evening prayers till dawn (ibid., 2:252–53).

Figure 13.3 *Rapa'i dabôh*, front and back view

The colonial Dutch administration sometimes banned *dabôh* performances (Snouck Hurgronje 1906, 2:252), presumably because they feared they might inspire or increase feelings of violent unrest. Daud Beureueh, the leader of the Darul Islam rebellion who was fighting for an Acehnese Islamic state during these years, also banned *dabôh* in the 1950s–60s claiming that it was out of step with Muslim modernism. Other local *ulama* who supported the modernist Muhammadiyah movement agreed. The number of performances had declined in the 1970s and 1980s, but the government registered many *dabôh* groups in the early 1980s (Isjkarim et al. 1980–81, 69).

At a *dabôh* performance, scores of cross-legged *rapa'i* players and singers sing *liké*, recite the names of Allah and the prophets, and invoke saints such as Abdul Qadir Jaelani and Sulaiman as they come to feel close to Allah and reach a trancelike state of religious ecstasy. They are led by a Muslim mystical leader (*kalipah*). The tempo, dynamic level, and excitement rise to an especially high level as they sing the names of the prophet Muhammad; it subsides as they mention other prophets, and increases again when they mention the Prophet again. Some of the devotees who feel they have reached a state of trancelike closeness to God then request the *kalipah*'s permission to allow them to show their religious commitment by stabbing themselves with awls, metal spikes, and the like; when they do so, they apparently do not wound themselves or feel any pain (audiovisual example 13.2).

In competitions (*rapa'i dabôh uruoh*) held in the 1970s and 1980s, two to twelve *kru* (crews) of about twelve *rapa'i* players each took part. Each *kru* was led by an *aneuk syéh* (dance leader) and an *aneuk apét* (*syéh*'s helper) under the direction of a *kalipah*, usually with two (or occasionally three) sides competing at a time (Isjkarim et al. 1980–81, 69–70), sometimes totaling as many as sixty players in the arena at the one time.[30]

At a *dabôh* performance that I witnessed in Lhokseumawe in 1982, the participants began by sitting cross-legged and placing their *rapa'i* on the floor in a large hall (other performances may be held outdoors).[31] After playing a series of opening drumrolls (*peureuk phōn*), both sides sang the confession of faith in slow (*jareueng*) and then fast (*bagah*) tempo. The lead singer sang a religious phrase and a welcome verse to the honored guests present, whereupon the players joined in, alternating between singing songs and playing *rapa'i* episodes. After a moderately slow section, they increased the tempo, and four devotees requested and were granted the permission of the *kalipah* to perform *dabôh apui* (fiery *dabôh*). They each picked up and danced with a red-hot awl (*dabôh*) or a dagger (*reuncong*), stabbing themselves without feeling pain because they were in a trancelike state of religious concentration (M. Kartomi 1991). Then a solo vocalist sang a verse containing a question, listened hard to his opponent's sung answer, and sang another response when it was his turn, providing witty answers to the questions posed to him. (This practice is called *tulak kisah*, "prose singing exchange"). Finally, the men played a loud, fast, unison passage on their *rapa'i* before stopping suddenly, as is the norm.

On the same occasion, I recorded a competitive performance between two *kru*. Both sides played the same repetitive rhythmic pattern for around forty minutes, and some devotees on both sides began to stab themselves. One side then tried to destroy the other's concentration by playing a disruptive rhythm (*lagèe pét peureuk aké*), forcing the opposing side (*lawan*) to try to find a coping strategy, such as consolidating the newly imposed rhythm in a transition passage. However, the *lawan* side failed to reestablish its rhythm and was forced to stop playing altogether. The *kalipah* called the performance to a halt to prevent the self-stabbing devotees from wounding themselves, and the *lawan* side lost the contest. In the following contest, one side lost points because its lead singer could not satisfactorily answer the questions posed in verse by his opposite number (M. Kartomi 1991).

Rapa'i geurimpheng

A *rapa'i geurimpheng* (meaning unknown) has a medium-sized goatskin head that ranges between approximately thirty-five and thirty-eight centimeters in diameter and is attached to a thin, receding body that is about eight to ten centimeters deep. Its body is cut from the lower trunk of a *bak panah* (jackfruit) tree (Idris 1993, 69–72), and its two separate pairs of metal disks built into its body provide a metallic jingling sound when it is beaten by hand. Two or three rectangular holes (measuring about 6 cm x 2 cm) are cut on the sides of the wooden frame, and a metal pin is inserted vertically across the middle of each to hold a pair of copper-disk jingles (measuring about 4–5 cm in diameter). As with other variants of the *rapa'i*, a rattan ring is inserted into its inner rim just before it is played.

In the Langsa area, *rapa'i geurimpheng* have two or three pairs of metal disks called *keuring-keuring/ceuring-ceuring* or *phring-phring* attached to them. When the instrument is shaken, the disks rattle against one another to produce a jingling sound. In the last decade, it has become common for some *tambo*, that is, skinless wooden or plastic frames with jingles attached, to be played with the *rapa'i geurimpheng* to augment the sound of their jingles.

The genre has a distinctive group performance style, alternating between *rapa'i geurimpheng* playing by a row of around twelve men (plus some optional *rapa'i pulot* or *rapa'i aneuk* playing) and body-percussion episodes, with the solo singer of one side spontaneously performing love poems and riddles (*h'iem*) that are answered by his opposite number in some of the other episodes (Idris 1993, 72). In modern

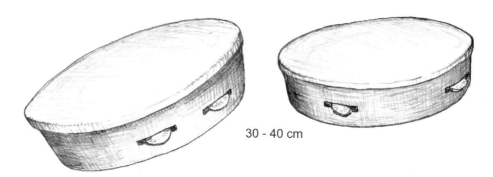

30 - 40 cm

Figure 13.4 *Rapa'i geurimpheng*

practice as well as in Snouck Hurgronje's time, two or three virtuoso *rapa'i pulot* players (see below) often sit behind the main row of *geurimpheng* drummers and play their high-pitched, sharp, loud jagged rhythms or smoothly interlocking rhythms in virtuoso style.[32]

Performances vary structurally, but they may begin with a pair of solo singers standing to one side of the row of musicians and singing 'salamulaikum (peace be with you) in free meter, followed by a refrain in strict meter. Kneeling in a row, the players then repeat the refrain and bow to the audience. In a performance I saw in Lhokseumawe, the men divided into two groups, one led by the *syéh* and the other by the *apét*, who sang secular or sacred texts after which the row of men sang refrains. The musicians then rested their instruments vertically on the floor and swayed them back and forth as they played a repetitious rhythmic pattern.[33] Between bouts of frame-drumming, the men played short episodes of rhythmic jingle sounds called *rapa'i lipéh* (thin beating) or *pukulan kosong* (I., "empty beating"), produced by beating on the upper edge of the *rapa'i* or playing the *tambo*. The solo singers then improvised some poetic texts, for example, about building up a patriotic spirit and praising the custom of mutual help (I. *gotong royong*), and they told jokes and engaged in word play (I. *jenaka*). Alternately kneeling upright and back on the soles of their feet, they then performed concerted body movements (*lapih*) with repeated *geleng* head-turning movements and with several changes of tempo.

The standard upper-body dance movements, called *asék*, were performed in a sequence numbered from 1 to 8. However, different groups often astonished their audience by varying the movements or the formations, for example, by sitting in a straight row, then around two concentric squares (the *pharangkang* formation, Idris 1993, 69). The *rapa'i* playing also brought surprises; for example, after building up to a very fast instrumental episode, the musicians stopped suddenly, holding their *rapa'i* diagonally in the air, to audience acclaim.

In competitions between two groups, the lead singer must be able to improvise clever answers to puzzles posed by the other group, and vice versa. The jury also takes the compactness of the performance, the musical qualities, and the effectiveness of any surprises in the music and movement into account (audiovisual example 13.3).

At the time of writing, the *rapa'i geurimpheng* is the most commonly played variant of the frame drum in North Aceh (fig. 13.4).[34] Snouck Hurgronje did not mention it; however, we know that it was performed at least sixty years ago in a village square and in the rice field after a harvest in North Aceh (Ibu Aisyah Daud, pers. comm., 1982). It is generally believed to have originated in North Aceh in the 1930s and spread in the 1950s to Great Aceh, East Aceh, Pidie, and North Aceh (Isjkarim et al. 1980–81, 56).

Commercial organizations along the northern and eastern coasts began to hire *rapa'i geurimpheng* performing groups in the 1960s. In the 1970s and 1980s, the leading groups in North Aceh were located at Kandang village in Kecamatan Muara Dua and Paya Bakong in Kecamatan Matang Kuli, with groups also operating in Peudada, Jeunieb, and Samalanga village areas (Isjkarim et al. 1980–81, 56). *Rapa'i geurimpheng* groups were also numerous in Gampong Batèe, Gampong Krueng Seumideun, Gampong Busu Sangei, and Gampong Mutiara in the 1960s and 1970s (Ibu Aisyah Daud, pers. comm., August 1982). In 1993, *geurimpheng* groups were still frequently found in Muara Dua, Samalanga, and Muarabatu, with a new one starting in Gandapura (Idris 1993, 69–72). By the early 1980s, the number of active groups in operation in most parts of Pidie had declined, remaining strong only in Gampong Lhôk Kayèe, Kecamatan Indrajaya. The fact that several groups from Great Aceh, Pidie, and North Aceh performed in the 2003 Festival of Acehnese Dance and Oboes in Lhokseumawe suggests that despite the conflict, its popularity had been maintained to a degree in those areas.

Rapa'i pulot

Made of goatskin and very strong black wood (*kayu puno*) with metal-disk jingles, the *rapa'i pulot* is approximately the same size as the *rapa'i geurimpheng*. A row of players sit closely together in a row playing *rapa'i pulot* with skins that are rather black in color because they have often been heated over a flame to make the sound sharper and more brilliant. The performances are distinguished by the amazing feats of a pair of child or young adult acrobats who have at their disposal ten group formations called *salikih* 1–10, including horizontal and vertical row formations (Idris 1993, 80).

Rapa'i pulot is a form of "people's village art" that developed in the mountainous interior of Aceh Besar long ago (Ibu Aisyah Daud, pers. comm., August 1982). Snouck Hurgronje described the *ratéb pulèt* (using a spelling from another speech variety) as a popular, secular form, despite its supposed origin as a *ratéb* (Snouck Hurgronje 1906, 2:247–48).[35] The term *pulèt* (lit. "to twist") referred in his time to the conical wooden rings (*boh pulèt*) with which the performers danced, continually twisting them as they performed body movements (ibid., 2:247). Performances often took the form of competitions between two or more villages, lasting from evening prayers to dawn or even to midday the next day. Playing with wooden rings is now obsolete. Performances now alternate between bouts of frame-drum playing, body movement, and body percussion, with the men singing responsorial refrains to the *radat's* (lead singer's) or his assistant's singing of devotional *liké* or secular texts in Acehnese *sanjak* meters (featuring an internal rhyme scheme).

In a performance I saw, twenty young male *rapa'i* players aged around seventeen to twenty-five years old sat cross-legged on the floor in two parallel rows (*salikih*) with the left foot slightly extended toward the front. They were led by a *syéh rapa'i pulot* and two helpers (*peungapét* or *apét*), one on the left (*wie*) and the other on the right (*uneun*) (Idris 1993, 82). The men then rested their *rapa'i* on the left foot in vertical playing position. The *syéh* signaled to them to stretch their arms out to the right and the left, a movement that the audience understood to be the beginning of the performance. Then, while the soloist sang a greeting song, the seated men performed a bow (*saleum sapa*) to welcome the audience and any *roh* (supernatural beings) believed to be present.

Still holding their frame drums vertically on the left foot, the *syéh* beat out the first rhythm, then the players repeated it, after which they put their drums on the floor and performed an episode of body movements (*likok kunyeh* [lit. "chewing-betel nut-movements"]) while clicking their fingers rhythmically and performing other body-percussion sounds. This was followed by alternating episodes of singing and *rapa'i* playing. Sometimes the players damped the *rapa'i* skin with their left hands to prevent it from sounding as they beat out rhythms on the metal-disk jingles. Still playing a series of interlocking rhythms on their *rapa'i*, they divided into two-, then three-row formations. Starting at a medium tempo, their *rapa'i* playing gradually grew faster until the *syéh* gave a sudden signal to stop. They resumed and repeated the process several times, sometimes alternating episodes of *rapa'i pulot* playing with bouts of body percussion and body movement, with the lead singer intermittently improvising a new or preexisting text to a melody, the refrains of which were then repeated by the players.

Six acrobats (*aneuk pulot*) then entered and performed a series of ten exciting gymnastic feats, sometimes walking effortlessly along the extended, crossed hands of the row of men and then performing somersaults. Sometimes the acrobats helped the men stand on each other's shoulders or hands, to the amazement and appreciation of the audience. In the *salikih* 7 formation, for example, the acrobats stood on the *rapa'i* players' shoulders and then on their crossed hands. In the *salikih* 10 scene, the acrobats jumped onto the row of *rapa'i* players' shoulders, with one on top to form three levels up in the air. Sometimes they tied a fence- or boat-shaped rope around the long line of players, on which the acrobats showed their balancing skills as they walked along it.

Rapa'i pulot are still played as a self-sufficient stage instrument in competitions.[36] Usually they contain minimal religious content and emphasize acrobatic display, especially when performed at government, media, or commercial functions. When taking part in a competition, one pair of solo singers improvises poetic questions or comments which the pair on the other side must answer.

Rapa'i geleng

Rapa'i geleng is a dynamic, virtuoso sitting dance with group singing, body movement, and frame-drum playing that may have been inspired by *diké angguk* (chanting with the rhythmic nodding of the head, audiovisual example 13.4). *Geleng* (I., "turn one's head") refers to the participants' repetitive movements of the head and the neck from left to right as they perform their upper-body movements (fig. 13.5). A *rapa'i geleng* is smaller and lighter than a *rapai pulot* and therefore more easily manipulated when played at a very fast tempo.

A performance begins with a row of eight to twenty singer-dancers (including their *syéh*) entering the stage, bowing to the audience, and sitting close together on the floor. They start beating their *rapa'i* (or optionally a *dab*) in unison, at first slowly, then at an increasingly fast tempo, usually ending the episode at a breathtakingly fast pace, and then suddenly stopping and placing their *rapa'i* horizontally on the floor in silence. The next episode may consist of a range of group body movements, followed by the singing of a religious or patriotic text in powerful unison. The text in Acehnese may be *Alhamdulilah pujo keu Tuhan Nyang peujeut alam langet ngon donya* (All praises to God who created sky and earth), or in another episode, *Nanggroe Aceh nyo tempat loun lahee, bak ujoung pantee pulo Sumatra, dilee baro kon lam jaro kaphe, jino hana lee aman sentosa* (Aceh is where I was born, on the coastal tip of Sumatra, formerly in the hands of the colonizers, now safe and peaceful) (Ara 2009, 162). In some episodes the players place their frame drums in vertical position on the floor, then move them up above their heads, down to each side, diagonally back to the left, then the right, and so on.

A *rapa'i geleng* performance requires the group of musicians to rehearse copiously to achieve the required powerful group vocal sound and compact movement, which often accelerate till they reach a lightning tempo. In some episodes, all the

Figure 13.5 *Tari rapa'i geleng*, Lhokseumawe, 2003. A row of fourteen *rapa'i geleng* players from Sanggar IAIN, Banda Aceh, turn their heads (*geleng*) to the right, then to the left, and so on.

odd-numbered men sway their upper bodies to the right, then to the left, to the back, to the front, and diagonally to the right and the left, while each even-numbered man sways in the opposite directions while performing the same sequence of body movements. In figure 13.5, the row of even-numbered players raise their *rapa'i* up high with both hands while singing in unison, after which the odd-numbered men raise their *rapa'i* to shoulder height while the even-numbered men lower theirs to lap level, repeating the formation many times.

The *rapa'i geleng* genre developed in the 1960s in Aceh Barat Daya and spread widely throughout Nagan Raya, Aceh Barat, and other areas of western Aceh before becoming a highly popular performance genre among university student groups in Banda Aceh and elsewhere in the 1980s and frequently appearing in government-organized competitions. The men usually wear matching trouser suits with *kain songket* in a color from the Acehnese flag: black, red, yellow, or a combination of these.

DAP OR RAPA'I ANEUK

The tiny *dap* (pronounced *dab* in some areas), the smallest member of the *rapa'i* family, is usually played with medium-size frame drums such as the *rapa'i geurimpheng* or *rapai geleng*. Beaten by hand, it produces a medium- to high-pitched sound. Its goatskin head is tautened with rattan, and its body is made of finer, more thinly cut (jackfruit) wood than any of the other frame drums (fig. 13.6).

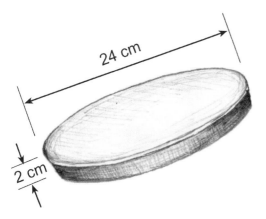

Figure 13.6 A *dap*

Dap musicians usually beat out loudly penetrating, interlocking rhythmic-timbral configurations and are therefore also called *rapa'i tingkah* (Ma., "interlocking *rapa'i*") and *rapa'i aneuk* (Ac., "child drum") players (Idris 1993, 80). Their rhythmic flourishes rise over the rhythmic cycles played on the lower-pitched frame drums with brilliant effect. In the standard Acehnese ensemble, one or two *dap* or *rapa'i aneuk* are normally played with an oboe (*seuruné kalée*), a pair of double-headed drums (*geundrang*), and a *rapa'i geurimpheng* or *rapa'i dabôh*. A hundred years ago, however, ensembles of five to seven "*dab*" with "bells" (built-in metal plates) were played with a Western violin (*biola*) and a "gong" (a metal disk used for official proclamations) to accompany *panton* verse recitations and dancing by a boy or an adult female soloist (Snouck Hurgronje 1906, 2:265). Since the 1930s, such performances have been called *biola Aceh* (fig. 13.7).

SOLO OR SMALL GROUP INSTRUMENTAL
ENSEMBLES WITH *RAPA'I*

In all the above genres, *rapa'i* are played by groups of about eight to twenty men. However, single *rapa'i* or small groups of *rapa'i* are also played in ensemble with other instruments to accompany female welcome and other dances, not only in traditional practice but also more recently at government and tourist functions, on international tours, and in the media. These dances with *rapa'i* and other instrumental accompaniment lent luster to formal occasions and peasant and working-class people's celebrations in the colonial period until the 1940s, when they were favored by the former Acehnese petty aristocracy (but not the fundamentalist *ulama*) as well as by the Dutch government, and thereafter by Indonesian government officials and commercial businesses.

Figure 13.7 A *biola Aceh*
player, Pidie, 1982 (see n. 33,
p. 406)

In Aceh Besar, the main instrumental ensemble played on formal occasions includes one or two medium-sized *rapa'i*, a pair of *geundrang* (double-headed drums),
a *tambo*, and a *seuruné kalée* (oboe). The Daya and West Acehnese form of this
ensemble also often includes a *canang* (a small, handheld gong). Among the dances
that are accompanied by these ensembles are the *ratôh pulo* (bubbling talk island), in
which eight men perform *saman* or *ratôh duek*–like body movements accompanied
by two *rapa'i* players, sitting apart. While the *ratôh pulo* is said to have originated in
Aceh Besar, the *likok pulo* (island movements) dance is attributed to Pulau Breueh,
an island located off Great Aceh's northern coast. Eight, ten, or twelve boys (the
rakan) sit in a row performing body movements and body percussion, accompanied
by musicians playing three small *rapa'i* (of approximately 20 cm in diameter) with
a solo singer and the *rakan* singing the refrains in unison.

Similar vocal-instrumental combinations accompany many *kreasi baru* ("new creations" of music and dance). In North Aceh's *alèe-alèe tunjang* (rice-grain stamping) dance for young women—a "new creation" that developed in the 1960s—the accompanying ensemble comprises one or two *rapa'i geurimpheng*, a pair of *geundrang*, an optional voice, and a *seuruné kalée*. The recently developed *piasan raya* (great festival) dance, with mixed couples performing hand movements and finger-snapping sounds, is accompanied by one or two solo singers and three men playing *rapa'i pulot*; it is especially popular today in Greater Aceh and said to have been favored by the petty aristocrats or district heads (*ulèëbalang*) in the colonial era. Choral songs by post-1940s Acehnese composers such as Syaiful Idris are also often accompanied by traditional Acehnese instrumental ensembles, including one or more *rapa'i*.

||||

The *rapa'i* serves as a potent symbol of Acehnese identity, especially the male view of identity, as symbolized by the physical strength and endurance required of the performers of the *rapa'i* genres, who are only men. The *rapa'i Pasè*, which is associ-

Figure 13.8 A *rapa'i* or *geundrang* ensemble, Pidie, 1982

Figure 13.9 A *geundrang keling* player, Sigli, Pidie, 1982

ated with the memory of Samudra Pasai—the first Muslim kingdom in Southeast Asia—symbolizes the people's pride in Aceh's glorious past, especially when it became a great regional power in the sixteenth and seventeenth centuries. Moreover, the Muslim devotional genre and martial art, *rapa'i dabôh*, serves as a reminder of the saying that Aceh is "the land of the dagger," a great warring nation of heroes who engaged in protracted struggles with their oppressors. Yet the *rapa'i geurimpheng* and *rapa'i pulot* are also a reminder of the mystical values of Sufi Islam and the traditional veneration of the ancestors and spirits of nature, as are apparent in the ritual making of the *rapa'i Pasè* and the esteem in which they are held as ancestral heirlooms and works of art. Not least, the uses and functions of the family of *rapa'i* instruments among the Acehnese musico-lingual group are a symbol of the spread of Islam in Aceh, in part through these performing-art genres.

The *adat* beliefs that were attached to the *rapa'i* genres handed down from the ancestors were gradually transformed in the twentieth century as Indonesian and local Acehnese government officials used them for their official functions and election campaigns. Throughout Indonesia the policy was adopted to transform, shorten, and aestheticize select traditional genres to make them suitable for political and commercial functions, the media, and the national and international stage. Some artists complied with the policy and produced songs and choreographies that official circles could use, while others resisted this tendency, either by maintaining the traditional religious- and/or Muslim-associated artistic expressions as they were or by subversively satirizing the horizontal and vertical conflicts affecting Acehnese society via military oppression and authoritarian governance.

Also the twenty-nine-year-long conflict between the Indonesian military and members of the Free Aceh Movement severely reduced the frequency of publicly organized artistic performances and the normal expressive, cathartic, and celebratory role of performance and entertainment in the community. However, this value was apparently restored after the peace accord in 2005, as people expressed their relief that the war was over by holding long postponed celebrations with traditional performances, and the dance schools and *sanggar* reopened.

Thus *rapa'i* music-culture at the time of writing continues to serve as a lens through which the changing identity, values, cultural style, gender relations, class distinctions, and historical experience of the whole Acehnese society may be viewed.

ACKNOWLEDGMENTS

During our travels throughout Aceh in 1982 we were kindly assisted in our *rapa'i* research by the late master musician Abdullah Raja and his sons in Gampong Pande, Kecamatan Mesjid Raya, Banda Aceh; artists Drs. Athaillah, Bp. Suhaina, Ibu Faridah Eriany, Bp. Rosna, and Bp. Hasanuddin Daud of Banda Aceh; and the Bupati of Aceh Pidie—Drs. A. R. Nurdin—and Drs. Muchtar Djalal in Sigli. In north Aceh, Ibu Aisyah Daud of Kecamatan Perusangan and musicians M. Husin Amin of Kecamatan Samalanga and Kalifah B. A. Kalisyik were very helpful, as were Ibu Cut Asiah and her team in West Aceh.

In our 2003, 2005–6, 2008, and 2010 trips, we were especially grateful to the fine dancers and choreographers Noerdin Daood of the Jakarta Arts Institute (IKJ) and Syéh Lah Geunta from East Aceh, who were very helpful in our visit to Lhokseumawe for the Festival of Acehnese Dance and Oboes, as were the then-Bupati of North Aceh, Tarmizi A. Karim, festival director M. Rizal, Lhokseumawe museum director

Ali Akbar, and Samsuddin Jali. In the Acehnese diaspora community in Jakarta, Agus Noor Amal, Iskandar, Dek Gam, Si Boss, Ucok, Jaya and Ibu Erlyin of the Acehnese artists' organization Perhimpunan Seniman Aceh Se Jabotabek (SAJAK) assisted us in 2003. In 2007 the other main Acehnese artist and lecturer at IKJ, Marzuki Hassan, accompanied us on our trips around Aceh Barat Daya and Aceh Barat, where we were able to record the various *rapa'i* genres.

14

CONNECTIONS ACROSS SUMATRA

This concluding chapter will draw together some of the connections between the traditional styles and genres of the performing arts across Sumatra, focusing on the impact of indigenous religion and Islam; classification of the musical instruments and ensembles; myths and legends; dances and music-dance relationships; social classes; gender factors; signal items of identity; and major changes since around 1900. To what extent an understanding of these connections can contribute to a concept of Sumatra's performing arts as a unified whole will become clearer when more research into the whole of greater Sumatra is completed.

INDIGENOUS RELIGIONS AND ISLAM

Religious beliefs and practices have inspired, modified, or transformed many music, dance, and theater genres in Sumatra. Though the indigenous religions differ in their detail in each area, they are all based on a reverence for the spirits of nature and the ancestors, and they tend to absorb elements of Islam and other world religions when engaged in artistic practices.

Among some modernist Muslims, songs involving black magic (*ilmu jahat*) practices are unacceptable (Sanday 2002, 72), but if white magic (*ilmu halus*) is blended with Muslim prayers or sayings at the beginnings and ends of the songs, as in the tiger-capturing rituals, they may be tolerated. In northern Aceh a tree may only be felled to make a frame drum after respectful incantations are sung to its spirit and care is taken to avoid destroying the surrounding trees and undergrowth (chap. 13). In parts of South Sumatra, animist and/or Muslim prayers need to be said before a pair of shamans perform the dangerous task of climbing a tall *sialang* tree to collect honey from the hives (chap. 7), and similar rituals are held in other areas (e.g., in east-coast North Sumatra, Goldsworthy 1978). Sometimes shamans refer to local ancestral spirits and Hindu-Buddhist deities such as Batara Guru (the Lord of the Universe) as well as to Allah and his Prophet to improve their chances of obtaining supernatural assistance for their efforts.

The ancestral spirits at a ritual performance with dancing and music are believed to contribute to the occasion not only spiritually but aesthetically as well, as their presence beautifies the dancing, singing, and instrumental sounds. In Mandailing, mystical rituals are performed while drums are being made, and they are played to invite the spirits to come down and inhabit them. However, the spirits are only attracted to join in if the correct drum rhythms are played; otherwise they will not recognize them (chap. 11). Dancers and musicians can also represent, or be inhabited by, the spirits of the ancestors, as in the case of the Seven Angels dance, based on the "Bitter Tongue" legend, in Besemah, South Sumatra (chap. 7).

Rituals often focus around inherited sacred objects, including musical instruments and weapons that are treasured in their own right, such as the great *rapa'i Pasè* drums in northern Aceh (chap. 13). Such objets d'art are made by spiritually gifted wood-carvers and smiths (e.g., *pande bosi*, "iron experts" in the Mandailing language), who are often also shamans. When a father presents an heirloom—such as a Malay *keris* (short dagger) or a Komering gong—to his son, he expects him to inherit the *ilmu* (mystical knowledge) of the spirit inhabiting the object. Inherited *ilmu* can also guide a musician as he performs, sometimes causing him to enter a state of trance and even to feel on occasion that his instrument is actually playing itself. Thus, the *nobat* ensemble in Riau's former Indragiri palace was reportedly heard playing itself in sympathy on the day of a sultan's funeral (chap. 6). Inherited objects (*pusaka*) need to be ritually cleaned every year. This is done rather clandestinely at the Indragiri royal descendant's home in Rengat, lest it offend some of the local *ulama*.

Such mystical practices are diminishing at a fast rate, however. The logging of large areas of Sumatra's primal forests since the 1980s has resulted in massive plant and forest destruction and long-lasting fires in the forest undergrowth, which have in turn disturbed the tigers, elephants, and other wild animals, some of which have rampaged villages and been killed without the traditional respect or ceremony, and have become endangered species. It has also forced whole villages to leave their agricultural land and move to urban areas. Among the human victims are the forest-dwelling communities, such as the Suku Kubu in Jambi and South Sumatra (chap. 7), and the hunter-gathererswidden agriculturalists such as the Suku Mamak in Riau, many of whom have been forced over the past half century to abandon their way of life (chap. 6).

ISLAM

The conversion of the majority of Sumatra's communities to Islam over the centuries had a major impact on their artists' creation and continued performance of the Muslim-related performing arts. The early proselytizers and returned pilgrims taught the people how to perform the call to prayer, recite the Qur'an, and carry out the verbal and physical religious exercises of prayer.[1] Male and female devotional groups who formed the habit of practicing such exercises developed some of them into art forms, in some of which a soloist and chorus sang either religious or secular lyrics and performed body movement or dance, and (in some Acehnese forms) body percussion (M. Kartomi 2010a). The proselytizers also introduced a number of other Sufi-influenced Shafi'i-Muslim genres (such as *dabus*, chap. 5) and a Shi'a genre (*tabut*, chap. 4).[2] Some secular forms of Arab culture were transplanted too, for example, the *zapin* dance with *marwas* drums and a large-bodied *gambus* (lute) in its instrumental ensemble (chap. 7), a form that probably derives from the Hadhramaut/Yemen (Nor 1993, 6, 7).

The historical details of the ways in which *dakwah* (conversion and continuing piety) occurred in Sumatra may never be known, but the legends suggest that the faith spread peacefully along the rivers and seacoasts and thence into the inland areas. In some cases, conversion occurred by force, as in the early-nineteenth-century Muslim Padri war in Minangkabau and south Tapanuli (chap. 11).[3] Dates of conversion vary from area to area. For example, the palace (*istana*) and people (*rakyat*) of the kingdom (*kerajaan*) of Pagaruyung in the Minangkabau heartland had been converted to Islam by the sixteenth century (chap. 5), while large areas of highland South Sumatra were converted only by the latter part of the nineteenth century and the early twentieth century (chap. 7). In some areas conversion appears to have occurred by contact with foreign Muslim traders and visitors, as in the late-thirteenth-century Acehnese kingdom at Samudera Pasai (located near present-day Lhokseumawe, chap. 13). To this day the people in the Pasai area proudly draw attention to their early conversion by noting that the *rapa'i Pasè* is now the main musical symbol of Aceh's identity (chap. 13). By the early twentieth century, the great majority of Sumatran communities had converted to Islam, and a few to Christianity, while the Chinese Indonesian minorities mostly remained Confucian or converted to a world religion.

Sumatra's early Muslim leaders encouraged communities of village men to form Sufi brotherhoods (Ar. *tarikat*), such as the Rifa'iyah, the Qadiriyah, the Naqsabandiyah, the Shatariyah, and the Sammaniyah. They established prayer and meet-inghouses (*surau, dayah, pesantren*), where they taught their pupils the tenets of the Muslim faith and encouraged members of the local brotherhood to perform religious exercises there or in one another's homes, usually on a Thursday from midevening and lasting all night. As in Sufi groups the world over, they believed that humans can come close to Allah by religious exercises that involve music and movement or dance, especially if they include the repetitious reciting of the *dhikr* (Sumatran-Malay; Ar. *zikr*; Ac. *liké*), for example, the first part of the confession of faith: *lā ilha ill 'llāh* (there is no God but God). Thus, various Sufi-oriented genres such as *hadra, rodat, serapal enam*, and since the 1970s *nasyid/nasit* spread through-out most parts of southern and central Sumatra and are still practiced to this day. Members of loosely organized brotherhoods still meet on Thursday evenings in some areas to sing devotional lyrics or the ninety-nine names of Allah with frame-drum accompaniment. In Aceh the men of a village sing devotional *dala'il* songs in soaring unison, reserving their frame drums for a great variety of other genres that have religious or secular lyrics. They also perform vocal genres with their own body-percussion music and movement, such as *ratéb duek* (a "sitting dance" with religious texts), *ratôh duek* (a sitting dance with secular texts), and *saman* (a sitting dance with either religious or secular texts), the latter genre being popular in the Gayo uplands and parts of West Aceh.

One of the leaders who promoted the values and practices of the Sufi brotherhoods was the famous scholar and poet Hamzah Fansuri (d. ca. 1590), who had been a member of the Qadir'iyyah order in Arabia. Other important religious figures reportedly include the poet Abdur'rauf of Singkel in the second half of the seventeenth century and his former student Syéh Burhanuddin, who is credited with the spread of Islam and its culture—including the chanting of holy names and frame-drum playing—in Pariaman. Followers of Syéh Samman spread Sufi practices in parts of Aceh in the first half of the eighteenth century, performing their *dhikr* loudly and at a frenetic tempo, for Samman had held that noise and motion were "powerful agents for producing the desired state of mystic transport" as opposed to other leaders who made "quiet and repose the conditions for the proper performance of their *dikrs*" (Snouck Hurgronje 1906, 2:219). Acehnese followers of Ahmad Qushashi also chanted the holy names of Allah and the prophets and followed the prescribed prayers.[4] The *saman* genre was "one of the devout recreations in which a religiously inclined public [took] part" (ibid., 2:216–17). Though most genres are for men to perform, even the women had their own form of Sufi religious devotions in the 1890s: a female *ratéb saman* (ibid., 2:216, 219), and women continue to perform such genres (e.g., *ratéb meuseukat*, M. Kartomi 2010b) to this day.

It is widely believed that early Muslim proselytizers expanded the repertory of the bards who performed the traditional stories, such as the Minangkabau "Cindua Mato" legend (chap. 3) and the pan-west-coastal "Sikambang" cycle (chaps. 3 and 10), by teaching them legends about the Muslim prophets and stories that came from the Middle East and Muslim India, such as the "Abdul Muluk" cycle (chap. 7).[5] The bards also inserted Muslim prayers and sayings at the beginnings and the endings of sections of their stories, as did the shamans who led ritual performances and singers of songs with a non-Muslim content, as in *phô* (chap. 12).

Centuries ago the frame drum became the Muslim musical instrument par excellence throughout Sumatra, and groups of male musicians developed a variety of genres that included the singing of religious and secular lyrics while playing them. Some artists believe that their frame drums were transplanted—along with Islam itself—from the Arabian Peninsula, Egypt, Persia, and beyond, perhaps at the time of the Pasè-Samudera kingdom (in present-day Aceh), which converted to Islam in the 1290s. However, the instruments could of course have been developed locally in pre-Islamic times or have been transplanted to Sumatra before the religion itself reached its shores. More likely still, the playing of locally made frame drums may have become more important in the culture as foreign Muslim genres were introduced and spread (chap. 13). In any case, the demand for frame drums and the associated ergological skills must have radically increased as the men of many villages joined Sufi brotherhoods and sang Sufi-style songs of praise while playing the instruments in devotional gatherings at home or in the *surau* (prayer and meetinghouses).

From the 1970s to the mid-1990s, some artists in Sumatra tended to classify their musical arts into two *aliran* (I., "streams"): (1) the stream of the *adat* or *asli* arts, or the "stream of spirit veneration . . . [that was] linked to Hindu culture brought . . . by Indian traders and migrants" (Isjkarim et al. 1980–81, 94), and (2) the stream of Islamic arts that "probably originated in the Middle East" and developed when the people were "convinced they should accept the teachings of Islam" (ibid., 191). Some extended the second category to include art forms associated with other world religions (I. *agama*), that is, Hinduism, Buddhism, Christianity, and Confucianism, and added a third category: the *aliran* of Western-influenced art forms (Mursal Esten, pers. comm., Padangpanjang, November 1990). Thus in the Chinese Indonesian community on the island of Bangka, for example, the relevant *aliran* are the *asli* Malay arts, the Confucian temple arts (e.g., the *wayang gantung* marionette puppet theater), and the arts that Dutch and other plantation owners promoted in the plantation and mining communities (the *tanjidor* bands) (chap. 9).

The problem with this classification, however, was that members of the second—Islamic—stream needed to differentiate between genres with a predominantly devotional religious purpose, on the one hand, and adaptations of the so-called animist forms to suit Muslim sensibilities, on the other. So in the late 1990s, some artists began to distinguish two subcategories: *kesenian Islami* (art with an Islamic theme) and *kesenian yang bernafaskan Islam* (art with an Islamic flavor). *Kesenian Islami* includes traditional and popular songs and song-dances with moral or religious texts, for example, *qasidah* (Ar. *kasidah*; I. *nasit*), and *lagu Islami* ("songs with a Muslim theme," especially *hadra, rodat*, and *serapal anam*, chap. 7). The songs are usually sung by a male or female soloist and response group, though modern urban performances and commercial recordings sometimes mix the sexes. The melodies are usually in a perceived Middle Eastern style, based on an "Arabic-sounding" heptatonic scale or more frequently its lower or higher tetrachord, and featuring melodic sequences and repeated phrases. Some are in quadruple meter and unornamented, while others are unmetered and sung with considerable melodic ornamentation.

"Art with an Islamic flavor" or "art associated with an Islamic lifestyle," on the other hand, does not necessarily have an explicitly religious theme, for it simply means praying regularly and wearing Islamic dress (Noerdin Daood, pers. comm., Lhokseumawe, 2003). When western Acehnese women perform *meuseukat* song-dances, they sometimes choose to sing religious texts, in which case the items are classified as *kesenian Islami*, but when they start with a Muslim phrase (such as *Asalamalaikom*, "Peace be with you") and then sing songs about secular themes such as romantic love, school, sailing, or the beauty of nature, the performance is said to "have an Islamic flavor."

Although all genres are similar in that they can be performed either in strict or free meter, with simple or complex melodic ornamentation, by solo or group artists, and with or without instrumental accompaniment, they always differ from one another in their stylistic details and performance practice. While performers of genres with an "Islamic flavor" tend to add Muslim phrases to their *adat*-related or secular texts and feature either traditional or modern popular music and dance styles, performances of the *kesenian Islami* genres focus on the delivery of Muslim-related texts, avoid dancing, and feature Muslim dress and Middle Eastern–related melodic attributes, gestures, and posture, such as kneeling and holding out the hands in a prayerful, cupped position in front of the body.

MUSICAL INSTRUMENTS AND ENSEMBLES

Notionally, Sumatra's traditional instruments may be classified into those played in upstream versus downstream areas or by their use in the various musico-lingual groups or subgroups. However such classifications would have little explanatory power, given that the instruments are portable and frequently cross borders. The instruments could also, of course, be classified by organological type into idiophones, membranophones, aerophones, and chordophones, but this would tell us nothing about their distribution and their musical and functional significance in Sumatra. More appropriately in the Sumatran context, the instruments can be classified according to religious association, given that each instrument is associated primarily with a particular set of religious beliefs. Many instruments are attributed with mystical power through the spirits believed to live in them, a belief that is subscribed to by adherents of not only the local variants of the indigenous religions and Confucianism but also of a Sufi brand of Islam; even modernist Muslims associate certain instruments with Islam and others with indigenous or other, for example, Christian, religious beliefs.

Seen in this light, the instruments of Sumatra divide into five main categories, beginning with the indigenous religious category, the origins of which date from before the Common Era to this day, followed by the Hindu-Buddhist category dating from the early centuries C.E. to circa the fifteenth century. The third category, associated with Islam (of whatever sect), dates from around the thirteenth century, while the fourth—European or Western—category, is associated with Christianity in Christian areas dating from around the sixteenth century, and also with Western secularism in the twentieth. The fifth—Chinese Indonesian—category is associated with Confucian and Buddhist belief, belonging to the bilingual Hakka- or Hokkien- and Malay-speaking descendants of immigrants from China in the cities and some rural areas, despite the periodic anti-Chinese pogroms, for example, as part of the anti-Communist purges across Indonesia in 1965–66.

The first class of instruments, associated with indigenous religion, includes the Dōng-son drums that are found in the mountainous Besemah area of South Sumatra, which are no longer played today. It also includes conch shells for signaling, for example, the *tentuang* found in offshore Riau; snake- and lizard-skin drums and fiddles found, for example, along the Kampar River in Riau; bamboo string instruments, for example, the tube zithers played in Mandailing; Jew's harps, bullroarers, and coconut-leaf horns that are found, for example, in Minangkabau; percussive instruments such as bamboo buzzers attached to drums in Mandailing; wooden rice-block stamping instruments found in South Sumatra (the Lahat area); and wood or bamboo wind instruments such as flutes, clarinets, and oboes that are played throughout Sumatra.

The second category, comprising instruments associated with Hindu-Buddhist belief and healing rituals, includes E-shaped strings of pellet bells (*genta*) among the Suku Kubu/Anak Dalem forest-dwellers; plucked strings, for example, the *hasapi* in

Batak Mandailing and Toba; sets of tuned, single-headed *gordang* drums in Mandailing; xylophones, for example, the *garantung* played near the Buddhist temple ruins in Portibi/Angkola; sets of tuned kettle-gongs, for example, *talempong* in Minangkabau and *momongan* in Mandailing; and for some observers, the bowed fiddle with an animal skin–covered body, for example, the *rabab* in Riau and Minangkabau and the *hareubab* in Aceh and *arbab* in the Batak lands.

The third, Muslim, category includes the suspended slit drums to call people to prayer, for example, the *kotuk-kotuk* in the Indragiri area of mainland Riau; indigenous plucked *ud*-like lutes, for example, the *gambus*; the small double-headed *marwas* (pl. *marawis*) drums imported from the Middle East; and the earthenware *tasa* and barrel-shaped *dol* drums transplanted from Shi'a India and Persia. Sumatra's many kinds of frame drums, ranging from the tiny *rapa'i* in Pariaman (Minangkabau) to the great *rapa'i Pasè* of northern Aceh, are generally associated with Islam, though some observers believe that the instruments predate the Muslim conversion.

The fourth category of instruments, transplanted from Christian Europe, includes the *biola* (violin), which is played in Malay ensembles such as the *orkes gamad* in Minangkabau; a melodeon-style *harmonika* played in Besemah-South Sumatra; the *harmonium* in the *Dul Muluk* theater in eastern South Sumatra and Jambi; Western brass instruments such as trumpets, saxophones, trombones, tubas, clarinets, string basses, kettledrums, cymbals, and *dramkit* (drum kit) played in *tanjidor* bands in South Sumatra and Bangka; and Western pop band instruments that are played, for example, in *pop Minang, pop Melayu*, and *dangdut* (Indonesian popular music) bands.

The fifth, Confucian, category of instruments played by Chinese Indonesians, includes the *tambur* (local double-headed drum), *so na* (oboe), and *po* (flat gongs), which accompany the *barongsai* and *liong* dancers, and the *pa tim* ensemble, comprising a Chinese oboe (*so na*), double-headed drum (*ta ku*), large cymbals (*cem*), flat gongs (*po*), three-string long-necked lute (*sanhian*), a two-string fiddle (*nanhu*), and a flute (*hsiao*), played in temple rituals (e.g., Raja Jin), Chinese theater forms, and funeral processions. Till the 1940s, bowed string instruments with coconut-shell bodies (Ma. *rebab batok besar* and *rebab batok kecil*) were added to this ensemble (chap. 9).

CONNECTIONS BETWEEN THE MYTHS AND LEGENDS AND THE MUSICAL ARTS

Like the instruments, the myths and legends and the attached art forms may be classified according to their religious association. The great majority of stories are linked to indigenous religious belief, and a few to Hindu sources. A substantial number have Sunni or Shi'a Muslim connections due to their Middle Eastern, Indian, Iraqi, or Iranian backgrounds, and some have been adopted from European and Javanese sources. Many of the genres performed in the musico-lingual subgroups are linked to legends that are told by bards at all-night celebrations during weddings, circumcisions, other life events, and on holy days.

Space prevents the inclusion here of a structuralist analysis of Sumatra's myths and legends as a whole. If one were to be attempted, however, many commonalities would doubtless be found in the myths' and legends' empirical references to rivers, forests, eagles, buffaloes, tigers, and such; types of subjects; plot structure; actions of the characters; and significant dialectical oppositions, for example, between upstream versus downstream peoples, village life versus town life, and male-female relationships.

Most of Sumatra's many hundreds of folk stories are mythical in that they refer symbolically to timeless events and the origins of things, while a few are legends told as if they were events in a definite historical period. Traditional audiences regard the myths, legends, and the music, dances, and rituals inspired by them, as sacred gifts of the ancestors. As they perform the stories, some bards emphasize explicit moral or religious messages, but most seek primarily to entertain, focusing on episodes that allow them to expand on such entertaining topics as female beauty or to bring in comic characters around which they can make ironic comments.

Most myths and legends are parts of indigenous epics known as *hikayat, kaba, haba dangdeuria, nyanyi panjang, sijobang*, and *turi-turian*. Others are imaginary tales (*kisah*), morality stories or parables (*hadih*), and fables that often feature personified animals. Some legends have been borrowed from foreign—mostly Middle Eastern and European—sources, especially those performed as part of theater forms that spread in the late nineteenth and the twentieth centuries. Normally the stories are orally transmitted, though a few have been written down, either in indigenous scripts (as in the bark books of the Batak and Besemah people), or in Arabic script, in publications by colonial and postcolonial-era scholars, for example, the *Muko-muko Chronicle*, which describes a royal funeral and aspects of the lifestyle in the former Malay court at Muko-muko.

MYTHS AND ART FORMS LINKED TO INDIGENOUS RELIGIOUS BELIEF

Although the myths are temporally vague, they often include precise mention of local rivers, mountains, and hills. Myths told by the healing and exorcizing shamans of the "Isolated Peoples" of the forests and the seas mention local hills and rivers, and they help them deal with environmental forces. For example, Suku Sekak shamans tell myths that explain how the sea spirits call the wind or calm the waves (chap. 9). Their rituals include sending model spirit boats out to sea as they sing songs addressed to the spirits of the sea and the land and perform circle or couple dances (e.g., *tari cakter*) on the beach, for example, to thankfully celebrate a good catch.

The South Sumatran myth about the primal ancestor Bitter Tongue (Pahit Lidah) also has an environmental emphasis. It relates the ancestral significance of the sacred Seguntang Hill near Palembang on the Musi River. Parts of it explain the origin or significance of local natural features and carved rock art. Thus one episode tells how Bitter Tongue turned a slit-drum player into a stone figure found among the rock art in the Besemah area of South Sumatra. Some episodes mention attributes and names of the ancestral founders of a village or area, such as the South Sumatran culture hero Atung Bungsu, who was guided by the legendary Seven Angels as he founded settlements at the estuaries. Others mention creator gods, for example, Gajah Mada, who is revered by the Lom in Bangka, or the good and evil spirits. Other commonly found characters are beautiful girls, heroic princes, kind grandmothers, ungrateful sons, and victims of slander. Some folk stories are attached to popular shamanic song-dances, such as *rantak kudo* in south-coastal Minangkabau, or to comic trance dances such as *gilo lukah*, found in Minangkabau and western Riau.

The most famous set of episodes from the "Bitter Tongue" legend tells the story of Malem Diwa (or heroes with other names) who falls in love with the Youngest Angel (Putri Bungsu) while she is bathing with her six sisters in a lake in the forest. In an Acehnese version of the myth, the hero finds a strand of the Youngest Angel's hair, which transforms him into a fish, and on swimming near where she is bathing, he comes across her clothes and the shawl that enables her to fly. He hides her clothes and shawl, thus preventing her from flying with her sisters back to heaven. With the help of an old grandmother, Ni Kebayan (Acehnese Ni Keubayan, who appears in many Malay legends), he marries her, and she gives birth to their son, Ahmat. One day she accidentally finds her shawl again and flies back to heaven. Her husband follows her, and after fulfilling difficult tests imposed by her father—the king of heaven—he is eventually reunited with her.

Many episodes of this story are told for whole nights on end. One tells of Malin Deman's romantic adventures and eventual marriage to a princess at Lunang in south-coastal Minangkabau. Several versions of the Youngest Angel myth recount how the hero travels on a mythical mount (*burak*) to China, Java, and beyond as he searches for her after she has flown away.

A good storyteller can keep his audience enthralled as he describes the heroine's beauty while bathing naked in the lake, draws out the erotic aspects of the story, and makes one-liner jokes about the couple's potential and real sexual encounters. Among the many songs and dances that derive from the myth are the *gandai* dances of Minangkabau's south coast and northern Bengkulu, and the eagle and wave dances (*tari lang, tari kebar*) in the highlands of South Sumatra. Indeed "The Youngest Angel" is the most widespread myth in Sumatra, with variants told in most Malay, Minangkabau, Batak, and Acehnese subgroups, but it is also well known in many other parts of Southeast Asia and beyond, for example under the name of "Jaka Tarub" in Java and Bali.

Similarly, many other myths and legends combine stories about the romantic adventures of a local hero with his amazing exploits as he rescues a princess or fights in battle against evil opponents, as in the legend of the first king of all Minangkabau, Cindua Mato. In one episode, Cindua Mato succeeds after several attempts to capture the Youngest Angel, Putri Bungsu, so that his master, King Dang Tuanku of Pagaruyung, can marry her. Many stories are rags-to-riches tales; for example, the commoner Cindua Mato carries out the wishes of his king and ascends through the ranks, by means fair or foul, to become the first king of both upstream and downstream Minangkabau.

Some myths deal with emotional parent-child relationships, the most famous one being about a newly rich son denying and spurning his mother in all his wealth at his marriage celebration. Variants of the story are told in many versions throughout central and northern Sumatra, where it forms part of the cycle called "Malem Diwa" in Aceh; "Malin Kundang" in Minangkabau, Gayo, and some Batak areas; and "Sampuraga" in Mandailing. Though some stories have an aristocratic bias and focus on extravagant praise of a royal personage, others are critical of those who obtain royal power, as in the Sampuraga myth.

Many myths along Sumatra's west coast are tragic in content. The Malelang myth, found in upstream central Aceh and North Sumatra's central highlands (Gayo and Mandailing), tells of the slander and execution of a boy and a girl for alleged sexual misconduct. The laments (*ratap*) sung during the *malelang* dancing episodes are performed in a very emotional, heavily ornamented style, as are the laments sung during the Acehnese *phô* song-dance. Originally a lament dance around a corpse, *phô* was transplanted long ago by *perantau* immigrants from the Pidie area of North Aceh to Aceh Barat Daya, where it was transformed under religious pressure in the 1960s into a medley of dances portraying stages of a young woman's life; it is performed to this day, though its original North Acehnese form no longer exists.

Myths about the illness or death of babies are prevalent. One of these describes a husband sadly saying farewell to his wife as he departs on a voyage from Sibolga to sell coffee in Penang, returning seven months later to find that his wife has given birth to their son, who is ill. The couple give a feast at which a shaman performs magic acts and sings healing songs, and the child either recovers (according to one version) or dies (in another version). If the latter, sad ending is told, heartrending laments are sung in a high-pitched, loud vocal style that is typical of west-coast songs sung at sea to call the wind, control one's fear in a storm, or avert feelings of loneliness. If the happy ending is told, the artists sing *sikambang* songs set to Malay *pantun* quatrains with a violin and a vocal part performing in Western implied harmony with a cyclic drum and frame-drum accompaniment. Traditionally mixed couples flirted with each other by dancing Malay *joget*-style dances (such as the handkerchief dance) to ensemble music played by male musicians while exchanging *pantun* verses, sometimes with the female partners coming from an itinerant *joget* troupe. However, since the 1950s, women were forbidden to perform these dances at local celebrations. Men performed both the male and the female dance roles, with the "female" partner performing hand movements with both ends of a long female *slendang* shawl around his neck.

The *joget*-style song-dances are based on the Malay Sikambang myth in which Sikambang is usually portrayed as a mermaid and *dayang* (lady-in-waiting) with a breathtakingly beautiful voice. Sad variants of the myth are sung about her right along Sumatra's west coast between Singkil and Krui. Some episodes tell of her queen's rejections of suitor after suitor, till the queen finally drowns herself. Others tell of the magical creation of offshore islands, some of which are destroyed or created by tsunamis or earthquakes.[6] Attached to the myth is a large repertory of *joget*-style song-dances for couples with violin and frame-drum accompaniment, such as the shawl dance (*tari salendang*) and the umbrella dance (*tari payung*) performed to the accompaniment of the Penang Island song. Sailors and fisherfolk report that they sometimes hear Sikambang singing beautiful songs while at sea.

Variants of at least one myth told on both sides of the Strait of Malacca have found their way to the Malay coast of western North Sumatra. They include a story about a son of the Malay Peninsula's hero Hang Tuah, who sailed upriver and walked with his followers from Indrapura on Sumatra's east coast through Tarutung in Batakland to the west coast, where he settled. One day the local Batak chieftain asked him in the local Batak language by what right he was occupying the land, to which he replied in Malay (not understanding the question): *Kita seribu* (We are a thousand), which the Batak king interpreted to mean that he and his followers were members of the (Batak) Pasaribu clan, and so he welcomed them as relatives.[7]

Some myths attribute genealogical meanings to sets of instruments. Thus, a local myth in Pakantan, Mandailing, tells how members of the two founding clans—Lubis and Nasution—were originally represented by two drums in ensembles played at their ceremonies, and as more clans came to settle there, more drums were added, five, seven, and finally nine drums, each representing a clan.

Sumatra's musico-lingual groups in all provinces share similar indigenous religious-associated rituals, myths, legends, music, dance, and theater forms, though each has its distinctive local qualities. A common feature among virtually every musico-lingual group is the opening purification ritual at a ceremony, usually with incense, offerings, shamanic or Muslim prayers, and a female song-dance performed around the ritual subject, such as a bride, who is ritually washed with scented water. The rituals are called *turun ke air* in Malay, *turun ke aiya* in Minangkabau, *turun ke aek* in Mandailing, and *peusijeuek* in Acehnese. Equivalent agricultural rites, called *turun ke sawah* (Ma., "go down to the rice field"), are performed at important moments such as planting, transplanting, and harvesting. Chinese Indonesians usually hold similar purification rites in agricultural areas such as Bangka's and when opening a business venture in urban areas, usually with incense, offerings, prayers, and, if a permit is issued, a performance of the *barongsai* or *liong* processional dance to wish the venture well (Nor 2000).

HINDU MYTHS AND ART FORMS

Hindu-Javanese myths were told in Javanese-style shadow-puppet plays (*wayang purwa*) with *gamelan* accompaniment in the former palace in Palembang from around the sixteenth to the early nineteenth century, and a puppeteer (*dalang*) and *gamelan* musicians were maintained by a descendant of royalty in Palembang until the 1990s. The myths performed derive from Demak-Javanese versions of episodes from India's *Ramayana* and *Mahabharata* epics, especially the latter's stories of the five Pandawa brothers in their battles against the ninety-nine Kurawa brothers, with local clown figures playing a prominent role.

MUSLIM-ASSOCIATED MYTHS AND LEGENDS AND ART FORMS

Some Muslim-associated myths tell of the origin of certain venerated musical instruments, for example, about how the Persian-born Muslim saint Abdul Qadir al-Jaelani miraculously brought the *rapa'i Pasè* down to earth at the moment of his birth (M. Kartomi 2004, 53). Some individual specimens of instruments are named after legendary figures, for example, one venerable *rapa'i Pasè* in Pidie (Aceh) is named after the Baghdadi princess, Putroe Cut Barén.

Some legends with a Muslim flavor look back to a particular period of heroic endeavor, as in the case of North Aceh's *Malem Dagang* epic about the exploits of Sultan Iskandar Muda's fleet in the sixteenth century. Another example is the story told in Pariaman about the exploits of Sutan Pangaduan, who is described as a Saudi-born hero who led local fighters in battle against the Portuguese and British on the Minangkabau coast. The Acehnese *Pocut Mahomet* chronicle tells a story in fine Acehnese literary style about Prince Mahomet's military exploits in seventeenth-century Pidie, in the course of which mention is made of tragic female *phô* lament singing and dancing with breast-beating at a hero's funeral. Another popular Acehnese legend that has inspired many songs and dances is the Iraqi epic about the seductions and abductions of the princess Putroe Cut Barén of Baghdad, including episodes mentioning her kingdom's conversion to Islam.

Probably the most popular legend in Aceh in the twentieth and early twenty-first century is the Muslim-inspired *Hikayat Perang Sabi* ("Holy War Story") about the Acehnese war against the Dutch (1873–1910), with references made in some versions to the Darul Islam rebellion in the 1960s and, since the 1980s, to the conflict between the Free Aceh Movement and the Indonesian army (1976–2005). The bards also describe in full erotic detail the joys to be expected of martyrs who die in battle as they encounter the seventy-seven damsels waiting for them in heaven.

In parts of eastern South Sumatra, Bangka, and Jambi from the early twentieth century until the 1990s, itinerant *Abdul Muluk* (*Dul Muluk*) theater troupes performed theater pieces based on Perso-Arabic legends about the adventures and amorous exploits of the hero from the epic *Hikayat Abdul Muluk*, accompanied by an ensemble comprising violins, *gambus*, and Middle Eastern and western percussion instruments. From the late nineteenth to the mid-twentieth century, other itinerant troupes performed Middle Eastern, European, Chinese, Indonesian, and other tales including "The Thousand and One Nights" in urban commercial theater forms such as *bangsawan, mendu,* and *komedie stambul* in many parts of eastern Sumatra, with stars of Malay, Arab, European, Chinese, and other ethnic backgrounds. Performances were given in some areas until the 1970s, but they became virtually obsolete in the television age.

CHINESE MYTHS AND ART FORMS

Since around the mid-seventeenth century, Chinese Indonesian artists in Sumatra have recounted their ancestral myths, including Hakka and Hokkien stories about the goddess of the sea—Dewi Kwan Yim—who protects voyagers, sailors, fisherfolk, and sea traders. Except when they were banned, for example, in the Suharto era, they also gave myth-related performances in musical, dance, and pageant forms. Traditionally, *barongsai* (dragon) and *liong* (lion) dances were performed in Confucian temple processions at Chinese New Year, *rebutan*, and other religious festivals. Episodes from such ancient epics as "The Three Kingdoms" were told and retold in marionette puppet and Chinese opera forms with oboe, drum, gong, and cymbal music, for example, in the temples in north and south Bangka. Over the centuries, Indonesian Chinese individuals and communities also participated as patrons, organizers, and artists in mainstream Sumatran artistic activities, such as in the annual *tabuik* ceremonies in Pariaman and Bengkulu. Their activities were severely limited, however, by periodic, racist pogroms against them, for example, during Suharto's ascent to power in 1965–66, resulting in bans on Chinese Indonesian artistic activity in the following decades (M. Kartomi 2000; Chan 2009).

DANCES AND MUSIC-DANCE RELATIONSHIPS

In general, the dances of all the musico-lingual groups divide into three categories: the male, the female, and the mixed-sex dances, which may be subdivided into two subcategories, the sitting and the standing dances. They may then be divided into three further subcategories: dances with musical accompaniment (i.e., with music played by a separate group of male or female musicians), self-accompanied dances with the dancers singing and/or performing body-percussion music, and displays of body movement with optional instrumental music.

Dancers in each musico-lingual group wear their own unique male and female dance costumes, but it is very common for female dancers to wear their hair in a bun with flower or metallic decorations and to flip over and otherwise manipulate the ends of a long dance shawl worn around their shoulders, which emphasizes the intricate movements of their hands and fingers. Men usually wear trouser suits with a sarong (*kain*) wrapped around the waist and a form of headdress, and they often attach a sword or other weapon.

Many male dances are based on movements of the art of self-defense (*pencak silat*), especially in the Malay, Minangkabau, and Riau subgroups and to a lesser extent in Batak Mandailing communities. Such displays usually comprise two parts: *pencak*, which is a "warming-up" display of elegant martial movements, and *silat*, which is a mock hand fight between two opponents, with an optional *keris* or other weapon. *Silat* is believed to have developed from forest-dwellers' observations of the attack and defense movements of tigers, for example, among the Suku Mamak people in Riau (M. Kartomi 2011b). Artists typically wear loose trouser suits with a wraparound *kain* and a headdress. In art-of-self-defense displays, drums or drum, gong, and optional oboe ensembles in some areas can be played to intensify the excitement or dispensed with altogether as a nonessential element.

Most of the female dances in southern and mountainous Sumatra are based on movements of eagles or angels hovering or flying and are associated with myths such as "The Youngest Angel" (e.g., *tari kebar*). The dances focus on their highly intricate arm, hand, and finger movements, emphasized by the movements of the ends of the dance shawl held in each hand. In some South Sumatran dances (e.g., *tari tanggai*), the dancers attach metal fingernails to their fingers, which emphasize the elegance of their hand and finger movements even more. The female dancers usually take relatively small steps, with downcast eyes, looking only indirectly at their onlookers or partners (if present). In some Minangkabau and Malay dances, for example, the *tari piring* (plate dance), the women hold a plate in each hand and rotate or half-rotate them in various formations, or roll over with them as they dance, sometimes with a lit candle attached to each plate, as in the *tari lilin* (candle dance). These and other female dances are often presented as welcome dances to the elders and guests at a life-event or official ceremony, with or without betel nut offerings. Some female dances depict cloth-weaving movements, while others enact the hoeing of the land, tilling, planting, and harvesting. Generally female dances are more spatially confined in their arm movements and steps than the male dances. All Malay dances are accompanied by some kind of instrumental ensemble played by a group of men or women, and some with two-way *pantun* response singing added.

Traditional "mixing" dances (*tari pergaulan*) are allowed in a few upstream areas if an elderly chaperon is present, and the mixed couples avoid physical contact, overly sensuous gestures, and a direct gaze at each other. The man dances protectively behind or beside the woman, making more-expansive arm movements and taking longer steps than hers, and performing arm, hand, and finger movements that are larger than her delicate and intricate ones. In some Malay and Minangkabau dances (Ma. *tari payung*; Mi. *tari payuang*), the male partner holds an umbrella over the woman as a sign of his regard and protection. In orthodox Muslim areas, men play both the male and the female role, with the latter played by a man wearing a long dance shawl.

While the standing dances are often based on the symmetrical repetition of dance motives with a prescribed floor plan, and although they focus on arm and hand movements rather than stepping routines, the sitting dances focus on movements of the torso and upper body, including movements of the arms and hands if the dancers are not playing frame drums. The sitting dances are performed by a group of men or women who are "sitting" close together (they are actually kneeling on their heels in a row), while the "standing" dances are performed in upright, stepping position. The former often involve solo and group singing of Muslim or secular texts, while the latter are usually linked to indigenous religious rituals or secular contexts.

Sumatra is particularly rich in male or female group song-dances, in which a solo singer performs the leading vocal role and/or alternates with the singing of the dancers in chorus, with or without instrumental or self-accompaniment. Most other traditional dances are accompanied by an instrumental ensemble that includes at least one drum and melodic instrument and a small gong component, though gongs are rare in Aceh and most northwest coastal areas.

"Body percussion," which denotes sounds made by beating two body parts together, is an important component of several standing and sitting dances in Aceh (e.g., *seudati* and *meuseukat*) and to a much lesser extent, the sitting dance called *indang* in Minangkabau and related dances (e.g., *rodat*) in South Sumatra, Riau, and elsewhere. In Aceh it includes finger-snapping, hand-clapping, beating the breasts, slapping the thighs, and tapping the shoulders, as distinguished from "quasi-body percussion," which denotes sounds made by beating a body part on another surface, for example, clapping a neighbor's hand or stamping a foot on the floor.[8] In Aceh it may be performed in a sitting or standing position, as in the *meuseukat* and the *seudati* dances respectively. A body-percussion episode may simply punctuate a group's singing and movement, or it may constitute a short composition with varying rhythmic figures, timbres, dynamic levels, tempi, and cadences, with an independent structure in its own right. For example, an episode may start with a repetitive rhythmic figure at a medium-loud level and moderate tempo; build up to a fast, loud texture of densely interlocking sound; and end suddenly (chap. 13).

Since Indonesian independence, choreographers in official government and private troupes have developed some elaborate choreographies of select traditional dances for use on grand occasions and to serve as displays of provincial or ethnic identity at festivals, on artistic missions, and on the media.

Research into ways in which musicians and dancers conceive of and perform their joint compositions is not yet highly developed methodologically, though both ethnomusicologists and ethnochoreologists have long acknowledged that musicians and dancers handle similar syntactic elements—such as rhythm, meter, tempo, formal structure, and dynamics—in their joint compositions, which need to be studied together (Kealiinohomoku 1965, 292–95). Many diverse practices are in operation. In Acehnese *seudati* performances, for example, the lead dancers and vocalists usually collaborate with each other and their group of artists before a performance to decide on the precise details of floor plans, movements, tempo changes, and sound effects that help build up and release tension.

When the dancers provide their own instrumental accompaniment in a performance, the dance and the music need, of course, to be studied in tandem. When a troupe of dancers accompany themselves by clicking their rings on plates in the

Minangkabau plate dance or by performing body percussion and quasi-body per-cussion music in the Acehnese *seudati, phô, meuseukat,* and *ratôh duek* dances, the integration of the aural components, text, and visual movement can be depicted in a multiple-stave score, in which the dance formations are presented in diagram-matic form on one stave, a set of stick figures represents the body movements or dance (Kaeppler 1998, 314–16) on another stave, a system of rhythmic-timbral signs represents the body percussion on yet another stave, the lyrics appear in poetic or prose texts with English translations between staves, and a separate stave (or staves) presents the vocal melodies in Western musical notation. An example is the multiple-stave score of *phô* in chapter 12. It was devised to maximize readability for those who know the Western staff notation system, while acknowledging that these song-dance genres are so complex that no notational method can ever do them justice.

Many more studies are needed before a picture of the wealth of Sumatra's dances can emerge. A preliminary study of spatial designs, floor plans, and movements of Aceh's standing and sitting dances in comparison to other visual arts has appeared (M. Kartomi 2004), and the ethnochoreologist and ethnomusicologist Mohd. Anis Md. Nor has made detailed studies of the syntax and dance-music relationships of two important male dance forms—the Minangkabau *randai* circle dance (1986), and the Malay *zapin* dances that are performed in many areas along Sumatra's east coast and in Malaysia (1993). He has also studied the structural characteristics of stylized dance gestures and the symmetrical repetition of arabesque and curvilinear dance motives in indigenous and Muslim-associated Malay dances (2003, 179–81). Mauly Purba has described Toba Batak ritual dancing (2002–3), and Ashley Turner has referred to Petalangan Malay shamanic dancing in Riau (1991), though these ethno-musicologists' main focus is on the accompanying music. A fruitful methodology in future studies might be to compare a musico-lingual group's dances with its visual arts, including designs woven in fabrics, painted on adornments, and constructed in architectural monuments of the musico-lingual groups (as in Nor 2003, 179–81).

CONNECTIONS BETWEEN THE PERFORMING ARTS IN SUMATRA'S MALAY SUBGROUPS AND SOCIAL CLASSES

From the early first millennium C.E. till the end of the colonial era, indigenous Malay societies throughout Sumatra and Malaya were divided into three main classes: the aristocratic class; and two subservient social classes: the settled agricultural people and the nomadic or seminomadic Suku Dalem and Suku Laut.

The oldest Malay courts were located at Sriwijaya-Palembang and Melayu-Jambi from approximately the seventh to the thirteenth centuries C.E. Following their demise, another palace was built at Palembang (possibly in the fourteenth century), which assumed a mixed Javanese-Malay orientation beginning around the sixteenth century. A polity was established at Malayupura in upstream Minangkabau in the fourteenth century, after which the main Minangkabau palace was established at Pagaruyung. The south-coastal Minangkabau palace was subsequently built at Indrapura and other great houses in such port towns as Padang and Painan. The plethora of coastal Malay courts that were subsequently established, including Deli, Serdang, Asahan, Langkat, Daik-Lingga, Siak, Pelalawan, Indragiri, and Daik-Lingga on the east coast, and Barus, Indrapura, and Muko-muko on the west coast, revered Pagaruyung for its supreme mystical power. In Aceh the aristocracy (*ulëëbalang*) ruled in the countryside under the nominal power of the sultan at Kutaraja, while in the Batak Mandailing area, chieftains (*raja*) ruled in the villages over a population of free commoners and slaves. The aristocratic lords everywhere encouraged artists to perform music, dance, and theater at their official, family, and religious holy day events, to which Dutch officials in the colonial era were often invited. Although village artists were not allowed to perform inside the palace grounds on important palace occasions, they provided a *ramai* (I., "lively") atmosphere by performing musical, dance, and theatrical items and setting up food stalls just outside them.

Unlike the Javanese-oriented Palembang palace, each of the larger former Malay courts in Sumatra and peninsular Malaya possessed a special instrumental ensemble—a *nobat*—as an essential part of the king's regalia. It marked his sovereignty and could only be played in his presence. The ensemble is related in instrumentation and function to the *naqqarakhana*, a ceremonial, military and political kettledrum-oboe ensemble of Mughal and Rajput India. Local *nobat* were played in the courts of Sumatra and peninsular Malaya at a sultan's installation and weddings or funerals of the royal family and on Muslim holy days, such as when breaking the fast on Idulfitri. The *nobat* orchestras of the east-coast Sumatran Malay courts at Deli, Serdang, Asahan, Langkat, Siak, Pelalawan, and Indragiri and the upstream and coastal west- and north-coast courts at Pagaruyung, Muko-muko, Indrapura, Painan, Barus, and Kutaraja/Aceh consisted of a trumpet and sets of drums, oboes, and gongs, as did the original *nobat* at Malacca in the early fifteenth century. At the palace of the former kingdom of Daik in the Riau Archipelago, the *nobat* comprised a metal kettledrum (*nekara*), a pair of double-headed drums (*gandang panjang*), a pair of small copper drums (*gandang penganak*), a pair of frame drums (*kencane*), a long silver trumpet (*nafiri*), two oboes (*sarunai*), a pair of small handheld gongs (*mong*), a small suspended gong (*tawak*), and three larger suspended *gong*. Malaysia's royal Malay courts at Kedah, Perak, Selangor, and Trengganu today still perform their respective *nobat* ensemble in the presence of their reigning king, but the remaining *nobat* in Sumatra are never played, because Sumatra no longer has any kings.

Elaborate rituals were performed before and after the *raja* installations and other court ceremonials. In the two Malay courts at Barus from the seventeenth to the nineteenth centuries, the installations were marked by *joget*-style *dayang-dayang* (ladies-in-waiting) and *panginang* (wet-nurse) dances that featured *joget*-style steps. The *panginang* dance referred to in Barus's *Asal* chronicle (Drakard [1988] 2003, 156–57) was probably a precursor of Barus's modern *panginang kapri* song-dance, because the former was danced only by females, and the latter is performed today by mixed couples, or more commonly, by men playing both gender roles, with violin and frame-drum accompaniment. Possibly the *panginang* dance was a female welcome dance with flute, bowed string (*arbab*), and frame-drum accompaniment, like the *joget inang* dance in the Riau-Lingga court at Daik in the Riau Archipelago and other *panginang* welcome dances performed in several Malay courts in eastern Sumatra and Malaysia.

Royal funerals were also regarded as special occasions in the courts. The lengthy funeral of a Barus king involved a royal *nobat* being played on the Acehnese sultan's ship that was carrying his corpse all the way from Aceh to Barus, where it was received with lament (*ratap*) singing and the playing of flutes (*bangsi*), suspended gongs (*agung*), small gong(s) (*canang*), drums (*gandang*), oboe (*sarunai*), bowed and plucked strings (*arbab* and *kucapi*), Javanese gong-chimes (*telempung jawa*), and cymbals (*bacecer*). Moreover, the royal mosque drum (*tabuhan larangan*) and the Friday mosque drum (*tabuh Jumat*) were played in interlocking fashion, and prayers were said. It is likely that the populace gathered from far and wide for the event and contributed performances on the outskirts of the palace grounds, as was the usual practice in all the former Malay courts I have visited. The people gathered to pay tribute to the ruler, and their artists performed music and dance, motivated by the blessings they believed they received from being in the sacred proximity of royalty.

Among the common people, performances of female *joget*-style dances and music were very popular, including couples dancing and response singing led by itinerant *joget* troupes who were accompanied by a vocalist, a melodic instrument such as a fiddle or a flute, an optional small gong, and drums. It was probably in the eighteenth century that the versions of the homegrown bowed-string instrument (*arbab, rabab, hareubab*) were gradually replaced by the violin (*biola*) because it is easier to play. The advent and spread of the *biola* was a transformational turn of events in that it brought in harmonically generated melodies and double-stopping techniques, which are typical of *biola* playing in the Malay *sikambang kapri* couples song-dance repertory that is dominant along Sumatra's west coast (between Singkil and Natal) today. That repertory is related to the *joget*-style dancing and music on Sumatra's east coast, which in turn probably originated in Malacca and was then transplanted upriver and on foot by itinerant *joget* troupes to Sumatra's east and west coasts. Such three-way musical links offer proof of the long-standing artistic and other contacts between the Malay *rakyat* and courts on each side of the Strait of Malacca and Sumatra's west coast.

Some of the chronicles and *hikayat* also refer to members of the local *rakyat* coming to help celebrate royal life events and Muslim holy days, staying outside the palace grounds, and joining in the laments at a funeral or performances of music and dance at a happy event. In return they obtained mystical blessings believed to be bestowed on them by their proximity to the king. Itinerant Malay *joget* song-dance troupes performed with violin and drum accompaniment near the palaces on their journeys, and princes sometimes fell in love with and followed the dancers on their journey. Several kings are known to have given titles to and maintained a special relationship with their local Suku Terasing, whose preferred lifestyle in the forest or in boats at sea privileged them as barter suppliers of coveted forest and sea products for international export, and who were—among other things—the trusted makers, maintainers, and players of the royal *nobat* instruments. The Suku Terasing performed their healing and exorcistic rituals with song, dance, drumming, flute playing, and bell ringing.

Minangkabau artists may increasingly have differentiated their artistic styles and identity from those of the Malay after Pagaruyung was founded and a distinctive sense of Minangkabau sociopolitical identity developed, or so the historical evidence suggests. The Minangkabau people share with the Malays a preoccupation with *pencak silat* and art-of-self-defense-based dances, which are differentiated in Minangkabau in the form of their distinctive plate and candle dances. They are usually performed either with a *talempong* gong-chime and drum or a violin and drum ensemble. Sumatra's Malay culture shares part of its *dendang* (traditional song) repertory with the Minangkabau, but the latter's *saluang jo dendang* (flute with vocal music) genre is quite distinctive in style and content. The Minangkabau probably developed their Sufi devotional forms and Muslim-associated sitting song-dances (*indang*) with frame-drum playing following their conversion to Islam in the sixteenth century.

The Batak subgroups in the mountains and eastern plains of North Sumatra probably developed their tuned drum and *tortor* culture quite independently from that of the Malays, though their forest-product collecting and trading activities ensured that they were in constant touch with Malay communities. Similarly, the Acehnese standing and sitting dances with frame-drum playing and body percussion probably developed quite independently of any external influence. Though the Indonesian Chinese were noted for their patronage over the centuries of both local Sumatran and Indonesian Chinese performing arts, their artists developed their cultures separately, given the long-standing political barriers between Indonesian Chinese and other Sumatrans. There is evidence, however, that neighboring communities usually attended their feasts and celebrations too.

In colonial times a new racially based class structure emerged in Indonesian societies, with the highest echelon comprising the Dutch and other Europeans, the second rung the "Foreign Orientals"—consisting mainly of Chinese Indonesians—and the bottom rung reserved for the "Natives" (*pribumi*). The Dutch maintained political power in part by collaborating with the sultans and chieftains in the towns and villages, supporting the aristocrat-sponsored indigenous performing arts by attending the aristocrats' functions, and promoting military and *tanjidor* brass-band music of Western origin among the people. They treated the Foreign Orientals as a pariah-diaspora group and tried to settle the Suku Terasing.

After 1945, the aristocratic class formally disappeared, though its descendants often joined the new ruling class, while the Indonesian Chinese remained a pariah-diaspora group. After the kings lost their power, the Suku Terasing were no longer seen as necessary to the Malay economy, and they suffered the ignominy of having their lifestyle ridiculed (Chou 2003). They were further marginalized in the latter half of the twentieth century as attempts to settle (and Islamize) them continued.

Among the settled subgroups in the former kingdoms and in the other Malay subgroups across a large part of Sumatra, the Malay genres are performed in their local diversity to this day. Similar genres are performed on Sumatra's west and east coasts, indeed right around Sumatra's coastline. There are also important similarities between the arts of the Malay forest and sea peoples that correspond to their partly similar lifestyles. Similarly, the rituals and associated arts of the majority agricultural and working-class communities across Sumatra resemble one another, ranging from the compulsory cleansing rituals to the ceremonial dances and ensemble music played heterophonically and with cyclic interpunctuating patterns and complex interlocking drumming. Of course some genres of the performing arts of the Sumatran Malays are also closely linked in repertory and style to those practiced across the Strait of Malacca in west-coastal Malaya, but these relationships go beyond the scope of this book.

It is important, however, to look beyond royal patronage when examining matters of style and genre. Class is not a decisive indicator of the creation or development of genres and styles in Sumatra, though in a few cases a small number of court musicians are attributed with having developed particular choreographies of existing rural or seaborne styles (e.g., a *sikambang* dance in the nineteenth-century Indrapura palace, chap. 3). Nor, given that most kingdoms in the past few centuries were relatively small, can royal patronage have been largely responsible for the dissemination of the various styles and genres. Some Malay song and dance styles (e.g., *lagu sinandung* texts and melodies) are performed to this day in the areas of the former kingdoms on both the east and west coasts of North Sumatra, but this is evidence of contact between the former courts, not of creative synergies between the courts and the villages. The fact that some royal families had the means to preserve aspects of their heritage tempts some observers to present court-centric theories about the origins and history of styles and genres that are practiced in large rural areas. The evidence overwhelmingly suggests, however, that those styles and genres, together with the associated legends and myths, spread mainly through the movements of itinerant troupes of ordinary artists or by migrations of kinship groups from area to area in search of land and opportunity, not by the courts. It also indicates that the styles and genres associated with indigenous religion were modified by the spread of the world religions, for example, of mixed Hinduism-Buddhism and later Sufi-style Islam in the case of the art of self-defense, and that conversion to new religions resulted in the development of new styles and genres, such as the sitting dances (e.g., *rodat*, *indang*, and *meuseukat*), which were apparently inspired by experiencing the sitting position of Muslim prayer.

GENDER FACTORS

The roles of and interrelationships between Sumatra's male and female artists vary across class and musico-lingual divides. My limited impression of the relatively isolated, Malay-speaking Suku Dalem and Suku Laut subgroups (Kubu, Mamak, Lubu, Lom, Kuala, and Sekak) leads me to think that the men play a slightly dominant role in the musical arts, with (usually) male shamans leading the exorcistic and healing rituals in the villages on the outskirts of the forest or on the beach respectively. Both male and female members of the Suku Dalem subgroups sing lullabies and children's songs and play the bamboo flute informally to their children and others, and the men play their paired double-headed drums and perform the art of self-defense (*pencak silat*), which is related to tiger and other animal movements in the forest. The Suku Laut women play an important role in the arts, performing mixed circle or line dances (e.g., *tari campak, tari cakter*), singing responsive *saut-sautan* verses with their male partners, and enjoying mixed-couples *joget/ronggeng* dancing with violin and frame-drum accompaniment on the beach. Until the 1950s, itinerant troupes of female Suku Kuala *joget* singer-dancers and male musicians and managers sought their livelihood by sailing up and down the Kampar and other east coast rivers to present all-night performances in river towns and villages, with male clients giving small payments for the privilege of singing and dancing with the female partner of their choice (chap. 10).

The patrilocal Malay, Batak, and Acehnese subgroups and the matrilineal Minang-kabau communities generally confine their women to the home, with a few women becoming semiprofessional shamans and lament singers in their own villages. Female artistic activities include singing and/or dancing at ritual events, singing romantic love poems and lullabies informally, and playing select nonritual instruments for their own amusement, such as xylophones (*garantung*) in Mandailing and Jew's harps (for and with potential husbands) in South Sumatra's Besemah area. Until the early 1980s, female solo dancing and mixed young-couples dancing with a chaperon for mixed audiences were also common at life-event ceremonies in the Besemah and other highland areas, but this was then gradually discouraged as the arts were increasingly Islamized. Muslim genres such as *nasyid* and *qasidah* replaced these non-Muslim art forms on the grounds that they belonged to the indigenous religious sphere and inappropriately allowed the mixing of the sexes. Moreover, the modern media provided other attractive entertainment.

In some parts of Minangkabau, women still play the *talempong* gong-chime and drum ensembles and perform traditional dances, for example, the plate dances, including in processions to and from the rice fields or at life-event ceremonies (e.g., in the Pariaman and Unggan hinterlands). However, in modernist Muslim areas (such as along much of Sumatra's west coast), women are not allowed to dance with men, and the men take both the male and the female dance roles, including wear-ing female dance shawls (*slendang*). In Minangkabau, all-female troupes of *indang* singer-dancers have multiplied since the 1980s, as have the male *indang* troupes. Male *pencak silat* performances among Malay, Minangkabau, and Mandailing musico-lingual groups are still frequently presented, but it is no longer compulsory for boys to learn the art, and some girls now take part. The devotional Sufi-style genres, traditionally played all night, are male-only pursuits that are still practiced in some Malay and west Acehnese areas of Sumatra, as is the devotional *dalai'l* group singing in northern Aceh.

Very little is known about the artistic contributions of particular, leading female artists throughout Sumatra over the past century, and virtually nothing is known about the times before that. In western Aceh, however, the culture memory has preserved the names of some leading female artists over the past century, one of whom is attributed with creating the techniques of the *ratéb meuseukat* sitting dance around the 1890s, with some other women reviving it in the 1960s and developing the secular, female *ratôh duek* song-dances. Still other women rechoreographed and promoted the female west Acehnese and Aneuk Jamée standing dances—*phô* and *malelang*—that had been performed at funerals until modernist religious leaders successfully discouraged performances of all the funeral arts since the 1950s (chap. 12).

The remnants of a once-strong funeral culture still exist in Batak subgroups, however, with descendants of male aristocrats in Mandailing's Pakantan area still being entitled to large-scale funerals with ritual dances accompanied by a nine-drum ensemble and the descendants of free commoners accompanied by a two-drum ensemble.

Traditionally male artists in northern Aceh have performed a range of vocal and frame-drum genres (with or without acrobatics), comic sketches (*biola Aceh*) by a mixed couple of singer-dancers (or two men playing both roles) with violin and frame-drum accompaniment, and sung recitations of epics and legends (*hikayat*, *haba*). The main male song-dances performed in standing position are *seudati*, traditionally performed all night in intervillage competitions, and the sitting dances, *ratôh duek*. *Seudati inong* (female *seudati*) dancing at celebrations was common in northern Aceh until the 1940s but was then banned by the religious leaders, whereupon some female artists developed a new female standing dance called *laweut* with mainly devotional Muslim song texts that virtually replaced *seudati inong* in most areas. Since the 1950s, both sexes also developed a number of other male and female dances at the instigation of the government for use at official functions, election campaigns, and festivals, and in national or international tours.

SIGNAL ITEMS OF IDENTITY AND LOCAL UNIQUENESS

Since the 1950s, governments and ethnopolitical entrepreneurs have chosen to promote some signal items of music and dance as prestigious icons of identity in order to lend grace to political campaigns, cultural displays, and artistic missions (*misi kesenian*); to add ethnic legitimacy at fashionable weddings in urban areas and in the diaspora; and for the development of tourism. Thus each signal item is widely recognized as an emblem of a particular province or an ethno-lingual group within it.

For West Sumatra it is the plate or candle dance (*tari piriang* or *tari lilin*), with a traditional or modern diatonic *talempong* or violin-frame-drum ensemble accompaniment. For Riau it is the *zapin* dance, with a Malay vocal, *gambus*, and *marwas* ensemble. For South Sumatra it is the Sriwijaya song-dance, with Malay or pop ensemble accompaniment. For the six Batak musico-lingual subgroups in North Sumatra, it is a Batak *tortor* dance adapted for the stage, with tuned drum ensemble

music (e.g., *gordang sambilan* in Mandailing), while for the west-coast Malay populations of the province, it is the *joget*-style *sikambang* song-dances and for the east-coast
Malays the *tari serampang duabelas* and other former east-coast palace dances, both
performed with violin and frame-drum accompaniment. The identity signifiers for
the Acehnese and Gayo are the famous sitting dances (*ratôh duek, meuseukat*, and
saman Gayo) with body percussion, though the *seudati* standing dance, along with
the *rapa'i geleng* sitting dance, which has been repressed at times by governments
and religious leaders, is still a contender. The state usually excludes the Indonesian
Chinese arts from identity symbolization, though most of the people would recognize the various local versions of the *barongsai* and *liong* processional dances as their
signal items. Official portrayals of Suku Terasing artistic genres often feature male
dancers wearing loincloths with smoke bombs and other theatrical effects to evoke
the atmosphere of their forest or sea environment.

Some of Sumatra's artistic practices and instruments are unique by world standards. They include Aceh's complex set of body-percussion techniques, which are
among the most developed and virtuoso of body-percussion genres in the world,
including Spain's flamenco genre. One distinctive type of musical instrument is the
great *rapa'i Pasè* of North Aceh, some specimens of which are larger than any other
large frame drums in the world, and their ergology and timbre are unique. In Aceh
government officials usually start their functions or mark an important political moment by beating a *rapa'i Pasè*, just as officials beat a bronze gong in Java and many
other parts of Indonesia.

OTHER CHANGES IN THE PERFORMING ARTS IN THE
LATE NINETEENTH AND THE TWENTIETH CENTURIES

The late nineteenth and the early twentieth centuries brought profound political,
economic, social, and artistic change to Sumatran societies. The lengthy Dutch-
Acehnese war ended in 1910, thereby completing Holland's nominal control of most
of Sumatra. While the traditional Sumatran arts continued to be performed, many
popular Malay, Minangkabau, and Chinese theater forms developed and gained
popularity in the first half of the century, as did *joget*- and *zapin*-style dancing and
American-style pop bands. In South Sumatra and Bangka, *tanjidor* brass bands
were established among workers in the plantations that were owned by Europeans
and others. In many areas indigenous religious communities were being converted,
sometimes forcibly, to Islam or Christianity. The available evidence suggests, however,
that a relatively relaxed relationship existed between rural and urban men and the
women, who often danced and sang together at ceremonies.

The end of colonial rule came with Sukarno's proclamation of Indonesian independence in 1945, following the defeat of the Japanese invaders in the Second World War. All the courts throughout Sumatra were abolished during the social revolution of the mid-1940s, and the aristocratic patronage of the arts ceased. The new Indonesian state apparatus took over the production and promotion of new songs, dances, and theater and the preservation of the older forms. The regional rebellions led by some *ulama* in Minangkabau and Aceh in the late 1950s failed, but they succeeded in politicizing some of the art forms, which resulted in some bans on genres, such as on Aceh's female *seudati* song-dance. Members of the leftist arts organization LEKRA and similar nationalist art organizations were prominent in the promotion of new nationalist song-dances, some of which could be performed in traditional, Malay pop, or international pop styles. Chinese Indonesian art organizations and patrons were actively involved in temple and national day processional arts and contributed to the development of the nationalist and new Chinese Indonesian arts. The government's Department of Education and Culture groomed leading artists to create and present polished performances of the other regional traditional arts, which were molded to express Indonesian nationalism and for display on international *misi kesenian* (artistic tours) and in the media. This represented the beginning of the modern professionalization of the performing arts.

Sumatran societies and the practice of the arts radically changed after Suharto's ascent to power in 1965–66, which led to the large-scale killings of many leftist-associated and Chinese Indonesian artists, and the exodus of the entire Chinese Indonesian population of Pariaman and some other towns. New anti-Chinese regulations and forced cuts in the land size of Chinese Indonesian temples contributed to the abolition of temple processions and other performances over the next three decades.

Under Suharto, the state was encouraged to promote the performing arts as instruments of political programs and election campaigns, regional identity, and national pride. These activities raised the status of many artists. The government established Sumatra's two performing-arts colleges in Padang Panjang in 1969 and Medan in 1979, thus professionalizing the arts further and helping to forge new career paths for artists and art administrators. Officials of the state Department of Education and Culture were required to conduct arts research projects throughout Sumatra, list the details of all performance organizations, and produce an arts encyclopedia.

The late 1970s also saw the renewed interest of provincial governments in cultural tourism, and the rise of *sanggar* art troupes, and the ethnopolitical entrepreneurs who manage them, to present "packaged ethnicity" for tourist audiences at festivals, theme parks, and weddings (Fraser 2007, 427–30). For example, these entrepreneurs have helped create icons of South Sumatran identity with a standard Sriwijaya dance and

Malay ensemble music of remarkably similar content and the same tunes in various contexts, thus regularizing and limiting the knowledge of the indigenous repertoire.

Meanwhile, the growing forces of globalization, industrialization, and modernization contributed to the spread and diversification of Sumatran, Indonesian, and international popular culture, mainly through cassette and compact disk sales, tours, and the media. Artistic authority began to diversify among not only leading traditional artists but also pop stars and entrepreneurs who became active as music producers and contributed performances in the tourist and media industries, government-run competitions and festivals, and the multiethnic theme parks. New ways of making music emerged among Sumatran communities, which diversified and enriched the musical scene, while some of the older styles and contexts weakened, and others continued to coexist alongside newer ones.

Sumatra's many musico-lingual groups and subgroups struggled to define their identity vis-à-vis other groups, including the politically dominant Javanese, who sometimes tried unfruitfully to direct the arts of Sumatran communities from Jakarta to Yogyakarta. In 1982, for example, the Jakarta-based Department of Education and Culture required each region to produce a Javanese-style dance drama based on a local legend, even if the area had no tradition of dance drama whatever, as in the case of Pakan Baru in Riau.

Since the late 1980s a strong Islamization movement throughout Sumatra and some other parts of Indonesia has resulted in a proliferation of segregated male or female troupes that specialized in performing *Islami* repertories, including vocal *nasyid* and *qasidah* groups, and song-dances in the sitting position of Islamic prayer, such as *rodat* in South Sumatra, *indang* in West Sumatra, *meuseukat* and *ratôh duek* in Aceh, and *saman* in Gayo. The melodic styles of some new songs were tonally and rhythmically influenced by the call to prayer, Qur'anic recitation, and returning pilgrims' musical experiences in the holy land. Dances "with an Islamic flavor" performed in standing position such as *zapin Melayu* also proliferated. Women's costumes changed, with the *jilbab* often replacing traditional headdresses and with Arab-influenced costumes that cover the whole body replacing the traditional costumes. Male and female performing troupes expanded greatly in number, and their performances at local celebrations replaced many traditional dances. To this day the groups frequently take part in competitions at the local, regional, regency, state, and international levels.

The assimilation laws targeting Chinese Indonesians and other discriminatory regulations eased after the May 1998 riots, which began as anti-Suharto protests in Medan and some Javanese cities, but developed into pogroms and rapes victimizing Chinese Indonesians. Suharto's fall from power in that year ushered in the Reformasi

(Reformation) period, which was marked by greater freedom of self-expression and a degree of artistic liberation, including a rediscovery of Chinese Indonesian culture, with street processions that included the lion and dragon dances. Chinese Indonesians at the time of writing continue to be regarded as the *pribumi*'s "Essential Other" in many respects, but the time is apparently ripe at last to carry out research projects on the substantial Chinese Indonesian contributions to Sumatra's performing arts.

POSTSCRIPT

Not surprisingly, since Mas Kartomi and I first began to travel around Sumatra forty years ago, some profound social and artistic changes have occurred within and between its many musico-lingual groups and subgroups, caused by such factors as shifting government policies, war, modernization, secularization, heightened religiosity, and the aestheticization of the arts for political, commercial, and touristic ends.

Throughout this book I have tried to explain some of these factors and their artistic outcomes. However, they clearly require much more research and examination throughout greater Sumatra than space in this book allows.

I am conscious that many young Sumatrans of the twenty-first century, who grew up in a world different from that of their parents and grandparents, may not recognize all, or any, of the performing arts described and interpreted in this book. Yet I have written it in the hope that it will provide present and future generations with knowledge of an artistic heritage of which they are not fully aware. I shall be delighted if it elicits their critical comments about my understandings of the topic and, more importantly, by the appearance of many other detailed, critical studies of Sumatra's musical arts and the factors that have led to, and continue to lead to, artistic change and its aesthetic and sociopolitical causes.

Detailed ethnographic research into the languages and peoples of Sumatra largely began in the twentieth century, with the Dutch ethnographer C. Snouck Hurgronje working on Aceh (1906) and Gayo (1903). Colonial-era and other subsequent linguistic research projects were summarized by P. Voorhoeve (1955). Anthropological studies of Rejang folk literature were carried out by M. A. Jaspan (1964) and P. Voorhoeve and M. A. Jaspan (1980), and the linguistic study of Besemah Malay by William Collins (1998).

In recent years, most areas have been surveyed, resulting in the 1981 Wurm and Hattori (W-H) and 2005 Ethnologue linguistic maps of Sumatra.[1] Map 1.1 in the present book is based on a combination of these two maps, though it adds the Aneuk Jamée and Pasisir Sumando speech varieties of Malay according to the results of my fieldwork on Sumatra's northwest coast. Linguistic studies of transmigrant Javanese groups and bilingual Malay- and Hakka- or Hokkien-speaking groups in Sumatra are yet to be made.

The W-H map uses the terms "language groups" (e.g., Malay and Batak), "language subgroups" (e.g., the northern, the southern, and Simelungun Batak), "dialects," "subdialects," and "group-level isolates" (e.g., Acehnese). However, the Ethnologue/Summer Institute of Linguistics (SIL) linguists prefer the term "speech variety" to "dialects" and "subdialects" to avoid implications of unproven genetic-lingual relationships between them (Paul Lewis, pers. comm., 2010). When SIL started research on Sumatra in 2001, fifty-two languages were listed, but when some were found to be speech varieties/dialects or subdialects, the total was reduced to thirty-five.

Several linguists agree that Sumatra has six main language groups, all of which belong to the (west) Malayo Polynesian branch of Austronesian (Adelaar 1992).[2] They are the Malayic, Acehnese, Batak-Gayo-Barrier Islander, Enggano, Rejang, and Lampungic groups. The term "Malayic" is a genetic grouping that includes the many scores of speech varieties of the Malay and Minangkabau groups and the Orang Laut and Orang Dalem subgroups, and excludes the Batak, the Acehnese, the Lampung, and the Rejang (see map in Bellwood 1985, 121).

According to W-H, the Malayic group includes the Minangkabau, with six main dialects: northern, central-northern (i.e., the *tigo luhak* heartland), central, central-eastern, southeastern, and southwestern, of which the northern (around Pariaman), central northern, central (around Solok), and southwestern areas are discussed in this book (chaps. 2–5). It also includes the Malayu Pasisir/Malayu Sumando (Coastal Sumando Malay) group from around Singkil south to around Natal (discussed in chap. 10); the Tamiang Malay in southeast-coastal Aceh; the east-coast Malay in the Deli, Serdang, Langkat, and Asahan areas (also referred to in chap. 10); and the Orang Laut subgroups (some of which are referred to in chap. 9). W-H refer to speakers of "Sumatra Malay" along Sumatra's east coast, a strip along most of its west coast, and almost all areas of Sumatra's large provinces of Riau, Riau Islands, Jambi, and South Sumatra, as well as almost all of the province of Bangka-Belitung. Varieties of Malay are also spoken by the nomadic or seminomadic Petalangan,

Mamak, and Sakai subgroups (referred to in chap. 6), members of which have traditionally spent part of each year in the forest, collecting and gathering forest products, and the rest of the year in their villages, engaging in swidden agriculture in their dry rice fields (*ladang*). Others are the still largely nomadic Kubu, who live in select forest areas of South Sumatra and Jambi (chap. 7), the Lubu forest-dwellers around upper Mandailing, and the Orang Laut or sea-boat-dwelling nomads/seminomads, including the Sekak and the Mapur, who live in coastal and offshore island areas of Bangka, Belitung, and the Riau Islands (see dotted-line areas on map 1.1); and the Bajau on the northwest coast near Barus and the nearby Banyak Islands (Voorhoeve 1955, 24), many of whom have settled in coastal areas in recent years. The Malays of South Sumatra province alone speak seventeen dialects: Kubu, Lematang, Palembang, Sekayu (in the western part of the Musi Banyuasin regency), Sindang Kelingi, Lembak, Lintang, Besemah, Ranau, Daya, Aji, Lengkayap, Semando, Enim, Belide, Penesak, and Ogan around Baturaja (north and west of Kayuagung).

In the W-H map, the Lampungic/Lampung group comprises the Komering and the Lampung languages, the latter including the Northern Lampung Abung and the Menggala speech varieties. The Rejang group is not Malayic (as portrayed in the W-H map) but an independent language group S. Adelaar (pers. comm., 2009). The W-H map classifies the western offshore islands as "language group-level isolates," including Enggano, Simeulue (with two dialects), Niasan (with two dialects), and Mentawei (with three dialects). The Batak component of the Batak-Gayo-Barrier Islands group includes the Alas-Kluet, the Pak-Pak Dairi, the Karo, and the Simalungun subgroups in the north and the Toba, the Angkola, and the Mandailing subgroups in the south (the latter is discussed in chap. 11), while the Gayo includes the northern and southern subgroups. The Acehnese language, which belongs historically to the Chamic family, is spoken in two groups of speech varieties: (1) the northern Acehnese group, including Aceh Besar, Pidie, Pasai, and Lhokseumawe (chap. 11), and (2) the western Acehnese group, including Singkil, Jaya, Nagan Raya, Aceh Barat, and Aceh Jaya (chap. 12).[3]

Three historians recently published books on aspects of the history of Sumatra as a whole: Anthony Reid (2005), Anthony Milner (2008), and Leonard Andaya (2008), the latter two including Malaya in their purview as well. Because Andaya's historical hypothesis is particularly relevant to the musico-lingual identities of the various groups discussed in this book, I shall outline it briefly here.

The hypothesis holds that the nascent ethnicization of the people of Sumatra rests fundamentally on the economic advantages arising from the international trade flowing between Sumatra's metropolitan seaport kingdoms and Arabia, India, and China in the first millennium C.E. and with Europe in the past half-millennium. Sumatra's two oldest kingdoms—Sriwijaya (centered near present-day Palembang) and subsequently Malayu (centered near Jambi) from the seventh to the twelfth century—spoke Old Malay, were internationally famous as centers of Buddhism, and attracted many foreign merchants and pilgrims, which resulted in the expansion of Malay economic power and the politicization of the Malay communities, serving as a catalyst for their differentiation from other groups in Sumatra.

The name Malayu persisted in inland Jambi, where an inscription attributed to king Adityawarman in 1347 refers to Malayupura (the Town of Malayu) as a polity in the Minangkabau highlands. Its artistic remains, inscriptions, and archaeological finds suggest that the people began to assert a separate Minangkabau identity and economic force between the fourteenth and the sixteenth century. Moreover, Portuguese documents in the early sixteenth century mention the Minangkabau people by name and the supernatural power of its king, at Pagaruyung. Their economic advantage increased when they decided to collaborate with the Dutch to free themselves of the oppressive control of the Acehnese at the time, which enabled them to increase their foreign trade via the nearby rivers that led down to the Strait of Malacca. Gradually they saw the value of detaching themselves from the Malay linguistic, artistic, and politico-administrative power system to the east and established their own identity in the Minangkabau heartland (L. Andaya 2008, 3).

After the Portuguese conquered Malacca on Malaya's west coast in 1511, the kingdom of Aceh became the leading Malay-speaking entrepôt in the region, following in the traditions of its predecessors at Pasai (in present-day Aceh from ca. the 1290s) and Malacca. Aceh reached the zenith of its fame as an international entrepôt and center of Islamic knowledge in the early to mid-seventeenth century. Its military strength under Sultan Iskandar Muda (1607–36), supported by Turkey and other allies, enabled it to expand its authority in Malaya and along Sumatra's west and east coasts as far southwest as Muko-muko and as far southeast as Riau (Lombard 1967, 91–98). Unable eventually to feed its commoner subjects on whom it relied for its wars and commerce (Ricklefs 1981, 32), Aceh's central role in the Malay world passed to Johor in the mid-seventeenth century. Aceh then found it economically and politically expedient to pursue a cultural, lingual, and literary identity of its own (L. Andaya 2008, 138–43).

Meanwhile, the people of North Sumatra's interior, known eventually as the Batak, had established a reputation for collecting high-quality camphor, benzoin, and other forest products, which they sold at Barus and other west-coastal entrepôts, and beginning in the eleventh century on the east coast at Kota Cina, whence their products were exported to China, India, and the Middle East in return for luxury goods. By the fourteenth century, they had established a cluster of clans (*marga*) and new settlements based on the idea of a common Batak ancestor, and the cluster became the basis for the division of the six Batak subgroups that are known today as the Toba, the Karo, the Pakpak Dairi, the Simelungun, the Angkola-Sipirok, and the Mandailing.

Sumatra's economy changed radically in the fifteenth century when the black pepper cash crop that was grown in the plantations owned by the sultanates of Aceh, Palembang, and Jambi for export to China and then to Europe radically increased in volume, which created a heavy local demand for rice, with the Batak providing the labor. However, it was not until the sixteenth century that the people of North Sumatra's interior established a distinct identity based on their language and indigenous religion. European contact resulted in subsequent divisions of the Batak subgroups when the Mandailing and the Angkola-Sipirok were forcibly converted to Islam during the early-nineteenth-century Padri war, and the other subgroups were converted to Christianity in the mid-nineteenth century.

The Malay ethnicity that had developed in Sriwijaya and among subsequent palace elites at Riau and elsewhere also spawned the creation of the Malay sea- and forest-dwelling ethnicities known as the Suku Laut and the Suku Dalam respectively. Because they rejected a settled lifestyle and its attendant feudal and subsequently colonial and Indonesian government controls, they are referred to collectively as the Orang Terasing (Isolated Peoples). For centuries they loyally defended and served the Malay kings, who rewarded them with special favors, thus encouraging them to maintain their preferred lifestyles.

The other two contemporary historians of Sumatra, Reid and Milner, argue that the evidence of the development of Sumatra's ethnicities before the rise of nationalism in the early twentieth century is too slight to serve as a credible basis for Andaya's hypotheses (Anthony Reid, pers. comm., February 2008; Anthony Milner, pers. comm., March 2008). Indeed, Reid argues that ethnicity only makes sense as part of the development of nationalism in Sumatra since the early twentieth century. Ethnicity is indeed a potentially slippery concept for which it is difficult to assemble sufficient evidence, and I have avoided using it. Yet Andaya's hypothesis contains considerable conceptual and explanatory power, and it resonates with my field experiences of Sumatra's musico-lingual groups and subgroups as a whole.

Another Sumatranist historian, Barbara Andaya (1993), wrote a detailed history of the Malays of South Sumatra and Jambi in the seventeenth and eighteenth centuries, emphasizing the importance of ancient and modern trade routes between the upstream and the downstream peoples in the Musi and the Batang Hari river systems, a theme that also applies to Sumatra's other great river systems in eastern Lampung, Riau, and North Sumatra. While most scholars have neglected the Indonesian Chinese component of Sumatra's history, she has also presented considerable evidence of Chinese contact and intermarriage with Sumatran royalty. The anthropologist Bart Barendregt carried out detailed research in the mountainous Besemah area of South Sumatra (2005) and linguist Karl Anderbeck on Jambi (2008), both emphasizing the historical role of the Musi and the Batang Hari river systems in communications across those areas throughout the past two millennia.

Largely because of poor communications and the lack of opportunities for fieldwork, sustained research into Sumatra's music began as late as the 1970s, a good fifty years after detailed research had begun into Javanese and Balinese music. Early contributions include Dutch ethnographer Christiaan Snouck Hurgronje's brief descriptions of musical instruments, musical genres, and song texts in a small part of Aceh where he lived in the early 1890s (see his *The Acehnese* 1906). Erich von Hornbostel gave an armchair account of the music of the Kubu (Suku Dalem) forest-dwellers near Palembang in 1908. R. von Heinze described Toba Batak instrumental and ensemble music in 1909, J. S. Brandts Buys and A. van Zijp Brandts Buys surveyed the vocal and instrumental music of Nias in 1942, Jaap Kunst surveyed Niasan music in 1938, and South Sumatran music in 1950, and Claire Holt and Rolf de Maré filmed dances in Nias and Batakland in 1939 (see Holt's posthumous notes: 1971a, 1971b).

The Ethnomusicological Archives at the University of Amsterdam and Amsterdam's Tropenmuseum contain recordings and instruments collected by Kunst and others, and various museums in Amsterdam, Leiden, Leipzig, Wuppertal, Tanjung Pinang, Banda Aceh, Padang, and Jakarta contain substantial holdings of Sumatran musical instruments. Archival music recordings and a few instruments from various provinces of Sumatra are held in the Sumatra Music Archive at Monash University's School of Music-Conservatorium, collected between 1970 and 2010 by Margaret Kartomi, David Goldsworthy, Lynette Moore, Ashley Turner, and Mauly Purba. Berlin's Museum fuer Voelkerkunde holds archival musical recordings from all Batak subgroups, mostly collected by Artur Simon in the 1970s and early 1980s.

Publications since the 1970s include Liberty Manik's article on Toba Batak music (1973–74); Artur Simon's sound recordings with liner notes and articles on Karo, Toba, and other Batak groups (Simon 1984a, b; 1987) and Sembiring's article on a Karo Batak song text (1981). The present author published articles on Mandailing Batak music (1981a, 1981b, 1983a, 1983b, 1990), and west coast Malay (1991), Minangkabau (1972, 1979, 1998–99), Acehnese (1991, 1992, 2004a, 2004b, 2005, 2006, 2007), and South Sumatra (1993a, b; 1998a, b) music, as well as articles on the musical instruments in all provinces of Sumatra in *The New Grove Dictionary of Musical Instruments* (1984) and the book *Musical Instruments of Indonesia* (1985). David Goldsworthy wrote on North Sumatran east-coast Malay music (1978), Ashley Turner on the music culture of the Petalangan people of mainland Riau (1991), Bart Barendregt on Minangkabau dance, theater, and martial arts in West Sumatra and on the Besemah, Semende, and Serawai people of South Sumatra's highlands (2005), Kirstin Pauka published a book (1998) and a DVD (2002) on Minangkabau *randai* theater and the art of self-defense, and Mauly Purba published on the *gondang sabangunan* music of the Batak Toba (2002, 2002–3, 2005). Also Rainer Carle published on Batak opera (1987, 1990) and Nigel Phillips on Minangkabau *kaba sijobang* singing (1980). Dissertations have been written on the traditional music of the east-coast Malays of North Sumatra (Goldsworthy 1979), southern Niasans (A. Turner 1982), the Simalungun Batak (Jansen 1980), the Pakpak-Dairi Batak (Moore 1985), Minangkabau *kaba sijobang* singing (Hajizar 1988), Toba Batak Catholic music (Okazaki 1994), and Batak *gondang sabangunan* music (Purba 2002, 2005). Mohd. Anis Md. Nor has published on Minangkabau *randai* dance (1986) and *zapin* dance of the Malay world (1993), and Matthew Cohen on colonial-era popular theater (*komedie stambul, bangsawan,* and *Abdul Muluk*) in Indonesia (2006). The present author produced vinyl disks of Mandailing and Angkola music on the Baerenreiter Musicaphone label (1983a, b) and compact discs of Acehnese and Minangkabau music on the Celestial Harmonies label (1998). Philip Yampolsky issued a series of compact discs of traditional music of the Toba Batak, the Karo Batak, and the Niasans (vol. 4, 1982); Minangkabau (vols. 6, 1994; vol. 12, 1996), Riau and Mentawai people (vol. 7, 1995); and Gayo and Lampung communities (vol. 12, 1996) on the Smithsonian Folkways label.

No single tone system prevails over large areas of South Sumatra, or in many cases within the practice of particular musico-lingual groups. Tunings of the one type of ensemble tend to vary even within and between neighboring villages.[4] This is especially so in the case of the metal gong-type instruments, due to the vagaries of forging and the fact that they tend to change pitch over the years and are not necessarily retuned. Each group of musicians possesses a remarkable tolerance of pitch variability. Given this aesthetic attitude, exact pitches of tones in cents or cycles per second are therefore not given in that book; it suffices to notate their approximate pitches by a capital letter (e.g., C D E♭ F G A♭ B C for a Western harmonic minor scale) and to add a plus or minus sign over or under a note if it sounds up to an approximate quarter tone above or below the designated pitch, respectively. C^1 designates the octave above "middle C" and C_1 the octave below it, and so on.

The following observations are based on the tunings of fixed-pitch instruments (gong-chimes) and scales used by vocalists and instrumentalists who imitate them (especially strings, winds, and even an accordion/*harmonika*) among a few groups of musicians in the South Sumatran countryside. Reference is also made to a historical Javanese *gamelan* set tuned in the Javanese *pélog* and *sléndro* tone systems from the former Palembang sultan's palace (chap. 7).

Gong-Chime Ensembles in South Sumatra

A variety of single- or double-row gong-chimes (sets of small kettle-gongs) are found among many upstream and downstream musical-linguistic groups in South Sumatra. The single-row instruments are variously called *kenong, tabuhan*, or *kromongan*. Double-row gong-chimes called *kromongan* or *kromong* occur in some parts of the downstream Kayuagung area, comprising a lower-pitched *ngeromong* row and a higher-pitched *ngelitang*. The gong-chimes are found in ensembles of the same names, that is, *kenong, tabuhan, kromong*, or *kromongan*.

Approximate tunings and tone systems employed by some groups of instrumentalists are notated below either at actual pitch or transposed to the octave on middle C (and marked *) to facilitate comparison of intervals. The tunings of the gong-chimes, which are arranged in a row resting on crossed cords in their frames, are given from left to right of the player.

Some gong-chime tunings are tuned to hemitonic pentatonic scales, including {E F G B C} and {E F A B C} (e.g., as recorded in the town of Tanjungsakti in 1989), while others have an anhemitonic four-tone palette, including {C^1 D^1 G^1 A^1} (e.g., as recorded in Sukajadi [Pageralam] in 1989), or a hemitonic four-tone palette, including {D♭ C^1 E D} (also occurring with the gong-chimes arranged in the order {D♭ D E C^1}, as recorded in Jokoh [Pageralam] in 1989). Tonal hierarchies mainly favor the tonic (notated as C) as the central tone and the fifth and the third above it respectively as the second and third most important tones, as in the *kenong* tuning {G_1 C D E G A C^1} (in Tanjungsakti in 1989, where the final and most frequently used tones are C, E and G), or the tonic and the fourth and fifth above it, as in the *tabuhan* tones {G¹ D¹ C¹ G C¹ D¹} (in Jokoh in 1989). Some gong-chime ensembles are tuned to a hexatonic scale. For example, the double row of kettle-gongs in the *tabuhan* in Kayuagung in 1971 is tuned to {G¹ A D¹ G¹ C¹ A¹ G} (in the *ngeromong* row) and {G E¹ D C¹ B A D¹} (in the *ngelitang* row), that is, in ascending scalic order, {A B C D E G}, in which the final tone on {C} is emphasized by four gongs tuned to that pitch, three gongs tuned to D, and two gongs tuned to {G}; thus, the tonal hierarchy ranks the tones in the following order: {C D G A E}. Other gong-chimes (arranged from left to right) have three-tone scales, for example, {E C♯ C♯ A} and {C♯ A C♯ A E C♯} (transposing to C♯ E G *) in the *tabuhan* in Burai Lama recorded in 1971.

Some Scales Used by Vocalists and Instrumentalists

The limited tonal evidence at hand suggests that highland bards, singers of lullabies and responsive ,courting songs, and players of Jew's harps tend to use the anhemitonic pentatonic scale {C D E G A}, with the tonal center on C or G, as in the cases of the male and female bardic singers recorded in Tanjungsakti in 1989. The players who adapted the same songs and Jew's harp melodies to their German-made chromatic button accordion (*harmonika*) in Tanjungsakti in 1971 used the same scale. Sometimes singers and string and wind players use the hexatonic scale, C D E F G A, as in the case of the lullaby singer recorded in Burai Lama in 1971, where the final tone alternated between the second and the fourth degree.

Singers accompanied by *biola* (violin) and *gambus* (pear-shaped lute) players usually perform Malay melodies in a heptatonic major or minor scale, with or without an approximately half- or quarter-tone raised or lowered second, third, sixth, or seventh degree, or combinations of these altered pitches. For example, a *biola* player in Endikat Ilir (near Lahat) in 1989 played melodies in a Western major scale to which he added a lowered third (C D E♭/E F G A B [C¹]). When playing melodies "with a Muslim flavor," vocalists and *serdam* (flute) players often use the major or minor scale, with or without the above-mentioned raised or lowered pitches.

Many modern bronze and iron *gamelan* ensembles have been imported by Javanese transmigrants into their many settlements throughout Sumatra. Historically, however, only one *gamelan* from Java is known to have been accepted into traditional practice by a Sumatran musical-lingual subgroup, namely, the seventeenth-century *gamelan* from Demak played by Javanized Palembang Malay (Orang Jawa-Melayu Palembang) musicians.

Different *gamelan* ensembles made in Central Java vary from one another slightly in their tunings, due mainly to the tuning preferences of their makers. However, all *gamelan* are tuned in one of two basic intervallic structures: the seven-tone *pélog* and the five-tone *sléndro*. The following is presented as a background to the discussion of the tunings of the Palembang court *gamelan* (chap. 7) and the song "Gending Sriwijaya" compared to other tone systems found in Sumatra.

The basic *pélog* tones are 1 2 3 4 5 6 7, from which three modes (*pathet*), namely, *nem, lima,* and *barang,* and four five-tone modal scales derive:

$$
\begin{array}{llcccccc}
\textit{Bem} \text{ I:} = & (\dot{6}) & 1 & 2 & 3 & 5 & 6 \\
& & \text{L} & \text{S} & \text{S} & \text{L} & \text{S} \\
\textit{Bem} \text{ II:} = & (\dot{6}) & 1 & 2 & 4 & 5 & 6 \\
& & \text{L} & \text{S} & \text{L} & \text{S} & \text{S} \\
\textit{Barang} \text{ I:} = & (\dot{7}) & 2 & 3 & 5 & 6 & 7 \\
& & \text{L} & \text{S} & \text{L} & \text{S} & \text{S} \\
\textit{Barang} \text{ II:} = & (\dot{7}) & 2 & 3 & 4 & 6 & 7 \\
& & \text{L} & \text{S} & \text{S} & \text{L} & \text{S} \\
\end{array}
$$

Where S = small interval, L = large interval, numerals = pitch degrees, superscript/subscript dots = higher/lower register, and *bem* = a combination of *nem* and *lima* modes.

The basic *sléndro* tones are 1 2 3 5 6, from which three *pathet,* that is, *nem, sanga,* and *manyura,* with three five-tone modal scales derive:

$$
\begin{array}{llcccccc}
\textit{Nem} = & (\dot{1}) & 2 & 3 & 5 & 6 & \dot{1} \\
& & \text{L} & \text{S} & \text{L} & \text{S} & \text{L} \\
\textit{Sanga} = & (\dot{3}) & \dot{5} & \dot{6} & 1 & 2 & 3 \\
& & \text{L} & \text{S} & \text{L} & \text{S} & \text{S} \\
\textit{Manyura} = & \dot{5} & \dot{6} & 1 & 2 & 3 & 5 \\
& & \text{S} & \text{L} & \text{S} & \text{S} & \text{L}^5 \\
\end{array}
$$

Approximate pitches:

$$
\begin{array}{ccccccc}
1 & 2 & 3 & 4 & 5 & \dot{6} & \dot{7} & \textit{pélog} \\
\text{E} & \text{F} & \text{G} & \text{A} & \text{B} & \text{C}^1 & \text{D}^1 \\
2 & 3 & 5 & 6 & \dot{1} & \textit{sléndro} \\
\text{D} & \text{E} & \text{G} & \text{A} & \text{C}^1 \\
\end{array}
$$

The Palembang Court *Gamelan*

The gong-chimes (*bonang*) of the *pélog* half of the seventeenth-century *gamelan* from Demak in the former palace in Palembang are tuned to a hemitonic pentatonic scale, the approximate pitches being {C D E♭ F A♭}. (The *sléndro* half was not available for scrutiny.) Although this *pélog* scale occurs in modern Java *gamelan* music (app. 3), it is not frequently used. The instruments are retuned when deemed necessary (R. M. Husin Nato Dirajo, pers. comm., Palembang, 1988).

Unlike in Central Java, where tunings of very old *gamelan* ensembles owned by the former regents and royal courts seem to have provided a model for some noncourt *gamelan* (Kunst [1949] 1973, 1:43), the tuning of the Palembang *gamelan* apparently had no impact in South Sumatra beyond the palace, since it was the only known historical *gamelan* in the region. The sultanate certainly did not encourage norms of tunings among makers of the various gong-chime ensembles in the countryside. Although different Javanese *gamelan* may vary slightly in their tunings, all must be in one of two basic intervallic structures, namely, the five-tone *sléndro* or the seven-tone *pélog*. Neither of these tunings is compatible with the Western tuning system. The term *gamelan* in Sumatra is not to be confused with *gamolan*, which is the name of a single xylophone played solo or an ensemble in parts of Lampung province (Kartomi 1985, 31). Its seven or eight bamboo keys, which roughly range over an octave, are freely suspended by rattan lacing to a trough, and are beaten by two performers with a pair of sticks each.

The following audio and audiovisual examples can be viewed or listened to at http://profiles.arts
.monash.edu.au/margaret-kartomi. Click on Books & Book Chapters and the link for this book's
Audio and Audiovisual Examples. Select a media example, scroll to the Description section, and
click on View/Open.

Audio Examples

2.1 Prayer chant followed by *dendang marindu harimau*

3.1 Excerpts from a Cindua Mato performance

3.2 A *rantak kudo* excerpt

3.3 *Tari piriang diatas piriang*

3.4 A *talempong pacik* excerpt

3.5 Four *talempong duduak* excerpts

4.1 Excerpt of sections 1 through 10 of a *tabuik* drumming performance

5.1 *Aluambek* dancing accompanied by an *indang* group's vocal excerpts

5.2 *Salawek dulang*

5.3 *Dikia Mauluik*

5.4 *Dabuih* excerpts

6.1 "Nyanyi Panjang Bersahutan"

6.2 "Lagu Gadiombi"

6.3 *Sama Sepukul*: music accompanying displays of self-defense

6.4 *Ratip* (healing song)

7.1 Excerpt from a *guritan* performance

7.2 *Tari adat Besemah*

7.3 A *rejunk* excerpt based on *cang-incang* verses, sung by a male vocalist at a wedding in
     Kayuagung, 1971

7.4 "Mantau Kundang" played on a *ginggung*

7.5 "Mantau Kundang" played on a *harmonika*

7.6 "Lagu Tari Tanggai" played on a *harmonika*

7.7 "Irama Mayok-Tari Penguton" played by an *orkes gambus*

7.8 *Tari tanggai* played by an *orkes gambus*

7.9 "Tari Zapin Lagu Alaika"

7.10 "Tari Zapin Lagu Pulut Hitam"

7.11 "Siti Zubaidah"

7.12 "Wayang-Lagu Bertempur"

8.1 "Tari Gending Sriwijaya"

10.1 "Lagu Pulau Pinang Tari Payung"
11.1 "Gordang Sambilan Irama Pamilihon"
11.2 "Gordang Sarama" played on a set of *gordang lima*
11.3 "Irama Alap-Alap Tondi" played by a *gondang dua* ensemble
11.4 *Gondang buluh irama Mandailing* (Mandailing bamboo drum rhythm)

All reasonable efforts have been made to acknowledge the moral rights of the performers of the recordings. If any details about them are incorrect or incomplete, I would be grateful to receive any further information at the School of Music-Conservatorium, Monash University, Clayton 3800, Australia.

Audiovisual Examples

9.1   *Tari campak asli* dancing outside the pavilion
9.2   Ensemble accompanying the *campak asli* dancing
9.3a *Campak asli* dancing on the beach
9.3b *Campak asli* dancing on the beach with camera focusing on the instrumentalists
9.4   *Tanjidor* band
IV.1 *Seudati*—rapid movements
IV.2 *Seudati*—slower movements
IV.3 A performance of *meuseukat*
IV.4 *Seudati* demonstration of Keutep Jaro
IV.5 *Seudati* demonstration of Dada Seribu
12.1 Segment of a *phô* dance performance
12.2 A *phô* dance performance at a government function
13.1 *Rapa'i Pasè*
13.2 *Rapa'i dabôh*
13.3 *Rapa'i geurimpheng*
13.4 *Diké angguk*

Note on Informal Learning, Musical Notation, and Transcription

1. Tan Sooi Beng (1993, 93) uses the term "intervallic succession" in lieu of the Western musical term "scale." Because of its common usage in discussions with Sumatran musicians, however, the latter term is used in this book, despite its arguably inappropriate cultural connotations in a Sumatran context.

Acknowledgments

1. The first part of the digitized and annotated Kartomi Collection of Traditional Musical Arts in Sumatra, recorded in all of Sumatra's provinces, can be accessed through the Sumatra Music Archive, the ARROW Repository at Monash University, and Music Australia at the National Library of Australia.

Chapter 1. Sumatra's Performing Arts, Groups, and Subgroups

1. In 2000 the population of Sumatra was 43,309,707 (Badan Pusat Statistik, 2001).
2. Other offshore islands visited include the Pulau Banyak archipelago, Nias, Siberut (Mentawei Archipelago), Belitung, Penyelai, Bengkalis, and Bintan in the Riau Archipelago.
3. "Lingual" means "pertaining to language"; cf. "linguistic," which means "pertaining to the study of language" (Arps 1992, 9).
4. The Wurm-Hattori map is from Wurm and Hattori 1981, 1983 and is available online at http://tinyurl.com/44porat. The Ethnologue map is from Lewis 2009 and is available online at http://www.ethnologue.com/.
5. Some colonial-era linguists wrote about a Orang Suku Laut group known as Loncong, but modern ethnographers and linguists have not found any evidence of its existence (Karl Anderbeck, pers. comm., 2010). A Loncong category is included in the W-H map.
6. Victor Turner (1982, 79) defines ritual as "prescribed formal behaviour for occasions not given over to technological routine, having reference to beliefs in invisible beings or powers regarded as the first and final causes of all effects."
7. Regarding battle-related rituals, until the nineteenth century, petty battles between neighboring groups over land and honor issues occurred regularly in parts of Sumatra.
8. *Animisme* derives from the Latin *anima*, meaning "breath" or "soul."
9. "In earlier times *silat* education appears to have been closely bound up with the belief in tiger-spirits. . . . Between the eighth and the thirteenth centuries . . . Hindu-Buddhist influences enriched the etiquette of the *silat* world with new concepts. . . . Both *adat* and Islamic education serve in making each Minangkabau person into a full-grown human being. . . .

The true *silat* fighter is like a pencil in the hand of Allah. He moves in accordance with "His will." . . . This is the work of the inner force (*kebatinan*): a life in accordance with the will of Allah grants the fighter immunity" (Barendregt 1995, 114, 117, 128).

10. The *adat/agama* controversy resulted in some artists adding Muslim phrases and prayers to *adat* forms to make them acceptable, a practice termed "syncretic" by some scholars and observers. The term "syncretism" has been viewed with suspicion by some Indonesian Muslim and Christian religious leaders, especially in the more intensely religious 1980s and 1990s. It has also been attacked by a number of scholars, though others find that the word "remains productively problematic" (Stewart and Shaw, 1994). "It not only conjures up an orthodoxy against which deviations can be measured; it also tempts us to presume we can identify the ingredients in any particular mixture, and that we know in advance how and why synthesis occurs" (Rutherford 2002). This is not the place, however, to contribute to the decades of scholarly debates about the merits and demerits of the term.

11. Adherents of Confucianism, which itself contains strong elements of ancestral veneration for human welfare, tend to fuse the Chinese deities with local ancestral and nature spirits in the respective Sumatran communities.

12. They were mainly the Indonesian Communist Party's art organization LEKRA (Lembaga Kesenian Rakyat Indonesia), though the Indonesian Nationalist Party was also active in the arts.

13. However, Dick discusses tensions between rich and poor and between the globalized urban middle class and the mass of people still living around the poverty line (Dick et al. 2002).

14. The late Isjkarim was one of the artists and state-employed music researchers in Aceh who wrote about the Acehnese arts in the 1970s and 1980s in mimeograph booklets prepared for the local branch of the Department of Education and Culture, which compiled such entries and published them in a multivolume *Encyclopedia of the Indonesian Performing Arts* in the 1990s.

Part I Introduction. West Sumatra and Riau

1. Our main Minangkabau field trips were in 1972, 1978–79, 1981–82, 1985–86, and 1992; our trips in Riau were in 1980–81 and 1984.

2. See M. Kartomi (2010c), review of Reimar Schefold's and Gerard A. Persoon's CD album of music from Siberut Island, Mentawai, 2009

3. Mpu Prapañca 1995, 33, canto 13.1.

4. As I have argued in chap. 1, Sumatra's western coast may be regarded as a corporate musico-lingual unit that divides into five subunits, of which the Minangkabau southern and northern coastal districts are two (see chaps. 3 and 4). The cultural unity of Sumatra's west coast has resulted from the impact on the musical arts of the people's mainly Muslim beliefs, the Malay lingua franca, the sea-based legends, the history of its local and international trading activity since the early centuries C.E., the European colonial conquests from ca. the fifteenth century, and the establishment of the national government since 1945.

5. Soon after the Dutch capture of Malacca and the renewal of pepper exports in 1634, "Batavia received a letter from the 'old king' of Indragiri offering to supply the company with pepper in exchange for items such as armour, bullets and cannons" (Barnard 2003, 36).

6. Other Sumatran palaces that possessed a *nobat* included Aceh's Malay sultanate in ca. 1600–ca.1750, Barus in the eighteenth and nineteenth centuries, Pagaruyung in around the sixteenth–nineteenth centuries, and the east-coast palaces at Asahan, Deli, Serdang, Langkat, Langsa, and southeast Aceh's Langkat in the eighteenth–twentieth centuries.

Chapter 2. Upstream Minangkabau

1. When two parties meet at a wedding or other function, they may address each other formally in *pantun*, making jokes or verbally attacking and counterattacking each other for prolonged periods. The guests may be welcomed in *pantun* and reply with other suitable *pantun* after which the host may then continue polite conversation, still in *pantun* form.

2. Some *silek* movements reflect a tiger's fierce attack, others an eagle swooping on its prey, and yet others the snatching of a monkey, three animals whose movements I have found are imitated in many *silek* dance choreographies throughout Sumatra.

3. Fraser (2007, 432) gives the Minangkabau term *gerinyak* as a type of ornament in *saluang jo dendang* performance.

4. wwf.org.au/news/illegal-coffee-grown-in-tiger-habitat, accessed 22 July 2010.

Chapter 3. The Minangkabau South Coast

1. One reason for the faulty view that the south coast is a mere backwater of the heartland is that it is comparatively underresearched. The colonial and postcolonial literature consists of only a few brief references to its geography, history, and anthropology (e.g., in Marsden 1966 [1811], 353–55), and it virtually ignores the performing arts. Ethnomusicological, anthropological, geographical, and historical research to date has focused mainly on the *darek* and neglected the south coast. In 1811, William Marsden published an account of the history of the kingdom of Indrapura, in which he mentions a wedding in 1400 between an Indrapura princess and a prince from Bantam in northwest Java. It drew attention to the kingdom's former wealth gained mainly from taxes imposed on the local trade in pepper and gold, which it acquired by river from the hinterland, and its historical link with the Muko-muko sultan's palace in the south (ibid.).

2. This enduring belief is according to two descendants of the Indrapura palace, Pandekar Sutan Sabarudin and Tengku Regen of Kp Muara Sakai in Indrapura in 1985. They said that a descendant of Bundo Kanduang lives in the royal house at Lunang to this day and claimed that Indrapura is older than Pagaruyung and that the ancestral hero Cindua Mato was born and died nearby.

3. South-coast Minangkabau artists regard both nonharmonic and harmonic styles as *asali* (authentic). However, as there is a strong musical difference between the two styles, the former will be called "*asali* Malay" and the latter "*asali* Malay-Portuguese." As explained in chap. 1, Sumatra's first significant contact with Europeans in the sixteenth century was with the Portuguese, whose main lasting musical influence was the introduction of the violin (*biola*) along with the associated European major and minor scales, tuning system, and musical harmony.

4. References to the traditional and Muslim arts in the former Muko-muko palace are made in the nineteenth-century court chronicle: *Syair Mukomuko* (Kathirithamby Wells and Hashim 1985).

5. These and other terms are given in the local speech varieties of south-coastal Minangkabau.

6. I am indebted to the *tegenai* Bp. M. Noerdin of Kampuang Painan Timur and Bp. M. Anas of Sungai Kuok, Kecamatan Batang Kapas, for information on the south-coast shamanic arts.

7. The main flutes in the *darek* are the very long, open bamboo *saluang* and the short, thick-bamboo flute called the *simpelong*. On the south coast another type is the *serdam*, which in some cases is a fipple flute, and in others a ring flute.

8. This ring-stop flute is also found in Sulawesi, Flores, and some other parts of the archipelago (Kaudern 1927, 243).

9. This *gilo lukah* performance was led by Bp. Sjamsun in Kampuang Pasar Sirantih, Kecamatan Batang Kapas. We recorded a similar *gilo lukah* performance along the Kampar River in Riau (chap. 6).

10. Besides the European violin (*biola*), which is played to accompany coastal Sikambang singing, Minangkabau has three types of traditional bowed string instruments: the south-coast *rabab*, which is described above; the north-coast *rabab Pariaman*, which has three strings; and the *rabab* in the *darék*, which has only two strings. All three types are associated with different repertories and styles (M. Collins 2003).

11. In 1983 Bp. Aslim was paid Rp 25,000 (worth $US18 at the time) for playing in the town of Painan, Rp 50,000 for playing in the capital city of Padang, and less than Rp 15,000 for performing in nearby villages. He was also a *rabab* maker, who received Rp 35,000 ($US25) in payment for a *rabab* that he made in his home in Salido.

12. Some other *kaba* that Bp. Aslim performed were named after heroes, such as "Sutan Palembang," "Abu Sama," and "Bujang Juah." However, "Anak Raja Tuo Sutan dan Putih Lindung Bulau" is a love story, "Gadis Abaidah" is the name of a beautiful heroine, and "Raja Sipatoka" is the name of a local chieftain.

13. For a different version of the Sikambang legend on North Sumatra's coast, see chap. 10.

14. Male dancers play both male and female roles in couples dances, in accordance with the Muslim prohibition of married women performing before an audience. In Sibolga in the 1970s and 1980s, however, we recorded a female Sikambang dancer performing Sikambang song-dances partnered by a male dancer (chap. 10).

15. See a description of a ceremony similar to the bride's ceremonial wash at Barus in chap. 10.

16. The *nenet* oboe, described later, is played only in the southernmost area, around Silaut.

17. In the early 1980s, the local Department of Education and Culture office responded to directives from Jakarta to "develop" their local dances for official occasions.

18. The Minangkabau plate dance is now world famous, occurring in many variants on the coast and in the *darék*. A relatively modern variant of the dance is the *tari piriang diatas kendi* (plate dance on a water jug), in which a dancer balances herself athletically on a water jug while rotating a plate in each hand in fast motion.

19. The names of the numbers one through four in Minangkabau are *ciek, duo, tigo, ampek*.

Chapter 4. *Tabut*

1. This view was expressed in my discussions about *tabut* with government and religious leaders in Jakarta, Pariaman, and Bengkulu in recent years.

2. The term *orang Kling*, meaning "a person of Indian descent," derives from the name of the early central-eastern Indian kingdom of Kalinga. Normally the term does not carry derogatory overtones in Sumatra, though it has at times elsewhere in recent decades. In our experience, a considerable number of people living in coastal Sumatra are descendants of Indian traders and soldiers and are proud to be called *Kling*.

3. Teungku Shak (Ishak) Marikam, who led a group of Acehnese *orang Kling* musicians of Shi'a heritage in the annual *tabut Hosan-Husen* festivals in Lembutu village, Kecamatan Pandar Baru (coastal Sigli, Kabupaten Pidie), told us in 1982 that his father had taught him to perform *tabut* music on two *geundrang kling* (Indian drums), a *seuruné* (Indian oboe), and a pair of *rapa'i* (frame drums), and that he had played in small *tabut* processions in Sigli whenever the Dutch or Indonesian governments allowed them to be held. Although they performed in the early years of Indonesian independence, many of their ritual *tabut* objects were destroyed by separatist Darul Islam leaders in 1953, after which *tabut* performances never returned.

Though no longer involved in *tabut*, Marikam and his troupe were still playing *tabut*-related oboe, drum, and frame-drum ensemble music in 1982, usually in a *lelucon* (comedy act) with two clowns, one of whom wore a comical imitation of an aristocratic English military hat.

4. See Pelly (1879) and Caron (1975) for two reports—separated by a century—of *ta'zia* in Iran; also Shurreef and Herklots ([1832] 1895, 119–23) and the *Census of India* (1961) for two reports (also separated by over a century) in the Deccan and Gujarat in the former and Lucknow and Delhi in the latter.

5. References to sepoy troops were made in the British colonial reports from the seventeenth century (John Bastin, pers. comm., 1983). The presence of sepoys in Sumatra is documented by Bastin in a print of a drawing of Fort Marlborough, Bengkulu, by Samuel Andrews (ca. 1767–1807), published in 1799 in London (Bastin and Brommer 1979, plate 3), and by reference to thirty or thirty-five "Seapoys" in Tapanuli in 1801 (Bastin and Brommer 1979, note 330). Sepoys were also stationed in Java in 1811–16 (Merle Ricklefs, pers. comm., 2008).

6. Bird-shaped biers called *burak* are also found in similar festivals in Lucknow and Delhi (see *Census of India* 1961, 3, plate 6).

7. In the *tabot* of 1981 in Bengkulu, by comparison, eight neighborhoods each built a *burak*, namely, in Pondok Besi, Kebun Ros, Tengah Padang, and Bali on one side (all sharing one permanent *gerga* shrine) and Berkas, Pasar Baru, Kepiri, and Melaboroh on the other (sharing another permanent *gerga*). In 1979, fifty *burak* appeared on the final day, including (1) the oldest and highest *burak*, which is called *tabot coki berkas*; (2) the leader of the final procession, called *tabol bangsal*; and (3) several biers called *tabot coki* (*tabot* is the Bengkulu spelling). Until *tabut* ceased to be performed in Sigli in 1953, two opposing villages took part, building *burak* cenotaphs in Gampong Gigin (Kecamatan Simpang) and Gampong Lembutu (Kecamatan Pandar Baru) respectively and on the tenth of Muharram throwing their *burak* into the sea (Teungku Shak Marikam, pers. comm., 1982). In Pariaman's 2009 *tabuik* festival, the two rival neighborhoods were Pasar and Subarang (Paul Mason 2010).

8. In Bengkulu there are two permanent cement shrines (called *gerga* or *gurga*) for each of the two main neighborhoods that participate. Temporary shrines are also made in the less important villages for use during the festival. In Pariaman there are no permanent shrines, though some say there were once.

9. Bonfires in pits play a more important role in the Indian proceedings than in their Sumatran counterparts, however (see Shurreef and Herklots [1832] 1895, 113). In India the participants may also walk on fire during *tabut/ta'zia* to prove their faith.

10. In Bengkulu the clod of earth is also said to symbolize the earth of India.

11. Breast-beating, which is typical of Iranian mourning in Muharram, is replaced in Pariaman by these rhythmic hand movements.

12. *Ratap* (sad songs) sung while, or as if, crying are sung mainly at funerals and palm-sugar collecting expeditions; it is believed that more sugar will be obtained if one cries while collecting.

13. Formerly *maratapi jari-jari* consisted of long song texts in Urdu, but only a few Urdu words are now included, and their meanings are no longer remembered.

14. Possibly the fish symbolizes the silver or gold fish mounted on a pole and used traditionally as a standard by the forces of Indian princes (see Shurreef and Herklots [1832] 1895, 115).

15. *Pedang Jenawi* are heirloom swords said to be made in Jenawi, Central Java.

16. *Maradai* performances have become a major feature of *tabuik* festivals in the twenty-first century. In 2008, there were kite races, traditional plays, speeches by political leaders, prayers, and the street processions that included performances of the *galombang* dances, the art of self-defense, the plate dance, *indang*, and other traditional and modern Minangkabau arts (see Paul Mason's video described later in this chapter).

17. *Basosoh* is a Minangkabau word used to describe a situation where two warring sides meet and the battle begins to become *ramai* (heated) (Ibu Wahidar Anwar, pers. comm., 1982).

18. In Bengkulu, the procedures differ from Pariaman in that the main *tabot* are carried in processions to Syek Burhanuddin's seaside grave for a memorial service attended only by the *tabot* families; the lesser *tabot* are thrown into the sea for children and adults to dive in and retrieve parts as souvenirs.

19. In the Pariaman hinterland, musical repertories played at weddings and circumcisions include "Anak Daro" ("Bride"), which is played to accompany the procession of a bridal couple.

20. For example, in villages around Lake Maninjau (Kampuang Pandan, Sungai Batang, Tanjung Sani, and Galapu), troupes comprising *tasa* and *dol* players perform regularly at weddings and other celebrations throughout the year, as well as taking part in *dol-tasa* competitions (in 1984, the Sungai Batang village group won). *Tabuik*-related titles of pieces played included "Atam" (i.e., "Matam") and "Basosoh" in Pariaman, while traditional Minangkabau titles included "Siamang Tagagau" ("Shocked Monkey"), "Riak Pandan" ("Rippling Grass Mat"), and "Ombak Baralun" ("Large Moving Wave").

Chapter 5. Four Sufi Muslim Genres in Minangkabau

1. *Mauluik* in Minangkabau, or *Maulid* as it is usually called in Indonesian, is the third month of the Muslim calendar, *rabii' ul-awal*.

2. Several musicians and academics who teach at the Sekolah Tinggi Seni Indonesia (STSI) in Padangpanjang use this classification, including Prof. Dr. Daryusti MH, Bp. Firdaus Muhammad Halim, and Bp. Asril Muchtar (pers. comm., Daryusti, 2009).

3. The frame drum is said to have been the only instrument to have been approved by the Prophet, Muhammad. This is according to a reference in a *hadith* (document containing written sayings of the Prophet) by his youngest wife, Aisha.

4. The traditional Minangkabau marriage arrangement, sometimes called *semando*, is matrilocal, i.e., the bridegroom marries into and lives with the bride's family. However, the mother's brother (*mamak*) has ultimate power in the family, and it is he who initiates his nephews into adulthood. The family's land, house, and goods are inherited through the female line; thus young men leave Minangkabau to go abroad (*merantau*) in order to acquire wealth. Traditionally, the young men sleep in the local *surau* (male meeting and prayer house) and are educated separately from the young women in religious and other matters, including the devotional art forms.

5. For a nineteenth-century account of these dances, see Hasselt (1881a).

6. Other popular male devotional genres include *hadra* or *barodat* incorporating solo and group-responsive singing of songs of praise and other religious (or secular) texts such as "Salla Rabbuna," "Salyarab," and "Sallalatullah," with group frame-drum playing and rhythmic clapping by those who do not play the frame drum, plus dancing in a row in sitting or standing position.

7. The latter possibility seemed particularly feasible to us after we sailed the course of the long Kampar River from its source in the Minangkabau highlands to its mouth, passing through the *bono* tidal wave near the river mouth into the Malacca Straits in November 1984 (with Bp. Tenas Effendi of Pekan Baru and former Monash University student Ashley Turner). Jane Drakard argues that Aceh may *not* have been a major source of conversion in West Sumatra given the Minangkabau people's memory of and mixed feelings about the harsh Acehnese regime under which they suffered, especially under Sultan Iskandar Muda (pers. comm.,

September 2007). Local anecdotal and musical evidence, however, suggests that Islam and associated musical genres were introduced both from Aceh and via the rivers from the east.

8. *Barzanji* refers to poetic songs sung in the month of Maulud about the Prophet's birth and praises of his life and teachings written by Jafar al Barzanji. Devotees usually sing from a copy of the *Kitab* (book) *Buchari*, or *Maulid Syarafil Anam*, on the Prophet's birthday (Sinar 1986, 70). They are very popular throughout Indonesia (Gade 2004, chap. 1).

9. Arguably, the *kaba* legends told by storytellers (*tukang kaba*), which contain cosmological, Muslim, and secular interspersions in clients' all-night celebrations (see, e.g., the Sikambang and the Malim Deman legends recounted in chap. 10), are another form of expression of that philosophical knowledge and ancestral "history."

10. These body-percussion patterns are much less rhythmically complex than in the main Acehnese body-percussion genres described in chaps. 12 and 13. They focus on dexterous group movements that frequently build up to a breathtakingly fast tempo.

11. In this and some other respects, *indang* resembles *ratōh duek* (group sitting dances) in Aceh (chap. 13).

12. *Maimbau* means "to call," "to cry"; *lapak* means "sound of blow made with flat of hand" (Toorn 1891).

13. Information in this paragraph is from an interview with the famous musician Bp. Islamidar in his home near Payakumbuh in December 1985.

14. When a new branch of Sufism is established, an individual teacher is initiated into the teachings of the order and then becomes a *khalifah* (*kalipah*) (Trimingham 1971).

15. He sang the confession of faith: "There is no God but God" (*Lāillāh' hailillāh Lā ilāha illā 'llāh*) and the salutation "Peace be with you" (*Assalamū 'alaikum*), followed by: "With my left and right hands I greet you and request forgiveness," after which the men sang, "Yes, peace be with you" (in Minangkabau) to a six-tone melody.

16. Among Sufi fraternities, the use of fire is restricted to Rifa'iyya devotions (Hughes [1885] 1976, 705).

17. For a recording of a Rifa' ceremony by the Islaamia Refia Jamaa Association in South Africa, see Folkways Record FR8942 with notes by Joseph Schacht (1959).

18. In North Aceh (in and around Lhokseumawe), for example, *dabôih* (Ac.) is mostly performed on government-organized occasions or by companies such as Mobil Oil, and less often now for village celebrations.

19. We attended devotional *indang* or *hadra* (also named *radat*) gatherings in several villages in Minangkabau (Payakumbuh, Sijunjung, Solok, Painan, and Talang Maur in 1972, 1985, 1986, and 1992). For a photo of an all-night *hadra* or *radat* session held in Liwa, Lampung, in January 1981 (similar to those in Minangkabau), see M. Kartomi (1985, 16).

Chapter 6. The Riau Indragiri Sultanate's Nobat Ensemble and Its Suku Mamak Stalwarts

1. Sumatran literary sources provide evidence that the palace in the Minangkabau heartland at Pagaruyung once had a *nobat*, as did the court at Aceh (Lamri) and the two palaces at Barus in the seventeenth century (chap. 10). The *nobat* in the former Riau-Lingga palace included a pair of frame drums (*kencane*), a pair of hand-held suspended gongs (*mong*), and a kettle-gong (*tawak*). The Siak palace, near the mouth of Riau's Siak River, and the Pelalawan court, in the middle reaches of Riau's Kampar River, also possessed *nobat*, and at the time of writing, the one at Siak is on display in the palace museum. Pelalawan's *nobat* may have

been established by Sutan Mahmud, who fled from the Portuguese invaders of Malacca to Kampar and died there in 1528 (Tenas Effendi, pers. comm., Pekan Baru, November 1984). With the Kingdom of Malaysia's system of rotating kings, *nobat* are still found in the royal courts at Perak, Kedah, Selangor, and Trengganu, and one of them is always played at a king's installation every five years. Their instrumentaria are similar, minimally featuring the royal drums (*nekara, nengkara*), the silver *nafiri* horn, a *sarunai* (oboe), and frame or goblet drums. The *nobat* in the palace in Brunei, like the *nobat* at Kedah, contains gongs, and at Trengganu, a pair of cymbals.

2. The *Sejarah Melayu* is a historical text in Malay that may have been completely rewritten several times from the seventeenth century onward (Teeuw and Situmorang 1952, 35). Wan Sri Benian, rule of the Riau kingdom of Bentan is mentioned in this source as being the first person to use the *nobat* (Brown 1953).

3. *Idulfitri* (Indonesian spelling) is the Muslim holiday that marks the end of the fasting month (Ramadan); *Iduladha* marks Abraham's willingness to sacrifice his son for Allah.

4. Marsden ([1811] 1966) mentions the existence of a *nobat* at the Minangkabau court in his book *The History of Sumatra*.

5. The official Indonesian name for these forest-dwelling people is Talang Mamak, one of the so-called *Suku Terasing* (Isolated People) in Indonesia. However, several of the Talang Mamak's *penghulu* (leaders) reject the name because the word *talang* implies that they are "primitive." The correct name, they say, is either Suku Mamak (Mamak ethnic group), in which Mamak refers to the royal ancestors they revere, or Suku Dalem (but also Anak Dalem, meaning "child" or servant of the palace; cf. *abdi dalem*, "devoted servants" in courts of Java). These "isolated peoples" performed a special legitimizing role in the Malay kingdoms based on their prior occupancy of the relevant lands (A. Turner 1997, 8). The sultan of Rokan/Kuantan claimed that the Suku Mamak stemmed from the family of his maternal uncle in pre-Islamic times and therefore served to preserve the pre-Islamic *adat yang sebenar adat* (lit. "the *adat* that is really *adat*"), which deals primarily with the sanctity and correct usage of land (Ashley Turner, pers. comm., 1988).

6. The drums and their context are described in detail in A. Turner (1991, 121–46).

7. The Temenggung was a "high official"; the word was originally a military predicate meaning "commander-in-chief." The information about these earlier practices was given to me after a brief private ceremony to show reverence for the ancestors by the son-in-law of the late Sultan Mahmud Indragiri, Bp. Tengku Hamat. *Adat* heads in the Pelalawan sultanate on the Kampar River were also called *pamangku adat* or *ketiapan*, while the administrative nobles were called Batin (Effendy 1997a, 632).

8. On visiting the graveyard at Kota Lama, we were informed that Sultan Mustafa, the sixth sultan of Indragiri (1559–1658), was buried in the largest of the graves. Next to it is the grave of the first sultan of Indragiri, Sultan Narasinga, who was buried next to a grave reputed to be that of a Portuguese general of the sixteenth century. According to legend, a Portuguese fleet had been destroyed in the river by Narasinga's father, Raja Gedombah, in the early sixteenth century.

9. See Ashley Turner (1991, 127). The *obab* is also used in trance art forms, such as healing ceremonies, in which a dancer enters into a trance identified with the possessing spirits.

10. However, the Suku Mamak *silat* performance described in Kartomi (2011, 50–55) was accompanied on a pair of handmade double-headed drums, *gendang ibu* playing to *peningka* (lead rhythm) and the *gandang anak* playing the *pengelalu* (continuing rhythm) (ibid., 50).

11. All the musicians are male, but females may dance and sing.

12. Effendy (1997a, 642) describes the honored social position of the *tukang nyanyi panjang* (singers of long songs) in traditional practice.

Chapter 7. South Sumatra

1. Our fieldwork was carried out among the musico-lingual groups in South Sumatra in 1971, 1988, and 1989.

2. People in different parts of the province tend to name their own group of rivers to make up the metaphorical nine, which is symbolically an important number in Malay cultures generally. Many groups mention the Musi, Banyuasin, Batang Hari-Leko, Komering, Ogan, Lematang, Enim, Rawas, and Lakitan as being the most important, but the highlanders mention only seven rivers (W. A. Collins 1998, 299). The social and mystical implications of the term Batang Hari Sembilan/ "The Realm of Many Rivers" are discussed at length in Barendregt (2005, 13).

3. In 1902, F. Heger grouped a collection of 165 Dōng-son drums into four types, of which the waisted drums were dubbed Type 1. As the heads of the Dōng-son drum are made not of skin but of metal, technically they are not drums, though they are believed to have functioned as drums. Several scholars have speculated that the Type 1 bronze timpani found in Besemah were played at rain-making and other mystical ceremonies or to rally men for war (e.g., Higham 1996, 124).

4. They are proof of an ancient civilization in Besemah that may have been contemporaneous with Austronesian migrations to the area ca. 500 b.c.e. (Bellwood 1995). Moreover, Chinese earthenware fragments found there possibly date back to the seventh century c.e. (Thomassen à Thuessink van der Hoop 1932, 136).

5. Thai centers included Pattani, Nakorn Sri Thammarat, and Chaiya. See Manguin, map 1, in Coedès and Damais (1992, ix). Trade with China is documented from as early as the fifth century c.e. Between 455 and 563 Kan-t'o-li (Jin Tuo Li) is reported to have sent five emissaries from the southeast coast of Sumatra to China (Wolters 1960, 343–44).

6. In the late first millennium c.e., Palembang and Jambi-Sumatran and Javanese Buddhists were in contact with the Nālandā college in Bihar where a special monastery was built to house Indonesian pilgrims, monks, and scholars (Fontein 1990, 35). After Nālandā declined around the tenth century, Sriwijaya-Palembang rose again in prominence, and the reformer-saint of Tibetan Buddhism, Atīśa came to study at Sriwijaya in around 1011–23, bringing some Tibetan canon texts from Sriwijaya to Tibet, it is said (Chattopadhyaya 1981, app. B, sec. 4; Becker 1993, 182).

7. Some bards hold that early efforts to convert the highlanders to Islam were made by the late-eighteenth-century Muslim leader Buyang Awak, but that they were converted in substantial numbers only from the early twentieth century, mainly due to the efforts of a Javanese proselytizer, Radin Gunawan (pers. comm., Bp. Saman and Bp. Surfai B.A. in Pagar Alam, 1988).

8. In 1983 Olaf Smedal visited Suku Lom resettlement projects in Kedimpul (near Jebus) and south of Pangkalpinang on Bangka and found that their resettlements were almost complete failures, for it is not possible to prohibit forest nomads from returning to the forest or to prevent fishermen from going to sea (Smedal, pers. comm., February 2010). Since then, however, progressive deforestation and depletion of ocean fish have brought even greater threats to the survival of both the forest and the sea peoples.

9. Of all the upstream groups, the greatest amount of scholarly attention has been paid to the thirty-eight or so local Besemah Malay language varieties/groups, the exact number of which

remains a matter of debate (Jaspan 1976, 163; W. A. Collins 1979, 14–16; Bowen 1993, 197; Barendregt 2005, 4–21). Most upstream groups share the same indigenous concepts, cultural ties, and system of social organization, including the kinship groups that provide the brides ("bride-giver groups") and those that receive them (the "bride-taker groups"). Patrilineal/virilocal, matrilineal/uxorilocal, and bilinear marriage types coexist in some villages or areas (Barendregt 2005, 7). Apart from the Enim, Lematang, and Ogan groups, the upstream people also share essentially the same history (Barendregt 2005, 6).

10. Barendregt distinguishes three "culture areas" in the southern Sumatran highlands (2005, 4). They comprise parts of Lampung, Bengkulu, and South Sumatra: the Rejang-Lebong and Musi areas bordering Kerinci and Minangkabau; the Ranau and Komering areas between the South Sumatra highlands and the Lampung groups to the east; and the highland communities of southern Sumatra, all of whom apart from the Rejang-Lebong speak local variants of Malay (Grimes 1996). Nineteenth-century Dutch linguists defined the language variants as belonging generically to Middle or Highland Malay (Voorhoeve 1978), which was possibly based on a putative Malay variant that was initially an intermediate between Riau-Lingga Malay and Minangkabau Malay (Brandes 1887, 75). Both the *ulu* and the *ilir* legends portray the foreign ancestors from downstream as being superior to the upstream ones from whom they took over (Barendregt 2005, 60–67). Indeed, the legends present the succession of legendary foreign contacts in a positive light.

11. The narratives often take the form of *andai-andai* verses, which typically contain philosophical statements and sometimes simply repetitious syllables (Collins 1979, 301).

12. At a communal ceremony the wife-taking clan carries out all the work for the wife-giving clan, who is given pride of place in the proceedings.

13. A large collection of highland letters is held at Leiden University, KITLV H799, and was assembled by O. L. Helfrich (1860–1958). Another large collection is held in the Leiden University Library (at shelfmark LUB Or. 8447), which was assembled by Voorhoeve (1899–1996) (Jaspan 1964, 6). They comprise clan chronicles, love poetry, and *pantun*-like riddles written in the South Indian–derived *ka ga nga* script used to write texts in Malay and Rejang.

14. The idea of weighing a lump of soil and comparing it to the weight of a select amount of water at a potential settlement site is widespread in Sumatra; for example, it features in a West Sumatran origin legend about the choice of a site for a settlement on the Kuantan River (Barendregt 2005, 64) and is mentioned in the *Sejarah/Hilir Chronicle* of Barus as a motif for a choice of place to settle (Drakard 1990, 75).

15. Variants of this legend are found in many parts of Sumatra.

16. The gong-chime melody focuses on the interval of a seventh: //:55 11 5 11://or //:AA B_1B_1 A B_1B_1://, where B_1 is in the lower octave. This interval is commonly dwelled on in other gong-chime music in the area as well and even occurs in some *gamelan Palembang* playing, e.g., the seventh between gong tone $B^\flat$ and saron tone $A^\flat$ in audio example 7.9.

17. In Pagaralam, however, there are only two routines. The first is named *netak* (flying very low), and the second *nendang terbing tinggi* (flying up high) (Bp. Saman, Bp. Y Herman Jentamat, and Bp. Surfai BA, pers. comm., Pagaralam, 1989).

18. The *tari Inggeris* is also performed on the Besemah border with Bengkulu and in parts of southern highland Bengkulu. We saw a stage performance of it by a group of ten young highland women from the Misi Kesenian (Artistic Mission) troupe in Melbourne in the mid-1970s. The dance is also mentioned in Kunst (1950, 167).

19. This information was provided by Bp. Saman Loear, Haji Dur, and Bp. Bujang in Jokoh and Bp. Y. Herman Jentamat in Tanjungsakti, 1989.

20. These three pieces feature fast, elaborate interlocking on the *kenong*. Reportedly, for many centuries, they accompanied flirtatious Malay *joget* dancing, with male participants giving coins to the professional female dancers for the privilege of singing responsive *pantun* and dancing with them. Travelling *joget* troupes consisted of young female singer-dancers, male instrumentalists, and a manager, who used to sail from village to village along the rivers. The troupes were reportedly members of the Orang Suku Laut. They are extremely rare, if not obsolete, today (Moh Bujang, pers. comm., Jokoh, 1989).

21. This dance is related to the abovementioned *gandai* dance of the Rejang people, accompanied by the singing of *sambai* songs (Jaspan 1964, 89). The Rejang speak a language isolate and live on each side of the border of South Sumatra and Bengkulu.

22. Information in this paragraph was supplied by musicians Bp. Haji Teman and Bp. Haji Abdul Halim in Tanjungsakti and Bp. Haji Dur and Bp. Moh. Bujang in Jokoh in 1989.

23. The male costume comprises a *baju tulak belanga* (trouser suit), *ikat pinggung* (wraparound waist cloth), and *ikat kepala* (cloth headdresses), while the female costume comprises a *baju kain songket bumpak* (silver or gold woven wraparound skirt), *baju kurung* (three-quarter-length long-sleeved blouse), *selendang jung sarat* (shawl), *ikat leher* (cloth neck piece), *kalung gelang temanggung* (ancestral jewelry), *ikat pinggung* (waist wraparound), and *ikat kepala* (headdress).

24. In our recording of an *erai-erai* dance in Endikat Ilir village (near Lahat), the violin was tuned to G D D¹ and the melody was based on the tones {F G A♭ A B♭ B C¹ D¹ E¹ F¹}. Another mixed-gender dance, performed when a host receives important guests, is called *gumai* (the name of a local area), accompanied by the same kind of *tabuhan* ensemble as in the *tari gegerit*. The melody of "Tembang Rai-rai" ("Batch of Lemongrass Song") recorded at Merapi village near Lahat in 1988 was based on the pitches {F, G, A♭, B♭, B, C_1, D_1, E_1, F_1}.

25. For example, the song text of "Umah Ui Umah" ("Mother, Oh Mother") requests a deceased mother to help her child gain friends and a home; "Pisang Raya" (a type of banana) deals with a boy's love for a girl; and "Air Selabu" ("Gourd Container of Water") deals with the observation that the rich get richer and the poor get poorer.

26. At a gathering, individuals sing or improvise amusing substitutes for the third line with the whole gathering joining in to sing the *Ra-sa sa-yang-sa-yang-é* refrain

27. The small locally made *gembos* is clearly a local predecessor of the large Arabic *ud*-like *gambus*, which has now largely replaced the indigenous instrument in modern Arab-influenced singing and dancing, including the *zapin* dance ensembles. On this point, also see Yampolsky 1996, CD 11 notes.

28. This couple, who were well-respected singers in their fifties, were not married to each other. But as the young people in the village could no longer sing *rejunk*, the middle-aged couple sang as if they were young potential lovers, so that our recordings could preserve knowledge of the genre.

29. *Rejunk* sung in this scale, which resembles a Javanese *pélog* scale in *nem* or *lima* (*bem*) mode, may have led Ahmad Dahlan Mahibat to compose "Gending Sriwijaya" in *pélog* (Hadji Wan Tjik, pers. comm., Palembang, 1971).

30. *Rejunk*, the generic term for singing, is associated with *junk*, a ship that sails the rivers and the sea; indeed water and the voice of poetry are connected in many poetic images (Barendregt 2005, 382–83).

31. Our recording of one such lullaby in Burai was set to the hexatonic scale: {1 2 3 4 5 6} or {A B C♯ D E F♯}, with the tonal center and final tone alternating between 2/B and 4/D and the text consisting of terms of endearment for the baby present.

32. The maker of a *serdam* measures the circumference of a piece of bamboo and multiplies it by 1.5 to obtain the required distance between the top and the second front hole, then multiplies it by 2 to obtain the distance down to the third hole. Pieces recorded were "Cintok Rawas" ("Rice-Stamping"), "Ayam Setalang" ("Chicken under One Roof"), "Raunggah" ("A Medley"), and "Tangis Anak Belai Jauh" ("Tears of a Bride Far from Her Home Village"). The same pieces are also played on the *harmonika*, and some (e.g., "Cintok Rawas") are played on the rice-stamping trough. Information on the *serdam* was provided by Bp. Mesulut and on the *harmonika* by Bp. Menalis, both of Dusun Gunung Kumbang, Tanjungsakti.

33. The instrument is described by Smith (2003, 308), under "Melodeon"; and in Kartomi (1985, 39), under "Harmonika."

34. Other pieces played were titled "Asasi" ("He's Not Sure"), "Bidodari Bekindon" ("The Angel Sways a Baby"), and "Air Umban" ("Water Falls into a Stream").

35. Basic music-ethnographic fieldwork among South Sumatran Kubu people still remains to be done. I have recorded only a small amount of Kubu music, and only on the outskirts of the city of Jambi. Erich von Hornbostel is the only musicologist to have published—and only briefly—about a few aspects of their music (Hornbostel in Hagen 1908a, 265), but his work was "armchair musicology," based on recordings made by Hagen (an anthropologist) on a journey between Palembang and Jambi. Loeb gave a general description of Kubu culture without mentioning the location of the people he was describing or his sources of information (Loeb [1935] 1972). In 1984, Sandbukt described the cosmological beliefs of a Kubu enclave, in a central part of Jambi province, who still remained outside the monetary economy and the reach of the administrative apparatus.

36. See a photo of a Kubu woman playing a *damuk* (flute) and description in M. Kartomi 1985, 27–28.

37. The term *tanjidor* derives from the Portuguese word *tangedor* (player), a derivative of *tanger*, meaning "to make a twang" (as on plucked strings). The Portuguese were Indonesia's first colonizers from the sixteenth century until the Dutch took over a century later. In the Dutch colonial and postindependence periods, *tanjidor* was outdoor brass-band music for processions and military displays (Heins 1975; Yampolsky 1994).

38. I Tsing, the Chinese Buddhist pilgrim who visited Sriwijaya-Palembang in 672, and who may have stayed there for six months with the thousand monks who were reportedly studying and translating texts in Sanskrit, mentioned in his chronicle the Chinese name of a place that may have stood for Tulung Bawang, the name of the court and river located near Menggala, as mentioned by the early-nineteenth-century document by the Dutch administrator W. Naarding.

39. We recorded various musical performances in Menggala and other parts of Lampung in 1981 and 1983.

40. In 1971 the two rows of kettle gongs in the Kayuagung *tabuhan* ensemble accompanying the *tari penguton* were tuned (from the right to the left of the player) approximately to {G_1 A D^1 G^1 C^1 A^1 G} (i.e., the *ngeromong* row) and {G E^1 D C^1 B A D^1} (i.e., the *ngelitang* row). Thus the basic scale was G A B C^1 D^1 E^1 G^1, with added gongs D, G, and A^1. The two big gongs (*tale*, *balok*, tuned to B_{111} and G_{11}) were struck alternately every four beats, the two lap-played small gongs (*bebondi*) alternately on every two beats, and the cymbals (*rujih*) on or between every beat.

41. This area exhibits a high degree of tolerance of pitch diversity. The tuning sequence of one *tabuhan* gong-chime that we recorded in Burai Lama is approximately {E¹ C♯¹ C¹ A A C♯}. Another set in Burai is tuned to C♯¹ A¹ C♯¹ A E C♯, while a set in Kayuagung is tuned to E¹ {D¹ C¹ B A G D₁}.

42. According to the Palembang office of the Department of Education and Culture, in 1978 there were more than a hundred *serapal anam* groups in Palembang alone. Some performances raised funds for mosque-building projects.

43. The *taqsim* was introduced into Arabic suites (*nauba*) from sixteenth-century Turkey and nineteenth-century Egypt (Farmer 1957, 421–77).

44. This recording was made in Riau, but it is stylistically similar to performances in Palembang.

45. A recording of "Lancing Kuning" and other Malay songs for *zapin* performance and "Serampang Laut" for *ronggeng* performance are to be found in Yampolsky 1996, CD 11 (track 1 was recorded in Palembang).

46. *Lancang kuning* is also "considered the basic, indispensable *gambus* song in mainland and island Riau" (Yampolsky 1996, CD 11 notes, 18). Some unorthodox beliefs are attached to it. It is regarded as *kramat* (sacred), and if it is performed without the required observances, there can be a storm, or someone may die. Yet its melody, which "uses an ordinary major scale, at one point altered in a way that suggests modulation from the tonic to the dominant, . . . sounds surprizingly European." Despite its non–Middle Eastern sound, it is nevertheless the preeminent *lagu gambus* (ibid., 8–9).

47. This research supports the suggestion "that the *zapin* dance and the strong Islamic connotations of *gambus* music may be a comparatively recent overlay on an earlier rural tradition of lute-playing" (Yampolsky 1996, CD 11 notes, 9). The early tradition may have been strengthened by the *zapin* dance and music that was transplanted via Hadramaut immigrants (from present-day Yemen) to Sumatra and the Malay Peninsula (cf. Nor, 1993; Capwell 1995, 76–89).

48. We recorded *Dul Muluk* shows in Kayu Agung, and Dumas recorded his in Bangka in the 1980s (Dumas 2000). The scholarly consensus holds that the medieval Arabic tales called *One Thousand and One Nights*, which were collected over the centuries from ancient Arabic, Syrian, Indian, and Persian sources, were probably created in 800–900 C.E. They served as a basis for several Malay theater forms such as *bangsawan* and *komedie stambul* from the turn of the twentieth century (Cohen 2006, 45–49), including *Abdul Muluk* theater. Performances of *Abdul Muluk* theater were banned in Batavia in 1882 for "undermining public morality by attracting female fans who became lovers of actors, resulting in marital and family crisis" (Cohen 2006, 207).

49. In audio example 7.11 the vocalist sings a melody based on the American "Battle Hymn of the Republic."

50. Songs still performed in Kayuagung and Bangka (the latter by the Fajar Timur group in Lima Ulu) during the 1980s and 1990s included "Sultan Baghdad," "Sultan Palembang," "Sultan Budiman," "Siti Zubaidah," "Sultan Abdul Muluk," "Tajul Muluk," and "Indera Bangsawan," accompanied by a *viol, gong*, and *gendang*, and from the 1980s by a band in modern *dangdut* style (Dumas 2000, 184–215). "Lagu Stambul Dua" is also popular as the only surviving song from the urban *stambul* theater; it was popular in Java and parts of eastern Sumatra from the 1890s to the 1930s (ibid.)

51. One *orkes gambus* that we recorded in Palembang comprised a *gambus*, a *gung*, a *gendang*, and a pair of medium, two-headed *ketipung* drums.

52. In 1988 the royal Palembang family tree and other cultural objects of the former palace were

in the possession of royal family descendant Raden Moh Husin Nato Dirajo of Kelurahan Sungai Tawar, whose title is a local Muslim adaptation of the Javanese title, Raden Mas.

53. It is reported in the *Hikayat Banjar* ("Banjar Chronicle") that the sultan of Demak also gave *gamelan* and *wayang* sets to the newly converted Sultan Suriansjah of Banjar, south Kalimantan, in the 1590s (Kartomi 2002, 22), i.e., just a few decades before Palembang is said to have received its sets, which corroborates the Palembang palace's claim that *gamelan* and *wayang* came from Demak. However, Palembang's *gamelan* sets have been much less well maintained than the Banjar sets, and the *pelok*-tuned half is rarely played at all (if it still exists; I was shown only the so-called *selindero* half). The tuning of Banjar's *selindero* instruments still somewhat resembles Java's *slendro* tuning, and its *pelok* instruments resemble Java's *pélog*, while the set currently used for *wayang* shows in Palembang is in neither *slendro* nor *pélog*, but something in between. Unlike the *gamelan selindero Banjar*, it has only one *saron* (cf. Banjar's three), two (cf. one) cylindrical drums, and one (not two) gong-chimes. Moreover, the *sarons* in the Banjar set, played loud and fast like Balinese *gangsa* (metallophones), have quite a different timbre from the Palembang ones and the usual Javanese ones. Some instruments have different names (e.g., the gong-chime is called *bonang* in Banjar and *kromongan* in Palembang), and the drums have different shapes, factors that are likely due to local adaptations. Whether the instruments have retained their original tunings is unknown, though they are believed to be original, as the instruments were apparently retuned when deemed necessary (RMH Nato Dirajo, pers. comm., Palembang, 1988).

54. In 1629, the Dutch began trading in the deepwater port of Palembang, located approximately eighty kilometers from the sea on the Musi River. It was intermittently under British or Dutch rule. The city became the administrative center of Dutch colonial South Sumatra in 1823, and capital of the province of South Sumatra in 1945. In 2007 its population numbered around 1.8 million people.

55. Javanized Palembang Malay, which is one of three or more Palembang Malay dialects, is waning rapidly. The core vocabulary and morphological elements "exhibit a comparable proportion of Malay and Javanese" (Tadmor 2002, 1–2).

56. Regarding Palembang Ilir, Palembang's villages were called *ilir* (downstream) if built on the *kraton* (palace) side of the Musi River (on the left bank if one is looking downstream) and *ulu* (upstream) if on the other bank. The bride at a village wedding to which I was invited in Palembang wore a Javanese bridal costume on one day, with her forehead hairline painted in a series of black V shapes as in Java, and a Sriwijaya-style Malay bridal costume with *songket* and golden headdress on the next.

57. In a recording of a *wayang* show that we made in Kampung 28 Ilir, the *dalang* (puppet master) made reference to the nine Muslim saints (Wali Sanga).

58. The working women included 1,053 spinners, 131 cotton weavers, and 78 silk *songket* weavers as well as yarn dyers, needlewomen, veil makers, embroiderers, *kemiri* nut oil pressers, etc. In 1870 there were 64 male and female healers (*dukun*) (C. F. E. Praetorius, JV Palembang 1832, ANRI Palembang 62–61, in Columbijn 2002). A total of 155 blacksmiths, who lived together in Kampung 18 Ilir near the palace, used to float upstream on their rafts to forge their products on the spot. After buying their daily needs, they floated home again (Colombijn 2002, 289, based on Praetorius).

59. Offerings before a performance consist of *nasi gemuk* (chicken and rice), but no incense is burned (Dalang Sukri Rasjid, pers. comm., 1973).

60. In the opening and fighting scenes, the *gamelan* played "Lagu Bertempur" ("War Piece") with an accelerating tempo; when the *dalang* described the rooms and furniture of a palace (e.g., the

palace of Astina), it played a quiet "Lagu Caturan" (BI, "Lagu Cerita," "Story Song"); during court audience or *wawancara* (discussion) scenes, it played a calm piece; when characters were relaxing, it played the "Lenggang Kangkung" ("Swinging Walking") piece; and when the hero went traveling, it played "Lagu Perjalanan" ("Traveling Piece").

61. No direct link was observable between the Palembang *kraton*'s Javanese-derived *kromongan* or *gamelan* orchestra tunings and repertoires and those of the Ogan Komering area's *kromongan* ensemble, which the local musicians believe was developed by their ancestors' contact with the Menggala kingdom in Lampung.

62. Usually the hand-played *gendang induk, gendang paningkah, kromongan* and *gambang* are included, but they were missing in this recording.

63. In Java, the term *sintren* can refer to the female court *serimpi* dance or to a folk magic show. In Palembang, it refers either to a solo singer in a *gamelan* performance or to the *serimpi* dance.

64. People of Arab descent traditionally lived in Kelurahan 13 Ulu, 14 Ulu, 8 Ilir, and 10 Ilir, Palembang.

65. Mohd. Anis Md. Nor (1993, 25) suggests on the basis of popular belief that Hadramaut Arabs brought *zapin* to Melaka and that it then spread as a court art to Malay sultanates in Malaya, the Riau Islands, and beyond. As Yampolsky points out, however, there is no evidence that *zapin* was actually performed in Malacca before the nineteenth century nor of how it spread in rural areas (Yampolsky 1996, notes to CD 8).

66. Yampolsky further suggested that *zapin* was able to escape the hostile attitude that some Islamic leaders cast on other secular music and dance by virtue of its presumed Arab origin (Yampolsky 1996, notes to CD 11).

Chapter 8. The Wartime Creation of "Gending Sriwijaya"

1. The second verse of the song is rarely sung and is not included here.

2. Sukarno, whom the Dutch had interned in Padang in 1942 (after his internment in Bengkulu from 1938), strongly influenced his West Sumatran colleagues when he declared that Indonesians should make use of the Japanese to achieve their own goal of national independence, and that strategic cooperation with them could diminish the harshness of their behavior during the occupation (Kahin 1999, 96).

3. In 1025, Sriwijaya-Palembang was seized and sacked by the Cōḷa, and by the late twelfth century it was reduced to a small kingdom, with its dominant role in Sumatra taken over by the Sriwijaya-Malayu kingdom based in Jambi and a vassal of Java. In the thirteenth century, the Javanese kingdom of Majapahit took advantage of Malayu's weakening naval strength, gained power over it, and subsequently came to dominate the political scene. By the fourteenth century, Malacca had become the dominant power in the region, and Sriwijaya had become a remote backwater (Coedès 1918, 4–10; 1964, 262; Nilakanta Sastri 1940, 285–86).

4. Legends in the Besemah highlands refer to this twenty-seven-meter-high hill as Bukit Si Guntang, Gunung Meru.

5. It is unlikely that Mahibat ever saw or heard the *gamelan pélog* that is reputed to have been given to the king of Palembang by the sultan of Demak in the seventeenth century. Even if he did hear the *pélog* half (i.e., if it still exists), its tuning may not have been in modern Javanese *pélog*. The tuning of the palace's *gamelan sléndro*, which Mahibat did hear played in accompaniment to a shadow-puppet show (Hadji Wan Tjik, pers. comm., 1971), has a tuning that lies somewhere between *sléndro* and *pélog* (see chap. 2). He may also have heard a

pélog-like vocal scale used in *rejunk* epic and response singing in upstream Besemah (Hadji Wan Tjik, pers. comm., 1971).

6. The weaving of *songket* brocade was probably introduced to the Sriwijaya kingdom from India or China and has developed a wealth of local designs and colors. It was worn by the king and the nobility (Gittinger 1979, 102) as well as dancers and bridal couples, who are treated like *raja sehari*, "king and queen for a day," as the Malay saying goes.

7. Semando is the name of an musico-lingual group in the South Sumatra's upstream northwest.

8. In 1944–45 the Japanese also patronized a theatrical troupe called Sandiwara Ratu Asia (lit. "Theater of the Ruler of Asia"), which toured for several months in many parts of West Sumatra, South Sumatra, and Lampung, and then in parts of Java.

9. See Tan (1993) for a detailed history of *bangsawan* in Malaysia and, to a lesser extent, in Indonesia.

10. They could have chosen an item from the many traditional dances that were formerly patronized by the petty princes in the countryside (Mochtar Madjid, Bupati of Lahat, pers. comm., December 1971). In the Tanjungsakti area, for example, guests are still welcomed with the *tari sirih* (betel nut dance), *tari tanggai*, and the related *tari gegegrit,* accompanied by a *tabuhan* bronze ensemble or an *orkes Melayu* comprising a *gambus*, drums (*marwas* and *gendang*), and a pair of suspended gongs.

11. The fact that female long-fingernail dances are also found in southern and northern Thailand was not seen as diminishing the case for "Tari Gending Sriwijaya" serving as South Sumatra's provincial symbol, for the cultural memory holds that Thailand was a vassal state of Sriwijaya-Palembang and that the idea of the dance could have been transplanted from Sriwijaya to Thailand. In recent correspondence, the archaeologist Edmund Edwards McKinnon writes: "The legendary dance connection between Śrīvijaya and Thailand could well be of substance, but I would not know how to prove it. That there was considerable cultural and commercial interaction between the various contemporary polities in Southeast Asia seems to be true, but tangible evidence is difficult to pinpoint. The recently discovered Cirebon (Rembang) wreck had an extremely varied cargo from all over the Middle East, Indian Ocean, China, and Palembang, so from that point of view one can say there were extremely widespread and intricate networks of trade contact after Śrīvijaya and very probably before it" (pers. comm., 31 March 2009).

12. Following the coup d'état in 1965 that resulted in the demotion and subsequent death of President Sukarno, an estimated half a million to a million people were systematically killed during Suharto's anti-Communist witch hunt in 1965–66. According to the new president, Suharto, the coup had been perpetrated by the Indonesian Communist Party (PKI), so he dubbed the movement Gestapu-30S, an acronym for the Gerakan September Tigapuluh (30th of September Movement), which refers to the date of the 1965 event and suggests a parallel to Hitler's Gestapo, though many suspected the event was masterminded by Suharto himself.

13. For a discussion of the history of *ronggeng*, see chap. 10.

14. From the late nineteenth to the mid-twentieth centuries, *ronggeng* dances were also performed in the context of *bangsawan, opera stambul*, and *Dul Muluk* theater, with traveling troupes performing in the towns and the countryside. However, as noted earlier, these theater forms are also almost obsolete, surviving to this day only in rare performances of *Dul Muluk*, for example, on Bangka.

15. There is insufficient space here to discuss *orkes Melayu, kromongan, gamelan*, and pop band arrangements of the song, but the brief analysis of the unaccompanied melody and chord chart in music example 8.1 indicates why *orkes Melayu* and pop band arrangements are perceived

to "sound Malay-Western," and the analysis of the interlocking multiphonic techniques used in a choral and a piano arrangement in music examples 8.2 and 8.3 show why these and other similar arrangements are perceived as "sounding Javanese."

16. Audio example 8.1 contains only seven rather than the usual eight phrases, to match the requirements of a particular choreography of "Tari Gending Sriwijaya."

17. "Colotomic" is a term invented by Jaap Kunst to denote the punctuation of a melody by a preconceived sequence of different gong strokes.

Chapter 9. The Island of Bangka

1. The chapter is based on our 1981 and 1994 fieldwork in northern and western Bangka and updated information since then. For reasons of space it does not include the island of Belitung.

2. According to legend, there were four chiefdoms on Bangka: east, north, central, and south.

3. The history of Bangka's chiefdoms and conditions during the Dutch period are discussed in Smedal (1989), Somers-Heidhues (1992), and B. Andaya (1993).

4. The temple arts and *tanjidor* brass bands in the Hakka-speaking north and the Hokkien-speaking south are similar, and the two communities shared visits of Chinese opera and Malay *bangsawan* theater troupes until the mid-twentieth century, but the south also became known for its elaborate mass weddings, as briefly discussed later in the chapter, and may therefore eventually be counted as a separate musico-lingual subgroup when more research is done.

5. In 1753, for example, Sultan Mahmud sent twelve ships loaded with tin to Batavia and another five carrying pepper to Canton, Amoy, and Ningpo (B. Andaya 1993, 191).

6. The Dutch divided the population of the Indies on racial grounds into the Europeans, the "Foreign Orientals" (mostly descendants of Chinese immigrants), and the "Natives" and banned most "Foreign Orientals" from owning land. However, people of Chinese descent on Bangka were one of the few exceptions, and many established farms or gardens on their own land (Kartomi 2000, 271–76, 305–8).

7. In 1998, 84 percent of Bangkans were Muslim, 6.5 percent Confucian, 5 percent Buddhist, 4 percent Christian, and 0.55 percent Hindu (Somers Heidhues 1996, 196). The latter two religious groups are not artistically significant.

8. Under Suharto, all Chinese cultural expressions were banned, and racial prejudice was rife.

9. Traditional Bangkan brides wear Chinese influenced *baju kurung* (BB) costumes made of red Bangka (Muntok)-made *songket tual* material trimmed in gold and red slippers.

10. According to the Ethnologue map of Sumatra (2010), the Sekak who live at the mouths of the Kampar and Indragiri Rivers and western Riau archipelagos are also known as Suku Loncong. However, the linguist Karl Anderbeck (pers. comm., 2010) doubts that the name is known or used today, because it occurs only in nineteenth-century sources.

11. Government officials encourage Suku Sekak artists to perform for their guests in a pavilion built for the Suku Lom in north-coastal Dusun Pejam, Kecamatan Belinyu, as on the occasion of our recording session in 1994. The performance we recorded was performed by the Sanggar Mekelin group, led by the choreographer Ibu Su'eryanti.

12. In 1983–84 there were only 752 Lom individuals (in 176 households) in Air Abik village and other areas of northern Bangka (Smedal 1989, 7). The Lom are listed in the Wurm and Hattori map of Sumatra as speaking a language isolate; however, anthropologist Olaf Smedal (1989) has shown that Lom is a distinct dialect of the Bangka Malay network, though it contains many local vernacular terms. He notes that they use "fast, syncopated" speech patterns (Smedal 1989, 7).

13. This source, a manuscript written by Bangka's late-nineteenth-century Kontroleur Kroon, was referred to by B. Hagen (1908b), who translated a funeral speech from the Lom-Mapur language into German (*petunjuk jalan*: "to show the path" to the hereafter). Smedal discussed this source and another literary funeral text (Smedal 1989, 125–34) and also gave an ethnographic description of Mapur/Lom life in Air Abik and Pejem villages, including their complex burial and funeral rites (Smedal 1989, 114–34).

14. In 1983, Olaf Smedal visited some Suku Lom settlement projects in Kedimpul (near Jebus) and south of Pangkal Pinang and found that they were almost complete failures. This is largely because it is not possible to prohibit forest nomads from returning to the forest (Smedal, pers. comm., 2010). Since then, however, progressive deforestation has brought even greater threats to their survival.

15. The once popular *wayang gantung* (Chinese marionette puppet theater) performed by traveling troupes from western Kalimantan has died out on Bangka (Khonghucu leader Bp. Lak Sak Soi, pers. comm., Desa Parit Empat, 1994), though it is still performed in Singkawang, western Kalimantan (Kartomi 2000, 304–5). Its ensembles include the *rebab batok* coconut shell fiddles.

16. Periodic repression of activities practiced by the "Foreign Oriental" population in the colonial era has been documented elsewhere (Kartomi 2000), as it has in the postindependence era (e.g., Coppel 1983).

17. This point was made by Margaret Chan in her analysis of Chinese Indonesian–Malay relations at the Capgomeh New Year celebration in Singkawang, west Kalimantan (Chan 2009, 141).

Part III Introduction. North Sumatra

1. In Minangkabau, *sumando* means "son-in-law," or it can denote a form of matrilocal marriage (Drakard 1990, 94, 178–79).

2. The Batak ethnonym is probably ancient, though no satisfactory derivation has been found (L. Andaya 2008, 146). A thirteenth-century Chinese source, the *Zhufan Zhi* by Zhao Rugua (a foreign trade inspector in Fujian), mentions a dependency of Sriwijaya called Ba-ta (ibid.). Panai (at Padang Lawas) was one of the areas mentioned in the Majapahit court epic poem the *Nagarakrtagama* (written in 1365) as part of *bhumi Melayu*, which suggests that the Javanese in the fourteenth century regarded the areas occupied by the Batak as part of the Malay world.

Chapter 10. From Singkil to Natal

1. Many Pasisir Melayu are descendants of *perantau* from Minangkabau and are therefore also known as Sumando/Semando (lit. "son-in-law" and a form of matrilocal marriage (Mi.); Drakard 1990, 94, 178–79). The Hilir chronicle of the Barus Hilir palace, *Sejarah Tuanku Batu Badan, Tambo Barus Hilir* (History of the downstream ruler of Barus) begins with praises of Allah in Arabic and Malay and then states the Tuanku's descent from Pagaruyung (Drakard [1988] 2003, 283).

2. Upstream and downstream in the titles of the rulers refer to the two kingdoms' orientations, not their locations, as they were barely two kilometers apart (Drakard [1988] 2003, 77–80). In the second century C.E., Ptolemy mentioned "Barousai," which may have been a precursor of Barus. Barus (alias Fansur, Pansur) became well known in the first millennium as a major supplier of camphor, with merchants from the Middle East and China visiting and a Tamil-speaking colony residing "more or less permanently" at nearby Lobu Tuo in the tenth

century (Nilakanta Sastri 1932, 326). The two rulers in Barus—the Raja di Hilir ("upstream ruler," who claimed Malay-Batak ancestry) and the Raja di Hulu ("downstream ruler," who claimed south-coast Minangkabau Tarusan ancestry)—presided over a culture that included a royal orchestra (*nobat*), laments (*ratap*), bowed (*arbab*) and plucked string (*kucapi*) instruments, flutes (*bangsi*), drums (*gandang*), oboes (*sarunai*), female *dayang-dayang* (ladies-in-waiting) and *inang/panginang* (wet-nurse) dances, and *tabuhan or telempong Jawa* ensembles comprising a gong (*agung*) and kettle-gong (*canang*) instruments (see translation of the *Asal Keturunan Raja Barus, Tambo Barus Hulu* (Origin of the descendants of the upland ruler of Barus) chronicle in Drakard [1988] 2003, 156–57). The *nobat* and gong ensembles are now obsolete and the *arbab* replaced by the more playable violin, but the other forms are still extant. The female *inang* song-dance of Malay origin is only rarely performed now, but its lively (*lincah*) movements and distinctive rhythmic pattern live on in the *sikambang kapri* dances, one of which is called *tari inang*. *Joget* dancing and *biola* playing are not mentioned in the chronicles, but we know that singers in mixed *joget* troupes exchanged *pantun* accompanied by *biola* and *gandang* in all-night *joget* shows in the 1930s (Tamar Sinaga, pers. comm., 1981).

3. These vocal and vocal-instrumental genres performed along the coast from Singkil to Natal, including Singkil's offshore Pulau Banyak ("Many Islands") archipelago, and closely related repertories, are performed south to the Minangkabau and Bengkulu coasts and down to Krui in Lampung (according to my fieldwork between 1977 and 2011). Of the several former royal courts along the west coast, the history of the dual court at Barus has been most extensively studied (Drakard 1999 and 2003). These terms *lagu sikambang asli* and *lagu sikambang kapri* are used only by some musicians in Barus and Sibolga; most people simply refer to both genres as *sikambang*.

4. *Kroncong* and *dendang sayang* are of Javanese and Sumatran/Malaysian origin respectively, usually with a vocalist, drum, and harmonically generated string accompaniment, and couples dancing. Both genres are widely believed to have originated through contact between Malay and Portuguese artists in the Portuguese colonial era (1511–1641).

5. European contact with Barus began in the early 1500s. The visiting Portuguese traveler Pires wrote that "the very rich kingdom of Baros, which [was] also called Panchur or Pansur," was visited by Indian Gujarati, Persian, Arabian, "Kling Bengalee," and other merchant ships and exported goods from Minangkabau and elsewhere (Cortesão [1944] 1967, 1:161–62).

6. *Talibun* and *gurindam Barus* are poetic verse forms featuring an indirect allusion (*sampiran*) and a main intent (*isi*), used by singers and storytellers along Sumatra's west coast. Some *tukang sikambang* are also called *tukang bergurindam* (*gurindam* performers).

7. A performance usually begins with "Lagu/Tari Adok" ("*adat* song-dance" in couples), followed by selections from the following couples dances: *saputangan* (kerchief), *kapri* (non-believer), *payung* (umbrella), *anak sikambang* (*sikambang* performers), *gelombang duobale* (twelve waves), *dua* (two [step]), *perak-perak* (silver), *rantak kudo* (horse stamps), and *langser madam* ("madam walks back and forth," of possible Dutch or Portuguese origin), and the songs may include "Mencerai Kasih" (Ending Love), "Pulau Pinang" (Penang Island), *kapri*, etc. I recorded these song-dances, performed by mixed teenagers on two occasions and adult males on two other occasions, in Singkil and Pulau Banyak in 2010.

8. Played by a *pawang* to call the wind or attract a potential lover, the body of a *singkadu* duct flute is cut from a rare type of bamboo (Ma. *buluh Cino*, "Chinese bamboo") found floating downstream from the forest. An instrument maker, Bp. Darus, whom I met in 1981 made a *singkadu* by measuring its length and the placements of its back finger hole and seven front

holes (three of which are burned out with a hot iron in a slanted shape) according to the width of his thumb.

9. Traditionally, the procession went to the local river, but nowadays a bowl of water (*galeta, tempat ai*) frequently substitutes by being blessed and sprinkled over the bride or the baby.

10. The "thin harmony" is played only on the violin, which implies IV-V-I harmonies and modulations mainly by a harmonic use of the leading note and double stopping.

11. Instead of using the Southeast Asian convention of placing the bar line after the metric stress, the transcriptions of the *sikambang kapri* songs use the Western notational convention of placing the bar line in front of the main metric stress, which usually occurs on the last note of a rhythmic/metric cycle of, say, sixteen beats. Microtonal intervals are depicted in the transcriptions with a flat sign for a slightly lower pitch and a sharp sign for a slightly higher pitch (e.g., an E-flat is around a quarter-tone lower than a note depicted as a D-sharp). Western notational conventions are used in the harmonically generated violin part as the alternative of writing the ornamentation in solfa number script would be difficult to read.

12. Some artists in Barus and Sibolga call the violin-accompanied songs *sikambang kapri*, but the term is unknown in southwestern Aceh (Singkil and Pulau Banyak) and other areas of Sumatra's west coast, unless it is used in a song title, e.g., "Lagu Kapri." In addition to the violin, the harmonium and the accordion are frequently played in ensembles in Minangkabau, east-coast North Sumatra, the Riau islands, and west-coast Malaya. In Barus, a pair of *gandang* usually suffices, while in Sorkam up to twelve are commonly played. In Natal, the *gandak bulek* (round drum) or a two-headed cylindrical *gondang* drum may be used.

13. The frame drums have goatskin heads and softwood (*lunak*) bodies. In this case, the larger one, called *gandang*, measures about 45 cm x 10 cm, while the smaller, called *gandang anak* (child drum), measures about 26 cm x 10 cm. Around Natal, a cylindrical, two-headed drum (*gendang bulek*, "round drum") is used in *kapri* ensembles, also known by the Mandailing name of *gondang* (Goldsworthy 1979, 68).

14. The violin modulations are from C to G, to C, to G minor, and thence to F, G, F, G, C, G, C, G, G, C, G, F, C, G, and C.

15. These onomatopoetic terms, which vary from area to area in the Pasisir, were used by our informants in Jago-Jago and Sorkam. In Barus, a musician referred to the high-pitched sound as *tak* instead of *tang*. There is no generally accepted set of terms denoting drum timbres for the whole of the Pasisir.

16. Indonesia's New Order government (1965–97) required that artists in all of Indonesia's provinces rechoreograph selected items for events such as formal government receptions and the election campaigns of Golkar, Suharto's government party; it also decreed that regional culture and education ministry offices document their traditional music and dance genres.

17. Another version holds that Sikambang sang the song out of grief at the death of her mistress. The queen had avoided marrying her hopeful suitor Raja Jonggi by insisting on his fulfilling impossible conditions, one of which was to bring a barge full of the rare *manau* variety of rattan from the hinterland to her on Musala Island. When he did so, she disappeared to the bottom of the ocean and ascended to heaven. When he heard of her death, he was so angry and upset that he threw a large piece of rattan into the sea, and it became Bilalang Island.

18. The pineapple and the banana symbolize the delicious sensuousness of the girls, and the see-through blouses suggest they are targets for seducers.

19. The former palaces were at Siak, Asahan, Deli, Serdang, Langkat, and Langsa on the east coast and at Daik (Lingga) and Penyengat in insular Riau (Kepulauan Kapri).

20. Ibu Maimunah Mochtar, of Binjai, Kabupaten Langkat, aged sixty-three in 1972, was a pro-

fessional theater troupe singer and violinist in her youth at the Langkat palace. She sang to the accompaniment of Bp. Abdullah Rachinur on the *gendang induk* and *gendang anak* frame drums and Bp. A. Manan, on the *akordian* (accordion). The four east-coast palaces, at Langkat, Deli, Serdang, and Asahan, lost their power in the social revolution of 1945.

21. These and other dances that were once performed in Riau's former courts at Lingga and Penyengat have been preserved and performed by choreographer Ibu Raja Ketiga and her troupe in Tanjung Pinang (we recorded some in Tanjung Pinang in 1981). *Ronggeng* performances were commonly presented at weddings on the east coast and in the Riau Archipelago until the early 1980s. Since then, they have usually been restricted to Indonesian Independence Day celebrations (Raja Ketiga, pers. comm., Tanjung Pinang, Riau, 1981). As Nor has observed, these *ronggeng* dances, which included *tari joget* and *tari inang*, were as popular in east North Sumatra in the 1930s and 1940s as they were in Johor, and they were especially popular in Sumatra "in the 1950s when singing contests between individual contenders from the audience and the *ronggeng* singers were presented on stage. They danced to the tunes of songs entitled 'Gunung Sayang,' 'Lagu Dua,' 'Inang,' and 'Zapin,' while improvising on pantun or Malay quatrains" (1993, 3).

22. In Aceh, a *ronggeng*-like genre with *lawak* (comedy), repartee *pantun* singing/dancing by a man dressed as a woman and "her" male partner, accompanied by a violin (now called *biola Aceh*), *dab* (frame drum), and gong resembled the *pelanduk* genre in Palembang, in which women danced with male partners.

23. *Kroncong* is a popular musical style usually performed by a vocalist with bowed and plucked string instruments in Java. It is believed to have developed as a result of Malay-Portuguese contact beginning in the sixteenth century (Kornhauser 1978; Abdurachman 1974, 1982).

24. In 1519 a Portuguese visitor to Barus mentioned that he had found five ships there from Gujarat, which treated him in hostile fashion (Tiele 1877, 354–55).

25. Bantus were captured in Africa and India and sold into Portuguese households in such places as Malacca, Macao, and the Cape of Good Hope, for Portugal needed to maintain her "shoestring empire" (Boxer 1969, xi) partly by profits from the slave trade. Gold, ivory, and slaves were the "principal products which Swahili settlements secured from the Bantu, or Kaffirs ('unbelievers') as they called them" (ibid., 40).

26. In Malay and Indonesian languages, the labial-dental voiceless fricative *f* in words of foreign origin is often replaced by the bilabial voiceless stop *p*. Vowel changes from the front, middle vowel *e* to the front high vowel *i* also often occur.

27. The evidence that Portuguese violins were brought in quantities to the Malay world is circumstantial only. However, the Portuguese writer Philipe de Caverel mentions that ten thousand guitars went with the Portuguese to Morocco in 1582, according to E. V. de Oliveira of the Centro de Estudos de Antropologia in Lisbon, as documented in an embassy report to Lisbon in 1582 and referred to in Pinto ([1653] 1969).

28. The British governor of Penang asked Anderson to visit some east-coast Malay palaces in 1823 to promote trade contact. He reported that he saw the violin, viola, *gendang*, gong, *gambang* (xylophone), *cromong* (gong-chime), *rebana* (frame drum), *sarunai* (oboe), *bangsi* (flute), *suling* (flute), *tetawak* (gong) and other brass instruments, *kacapi* (plucked lute), and other instruments (Anderson [1826] 1971, 291–92). He presented his own violin to the "rajah" of Siak "with a complete set of spare strings" when he departed (ibid., 183). The violin may have replaced the *rebab, arbab*, and other local bowed strings in many coastal areas as it is more versatile, has a wider timbral and dynamic range, and stays in tune better, and its bowing across the strings is more efficient (Catherine Falk, pers. comm., 1975).

29. In Portugal, laws were passed in 1562–82 mandating that all Asians who converted to Christianity would become Portuguese nationals and be treated as equals of their Portuguese coreligionists (Boxer 1965, 43; Abdurachman 1982, 2).

30. The oldest known reference to *kroncong* music is in Schuchardt (1891). The title of an extant *kroncong* song, "Cafrinyo" (with a text about a Goanese Eurasian girl), is related to the term *kapri*, which may have been derived from "a 'cafre' (Negro), with a lot of jumping and intricate dance figures" (Abdurachman 1974, 10), or from *capriol*, a European dance that was popular during the Portuguese colonial period (see Arbeau [1589] 1967, 103). *Kaparinyo* is the name of a related song on Sumatra's Minangkabau coast.

31. Representative recordings of performances by former royal and "commoner" artists in Binjai (near the former Langkat palace), Deli, Serdang, Asahan, and Siak Sri Inderapura are held in the Monash University Music Archive (recorded by myself and David Goldsworthy). I recorded the Serdang palace variants of some songs and dances believed to be of Malay-Portuguese origin, performed by a troupe led by the historian and royal descendant of the Serdang palace Tengku Luckman Sinar SH, in his home in Medan in 1972 and 1981.

32. The Dutch were probably responsible for introducing what became the *tanjidor* brass and percussion bands in Java and Sumatra from the eighteenth to nineteenth centuries. The British, under Raffles—while running the nineteenth-century fort at Bengkulu—were the probable source of the maypole dance, a version of which is still performed in Lahat and other areas of South Sumatra (see chap. 7), and the sepoy soldiers whom the British transplanted to man their fort spread *tabut* and related Shi'a practices around Sumatra's west and north coasts beginning in the early nineteenth century. Spanish and French cultural influences were minimal in Malay areas.

33. This is the oldest known reference to the *biola* in a Sumatran source: *geuseupot kudang deungon kucapi, ji muba'e ngòn biula* (consulted by courtesy of and translated in the text by Lance Castles). As this literary work describes events in early-sixteenth-century Aceh, including the wars of Sultan Iskandar Muda (reign 1607–41), it was probably written in the early 1700s. Snouck Hurgronje refers to a European violin called *biula*, which was "much beloved by the Achehnese, and on which some of them perform[ed] very creditably" (Snouck Hurgronje 1906, 2:265). (This was probably a *biola Aceh*; see fig. 13.7, p. 338).

34. The two Barus chronicles' accounts of the legendary war with Aceh in the seventeenth century mention the arts. After the Acehnese decapitated Sultan Ibrahim of the Barus Hilir palace, his son, Raja Usuf, went to Aceh to protest and seek compensation. The sultan of Aceh showed regret for Ibrahim's death and decreed that his corpse would be brought back in state by sea to Barus with the royal *nobat* orchestra, mourning songs and flute sounding all the way. The chronicles describe the intensely emotional reaction when the corpse arrived in Barus, with local artists singing mourning songs (*ratap*) and playing flutes (*bangsi*) along the road in the funeral procession (*Sejarah Chronicle*, Drakard [1988] 2003, 246), and with "even the Bataks paying tribute" (ibid., 255). There were sounds of gongs and kettle-gongs (*berbuni agung dengan canang*), drums and oboes (*berbuni gandang dan sarunai*), a bowed-spike string instrument and plucked zither (*berbuni arbab dan kucapi*), interlocking Javanese gong-chimes (*maningkah telempung Jawa*), the royal mosque drum (*berbuni tabuhan larangan*), interlocking Friday drum (*maningkah tabuh Jumat*), cymbals (*bacecer*), a small summons gong (*canang mamanggil*), and the sound of Muslim prayers (*membaca do'a*) (ibid., 254).

35. In his description of west Sumatra in 1761 (in *Raakende de Gesteldhijd van 't land en desselfs bewoners* [About the situation of the country and its inhabitants], Huybert van Basel wrote that the coastal population included Chinese, Siamese, Javanese, and Malaccans as well as

Sumatran Malays and Bataks who had accepted Islam (Van Basel's report is summarized in Kielstra 1887, 499–599).

36. Female Malay welcome dances accompanied by violin, harmonium, drums, and gongs entertained in the palaces at Daik on Lingga Island and at Penyengat palace in insular Riau (Ibu Raja Ketiga, pers. comm., Tanjung Pinang, 1981) and at the palace at Siak (Bp. Ismet, pers. comm., 1984). I also recorded such violin-accompanied dances in Tanjung Pinang in 1981, including "Lagu/Tari Inang," "Lagu Dua," "Sinandung," and "Laksamana Dibunoh." Goldsworthy (1979) recorded the same titles and other related ones in the areas of the former Langkat and Binjai palaces and elsewhere on North Sumatra's east coast.

37. *Gamad, badendang*, and *japri* song-dances are often accompanied by violin and drums.

38. Orang Melayu Pulau (Malay Island People), alias Orang Kuala (Mouth People), prefer to be called Orang Penyelai or Orang Melayu Asli rather than Orang Laut (Sea People) because of the term's pejorative implications among former royalty and strict Muslims. This is according to a personal communication from members of the troupe that I recorded, including the female singers Mak Minah, Mak Tayek, Mak Siti, and Mak Tene, and the male instrumentalists Bp. Hassan (leader), Bp. Buli, and Bp. Rasa.

39. The people's indigenous religious beliefs with a Hindu flavor are expressed in their healing ceremonies, where words of Sanskrit origin appear, e.g., *gento* (bell), *monto* (from *mantra*, "prayerful chant"), and *dewa* or *orang bunyian* (spirit), whose singing is accompanied by the magically powerful flute, *sempelong*.

40. Bp. Tenas Effendy saw a similar itinerant *joget* performance on distant Bintan Island, Riau Archipelago (pers. comm., 1981).

41. For a full description and discussion of Malay *zapin*, see Nor (1993).

42. These songs were accompanied by guests throwing rice grains on a couple at a wedding or baby at a baby thanksgiving and other rituals that resemble those normally practiced on the east and west coasts of Sumatra.

43. Royal Barus descendant Bp. Zainal Arifin Pasaribu of Barus and Bp. Tamar Sinaga of Sorkam, pers. comm., 1984.

Chapter 11. The Mandailing *Raja* Tradition in Pakantan

1. We made our recordings during field trips to several Mandailing and Angkola-Sipirok villages in the 1970s and the diaspora in Medan focusing on the Mandailing Gunung Kulabu troupe between 1971 and 1981. Experiences on our 1978 trip, which included the Mandailing na Menek villages of Pakantan, Tamiang, Huta na Godang, Muarasoma, and Batang, and Angkola villages in and around Padangsidempuan, made it clear that the details of the musical styles, ensemble types, and repertoires differed in each Mandailing na Menek village (though this was only to be expected, given their oral transmission across the generations).

2. According to the Sampuraga legend, which is known as "Malin Kundang" in some other Batak areas and Minangkabau and as "Malem Diwa" in Aceh, a young man named Sampuraga lived in Padang Bolak with his elderly mother. He wanted to escape poverty, and he tearfully bade her farewell as he departed to seek his fortune. After walking to Pidolo, he settled in Sirambas, which was ruled by Raja Silanjang. Impressed with Sampuraga's capacity for hard work, the king agreed that he should marry his daughter, and the news of the planned palace wedding party spread far and wide. On hearing of his success, Sampuraga's mother walked a long distance to attend the wedding. However, on meeting her face-to-face, Sampuraga felt ashamed of her poor clothes, and he expelled her from the palace saying: "You are not my mother, old woman! She died long ago." In tears the elderly mother prayed to Allah that he

be punished for being blinded by wealth and betraying his mother. A great flood struck the palace, drowning Sampuraga and everyone else in it, turning the area into the eternal hot springs found to this day in Sirambas village.

3. A *huta* was a self-governing unit headed by the *raja*, who came from the land-owning clan (*marga tanah*). In 1854 each *huta* comprised about three hundred to four hundred people. By the 1980s, the *huta* of Pakantan comprised approximately nine hundred (A. P. Parlindungan, pers comm., 1984). In Upper "Small Mandailing," the Lubis clan owned the land, and in Lower "Great Mandailing," it was the Nasution clan.

4. The term *namora natoras* refers not only to the (all-male) nobles and elders but also to the "parliament," governing council, and judicial assembly that they represent. The parliament is headed by the *raja panusunan buluk* or *raja pamusuk*.

5. In Pakantan, *gordang* are sets of either five or nine tuned, single-headed drums in the *gordang lima* (five *gordang*) or *gordang sambilan* (nine *gordang*) ensembles respectively, while *gondang* are pairs of untuned, two-headed drums in the *gondang* or *gondang duo* ensemble. Nasution's fieldwork took place in Sayurmaincat, Kotanopan, and Mandailing in July 1999. He found a variety of *adat* and musical terms, ensembles, and musical concepts in these different villages (Nasution 2007). Systematic study of instrumental tunings has not yet been carried out, but the tunings clearly vary in different villages from my experience.

6. The differences include the drum rhythms and their names, the relative importance of the different instruments, and the greater prevalence of the Muslim-associated female arts such as *nasit* in Angkola vis-à-vis Mandailing (see the contents of my two Baerenreiter disks: *Music of Mandailing* and *Music of Angkola* [Kartomi 1983 a and b]).

7. The names of the *gondang, gordang lima*, and *gordang sambilan* ensemble rhythms in Pakantan and Huta na Godang are essentially similar, though the latter lacks the *gondang Mandailing* rhythm and has some unique rhythms of its own, e.g., *gondang maturepek* and *riang-riang*; moreover, Pakantan's *gordang Roto* rhythm is called *gordang pandasdas* in Huta na Godang. While in Pakantan and Huta na Godang, the chieftains' family heads were allowed to have a *gordang sambilan* played at their life-event ceremonies; in Tamiang only the Raja Panusunan Bulang (head *raja*) and Raja Pamusuk (village chieftain) were allowed to do so.

8. Some other Mandailing clans are the Dalimunte, the Mardia, the Pulungan, the Rangkuti, the Parinduri, the Daulae, the Matondang, the Batubara, and the Tanjung.

9. Due to the growing prosperity in West Sumatra from the late seventeenth century onward, an increasing number of Minangkabau men made the hajj to the holy land and were influenced by its politico-religious trends, including the puritanical Wahhabi movement, which passionately desired to resist mystical beliefs and took up arms to "purify" Islam in the Muslim world. In the early 1800s, Wahhabi-inspired Minangkabau forces tried to abolish royalist and animist ideas and to destroy the members of the royal court center, who scattered after a failed rebellion against the Dutch in 1833, and the court's culture at Pagaruyung. They also destroyed much of the Mandailing, Angkola, and Sipirok areas and converted the population to Islam (L. Andaya 2008, 106–7). Raja Junjungan of Huta na Godang, whose great-great-grandfather (d. 1835) was a *pande bosi* (mystically gifted metalsmith), told us stories about his ancestors who were sent to Bonjol in the 1820s to be converted to Islam during the Padri occupation. He claimed that his great-great-grandfather made some of the bronze *canang* (kettle-gongs) in the *gondang, gordang lima*, and *gordang sambilan* ensembles in Huta na Godang in the early 1800s.

10. For a summary of Padri and Dutch activity in early-nineteenth-century Mandailing, see Castles (1972, 19–24).

11. For the location of the Lubu people, whose language is related to that of the Kubu in Jambi and South Sumatra, see the map of Sumatra in Foley (1981) and Map 11.1 above.

12. The ergology, organology, and social role of *tulila* playing in the courting process are described at length in Nasution (2007). Only fine, thin bamboo (*bulu sorik*) is used to make this flute, in order that it make a sweet (*merdu*), delicate sound that "expresses the emotion of longing" (Nasution 2007, 157). The flute has four front finger holes and plays a free-meter melody that moves in tones, semitones, and microtones within a range of a fourth or a fifth.

13. Lévi-Strauss distinguished between diametric and concentric dualisms in both territorial and social-structural terms. Thus villages that exhibit characteristics of diametric dualism usually divide into two hemispheres, e.g., among the Winnebago people in the Great Lakes area. Those that exhibit qualities of concentric dualism have a sacred inner circle surrounded by a profane outer circle, which is surrounded in turn by uncleared land, as among the Badui in West Java; structurally they comprise a triad disguised as a dyad (Lévi-Strauss 1963, 133–39).

14. Mandailing house decorations consist only of geometric and animal designs, which according to Thomassen à Thuessink van der Hoop (1949, 23), are the most ancient of all Indonesian designs, preceding the development of the other leaf and vegetable designs that entered the region with the advent of Hinduism.

15. The Javanese *gunungan* (*kayon*) and the Mandailing *tutup ari*, which are the most significant symbols of Javanese and Mandailing thought respectively, are both mountain shaped.

16. Ancestors of present-day Indonesians worshiped the buffalo as a sacred animal in the latter Stone Age (Neolithic). The motive of the buffalo head still symbolizes the fruitful earth and protection against evil (Thomassen à Thuessink van der Hoop 1949, 130).

17. "By the shape of its horns the kerbau (buffalo) is related to the moon" (Thomassen à Thuessink van der Hoop 1949, 130).

18. The concept of dualism is arguably too simplistic and indiscriminate to explain the underlying structure of Mandailing society as a whole (or even of Pakantan within Mandailing), because symbolic binary distinctions are made in many cultures and cannot therefore serve as a distinctive tool on their own. The dualism-based approach to analyzing the structure of society was used by several structuralist scholars of the Indies who have been criticized for being preoccupied in an ahistorical way with cultural totalities. My purpose, however, is not to offer a binary-based theory of the structure of the whole society but to draw attention to the dualisms in the performing arts that village elders and artists choose to emphasize in their explanations of the aesthetics of their performing and visual arts. The structure of the three instrumental ensembles and the visual arts, for example, are replete with dualisms.

19. Like the *tulila*, the *sarune buluh* plays tonal, semitonal, and microtonal melodies in a range of a fourth or a fifth. A specimen from Pakantan measures 23 cm x 3 cm. The *preret* (oboe) in Lombok is attributed with similar sonic power to attract (Harnish 2006, 153).

20. The drum was also regarded as a sacred instrument in the entire Batak area and in other parts of Southeast Asia, for example, in central Thailand (see Morton 1976, 68). The oldest known musical instruments in Southeast Asia are the revered Dōng-son kettle "drums" (so named despite their metallic, not skin, heads), which may have been played at religious rain-making ceremonies (see also chap. 7).

21. A slightly different view of the matter has been described by Roheim: "The penis is the small part of the body that penetrates deeper into Mother Earth . . . than any other part of the body" (1972, 325).

22. The bodies of the drums are made of *ingul* wood (a Mandailing term), and the dried cow-skin membranes on the top end are laced to the body with rattan. In Pakantan today, *gordang* are

played consistently loudly (*gogo*), but the elders claim that in the past they were performed in a more *haripian* (peaceful, quiet) way in order to attract the benign spirits. People in the village of Tamiang today alternate between loud and soft *gordang* playing but agree with the statements about changes in dynamic levels given by the Pakantan elders.

23. In Gunungtua-Muarasoro, however, the pairs of drums—from large to small—are called *panjangati, paniga, panulus,* and *eneng-eneng* (Nasution 2007, 28).

24. "De instrumentale muzijk bepaalt zich bij een stel trommen van verschillende grootte, dat men in het voorhuis van den *pamoesoek* ziet hangen; een dergelijk stel gongs en bekkens, date en voornaam gedeelte van den rijkdom der hoofden uitmaakt; de *seroeneh* of *hobo*" (Willer 1846, 350–51). "The instrumental music consists of a set of drums of different sizes that hang in the pavilion of the *pamoesoek*; also a set of gongs or cymbals[and] the sarune or oboe."

25. A detailed description of a funeral in the mid-nineteenth century is given in Willer (1846, 321–23).

26. The "howling ululantes" refers to the sorrowful singing by women at a funeral, called *mangandung hamatian*. This practice has almost ceased because of the disapproval of Muslim leaders who teach that one should not indulge in mourning because death is the will of Allah. The "*kalintangs*" Marsden mentions is a reference to *kulintang*, a name used in parts of Minangkabau, South Sumatra, the southern Philippines and elsewhere for the gong-chimes that are called *momongan* in Mandailing.

27. *Topak* compares with the Javanese (Yogyakarta) term *tepak*, meaning a quiet sound made by curved fingers on the left head of the drum, or a "flyswatter."

28. This rhythm was transcribed from a performance on a two-drum *gondang* ensemble, but it is also used in *gordang* performances of this piece. The timbral notation system used here is an adaptation of Parlindungan's system, which he outlined in a letter to me in 1972.

29. Today dancers wear trousers and shirts in red, white, and black (a dualism of male/white and female/black, which becomes a triadism when the redness of danger is added), or simply red, with turban-like head-rolls and an *ulos Patani* (a long, traditional shawl of a type believed by elders in Pakantan to have originated in Pattani, southern Thailand). This description is based on an interview with Bp. Burhan Nasution in Pakantan.

30. Traditional belief holds that the institution of *sibaso* predated that of *raja*. In each generation, the *sibaso* and the *raja* usually belonged to the same family. According to the legendary songs in Pakantan, the first *sibaso* was the primal ancestor of the Lubis clan, Na Mora Bosi, a master metalsmith and mystic hailing from the Bugis region of Sulawesi who founded the ancestral village of Hatonga in Padang Lawas (to the northeast of Mandailing na Menek), from whence his two younger sons—Si Langkitan and Si Baitang—were sent to "the land of gold" (Mandailing na Menek). Here they defeated the local people in battle and married into the family of the *raja* of the local Nasution clan, Na Mora Sutan, who fled to Pakantan. Moreover, a grandchild of the primal ancestor became known as Raja Mangalaon (after whom a drum rhythm is named). He married a woman from the Harahap clan, and one of their children went to live in Pakantan.

31. Unlike performances in my recordings of "Jolo-Jolo Turun" and "Ideng-Ideng," which showed very slight variation in the second metric unit (bar), no motivic variation whatever occurred in my recordings of "Alap-Alap Tondi."

Part IV Introduction. Aceh

1. Much of the forest has been depleted in the early twenty-first century due to extensive illegal logging.

2. As the linguist Thurgood points out, the second migration correlates with the fall of the southern Champa capital in 1471, and with the same migration from Champa referred to in the *Sejarah Melayu* (Shellabear 1909, 10).

3. There are also several nonindigenous minorities, the largest of which are settlers from Java. For an anthropological study of the Alas minority, see Iwabuchi (1994); for the Gayo, see Bowen (1993).

4. The wars included the Dutch-Aceh war (1873–ca.1910), the Japanese occupation (1942–45), the Indonesian War of Independence (1941–49), the Cumbok war (1946–47), the Darul Islam rebellion (1953–59), and the conflict with the Gerakan Aceh Merdeka (Free Aceh Movement) from 1976 to 2005. They also suffered mass killings during Suharto's anti-Communist purges beginning in 1965. The Free Aceh Movement was formed largely as the result of Indonesian policy actions (Miller 2009, 4), including Jakarta's siphoning off of the vast reserves of natural gas and oil discovered in Aceh in the early 1970s (Kell 1995, 13–28). The conflict ended in 2005 following the shock of the massive Indian Ocean tsunami in 2004.

5. There are two forms of *meuseukat*, one that is part of praying and the other that constitutes a performance art (Ibu Cut Asiah, pers. comm., March 2007). Groups of men also pray or perform in this way, and both sexes may also read religious texts silently (Amir 2006, 190–91).

6. The litany recited in *ratéb meuseukat* includes the *sifeut* (recitation of characteristics of God), *angguk rabani* (praises of Prophet Muhammad), *rukon* (recitation of principles of Islam), and *dala'il khairat* (recitation of the principle religious teachings) (Amir 2006, 41).

7. This account is based on my interviews with elderly members of former west- and north-coast, including *ulèëbalang* families who celebrated their weddings in the 1930s.

8. For an account of the trend toward "a harsh and puritanical Islam, fed by modern uncertainties, [that] was driving young women to wear the veil and young men to renounce the old rituals" in Java since the 1990s, see Beatty (2009). He argues that "with the rise of assertive piety, neighbourhoods and communities were splitting. . . . That diversity and respect for pluralism are now under threat" (2).

Chapter 12. Changes in the Lament Dances in Aceh

1. In a *peusijuek* (Ac.) "cooling" ritual, scented water, rice grains, and leaves are sprinkled over the ritual subject, e.g., a bride, as in the Malay *turun ke air* ritual. Muslim prayers are usually added.

2. This chapter is based on field work in and around Meulaboh in 1982; Kabupatens Aceh Barat, Aceh Barat Daya, and Nagan Raya in 2007; and Nagan Raya and Aceh-Singkil (including Pulau Banyak) in 2010.

3. The Acehnese musico-lingual subgroup is dominant in Kabupatens Aceh Barat, Nagan Raya, and Aceh Barat Daya, and the Aneuk Jamée subgroup is dominant in Kabupatens Aceh Jaya, Kecamatan Tapaktuan, Susoh and Kandang, and Kabupaten Singkil. One third of the inhabitants of Meulaboh are Aneuk Jamée (Nyak Cut Syam, pers. comm., 2007).

4. "Cosmology" is defined as a system of beliefs about the natural order and the character of the universe as a cosmos. Isjkarim and his coauthors write about an *aliran* (layer) of "spirit veneration" that was "linked to Hindu culture brought to Aceh by Indian traders and migrants," as distinct from the time when Acehnese were "convinced they should accept the teachings of Islam" (trans. of Isjkarim et al. 1980–81, 94).

5. *Haba Dang Deuria* is a spontaneous bardic performance of local *cerita rakyat* (I., "folk stories") in Acehnese sung poetry, usually with the aid of properties such as a sword, flute, and cushion

for beating out rhythms, ending scenes, and expressing emotion. In the early nineteenth century a Jeuram-born bard named Tok Tek (whose title was Tok Dang) told the original story about the hero Dang Deuria, of the kingdom of Jeuram (Nagan Raya), performing all night for seven nights in a row. It was then further developed across the generations by Pang Kaun, Waki Nu, Udan, and M. Yahya, all of whom were known by the title of Mak Lapèe. The favorite story of the current Mak Lapèe (Bp. Muda Bahlia), whom I visited in Manggeng in 2007, was "Malem Diwa" (Ac.). The form was further developed and popularized by the late Bp. Adnan, alias PMTOH (Isjkarim et al. 1980–81, 220).

6. The Malelang legend is only told in Aneuk Jamée communities, not along Sumatra's west coast. However, a rather similar legend is told in the neighboring Gayo musico-lingual group.

7. Lyrics combining pre-Muslim and Muslim terms or references were sung at least as long ago as the 1890s (see Snouck Hurgronje 1906, 2:253–56).

8. The Malay equivalent of the west Acehnese term *manoe pocuk* is *turun ke air*, "go down to the water (river)."

9. At some Blangpidie weddings, a *syéh* sings *meubaʾeu* (laments) and performs *manoe pocuk* with seven other women around the bride and groom (Marzuki Hassan, pers. comm., Blangpidie, 2007), but in many other areas only the bride is ritually washed. The Malay equivalent of the western Acehnese term *manoe pocuk* is *turun ke air*, or *turun mandi*, "go down to the water/the river for a ritual wash."

10. Ibu Mariam was seventy years old in 1982 when interviewed by Mursalan Ardy about *malelang* in her village, Ujung Padang, Kecamatan Susoh, in 1980 (Burhan and Idris 1986–87, 131–33). Ibu Cut Asiah knew her.

11. In 2007, Mas Kartomi and I visited the descendants of *ulèëbalang* who live in the White House (Rumôh Putéh), which was built by their antecedents at Gampong Kuala Batée in 1924. Besides ruling the local Kuala Batée chiefdom with Dutch support, their forebears served as patrons of the arts, providing the White House as the most prestigious venue for local performances, with Dutch administrators sometimes invited to attend their feasts (Ibu Cut Putéh, pers. comm., 2007). In 2007 we videoed in the White House the performances of the *malelang* and *phô* song-dances by groups of teenage girls under the leadership of Ibu Nurhayati and Ibu Hanila YS respectively.

12. The Aneuk Jamée *malelang* dance and legend are somewhat similar to the *bines* dance and legend in the mountainous Gayo region of Aceh. In that legend, a girl named Odeni Malelang is whipped for alleged sexual relations with a young man, and although her mother pleads for compassion, she is sentenced to death (or in another version, she commits suicide). The mother sings laments while dancing with some other women around her daughter's corpse, with the group's rhythmic stamping on the floor intensifying her laments. A *bines* performance starts with the *syéh* singing *salam alaikom*, followed by sections from the legend in verse, including advice about moral behavior, after which a group of at least twelve (or even more than forty) women perform the dance. *Bines* groups have competed in the Festivals of Acehnese Arts (PKA) since 1972 (Isjkarim et al. 1980–81, 120–23).

13. *Salam alaikom* is a local Aneuk Jamée pronunciation of the Arabic *Assalamū' 'alaikum*, meaning "peace be with you."

14. These words are sung. The gesture is clearly of indigenous, not foreign Muslim, origin.

15. I was told about the *fatwah* (a religious opinion about Islamic law issued by *ulama*/Islamic scholars) by Teuku Tjut Mohamad Hoessin in Meulaboh in 1982.

16. Aboe Bakar's dictionary definition is based on Djajadiningrat's (1934), who worked in close contact with the Dutch ethnographer and scholar of Aceh, C. Snouck Hurgronje (1906).

17. Ibu Cut Asiah's grandfather was T. Thjik Nagor, the *raja* in Meulaboh in the second decade of the twentieth century. His descendant Cik Ali Akbar ran the chiefdom till he was exiled to Sabang upon the departure of the Dutch and during the three and a half year Japanese invasion (1942–45), while the chiefs at Jeuram and Blangpidie were killed. Because she was a talented singer and dancer, she was awarded a scholarship.

18. *Hikayat Pocut Mahomet* (trans. by Drewes 1979 and Siegel 1979) was an orally transmitted epic (*haba*) written down by a religiously learned man, Teungku Lam Rukam, who hailed from or lived in Lam Rukam, a village in the province (*sagoe*) of the Mukim 35. Leubè Beu'ah was his informant and Pakèh Salikan his transcriber (Drewes 1979, 7). The work was written in the Acehnese *sanja'* meter (see Drewes 1979, 7). The manuscripts are held in the university library in Leiden and elsewhere.

19. In line 1, "pounding the breasts" is given as *leumpah dada,* while in the last line it is given as *djipoh droe tumba dada.*

20. As mentioned earlier, Brakel notes evidence that Aceh experienced waves of Shi'a influence in the fourteenth and eighteenth to nineteenth centuries respectively (1975b, 1–6).

21. The Acehnese text reads: *Adat maté aneu' gata di leupu, lhèe uroë kumuphô kuleumpaih dada* (Drewes 1979, 188–89, line 1865]).

22. Snouck Hurgronje, who never visited western Aceh himself, wrote this footnote on *muphô* on the basis of secondhand information.

23. Snouck Hurgronje refers to the dancing as *muphô*, in which *mu* or *meu* serves as a prefix meaning "to carry out" and *muphô* is "a lascivious dance performed after a funeral" ([1894] 1906, 2:372). No weeping was allowed in the presence of the dying, but tradition required that all wail loudly in chorus when someone dies, serving also to announce the death to the neighbors (Snouck Hurgronje 1906, 1:419). After the funeral, men came to offer condolences in the space beneath the house while the women came into the house. They performed a *muphô* ceremony, in which a female relative "made the visitor wail" by crying and lamenting (*mòe*, "to weep"; *ba'e*, "to lament") with her (ibid., 424).

24. According to a similar northern Acehnese account, *phô* originated as a dance around a coffin in the northern Acehnese chiefdom of Kuala Batée under the *ulèëbalang* ruler Teuku Tjoet Putéh and spread from there along the north coast into other great houses. During a performance, the solo singer always sang excerpts from a legend about a royal death (*kisah kematian*), and the dancers stamped their feet and beat their breasts in grief (Dr. A. R. Nurdin, Bupati of Pidie, pers. comm., 1983). Members of the Putéh family still live in the White House, which is used for government functions. On the walls hang photographs, mainly of female descendants such as Tjoet Derna Intan binti Teuku Tjoet Dhien (1928–72), Tjoet Putéh binti Teuku Tjoet Dhin (taken in 1929), Tjoet Meurah Awon binti Teuku Tjoet Dhin (dates unknown), and Cut Ita binti Teuku Radja Kasjah (d. 2004).

25. The Wahhabi (Salafi) reform movement, which began about 260 years ago and aimed to cleanse Arab Bedouin society of Sufism, became moderately influential in some parts of Aceh at the turn of the twentieth century (the late Teuku Tjut Mohamad Hoessin (b. 1910), pers. comm., Meulaboh, 1982). It was opposed to Shi'ism and the performing arts and prescribed modest dress, especially for women.

26. Several artists and Department of Culture and Tourism officials told me in 2010 that T. Rukibah had invented the techniques of the *meuseukat* song-dance techniques at Seunagan at the turn of the twentieth century. Her father was one of a succession of famous religious teachers called Habib Muda Seunagan who promoted activities of the Sufi brotherhood, Naqsabandiyah, the incumbent in the early twenty-first century being Habib Abu Qudrat.

27. Teuku Tjut Mohamad Hoessin and Ibu Cut Asiah informed me in 1982 that they witnessed several aristocratic weddings in the 1930s, including at the great house in Blangpidie and Meulaboh, and had also visited the White House in Kuala Batée.

28. Dutch administrators disapproved of *dabôh* and sometimes banned it in west Aceh in the 1920s and 1930s (Bp. Teuku Tjut Mohamad Hoessin, pers. comm., 1980). *Daboih, dabôh* (Ac.), *dabus* (Ar.) is a dance of religious concentration to induce physical invulnerability, including in battle. An East Acehnese performance is described in M. Kartomi 1992, while a Minangkabau-style performance is described in chap. 2 of this volume.

29. In the 1950s and early 1960s, female dances were discouraged in the villages of western Aceh, though they were allowed in government and business circles in the cities. All over Aceh, including the west, the female *seudati* song-dance was banned, and even male *seudati* was barely tolerated.

30. A rebellious movement against the republic that accused it of breaking its promise to give Aceh real autonomy was led by T. M. Daud Beureueh between 1953 and 1957.

31. A booklet was published titled *Mengapa Seudati itu Tidak Haram* ("Why Seudati Is Not Forbidden") (Departemen Agama [Department of Religion] 1972, 3–4).

32. One text translates as follows: "Now let's tell a story about education in the region of Aceh. The region of Aceh is developing. There is much activity and progress is in train. Primary and upper secondary schools are provided in almost every area" (M. Kartomi 1998 (recording), Aceh CD, track 4).

33. For other descriptions of performances of *phô* in the 1970s–1980s, see Isjkarim et al. 1980–81, 179–85; Idris 1993, 122–24; for *malelang*, see Burhan and Idris 1986–87, 131–32.

34. The *peuleuet manok* dance depicts the movements and duels of roosters in the farmyard. Cockfights were popular in Aceh in the precolonial, colonial, and postcolonial periods, though they were frequently banned by the authorities on the grounds that they encouraged gambling and were cruel to the animals.

    The text of *thum bédék* reads as follows:

Thum bédék thum bédék thum bédék	Sound of cannon shots
Bila negara bila negara	Country's revenge
T. Umar Johan Pahlawan	T. Umar Johan Pahlawan
Syahid di gotnya di Ujung Kalak	The martyr was taken in Ujung Kalak
Di ujung kalak tugu pahlawan	His gravestone is at Ujung Kalak
Tanda di sinan syahid panglima	Sign of the martyr-general

35. Male *syahé* singers are notorious to this day for their inclusion of ribald or lewd improvised song texts, whether in village-style *seudati* (their main standing and stepping dance) or the *ratôh duek* (secular sitting dance).

36. The body-percussion classification includes my invented symbols for use in notating body percussion episodes, as in music example 12.1.

37. Artists and officials were asked to aim to achieve "national" quality (i.e., suitable for participation on national tours or on the national media) by focusing, for example, on impressive costumes and stagecraft, varying in duration from short (say, three-minute) to long (say, twenty-minute) versions suitable for different occasions, and then to achieve an "international" quality, which if recognized as such, might result in their performing for an international audience. In the 1980s, companies such as Mobil Oil hired such high-quality troupes to perform at their commercial functions. When the security situation permitted, troupes competed for invitations to and prizes awarded at festivals.

38. In some modern *phô* performances, instruments such as the *rapa'i* and *seuruné kalée* are sometimes added. However, traditionalists do not approve of such additions because they obscure the sound of the body percussion, especially the foot-stamping which is a key feature of the style.

39. Alongside the roads in rural areas, I saw *phô, malelang, manoe pocuk*, and *meuseukat* dances being performed again at village celebrations, for example, in a circumcision ceremony I attended at regular rehearsals in various village *sanggar* and in the White House (see the above photos, figs. 12.2, 12.3, and 12.4, taken in 2007).

40. In 2010 Syéh Indah was a twenty-eight-year-old mother of two who did not have the opportunity to attend school, having married at age twelve. She inherited her singing and dancing interest from her mother, Syéh Lima (alias Ibu Nurulala), who had been the leading *syéh* in the village before her daughter was ready to form her own troupe. She developed her own traditional-style version of *phô* to perform at SMA-V in 2009, where it won first prize for its *keaslian* (authenticity).

Chapter 13. "Only If a Man Can Kill a Buffalo with One Blow Can He Play a *Rapa'i Pasè*"

1. Field materials for this chapter are from our 1982 (August and November) and 2003 (February–March) trips to Aceh, while written data on Aceh's music cultures are mainly from a few colonial-era Dutch authors, especially Snouck Hurgronje (1906), whose field experience in Aceh in the 1890s was limited however to Greater Aceh and perhaps part of Pidie. I was also informed by three booklets on Acehnese performing arts published by research committees established by the Department of Education and Culture in Aceh (Isjkarim et al. 1980–81; Burhan and Idris 1986–87; Idris 1993).

2. The first Muslim king in Southeast Asia was Sultan Malik Saleh, who died in 1297, as his tombstone in Pasai indicates. The kingdom was engaged in soliciting trade commodities from the unconverted people of the hinterland (Abdullah 1989, 21). Literary sources show that medieval-era Acehnese lived mainly in Great Aceh (Aceh Besar) but also probably in parts of Pidie and Daya (Mark Durie, pers. comm., 1995).

3. This Acehnese saying reads: *Soe nyang jeuet poh keubeue sigo mate, ureueng nyan jeuet meu'en rapa'i Pasè* (Ibu Aisyah Daud, pers. comm., Sigli, 1982; Sri Hastanto, pers. comm., Jakarta, 1994; Ali Akbar, pers. comm., Lhokseumawe, 2003). It refers to a traditional method of killing a water buffalo (*keubeue*), an animal that is widely believed across the archipelago to be a mystical mount to transport a deceased person to the upper world. For Muslim feast days, it is usual to sacrifice a domesticated oxen (*lieu lumo agam*) rather than a water buffalo, killed in the Muslim way under an *ulama*'s supervision (Snouck Hurgronje 1906, 1:243).

4. The Acehnese frame drums are subdivided into organological variants of a standard single-headed, framed membranophone. All the variants together make up an organological type (i.e., they possess a bundle of attributes; see M. Kartomi 1990, 17).

5. Bruner (1979) and Acciaioli (1985) have described the Indonesian government's secularization and aestheticization of the traditional arts in selected areas for political and commercial purposes, where aestheticization means the replacing of an art form's traditional meaning with a formal artistic emphasis.

6. The *rapa'i kisah* is of medium size (ca. 38 cm x 8 cm) and is played to accompany storytelling (*kisah*). In *rapa'i kisah* or *rapa'i hajat*, a pair of soloists alternate with a group of *rapa'i geurimpheng* or *rapa'i pulot* players to sing poems of advice or religious *dakwah* texts (i.e.,

texts that strengthen the faith), humorous puzzles, historical stories, or comments on the current political situation, depending on the request from the host at a gathering (Idris 1993, 79–80). Malay groups in Aceh play three other organologically distinctive forms of *rapa'i*, two of which are found along the Malay southwest and southeast coastal areas of Aceh. The two Malay varieties are called the *rabana Barus* or *rabana Singkel* and the *rabana Sumatra Timur* respectively. In both of these areas, the Malay name of *rabana* is usually used to refer to the frame drums, though they are also sometimes referred to by their Acehnese name of *rapa'i*. Another structurally different form of frame-drum, *rapa'i guwel*, is played by the Gayo musico-lingual group in the highlands of Aceh.

7. Among my artist colleagues who linked the *rapa'i* to Acehnese identity in interviews were Ibu Aisyah Daud in Langkat in 1982 and Bp. Ali Akbar in Lhokseumawe in 2003.

8. Horizontal conflicts within the contemporary Acehnese elite, such as between the *ulama* and the technocrats (sometimes dubbed "the new *uleëbalang*," the descendants of aristocrats), and vertical conflicts between the Acehnese elite and the Indonesian state have resulted in various different narratives being told about, or emphasis being given to different aspects of, Acehnese identity (Nielsen 2002, 4, 19). Vertical conflict is a conflict between two hierarchically different actors (e.g., between a regional and a central authority, such as Aceh and Jakarta), while horizontal conflict manifests itself between two hierarchically similar actors (e.g., within the regional elite in civil Acehnese society) (ibid., 4).

9. *Timpan* is a special sticky rice cake with desiccated coconut inside, wrapped in a piece of young coconut leaf. Teuku Tjeut Moh. Hoesin recounted this verse in his home in Meulaboh in 1982.

10. Quoting a *hadith* (a narrative record of the sayings of Muhammad and his companions), Doubleday shows that the prophet Muhammad allowed women to play frame drums at weddings and probably other festivals as well, and that in Muhammad's time they also played the instruments at battle time, singing to encourage their warriors (1999, 109–12). Moreover, the *hadiths*, including those by the prophet's wife Aisha, attest to the fact that Muhammad enjoyed listening to music, with women being the main performers (Roy Choudhury 1957, 66–70).

11. The term *Serambi Mekah* is used in the monumental court chronicle, *Bustanussalatin* (1649) written by the Gujerati-born Arab *ulama* Nuruddin ar-Raniri, written during the reign of Iskandar Thani (1636–41).

12. As the saying *bruek lakèe ujeuen* (beat a coconut shell to request rain to fall) suggests, one function of making *rapa'i* music and other sounds in a rice field in times of drought is to make rain fall (Bakar et al. [1985] 2001, 688) with a *rapa'i* sometimes substituting for a coconut shell (Ali Akbar, pers. comm., 1983).

13. Recent Indonesian military activity against Acehnese separatists was most intense between 1989 and 1998 and again from 1999 to 2004.

14. As Daud and Durie (1999, 1) point out, the Acehnese lexicon includes borrowings from Arabic, Malay, Indonesian, Sanskrit, Persian, Tamil, Dutch, Portuguese, English, and Mon-Khmer languages of Southeast Asia.

15. The form of the eggcup-shaped trough in which the husks were stamped off the rice grain in Aceh and parts of mainland Southeast Asia differs from that of the larger, rectangular group rice-stamping trough used in most other parts of Indonesia. The same troughs are used in the *alèe-alèe tunjang* (rice-stamping) dance in northern Aceh.

16. *Indang* in Minangkabau has some points of similarity with Aceh's *rapa'i* genres, but each has its own unique stylistic quality. As noted in chap. 5, some Acehnese and Minangkabau artists

believe that *indang* originated in northwest Minangkabau when under Acehnese control in the sixteenth–seventeenth centuries.

17. Doubleday (1999, 105) has noted that frame drums (some with metal plates attached) were played by men and women in Mesopotamia (present-day Iraq) for religious parades and lament singing at least as long ago as 4000–3000 B.C.E.

18. The oldest evidence of the frame drum in the Indonesian archipelago appears in the Javanese literary source *Smaradahana* 4:10, dated 1135 C.E. (Kunst 1949 [1973], 1:iii), in which the instrument is referred to as *tabang-tabang*. The *redep* frame drum, a name used throughout the twentieth century in Bengkulu and other parts of Sumatra, is mentioned in the *Harivangca* 20:17 (Kunst [1949] 1973, 1:218). A report dated 1723–26 by the Dutch traveler Valentijn mentions the "*rabana*" (*terbang*) and the "*bodoc*" (*bedug*) drums that accompanied female singing in Java (ibid., 1:114). The early-nineteenth-century Javanese romance-poem *Serat Centhini* mentions various sizes of *terbang* in rural ensembles that accompanied popular Middle East–influenced singing along Java's north coast (Pigeaud 1967, 229). In early-twentieth-century Java, religious groups also played *terbang* to accompany their songs of praise, especially on the Prophet's birthday (Kunst [1949] 1973, 1:217).

19. This popular belief about the origin of the *rapa'i* has been immortalized in the following Acehnese *panton* verse (Isjkarim et al. 1980–81, 253, translated by Mark Durie):

> Di langèt manyang bintang meublè-meublè
> Cahya ban kandé leumah u bumoe
> Asai rapa'i bak Syéh Abdul Kadé
> Masa nyan lahé peutreun u bumoe
>
> [Stars shine forth in the heavens.
> Lamplike rays are visible from the earth.
> The *rapa'i* originated through Syéh Abdul Kadir.
> When he was born, he brought it down to earth.]

20. According to Snouck Hurgronje (1906, 2:249), the Sufi fraternity Rifa'iyah was once strong in parts of Aceh, though only some of the religious leaders in Aceh now appear to know of the connection, according to my field experience.

21. Followers of Syéh Sammān are believed to have composed the *ratéb/dhikr* words to be sung and laid down the rules of the movements of the body and the postures to accompany them (Snouck Hurgronje 1906, 2:217).

22. Snouck Hurgronje wrote that *saman* is "one of the devout recreations in which a religiously inclined public takes part," but he criticized some performances for having little real religious content or significance. He also mentioned that women had a *ratéb saman* of their own (1906, 2:219).

23. The largest frame drums in Java (Sumedang, West Java) in the early twentieth century were the deep-rimmed *terbang besar*, with their skins nailed onto their wooden bodies and measuring 60–75 cm in diameter. Next in size were the deep-rimmed *terbang gembrang*, with their skins tautened by a rattan hoop and wooden plugs, measuring 25–30 cm in diameter. The much flatter *terbang ketimpring* were fitted with three equidistant tinkling plates/jingles on their side walls. A small *terbang*, a *kemprang*, had a bright sound (Kunst [1949] 1973, 1:368–89).

24. This account is based on Basri Daham's interview article with Utōh Taleb (2003, 4), consulted per courtesy Iwan Amir.

25. This is according to Helmut Hass, the chairman of the Dewan Kesenian Aceh (Aceh Arts Council) in Jakarta (Daham 2003, 4).

26. The *tualang* (Latin: *Koompassia malaccensis, Koompassia parvifolia*) is a tall tree that often contains beehives, found in the jungles in Sumatra (Bakar et al. [1985] 2001).

27. Elsewhere in Sumatra this black monkey is known as *siamang*.

28. In Java, too, large frame-drums (*terbang*) may be given proper names, such as Macan Garongan (Roaring Tiger), which the nineteenth-century text *Centhini* quoted (Kunst [1949] 1973, 1:217). In early-nineteenth-century Java, a large, deep-voiced frame drum called *angguguk imbal gedhug* was played (*Centhini*, canto 37, stanza 223, in Kunst [1949] 1973, 1:217). Proper names are also given to great gongs. Regarding the name Si Mirah, *Si* in Acehnese can mean *Sri*, the name of a Hindu divinity (Bakar et al. [1985] 2001, 897).

29. There were two *rapa'i Pasè* in Syamtalira Aron, two in Matangkuli, two in Baktiya, two in Tanah Jambo Aye, and two in Lhok Sukon, as well as a much larger number in Kecamatan Gedong and Kecamatan Samudera, the site of the former Pasai kingdom (Idris 1993, 80).

30. Teams of uniformed *rapa'i* players tend to wear dark red, leaf-green, dark bean-green, or sea-blue shirts with narrow cuffs and loose armholes and baggy black trousers, belts, and a cloth headdress tied jutting up at the back (Isjkarim et al. 1980–81, 69).

31. Another way of starting is for the players to stamp out a rhythm on a mat and the *kalipah* to call out a command, raising his hands above his head (Isjkarim et al. 1980–81, 69).

32. The sound of the *rapa'i pulot* resembles the sharp, brilliant, penetrating timbres produced by the small, double-headed Malay *marwas* drums. The sound may also resemble the small, early-nineteenth-century Javanese frame drums called *kempyang* (bright). Kunst ([1949] 1973, 1:217) mentions that it was referred to in the *Centhini*, canto 37, stanza 226.

33. For example, the player may beat on the tenth and twelfth beats of a sixteen-beat cycle, notated as {h h h h l l l l h . h . l l l l}, where "h" indicates a high-pitched *rapa'i* sound, "l" indicates a low-pitched sound, and the dots indicate the jingle sound, as demonstrated by Jakarta-resident Acehnese musicians (SAJAK) in video recordings that I and my team made in 2003.

34. *Rapa'i geurimpheng* are also called *rapa'i macam* (kind of *rapa'i*) or *rapa'i lagèe* (melodic *rapa'i*).

35. Other early Dutch writers refer to "*rapa'i poelet*"; Kreemer mentions that two different *kampong* groups would play them in the village *meunasah* and sing *panton* (quatrains, each comprising an allusive and a clearly meaningful couplet), *kisah* (a greeting and question or other dialogue), and *nasib* (answering verse), while moving their arms and snapping their fingers and would then break into a *sadati* performance (Kreemer 1922, 1:424). Jacobs also mentioned that performers (*anek poelet*) would play four to five *rapa'i* of different sizes as well as Malay *rabana* (Jacobs 1894, 160, 171).

36. In 1982, some of the most competitive *rapa'i pulot* groups were located in Kecamatan Samalanga and *Peusangan* (Ibu Aisyah Daud, pers. comm., 1982). In Peureulak and eastern Gayo (Lokop), a genre similar to *rapa'i pulot* but without swaying body movements is called *cuwek*, performed in a rice field after a harvest (pers. comm., Noerdin Daood, pers. comm., 2003).

Chapter 14. Connections across Sumatra

1. As in some other predominantly Muslim countries, calls to prayer and the recitation of the Qur'an are important musical expressions, but they are not usually referred to as music because their musical quality is regarded as unimportant compared to the religious message they convey. Yet talented muezzins and Qur'an reciters who perform with great skill and beauty of sound are highly praised for their style.

2. *Dabus, tabut*, and other transplanted forms were probably introduced into Sumatra from different areas in the Arabian Peninsula, northern India, and Persia, as suggested by the fact that versions of *dabus* are performed very differently in North Aceh, West Aceh, and Minangkabau, and that the version of *tabut* performed in Pariaman differs strongly in style from the version in Bengkulu.

3. Minangkabau pilgrims to Mecca in the late eighteenth century experienced its occupation by the fundamentalist Wahhabi movement. On their return to West Sumatra, some of them founded the military Padri movement, which aimed to purify Islam of superstitions. Moderates who opposed the Padri sought refuge with aristocrats who were supporters of *adat* practices and asked the Dutch for help. The war spread to neighboring Mandailing and Angkola, where most of the people converted to Islam under duress.

4. Snouck Hurgronje criticized the performances on the grounds that they had no real religious content or significance for the participants (Snouck Hurgronje 1993–94, 2:216–17), a view that was arguably based on an incorrect interpretation of song texts due to Snouck Hurgronje's ignorance of the local Kluet language (Amir 2006, 123–30).

5. Taufik Abdullah hypothesized that the Minangkabau "Cindua Mato" legend was created in the sixteenth century when Islam was still being integrated in the countryside (1970, 10).

6. While we were sailing around the Pulau Banyak archipelago in 2010, some boatsmen told me several myths about the creation of islands that we passed, including some new ones that arose after the 2004 tsunami.

7. According to another version of this myth, Hang Tuah's son began his journey from Tarusan near Indrapura on Minangkabau's southwest coast.

8. In Vietnam, Mongolia, and elsewhere, body percussion can include tongue and mouth clicking. However, they are not common techniques in Sumatra.

Appendixes

1. The former are a little more language-agnostic than the latter, that is, they do not classify their speech varieties into dialects, languages, and families of languages (Paul Lewis, pers. comm., 2010).

2. Linguists have recently shown that the Batak-Gayo-Barrier Island language group exists and that Rejang is a linguistic isolate (Adelaar 2005, 22).

3. A form of Chamic, which became the lingua franca of the Champa kingdom of southern Vietnam in the sixth century C.E., became Acehnese when their forebears migrated to Aceh some time later (Adelaar 2005, 17)

4. Variability of pitch in Javanese *gamelan* tunings has also long been noted, as has the local desirability of imitating certain *gamelan* tunings (e.g., the *gamelan sléndro Layem* of the Regent of Tasikmalaya and one of the two three-toned *gamelan Munggang* of the Susuhunan of Solo; see Kunst [1949] 1973, 1:48).

5. Based in part on Sutton (1998, 657).

English Terms

colotomic pattern   a pattern of sounds that divide or subdivide a rhythmic cycle (e.g., if the cycle comprises eight beats, the fourth and eighth beats normally coincide with a deep stroke on a drum or gong, or a deep body-percussion sound).

culture memory   a view of an earlier period or period, based on reports and experiences by people from different walks of life who remember what their forebears and teachers told them about it

drum-chimes   sets of drums tuned in a row

gong-chimes   sets of small kettle-gongs tuned in a row

indigenous religion   veneration of the spirits of nature and the ancestors to gain inner strength (*tenaga dalam*) and promote the welfare and safety of one's community. Many writers refer to the indigenous religions as a whole under the name of animism (I. *animisme*), though it is generally known by different names in different areas, e.g., *perbegu/pelebegu* in the Mandailing area.

keynote   the most important tone of the scale in nonharmonically conceived music; usually the final note of a number of melodic phrases in a song or piece, and sometimes the final note of a recurring three- or four-note melodic formula

legend   a story told as if it were a historical event in a definite period of time

melodic formula   a pattern of notes that frequently occurs at cadential points (e.g., A G E D, where D is the final tone)

musical arts   performing arts containing music, including vocal, chanted, instrumental, theatrical, art of self-defense, and dance genres with music

musico-lingual groups   population groups and subgroups that are primarily distinguished from one another on the basis of the musical and lingual attributes of their vocal-musical genres (including songs, ritual/religious chanting, song-dances, and intoned theatrical monologues or exchanges), and only the second level of division on the basis of their musical instruments

myth   a symbolic narrative that explains the origin of things, without a coherent chronology

semiprofessional artist   a leading artist (often a shaman) who is asked to perform at a celebration in return for food or other payments, or who receives compensation in kind for expenses incurred, and whose main sustenance comes from other work

speech varieties   varieties of language spoken, without implying any specific lingual relationships between them

synthesis   a blend or combination of elements from a variety of phenomena

tonic   the key note of the scale in harmonically conceived music (e.g., F in F major)

weretigers   shamans who can turn into tigers

Sumatran Languages and Indonesian

adat   I., custom, a set of cultural practices

adat-istiadat   I., custom, tradition

aguang   Mi., gong

Akademi Seni Karawitan Indonesia (ASKI)   I., Academy of Indonesian Traditional Music

akordion   I., piano accordion

Alam Melayu   Ma., "the Malay world," areas of Southeast Asia where Malay is spoken.

Alam Minangkabau   Ma., "the Minangkabau world," areas of West Sumatra and beyond where Minangkabau is spoken

alek   Mi., celebration, party, festival; *baralek*: to engage in an *adat* celebration

aliran   I., Mi., Ac., stream or branch of Islam; pre-Muslim, Muslim, or pop style of performance; school of *rabab pasisia* playing (Mi.), musical or dance style inherited from older performers

anak daro   Mi., Ac., bridegroom

aneuk diké   Ac., child of *dike*. See also *radat*

Aneuk Jamée   Ac., lit. "Descendants of the Guests," people who have migrated from along Sumatra's west coast to west- and south-coastal Aceh, and who speak a patois of Malay and Minangkabau, whence many of their antecedents migrated since approximately the eighteenth century. Their culture is strongest in Singkil and Kepulauan Banyak. See also *Pasisir Malayu*

aneuk pulot   Ac., acrobat in a *rapa'i pulot* performance

aneuk syahé, or *syahé*   Ac., lead vocalist in a song-dance performance

angguk rabbani   Ac., Praises of the Prophet Muhammad

Angkola-Sipirok   people of Batak Angkola descent, mostly living in areas of North Sumatra where Angkolan and Sipirok speech varieties are dominant

animisme   indigenous religion. See also *perbegu,* indigenous religion

Arab   I., people of Arabic descent, speakers of varieties of Arabic who live in many (especially coastal) areas of Sumatra

arbab   Ma., a now-obsolete bowed string instrument in Aceh and in Malay and Batak areas of North Sumatra

ashar   I. (Ar. *Asr*), the third of the daily Muslim prayers, in the afternoon

asli   I., "original" Malay song-dance genre in slow tempo usually accompanied by a *biola, rebana*, and a gong that is struck on every eighth beat; performed in Riau and Malaysia

ayeun aneuk   Ac., swaying a child (in a hammock), usually with lullaby singing

ayun-ayun   Mi., melismatic singing, tremolo oscillation singing on a particular vowel or consonant

azan   I., call to prayer

badendang   Ma., song-dances with violin and frame-drum accompaniment on Penyelai Island at the mouth of the Kampar River

bagurau   Mi., enjoy a performance of music, dance, or theater. *Malam bagurau*: "fun night," e.g., to raise funds for a new mosque or other facility

bahasa hutan   Be., Ma., Mi., taboo language used on entering the kingdom of weretigers

balabeh   Mi., a posture assumed by a fighter as he faces his opponent in an art-of-self-defense performance. Concentrating mentally and holding a hand in front of his chest, he lowers his body with his weight resting on his knees in the so-called horse (*kudo*) stance.

bangsa   I., nation

bangsawan   Ma., lit. nobility, a type of Malay popular theater or opera *bansi, bangsi*   Ma., Mi., small (e.g., 20 cm by 1.5 cm), recorder-like, end-blown bamboo flute, often with seven front holes and one rear hole

bararak babako   Mi., procession from bride's paternal home

barzanji   Mi., Muslim religious text performed vocally, sometimes with frame drumming

baselo   Mi., to sit cross-legged

batagak panghulu   Mi., ceremony to bestow an honorable title on a man

Batak   I., a major ethnic and musico-lingual community in North Sumatra, comprising the mainly Muslim Mandailing and Angkola-Sipirok, and the mainly Christian Toba, Simalungun, Karo, and Pakpak Dairi subgroups.

Batang Hari Sembilan   Be., Ma., symbolic Besemah-Malay region with nine major rivers

Besemah   Ma., people of Besemah descent, most of whom live in areas of South Sumatra where Besemah speech varieties are spoken

beuet Qur'an   Ac., solo recitation of the Qur'an

biola Aceh   Ac., Acehnese violin, comedy act by two male comedians—one acts the part of a husband and the other his wife dressed in female clothes—and a *biola-* playing singer

Bukit Barisan   Ma., the great dividing range that runs inland along Sumatra's west coast

Bundo Kanduang   Mi., senior woman in a matrilineal household, legendary matriarch in various *kaba*, the first queen of Pagaruyung palace in the *luhak nan tigo*

bupati   I., regent, administrative head of a region (I., *kabupaten*)

canang   Ma., small, flat, or bossed gong

carano   Ma., Mi., a metal ceremonial container, usually containing betel for chewing at ceremonies

celempong   Mi. (cf. *talempong, caklempong, calempong, kelintang*) gong-chime in South Sumatra

cerita puyang   Be., Ma., ancestral narratives

cuwek   Ac., dance by six men led by syéh accompanied by group *rapa'i* frame-drum playing in a rice field after a harvest in Peureulak, East Aceh; often performed in competition between villages

dabus Ar., I.; *dabôh/dabôih* Ac.; *dabuih* Mi.   (1) awl; (2) a mystical Sufi art form in which religiously inspired performers display martial prowess and invulnerability through expressions of religious devotion, led by a *kalipah*, accompanied by mass frame-drum playing

dakwah   Ar., the early outreach and conversion to Islam and the continuing call to believers to deepen their faith and piety

dala'il khairat   Ac., recitation of the main Muslim teachings

Dalem   Ma., the court of the former Sultanate of Palembang

dampeng Ma.; *dampiang*, Mi.   an art-of-self-defense-based dance performed by two men in a bridegroom's procession to the bride's house or for a circumcision celebration

dangdut   I., a pop music and dance genre and style first developed in the 1970s, usually with Hindi film and Arabic and Western pop elements

dap (dab) or *rapa'i aneuk*   Ac. a tiny frame drum

darek Mi.; *darat* I.   the hilly or mountainous cultural hinterland of West Sumatra where the Minangkabau first settled, including the *luhak nan tigo* districts

dayah   Ac., Muslim religious school

dendang   Mi., solo song performed with improvised or memorized poetry, sometimes with flute accompaniment. *Padendang*: singer, *badendang*: to sing. *Dendang Pauah*: a genre of *kaba* performance with a block *saluang* flutist in Padang and surrounds

dhikr Ar., *diké* Ac.   lit., "remembrance" (of Allah), to chant/sing the Muslim litany, or phrases from it. See *liké dikia rabano*   Mi., a Muslim vocal genre with large frame-drum playing

dol   Mi., a large, cylindrical double-headed drum of Persian origin, also known as *tambua*

dukun   Ma., Mi., Ac., traditional healer, often a shaman as well

estra or *lanie*   Ac., an extra dance and/or song item added to the standard sections of a *seudati, ratôh duek, phô,* or *meuseukat* performance, usually a popular song

gamad   Mi., Bengk., harmonic Malay music performed in coastal Minangkabau or Bengkulu, usually featuring a vocalist, a hybrid Malay-European instrumental ensemble, and couples dancing

gambus   Ma., plucked or strummed lute played in Malay music

gamelan   Jav., a Javanese orchestra mainly comprising percussion instruments including metallophones (especially gongs, gong-chimes), xylophones, drums, and a solo voice, flute, and bowed string instrument

gandang Mi., *gendang* Ma.   a generic term for a double-headed drum of any type or size

gandang sarunai   Mi., Be. a musical genre played on a pair of drums and a *sarunai*

gandang tambua   Mi., group drumming ensemble in the Maninjau area, offshoot of the *dol-tasa* drumming in the *tabuik* ritual

gelombang duabelas/duobale   Ma., lit. "twelve waves," *rondai*-like circle dance by twelve men at a (west) Pasisir wedding (between Singkil and Pariaman) after the bridegroom arrives in procession at the bride's house

genggong   I., Ma., Jew's harp

geudam gaki   Ac., a quasi-body-percussion technique, i.e., stamping or tapping the floor or ground with the left (*wie*) or right (*uneun*) foot, often with finger-snapping to accentuate the sound

geundrang   Ac., a two-headed cylindrical drum measuring ca. 40–50 cm length and ca. 18–20 cm diameter, made of *nangka* wood and goatskin, or thin cowskin, beaten by hand or with a wooden stick. Usually maintains the rhythm of a piece with an optional *gedombak* (hourglass-shaped) drum and an oboe (*seuruné kalée*)

gondang   Mand., (1) a double-headed drum played in pairs in a *gondang* ensemble; (2) an ensemble in Pakantan comprising a pair of *gondang* drums, an oboe (*sarune*), two to six kettle-gongs (*momongan*), a *doal* (small suspended gong), a pair of hanging gongs (*ogung*), a pair of small vertically played cymbals (*talisasayap*), and optional vocalist

gong   Ma., a small to medium bossed gong

gordang   Mand., (1) a large, single-headed, tuned drum; (2) a set of *gordang* drums; (3) an ensemble comprising a set of *gordang* and other instruments in Pakantan and some other villages

gordang lima   Mand., (1) a set of five tuned *gordang* drums; (2) an ensemble that contains a *gordang lima* and other instruments in Pakantan and some other villages

gordang sembilan   Mand., (1) a set of nine tuned *gordang* drums; (2) an ensemble that contains a *gordang sembilan* and other instruments in Pakantan and some other villages

gurindam   Ma., (1) a Malay poetic form that usually comprises two pairs of two-line verses; (2) a song style with a Malay solo singer accompanied by an *orkes gambus* or similar ensemble

guritan,   Ma., (1) a storytelling genre; (2) a poetic form in upstream South Sumatra, Bengkulu, and West Sumatra

haba dang deuria   Ac., a spontaneous bardic performance in Acehnese poetry of various *dongeng* (*cerita rakyat* folk tales), usually sung with the aid of properties such as a sword, a flute and a cushion for beating out rhythms, ending scenes, and expressing emotion. According to legend, it was originally a story told about people in the kingdom of Jeuram (in Nagan

Raya) in the early nineteenth century by a Jeuram-born man named Tok Tek, who became known as Tok Dang, after which it was developed into a dramatic form by Pang Kaun, Waki Nu, Udan, and M. Yahya, all of whom were known by the title of Mak Lape. Dang Deuria was the name of the hero in the Dang Deuria story. The form was further developed and popularized by the late Bp. Adnan, alias PMTOH (Isjkarim et al. 1980–81, 220).

hadith, hadis Ar., a collection of reports about the sayings, customs, and deeds of the Prophet and his companions

haram Ar., forbidden, especially in context of Islam

hareubab Ac.; *arbab*, Batak three-string spiked fiddle with a horsehair bow, now obsolete. In Aceh it is around 120 cm long and with a skin-covered bowl-shaped body of approximately 23 cm diameter; its gut strings are wound around the two tuning pegs jutting out to left and right.

harmonika I., a rectangular, chromatic button accordion (melodeon) with bellows and a free-reed made by the German Hoehner Company, which became popular in Besemah, South Sumatra, in the early twentieth century

hikayat Ma., Ac., orally performed or written epic or literary work, often with a legendary, religious, or moral character

iblis Ma., a disputative spirit

ilir Ma., downstream

inang a Malay song-dance genre in quick tempo that portrays the swaying movements of ladies-in-waiting (*inang*), traditionally accompanied by a *biola*, a *rebana*, and a *gong*

indang Mi., (1) a small, goatskin frame drum of approximately 10–12 cm diameter or a medium-size frame drum of approximately 20–25 cm diameter; (2) a sitting song-dance genre with group frame-drum playing and singing of Muslim or secular texts

isya I., *ishaa* Ar. last of the Muslim daily prayers, in the evening

japri Ma.. See *kapri*

jilbab I., female Muslim head scarf

joget, ronggeng, rentak lagu dua Ma., I., a medium- to quick-tempo Malay song-dance for mixed couples, traditionally accompanied by a violin and a drum (and other optional instruments), with a professional female singer-dancer accepting paying male partners with whom they exchange *pantun* verses and dance in couples without touching. In the past few decades, pious communities banned mixed couples dancing except among teenagers and children and substituted male dancers for the female role. See *Serampany 12*

kaba Mi., epic story, myth (oral or written)

Kabupaten I., an administrative area, a regency

kacapi Mi., zither

kain kabaya female Malay/Indonesian costume comprising a wraparound skirt (*kain*) and long-sleeved blouse (*kabaya* Mi.; *kebaya* I.), usually with a long shawl (*slendang*) worn around the shoulders

kalipah Ac., Muslim mystical leader of a *dabus* performance

kampung I., *kampuang* Mi. village, a complex of houses and fields

kaphé Ac., infidel, from *kaffir* Ar.; *kafir* I.

kapri Ma., (from *kafir*, "infidel"), a hybrid Malay-European style of vocal, violin, and drum music and dance in Sumatra's west Pasisir, especially between Singkil and Natal

Kecamatan I., an administrative district within a Kabupaten

kelintang, kelittang Ma., a gong-chime, a gong-chime and drum ensemble in South Sumatra *kenduri*   Ac., Ma., Mi., a commemorative celebration

kesenian Islami   I., performing arts with doctrinal, *zikir*-based texts and Arab-sounding scales and musical style, often accompanied by frame drums and a *gambus* (lute)

kesenian yang bernafaskan Islam   I., performing arts with an Islamic flavor

ketebung   Ma., a double-headed drum in the Petalangan and Suku Mamak areas of Riau

kisah   Ac., the story-singing section of a dance (e.g., *phô, seudati*) sung by a *syahé*

kreasi baru   I., a new creation

kroncong   I., a popular musical style with probable Portuguese/Malay roots, usually performed by a vocalist with bowed and plucked string instruments in Java

kumantan   Riau Ma., a person who can enter into a psychic state in which she or he becomes possessed by a spirit or journeys into the spirit world on behalf of members of her or his Petalangan community

langkah   Ma., Mi., Ac., steps in a dance; *langkah silat* Ma. (*silek* Mi.) steps in the art of self-defense

laweuet   Ac., modern form of the female *seudati* dance (since the early 1970s), short for *seulaweuet* Ac., from *shalawat* Ar., praises of the Prophet

Lebaran   weeklong celebrations at Idulfitri, the end of the fasting month (Ramadan)

lesung   I., percussion instrument that resembles a trough for husking rice

liké   Ac., from Ar. *dhikr*, to chant, to chant in *ratéb*

luhak, luhak nan tigo   Mi., lit. "the three areas" of the *darek*, the Minangkabau heartland: Agam, Tanah Datar, and Lima Puluh Koto

madrasah   I., Islamic boarding school run by one or more *ulama*

magreb   I. (Ar. *maghrib*), fourth of the daily Muslim prayers, at sunset

majlis   Ar., lit. "place of sitting," a form of Shi'a chant, sung in *tabuik/tabut*

malelang   Ac., traditional female circle dance with vocal music and body percussion attached to the legend of Malelang and Madion in South Aceh

Mandailing   I., people of Batak Mandailing descent who live in areas of North Sumatra or diasporas where speech varieties of Mandailing are dominant

manoe pocuk/peutron manoe   Ac., a traditional female circle dance around a ceremonial subject (e.g., a bride, or a boy about to be circumcised) before being ritually washed (*turun mandi*) or to celebrate a good harvest

marga   Ba., Ma., a genealogical unit

matam (*mahatam*)   Sa., Urdu, name of a dirge in Urdu sung and a drum rhythm/piece played in *tazia* (Persian), known as *tabuik/tabut* in Minangkabau

Maulud Nabi, Maulud, Mauludan   celebration of the Prophet's birthday, third month of the Muslim year

Melayu   I., a major ethnic and musico-lingual group living in parts of all provinces of Sumatra, other parts of Indonesia, and Malaysia, and comprising many subgroups; an area where Malay or a variant of Malay language is spoken; a person of Malay descent

merantau I., Mi.; *meurantoe* Ac.   to seek one's fortune abroad, out-migrate; also *rantau*, meaning migration, place of migration

meuseukat   Ac., a female sitting dance with religious or secular texts from western Aceh. See also *ratéb meuseukat*

muphô   Ac. to perform the *phô* dance (see Snouck Hurgronje 1906, 1:428). See *phô*

nasib   Ma., Ac., religious stories sung by a group, e.g., in a *madrasah*, led by one or two solo singers

nagari   Mi., a village federation, indigenous political unit

nenek mamak Ma.; *niniek mamak* Mi.   village elders

nobat   Persian, a royal court ensemble, usually comprising a metal kettle drum (*negara, nakara, nahara*), a pair of double-headed drums (*gendang*), a long silver trumpet (*nafiri*), an oboe (*serunai*) and a suspended gong (*gong*). It marks a ruler's sovereignty, forms an essential part of his regalia, and is only played in his presence, including at his installation and royal life events. Its first recorded use (mentioned in the *Sejarah Melayu*, "Malay Annals") was during the reign of Sultan Muhammed Shah (1424–41). It is still played in royal Malaysian courts but not in Indonesia's former Malay palaces, as there is no longer a sovereign.

obab   Riau, Ma., a bowed string instrument with a snakeskin and half-coconut-shell body along areas north and south of the Kampar River in Riau. See also *rebab*

Orang Dalem   Ma. See Suku Dalem

Orang Suku Laut   I., Ma., lit. "People of the Sea," nomadic or seminomadic fisherfolk who prefer to live in relative isolation on houseboats at sea, returning to their coastal shacks in inclement weather

orkes talempong   Mi., a *talempong* (gong-chime) orchestra in Western diatonic tuning, comprising many types of Minangkabau instruments, developed in the late 1960s

pantun Ma.; *panton* Ac.   a Malay poetic form/quatrain comprising a b a b rhyming couplets, normally with a poetic allusion (*sampiran*) in the first couplet and the poet's main message or intent (*isi*) in the second

pasar   I., permanent marketplace (compare with *pecan*, "weekly market")

pasisia   Mi., the southern and northern coastal areas of Minangkabau

pasisir   Ma., the coastal areas of Sumatra, especially the western coast

Pasisir Malayu ("coastal Malay") or *Aneuk Jamée/Jamu*   a Malay-Minangkabau lingual patois containing some Acehnese words, spoken in coastal Aceh and North Sumatra; a term applied to people who speak varieties of Malay along the western coast of Sumatra

pelaminan Ma., *palaminan* Mi.   bridal alcove

pélog   Jav., a heptatonic tone-system, with three pentatonic modal scales

pemangku adat   I., government-appointed expert in customary law

pencak silat Ma., *pancak silek* Mi.   martial arts/art of self-defense, usually including a display of skills and a fight between two performers

penghulu Ma., *panghulu* Mi.   male leader of a clan or lineage *perbegu* (Mand.); a person who venerates the ancestors and spirits of nature

peningka Ma.; *paningka* Mi.   lit. "interjector," a drummer or kettle-gong player who interjects unexpected patterns or accents into the leader's (*penyelalu's*) more continuous rhythmic ground

penyelalu   Ma., a continuous rhythmic ground. See *peningka*

perbegu   Mand., a person who venerates the ancestors and spirits of nature

peumulia jamée   Ac., traditional female dance to welcome guests (without betel nut). See also *ranub lampuan*

phô   Ac., western and southern Acehnese group song-dance with stamping and other body percussion, performed by unmarried girls in western Aceh

piyasan   Ac., festival

pribumi   I., lit. "sons of the earth," a racial classification of indigenous Indonesians as opposed to people of Indonesian Chinese descent, etc.

pukulan kosong   I., lit. "empty beating," a sharp sound beaten on the upper edge of a frame drum

pupuik gadang, pupuik batang padi   Mi., an aerophone made of coconut palm frond or rice stalk

pusaka   Ma., Sa., a family heirloom that must be treasured and protected as a gift from the ancestors; inherited royal regalia

puyang   Be., Ma., ancestor, cultural hero, founder of a settlement

qasidah   I., Muslim group song type

rabab Mi., fiddle, occurring in three types: *rabab darek, rabab Pariaman*, and *rabab pasisia*

rabab darek Mi., lit. "upstream fiddle": a spiked, 60–70 cm high fiddle with two strings tuned a fifth apart and a carved wooden body of 25 cm diameter found in the *darek*

rabab Pariaman Mi., a spiked, 40 cm high, short-necked fiddle with a half-coconut body (ca. 16 cm diameter) and three strings tuned in fourths, found in the north-coastal area

rabab pasisia Mi., lit. "coastal fiddle" found along the south coast. It resembles a viola, stands ca. 60 cm high, is 16–18 cm wide at the base, and has four strings, three of which are tuned in fifths and the lowest is untuned.

radat, rodat Ma., Ac., lit. "word-giver"; lead vocalist in a group *diké/dala'il* performance. He usually sings a phrase or section of the Qur'an or a *hadith* with one or two assistants, who pass on verbal cues to the group, e.g., to change to a different tempo or chant (*witr*) or prepare to end a session or section.

rakyat I., M., the common people, the working class and the peasants

randai Mi., a form of Minangkabau theater since the 1930s with *galombang* dancing in the round, and with scripts adapted from a *kaba* story or created on an original topic

rantau Mi., coastal plains, lowland, area where young highland men sought their fortune. See also *merantau*

ranub lampuan Ac., female Acehnese dance to welcome guests with betel nut and accessories, created in the 1960s. See *peumulia jamée*

rapa'i Ac., Mi., frame drum

rapa'i aneuk Ac., lit "child frame drum," a small high-pitched frame drum

rapa'i dabôih/dabôh Ac., a medium-sized frame drum played in performances of the devotional *dabôh/dabôih* genre

rapa'i geleng, tari rapa'i geleng (1) a medium-sized frame drum; (2) a genre led by a solo singer in which a row of men in sitting position play frame drums as they turn their heads (*geleng*) to the right, then the left, etc., created in western Aceh in the 1950s

rapa'i geurimpheng Ac., (1) a medium-sized frame drum, usually with metal-disk jingles attached; (2) a genre led by a solo singer (*aneuk syahé*) in which a group play the frame drums with singing and body movement

rapa'i lipéh Ac., lit. "thin beating," a sharp sound beaten on the upper edge of a *rapa'i*

rapa'i Pasè Ac., a large, single-headed, waisted drum played in suspended position, named after Aceh's first Muslim kingdom of the 1290s: Pasè (Ac.), Pasai (Ma)

rapa'i pulot (1) a medium-sized frame drum; (2) a genre with vocal and frame-drum music, usually with acrobatics

ratap, ratok Ma., Ac., to wail, lament; formerly a death rite used in the *phô* song-dance of western Aceh

ratéb Ac., (from *ratib*, Ar.) chants/songs of praise, Qur'anic teachings or litany (*diké* or *liké*) with body movement, occurring in a variety of genres, e.g., *ratéb meuseukat, ratéb*

ratéb dong Ac., *ratéb* performed in standing (*dong*) position

ratéb duek Ac., *ratéb* performed in sitting (*duek*) position

ratéb meuseukat Ac., a traditional devotional song-dance with body percussion from western Aceh normally performed by females, a form of *ratéb*

ratip Ma., healing songs performed in villages along the Kampar River in Riau

ratôh Ac., lit. "continuous chatter"

ratôh duek Ac., lit. "sitting *ratôh*," a dance genre performed in sitting position, with episodes of solo and group singing and body percussion

ratok Mi., a sad song in the *saluang* or *rabab pasisia* repertory, often in free meter

rebab Ma., a spike fiddle with a half-coconut-shell body and two strings tuned in fourths or fifths in a few Malay areas of Sumatra

rebana Ma.; *rabano* Mi. a large frame drum

Reformasi I., the "reformation" era in Indonesia, beginning with Suharto's fall in 1998

rejunk Ma., exchange of sung poetry by lovers and others in the Besemah area of South Sumatra

roh I., Ma., spirit

rondai Ma. Pasisir, a male dance performed outside the bride's house at a Pasisir wedding (between Singkil and Pariaman)

ronggeng See *joget*

rumah gadang Mi., lit. "large house," a house with traditional architecture featuring buffalo horn–shaped roofs

salam Ma., *saleum* Ac. greeting, the opening gesture in a dance

salawat/salawek dulang M., a vocal genre with religious and secular texts accompanied by beating brass trays (*dulang*), usually performed by a pair of men

salendang Mi., *slendang* I., Ma. a long dance shawl that is normally worn around the shoulders, extends to knee length on both sides, and serves as an adjunct to the arm and finger movements in a dance. Sometimes its movements depict a bird flying (e.g., in Besemah and south-coast Minangkabau).

saluang Mi., generic term for a bamboo flute; an end-blown, ring-stop flute

saluang darek Mi., the standard end-blown bamboo flute of the *darek*, an open tube with four finger holes, ca. 70 cm long and 1.5–2.5 cm wide, played on the slant because of its length

saluang panjang Mi., an end-blown bamboo ring flute with three holes and a node at the top, 60–70 cm long and 2–2.5 cm wide, played horizontally

saluang jo dendang Mi., lit. "flute and vocal music"

saluang panjang Mi., an end-blown bamboo ring flute with three holes and a node at the top, 60–70 cm long and 2–2.5 cm wide, played on the slant

saluang Pauah Mi., a whistle block bamboo flute named after the Pauah area (inland from Padang), with six finger holes (of which the top two are grouped together), ca. 40 cm long, like a seven-holed *bansi*

saman Ac., (1) a group performance in sitting position of songs of praise to Allah and the Prophet (a *ratéb*), with or without body percussion, reputed to have been developed in Gayo areas of central Aceh and upstream western Aceh by followers of the Arabic mystic Muhammad Saman centuries ago; (2) a section of a *seudati* performance with song and body percussion.

samman Gayo, a sitting song-dance with body percussion and body movement. See *saman* Ac.

sampelong Mi., *sempelong* Ma. broad, block bamboo flute with four holes (of which the top three are grouped together), 50–60 cm x ca. 4 cm, with mystical associations, from the Limapuluh Kota area in the *darek*. The player's lips must be placed inside the bamboo mouthpiece.

sanggar I., workshop, a semiprofessional or professional dance troupe and dance school

sarunai Ma., Mi., an oboe

saut-sautan I., M., exchange of improvised verses in performance with another singer

sendratari I., dance drama; combines *seni* (art), *drama* and *tari* (dance)

Serampang 12 a form of the Malay *joget* dance genre choreographed by Sayuti in 1934. It has twelve dance steps, said to depict a couple's love story from courtship to marriage.

serdam Ma., an end-blown bamboo ring flute in Minangkabau, South Sumatra, and Jambi

setan I., Ma., a malicious spirit

seudati Ac., an all-male or all-female song-dance genre performed by a pair of solo vocalists and eight solo dancers in standing and stepping formations with elaborate body percussion and body movement. At traditional feasts, performances last all night for several nights, with a solo vocalist singing entertaining and humorous *panton* on any topic, often making controversial political, social, sexual, or religious references.

seudati agam,   Ac., male *seudati* song-dance

seudati inong   Ac., female *seudati* song-dance

seudati tunang   Ac., a contest between two *seudati* troupes

seung   Ac., a makeshift wooden stage with a palm-leaf roof and decorations

seuruné kalée   Ac., an oboe played with circular breathing in ensemble with drums, frame drums, and an optional small *canang* kettle-gong. Its slightly conical hardwood pipe is ca. 40–45 cm long, and it has six or seven front finger holes, one back hole, and a 6–15 cm wide flare attached to its lower end.

sholat   I., five daily prayers

sibaso   Mand., traditional healer, shaman

sifeut   Ac., Ar., a recitation of the characteristics of God

sijobang   Mi., a vocal epic from Payakumbuh with matchbox percussion or *kacapi* accompaniment

sikambang asli   Ma., lit. "original *sikambang*," Malay spells sung by shamans to call the wind or calm the waves at sea (usually at a high pitch); songs sung by bards telling the "Sikambang" legend; formal lullabies by women at baby thanksgivings and weddings along Sumatra's west coast (between Meulaboh and Krui, including Pulau Banyak and other islands)

sikambang kapri   Ma., couples song-dances with vocal, violin, and frame-drum accompaniment performed at baby thanksgivings, weddings, and circumcisions on Sumatra's west coast between Sibolga and Barus, including on offshore Pulau Banyak and other islands, with texts on love, the mermaid Sikambang, nature, etc.

silat Ma.; *silek* Mi.   martial arts

sirih   Ma., betel leaf and nut

sléndro   Jav., pentatonic tone system, with three modal scales

songket   Ma., a luxury silk or cotton cloth woven with a supplementary gold or silver metal weft

suku   I., clan, extended family group who usually trace their descent to a common ancestor, ethnic subgroup

suku bangsa   I., ethnicity

Suku Dalem   Ma., lit. "People of the Forest," nomadic or seminomadic people who prefer to live in the forest

Suku Kubu   Ma., one of the *Suku Dalem* subgroups of South Sumatra and Jambi

Suku Laut   See *Orang Suku Laut*

Suku Lubu   Ma., one of the *Suku Dalem* subgroups near the Mandailing area in North Sumatra

Suku Sekak   Ma., one of the *Suku Laut* subgroups of Bangka and Belitung

Suku Terasing   I., Ma., lit. "Isolated People," including the *Suku Laut* and the *Suku Dalem* groups

suléng   Ac., bamboo flute

surau   Mi., village prayer house, Muslim school and boarding house for males

syahé   Ac., See *aneuk syahé*

syair   Ma., a quatrain with an a a a a rhyming scheme

syéh, céh, chéh   Ac., from *syaich* Ar., master, dance leader

tabuik, tabot   See *tabut*

tabut Ar. (coffin); *tabuik* Mi.; *tabot* Bengk.   a Shi'a ritual commemorating the battle of Karbala, with *dol* and *tasa* or *gandang tambua* drumming *talempong* (*caklempong*)   Mi., a single kettle-gong, a gong-chime, or an ensemble minimally containing a *talempong* set and drums

talempong duduak   Mi., lit. "seated *talempong*," a row of *talempong* kettles arranged in a wooden rack or frame and beaten by a player with one or two sticks

talempong pacik   Mi., lit. "held *talempong*," two, three, or more pairs of handheld kettle-gongs played by a group walking in a procession

talibun   Ma., a poetic genre performed by singers and bards along Sumatra's west coast and some inland areas, especially at weddings. In *talibun pasisir* or *ende-ende Tapanuli,* a man and a woman may exchange verses about love , longing, etc., in verses that may contain six, eight, ten, or twelve lines, including a *sampiran* (analogy) and an *isi* (main content). In some areas the verse has up to twenty lines.

tambo   Mi., a mythical history, or a skinless frame drum with jingles attached

tambua   Mi., large, cylindrical, double-headed drums

tarekat Ma.; *tarèkat* Ac., from *tariqa* Ar.   mystical path, a Sufi brotherhood

tari payung Ma.; *tari payuang* Mi.   umbrella dance

tari piring Ma.; *tari piriang* Mi.   plate dance

tari serampang duabelas   a traditional Malay social dance, especially popular on Sumatra's east coast

tari slendang I.; *tari salendang* Ma., Mi.   shawl dance

tasa pant   Mi., a kettledrum of Persian origin played in *tabuik/tabut*

tassawuf   Ar., litany, a mystical Sufi practice that aims to improve knowledge of the inner self (*'ilm al'batin* Ar.). It developed in the seventh century C.E. in the Middle East and spread to Southeast Asia and other areas of the Muslim world

tingkah   Ma., interlocking, e.g., *rapa'i tingkah* Ac., interlocking frame-drum playing

top padé   Ac., a rice-stamping trough, the name of a formation in the *seudati* dance

tukang   I., a skilled craftsman, including a musician; e.g., a *tukang rabab* is a professional or semiprofessional *rabab* player.

turun ke air I., Ma.; *turun ka aek* Mi.   lit. "go down to the river/water," a subject's ritual wash, e.g., a bride before her wedding, or a baby before his or her first haircut. A well or a bowl of water may substitute for the river.

ulama   Ma., a religious leader who may run a *madrasah* or *pesantren* (Muslim boarding school), give sermons (*kotbah*), or preside over Muslim rituals. The title may also be given to a re-spected old man.

ulèëbalang   Ac., from *ulèe* (head), *balang* (soldier); aristocrat and administrative/ military chief in colonial-era Acehnese chiefdoms

ulu   Ma., upstream

witr Ar.; *wird* Ac.   litany, chant

zapin Ar.; *japin* Ma.   a traditional Malay group or couples dance performed in the former Malay palaces in Sumatra, Malaya, and Kalimantan and still popular in east-coastal Sumatra and Malaysia. Traditionally performed by all-male groups or by pairs of girls assuming both the male and the female couples roles, at weddings, circumcisions, and other celebrations. Usu-ally accompanied by a Malay ensemble including a solo singer, violin, oboe, *akordion*, and drums (*gendang, ketipung,* and *marwas*).

Abdullah, Taufik. 1966. "Adat and Islam: An Examination of Conflict in Minangkabau." *Indonesia* 2 (October): 1–24.

——. 1970. *Some Notes on the Kaba Tjindau Mato: An Example of Minangkabau Literature.* Ithaca: Cornell University Modern Indonesian Project.

——. 1989. "Islam and the Foundation of Tradition in Indonesia: A Comparative Perspective." In *India and Indonesia: General Perspectives*, ed. J. C. Heesterman et al., 17–36. Leiden: Grafaria.

Abdurachman, Paramita R. 1974. "Portuguese Presence in Jakarta." Paper presented at the Sixth International Conference of Asian History, International Association of Historians of Asia, Yogyakarta.

——. 1982. "Portuguese Settlements and Christian Communities in Solor and Flores (1556–1630)." Paper presented at Asian Studies Association of Australia Conference, Monash University.

Acciaioli, Greg. 1985. "Culture as Art: From Practice to Spectacle in Indonesia." *Canberra Anthropology* 8:148–72.

Adam, Boestanoel Arifin. 1986–87. *Talempong: Musik tradisi Minangkabau.* Kokar: Padang Panjang.

Adelaar, Alexander. 1992. *Proto Malayic: The Reconstruction of Its Phonology and Parts of Its Lexicon and Morphology.* Canberra: Department of Linguistics, Research School of Pacific Studies, Australian National University.

Al-Faruqi, Lois Ibsen. 1981. *An Annotated Glossary of Arabic Musical Terms.* Westport, CT: Greenwood.

Amir, Iwan. 2006. "Sing, Adapt, Persevere: Dynamics of Traditional Vocal Performers in the Islamic Region of Aceh from the Late 19th to the Early 21st Century." PhD diss., Monash University.

Amirullah, Tgk H. M. Divah. 2006. "Musyawarah Ulama Kabupaten Aceh Utara dan Kota Lhokseumawe, Kesimpulan." Typescript.

Andaya, Barbara Watson. 1989. "The Cloth Trade in Jambi and Palembang Society during the Seventeenth and Eighteenth Centuries." *Indonesia* 42:27–46.

——. 1993. *To Live as Brothers: Southeast Sumatra in the Seventeenth and Eighteenth Centuries.* Honolulu: University of Hawaii Press.

——. 1995. "Upstreams and Downstreams in Early Modern Sumatra." *The Historian* 57.3:537–52.

Andaya, Leonard. 1975a. *The Kingdom of Johor 1641–1728.* Kuala Lumpur: Oxford University Press.

——. 1975b. "The Structure of Power in Seventeenth Century Johor." In *Pre-Colonial State Systems in Southeast Asia*, ed. A. Reid and L. Castles, 1–11. Kuala Lumpur: Malaysian Branch of the Royal Asiatic Society.

——. 2002. "Aceh's Contribution to Standards of Malayness." *Archipel* 61:29–68.

——. 2008. *Leaves of the Same Tree: Trade and Ethnicity in the Straits of Melaka.* Honolulu: University of Hawaii Press.

Anderbeck, Karl, R. 2008. *Malay Dialects of the Batanghari River Basin*. Jambi, Sumatra: SIL International.

Anderson, J. (1826) 1971. *Mission to the East Coast of Sumatra in 1823*. Kuala Lumpur: Oxford University Press.

Anon. 1918a. "Hasan-Hoesein of Taboet-feest." In *Encyclopaedie van Nederlandsch-Indië*, 2:63–64. The Hague: Martinus Nijhoff; Leiden: Brill.

———. 1918b. "Kouta Radja." In *Encyclopaedie van Nederlandsch-Indië*, 2:373–74. The Hague: Martinus Nijhoff; Leiden: Brill.

Apel, W. 1970. *The Harvard Dictionary of Music*. London: Heinemann.

Ara, K. L. 2009. *Ensiklopedi Aceh: Musik, tari, teater, Seni Rupa, Banda Aceh*. Aceh: Yayasan Mata Air Jernih & Badan Arsdip dan Perpustakaan Aceh.

Aragon, Lorraine V. 2000. *Fields of the Lord: Animism, Christianity and State Development in Indonesia*. Honolulu: University of Hawaii Press.

Arbeau, Thoinot. (1589) 1967. *Orchesography*. Trans. M. S. Evans. New York: Dover.

Arps, Bernard. 1992. *Tembang in Two Traditions*. London: School of Oriental and African Studies.

Aspinall, Edward. 2005. *The Helsinki Agreement: A More Promising Basis for Peace in Aceh?* Washington, DC: East-West Center.

Assman, Jan. 1988. "Kollektives Gedächtnis und kulturelle Identität." In *Kultur und Gedächtnis*, ed. J. Assman and T. Hölscher, 9–19. Frankfurt am Main: Suhrkamp.

———. 1992. "Collective Memory and Cultural Identity." *New German Critique* 65:125–33.

Badan Pusat Statistik. 2001. *Population of Indonesia: Results of the 2000 Population Census*. Series L2.2–L2.2.31. Jakarta.

Baily, John. 1988. *Music of Afghanistan: Professional Musicians in the City of Herat*. Cambridge: Cambridge University Press.

Bakar, Aboe, Budiman Sulaiman, M. Adnan Hanafiah, Zainal Abidin Ibrahim, and H. Syarifah. (1985) 2001. *Kamus bahasa Aceh-Indonesia*. Jakarta: Balai Pustaka.

Bambang Budi Utomo. 1985. "Karanganyar as a Srivijayan Site." Paper presented at the SPAFA [Seameo Regional Centre for Archaeology and Fine Arts] Consultative Workshop on Archaeological and Environmental Studies on Sriwijaya, Jakarta, Medan, Padang, 16–30 September.

Barendregt, Bart. 1995. "Written by the Hand of Allah: *Pencak silat* of Minangkabau, West Sumatra," *Oideion* 2:113–30.

———. 2002a. "The Sound of Longing for Home: Redefining a Sense of Community through Minang Popular Music." *Bijdragen tot de Taal-, Land- en Volkenkunde* 158.3, 411–50.

———. 2002b. "Representing the Ancient Other." *Indonesia and the Malay World* 30.88:277–308.

———. 2005. "From the Realm of Many Rivers: Memory, Places and Notions of Home in the Southern Sumatran Highlands." PhD diss., University of Leiden.

Barnard, Timothy P. 2003. *Multiple Centres of Authority: Society and Environment in Siak and Eastern Sumatra, 1674–1827*. Leiden: KITLV Press.

Bastin, John. 1965. *The British in West Sumatra (1685–1825): A Selection of Documents, Mainly from the East India Company Records Preserved in the India Office Library, Commonwealth Relations Office, London*. Kuala Lumpur: University of Malaya Press.

Bastin, John, and Bea Brommer. 1979. *Nineteenth-Century Prints and Illustrated Books of Indonesia with Particular Reference to the Print Collection of the Tropenmuseum, Amsterdam: A Descriptive Bibliography*. Utrecht: Het Spectrum.

Bauman, Richard. 1986. *Story, Performance, Event*. Cambridge: Cambridge University Press.

Beatty, Andrew. 2009. *A Shadow Falls in the Heart of Java*. London: Faber & Faber.

Becker, Judith. 1993. *Gamelan Stories: Tantrism, Islam, and Aesthetics in Central Java*. Tempe: Program for Southeast Asian Studies, Arizona State University.

Bellwood, Peter. 1985. *Prehistory of the Indo-Malaysian Archipelago*. Sydney: Academic Press.

———. 1995. "Austronesian Prehistory in Southeast Asia: Homeland, Expansion and Transformation." In *The Austronesians: Historical and Comparative Perspectives*, ed. Peter Bellwood, James J. Fox, and Darrell Tyron, 103–18. Canberra: Department of Anthropology, Research School of Pacific and Asian Studies, Australian National University.

Belo, Jane. 1960. *Trance in Bali*. New York: Columbia University Press.

Benda, H. J. 1958. *The Crescent and the Rising Sun*. The Hague: W. van Hoeve.

Benjamin, Geoffrey. 1976. "Austroasiatic Subgroupings and Prehistory in the Malay Peninsula." In *Austroasiatic Studies*, ed. Phillip Jenner, Laurence C. Thompson, and Stanley Starosta, 1:37–128. Honolulu: University of Hawaii Press.

———. 2002. "On Being Tribal in the Malay World." In Benjamin and Chou, *Tribal Communities in the Malay World*, 7–76.

Benjamin, Geoffrey, and Cynthia Chou, eds. 2002. *Tribal Communities in the Malay World: Historical, Cultural and Social Perspectives*. Leiden: International Institute for Asian Studies; Singapore: Institute of Southeast Asian Studies.

Besin, A. F. Kau. 1982. "Gending Sriwijaya" (piano arrangement). *Lagu-lagu Rakyat Indonesia untuk Piano Remaja*, 6–8. Jakarta: Penerbit PT Gramedia.

Blackwood, Evelyn. 1995. "Senior Women, Model Mothers and Dutiful Wives: Managing Gender Contradictions in a Minangkabua Village." In *Bewitching Women, Pious Men: Gender and Body Politics in Southeast Asia*, ed. A. Ong and M. G. Peletz, 124–58. Berkeley: University of California Press.

Boedenani, H. 1976. *Sejarah Sriwijaya*. Bandung: Tarate.

Bolle, Kees W. 1979. "Myth and Mythology." In *Encyclopedia Britannica*, 22:793–804.

Bosch, F. D. K. 1941. "Een Maleische inscriptie in het Buitenzorgsche." *Bijdragen tot de Taal-, Land- en Volkenkunde* 100:49–54.

Bowen, J. R. 1993. *Muslims through Discourse: Religion and Ritual in Gayo Society*. Princeton, NJ: Princeton University Press.

Boxer, Charles Ralph. 1965. *The Dutch Seaborne Empire, 1600–1800*. London: Hutchinson.

———. 1969. *The Portuguese Seaborne Empire, 1415–1825*. London: Hutchinson.

Brakel, Lode F. 1969. "The Birthplace of Hamza Pansuri." *Journal of the Malay(si)an Branch of the Royal Asiatic Society* 42.2:206–22.

———. 1975a. *The Hikayat Muhammad Hanafiyyah*. Leiden: Koninklijk Instituut voor Taal-, Land- en Volkenkunde.

———. 1975b. "State and Statecraft in Seventeenth-Century Aceh." In *Pre-Colonial State Systems in Southeast Asia*, ed. Anthony Reid and Lance Castles, Monographs of the Malaysian Branch of the Royal Asiatic Society, no. 6, 56–66. Kuala Lumpur: Royal Asiatic Society.

———. 1979a. "Notes on Yoga Practices, Lahir dan Zahir, the Taxallos, Punning, a Difficult Passage in the Kitab 'al Muntahi, Hamza's Likely Place of Birth, and Hamza's Imagery." *Journal of the Malay(si)an Branch of the Royal Asiatic Society* 52.1, no. 235:73–98.

———. 1979b. "Hamza Pansuri." *Journal of the Malay(si)an Branch of the Royal Asiatic Society* 52.2:73–98.

Brandes, J. L. A. 1887–1900. "Nog eenige Javaansche piagem's uit het mohammedaansche tijdvak, afkomstig van Mataram, Banten en Palembang." *Tidschrift voor Indische Taal-, Land- en Volkenkunde* 32 (1887): 553–601; 43 (1891): 605–23; 37 (1894): 121–26; 42 (1900): 131–34, 491–507.

Brandts Buys, J. S., and A. van Zijp Brandts Buys. 1928. "De toonkunst bij de Madoereezen." *Djawa* 8:61–349.

Brinkgreve, Francine, and Retno Sulistianingsih, eds. 2010. *Sumatra: Crossroads of Cultures.* Leiden: KITLV Press.

Brown, C. C. 1953. "Sejarah Melayu or 'Malay Annals': A Translation of Raffles MS 18." *Journal of the Malay(si)an Branch of the Royal Asiatic Society* 25.2:7–276.

Bruinessen, Martin van. 1994. "Origins and Development of the Sufi Orders (*Tarèkat*) in Southeast Asia." *Studia Islamika* (Jakarta) 1.1:1–23.

Bruner, Edward M. 1979. "Comments: Modern? Indonesian? Culture?" In *What Is Modern Indonesian Culture?*, ed. Gloria Davis, Southeast Asia Series 52, 300–306. Papers presented at the Indonesian Studies Conference 1976, Indonesian Studies Summer Institute, Madison, Wisconsin. Athens: Ohio University Center for International Studies.

Burckhardt-Qureshi, Regula. 1981. "Islamic Music in an Indian Environment: The Shi'a Majlis." *Ethnomusicology* 25.1:41–72.

Burhan, Firdaus, and Z. Z. Idris, eds. 1986–87. *Ensiklopedi musik dan tari daerah Propinsi Daerah Istimewa Aceh.* Jakarta: Department of Education and Culture, Inventory Project for Documentation of Regional Culture.

Capwell, Charles. 1995. "Contemporary Manifestations of Yemeni-Derived Song and Dance in Indonesia." *Yearbook for Traditional Music* 27:76–89.

Carey, Peter. 1984. "Changing Javanese Perceptions of the Chinese Communities in Central Java, 1755–1825." *Indonesia* 37 (April): 1–47.

Carle, Rainer, ed. 1987. *Cultures and Societies of North Sumatra.* Hamburg: Dietrich Reimer-Verlag.

———. 1990. *Opera Batak: Das Wandertheatre der Toba-Batak in Nord Sumatra.* 2 vols. Hamburg: Dietrich Reimer Verlag.

Caron, Nelly. 1975. "The Ta'zieh: The Sacred Theatre of Iran." *World of Music* 17.4:3–10.

Castles, Lance. 1972. "The Political Life of a Sumatran Residency: Tapanuli 1915–1940." PhD diss., Yale University.

———. 1975. "Statelessness and Stateforming Tendencies among the Bataks before Colonial Rule." In *Pre-Colonial State Systems in Southeast Asia*, ed. Anthony Reid and Lance Castles, 67–76. Kuala Lumpur: Malaysian Branch of the Royal Asiatic Society.

Census of India. 1961. *Moharram in Two Cities, Lucknow and Delhi.* Ed. Roy Burman. Monograph Series 1.3. New Delhi: Ministry of Home Affairs.

Chan, Margaret. 2009. "Chinese New Year in West Kalimantan: Ritual Theatre and Political Circus." *Chinese Southern Diaspora Studies* 3:106–42.

———. Forthcoming. "Nini Towong: The Chinese Connection."

Charles, Nickie, and Felicia Hughes-Freeland, eds. 1996. *Practising Feminism: Identity, Difference, Power.* London: Routledge.

Chattopadhyaya, Alaka. 1981. *Atīsa and Tibet.* Delhi: Motilal Banarsidass.

Chou, Cynthia. 2003. *Indonesian Sea Nomads: Money, Magic, and the Fear of the Orang Suku Laut.* London: RoutledgeCurzon.

———. 2010. *The Orang Suku Laut of Riau, Indonesia: The Inalienable Gift of Territory.* New York: Routledge.

Coedès, G. 1918. "Le Royaume de Sriwijaya." *Bulletin de l'École Française d'Éxtreme-Orient* 18.6:1–36.

———. 1964. *Les états hindouisés d'Indochine et d'Indonésie.* Paris: Editions de Boccard.

———. 1968. *The Indianized States of Southeast Asia.* Ed. Walter F. Vella. Trans. Susan Brown. Honolulu: East-West Center.

Coedès, G., and Louis-Charles Damais. 1992. *Sriwijaya: History, Religion and Language of and Early*

Malay Polity; Collected Studies by George Coedès and Louis-Charles Damais. Monograph no. 20. Kuala Lumpur: Malaysian Branch of the Royal Asiatic Society.

Cohen, Matthew. 2006. *The Komedie Stamboel: Popular Theater in Colonial Indonesia 1891–1903*. Athens: Ohio University Press.

Collet, O. J. A. 1925. *Terres et peuples de Sumatra*. Amsterdam: Societe d'edition "Elsevier."

Collins, Megan. 2003. "The Minangkabau Rabab Pasisia: Music, Performance and Practice in West Sumatra, Indonesia." PhD diss., Victoria University of Wellington.

Collins, William A. 1979. "Besemah Concepts: A Study of the Culture of the People of South Sumatra." PhD diss., University of California, Berkeley.

———. 1998. *The Guritan of Radin Suane: A Study of the Besemah Oral Epic from South Sumatra*. Leiden: KITLV Press.

Colombijn, Freek. 2002. "The Ecology of Sumatran Towns in the Nineteenth Century." In *The Indonesian Town Revisited*, ed. Peter J. M. Nas, 283–95. Münster: Lit Verlag.

Coppell, Charles. 1983. *Indonesian Chinese in Crisis*. Kuala Lumpur: Oxford University Press.

Cortesão, Armando, ed. and trans. (1944) 1967. *The Suma Oriental of Tomé Pires*. 2 vols. London: Kraus.

Daham, Basri. 2003. "Taleb, Seniman dan 'Utoh Rapai' dari Aceh." *Kompas*, 11 April, 4.

Daud, Bukhari, and Mark Durie. 1999. *Kamus basa Aceh = Kamus bahasa Aceh: Acehnese-Indonesian-English Thesaurus*. Canberra: Pacific Linguistics Research School of Asian and Pacific Studies, Australian National University.

———. 2012. *Acehnese Dictionary with Trilingual Thesaurus*. N.p.

De Casparis, J. G., and I. W. Mabbett. 1992. "Religion and Popular Beliefs of Southeast Asia before c.1500." In *The Cambridge History of Southeast Asia, from Early Times to c. 1800*, ed. Nicholas Tarling, 276–339. Cambridge: Cambridge University Press.

De Clercq, F. S. A. 1878. *Het Maleisch der Molukken*. Batavia: W. Bruining.

de Josselin de Jong, Patrick E. 1951. *Minangkabau and Negri Sembilan: Socio-Political Structure in Indonesia*. Leiden: Ijdo.

Departemen Agama. 1972, "Mengapa Seudati itu Tidak Haram." Internal paper.

Deutz, G. J. J. 1874. "Baros." *Tidschrift voor Indische Taal-, Land- en Volkenkunde*, 22:156–63.

Dick, Alistair. 1984. "Daf." In *The New Grove Dictionary of Musical Instruments*, ed. S. Sadie, 1:545. London: Macmillan.

Dick, Howard W., J. H. Houben, J. Thomas Lindblad, and Thee Kian Wie. 2002. *The Emergence of a National Economy: An Economic History of Indonesia, 1800–2000*. ASAA Southeast Asian Publication Series. Sydney: Allen & Unwin African Studies.

Djajadiningrat, Hoesein. 1911. "Critisch overzicht van de in Maleische werken vervatte gegevens over de geschiedenis van het Soeltanaat van Atjeh." *Bijdragen tot de Taal-, Land- en Volkenkunde* 65:135–265.

———. 1934. *Atjèhsch-Nederlandsch Woordenboek*. 2 vols. Batavia: Landsdrukkerij.

Djaruddin Amar, A Najir Yunus St. Tianso. 1989. *Pengantar Pengetahuan Adat*. Padang: CV Cahaya Matahari.

Dobbin, Christine. 1974. "Islamic Revivalism in Minangkabau at the Turn of the Nineteenth Century." *Modern Asian Studies* 8:319–45.

———. 1981. *The Minangkabau Response to Dutch Colonial Rule in the Nineteenth Century*. Ithaca, NY: Cornell University Press.

———. 1983. *Islamic Revivalism in a Changing Present Economy: Central Sumatra, 1784–1847*. London: Curzon Press.

Doubleday, Veronica. 1999. "The Frame Drum in the Middle East: Women, Musical Instruments and Power." *Ethnomusicology* 43.1:101–34.

Dournon, Genevieve, and Margaret Kartomi. 1984. "Tasa." In *The New Grove Dictionary of Musical Instruments*, ed. S. Sadie, 3:532. London: Macmillan.

Drakard, Jane. 1982. "The Upland and Downland Rajas of Barus: A North Sumatran Case Study." In *The Malay-Islamic World of Sumatra: Studies in Politics and Culture*, ed. John Maxwell, 74–94. Clayton, Victoria: Monash University, Centre of Southeast Asian Studies, 1982

———. 1984. "A Malay Frontier: The Adaptation of Malay Political Culture in Barus." MA thesis, Monash University.

———. 1986. "Ideological Adaptation on a Malay Frontier." *Journal of Southeast Asian Studies* 17.1:39–58.

———. (1988) 2003. *Sejarah raja-raja Barus: Dua naskah dari Barus*. Jakarta: Gramedia.

———, ed. 1989. "An Indian Ocean Port: Sources for the Early History of Barus." *Archipel* 37:53–82.

———. 1990. *A Malay Frontier: Unity and Duality in a Sumatran Kingdom*. Ithaca, NY: Cornell University Press, Southeast Asia Program.

———. 1999. *A Kingdom of Words: Language and Power in Sumatra*. Kuala Lumpur: Oxford University Press.

Drewes, G. W. J. 1968. *New Light on the Coming of Islam to Indonesia?* The Hague: Martinus Nijhoff.

———, ed. and trans. 1979. *Hikajat Potjut Muhamat: An Acehnese Epic*. The Hague: Martinus Nijhoff.

———. 1980. *Two Achehnese Poems: Hikajat Ranto and Hikajat Teungku di Meuké*. The Hague: Martinus Nijhoff.

Dumas, Robert Martin. 2000. *"Teater Abdulmuluk" in Zuid-Sumatra op de drempel van een nieuw tijdperk*. Leiden: Research School for Asian, African and Amerindian Studies, Leiden University.

Durie, Mark, 1990. "Proto-Chamic and Acehnese Mid-Vowels: Towards Proto-Aceh-Chamic." *Bulletin of the School of Oriental and African Studies* no 1:100–114.

During, Jean. 1984. "Dohol." In *The New Grove Dictionary of Musical Instruments*, ed. S. Sadie, 1:580. London: Macmillan.

Ediwar. *Indang Pariaman: Dari tradisi surau ke seni pertunjukan rakyat Minangkabau*. Bandung: Universitas Pendidikan Indonesia, 2007.

Effendy, Tenas. 1997a. *Bujang Tan Domang: Sastra lisan orang Petalangan*. Yogyakarta: École Française D'Extrême-Orient.

———. 1997b. "Petalangan Society and Changes in Riau." In *Riau in Transition*, ed. Cynthia Chou and Will Derks, Bijdragen tot de Taal-, Land- en Volkenkunde 153, no. 4, 630–47. Leiden: KITLV.

———. 2002. "The Orang Petalangan of Riau and the Forest Environment." In Benjamin and Chou, *Tribal Communities of the Malay World*, 364–83.

Fachruddin, Chalida. 1982, 1983. "'Mahoyak Tabuik': Kesenian Tradisonal Pariaman." *Waspada Daily*, Medan, 30 December 1982; 6 January 1983, 6.

Fansuri, H. Aspul. 1980. "Ikatan Keluarga Bear Pesisir Tapanuli Tengah." *Pembangunan Khusus Kecamatan Barus/Sorkam dan Sekitarnya*. Roneoed booklet, Jakarta.

Farmer, Henry G. 1952. "The Religious Music of Islam." *Journal of the Royal Asiatic Society* 1.2 (April): 60–65.

———. 1957. "The Music of Islam." *New Oxford History of Music*. Vol. 1. London: Oxford University Press.

Ferrand, G. 1913. *Relations de voyages et textes géographiques Arabes, Persans et Turks relatifs à l'Extrême-Orient du VIIIe siècles*. 2 vols. Paris: E. Leroux.

Flora, Reis. 1995. "Styles of the Śahnāī in Recent Decades: From *Naubat* to *Gāyakī Ang.*" *Yearbook for Traditional Music* 27:52–75.

Foley, William A. 1981. Map of Sumatra Linguistic Groups. In *Language Atlas of the Pacific Area*, ed. S. A. Wurm and Shiro Hattori, 38. Canberra: Australian Academy of the Humanities and the Japan Academy.

Fontein, Jan. 1990. *The Sculpture of Indonesia*. Washington, DC: National Gallery of Art.

Forbes, H. O. 1885. "On the Kubus of Sumatra." *Journal of the Royal Anthropological Institute* 15:121–26.

Forbes, Mark. 2007. "Pop Groups Fall Foul of Stricter Religious Climate in Aceh." *The Age* (Melbourne), 26 August, 10.

Fox, James. 1979. "The Ceremonial System of Savu." In *The Imagination of Reality: Essays on Southeast Asian Coherence Systems*, ed. A. Becker and A. A. Yengoyan, 145–73. Norwood, NJ: Ablex.

Francis, E. 1839. "Korte beschrijving van het Nederlandsch grondgebied ter Westkust van Sumatra 1837." *Tijdschrift voor Nederlandsch-Indie* 2:28–45.

Fraser, Jennifer A. 2007. "Packaging Ethnicity: State Institutions, Cultural Entrepreneurs, and the Professionalization of Minangkabau Music in Indonesia." PhD diss., University of Illinois at Urbana-Champaign.

Frey, Katherine Stenger. 1986. *Journey to the Land of the Earth Goddess*. Jakarta: Gramedia Publishing Division.

Funke, Friedrich W. 1961. *Volkstum Sued-Sumatras im Wandel*, vol. 2, *Das Leben in der Gegenwart*. Leiden: E. J. Brill.

Gade, Anna. 2004. *Perfection Makes Practice: Learning, Emotion, and the Recited Qur'an in Indonesia*. Honolulu: University of Hawaii Press.

Gallop, Rodney. 1933. "The Folk Music of Portugal—II." *Music & Letters* 14.4:343–54.

———. 1934. "The Folk-Music of Eastern Portugal." *Musical Quarterly* 20:96–106.

Geertz, Clifford. 1975. *The Interpretation of Cultures*. London: Hutchinson.

———. 1981. *Negara: The Theater State in Nineteenth-Century Bali*. Princeton, NJ: Princeton University Press.

Gittinger, Mattiebelle. 1979. *Splendid Symbols: Textiles and Tradition in Indonesia*. Singapore: Oxford University Press.

Goitein, S. D., ed. 1973. *Letters of Medieval Jewish Traders*. Princeton, NJ: Princeton University Press.

Goldsworthy, David J. 1978. "Honey-Collecting Ceremonies on the East Coast of North Sumatra." In *Studies in Indonesian Music*, ed. Margaret Kartomi, 1–44. Clayton: Centre of Southeast Asian Studies, Monash University.

———. 1979. "Melayu Music of North Sumatra." PhD diss., Monash University.

———. 1986. "The Dancing Fish Trap (*lukah menari*): A Spirit Evocation Song and Spirit-Possession Dance from North Sumatra." *Musicology Australia* 9:12–28.

Graves, Elizabeth E. (1971) 1985. *The Ever-Victorious Buffalo: How the Minangkabau of Indonesia Solved Their "Colonial Question."* Ann Arbor, MI: University Microfilms. (PhD diss., University of Wisconsin, Madison, 1971.)

———. 1981. *The Minangkabau Response to Dutch Colonial Rule in the Nineteenth Century*. Ithaca, NY: Cornell Modern Indonesia Project/Southeast Asia Program, Cornell University.

Grimes, Barbara F., ed. 1996. *The Ethnologue*. 13th ed. Dallas: Summer Institute of Linguistics, 1996.

Guillot, Claude, ed. 1998. *Histoire de Barus, Sumatra: Le site de Lobo Tua*. Vol. 1. Paris: Association Archipel.

———. 2002. *Lobo Tua: Sejarah awal Barus.* Archeological Translation Series 5. Jakarta: École française d'Extrême-Orient.

Hadler, Jeffrey. 2008. *Muslims and Matriarchs: Cultural Resilience in Indonesia through Jihad and Colonialism.* Ithaca, NY: Cornell University Press.

Hagen, Bernard. 1908a. *Die Orang Kubu auf Sumatra.* Frankfurt am Main: Joseph Baer.

———. 1908b. "Beitrag zu Kenntnis der Orang Sekka (Sakat) oder Orang Laut, sowie der Orang Lom oder Mapor, zweier nicht-muhamedanischer Volksstaemme auf der Insel Bangka." *Abhandlungen zur Anthropologie, Ethnologie und Urgeschichte.* Festschrift, 37–46, Frankfurt. Translated in Smedal, *Order and Difference.*

Hajizar. 1988. "Studi Tekstual dan Musikologis Kesenian Tradisional Minangkabau Sijobang: Kaba Anggun Nan Tunggal Magek Jaban." Sarjana (master's) thesis, Universitas Sumatera Utara.

Hall, Robert A. 1966. *Pidgin and Creole Languages.* Ithaca, NY: Cornell University Press.

Harnish, David. 2006. *Bridges to the Ancestors: Music, Myth, and Cultural Politics at an Indonesian Festival.* Honolulu: University of Hawaii Press.

Harrison, F., and J. Harrison. 1968. "Spanish Elements in the Music of Two Maya Groups in Chiapas." *Selected Reports* 1.2:1–44.

Hasselt, A. L. van. 1881a. "De talen en letterkunde van Midden-Sumatra." In *Midden-Sumatra: Reizen en onderzoekingen der Sumatra-expeditie, uitgerust door het Aardrijkskundig Genootschap, 1877–1879,* ed. P. J. Veth, pt. 3, no. 2. Leiden: E. J. Brill.

———. 1881b. "Reizen." In *Midden-Sumatra: Reizen en onderzoekingen der Sumatra-expeditie, uitgerust door het Aardrijkskundig Genootschap, 1877–1879, beschreven door de Leden der Expeditie, onder toezicht van P. J. Veth,* ed. P. J. Veth. Leiden: E. J. Brill.

———. 1882. "Muziek en Muziekinstrumenten: Spelen Dierenrechten." In *Volksbeschrijving van Midden-Sumatra,* ed. P. J. Veth, pt. 3, no. 3, chap. 4, 99–136. Leiden: Brill.

Hastrup, Kirsten. 1998. "Theatre as a Site of Passage: Some Reflections on the Magic of Acting." In *Ritual, Performance, Media,* ed. Felicia Hughes-Freeland, 29–45. New York: Routledge.

Heins, Ernst. 1975. "Kroncong and Tanjidor: Two Cases of Urban Folk Music in Jakarta." *Journal of the Society for Asian Music* 7.1:20–32.

Heinze, R. von. 1909. "Über Batak-Musik." In *Nord-Sumatra,* vol. 1, *Die Batakländer,* ed. Wilhelm Volz, 373–81. Berlin: D. Reimer.

Helfrich, O. L. 1904. *Bijdragen tot de kennis van het Midden Maleisch (Besemahsch en Serawajsch dialect).* Batavia: Landsdrukkerij.

Helfrich, O. L., W. R. Winter, and D. M. J. Schiff. 1888. "Het Hasan-Hosein of Taboet-feest te Bengkoelen." *Internationales Archiv für Ethnographie* 1:191–96.

Herklots, G. A., and Jaffur Shurreef. 1895. *Qanoon-e-Islam or the Customs of the Mussulmans in India.* 2nd ed. Madras: Higginbotham.

Heryanto, Ariel. 1998. "Ethnic Identities and Erasure: Chinese Indonesians in Public Culture." In *Southeast Asian Identities: Culture and Politics of Representation in Indonesia, Malaysia, Singapore, and Thailand,* ed. Joel S Kahn, 95–114. Singapore: Institute of Southeast Asian Studies; London: I. B. Tauris.

Higham, Charles. 1996. *The Bronze Age of Southeast Asia.* Cambridge: Cambridge University Press.

Hobsbawm, Eric. 1983. "Introduction: Inventing Traditions." In Hobsbawm and Ranger, *Invention of Traditions,* 1–14.

Hobsbawm, Eric, and Terence Ranger, eds. 1993. *Invention of Traditions.* Cambridge: Cambridge University Press.

Holt, Claire. 1967. *Art in Indonesia: Continuities and Change.* Ithaca, NY: Cornell University Press.

———. 1971a. "Dances of Sumatra and Nias: Notes." *Indonesia* 11:1–20.

———. 1971b. "Batak Dances: Notes." *Indonesia* 12:65–84.

———. 1972. "Dances of Minangkabau: Notes." *Indonesia* 13:73–78.

Hooker, Virginia Matheson. 1991. *Tuhfat al-Nafis: Sejarah Melayu-Islam.* Kuala Lumpur: Dewan Bahasa dan Pustaka.

Hornbostel, Erich von. 1908. "Ueber die Musik der Kubu." In Hagen, *Die Orang Kubu auf Sumatra,* 243–56.

Hughes, Thomas P. (1885) 1976. *A Dictionary of Islam.* Lahore: Premier Book House.

Hughes-Freeland, Felicia, and Mary M. Crain 1998. "Introduction." In *Recasting Ritual: Performance, Media, Identity,* ed. Felicia Hughes-Freeland and Mary M. McCrain, 1–20. London: Routledge, 1–20.

Husin Nato Dirajo, Raden Moh. 1978. "Wayang Palembang." Typescript.

Hymes, Dell, ed. 1971. *Pidginization and Creolisation of Languages.* Proceedings of a Conference held at the University of the West Indies, Mona, Jamaica, April 1968. London: Cambridge University Press.

Idris, Z. H., ed. 1993. *Peralatan hiburan dan kesenian tradisional Propinsi Daerah Istimewa Aceh.* Jakarta: Department of Education and Culture.

Idrus Hakimy, Dt. Rajo Penghulu. 1997. *Pokok-pokok pengetahuan adat alam Minangkabau.* Bandung: Pt. Remaja Rosdakarya.

Ileto, Reynaldo. 1992. "Religion and Anticolonial Movements." In *The Cambridge History of Southeast Asia,* ed. Nicholas Tarling, 197–248. Cambridge: Cambridge University Press.

Isjkarim et al. 1980–81. *Kesenian tradisional Aceh.* Banda Aceh: Department of Education and Culture, Art Development Project in the Special Region of Aceh.

Iskandar, Teuku. 1958. *De Hikajat Atjeh.* The Hague: Martinus Nijhoff.

———, ed. 1966. *Bustanu's-Salatin of Nuru'd-din ar-Raniri.* Vol. 2, fasc. 13. Kuala Lumpur: Dewan Bahasa dan Pustaka.

Ito, Takeshi. 1984. "The World of the *Adat* Aceh: A Historical Study of the Sultanate of Aceh." PhD diss., Australian National University.

Iwabuchi, Akifumi. 1994. *The People of the Alas Valley: A Study of an Ethnic Group of Northern Sumatra.* Oxford: Clarendon Press.

Jacobs, Julius. 1894. *Het familie—en kampongleven op Groot-Atjeh: Een bijdrage tot de ethnographie van Noord-Sumatra.* Vol. 2. Leiden: E. J. Brill.

James, K. A. "De geboorte van Singa Maharadja en het ontstaan van de Koeria [District] Ilir in de onderafdeeling Baros." *Tidschrift voor Indische Taal-, Land- en Volkenkunde,* 45 (1909): 134–45.

Jansen, A. D. 1980. "Gonrang Music: Its Structure and Function in Simalungun Batak Society in Sumatra." PhD diss., University of Washington.

Jaspan, M. A. 1964. *Folk Literature of South Sumatra: Redjang Ka-Ga-Nga Texts.* Canberra: Australian National University.

———. 1976. "Redjang Complex." In *Insular Southeast Asia: Ethnographic Studies,* section 1: *Sumatra,* ed. Frank M. Lebar. New Haven, CT: Human Relations Area Files.

Joustra, M. 1915. *Van Medan naar Padang en Terug.* Leiden: Doesburgh.

———. 1923. *Minangkabau: Overzicht van land, geschiedenis en volk.* The Hague: Martinus Nijhoff.

———. 1926. *Batakspiegel.* 2nd ed. Leiden: Doesburgh.

Kaeppler, A., and J. W. Love, eds. 1998. "Australia and the Pacific Islands." In *The Garland Encyclopedia of World Music,* 9:316. New York: Garland.

Kahin, Audrey. 1999. *Rebellion to Integration: West Sumatra and the Indonesian Polity, 1926–1998.* Amsterdam: Amsterdam University Press.

Kahn, Joel S. 1993. *Constituting Minangkabau: Peasants, Culture, and Modernity in Colonial Indonesia*. Providence, RI: Berg.

———. 1995. *Culture, Multiculture, Postculture*. London: Sage.

Kaplan, Mordecai. (1957) 1981. *Judaism as a Civilization: Toward a Reconstruction of American Jewish Life*. 2nd ed. Philadelphia: Jewish Publication Society; Reconstructist Press.

Kartomi, Karen. 1986. "Mendu Theatre on the Island of Bunguran, Sumatra." BA honors thesis, Monash University.

Kartomi, Margaret. 1977. "With Bells and Drums." *Hemisphere* 21:21–28.

———. 1979. "Minangkabau Musical Culture: The Contemporary Scene and Recent Attempts at Its Modernization." In *What Is Modern Indonesian Culture?*, ed. Gloria Davis, 9–36. Athens: Ohio University Press, Center for International Studies.

———. 1981a. "Randai Theatre in West Sumatra: Components, Music, Origins and Recent Change." *Review of Indonesian and Malayan Studies* 15.1:1–44.

———. 1981b. "The Processes and Results of Musical Culture Contact: A Discussion of Terminology and Concepts." *Ethnomusicology* 25.2:227–49.

———. 1982. "Javanese Gamelan Aesthetics: Some Preliminary Thoughts." In *Proceedings of the 30th International Congress of Human Sciences in Asia and North Africa, Southeast Asia*, vol. 1, ed. Graciela de la Lama, 217–26. El Colegio de Mexico.

———. 1984. "Nobat." In *The New Grove Dictionary of Musical Instruments*, ed. S. Sadie, 2:771–72. London: Macmillan.

———. 1985. *Musical Instruments of Indonesia: An Introductory Handbook*. Melbourne: Indonesian Arts Society.

———. 1990. *On Concepts and Classifications of Musical Instruments*. Chicago: University of Chicago Press.

———. 1992. "Experience-Near and Experience-Distant Perceptions of the *Daboih* Ritual in Aceh, Sumatra". In *Von der Vielfalt musikalischer Kultur: Festschrift für Josef Kuckertz, zur Vollendung des 60. Lebensjahres*, ed. Rüdiger Schumacher, 247–60. Anif/Salzburg: Verlag Ursula Müller-Speiser.

———. 1993a. "Revival of Feudal Music, Dance, and Ritual in the Former 'Spice Islands' of Ternate and Tidore." In *Culture and Society in New Order Indonesia*, ed. Virginia Matheson Hooker, 185–210. Kuala Lumpur: Oxford University Press.

———. 1998. "Sumatra." In *The Garland Encyclopedia of World Music*, vol. 4, *Southeast Asia*, ed. T. E. Miller, 598–629. New York: Garland.

———. 2000. "Indonesian-Chinese Oppression and the Musical Outcomes in the Netherlands East Indies." In *Music and the Racial Imagination*, ed. Ronald Radano and Philip V. Bohlman, 271–317. Chicago: University of Chicago Press.

———. 2002. "Meaning, Style and Change in *Gamalan* and *Wayang Kulit Banjar* since their transplantation from Hindu-Buddhist Java to South Kalimantan." *World of Music* 44.2: 17–55.

———. 2004. "Some Implications of Local Concepts of Space in the Dance, Music and Visual Arts of Aceh." *Yearbook for Traditional Music* 36:1–42.

———. 2005. "On Metaphor and Analogy in the Concepts and Classifications of Musical Instruments in Aceh." *Yearbook for Traditional Music* 37:25–57.

———. 2006. "Aceh's Body Percussion: From Ritual Devotionals to Global *Niveau*." *Musiké: International Journal of Ethnomusicological Studies* 1:85–108.

———. 2007. "The Art of Body Percussion and Movement in Aceh and Its Links in Countries around the Northern Rim of the Indian Ocean and the Mediterranean." Paper presented at the Congrès des Musiques dans le monde de l'islam, Assilah, August 2007. Available online at http://www.mcm.asso.fr/site02/music-w-islam/articles/Kartomi-2007.pdf , accessed 29 November 2011.

———. 2010a. "The Development of the Acehnese Sitting Song-Dances and Frame-Drum Genres as Part of Religious Conversion and Continuing Piety." *Bijdragen tot de Taal-, Land- en Volkenkunde* 166.1:83–106.

———. 2010b. "Toward a Methodology of War and Peace Studies in Ethnomusicology: The Case of Aceh, 1976–2009." *Ethnomusicology* 54.3:452–83.

———. 2010c. Review of *Songs from the Uma: Music from Siberut Island (Mentawei Archipelago), Indonesia* (2009, Ethnic Series. PAN Records PAN 2111/12). *Yearbook for Traditional Music* 42: 225–26.

———. 2011a. "'Art with a Muslim Theme'" and "Art with a Muslim flavor" in the Body Percussion Song/Dances in Aceh." In *Divine Inspiration: Music and Islam in Indonesia*, ed. David Harnish and Ann Rasmussen, 269–96. New York: Oxford University Press.

———. 2011b. "Traditional and Modern Forms of *Pencak Silat* in Indonesia: The Suku Mamak in Riau." *Musicology Australia* 33.1:47–68.

———. 2011. "Music: Muslim Women's Activities and Contributions to Modern Music." In "Contemporary Muslim Societies: Indonesia," *Encyclopedia of Women and Islamic Cultures*, ed. Suad Joseph. Leiden: Brill.

Kartomi, Margaret, with Iwan Amir. 2005. "The Female Vocal and Body Percussion Arts in Meulaboh, West Aceh: Song Texts and the Gender Divide." In *Bahasa Sastra dan Budaya dalam Untaian Karya: Sebuah Cemetuk Persembahan untuk Prof HTA Ridwan PhD*, ed. T. Thyrhaya Zein et al., 157–83. Medan: Universitas Sumatera Utara Press.

Kathirithamby-Wells, J. 1969. "Acehnese Control over West Sumatra up to the Treaty of Painan, 1663." *Journal of South Asian History* 10.3:453–79.

———. 1977. *The British West-Sumatran Presidency, 1760–1785: Problems of Early Colonial Enterprise*. Kuala Lumpur: University of Malaya Press.

Kathirithamby-Wells, J., and Muhammad Yusoff Hashim. 1985. *The "Syair Mukomuko": Some Historical Aspects of a Nineteenth-Century Sumatran Court Chronicle*. Kuala Lumpur: Malaysian Branch of the Royal Asiatic Society.

Kato, Tsuyoshi. 1980. "The World of Minangkabau Coastal Merchants in the Nineteenth Century." *Journal of Asian Studies* 39.4 (August): 729–52.

———. 1982. *Matrilineality and Migration: Evolving Minangkabau Traditions in Indonesia*. Ithaca, NY: Cornell University Press.

Kaudern, Walter A. 1927. *Musical Instruments in Celebes*. Ed. B. Hagen. Ethnographical Studies in Celebes 3. Göteborg: Elanders Boktryckeri.

Kealiinohomoku, Joann W. 1965. "Dance and Self-Accompaniment." *Ethnomusicology* 9.3:292–95.

Kell, T. 1995. *The Roots of the Acehnese Rebellion, 1989–1992*. Ithaca, NY: Cornell Modern Indonesia Project, Southeast Asia Program, Cornell University.

Keuning, J. 1953–54. "Toba-Bataks en Mandailing-Bataks: Hun culturele samenhang en daadwerkelijk antagonisme." *Indonesië* 7:156–73.

Kielstra, E. B. 1887. "Onze kennis van Sumatra's Westkust, omstreeks de helfd der achttiende eeuw." *Bijdragen tot de Taal-, Land- en Volkenkunde* 36:499–559.

Kipp, Rita Smith. 1974. "Karo Batak Religion and Social Structure." *Sumatra Research Bulletin* 3.2:4–11.

———. (1991) 1996. *Dissociated Identities: Ethnicity, Religion, and Class in an Indonesian Society*. Ann Arbor: University of Michigan Press.

Kornhauser, Bronia. 1978. "In Defense of *Kroncong*." In *Studies in Indonesian Music*, ed. Margaret Kartomi, 104–83. Melbourne: Centre of Southeast Asian Studies, Monash University.

Kreemer, J. 1922–23. *Atjèh, algemeen samenvattend overzicht van land en volk van Atjèh en onderhoorigden*. 2 vols. Leiden: E. J. Brill.

Krom, N. J. 1931. *Hindoe-Javaansche Geschiedenis*. 2nd ed. The Hague: Martinus Nijhoff.

Kunst, Japp. 1942. "Music in Nias." In *Internationales Archiv für Ethnographie*, trans. J. S. A. Carriene-Lagaay, 42:1–92. Leiden: E. J. Brill.

———. (1949) 1973. *Music in Java: Its History, Its Theory and Its Technique*. Trans. and ed. Ernst L. Heins. 2nd rev. ed. 2 vols. The Hague: Martinus Nijhoff. Originally published as *De toonkunst van Java* (The Hague: Martinus Nijhoff, 1934).

———. 1950. "Die 2000-jährige Geschichte Süd-Sumatras im Spiegel ihrer Musik." In *Kongressbericht Luneberg*, ed. Hans Elbrecht, 160–67. Kassel: Bärenreiter.

Langenberg, M. van. 1977. "North Sumatra under Dutch Colonial Rule: Aspects of Structural Change." *Review of Indonesian and Malaysian Affairs* 11.1:74–110.

Lasiyo. 1992. "Agama Khonghucu: An Emerging Form of Religious Life among the Indonesian Chinese." PhD diss., School of Oriental and African Studies, University of London.

Latham, Ronald. 1978. *The Travels of Marco Polo*. Middlesex: Penguin, 1978.

LeBar, Frank M., comp. 1976. "Sumatra." Sec. 2 in *Insular Southeast Asia: Ethnographic Studies*. New Haven, CT: Human Relations Area Files.

Lee Ham King. 1995. *The Sultanate of Aceh: Relations with the British, 1760–1824*. Kuala Lumpur: Oxford University Press.

Legge, J. D. 1964. *Indonesia*. Englewood Cliffs, NJ: Prentice Hall.

Lekkerkerker, Cornelis. 1916. *Land en Volk van Sumatra*. Leiden: E. J. Brill.

Lévi-Strauss, Claude. 1963. *Structural Anthropology*. New York: Basic Books.

Levtzion, Nehemia. 1997. "Eighteenth-Century Sufi Brotherhoods: Structural, Organizational and Ritual Changes." In *Islam: Essays and Scripture, Thought and Society; A Festschrift in Honour of Anthony H. Johns*, ed. Peter G. Riddell and Tony Street, 147–66. Leiden: E. J. Brill.

Lewis, Paul, M., ed. 2009. "Sumatra" (map). In *Ethnologue: Languages of the World*, 16th ed. Dallas: SIL International, 2001. Available online at http://www.ethnologue/com/, accessed 29 November 2011.

Loeb, Edwin M. (1935) 1972. *Sumatra: Its History and People*. New York: Oxford University Press.

Loeb, Edwin M., and R. Heine-Geldern. 1935. *Sumatra: Its History and People; The Archaeology and Art of Sumatra*. Vienna: Verlag des Instituts für Völkerkunde der Universität Wien.

Lombard, Denys. 1967. *Le Sultanat d'Atjéh au temps d'Iskandar Muda (1607–1636)*. Paris : École Française d'Extreme-Orient.

———. 1988. "Une autre Méditerranée dans le Sud-Est asiatique." *Hérodote: Revue de géographie et de la géopolitique* 88:184–92. Translated into English by Nola Cooke as "Another 'Mediterranean' in Southeast Asia," *Chinese Southern Diaspora Studies* 1 (2007): 3–9. An edited version is published in *Japan Focus* online at http://www.japanfocus.org/-Denys-Lombard/2371.

Lubis, Abdur-Razzaq. 2004. "The Transformation of Traditional Mandailing Leadership in Malaysia and Indonesia in the Age of Globalisation and Regional Autonomy." Available online at http://www.mandailing.org/mandailing/columns/autonomy.htm, accessed 27 January 2010.

Lubis, Mhd. Arbain. 1993. *Sejarah Marga-Marga asli di tanah Mandailing*. Medan: Departemen Pendidikan dan Kebudayaan.

Lubis, Raja Junjungan. 1980. "Sirih Adat Lambing Permusyawaratan Persatu Paduan dan Kegotong Royongan." In *Buku Warisan Marga-Marga Tapanuli Selatan Turun-Kemurun*, ed. H.

Anwar Harahap, 30–41. Medan : Yayasan Manula Glamur; punguan Manula Marga-marga Tapanuli Selatan.

Ma, Huan. (1433) 1970. *Ying-yai sheng-lan: The Overall Survey of the Ocean's Shores*. Trans. from the Chinese text and edited by Chengjun Feng. Introductory notes and appendices by J. V. G. Mills. Cambridge: Cambridge University Press/Hakluyt Society.

Manggis, M. Rasjid. 1979. *Randai Sebagai Teater Arena Minangkabau*. Padang: Department of Culture. Roneoed publication.

———. 1989. *Malin Deman*. Pustaka: Bukit Tinggi.

Manguin, P.-Y. 1993. "Trading Ships of the South China Sea." *Journal of the Economic and Social History of the Orient* 36:253–80.

Manik, Liberty. 1970. "Gondang-Musik als Ueberlieferungsgestalt altvoelkischer Lebensordnung." *Bijdragen tot de Taal-, Land- en Volkenkunde* 126:400–428.

———. 1973–74. "Eine Studienreise zur Erforschung der rituellen Gondang-Musik der Batak auf Nord-Sumatra." *Mitteilungen der Deutschen Gesellschaft für Musik des Orients* 12:134–37.

———. 1977. "Suku Batak dengan 'Gondang Batak'nya." *Peninjau* 4.1:66–76.

Mansurnoor, Lik Arifin. 2009. "Response of Southeast Asian Muslims to the Increasingly Globalized World: Discourse and Action." *Historia Actual On Line* (5 October 2004): 103–11. Available online at http://www.historia-actual.com/hao/Volumes/Volume1/Issue5/esp/v1i5c10.pdf, accessed 29 January 2010.

Manusuma, A. Th. 1922. *Komedie Stamboel of de Oost-Indische opera*. Batavia: Weltevreden.

Mariam, M. A. 2002. "Singapore's Orang Selatar, Orang Kallang and Orang Selat: The Last Settlements." In Benjamin and Chou, *Tribal Communities in the Malay World*, 273–92.

Marsden, William. (1811) 1966. *The History of Sumatra*. 3rd ed. Kuala Lumpur: Oxford University Press.

Mason, Paul H. 2008 "The End of Fasting, Inside Indonesia." *Inside Indonesia* 93. Available online at http://insideindonesia.org/content/view/1126/47/, accessed 21 September 2011.

———. 2009. "Gestures of Power and Grace." *Inside Indonesia* 96. Available at http://www.insideindonesia.org/edition-97/gestures-of-power-and-grace, accessed 21 September 2011.

———. 2010. "Islamic New Year in West Sumatra." *Inside Indonesia*, 9 December 2010. Available online at http://www.insideindonesia.org/stories/islamic-new-year-in-west-sumatra-09121378, accessed 29 November 2011.

Matheson, Virginia. 1975. "Concepts of State in the *Tuhfat al Nafis*." In *Pre-Colonial State Systems in Southeast Asia*, ed. Anthony Reid and Lance Castles, 12–22. Kuala Lumpur: Malaysian Branch of the Royal Asiatic Society.

McKinnon, Edmund Edwards. 1984. "*Kota Cina*: Its Context and Meaning in the Trade of Southeast Asia in the Twelfth to Fourteenth Centuries." 2 vols. PhD diss., Cornell University.

———. 1985. "Early Politics in Southern Sumatra: Some Preliminary Observations Based on Archaeological Evidence." *Indonesia* 40:1–37.

———. 1996. "Medieval Tamil Involvement in Northern Sumatra, c.11–c.14 (the Gold and Resin Trade)." *Journal of the Malay(si)an Branch of the Royal Asiatic Society* 69.1:85–99.

McKinnon, Edmund Edwards, and Tengku Lukman Sinar. 1974. "Notes on Further Developments at Kota *Cina*." *Sumatra Research Bulletin (Hull University)* 4.1:63–86.

McPhee, Colin. 1966. *Music in Bali: A Study in Form and Instrumental Organization in Balinese Orchestral Music*. New Haven, CT: Yale University Press.

Melalatoa, M. J. 1982. *Kebudayaan Gayo*. Jakarta: Balai Pustaka.

Meuraxa, Dada. 1966. *Atjeh 1000 Tahun dan Peristiwa Teungku Daud Beureueh*. Medan: Pustaka Hasmar.

———. 1973. *Sejarah kebudayaan suku-suku di Sumatera Utara*. Medan: Sasterawan.

Miksic, John. 1998. "Entrepots along the Melaka Strait." In *The Encyclopedia of Malaysia: Early History*, vol. 4, ed. Nik Abdul Rahman, 117. Singapore: Archipelago Press.

Miller, Michelle Ann. 2009. *Rebellion and Reform in Indonesia*. London: Routledge.

Milner, A. C. 1982. *Kerajaan: Malay Political Culture on the Eve of Colonial Rule*. Tucson: University of Arizona Press.

Milner, Anthony. 2008. *The Malays*. Oxford: Wiley-Blackwell.

Milner, A. C., E. Edwards McKinnon, and Luckman Sinar, Si. 1978. "Aru and Kota Cina." *Indonesia* 26:1–42.

Moens, J. L. 1924. "Het Buddhisme op Java en Sumatra in zijn laatste Bloeiperiode." *Tijdschrift voor Indische Taal-, Land-en Volkenkunde, Bataviaasch Genootschap van Kunsten en Wetenschappen*, 521–79.

Moore, Lynette M. 1979. "A Survey of the Instrumental Music of the Pakpak Dairi of North Sumatra." MA preliminary thesis, Monash University, 1979.

———.1981. "An Introduction to the Music of Pakpak Dairi of North Sumatra." *Indonesian Circle*, 24 March, 39–45.

———. 1984. "Music of the Pakpak Dairi." *Journal of the Australian Indonesian Association* (July): 9–11.

———. 1985. Songs of the Pakpak of North Sumatra. PhD diss., Monash University.

Morton, David. 1976. *The Traditional Music of Thailand*. Berkeley: University of California Press.

Mpu Prapañca. 1995. *Nagarakrtagama (Desawarnana)*. Trans. Stuart Robson. Leiden: KITLV Press.

Mursal, Esten. 1977. "Beberapa Informasi dan Catatan tentang Randai II." *Budaya Jaya* 112.10:537–43.

———. 1979. "Eksistensi Randai sebagai Teater Rakyat: Suatu Proses Perkembangan." Paper presented at Persidangan Antarabangsa Pengajian Melayu, Universiti Melayu.

Mus, Paul. (1933) 1975. *India Seen from the East*. Trans. I. W. Mabbett. Ed. I. W. Mabbett and D. P. Chandler. Monash Papers on Southeast Asia 3, no. 1. Clayton: Centre of Southeast Asian Studies, Monash University. Originally published as "Cultes indiens et indigènes au Champa," *Bulletin de l'École Française d'Extrême Orient* 33 (1933): 367–410.

Naim, Asma, and Mochtar Naim. 1975. *Bibliografi Minangkabau*. Singapore: Institute of Southeast Asian Studies, Singapore University Press.

Naim, Mochtar. 1973. *Merantau: Minangkabau Voluntary Migration*. PhD diss., University of Singapore.

Nas, Peter J. M., ed. 2002. *The Indonesian Town Revisited*. Singapore: Institute of Southeast Asian Studies.

Nasution, Edi. 2007. *Tulila: Musik Bujukan Mandailing*. Penang: Areca.

Neubauer, Eckhard. 1980. "Islamic Religious Music." In *The New Grove Dictionary of Music and Musicians*, vol. 9, ed. Stanley Sadie, 342–49. London: Macmillan.

Nicholson, Clara K. 1965. "The Introduction of Islam into Sumatra and Java: A Study in Cultural Change." PhD diss., Syracuse University.

Nielsen, Mette Lindorf. 2002. "Questioning Aceh's Inevitability: A Story of Failed National Integration?" *A Global Politics Network Report*, 44 pages. Available online at http://www.global-politics.net/essays/Lindorf_Nielsen.pdf, accessed 29 January 2010.

Nilakanta Sastri, K. A. 1932. "A Tamil Merchant-Guild in Sumatra." *Tijdschrift voor Indische Taal-, Land- en Volkenkunde* 72:314–28.

———. 1940. "Sri Vijaya." *Bulletin de l'Éçole Française d'Extrême-Orient*, 40:239–313.

———. 1978. *South India and South-East Asia: Studies in Their History and Culture.* Mysore: Geetha Book House.

Nor, Mohd. Anis Md. 1986. *Randai Dance of Minangkabau, Sumatra, with Labanotation Scores.* Kuala Lumpur: University of Malaya Press.

———1993. *Zapin: Folk Dance of the Malay World.* New York: Oxford University Press.

———2000. "Lion Dance for Hire: Performances for the Inauguration of Chinese Business Premises in Malaysia." *Journal of Asian Business* 16.1:85–94.

———2003. "Arabesques and Curvilinear Perimeters in the Aesthetics of Maritime-Malay Dances." *Yearbook for Traditional Music* 35:179–81.

Nothofer, Bernd. 1997. *Dialek Melayu Bangka.* Kuala Lumpur: Penerbit Universiti Kebangsaan Malaysia.

Oemarjati, Boen S. 1971. *Bentuk lakon dalam sastra Indonesia.* Jakarta: Guhung Agung.

Okazaki, Yoshiko. 1994. "Music, Identity, and Religious Change among the Toba Batak People of North Sumatra." PhD diss., University of California, Los Angeles.

Ooi, Keat Gin. 2004. *Southeast Asia: A Historical Encyclopedia, from Angkor Wat to East Timor.* 2 vols. Santa Barbara, CA: ABC-Clio.

Pamoentjak, Muhammad Thaib Sutan. 1935. *Kamoes bahasa Minangkabau-bahasa Melajoe-riau.* Batavia: Balai Poestaka.

Parlindungan, M. O. 1964. *Pongkinangolngolan Sinambela Gelar Tuanku Rao; Terror Agama Islam Mazhab Hambali di Tanah Batak, 1816–1833.* Jakarta: Tanjung Pengharapan.

Pauka, Kirstin. 1998. *Theater and Martial Arts in West Sumatra: Randai and Silek of the Minangkabau.* Athens: Ohio University Press.

Peacock. J. L. 1968. *Rites of Modernization: Symbolic and Social Aspects of Indonesian Proletarian Drama.* Chicago: University of Chicago Press.

Pelly, Lewis. 1879. *The Miracle Play of Hasan and Husain, Collected from Oral Tradition.* Notes by A. Wollaston. London: Allen.

Phillips, Nigel. 1980. "Tukang Sijobang Storytellers in West Sumatra." *Archipel* 20:105–19.

———. 1981. *Sijobang: Sung Narrative Poetry of West Sumatra.* Cambridge: Cambridge University Press.

Pigeaud, Theodore G. Th. 1962. *Java in the Fourteenth Century: A Study in Cultural History.* Vol. 4. The Hague: Martinus Nijhoff.

———. 1967. *Literature of Java: Synopsis of Javanese Literature, 900–1900 A.D.* The Hague: Martinus Nijhoff.

Pinto, Fernand Mendez. (1653) 1969. *The Voyages and Adventures of Fernand Mendez Pinto.* Trans. H. Cogan. London: Dawsons.

Pires, Tomé. 1944. *The Suma Oriental of Tomé Pires: An Account of the East from the Red Sea to Japan, Written in Malacca and India in 1512–1515; and The Book of Francisco Rodrigues, Rutter of a Voyage in the Red Sea, Nautical Rules, Almanac and Maps Written and Drawn in the East before 1515.* Trans. and ed. from the Portuguese MS, Bibliothèque de la Chambre by Armando Cortesão.

Poensen, C. 1888. "Het daboes van Santri-Soenda." *Mededeelingen van wege het Nederlands Zendeling Genootschap* 31:253–59.

Prapañca, Rakawi, of Majapahit. 1960–63. *Java in the 14th Century: A Study in Cultural History: The Nagara-Kertagama by Rakawi Prapañca of Majapahit, 1365 A.D.* Notes, translations, commentaries and a glossary by Theodore G. Th. Pigeaud. 5 vols. The Hague: Martinus Nijhoff.

Purba, Mauly. 1988. "*Gordang Sambilan*: Social Function and Rhythmic Structure." MA thesis, Wesleyan University.

———. 1998. "Musical and Functional Change in the Gondang Sabangunan Tradition of the Protestant Toba Batak 1860s-1990s, with Particular Reference to the 1980s-1990s." PhD diss., Monash University.

———. 1991. *Fungsi Sosial Ensambel Gordang Sambilan pada Masyarakat Mandailing di Desa Tamiang, Kecamatan Kotanopan, Kabupaten Tapanuli Selatan.* Utara: Universitas Sumatera.

———. 2001. *Maqam dalam proses transformasi sosiobudaya musik Islam di Asahan.* Universitas Sumatera Utara.

———. 2002. "*Gondang Sabangunan* Ensemble Music of the Batak Toba People: Musical Instruments, Structure, and Terminology." *Journal of Musicological Research* 21:21–72.

———. 2002-3. "*Adat ni Gondang*: Rules and Structure of the *Gondang* Performance in Pre-Christian Toba Batak *Adat* Practice." *Asian Music* 34.1:67–109.

———. 2005. "From Conflict to Reconciliation: The Case of the *Gondang Sabangunan* in the *Order of Discipline* of the Toba Batak Protestant Church." *Journal of Southeast Asian Studies* 36.2:207–33.

Raffles, Thomas Stamford. 1818. "On the Maláyu Nation, with a Translation of its Maritime Institutions." *Asiatic Researches* 12.

———. 1830. *The History of Java.* 2 vols. London: Murray.

———. 1835. *Memoir of the Life and Public Services of Sir Thomas Stamford Raffles, F. R. S. &c particularly in the Government of Java, 1811–1816, and of Bencoolen and Its Dependencies, 1817–1824; with Details of the Commerce and Resources of the Eastern Archipelago, and Selections from His Correspondence.* London: Duncan.

Rees, W. A. van. 1870. "Pasoemah." *Het Vaandel*, 35–49.

Reid, Anthony. 1969. *The Contest for North Sumatra.* Kuala Lumpur: University of Malaya Press; New York: Oxford University Press.

———. 1971. "The Birth of the Republic in Sumatra." *Indonesia* 12:22–31.

———. 1975. "Trade and the Problem of Royal Power in Aceh: Three Stages; c.1550–1700." In *Pre-Colonial State Systems in Southeast Asia: The Malay Peninsula, Sumatra, Bali-Lombok, South Celebes*, ed. Anthony Reid and Lance Castles, 45–55. Kuala Lumpur: Malaysian Branch of the Royal Asiatic Society.

———. 1979. *The Blood of the People: Revolution and the End of Traditional Rule in Northern Sumatra.* Kuala Lumpur: Oxford University Press.

———. (1988) 1993. *Southeast Asia in the Age of Commerce.* 2 vols. New Haven, CT: Yale University Press.

———. 2005. *An Indonesian Frontier: Acehnese and Other Histories of Sumatra.* Leiden: KITLV Press.

Ricklefs, M. C., 1981. *A History of Modern Indonesia since c. 1930.* London: Macmillan.

Ris, H. 1895. "De onderafdeeling Klein Mandailing Oeloe en Pahantan en hare bevolking met uitzondering van de Oeloe's." *Bijdragen tot de Taal-, Land- en Volkenkunde* 46:532.

Robson, S. O., ed. and trans. 1995. *Desawarnana (Nagarakrtagama) by Mpu Prapanca.* Leiden: KITLV Press.

Róheim, Géza. (1930) 1970. *Animism, Magic and the Divine King.* New York: International Universities Press.

Ronkel, Philippus S. van. 1914. "Nadere Gegevens om Trent het Hasan-Hoesain Feest." *Tijdschrift voor Indische Taal-, Land- en Volkenkunde* 50.6:334–44.

Roo de la Faille, P. de. *Dari zaman kesultanan Palembang.* Trans. from the Dutch by Soegarda Poerbakawatja. Jakarta: Bhatara, 1971.

Rouffaer, G. P. 1906. "De Hindostansche oorsprong van het 'negenvoudig' Sultans-zegel van Atjeh." *Bijdragen tot de Taal-, Land- en Volkenkunde* 59:349–84.

Royce, Anya Peterson. 1982. *Ethnic Identity: Strategies of Diversity*. Bloomington: Indiana University Press.

Roy Choudhury, M. L. 1957. "Music in Islam." *Journal of the Asiatic Society* 23.2:43–102.

Rutherford, Danilyn. 2002. "After Syncretism: The Anthropology of Islam and Christianity in Southeast Asia; A Review Article." *Comparative Studies in Society and History* 44.1:196–205.

Sakai, Minako. 2003. "Resisting the Mainland." In *Autonomy and Disintegration in Indonesia*, ed. Damien Kingsbury and Harry Aveling, 189–200. London: RoutledgeCurzon.

Salisbury, David A. 2000. "Aspects of Musical and Social Identity in the Talempong Musical Tradition of the Payakumbuh Region, West Sumatra, Indonesia." PhD diss., University of New England.

Sanday, Peggy. 1990. "Androcentric and Matrifocal Gender Representations in Minangkabau Ideology." In *Beyond the Second Sex: New Directions in the Anthropology of Gender*, ed. Peggy Sanday and Ruth Goodenough, 139–68. Philadelphia: University of Pennsylvania Press.

———. 2002: *Women at the Center: Life in a Modern Matriarchy*. Ithaca, NY: Cornell University Press.

Sandbukt, Øyvind. 1984. "Kubu Conceptions of Reality." *Asian Folklore Studies* 43.1:85–98.

———. 1988. "Tributary Tradition and Relations of Affinity and Gender among the Sumatran Kubu." In *Hunters and Gatherers*, vol. 1: *History, Evolution and Social Change*, ed. Tim Ingold, David Riches, and James Woodburn, 107–16. Oxford: Berg.

Santa Maria, Luigi. 1967. *I prestiti portoghesi nel malese indonesiano*. Pubblicazioni del Seminario di Indianistica, no. 1. Naples: Instituto Orientale di Napoli.

Sarkissian, Margaret. 2000. *D'Albuquerque's Children: Performing Tradition in Malaysia's Portuguese Settlement*. Chicago: University of Chicago Press.

Schechner R. 1993. *The Future of Ritual: Writings on Culture and Performance*. London: Routledge.

Schieffelin, Edward L. 1998. "Problematizing Performance." In *Ritual, Performance, Media*, ed. Felicia Hughes-Freeland, 194–207. London: Routledge.

Schnitger, F. M. 1937. *The Archaeology of Hindoo Sumatra*. Leiden: E. J. Brill.

———. 1964. *Forgotten Kingdoms in Sumatra*. Leiden: E. J. Brill.

Schreiner, Artur. 1982. "Altreligiöse und soziale Zeremonien der Batak." *Zeitschrift für Ethnologie* 107.2:177–206.

———. 1984. "Functional Changes in Batak's Traditional Music and Its Role in Modern Indonesian Society." *Asian Music* 15.2:58–66.

Schrieke, B. 1957. *Indonesian Sociological Studies*. Vol. 2, *Ruler and Realm in Early Java*. The Hague: W. van Hoeve, 241–60.

Schuchardt, Hugo. 1891. *Über das Malaioportugiesische von Batavia und Tugu*. Kreolische Studien 9. Vienna: Tempsky.

Sembiring, Terbit. 1981. "Song of Evacuation: A Song of Fighting for Independence in Indonesia." In *Cultures and Societies of North Sumatra*, ed. Rainer Carle, 394–428. Berlin: Dietrich Reimer Verlag.

Shavian, A. 1979. "Arts of Islamic Peoples: Music." In *Encyclopedia Britannica* 9:973–77.

Sheikh Abdl Qadir al-Jaelani. 2003. *Celebrations of the Desires*. Trans. from the Sudanese by Julian Millie. Bandung: Joseph Helmi Publications.

Shellabear, W. G., ed. 1950. *Sejarah Melayu or the Malay Annals*. Singapore: Malaya Publishing House.

Shellabear, W. G., with Sulaiman bin Muhammad Nor. 1909. *Kitab Kiliran Budi*. Singapore: Methodist Publishing House.

Shurreef, J., and G. A. Herklots. (1832) 1895. *Qanoon-e-Islam, or the Customs of the Moosulmans in India*. 2nd ed. London: Parbury, Allen, 1895.

Siegel, James. 1979. *Shadow and Sound: The Historical Thought of a Sumatran People*. Chicago: University of Chicago Press.

Simon, A. 1981. "Social and Religious Functions of Batak Ceremonial Music." In *Cultures and Societies of North Sumatra*, ed. Rainer Carle, 337–50. Berlin: Dietrich Reimer Verlag.

———. 1984. "Functional Changes in Batak Traditional Music and Its Role in Modern Indonesian Society." *Asian Music* 15.2:58–66.

———. 1985. "The Terminology of Batak Instrumental Music in Northern Sumatra." *Yearbook for Traditional Music* 17:113–45.

———. 1993. "Gondang, Gods and Ancestors: Religious Implications of Batak Ceremonial Music." *Yearbook for Traditional Music* 25:81–87.

Simorangkir, S., A. H. Lubis, H. Sihombing, and S. Silitonga. 1986. *Struktur bahasa Pesisir Sibolga*. Jakarta: Pusat Pembinaan & Pengembangan Bahasa, Departemen Pendidikan dan Kebudayaan.

Sinar, Tengku Luckman. 1986. *Sari Sejarah Serdang*. Jakarta: Departemen Pendidikan dan Kebudayaan.

———. 1993. "Musik dan Lagu Melayu." Radio Republik Indonesia broadcast, Bukit Tinggi, 12 January.

Siregar, Ahmad. 1977. *Kamus bahasa Angkola/Mandailing Indonesia*. Jakarta: Pusat Pembinaan dan Pengembangan Bahasa.

Smedal, Olaf H. 1989. *Order and Difference: An Ethnographic Study of Orang Lom of Bangka, West Indonesia*. Oslo Occasional Papers in Social Anthropology, Occasional Paper 19. Oslo: Department of Social Anthropology, University of Oslo.

Smith, Graeme. 2003. "Melodeon." In *Continuum Encyclopedia of Popular Music of the World*, vol. 2: *Performance and Production*, ed. John Shepherd et al., 308. London: Continuum.

Smith, R. B. 1968. *The First Age of the Portuguese Embassies, Navigations, and Peregrinations in Persia (1507–1524)*. Bethesda, MD: Decatur Press.

Snouck Hurgronje, Christiaan. 1903. *Tanah Gayo dan Penduduknya*. Jakarta: INIS.

———. 1906. *The Achehnese*. Trans. A. W. S. O'Sullivan. 2 vols. Leiden: E. J. Brill. Originally published as *De Atjèhers* (Batavia: Landsdrukkerij, 1893–94).

Somers Heidhues, Mary F. 1992. *Bangka Tin and Mentok Pepper: Chinese Settlement on an Indonesian Island*. Singapore: Institute of Southeast Asian Studies.

———. 1996. "When We Were Young: The Exile of the Republic's Leaders in Bangka, 1949." In *Making Indonesia: Essays on Modern Indonesia in Honor of George McT. Kahin*, ed. Daniel Lev and Ruth McVey, 81–95. Ithaca, NY: Cornell University Press.

———. 2010. "Chinese Presence in Malay-Indonesian Narratives: Founders and Heroes of Merchants and Wifegivers?" Hamburg: Asia-Africa Institute.

Stewart, Charles, and Rosalind Shaw, eds. 1994. "Introduction: Problematising Syncretism." In *Syncretism/Anti-Syncretism: The Politics of Religious Synthesis*, 1–24. London: Routledge.

Subhadradis Diskul, M. C., ed. 1980. *The Art of Srivijaya*. Melbourne: Oxford University Press and UNESCO.

Suleiman, Satyawati. 1976. *Monuments of Ancient Indonesia*. Jakarta: Proyek Pelita, Pembinaan Kepurbakalaan dan Peninggalan Nasional, Departemen P & K.

———. 1977. "The Archaeology and History of West Sumatra." *Bulletin of the Research Centre of Archaeology in Indonesia* 12:1–25.

———. 1980. "The Art of Srivijaya." In Subhadradis Diskul, *Art of Srivijaya*, 1–20.

Suryadi. 2003. "Minangkabau Commercial Cassettes and the Cultural Impact of the Recording Industry in West Sumatra." *Asian Music* 34.2:51–89.

Suryadinata, Leo, et al. 2003. "2000 Population Statistics." Indonesian Central Statistics Bureau, 30 June 2000.

Sutton, R. A. 1998. "Java." In *The Garland Encyclopedia of World Music*, vol. 4: *Southeast Asia*, 645. New York: Garland.

Taal, Sandra. 2002. "Cultural Expressions, Collective Memory and the Urban Landscape in Palembang." In *The Indonesian Town Revisited*, ed. Peter J. M. Nas, 172–200. Münster: Lit Verlag.

Tadmor, Uri. 2002. "Language Contact and Historical Reconstruction: The Case of Palembang Malay." Paper presented to the Fifth International Symposium on Malay/Indonesian Linguistics (ISMIL 5), Leipzig, 16–17 June.

Tambiah, S. J. 1981. "A Performative Approach to Ritual." In *Proceedings of the British Academy* no. 65, 113–69. Cambridge, MA: Harvard University Press.

Tan, Sooi-Beng. 1989. "From Popular to 'Traditional' Theatre: The Dynamics of Change in *Bangsawan* of Malaysia." *Ethnomusicology* 33.2:229–73.

———. 1993. *Bangsawan: A Social and Stylistic History of Popular Malay Opera*. South-East Asian Social Science Monographs. Singapore: Oxford University Press.

Tanner, Nancy Makepeace. 1981. "Rethinking Matriliny: The Case of the Minangkabau." In *Report of the IUAES Intercongress in Amsterdam*. Berkeley: University of California Press.

Teeur, A., and T. Situmorang. 1952. *Sejarah Melayu*. Jakarta: Djambatan.

Teeuw, A. 1967. *Modern Indonesian Literature*. The Hague: Martinus Nijhoff.

Temple, Sir Richard Carnac, ed. 1919. *The Travels of Peter Mundy in Europe and Asia, 1608–1667*. 3 vols. London: Hakluyt Society.

Thomassen à Thuessink van der Hoop, Abraham Nicolaas Jan. 1932. *Megalithic Remains in South Sumatra*. Trans. William Shirlaw. Zutphen: W. J. Thieme.

———. 1949. *Indonesian Ornamental Design*. Bandoeng: A. C. Nix.

Thurgood, Graham. 2007. "The Historical Place of Acehnese: the Known and the Unknown." Paper presented at the First International Conference on Aceh and Indian Ocean Studies, Banda Aceh.

———. 2010. "Hainan Cham, Anong, and Eastern Cham: Three Social Contexts, Three Patterns of Change." *Journal of Language Contact, VARIA 3*. Available online at http://www.jlc-journal. org, accessed 21 September 2011.

Tiele, P. A. 1877. "De Europeërs in den Maleischen Archipel, eerste gedeelte 1509–1529." *Bijdragen tot de Taal-, Land- en Volkenkunde* 25:321–420.

———. 1879. "De Europeërs in den Maleischen Archipel, tweede gedeelte 1529–1540." *Bijdragen tot de Taal-, Land- en Volkenkunde* 27:1–69.

Toorn, J. L. van der. 1891. *Minangkabausch-Maleisch-Nederlandsch Woordenboek*. The Hague: Martinus Nijhoff.

Trimingham, J. Spencer. 1971. *The Sufi Orders in Islam*. London: Clarendon Press.

Turner, Ashley. 1982. "Duri-dana Music and Hoho Songs in South Nias." Honors thesis, Monash University.

———. 1991. "Belian as a Symbol of Cosmic Reunification." In *Metaphor: A Musical Dimension* ed. Jamie C. Kassler, 121–46. Sydney: Currency Press.

———. 1997. "Cultural Survival, Identity and the Performing Arts of Kampar's Suku Petalangan." In *Riau in Transition*, ed. C. Chou and Will Derks, Bijdragen tot de Taal, Land- en Volkenkunde 153, no. 4, 648–72. Leiden: KITLV.

Turner, Victor W. 1982. *From Ritual to Theatre: The Human Seriousness of Play*. New York: PAJ Publications.

Tyler, S. R. 1979. *The Said and the Unsaid: Mind, Meaning, and Culture*. New York: Academic Press.

Uchino, Megumi. 2005. "Socio-Cultural History of Palembang *Songket*." *Indonesia and the Malay World* 33.96:205–23.

Voorhoeve, P. 1955. *Critical Surveys of the Languages of Sumatra*. Leiden: Martinus Nijhoff.

———. 1978. "Some Notes on South-Sumatran Epics." In *Spectrum: Essays Presented to Sutan Takdir Alisjahbana on His Seventieth Birthday*, ed. S. Udin, 92–102. Jakarta: Dian Rakyat.

———. 1985. *Südsumatranische Handschriften*. Verzeichnis der orientalischen Handschriften in Deutschland: Handschchriften aus Indonesien 29 (Bali, Java, and Sumatra). Stuttgart: Franz Steiner Verlag.

Voorhoeve, P., and Helen Jaspan. 1980. "M. A. Jaspan's Papers on Sumatra." *Indonesia and the Malay World* 8.22:3–6.

Vredenbregt, J. 1973. "Dabus in West Java." *Bijdragen to de Taal-, Land- en Volkenkunde* 2.3:302–20.

Wertheim, W. F. [1956] 1964. *Indonesian Society in Transition: A Study of Social Change*. Rev. ed. The Hague: Van Hoeve.

———. 1964. *East-West Parallels*. The Hague: Van Hoeve.

Wijaya, P.T., and F. A. Sutjipto. 1978. *Kelahiran dan Perkembangan Ketoprak*. Jakarta: Department of Education and Culture.

Willer, T. I. 1846. "Verzameling der Battahsche wetten en instellingen in *Mandheling* en *Pertibie: Gevolgd van een overzigt van land en volk in die streken*." *Tijdschrift voor Nederlandsch-Indie* 2:145–248.

Winstedt, R. O. 1938. "Sejarah Melayu." *Journal of the Malay(si)an Branch of the Royal Asiatic Society* 16.3:1–226.

Withington, W. A. 1967. "The Major Geographic Regions of Sumatra, Indonesia." *Annals of the Association of American Geography* 57:534–41.

Wolters, O. W. 1960. "The Po-ssu' Pine Trees." *Bulletin of the School of Oriental and African Studies* 23.2:323–50.

———. 1967. *Early Indonesian Commerce: A Study of the Origins of Sri Vijaya*. Ithaca, NY: Cornell University Press.

———. 1970. *The Fall of Srivijaya in Malay History*. London: Lund Humphries.

———. 1983. "A Few Miscellaneous *pi-chi* Jottings on Early Indonesia." *Indonesia* 36:49–65.

———. 1986. "Restudying Some Chinese Writings on Sriwijaya." *Indonesia* 42:1–41.

Wurm, S. A., and Shiro Hattori, eds. 1981. "Sumatra" (map comp. by W. A. Foley). In *Language Atlas of the Pacific Area*, 38. Canberra: Australian Academy of the Humanities and the Japan Academy.

Ypes, W. K. H. 1907. "Nota Omtrent Singkel en de Pak-pak landen." *Tijdschrift voor Indische Taal-, Land- en Volkenkunde* 49:355–612.

Sound Recordings

Kartomi, Margaret. 1983a. *The Angkola People of Sumatra: An Anthology of Southeast Asian Music*. Recorded, edited, and annotated by Margaret Kartomi. Bärenreiter Musicaphon, BM30 SL2568.

———.1983b. *The Mandailing People of Sumatra: An Anthology of Southeast Asian Music*. Recorded, edited, and annotated by Hidris and Margaret Kartomi. Bärenreiter Musicaphon, BM30 SL2567.

———. 1998a. *The Music of Islam.* Vol. 15: *Muslim Music of Indonesia: Aceh and West Sumatra.* Recorded, edited, and annotated by Margaret Kartomi. Celestial Harmonies 14155–2.

———. 1998b. *Kroncong Moritsku.* Vol. 6 of a 12-vol. CD set, *The Journey of Sounds.* Tradisom, Compact Disc VS06.

Pauka, Kirstin. 2002. *Randai: Folk Theater, Dance and Martial Arts of West Sumatra.* Electronic resource, CD-ROM. Ann Arbor: University of Michigan Press.

Schacht, Joseph. 1959. *Sufi Ceremony: Rifa' Ceremony of the Eleventh Day of Rabi-L-Achien Honouring Abdul Hadir Beker.* Recorded by the Islaamia Refia Jamaa sect of Malayan Mohammedans in the Union of South Africa. Smithsonian Folkways Recordings, FR08942.

Simon, Artur. 1984a. *Gondang Batak, Nord Sumatra.* Museum Collection, Berlin (West).

———. 1984b. *Gondang Toba/Northern Sumatra.* Museum Collection, Berlin (West).

———. 1987. *Gendang Karo/Northern Sumatra, Indonesia: Trance and Dance Music of the Karo Batak.* Museum Collection, Berlin (West)

———. 1999. *Instrumental Music of the Toba and Karo Batak, North Sumatra, Indonesia.* Berlin Phonogram Archive.

Yampolsky, Philip. 1991. *Music of Indonesia: Music from the Outskirts of Jakarta: Gambang Kromong.* CD 5, tracks 7–10. Smithsonian Folkways Recordings, with Indonesian Society for the Performing Arts (MSPI).

———. 1994. *Music of Indonesia: Betawi and Sundanese Music of the North Coast of Java: Topeng, Betawi, Tanjidor, Ajeng.* CD 5, tracks 4–7. Smithsonian Folkways Recordings, with Indonesian Society for the Performing Arts (MSPI).

———. 1996. *Music of Indonesia: Melayu Music from Sumatra and the Riau Islands.* CD 11. Smithsonian Folkways Recordings, with Indonesian Society for the Performing Arts (MSPI).

———. 1975. *Indonesian Popular Music: Kroncong, Dangdut, and Langgam Jawa.* Smithsonian Folkways Records, SFW40056.

———. 1982. *Music of Nias and North Sumatra: Hoho, Gendang Karo, Gondang Toba.* Music from Indonesia 4. Smithsonian Folkways Recordings 40420.

———. 1994. *Night Music of West Sumatra: Saluang, Rabab Pariaman, Dendang Pauah.* Music from Indonesia 6. Smithsonian Folkways Recordings, 40422 CD.

———. 1995. *Music from the Forests of Riau and Mentawai.* Annotated by Hanefi, Ashley Turner, and P. Yampolsky. Music from Indonesia 7. Smithsonian Folkways Recordings, 40423.

———. 1996. *Gongs and Vocal Music from Sumatra: Talempong, Didong, Kulintang, Salawat.* Music of Indonesia 12. Smithsonian Folkways Recordings, 40428.